ELCOME
CHICAGO
7091LB
COOPER
KT-445-066

Billy Connolly's Route 66

Billy Connolly's Route 66

The Big Yin on the Ultimate American Road Trip

Billy Connolly

***with* Robert Uhlig**

SPHERE

First published in Great Britain in 2011 by Sphere

A CIP catalogue record for this book
is available from the British Library.

ISBN 978-1-84744-521-6

Maps drawn by John Gilkes
Endpaper photographs by Tim Pollard

Typeset in Times by M Rules
Printed and bound in Great Britain by
Clays Ltd, St Ives plc

Papers used by Sphere are from well-managed forests
and other responsible sources.

MIX
Paper from
responsible sources
FSC® C104740

Sphere
An imprint of
Little, Brown Book Group
100 Victoria Embankment
London EC4Y 0DY

An Hachette UK Company
www.hachette.co.uk

www.littlebrown.co.uk

Contents

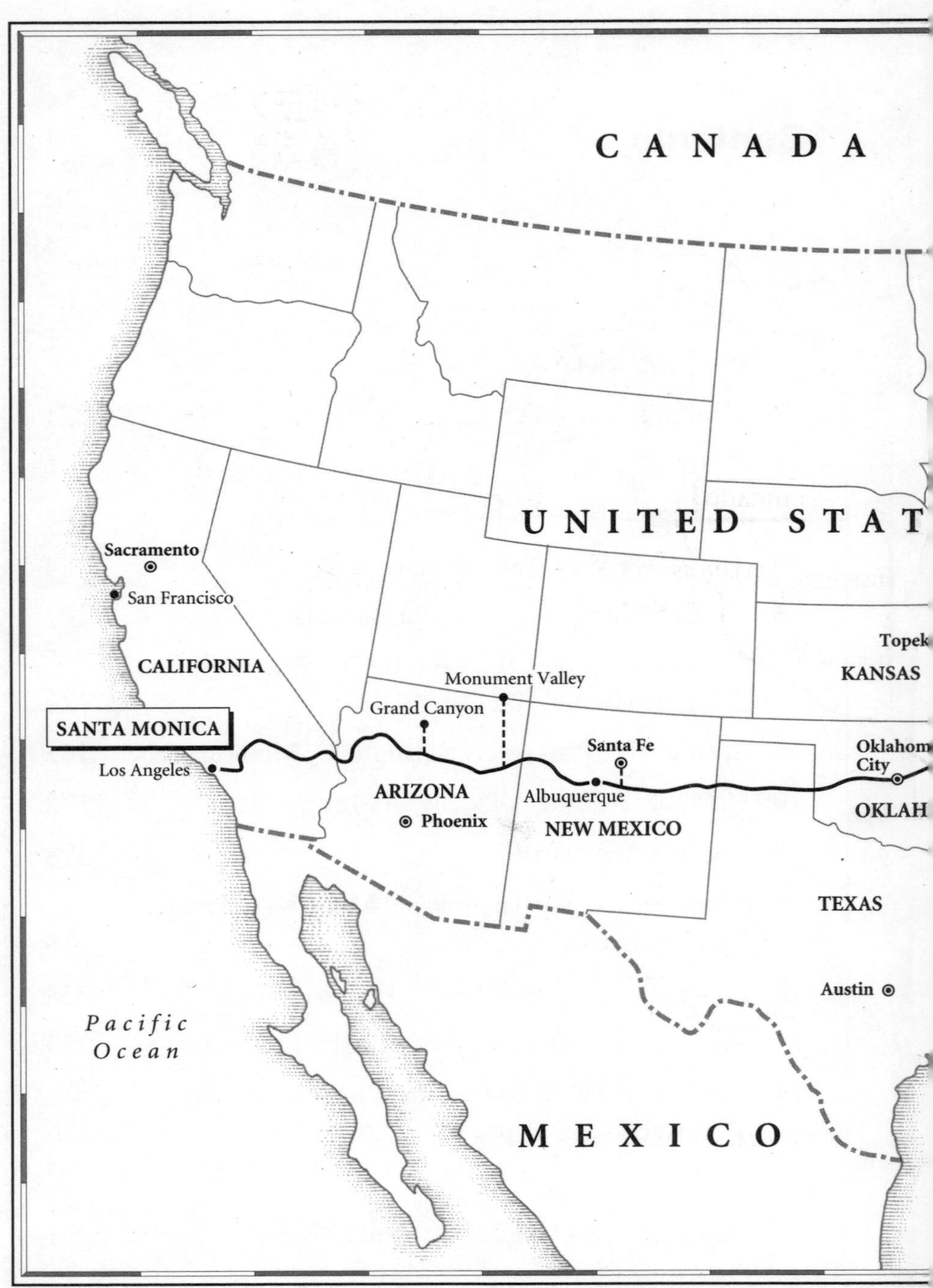
CANADA
UNITED STAT
Sacramento
San Francisco
CALIFORNIA
SANTA MONICA
Los Angeles
Grand Canyon
Monument Valley
ARIZONA
Phoenix
Santa Fe
Albuquerque
NEW MEXICO
Topek
KANSAS
Oklahom
City
OKLAH
TEXAS
Austin
Pacific
Ocean
MEXICO

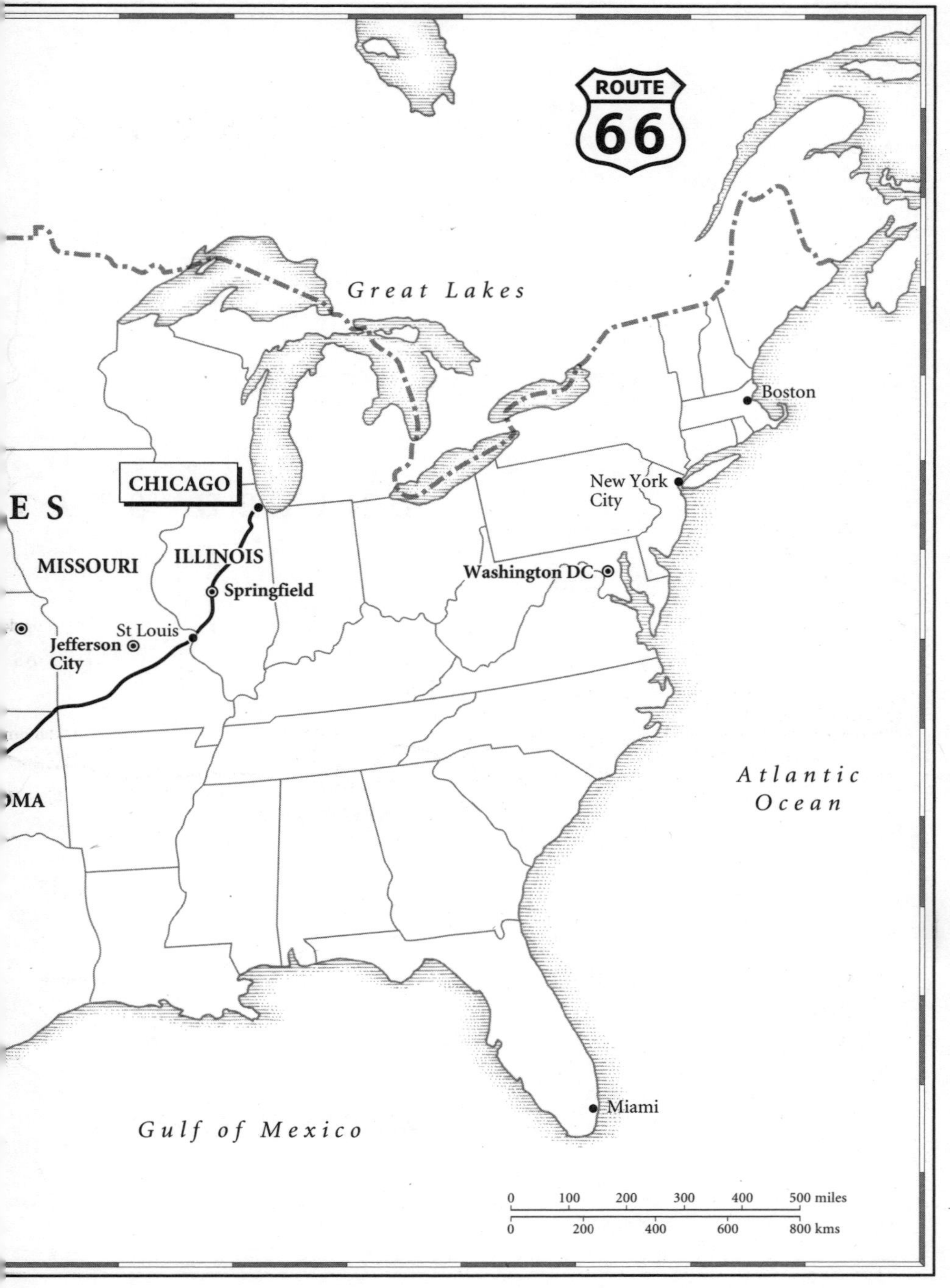
ROUTE
66
Great Lakes
Boston
CHICAGO
New York
City
E S
ILLINOIS
MISSOURI
Washington DC
Springfield
St Louis
Jefferson
City
Atlantic
Ocean
OMA
Miami
Gulf of Mexico
0 100 200 300 400 500 miles
0 200 400 600 800 kms

Billy Connolly's Route 66

1

Get Your Kicks

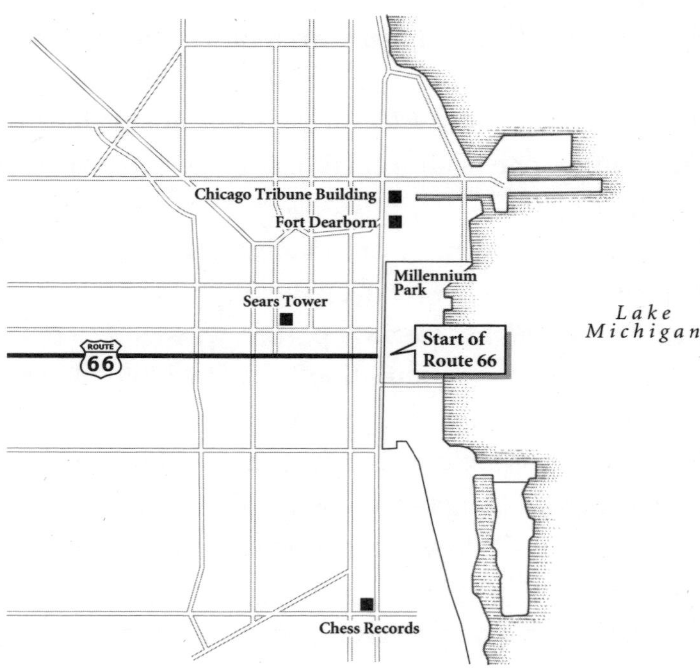

It was a moment I'll remember for the rest of my life. I'd been travelling along Route 66 for a few days, and I couldn't resist a quick detour to Arthur, a small community nearly two hundred miles south of Chicago. 'Population 800', it said on the sign at the edge of town. Beside it, another sign warned drivers that the roads might be busy with horse-drawn carriages. And with good reason: this was Amish country.

I didn't know what to expect. I'd always quite liked Amish folk; although, to be honest, I knew very little about them. It was just something about the look – the horse-drawn carriages, the hats, the plain, modest clothing, the way they carried themselves – that always led me to think they were really rather nice people.

I parked my trike outside a simple house that backed on to a large workshop. Waiting inside was a furniture-maker with the best haircut I'd ever seen – like Rowan Atkinson's pudding bowl in the first series of *Blackadder*. Beneath the mop of hair was Mervin, a man with a thick beard, no moustache and a slow, soft grin.

Mervin makes the most outstandingly great furniture: the kind of stuff that will last for ever; the antiques of tomorrow. He showed me around his workshop, then we stood in his office while he answered every question I asked with total honesty. I could tell immediately that this delightful, decent man was being absolutely straight with me. He had nothing to hide. Men like Mervin have a ring of truth about them.

'Why do you all grow beards and you don't grow moustaches?' I said.

'Well, I wouldn't want to grow a moustache when everybody just had a beard and no moustache,' said Mervin. 'We like to be the same and share and be equal.'

How humane. In this age of individualism, what a delight to find a community of people who strive for equality and lead their lives according to whatever is best for everyone. We talked some more and Mervin explained the rules of the community, although the way he told it, those rules didn't seem like restrictions but simple guidelines for a better, more harmonious way of living. With no sign of frustration about what he wasn't allowed to do, Mervin totally accepted the boundaries of his life. Then he asked me if I wanted to go for a ride on his buggy.

You know those black Amish buggies? I'd always fancied a ride on one of them, but first we had to get Mervin's horse out of the stable and hitch it to the front of the wagon. Now, I'm a wee bit frightened of horses – not terrified, just a wee bit wary. So I lurked behind Mervin until he'd got the beast out of the stable, then I led it to the buggy and Mervin showed me how to hitch it up. We climbed into the buggy and off we went. After about two minutes Mervin said, 'Here . . . ' and handed me the reins. I was in charge. I was in seventh heaven. Riding along in an Amish buggy, with an Amish guy, waving to Amish people. It was a wonderful moment. It might sound ludicrously inconsequential – and I suppose it was – but it pleased me so, so much.

Once we'd ridden in the buggy for a while, Mervin invited me and the whole film crew back to his farm for something to eat. And we're not talking a bag of crisps here. An amazing meal was prepared by Mervin's wife and mother, dressed in traditional long dresses, while a group of little girls, so beautiful in their bonnets, sang wee songs to themselves, completely oblivious to us.

Not everything that I experienced with Mervin was quite so idyllic, though. While we were in the buggy, he told me about a family tragedy that was so distressing it took my breath away. I'll not tell you any more about it until we come to that part of the story. All I'll say now is that it broke my heart. Yet Mervin had a stoicism about him that had kept him sane in the face of a terrible event. If something similar had happened to me, it would have haunted me for the rest of my life, and it might have changed me for the worse. But Mervin had an acceptance that allowed him to remain a lovely, honest, happy man.

Without any doubt, the time I spent with Mervin was one of the highlights of my life. I'll remember that afternoon clip-clopping through Arthur, Illinois, for ever. There wasn't much to it, but I think of my life as a series of moments and I've found that the great moments often don't have too much to them. They're not huge, complicated events; they're just magical wee moments when somebody says 'I love you' or 'You're really good at what you do' or simply 'You're a good person'. I had one that day with Mervin, the Amish furniture-maker.

The peace and simplicity of Mervin's little community stood in stark contrast to what I'd seen over the past few days along Route 66 – that mythical highway forever associated with rock'n'roll, classic Americana and the great open road. Most people, including me, would think of wisecracking waitresses and surly short-order cooks in classic fifties diners. Grease monkeys with dirty rags and tyre wrenches. Gas-pump jockeys and highway patrolmen. Oklahoma hillbillies in overalls and work boots. Stetson-wearing Texan ranch owners and cowboys at a rodeo. Idealistic hitch-hikers following in the footsteps of Jack Kerouac. Eccentric owners of Route 66-themed tourist haunts. Native Americans in the Navajo and Apache reservations of New Mexico and Arizona. Maybe even a few surfers, hippies or internet entrepreneurs in California.

I'd already met a few of them, but when I'd set out from Chicago a few days earlier, my greatest hope had been to make a connection with someone just like Mervin. I'd thought back to similar trips I'd made in the past, like my tour of Britain and my journey across Australia. Every journey had involved visits to historic sites, explorations of beautiful landscapes, and planned meetings with locals and various dignitaries. The itinerary had always been tightly scheduled, as it has to be when shooting a television series. But in every case the best moments had resulted from an unexpected encounter with an interesting character – like the time ten years earlier when I'd made a television series called *Billy Connolly's World Tour of England, Ireland and Wales*.

I met dozens of fascinating people and visited scores of locations between Dublin and Plymouth, but the highlight came when I visited the grave of Mary Shelley, author of *Frankenstein*, at the parish church of St Peter in Bournemouth. I suppose you could say I'm a bit freaky, because I've always been fond of graveyards. Many people think of them as morbid, sad places, but to me they're monuments to great lives lived and they provide a connection to our ancestors and heritage. They're full of stories about people. And the story of Mary and her fantastically talented husband, the poet Percy Bysshe Shelley, is as good as they come. Which was why, one sunny day, I was standing beside her grave with a television camera and a furry microphone pointing at me.

Just as I was telling the tragic story of how Percy Shelley drowned in Italy, a stooped figure appeared in the graveyard. Dressed in black, clutching a can of strong cider, and with a dirty green sleeping bag draped around his shoulders, he approached us with an admirable disdain for the conventions of television productions. Oblivious of the tramp's approach, I continued to talk to the camera, relating the story of Shelley's cremation on a beach. I'd just mentioned that Shelley's friend Edward John Trelawny snatched the poet's heart from the funeral pyre and passed it on to Mary, who then kept it in a velvet bag around her neck for thirty years, when the old fella stopped beside me and pointed at the grave.

'*Frankenstein*, wasn't it?' he interrupted.

For a moment I didn't know what to say. Then I caught on. 'That's right,' I said. 'Mary Shelley.'

'Her husband was a poet, wasn't he? Shelley . . . '

'Yeah, Percy Bysshe Shelley.'

Climbing on to the grave, the wino sat cross-legged on top of it and swigged from his can.

'Do you like Shelley?' I asked. 'Or have you just chosen to sit there?'

'I studied him at school.'

It was soon obvious that this was a bright guy who had fallen on hard times. We rabbited away about Shelley and Shakespeare – if you give people a chance, they shine – and then he told me he came from the Midlands.

'The Black Country?'

'Nearer Birmingham . . . You haven't got a cigarette on you, do you?'

'I don't. I don't smoke cigarettes.'

I liked this man. He was very straightforward. So I offered to get him some. 'What do you smoke?'

'Just ten. Ten cigarettes,' he said.

So I walked off to a nearby shop and bought him a packet.

When I got back we had a long chat. He was pleased with the fags and I was tickled to have made contact with such a lovely, open man. It was another of those wee unexpected moments that I'll always remember.

Something similar happened in 2009 when, during the making of *Journey to the Edge of the World* – my voyage through the North West Passage, deep within the Arctic Circle – I met Brian Pearson, the local undertaker, cinema owner and bed-and-breakfast proprietor. A former dishwasher, lord mayor and taxi driver, Brian was a complicated man who reminded me of plenty of people I'd known as a kid. He was well read, self-educated, but had a kind of grumpiness because he could see things turning to shit all around him. And his mood wasn't helped by the fact that nobody tended to listen to him. Sat behind the wheel of his hearse, he drove me around the streets of his small town, relating stories about what really went on in his community. I spend a lot of time on my own – even when I'm with people I often feel like I'm alone because I think differently to most of them – so I'm always thrilled when I manage to connect with another human being. That afternoon, I felt a real connection with Brian, an interesting and interested man.

So when I was preparing to spend six weeks travelling across the heartland of America, from Chicago to Santa Monica, I told myself that if I had one encounter that equalled the tramp at Mary Shelley's graveside or Brian Pearson, then the trip would have been more than worthwhile. Less than a week into my journey, I'd met Mervin, and everything I'd hoped for had come true.

My journey along Route 66 began long before the first wheel turned on tarmac beneath me. About a year after making

Journey to the Edge of the World, various television companies approached me with a load of ideas about where I could go next. None of their suggestions appealed, but then I mentioned to one of the producers at Maverick Television that I had always wanted to travel along Route 66. They leapt at it – after all, Route 66 is the most famous road in the world. Everyone's heard of it. My interest in it goes back to when I first heard Chuck Berry belting out one of the best rock'n'roll records of all time: '(Get Your Kicks on) Route 66'. Ever since, I've wanted to travel the length of Route 66 – just for my own enjoyment, without a film crew in tow, as a holiday. It's the grooviest road in the world.

Of course, many other roads have been made famous by songs. There's the road to the Isles and the road back home. There's Abbey Road and the Yellow Brick Road. And, as a Scotsman, I know all about taking the high road or the low road. But that song's all about being dead. (I don't mean to insult Scotland here, but it's true. In 'Loch Lomond', a dying soldier is talking to one of his comrades. The 'high road', travelled by the healthy soldier, will be slower than the 'low road' that the dying man's spirit will be able to take.) 'Route 66' is about being alive. It *is* rock'n'roll. From Nat King Cole and Chuck Berry to the Rolling Stones, Dr Feelgood, Depeche Mode and even Dean Martin, it's a classic. And because of the song, Route 66 has become one of those magical places that you've always longed to see if you've got any interest at all in rock'n'roll music and being alive.

None of the other songs urged people to hit the road simply for the pleasure of getting their kicks from watching the miles go by. With its exhortation to travel from Chicago through St

Louis, Joplin, Oklahoma City, Amarillo, Gallup, Flagstaff, Winona, Kingman, Barstow and San Bernadino to Los Angeles, the song is an open invitation to anyone seeking adventure to find their thrills and spills on a California road trip. Who could resist? Not me, that's for sure.

But it's more than just the song. Route 66 is special for many reasons. In America, all other routes, north–south and east–west, are pronounced 'rowt'. It's rowt this and rowt that. But thanks to the song, Route 66 has remained *Root* 66. And it's steeped in a potent mix of histories – of America as a nation and of rock'n'roll as a cultural force. So it is perhaps not surprising that Route 66 appeals to everyone. Americans, Europeans, Australians, Japanese and Southeast Asians, you'll meet them all along its 2,278 miles. It attracts car enthusiasts, motorcyclists, guitar players, people with long hair, silly people and dreamers. I hadn't quite realised the extent of this popular appeal until a few days after it was announced that I was going to ride its full length. From then on, people started telling me that they'd always longed to do the same thing. 'My wife and I have been saving up for five years to do Route 66,' wrote one guy. 'I hope you have a good trip,' wrote another. 'For me, it was the trip of a lifetime.'

Like the Silk Road or the salt and spice roads through Africa, the Pan-American Highway or the Trans-African Highway, Route 66 is one of those wonderful trails that will always exist. It's been called a road of dreamers and ramblers, drifters and writers. Well, I want to be part of that. I want to sit on my bike and ride Route 66. I want to go to Santa Fe and New Mexico. And I want to sing the song as I head down through the plains of Illinois and Missouri, the Oklahoma and Kansas prairies, the

Texas Panhandle, the deserts and mountains of New Mexico, Arizona and California. I want to sing along with Chuck Berry, the Rolling Stones, Nat King Cole and all the other guys who have recorded Bobby Troup's fabulous song. And when I do it, I want to be singing at the top of my lungs as the miles pass beneath my wheels.

More than anything, I want to reconnect with old small-town America. Like a lot of Britain, much of it has been smothered under a beige blanket of franchised coffee shops, fast-food palaces, faceless shopping malls and edge-of-town superstores with uninspiring, unimaginative corporate brand names above their doors. That's not real America. It's the creation of blue-suited marketing and advertising executives. Real America is to be found in all those small towns that have been bypassed by the freeways. That's where I hope to find the fragments of thirties, forties and fifties Americana that I love. Funky neon signs enticing travellers to pull in at motels and diners. Or the giant oranges that used to lurk along the highways of California, selling ice-cold, freshly squeezed juice to thirsty motorists. At one time there was a chain of them across the state and they did a roaring trade. In the days before air-conditioned cars and express freeways, a single stand could easily go through six thousand oranges in a week. Now there's just one left on Route 66 – and I want to see it before it's too late.

Representing freedom, migration and the empty loneliness of the American heartland, Route 66 is one of the essential icons of America – not just for Americans, but for anyone who, like me, is fascinated by the United States. Snaking across eight states, its concrete and asphalt was a ribbon that tied the nation together and enticed millions of Americans with a romantic ideal of adventure and an exodus to a better life.

To some, it's the 'Mother Road' immortalised by John Steinbeck in *The Grapes of Wrath* – an escape route for thousands of farmers and poverty-stricken families fleeing the barren dust bowl of Oklahoma and Kansas for the promised land of California during the Great Depression. To others – me included – just the mention of its name always evokes the birth of rock'n'roll and Chuck Berry urging us to 'get our kicks'. To the beatniks and hipsters, it epitomises the great American open road eulogised by Jack Kerouac in *On the Road*. To the generation of baby-boom Americans that I know, it will always be associated with a 1960s television series, called *Route 66*, in which two young men travelled across America, seeking adventure and getting caught up in the struggles of the people they met. And, like my grandson, many of today's youngsters know it from *Cars*, the Pixar animated film that was conceived as a way of making a documentary about the road and which features several businesses and residents along the route.

When I thought about it, it struck me that in many ways, roads like Route 66 are as significant to American culture and social history as cathedrals and palaces are to European history. For a young nation founded on exploration and migration west, these great arteries of transportation became a major agent of social transformation. They did more than just move people; they changed America. Among all those highways, Route 66 was the everyman's road that connected Middle America with southern California, a strip of hardtop that led to the birth of those icons of Americana I like so much: diners, motels and road food. Route 66's 2,278 meandering miles inspired thousands of cross-country road trips. And what fun it must have been to travel its length. Taking its travellers from Chicago on Lake Michigan to Santa Monica on the Pacific Ocean (and vice versa), it traversed prairie, open plains, desert, mountains, valleys and countless rivers and creeks. What a trip.

Now that much of it has been bypassed by faster, cleaner and more sterile interstate highways, the Mother Road has become, for me and countless others, a historically significant relic of America's past. To those of us for whom it was once small-town America's Main Street, Route 66 represents a simpler time when family businesses, not corporate franchises, dominated the landscape and neon motel signs were icons of a mobile nation on the road.

One of the things that fascinates me is that by following the rutted paths of Native American trails in some parts, Route 66 could even be said to pre-date the arrival of white colonists in the New World. And the road as we know it today can trace its origins to the great migration west beyond the Mississippi in the nineteenth century. When I set off from Chicago, I'd be riding along a route with a pre-history that began in 1853, when the American government commissioned a survey to build a transcontinental railway for military and civilian use. But when the survey was complete, rather than investing in steel tracks, the wise guys in Washington chose to construct a network of wagon trails. Even in those days, it seems to me that the American instinct was to empower the individual to make his or her own way in life. In 1857 a wagon trail costing $200,000 was extended from the New Mexico–Arizona border along a line close to the 35th parallel as far as the Colorado River and linked into other trails to create a route between the Arkansas

River in Missouri and the furthest reaches of American expansion into the southwest of the country.

Fifty years later, when the first motor cars started to chug along American dirt tracks, the Washington wise guys' attention turned to creating a hard-surfaced road right across the United States. At that time, the main coast-to-coast road was the ramshackle Lincoln Highway, which followed a northerly route from New York to San Francisco, but few people made the trip and even fewer could afford a car. In 1912 the federal government started building a road from Washington, DC to St Louis along the Cumberland Road, an old wagon trail. From St Louis, it was extended along a path following the old Santa Fe Trail to Albuquerque in New Mexico before veering southwards to Flagstaff in Arizona. Called the Grand Canyon Route, the road then passed through Ashfork and Seligman to Topock on the Colorado River, where cars were loaded on to railway trucks and transported to Needles in California. The last section of road ran through the Mojave Desert to San Bernardino before heading due south to San Diego.

Except for a few minor diversions, all of that route from St Louis to San Bernardino followed what would later become part of Route 66. Then in 1914, Henry Ford, that genius of mass-manufacture, applied the methods he'd seen in the Colt Revolver factory to making cars. Within a decade of Henry Ford inventing his Model-T, the number of registered vehicles on American roads had leapt from 180,000 to more than 17 million, and motoring had become a means of transportation for the masses. For American families and businesses, the automobile promised unprecedented freedom and mobility. By the early 1920s, they were demanding a reliable road network on which to drive their newly acquired vehicles. In response, the federal government pledged to link small-town USA with all of the metropolitan capitals.

At last Route 66's hour had come. In the summer of 1926 the first interstate highway connecting Chicago to the West Coast was finally authorised. Officially designated Route 66, it ran from Chicago to Los Angeles, linking the isolated, rural West to the densely populated, urban Midwest and Northeast. Chicago had long served as a central meeting and distribution point for goods and people moving to the West, so it made sense for it to be the starting point. A large part of the new highway followed the old Santa Fe Trail and Grand Canyon Route. Cobbled together from existing roads and designed to connect the Main Streets of remote local communities, much of it was in poor condition. Speeds above 20 m.p.h. were rarely possible in Oklahoma, Texas, New Mexico and Arizona, where the road was often little more than a dirt track cleared of the largest boulders. Nevertheless, by running south to avoid the high passes of the Rocky Mountains, Route 66 was the first road from the Midwest to the Pacific that was passable all year round.

By 1929, the whole of the Illinois and Kansas sections, two-thirds of the Missouri section and a quarter of the road in Oklahoma had been paved. Even bikers like me would have been happy with that. But across all of Texas, New Mexico, Arizona and non-metropolitan California only sixty-four miles had been surfaced. Nevertheless, businesses in the numerous small towns along the route prospered as local entrepreneurs built service stations, restaurants, motels, campgrounds and entertainment attractions.

When the Great Depression gripped America in the early

1930s, more than 200,000 people escaped from the dust bowl states of Kansas and Oklahoma. Strapping their belongings on to their flatbed trucks, they set off along Route 66 with dreams of a better life in the promised land of California. President Roosevelt's New Deal programme increasingly eased their way, as thousands of unemployed men were set to work on the road as part of a nationwide investment in public works. By 1938, all of the Mother Road was surfaced with concrete or tarmac, making it America's first transcontinental paved route.

The highway experienced its heyday over the next two decades. As soon as America entered the Second World War in December 1941, Route 66 became the primary transport route for millions of GIs and mile-long convoys of military supplies, and a string of new military bases soon sprang up along its length, particularly in New Mexico, Arizona and California. Meanwhile, an unprecedented movement of people began as several million more Americans headed west to work in weapons and munitions plants, with the vast majority of them making the journey along the Mother Road.

After the war, the road remained as busy as ever. Millions of Americans, among them thousands of soldiers and airmen who had done their military training out west, exchanged the harsh climate of the 'snowbelt' for the easy living of the 'sunbelt'. With more leisure time on their hands, millions of others spent their vacations on road trips and sightseeing. Catering to the holiday traffic and migrating masses, the motels, campsites, cabins, diners, petrol stations, mechanics, tyre dealerships and souvenir shops multiplied. The most iconic Route 66 landmarks – those neon-lit diners, gas stations and motels that I love – all date from this period.

However, the Mother Road's huge popularity sowed the seeds of its own downfall. Like many of the roads that were constructed in the 1920s and 1930s, it was too narrow and structurally antiquated for the fin-tailed gas guzzlers and vast 'humping to please' trucks of the 1950s. President Eisenhower had been impressed by the German autobahn network he'd glimpsed during the war and his government decided that the nation needed a similar network of multi-lane highways, as much for military purposes (this was the height of the Cold War) as for use by commercial freight and private vehicles. So, starting in the late 1950s, sections of Route 66 were replaced by four-lane interstate highways until, by 1970, travellers could drive the entire distance from Chicago to Los Angeles along Interstates 55, 44 and 40 without ever coming into contact with small-town America. In fact, the interstates made it possible to drive coast to coast without even speaking to another human being. Stop, swipe your credit card, pump some gas, buy a snack, then floor the pedal to the metal until the next stop.

Life was slipping out of the Mother Road and in 1979 the Route 66 designation started to be removed from the hodgepodge of Main Streets, farm-to-market roads and rural highways that had once linked the two seaboards of America. Thousands of businesses that had relied on it withered and died. Some entire towns ceased to exist. The death knell for Route 66 itself finally sounded in 1985, when the Mother Road was officially decommissioned.

Yet Route 66 refused to die. Realising its social significance in America's short history, a band of enthusiasts kept interest in the road alive. In 1990 the US Congress passed a law that recognised Route 66 as a 'symbol of the American people's heritage of travel and their legacy of seeking a better life'. A few years later an official preservation programme was enacted by the National Park Service, turning Route 66 into a de facto national monument.

Now it was my turn to set out on the legendary Mother Road and fulfil the dream of a lifetime. As I packed my bags and left home, my only hope was that I would experience proper emptiness – that sense of being the only human alive for tens or even hundreds of miles around. I wanted to be in the middle of nowhere, totally on my own, enveloped by silence, like those scenes in the movies when you see the homeward-bound GI step off the Greyhound bus into a vast empty plain beneath a big blue sky.

I had made it clear to Nicky Taylor, the show's producer, that although I would obviously have a documentary crew in tow, I was determined to travel with no preconceptions about what was lying ahead of me. I told Nicky I wanted to keep the experience as pure as possible. Even if it drove the crew doolally, I wouldn't allow myself to be barracked into visiting places that didn't interest me. There was no way I was going to take part in stunts or make detours simply because they'd look good on television. I didn't want set-up meetings with weirdos and professional eccentrics, the kind of people whose entire existence depended on promoting Route 66.

I wanted this to be a personal journey of discovery. I wanted to experience every mile as it came upon me. When I woke each morning, I didn't want to know what I would be doing that afternoon, let alone the next day. What would happen would happen. The serendipitous nature of the trip was everything to me. Planning ahead would kill the adventure and the excitement. If that happened, there would be no point leaving home.

A few days later, I was standing on a fishing boat on Lake Michigan in front of a spectacular view of Chicago. Spread out across the horizon were the Willis Tower (still known by most people as the Sears Tower), the Hancock Center, with its two pointy spires, and dozens of other skyscrapers. You might wonder what I was doing on that boat. Well, I was there to have a good look at Chicago before setting off – like getting the target in my sights. It wasn't my idea and, to be honest, I found it a wee bit pointless. But these things have to be tried. Nothing ventured, nothing gained.

Personally, I am not a boaty man. The rising and falling on the swell, the false horizon and the diesel fumes combine to do me no good at all. They make me bitchy. And on that windy, overcast afternoon in late April, I was even bitchier than usual because, for some reason, I was pissing like a racehorse. I'd gone about twelve times by the time I had to shoot the first segment for the programme, introducing Chicago. But in the midst of all this, I heard something that made me forget my foul mood. The skipper told me he'd recently caught twenty-nine salmon in a single day. In Lake Michigan, of all places! I'd always thought that the lake was so polluted that nothing could possibly live in it.

To an ageing hippy like me, the skipper's news was a bolt of joy. Then he told me that commercial fishing has been banned on the lake. Another wonderful thing. Sometimes old idealistic eco-heads like me can get kind of depressed when we switch on the television and are confronted by programmes about people killing crabs or hauling in swordfish or hoovering the bottom of the sea in Alaska. Those fishermen tend to be portrayed as macho heroes who do a very brave and wonderful job, but to my mind they are vandals. So when I heard that they are no longer allowed on such a vast expanse of water as Lake Michigan, my heart sang a wee song. After all, it wasn't so long ago that Lake Erie, another of the Great Lakes, was officially declared dead; and the Cuyahoga River, which flowed into it, was declared a fire hazard. Can you imagine anything more ridiculous than a river being a fire hazard? But it happened because they poured tons of shit – logs, oil, old tyres, paint, flammable chemicals and, literally, shit – into it. The muck decomposed and created methane and other flammable gases. Then, in June 1969, the inevitable happened and the Cuyahoga did indeed catch fire, devouring two bridges in Cleveland – a city that people started to call the 'Mistake by the Lake'. What in the name of God were we doing to ourselves?

Fortunately, the fire sparked so much public indignation that a legal framework for protecting watercourses and lakes – the Clean Water Act – was passed three years later. And now salmon were back in Lake Michigan, which would never have happened without that piece of legislation. We have our arses kicked on a daily basis by people who don't know what they are talking about, so it's lovely to hear something that makes me feel a wee bit proud to be a member of the human race.

By the time we were heading back towards shore, I'd totally shaken off my grouchy mood. It was still choppy on the lake, but now I was feeling good about the world and excited about the journey ahead. I was going to have lots of fun. Meet lots of people. See lots of things. And tell you all about it. So come with me. Join me on Route 66. We'll get our kicks together on the Mother Road. Come on, I dare you.

2

Winding from Chicago

First things first. If I was going to travel the length of Route 66, I needed the right kind of transportation. A sleek saloon car would have been too dull; a 4×4 too plush. In many people's eyes Route 66 requires either a convertible or a fat Harley-Davidson. But neither seemed right for me.

I did my time on bikes in my youth, but I felt that like most other things of joy, the motorbike had become lifestyled and corporatised, a packaged form of rebellion of which I wanted no part. So, with the Chicago skyline looming in the distance, in a dirty backstreet squeezed between semi-derelict buildings and empty spaces strewn with boulders and rubbish, I met my steed. One hundred horsepower of mean, throbbing heavenliness: a Boom Lowrider LR8 Muscle. Officially, it was a trike, but for some reason I'd never been able to say that word. I'd always said 'bike'. Whatever I called it, though, it was a thing of absolute beauty.

Water-cooled and fuel-injected, it had a 1.6-litre, four-cylinder Ford Zetec engine and it rode like a dream. Most of it was fairly standard, but I'd removed the leg guards and some tan-coloured panels along the side of the black seats, added a pair of extra headlights and adjustable suspension, and replaced some parts with chrome or polished stainless-steel equivalents. It looked the business.

Now the thing about trikes – especially a modern, low-slung one like the LR8 – is that my arse is only about eighteen inches off the tarmac. I reckon it's partly for this reason that they have such a profound effect on people in their nice, safe, grey cars. I'd watch them as they drew alongside me, gawping, mouthing, 'Shit, look at that!' and wishing they were me. It happened countless times every day. Sometimes they lowered their side windows and leant out. Then the questions start.

'Oh, *man*, where did you get that thing?'

'What kind of engine does it have?'

'*Jeez-sus!* What's that thing you're riding?'

I just make shit up. When they ask, 'How many cylinders?', I say, 'Eight,' then smile when they shout, 'Wow! No way, man!' (It only has four.) But the trike is so outlandish to most people that I could make almost anyone believe almost anything. Compared with anything else on the road, it looks like a three-wheel Batmobile. It's a joy, it's funky and it's designed for showing off. A total poser's machine. Some people mightn't like that, but I don't give a shit what they say, because I love it.

My trike was like a cross between a hot-rod car and a chopper bike, but in fact it had all the disadvantages of a motorbike and none of the advantages of a car. I couldn't squit through a static line of traffic like a motorcycle – I was stuck in the queue with the cars. But while I was sitting there, waiting, I couldn't listen to Radio 4. There was no heater, so I'd freeze my bum off; and if it rained, my crotch would get soaking wet. But that was also the great delight of a trike – I'd be at one with nature, out in the fresh air, smelling and feeling and hearing my surroundings, immersed in the landscape. A motorbike offered the same sensation, but on a trike I could enjoy all that *and* lean back and relax. Maybe that's why bikers hate them so much, particularly those Harley-riding weekend bikers (which, incidentally, is another reason why trikes appeal to me).

One final thing I had to make clear from the very beginning of the trip was that a bike was like a horse. It's *my* bike. The production company might have bought it at enormous expense, and the film crew might be filming me on it, but it wasn't *our* bike. And it certainly wasn't *their* bike. It was *my* fucking bike. So, if anyone fancied sitting on it, they had to ask me fucking nice. And if they dared to swing their leg over *my* bike without asking permission, they would get a very old-fashioned look from me. At one point in the trip one of the girls in the crew climbed aboard to turn off the lights and my immediate thought was: *Fuck!* She never asked me!

But you should see the looks I got from people when I parked it. They gazed at it enviously and I knew what they were thinking: Oh, I can picture myself rattling along Route 66 on that thing, headphones on, singing along to ZZ Top's 'Sharp Dressed Man' or the opening line from 'Born to be Wild' by Steppenwolf – '*Get your motor running* . . . ' The trike brings out that in all of us, which is no bad thing. Forget Viagra, get yourself a trike!

Before I took the beast out for the first time, I did something I'd never done before. I strapped on a helmet. That's right, I bought myself a crash helmet. I'd always thought I was the last person on earth who would do something like that. I didn't know whether it was my age or the age we lived in, but before I left home, I'd done a bit of serious thinking. Now, some American states allowed bikers to ride without a lid while others didn't, but I wasn't going to go splitting hairs over it. It wasn't like I wanted to be on some kind of bloody crusade. I'd always enjoyed the freedom of wearing only a wee leather hat. After all, I had three wheels, so it wasn't like I was going to fall off. But then I started thinking that somebody might thump into me. Don't be a bloody penny pincher, I thought. Just wear a helmet. Then my wife said, 'Wear a helmet,' and that sealed it.

I'll repeat that. I *thought*, Wear a helmet. My wife *said*, 'Wear a helmet.' So I did.

Actually, that's a complete lie. I didn't even consult Pamela about it this time. But she'd always thought I should wear a helmet, even on my own trike in Scotland. So I decided all by myself: Cut out the crap, Billy. Get a helmet.

Then I thought of two more good reasons for wearing a helmet.

Gary. And Busey.

In 1978, Gary Busey was nominated for an Oscar for his portrayal of Buddy Holly in *The Buddy Holly Story*. He also appeared in *A Star is Born*, *Top Gun* and *Lethal Weapon*. But in December 1988 he had a bike accident. He fractured his skull and suffered permanent brain damage because he was not wearing a helmet. In time, he recovered, but life was never the same for Gary.

So, I found myself in a Chicago motorbike store, looking for a helmet. The choice was overwhelming. First up was a whole-face helmet, like the ones that assassins wear. It was easy to decide against one of those because the camera crew and viewers needed to see my face when I was riding my bike. But that still left hundreds of open-face helmets. I asked someone in the store for advice.

'Does this look okay to you?' I said. 'Is it the right fit?'

'Yeah,' said the guy.

Then I realised he was carrying a bag of groceries and didn't have a clue what I was talking about. He'd just wandered in on his way back from the supermarket.

Eventually I found someone who actually worked there and was instantly reminded that most Americans are brilliant salesmen. Not only did this guy sell us a helmet; he ran out and bought cheeseburgers and soft drinks for all the crew, told jokes, had a laugh and made us all feel absolutely welcome. A great representative of an extraordinary country.

I'm one of those guys who looks slightly odd in a helmet, so I had to be careful about exactly which model I chose. I tried on one that was very popular with American bikers – it looked a bit like a Third Reich helmet. I was relieved when it didn't fit, because I thought the Nazi look was much better left under the bed. In the end I settled on a black open-faced number with a visor. And to my surprise, having bought it, I didn't feel any less cool. I was even looking forward to wearing it. It was fitted up electronically so I could hear music on the trike, which was brilliant, like having a jukebox wrapped around my head. And it was rather comfortable, as long as I didn't put the visor up. If I did that, it caught the wind, so I decided that I'd either have to remove the visor or keep it down at all times. No visor, I suspected, was going to win, and I'd wear the helmet with my fishing glasses. 'Wait till you see them,' I told the crew as I tried them on with the helmet. 'They will blow you away.

They're yellow, kind of amber, polarised lenses with silver sides.'

I checked myself in the mirror to see how the helmet looked with the glasses. Pretty groovy, I thought. Windswept, interesting and much better than I'd expected. The salesman tried to sell me a pair of motorcycle gloves, but I'd already decided I'd go to a cowboy shop. Cowboys do much better gloves than motorcyclists. The problem with most motorcycle gloves is they do this thing, the go-fast look. Well, I don't like it. I prefer it more casual, because a trike's different from a bike. Bikes are for going fast, making a lot of noise and all that. A trike's kind of laid back. As I've said, it's a posing machine. And I knew exactly what I wanted to wear on my hands while I posed: tan-coloured, deer-hide cowboy gloves. Oh yes.

Sorted with helmet and gloves, it was time to christen the trike. I'd been looking forward to this moment, but taking the beast out for its virgin ride was a nightmare. It had a different gearbox from mine back home, so I couldn't find the gears instinctively. But once I'd studied a diagram and learned how to go through the gears, it became a joy; although, for some reason, I still needed to know Serbo-Croat yoga to get it into reverse. I liked to think the soul of the bike didn't want to have a reverse gear. It just wasn't right – bikes shouldn't go backwards. So I thought the bike was fighting it all the way. But once I'd worked it out, I was as happy as a clam. And, as you know, clams are very happy things.

With the camera crew ahead of me in a car, we did a big tour around the outskirts of Chicago so that I could get used to the trike. It was fantastic to see the city looming up all around me, like in a science-fiction movie. Then I rode into town and it was just great. The trike ran like a cuckoo clock.

The only downside was the weather. It was a dodgy-looking day, with the weather neither one thing or the other. One of those greyish, yellowy, funky, funny days. Every time I phoned someone in Scotland, they told me they were in the middle of a searing heatwave and I seethed with envy. That morning, I'd seen a weather report from Britain. It was mid-April and seventy-five degrees Fahrenheit, and everyone was running around in their underwear. I love the British fervour for throwing off our clothes. And the first people to disrobe are always the ones with the grubbiest underwear, like the guys I knew in the shipyards who put on long johns in September and took them off in May. Meanwhile, we were freezing our balls off in Chicago.

As I rode through downtown Chicago, past the famous water tower, I tried out the communication link with the director, Mike. It worked like a dream, and it was great to show him that I could talk straight to the camera from the bike. It meant that I didn't need to stop at a location before explaining it to viewers. I was dead against television that spoon-fed information to people. If I said, 'There's a water tower over there,' as I drove past, I could then talk about it later, knowing that the viewers would remember it. I didn't have to stop, lean against it, point and labour the point that I was talking about a water tower. We shot a piece about the city from the bike as we drove along with all the other traffic flying around us, before eventually arriving at the shiny black monolith that dominates the Chicago skyline.

For twenty-five years, the Sears Tower in Chicago was the tallest building in the world. But it was overtaken in 1998 by those cheeky upstarts in Malaysia with their twin skyscrapers, the Petronas Towers. So these days it was just the tallest building in America, but that was more than good enough for me when I visited it. Built as the headquarters of Sears Roebuck and Co., the tower used nine exterior frame tubes of different lengths, from 50 to 110 storeys, bundled together to provide strength and flexibility, avoiding the need for interior supports. It was said that the architect conceived this technologically innovative building when he watched someone shake cigarettes out of a packet.

Officially, the building was rechristened the Willis Tower in 2009, but it would always be the Sears Tower to me. Willis, a London-based insurance broker, leased three of the tower's 110 floors and gained the naming rights to the whole shebang until 2024. The name-change was not a popular move. *Time* magazine said it was one of the top ten worst corporate rebrandings, while CNN reported that many Chicagoans were refusing to acknowledge the new title.

Whatever its name, though, the tower was a beauty and I loved it. Riding up in the lift – or, more appropriately, the elevator – a recorded message reeled off some very impressive statistics about this 1,450-foot 'modern marvel'. In just seventy seconds we shot past the height of the Great Pyramid, the Seattle Space Needle, the Gateway Arch in St Louis, Moscow State University, the Eiffel Tower and so on until we emerged 103 floors above ground level. There were still another five storeys above me, but this was the viewing floor, which has the most spectacular views, if you like that kind of thing. All of Chicago, a large chunk of Lake Michigan and a fair bit of the State of Illinois were spread out around the tower. It was stunning.

Much of what made the view so spectacular was there because of the events of four days in 1871, when Chicago was devastated by a massive fire. At that time, the entire city centre, stretching over four square miles, was built of wood. Eighteen thousand properties were destroyed, 300 people died and 90,000 were made homeless. Only the water tower that I'd ridden past earlier in the day was left standing. It was remarkable to think that all of central Chicago was rebuilt around that tower. Nowadays, it served as a monument to the Great Fire of Chicago. (Incidentally, on the same day that the fire broke out, not far from Chicago, a forest fire killed even more people, but few people ever mentioned or remembered it.)

Once the fire had burned itself out, Chicago's mayor, a guy called Roswell Mason, sent out an all-points bulletin. He said: 'Tomorrow, one hundred thousand people will be without food and shelter. Can you help?' It worked like magic. People responded unbelievably well. Millions of dollars flooded in, and the cash enabled the city authorities to rebuild Chicago from scratch, something that had never been done on such a large scale. Architects, builders and anyone else with a good idea flooded in from all over the world. There was no rule book in 1871, no health and safety officers or building regulation inspectors, so the rebuilding of Chicago was fast and furious.

But possibly the most significant factor in the whole process was that seventeen years earlier, a bedstead maker in New York – Elisha Otis – had designed a hoist for lifting heavy equipment around his factory. Otis's device had ratchets fitted to the sides of the hoist. These ratchets, which allowed a platform to move up and down smoothly, also snapped into action at any sudden downward movement, preventing a lethal plunge. Otis immediately realised that he had something special on his hands, so he urged the bed company to market his invention. At an impressive public display at New York's Crystal Palace in 1854, Otis ascended on his hoist to the height of a house, then ordered someone to cut the rope with an axe. The audience gasped as the ratchets sprang into action and Otis remained suspended in mid-air. Everyone was very impressed.

Three years later, Otis turned his invention into the first 'safety elevator', which was installed for passenger use in a New York department store. Of course, it was more than just a gimmick. By transporting people rapidly and effortlessly upwards, it made multi-storey buildings practical and safe for the first time. Thanks to Otis, no one needed to fear the vertical abyss opening up beneath their feet as they ascended a skyscraper like the Sears Tower in a high-speed lift. If the steel cables hoisting up the cart snapped, they'd feel nothing more than a slight wobble as the ratchets sprang into action. The lift would stay put, suspended in mid-air until help arrived.

So, when Chicago's leaders started rebuilding the city centre after the devastating fire, they had the opportunity to build bigger, better and especially higher. Land was expensive and scarce, so developers went upwards not outwards. The Home Insurance Company Building, a ten-storey office block completed in Chicago in 1885, was regarded as the first true modern skyscraper. It was the first to use steel girders, which were stronger than iron, and the first to hang an outer masonry curtain wall on the load-bearing steel skeleton. Sadly, it doesn't exist any more, but there is a wee plaque commemorating it on Route 66. Of course, at only ten storeys high, it would be considered a dwarf in comparison with today's skyscrapers, but after it was built it was clear that the only way the city could go was up. In Chicago, the sky was the limit.

Standing in the Sears Tower, there was a real sense of where Mr Otis's invention had taken us, particularly when I stepped into the wee glass cubicle that jutted out of the side of the building, more than a thousand feet above the ground. It was like a high version of the Pope-mobile, and stepping into it was a real nerve-tickler, the creepiest feeling I'd ever experienced. Looking between my feet straight down to the street, something inside me insisted I shouldn't be standing there. I felt my heart pumping, my nerves tingling and my body shouting, 'Don't do this. Please don't do this. This is wrong. This does not compute. Go back. *Go back.*' I didn't know what anyone hoped to achieve by offering visitors the chance to walk into that glass box, except for a celebration that they weren't dead.

Like anyone who had ever stepped into that wee glass box, I really had to fight the urge not to do it. And that fitted with something that had always amused and amazed me about human beings. If you go up to a baby and roar at it, the baby will show signs of being frightened and will close its eyes. But then it'll open its eyes and want you to do it again. Well, it was the same thing with the glass box. The floor was going 'roar' and I was going, 'Again, again!' for the same reason that people freefall parachute. So, even though something kept nagging at me to get out of the wee glass box right away, I stuck at it, not least because the view was so remarkable.

Far beneath me, I spotted a line of yellow taxis turning into Adams Street. Although it was just a regular Chicago street, it was also the start of Route 66, from where I'd soon be heading out west. But before I turned my trike towards California, I had to visit a few places in the Windy City. Incidentally, the Windy City nickname is believed to have come either from the propensity of Chicago's politicians to make long-winded speeches or from a New York newspaper editor's accusation that Chicagoans tended to boast about their hometown. It was apparently not a comment on the notoriously nippy winds that blasted from the plains and Lake Michigan through Chicago's concrete canyons. Chicago was not significantly windier than any other American city, such as New York or Boston, although when the Arctic wind came off the lake and blew down Michigan Avenue, it could cut you in half.

Before leaving the Sears Tower, I made it up the final five floors from the glass bubble to the roof. Standing on the very top of the building, I stood like a dooley while a helicopter swooped from a great distance and filmed me pointing to the west. Easy enough, but the highlight of the roof visit was the story I was told of a guy who was painting the antenna and was microwaved. It's said that he cooked himself, losing the use of his legs because of the sheer power of the transmitter. It had the ring of an urban legend about it, but it still amused me.

One of the best things about the Sears Tower was that whenever I saw the building again, I'd know I'd been on top of it. Having already stood on top of lots of things, it added to the collection, which included Sydney's Opera House and Harbour Bridge. Both of them reminded me of my daughter, who once said the nicest thing. She was on the back of my Harley trike as we were coming over the Harbour Bridge, driving towards the Opera House, where I was performing a gig.

'God I love it here,' she said. 'I love being here.'

'What do you mean?' I said.

'When you're here, you know exactly where you are on the planet.'

I thought, Oh my goodness, so you do. It was absolutely true. Since then, I've become more and more aware of how iconic landmarks could do that to you – let you know exactly where you were on earth. The Taj Mahal did it. The Empire State Building did it. The Houses of Parliament and the Eiffel Tower did it. And so did the Sears Tower. Most of the time we didn't know precisely where we were, but those buildings made us totally aware of our place in the world. It was no big deal, just a wee jolly, but it pleased me no end.

Before leaving the tower, I looked out one last time from the roof and gazed southwest. Seeing my journey laid out in front of me got me thinking of what lay further along the road – Illinois, Missouri, Kansas, Oklahoma, Texas, New Mexico, Arizona and California, then the Pacific. Far below, I could see the thick artery of eight lanes of Interstate 55 snaking through the conurbation – the most popular way out of Chicago. Since the mid-1960s, it had been the official replacement for Route 66. As I mused about starting the journey, I heard the whine of a train horn in the distance. The loneliest sound in the world, but also one of the most romantic, it beckoned me to venture out into the vast plains of America and explore what lay along the mythical highway. But first I wanted to go on another quick spin around central Chicago, one of my favourite cities.

Whenever I'm in Chicago, I make a point of visiting Fort Dearborn. Nowadays it's just some brass plates on the road and pavement outside Fanny Mae's sweet shop on the corner of two city centre streets. I always stop in the shop to buy a few sweeties. They do a lovely plain chocolate caramel. If I could force one through the pages of this book, I'd give you one. Those brass plates mark the point where Fort Dearborn used to be located. For some unfathomable reason, I've always had a romantic image of the fort, which I used to think was the site of the last Indian battle on American soil. But I recently discovered that it was actually the site of a massacre of French pioneers conducted by Native Americans, supported by the British.

In the 1670s, French pioneers were the first Europeans to travel along the Chicago River. They settled near its mouth and claimed a large surrounding territory for France. About thirty years later, they were driven out by Fox Indians during the Fox Wars, which continued until the 1730s. At the end of the French and Indian War (the North American portion of the Seven Years War between Britain and France) in 1763, the area was ceded to Britain, which in turn lost it to the United States at the end of the American War of Independence. As a result, in 1776 the mouth of the Chicago River was resettled by a new wave of pioneers. Among them was Jean Baptiste Point du Sable, a Haitian farmer and trader who, as the first permanent resident of Chicago, is regarded as the founder of the city. (In case you were wondering, the city takes its name from *shikaakwa*, the Miami–Illinois Indian word for the stinky, leek-like vegetables that can still be found rotting along the banks of the Chicago River.)

In 1804 US troops constructed a log fort at the mouth of the river. They named it after Henry Dearborn, the Secretary of War, and a small settlement grew around it. The village didn't last long, though. In 1812 war broke out again between the

United States and the British Empire, including Canada. General William Hull, the Governor of Michigan, ordered the evacuation of Fort Dearborn, but Potawatomi Indians ambushed the evacuees, killing eighty-six and capturing sixty-two soldiers, women and children, among them the commandant and his wife, who were ransomed to the British. A posse of five hundred Indians was sent to do the gig, so it was not a small skirmish. Those troops and pioneers got wellied, and their fort was burned to the ground. It was rebuilt in 1816, but it must have been a tough place to live, as various wars with Winnebago and Black Hawk Indians continued to rage. Most of the fort was again destroyed by fire in 1857, and what remained was razed to the ground in the Great Fire of 1871.

I always liked to stand at the crossroads outside Fanny Mae's for a wee while, imagining flaming arrows flying overhead. On one occasion a young woman came up to me, a kind of hippy girl, and asked what I was doing. I told her I was thinking of Indians ambushing the pioneers.

'Oh, you like all that kind of stuff about Chicago?' she said.

'Oh yeah,' I said. 'Love it.'

'Do you like architecture?'

'Oh yeah. You bet.'

And it's true – I do. The Michigan–Wacker Historic District in the centre of Chicago, where Fort Dearborn used to stand, is an amazing place for gazing at buildings. There's a remarkable line-up of world-class architecture on both banks of the Chicago River, such as the gleaming white art deco Wrigley Building, chosen by William Wrigley, the chewing gum magnate, to house his company. There are several other stunning granite skyscrapers built in the 1920s and 1930s. But smack in the middle of all that fabulous beauty is a glass monstrosity, erected where another lovely white stone building used to stand. The modern eyesore was built by Donald Trump and, in my opinion, it's a piece of shit, so I always just pretend it's not there. It looks totally out of place, and it makes me quite angry that Trump was allowed to build it. He wants to be President, but I can't help thinking that the whole country would end up looking like a public toilet if he was ever elected.

Gazing at all of the surrounding buildings with the hippy lass, I pointed at what looked like a big, skinny cathedral. 'That's my favourite,' I said.

'Oh, mine too,' she said.

So we started to walk towards the *Chicago Tribune* Building, and on the way over she asked, 'Do you have old buildings in Scotland?'

I'm still laughing about that question now, but at the time I just said, 'Yeah.'

'We've got buildings here a hundred years old,' she said.

'Ooh.'

'Oh yeah.'

'Do you know,' I said, 'in Scotland, there's a place called New Bridge. It's called New Bridge because they built a new bridge there . . . in the seventeenth century. Mind you, they're still driving over the old bridge.'

The girl looked kind of bewildered, then wandered off. I'm sure she didn't believe a word of it.

It was a short walk from the site of Fort Dearborn to the *Chicago Tribune* Building and I crossed the river on one of the many bridges that could be raised to allow tall shipping to pass into Lake Michigan. On St Patrick's Day, they dye the river green in recognition of Chicago's large Irish community. But the dye wasn't really necessary, as the river had a weird green tint to it all year round. Walking over the bridge, I again had reason to doubt the origins of Chicago's nickname. The city might have more than its fair share of gasbag politicians and boastful locals, but that morning it didn't seem that way. My hair was the clue: a horizontal haircut. Try telling me that Chicago wasn't windswept.

Approaching the *Chicago Tribune* Building, the first thing you notice is the vertical stripes, which makes it seem much taller than its 462 feet. But move closer and it looks more like a Gothic King Arthur's Castle. This combination might sound incongruous, but it works brilliantly. It's a most attractive building, built as a result of a competition held in 1922 to design the most beautiful office building in the world. The architects won a $100,000 prize and the commission to build the tower. If they held the same competition today, I think the same architects would win again. They would certainly get my vote. I love it. I know some breathtaking buildings are being constructed, especially in Spain, but I don't think any of them compare with the *Chicago Tribune* Building. To me, it's a thing of absolute beauty. But there's more to the building than just the original design, as brilliant as that is.

The original owner and publisher of the *Chicago Tribune*, Robert 'Colonel' McCormick, had been a war correspondent and he went to Europe early in the First World War to interview Tsar Nicholas II, Prime Minister Herbert Asquith and First Lord of the Admiralty Winston Churchill. While travelling around Europe, he collected chunks of historic buildings, including a lump of stone that had been blown off Ypres Cathedral by the

German artillery. Initially, he just kept these as souvenirs, but then he instructed the *Tribune*'s correspondents, wherever they were in the world, to start collecting pieces of other famous buildings 'by well-mannered means'. When the correspondents arrived back in Chicago with their booty, the pieces of masonry were implanted in the outer walls of the lower storeys of the *Chicago Tribune* Building.

Now, walking around the tower, I kept spotting them, and it was difficult not to exclaim whenever I saw a chunk: 'Ooh, look, a wee bit of Edinburgh Castle!' or 'Wow, a chunk of the Parthenon!' Quite how the correspondents managed to collect all of this stuff 'by well-mannered means' was a mystery to me. Did they sneak up Edinburgh's High Street in the middle of the night with a sledgehammer and smash a chunk off the castle walls? I didn't know, so I suppose it was better not to question their methods and just enjoy the result.

There were lumps of masonry from Tibet, the Great Wall of China, the Taj Mahal, the Palace of Westminster, the Great Pyramid, the Alamo, Notre-Dame Cathedral, Abraham Lincoln's Tomb, the Berlin Wall, Angkor Wat – the list went on and on. In all, there are 136 fragments of other buildings implanted into the walls of the *Chicago Tribune* Building. As I walked around the perimeter, I took a wee look at each piece of Colonel McCormick's grand haul: the Royal Castle, Stockholm; the Ancient Temple, Hunan Province; Fort Santiago; St David's Tower, Jerusalem; a piece from the Holy Door of St Peter's Basilica in the Vatican; a wee bit of Pompeii; the Badlands, South Dakota – that was a nice one; the Monastery of St Michael of Ukraine; the Old Post Office in O'Connell Street, Dublin, where the Irish rebellion started; the Temple of the Forbidden City,

Beijing; a roof tile from some Roman ruins; a tiny shard of stone from the Cave of the Nativity in Bethlehem; a rock from Flodden Field in Northumberland, where the English gave the Scots one hell of a doing; then, next to it, a piece from the Tower of Tears in Amsterdam.

But my favourite is a fragment of Injun Joe's Cave, a show cave in Missouri on which Mark Twain based the cave he described in *The Adventures of Tom Sawyer*. I'm a Twain fanatic, so I was really disappointed when it wasn't where I thought it would be. But then, at the very last second, I came around a corner and there it was, my old pal sticking straight out of the wall. Just seeing it made my day. The smallest things can make me happy. I gave it a little rub, just to check I hadn't imagined it. Phew. I wasn't senile like I thought I might be.

From my favourite building I walked a few blocks south down Michigan Avenue, one of my favourite streets, past more magnificent architecture to Millennium Park, which adjoins Grant Park, where Barack Obama held his victory speech after winning the 2008 presidential election. Still marvelling at the fabulous buildings, I reflected that Chicago was a very beautiful place – a stunningly good-looking city – and Chicagoans generally seemed intent on keeping it that way, making it more gorgeous as they went along. It wasn't like Edinburgh, where the city authorities were in the process of plonking a big bloody tram system down the middle of Princes Street, the jewel in the city's crown.

It seemed to me that most of the world's beautiful cities – Venice, Rome, Paris, even Glasgow, which was a gorgeous Victorian city – were constantly under pressure from cretins who wanted to build awful eyesores, or demolish the beauty and replace it with car parks. I could only assume that the people who found themselves in positions of authority, which they achieved because they were desperate for power, seldom had any aesthetic taste. Meanwhile, the people who did have taste didn't seek power. So cities were constantly under threat because the tasteless people were always in charge. It saddened me. But walking down the streets of Chicago really cheered me up, because it was a living example of how a city could improve and get better looking all the time.

Then I arrived at Millennium Park, which was the cherry on Chicago's icing. Close to the shore of Lake Michigan, right in the middle of the city, this was a stunning park, but there was a huge row about it when it was built. Although it covered only twenty-four acres, it cost $475 million, more than three times its original budget, which the people of Chicago funded through a combination of taxes and donations. To make matters worse, it opened four years late, in 2004, long after the New Year's Eve it was meant to celebrate.

However, in spite of its shaky beginnings and huge cost, I thought it was a triumph, and incredible value for money. It will last a long time and Chicagoans will keep reaping its rewards. I only wished we had something similar in Glasgow.

It reminded me of a story I once heard about a city that bought some Jackson Pollock paintings. The authorities were harangued and mercilessly ridiculed by everyone who thought the paintings were worthless junk. Then, ten or twenty years later, the ridicule stopped as those people who'd complained and grouched discovered what a wonderful investment the city had made on their behalf. I hoped the same thing happened with Millennium Park. It was already Chicago's second most popular tourist attraction, and the area around it had the fastest-appreciating real estate in America. But what really mattered was that it was such a life-affirming place, thanks in part to its designer, Frank Gehry – probably the most important architect of our age.

Built over rail yards and parking lots, the centrepiece of the park was an ultra-modern, vast open-air concert venue that accommodated 4,000 in seats and another 7,000 on a huge lawn. A field of thick grass sloped down towards the Jay Pritzker Pavilion, a stage surrounded by 120-foot-high slices of brushed stainless steel that looked like ribbons fluttering in the wind. Above it all, a spider's web of criss-crossing pipes housed hundreds of loudspeakers, suspended above the audience to distribute the sound as effectively as inside a concert hall. It was unbelievable.

Nearby, there was a great sculpture by the Indian-born British artist Anish Kapoor. Although called 'Cloud Gate', everybody knew it as 'The Bean'. If you saw it, you'd know why: it looked just like a 66-foot-long, 33-foot-high, shiny, metallic jelly bean. Created using a huge number of stainless-steel plates weighing more than 110 tons, 'The Bean' had been polished to such a fine degree that I couldn't see a single seam. Jesus only knows how Anish Kapoor managed to do it. But what everyone loved about The Bean was the way it stretched and distorted views of the Chicago skyline behind you when you stood in front of it. And when I walked underneath it, I saw myself multiplied, repeated and stretched. It was like looking into a psychedelic kaleidoscope.

The area around 'The Bean' is extremely beautiful, and when we filmed there it was full of people, even though it was a very cold day. A mass of really happy visitors were taking photographs, wandering around, and smiling and laughing when they saw their reflections in the sculpture – surely that was proof of its value. Young and old alike were tickled by it. People even did little dances to see how their reflections would move. It struck me that 'The Bean' had a quality like the *International Camera Dance Movie* that for years I've been threatening to make. My plan would be to take a movie camera out of its case, put it on a tripod in an urban area, and just leave it running. Children would jump up and down in front of it. Adults would stop and stare. And whatever country they came from, people's reactions would be the same. 'Ooh,' they'd say in their native tongue, 'look – a camera.' Then they'd shimmy around in front of it, moving in for a closer look. You might think I'm indulging in my habit of digressing, but there's a point here. Just like 'The Bean', and in the nicest possible way, my movie would have no point whatsoever. They're both just fun and interesting and they make us smile. And a lot of good things have no point at all.

So, if you ever get the chance, have a look at the views of Chicago that are reflected in 'The Bean'. There's no point to it, but just go and see if it has the same effect on you as it has on everyone else. I bet it does.

A short walk from 'The Bean' is something else that would blow anyone away. Called the 'Crown Fountain' and designed by the Spanish artist Jaume Plensa, it's a pair of 50-foot-tall glass towers that display video images of a thousand Chicago residents in what looks like a big picture frame. I won't even pretend to know how they superimposed the images on to the 50-foot-high glass towers, but it's fascinating to watch as the giant faces smile for a few minutes, then pucker their lips all kissy-kissy while pipes send out large streams of water, giving the illusion that the water is spouting from their mouths. Kids absolutely love it, me included.

Of course, there's always uproar when a government or a council spends public money on something like this, as if art wasn't worth the effort of spending money. But then a government will go and spend billions on nuclear missiles and hardly anybody lets out a squeak. What's wrong with the world? You get an atomic submarine that's good for nothing but maiming and killing, and people almost applaud the thing when it comes into harbour. But spend a few dollars on a beautiful work of art and people are outraged. 'The Bean', the 'Crown Fountain' and the other parts of Millennium Park are a joy, yet people always moan about how much it all costs. The park is a lovely place to be, dynamic and relaxing at the same time. It's great. And you know what? I think it's a snip at $475 million.

From the park, it's a very short hop, skip and jump across Michigan Avenue to the original start of Route 66 at the corner of Jackson Boulevard. It's traditional for Route 66 travellers to have their final meal in Chicago and their first on Route 66 at Lou Mitchell's, which has been at 555 West Jackson Boulevard since 1923. It's a nice enough place that does an all-day breakfast and very good Danish pastries, but I had an appointment to keep around the corner.

Although the junction of Jackson and Michigan was the original starting point in 1926, it's no longer the place where most people begin their journey. There are two reasons for this. First, in 1933, after the World Fair freed up some land to create Grant Park, the start was moved a few blocks to the east – to Lakeside Drive on the edge of Lake Michigan. Then, in 1955, the City of Chicago turned Jackson Boulevard into an eastbound one-way street, making it impossible to head west on the original Route 66. As a result, the start was moved a block north to Adams Street, another one-way street, but going in the opposite direction.

If all of that sounds complicated, it's nothing in comparison to what happened to the rest of Route 66. Throughout its history, the Mother Road was more akin to a meandering river than a fixed road: its source and destination remained constant, but its route frequently changed to suit local circumstances. So shifting the start from Jackson to Adams is a very apt harbinger of what will follow in the miles ahead.

I arrived on Adams Street without my trike, as I still wasn't quite ready to begin. First, we had to shoot some publicity stills beneath a sign that marked the start of Route 66. I've never been a big fan of having my picture taken. To me, it's as bad as going to the dentist, a kind of root-canal vibe. The photographers are usually really nice guys, but I can't help feeling – when I'm doing something with my face, my eyes, or the angle of my head – that the snapper is thinking, Is this how this prick sees himself? I know it's probably just paranoia, but I can never get shot of it, so I always find the whole process kind of awkward, and I'm usually very glad when it's over.

That evening, I was especially glad when we finished because it was bloody freezing, so much so that I went out and bought some thermals afterwards. Something weird was happening to the weather in the Midwest of America in late April 2011. To the east, west and north of us there were typhoons, hurricanes and probably fucking tsunamis by the dozen. I had no idea what was going on, but it did occur to me that it might be the end of the world.

The next day I was back at the corner of Adams and Michigan, now dressed in my leather jacket and leather chaps, with a nice big crutch cut out of them – just what I needed to let in the freezing-cold air. I pulled on my helmet and threw a double-six to start.

Leaving early in the morning, I didn't need to be told it was a Sunday – it's a strange day all over the world. I've got a theory that if you were unconscious in a coma for twenty years and you suddenly woke up, you might not know where you were, but you would know if it was a Sunday. It's got a particular vibe to it, just like Friday night – my personal favourite. I think that Friday night feeling comes from the days when I had my welder's wages in my back pocket, all aftershave and shoeshine, going dancing at the end of the week at the Barrowland or the Dennistoun Palais in Palermo shoes with inch-vents on the jacket and sixteen-inch drainpipe trousers. Happy days.

Riding off on the magic trike to the sound of a busker playing a saxophone – of all things, it sounded like 'Careless Whisper' by George Michael – we soon left Millennium Park and the Art Institute of Chicago behind us. I'd wanted to pop into the Institute to see a specific painting, Grant Wood's 'American Gothic' – the one with the guy in his overalls holding a pitchfork, standing next to his daughter. But we never made it, mainly because of all that weird weather. And it was still weird now – we were heading straight towards tornadoes. I dearly hoped we wouldn't run into one. I'd seen a tornado once before, and it was more than enough to last me the rest of my life.

3

A Royal Route

I was travelling light. My golden rule for any trip is to clear out my mind before I leave home. Empty it so that it's wide open to every experience during the journey. It's like travelling with an empty suitcase that I can fill with things I find along the way. I don't understand why anyone would want to gather up all the things that surround them at home – pictures and mementoes and life's little luxuries – and take them on the road with them. The only things from home that are essential to me are my banjo and an iPod packed with banjo music that I listen to when I'm on my trike.

Riding through the centre of Chicago, almost every time I stopped someone called out to me, like the taxi driver who wanted to know what I was riding. 'It's a trike,' I said. Then a young lad on a skinny bike remarked on the quietness of my engine. 'It's got four cylinders,' I replied. This makes it a lot quieter than the single- and twin-cylinder Harley-Davidsons that usually cruise the streets.

A woman crossing the road yelled, 'Hey, Billy!' I nodded and smiled at her. 'What are you doing here?' she asked as she whipped out a camera and took my picture.

'We're making a film about Route 66. That's why I'm in Chicago.'

It was nice to be recognised by fans and passers-by. It made me feel all famous and warm and cuddly.

At the end of the block I passed under one of the most iconic sights in Chicago – the cast-iron legs of the elevated train system. Or the 'El', as Chicagoans call it. Nelson Algren, the novelist who wrote *The Man with the Golden Arm*, called it Chicago's rusty iron heart. It works like a subway system, transporting people far away from the traffic of cars, buses and trucks on the roads, but it's above the ground rather than below. I think it's absolutely beautiful. It's like the Forth Bridge to me – all rivets and girders and proof of how clever men can be. And it has the same impact as a red London bus or a yellow New York taxi. As soon as you see any of those things in a movie, you know exactly where you are. Usually there's a car chase going on under the El. Or people running along with guns, with one guy on the road and another way up above him on the El, trying to hide, legging it up and down stairs, or sprinting along the tracks and past queues of commuters, shoving them out of the way.

I wish we had an El in Glasgow. We almost did once. In the 1930s a guy called George Bennie built a prototype rail system called the 'railplane' at Milngavie, just outside the city. It was on legs and rails, just like the El, but the cars hung from an overhead monorail and had propellers powered by on-board motors at each end of the carriage. They looked like cigar tubes. Bennie reckoned his trains could travel at up to 120 m.p.h., but he couldn't find someone to finance his great idea and build it in Glasgow. That was a shame, because we Glaswegians could have had something like the El, but even more swanky. Sydney's got something similar now – the overhead railway – and it's hugely popular. It makes the traffic flow better and people like it because they can get to work easily. It's comfortable, it's funky and it looks great.

Because I like the El so much, I'd persuaded the director that we ought to film something about it before we set off on Route 66. But when we went to do it I was a wee bit disillusioned because the director took us far down the line, where the El runs along rails at ground level, not suspended above the street. What I didn't realise was that it's difficult to get permission to film on the inner-city section that I like. But then the director told me he had a wee trick in mind. We boarded a train a long way out of town and I interviewed a supervisor called Jackie, who is some kind of expert on the system and its history. While I asked her all about her job and the El, the train started to rise above the streets, and before I knew it we were back in the centre of Chicago. I got off the train and walked down the stairs, with the crew filming me all the way. Result.

It made me very happy, not because we'd found a cunning way to bypass the restrictions, but because I like to celebrate the achievements of the human race. I like to show people at their best. And I think you often see people at their absolute best in engineering. Of course, the El is a staggering feat of engineering, especially the riveting. There must be a zillion rivets in Chicago, and most of them are on the El. Whenever I see something like the El, or a big ship or an impressive bridge, I get so proud of my species. Which makes a change. It's our fault that the jungle is on fire, although I never set fire to a jungle in my life. It's our fault that the spotted lemur has got nowhere to live, even though I couldn't pick out a spotted lemur in a police line-up. I'm a nice guy. I want the world to be beautiful. So I like to point out the beauty of human creations, like the El, to give the human race a nudge, as if to say, 'Just look what we can achieve if we put our minds to it.'

Thinking about celebrating the beauty of mankind's creativity got me thinking about another of my pet theories, which is that newspaper obituaries should be closer to the front because they are often stories about the great unsung heroes of the world. I realised this when a pal of mine died some years ago. I read his obituary; then I read all the others in the paper that day. And I thought: My God, these are extraordinary people. How come I've never heard of them? They had found cures for diseases or helped children and innocent people escape from dictators all over the world. But we rarely took any notice of them because they were old. If we saw them in a supermarket, we'd never give them a second thought.

So I'm on a little one-man crusade to bring the obituary closer to the front of the paper. Let's sing a bit louder about the unsung. Rather than spending all our time watching stupid people doing stupid things and being filmed by other stupid people on reality TV shows, why don't we spend a few minutes each day reading about good people doing good things? I'm not being a hippy. It's just that we've got to improve ourselves as a species or we are absolutely doomed.

I was thinking about all of this as I passed under the El. As I slipped between its massive iron legs, a train hurtled overhead, as if to say: 'Look what you're capable of. Look at *this*.' It really is a magic noise – the sound of trains right in the middle of town. I bet the wee boys in Chicago just love it. I reckon they're crazy about it. But not everyone's as jolly and happy about the El as I am. Way back in 1892, the New York Academy of Medicine claimed that 'the elevated trains prevented the normal development of children, threw convalescing patients into relapses and caused insomnia, exhaustion, hysteria, paralysis, meningitis, deafness and death. And pimples on the willy.'

I'm sure you can guess which of those ailments I added to the list.

Continuing on down Adams Street on the trike, I was enjoying every yard of it. The concrete canyons, where you have to look straight up to see the sky, are really amazing to ride along. But I was soon twisting and turning to follow Route 66 out of the Windy City, passing down streets and avenues with names like Ogden, Cicero, Nerwyn, Harlem and Lyons. I think a lot of people are a bit disappointed when they discover that Route 66 isn't just one long, straight road but all broken up into various chunks and sections.

Not so long ago, in the days of prohibition, these outer parts of Chicago were once undershot with a spider's web of tunnels used by gangsters and bootleggers to distribute their wares to the speakeasies. Chicago is such a beautiful town these days – good and interesting and clean and lovely – and the city authorities now seem very embarrassed by all that Al Capone stuff from the 1920s and 1930s. When you ask them about it, they say, 'Well, it was a long time ago. It was a period we'd rather just put behind us . . . blah-di-blah-di-blah.' But the truth is that the prohibition era was one of the most interesting periods in Chicago's history, which is why we stopped to investigate it. I reckon you have to go to a speakeasy if you're in Chicago, so we did.

The American government made a criminal mistake in the late 1910s, when it bowed to pressure from the Anti-Saloon League and the Women's Christian Temperance Union and enacted legislation to shut down boozers everywhere. Can you believe it: every bar in America was shut. For thirteen long years, until 1933, it was illegal to make, sell or transport alcohol. As a result – you know everybody needs a wee drinky-poo – speakeasies sprang up everywhere.

Everyone imagines every speakeasy had a wee hole in the door. You know, knock twice, wait for the wee hole to open just a whisker, whisper, 'Joe sent me,' and sneak inside. But there were thirty thousand of them in New York alone – twice the number of bars there had been before the ban on booze came into effect in January 1920 – so there was no such thing as a standard speakeasy.

The one we visited in Chicago was on Wabash Street, not far south of Adams Street and the start of Route 66. It's now a very good restaurant called Gioco, but you can still see remnants from its prohibition days, when the front was a restaurant but the rear was a boozer that became more and more secretive, and much more interesting, the further back you ventured.

Something many people don't realise about that period in America is that, in the midst of all that prohibition, you were allowed to brew a hundred gallons of beer and fifty gallons of wine in your own house, but you couldn't sell it. No one was allowed to distil hard liquor, but that didn't stop the bootleggers. They called it bathtub gin in northern cities like Chicago. In the rural southern states it was known as moonshine.

Even though people were allowed to make all the beer and wine they could possibly drink at home, they still wanted to go out for a bevvy. Just like now, they enjoyed mixing and doing the how-do-you-do when they were drinking. Seeing a good business opportunity, a guy in his twenties called Al Capone, with a big scar on his face and a white hat, convinced the authorities to let him sell non-alcoholic beer.

I mean, what a lame story.

Capone made thousands of barrels of non-alcoholic beer and delivered them to the speakeasy on Wabash Street, among others. As soon as the police had inspected the non-alcoholic hooch, Al's mates would show up with big veterinarian syringes – the type that you usually shove into a cow's bum – full of ethanol. Pure alcohol, in other words. The ethanol was sourced from all over America, but the bulk of production took place in the countryside. Capone used Route 66 to transport the moonshine from rural areas to Chicago in false petrol tanks. The ethanol would be injected into the barrels and – Ta da! Off we go! – happy days were back again. If the cops turned up when the speakeasy was in full swing, there were escape routes through which the VIPs could make a swift exit. The rest of the clientele would have to face the music. And probably stop dancing.

Prohibition was hugely counter-productive. It actually *increased* alcohol consumption and promoted crime by igniting the bootlegging moonshine and beer wars fought by the Chicago gangs. Capone became the biggest and most notorious gangster in America when he took over the running of the Outfit – the syndicate of Chicago organised crime gangs. He was a major villain – in addition to bootlegging, he was involved in prostitution and bribery of government figures – yet he didn't lurk in the shadows. On the contrary, he became a highly visible public figure. Many Chicagoans even admired him, seeing him as a self-made success story. And Capone responded by giving some of the money he made from his illicit activities to charity, creating the image of a modern-day Robin Hood.

He kept plenty of the cash for himself, though, and lived ostentatiously. He held meetings in the Jeweler's Building, a forty-storey neo-classical office tower in the heart of Chicago with an automated car lift that jewellery merchants used to make safe transfers of their merchandise. Capone would drive his car into the lift, rise to the top floor, and enjoy a few drinks in Stratosphere, the speakeasy with the best views in town.

But on St Valentine's Day 1929 Al Capone made a big mistake. He sent his boys down the road to wipe out seven Irishmen. Disguised as policemen, Capone's gang showed up with machine-guns and mowed down their Irish rivals. (Curiously, one of the Irish gangsters wasn't a gangster at all, but a doctor. He was a kind of hoodlum groupie – he liked to follow the gangsters around town and act tough.) When the press published pictures of the massacre, the people of Chicago thought Big Al had gone too far and started to turn against him. Eliot Ness and his 'Untouchables' in the Bureau of Prohibition took a look at Capone's activities, but they found it impossible to link him to any serious crime, let alone the massacre. He'd covered himself pretty well and had the police in his pocket. Then they had the bright idea of taking a look at Capone's tax records.

Here's a thing. In 1927 Capone had made $106 million, but

he hadn't filed a tax return. So they hauled him in for that. He was fined fifty thousand dollars and sent away for eleven years, most of which he served in Alcatraz. While in prison, he contracted syphilis, which affected his physical and mental health to such an extent that he was no longer able to run the Outfit. By 1946, he had the mental capacity of a twelve-year-old. Eventually, at the age of forty-seven, he died following a stroke and a heart attack brought on by the syphilis.

Amazingly, Al Capone left us with a legacy that has nothing to do with booze. One of his charitable donations was a million dollars to provide milk for schoolchildren. But he insisted that a use-by date must be put on each bottle because he'd always hated the sour milk he'd been forced to drink as a child. It was the first time that anyone had had this idea, and it set a standard that's endured to this day. Isn't that the strangest thing?

The side-effects of prohibition weren't all bad, particularly its influence on the music industry and specifically jazz. Because it was the music of the speakeasies, jazz became very popular very fast, and it helped integration by uniting mostly black musicians with mostly white crowds. Chicago played its part in the development of jazz, but it played an even bigger role in rock'n'roll, which you could say was invented by black men (and women) in a little room in South Chicago, where Muddy Waters and all the other greats – including Chuck Berry, Bo Diddley and Etta James – made their first records.

That room was the recording studio of Chess Records, a legend in the blues and rhythm'n'blues world. In 1928 two Jewish brothers, Leonard and Phil Chess, arrived in Chicago as Polish immigrants. They started a few bars and by the 1940s had a nightclub called the Macomba Lounge. One of the singers

Mike Reilly

The Windy City – the starting point for my Route 66 adventure.

Tim Pollard

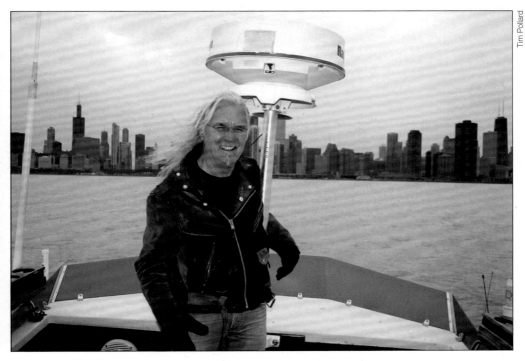

Lake Michigan. One of the best ways to see Chicago, as long as you don't get seasick.

Nicky Taylor

Me, director Mike (seated), and Mark, the sound guy, getting to grips with one hundred horsepower of mean, throbbing heavenliness – my Boom Lowrider LR8 Muscle.

Mark Atkinson

Mark Atkinson

Taking the trike for its first spin around Chicago. It ran like a cuckoo clock.

Maverick Television

The Willis Tower, or the Sears Tower as it will always be known to me and to many Chicagoans.

Maverick Television

Trying to overcome my nerves in the glass viewing box on the 103rd floor.

Maverick Television

The brass plates marking out the location of Fort Dearborn.

Maverick Television

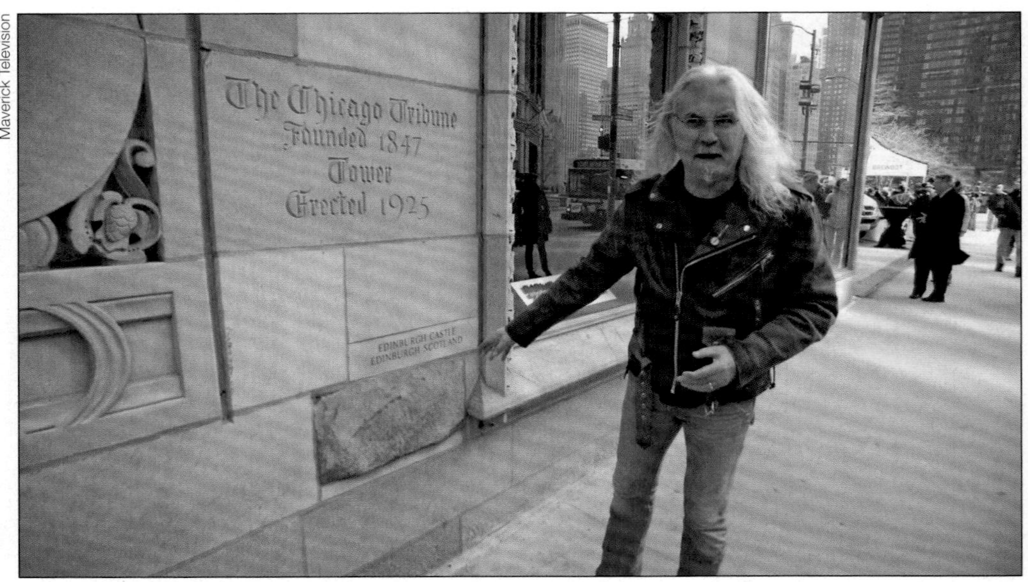

A wee bit of Scotland in Chicago – the *Tribune* Building, complete with chunks of historic buildings, including Edinburgh Castle.

Mike Reilly

Anish Kapoor's Cloud Gate (or 'The Bean' as the locals prefer to call it), and Jaume Plensa's Crown Fountain, both in Chicago's Millennium Park. I loved it here – a real life-affirming place.

Mike Reilly

Mike Reilly

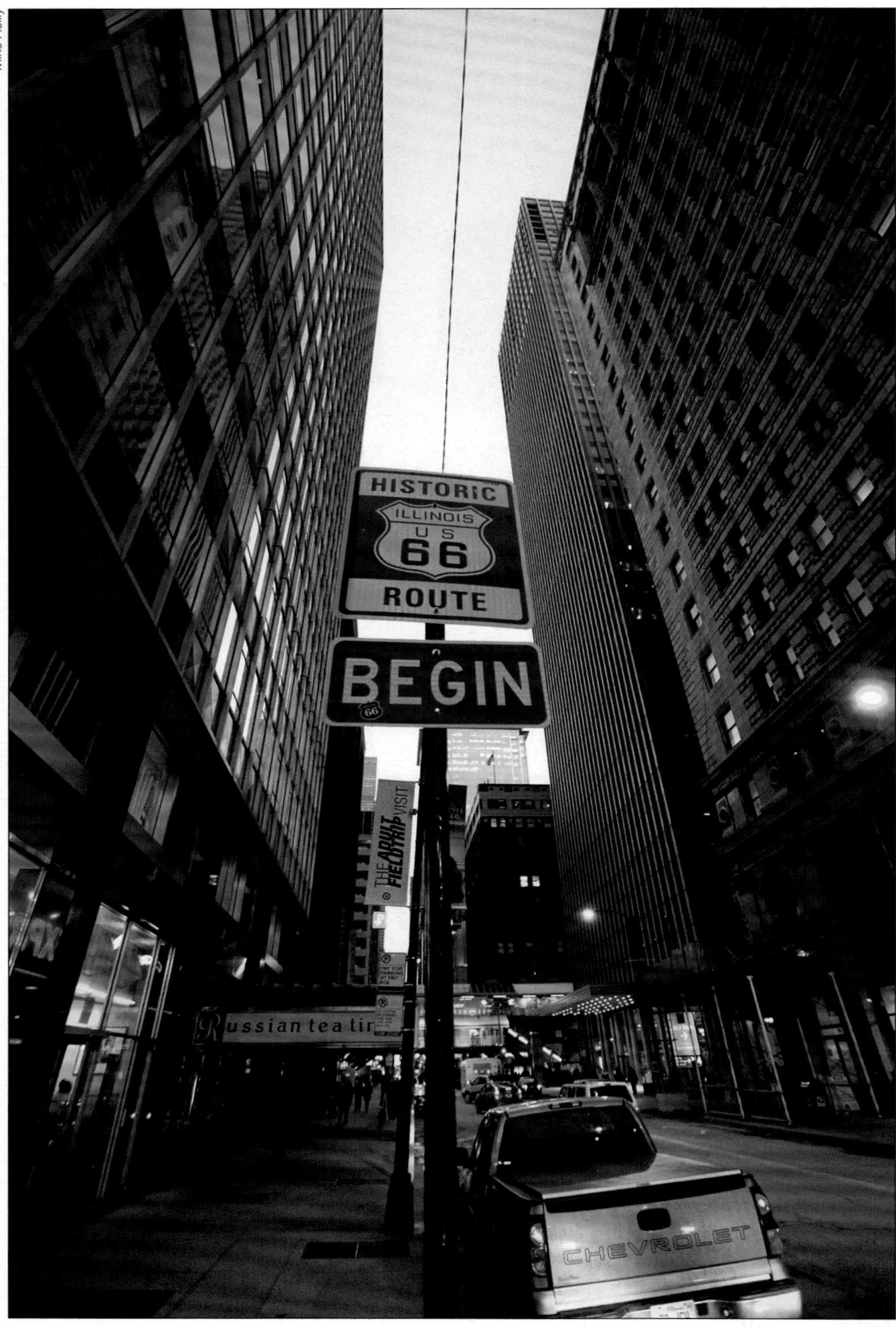

The sign marking the current start of the Mother Road on Adams Street – a block north of the original at the corner of Jackson and Michigan.

Mike Reilly

With supervisor Jackie, the tracks of the El Train in the background. I love the El – it's a staggering feat of engineering and really shows what the human race is capable of achieving.

Tim Pollard

The wall of fame at the Chess Records Building – the birthplace of rock 'n' roll.

Maverick Television

Heading out of the Windy City, and its gigantic palaces in the sky.

who performed there was a certain McKinley Morganfield, who boosted his earnings by busking around South Chicago during daylight hours. He was better known to everybody by his nickname – Muddy Waters.

The Chess brothers already had an interest in a record label called Aristocrat, so they used it to record Muddy's raw singing style, which perfectly reflected the spirit of the Chicago blues bars. The recordings were a great success, and soon Leonard and Phil were able to buy out their partners in Aristocrat and change the company's name to Chess Records.

Muddy's increasing fame drew other young Mississippi bluesmen to Chicago, such as Little Walter Jacobs and a twenty-stone farm worker named Chester Burnette, who soon became known as Howlin' Wolf. In their footsteps followed Sonny Boy Williamson, Memphis Slim, John Lee Hooker and Willie Mabon. All legends.

In 1955 Muddy introduced the Chess brothers to a twenty-eight-year-old singer and guitarist who was on holiday from St Louis. He sang 'Ida Red', a song he'd written himself. Leonard and Phil liked the song but suggested a new title. Renamed 'Maybellene', it was the first of many Top Forty hits for the guy from St Louis – Chuck Berry – who went on to write and record a string of hits that became signature songs of rock'n'roll: 'Roll Over Beethoven', 'Johnny B. Goode' and 'Sweet Little Sixteen'.

The studios and offices of Chess Records were based at several locations in South Chicago, but the most famous was immortalised by the Rolling Stones in their song '2120 South Michigan Avenue'. Nowadays, it's home to Willie Dixon's Blues Heaven Foundation. It's in a rundown neighbourhood that probably has never seen better days. It has that air of always having been a bit on the skids, but it's a real place with a proper sense of identity and a community that holds together when times are tough.

Walking up to the old Chess Records building produced a strange sensation in me. In a nondescript street with a wee garden on one side, initially it felt like a non-event. But then I noticed some iron figures set into the garden railings – like a guy playing guitar, who just happened to be Chuck Berry. Wandering along a wee bit further, I spotted another, recognised the guitar, and realised it was Bo Diddley. Before I knew it, I was standing outside the birthplace of rock'n'roll.

As soon as I stepped through the door, I knew I'd arrived somewhere special. It's holy ground – the Taj Mahal for anyone who likes rock'n'roll. Hallelujah central. And they let me in even though I'm about as black as snow. Then the funniest thing happened. Me and several of the crew all went very quiet and treated the place like a church. Nobody said 'Ssshhh!' or anything like that. A silence just fell upon us when we realised we were standing in the actual building where they recorded all those fantastic songs.

There's a wee museum with some posters on the wall from the old Blues Caravan tours. I remember those posters from when the tours came to Scotland in the sixties. They always looked great and the line-ups were terrific. I mean, can you imagine a show like the one I spotted on one of the posters: Jimmy Reid, John Lee Hooker, T-Bone Walker, Big Joe Williams, Curtis Jones and the Taylor Blues Band, all on the same bill? Even wee Mississippi John Hurt was there. And Memphis Slim. My God – what a night out. We used to love it whenever they came to town.

From the museum, I moved on into a large whitewashed room at the centre of the building. It was the room where all those hits – 'Johnny B. Goode' and the rest – were recorded. I touched a key on a piano, just to be sure I'd definitely touched something that one or more of the greats had once touched. Then I imagined Etta James and Bo Diddley singing, and Chuck Berry duck-walking across the floor, and all the others creating magic in that little room. Some of Ronnie Wood's drawings were hanging on one of the walls, but it was still quite hard to believe that the Rolling Stones had made an album in there. Can you imagine how that little room must have rocked over the years? I felt precious and churchy and I'm sure you would too if you visited Chess Records. It's a very special place.

I'd made my pilgrimage to Chess Records earlier in the week, before leaving Chicago on Route 66. But on the Sunday of my departure, a couple of hours before I left Adams Street, I returned to the neighbourhood for a unique experience. It had been a long time since I'd been to church on a Sunday morning, but now I was heading to Quinn Chapel, two blocks south of the old Chess Records building and an equally famous place in music and social history.

Quinn Chapel is the oldest black congregation in America. Services have been held there since the 1850s, when its congregation consisted mostly of freed slaves and abolitionists. When slavery was still a fact of life in the southern states, the chapel was a safe house on the Underground Railroad, a secret network of travel routes that were used to guide slaves to free states and territories in the northern United States and Canada.

In the years since then, a succession of black leaders and luminaries such as Martin Luther King, Booker T. Washington and Frederick Douglass, a former slave who became a leader of the abolitionist movement, have spoken from the pulpit at Quinn Chapel.

On its own that would be hugely significant, but Quinn Chapel is also where gospel music really began in America. I've always loved gospel singers, especially Ray Charles and Etta James. So I'd been looking forward to experiencing a service of the African Methodist Episcopal Church, but I was very nervous before entering the chapel because I'm as close to an atheist as you can get. I think I am, anyway. It's probably better to say I don't believe in religion. So I was nervous in case I offended the congregation by being a disbelieving voyeur sitting among them. Even though they didn't know it, *I* knew it. I'm not religious, but I'm not against people who are, and I don't believe in telling people that they're wrong. It's not the right thing to do. All of this was bothering me terribly, but as soon as I got into the church, a big whitewashed hall, I was so overwhelmingly and pleasantly surprised that I forgot all about my qualms.

First of all, there was a choir to one side of the altar and a girl standing front and centre, where the priest or pastor would normally stand. She was half singing and half talking, in that Aretha Franklin soul way. I nearly cried. My lip went all wobbly. I'm not joking, I had to tell myself to get a grip because there were a lot of people around me, singing, 'Hallelujah, hallelujah', and I didn't want to draw their attention.

I found a few empty seats and sat down to listen. Beside me was a chair with a Bible on it. After a while, a man in a light fawn suit picked it up, sat down beside me and started reading the Bible and mumbling. The service continued with more singing, more gesticulating and waving and praying, and I must say it pleased me greatly. A wonderful woman sitting behind the pastor was going, 'All right, all right' – agreeing with everyone – 'Yes, sir . . . yes, sir. All right. Yeah.' Then the man in the fawn suit turned to me. 'Would you like a Bible?'

I didn't like to say no.

He went off to get me one, returned, then pointed to his own so that I could find the appropriate page. I'm not a Christian now, and when I was a Catholic I didn't know the Bible – we used a missal to guide us through the mass (Catholics and the Bible have a funny relationship, but that's another story for another time). But I could follow the pastor's preaching. I was enjoying it and having fun with a little girl and her young brother who were sitting beside me, faffing around and getting them to laugh and joke and jest with me.

It was delightful. And what amazed me – even though it shouldn't have, because it's happened so many times when I've been among black communities – was the kindness and generosity of spirit shown to me.

The previous day I'd been to the oldest cigar store in America. It's in the centre of Chicago, next to the El. The crowd inside was mostly black and they were all watching the Chicago Bulls playing basketball. I had a shoeshine, bought my cigar and sat down. I'm not much of a basketball fan, but it was a very good game. One of the crowd of black guys recognised me while another thought I'd been in *Monty Python*. (It's a recurring disappointment for me in America. Maybe the association is because I did *The Secret Policeman's Ball* with some of the Pythons and that was a big hit in the States.) The guys were cracking jokes and having fun, then one asked if I'd like a drink.

'No, I don't drink,' I said. 'But I'd like to smell it, if you don't mind.' It was Maker's Mark, a Kentucky bourbon whiskey, and I had a sniff. 'Oh . . . memories. Memories.'

The guys all laughed and smiled. Then one of them stood up, came over and handed me a ten-inch-long Bolivar cigar. *A Havana*. 'Welcome to Chicago, Billy,' he said.

I nearly fell off my seat. Such friendliness, such overwhelming *bonhomie* and *joie de vivre*. And for *nothing*. All I had done was walk into the shop. And they had shown me such outstanding hospitality and kindness.

So I should have known better than to be surprised at the homeliness that was shown to me in Quinn Chapel as everyone who came near me shook my hand, wished me a good day and said they were glad I was there.

As I said, I'm not a believer any more and I don't think I ever will be again. I used to be quite a sincere Catholic when I was a boy, but it hasn't stood the test of time for me, especially when a child dies and some fool says, 'Jesus wanted him for an angel.' I just want to lash out when I hear something like that; I want to get violent. I think religion's time has come and gone. They're having a lot of fun just now throwing bombs at each other, aren't they, all the peace and love merchants. That said, the spirit and the sheer enthusiasm in that room persuaded me that if I was going to be religious again, that might be the religion I'd go for. I certainly came out feeling much, much better than when I went in.

It was just a joy watching that congregation of people at their best, worshipping as they saw fit. And what they saw fit, I saw fit. I wasn't jealous of their faith, but I admired it. I thought a wee bit of it would do me some good. It took me back to when I was a boy, when I had faith. And although that's gone now, visiting Quinn Chapel and being among a congregation of good people doing good was a happy experience, a wholesome thing to do. I'm glad I did it.

Chess Records and Quinn Chapel border on to a neighbourhood of Chicago called Bronzeville, which in the early twentieth century became known as the Black Metropolis after half a million African-Americans fled the oppression of the South and migrated to the city in search of industrial jobs. The city authorities confined the new arrivals to this borough, which extended over a very small area between 29th and 31st streets. The conditions were extreme at times. For instance, twenty thousand people were housed in four twenty-two-storey buildings within very close proximity to one another. However, this mass migration brought music into the area. Bronzeville was a haven for jazz, blues and gospel. The great Louis Armstrong's trumpet ignited the borough's many jazz clubs. Muddy Waters and Buddy Guy created electric blues here, while Quinn Chapel and the Pilgrim Baptist Church gave birth to gospel music.

Ever since then, Bronzeville has continued to bustle with celebrities, intellectuals, musicians and artists. The Regal Theater, located in the heart of the area, was demolished in the 1970s, but in its heyday it played host to the cream of twentieth-century American music. Nat King Cole, Ella Fitzgerald, Sarah Vaughan, Lena Horne, Dinah Washington, Miles Davis and Duke Ellington performed there frequently. The Supremes, the

Temptations, the Four Tops, the Jackson 5, Gladys Knight and the Pips, Count Basie, Dizzy Gillespie, Louis Jordan, Solomon Burke, Dionne Warwick, James Brown, the Isley Brothers, John Coltrane – the list of performers at the Regal is like a *Who's Who* of soul, rhythm'n'blues and jazz. What would anyone have given to be present at the Motown Revue in June 1962, when 'Little' Stevie Wonder, Smokey Robinson and the Miracles, Mary Wells and the Marvelettes and Marvin Gaye were on the bill? What a line-up.

But until the mid-1960s, when the Civil Rights Act was passed, travelling through America was frequently fraught for African-Americans. Restricted to segregated zones in the South and often discriminated against in other areas too, their journeys along America's highways – including Route 66 – were far from simple. Some motel and restaurant owners welcomed black Americans; others blatantly discriminated against them.

In 1936 a postal employee from Harlem, New York, came up with the idea of producing a guide to integrated or black-friendly establishments. Although initially it focused on businesses in New York State, Victor Green's guide was such a success that within a year its coverage had spread nationwide. Under a banner of 'Now we can travel without embarrassment', *The Green Book* was particularly helpful to African-Americans who travelled through what were called 'sunset towns', which publicly stated that 'Negroes' had to leave by sundown or face arrest. Known unofficially as 'The Grapevine', the book became the inspiration for that fantastic song, 'I Heard it through the Grapevine', recorded by Smokey Robinson and the Miracles, Gladys Knight and the Pips, and of course, in its definitive version, Marvin Gaye.

I went to meet Preston Jackson, an artist and activist who lives and works in Bronzeville, whose family made it across America using *The Green Book*. I'd intended to ask him about his family's experiences, but we ended up talking more about the effects of growing old – like those single hairs that grow out of your ears or eyebrows – and the absurdity of Pat Boone singing 'Tutti Frutti'. This lovely, intelligent, committed, talented man had come to the same conclusion as me and thousands of others: when Boone recorded 'Tutti Frutti', that paragon of clean living didn't have a clue that the song was about prostitution and gay sex. (The original opening lyrics were: 'A wop bop a loo mop, a good goddamn!/Tutti frutti, loose booty/If it don't fit, don't force it/You can grease it, make it easy'!)

Preston has remained militant in the most gentlemanly, pure way. He's a good man with a very good heart who cares deeply about the culture of his people and he tries to portray it through his art. He showed me his sculptures, many of which portrayed Harlem in its heyday and the years of its decline. We chatted about all sorts of things. Then, at the end of the meeting, my nemesis caught up with me again.

As I mentioned earlier, in America I am often mistaken for one of the Pythons. Don't ask me why, as I don't look anything like John Cleese, especially when my long, grey hair is down, as it was that day. Nevertheless, it often happens. People will come up to me and say, 'Excuse me. Are you John Cleese?'

Or they'll say, 'I love your work.'

'Oh, thanks very much,' I'll respond.

'So how are the other guys?'

'Who?'

'The rest of the *Monty Python* crew. Eric? Michael?'

And my heart sinks.

Sometimes I tell them I'm not John Cleese. 'No, I'm a Scottish comedian,' I say. 'My name's Billy Connolly.'

'Oh? Incognito?' And then they do the nudge, nudge, wink, wink thing.

As it happened, earlier that day I'd told the crew about being mistaken for John. I could see that some of them only half-believed me. After all, no Brit would confuse my Glaswegian brogue for John's clipped English vowels. But then, as I came downstairs from Preston's gallery, a big black guy tapped me on the shoulder.

'Are you John Cleese?'

'No, I'm Billy Connolly.'

'Oh . . . incognito?'

Nicky, the producer, just exploded. The truth was revealed before her very eyes.

Now I was back on my trike, heading southeast on Route 66, gradually coming to the edge of Chicago. It's always weird when you leave a city. No matter how much you like the place, the outskirts always suck. You go from these gigantic palaces in the sky, like the *Chicago Tribune* Building and the Sears Tower (which I could see in my mirrors for ages) and then the surroundings get more and more shabby and rundown. The Windy City is a brawny kind of place, and here at its fringes are the factories, slaughterhouses and foundries on which it built its industrial might and reputation. The road darts between warehouses and over railroad tracks and makes a few turns. Then, suddenly, we were out in the countryside, joining

Interstate 55 for about eight miles (it was built directly over Route 66 here, so you can't avoid it) before leaving it to rejoin old 66. Even here, out of town and in the proper outdoors, it was a bit shabby, largely because it was reclaimed mining land and there was still a kind of messiness to it. And the weather didn't help. It was another grey and windy day. Although I like rain and what it does, I was starting to feel we really hadn't been blessed with good weather since arriving in Chicago. A bit of sun would have been welcome, especially now that we were on Route 66. Everybody's image of the Mother Road involves bright colours – red and yellow, white and blue – rock'n'roll, hamburgers and hot dogs, Jerry Lee Lewis and Chuck Berry. But I was getting rained on all the time and somehow it didn't fit.

A few minutes later, I entered Romeoville, a town about thirty miles southwest of Chicago. Nestling between urban areas, this part of Illinois was mostly agricultural country, and Route 66 was flanked by wide-open plains that looked like potato fields, only occasionally broken up by sparse lines of trees or telegraph poles. Much of the produce from these fields used to be shipped from Romeoville along the Des Plaines River, which passes through the town, and the Illinois & Michigan canal system. Nowadays, nearly all of it goes by road.

Romeoville used to be called Romeo when it was part of a twinned community with Juliet, a few miles further down Route 66. That romantic association ended in 1845, when someone realised that Juliet was most likely a misspelling of the name of the French pioneer Louis Jolliet, who first explored the area in the 1670s. The town decided to change its name in honour of him, but it still didn't get the spelling quite right. It's now known as Joliet. Meanwhile, jilted by its twin, Romeo acknowledged the busted romance and became Romeoville. Nowadays, it plays very much second fiddle to Joliet, which is the first significant city beyond the sprawl of Chicago.

You might have heard Joliet mentioned in television crime programmes. It used to be a quarry town, nicknamed 'Stone City'. Much of that lovely white stone seen on skyscrapers like the Wrigley Building in the heart of Chicago came from Joliet's quarries. But these days the town is most famous for its prisons. They are the biggest industry in town. Imagine prison being your biggest industry – holy moly! – but that's one of the strangest things about America. The Land of the Free incarcerates more of its people than any other country on earth.

Joliet's most famous prison, the Joliet Correctional Center, is known to millions of *Blues Brothers* fans as the lock-up from which Jake Blues is released at the beginning of the movie. It is also name-checked in Bob Dylan's 'Percy's Song'. But it closed in 2002 and all the prisoners were moved to a much larger maximum-security facility, the Stateville Correctional Center, a vast compound on the edge of town that used to have a death row and conduct executions by lethal injection. It's the kind of isolated place in which the US government is hoping to house some of the terrorist suspects who are currently stuck down in Guantanamo Bay. There's another clink, the Will County Adult Detention Facility, on the other side of town, so you could say Joliet is book-ended by slammers.

Driving through the outskirts of town, I passed an ice-cream parlour with a couple of *Blues Brothers* figures on its roof. Gimmicks like those two figures have been features of Route 66 ever since its heyday, when restaurants and motels would go to extraordinary lengths to attract the attention of passing drivers.

There's not much more to say about Joliet. It's a pretty wee town with a river flowing through the middle, but, based on my experience, no people in it – except for one guy running along a pavement. I hope he hadn't escaped from prison.

4

It Starts in Illinois, Let Me Tell You Boy

A few more miles through the tall-grass prairies of Illinois, I arrived in Wilmington, turned a corner and came face to face with a wonderful sight – a twenty-eight-foot-high green spaceman in a silver helmet who advertised a drive-in restaurant called the Launching Pad.

Big guys like him are still common sights on Route 66. Some travellers make a thing out of trying to spot as many of them as possible. Originally, these giants were designed to catch the eye of potential customers who were driving past so that people would say, 'Gee look, a giant. Let's go and eat there.' Later, when the interstates bypassed a lot of the communities on Route 66, even bigger giants were built, to catch the attention and wallets of people cruising past.

The owner of the Launching Pad bought his spaceman at a restaurateurs' convention in 1965 for three thousand dollars. Which begs the question: what kind of person lugs a twenty-eight-foot spaceman to a convention? I always thought conventions were held in hotel suites, and I can't imagine anyone dragging a twenty-eight-foot astronaut into the Glasgow Hilton, no matter how much I stretch my imagination. But this fella had bought his giant spaceman for three thousand bucks and good on him, the entrepreneur that he was. I just wonder what he said to his wife when he brought it home. 'Darling, I've got you a present . . . '

When that fella bought the big guy, it was just a big semi-naked model. Someone used to make a standard roadside giant – they all had the same trousers and always held their hands out in front of them. So the owner of the Launching Pad held a competition to give his giant a name and decide how he should be dressed. A ten-year-old girl won the contest with her suggestion of Gemini – after the Gemini space programme, which was all the rage at the time. They made a big space helmet and a rocket, which they put in his hands. The helmet made him look a bit like a giant welder, but maybe that's just me. Strangely, two rockets have been nicked from his hands so far, although I can't imagine what the dirty swines do when they steal a six-foot polystyrene rocket. It's rather tragic. Did they take them home and play with them?

As far as luring people off the interstate, the Gemini Giant would certainly work for me. I can just imagine my kids when they were younger – 'Dad, take us there. I wanna go to where the rocket man is. Take us there, Dad. Come on, Dad, *come on*.' I'd cave in. And anyway, I've always loved that kind of thing myself – that part of America that's always viewed as big and vulgar, but which really appeals to me. Things like the biggest chair in the world, the biggest frying pan and the tallest thermometer. I love all that. There's something of the sideshow about it, something Coney Island, that tickles me. It's fun and Americans know what fun is. After all, they've got the only constitution in the world with the word 'happiness' written into it.

American adults believe in having fun. They've got more toys than us Europeans. If you go into an American's garage, you'll find a four-wheeled vehicle and a three-wheeled vehicle and bicycles and boats and dirt bikes and a motor home. I'm in total agreement with them. Life is supposed to be fun. It's not a job or an occupation. We're here only once and we should have a bit of a laugh. So these big men by the side of the road totally appeal to me.

Wilmington itself is a nice enough place. There's a dinosaur model on top of a tyre garage and a few other remnants of Route 66's heyday in the main street, such as a boarded-up drive-through restaurant.

Pushing on, heading for Pontiac, I was cruising happily when my eyes darted from the road and right there, in a diner's car park in Bramlington, I spotted Elvis, James Dean and Betty Boop. Yelling at the crew, who were driving ahead of me in the truck, I pulled over. The Route 66-themed, 1950s-style joint – the Polk-a-Dot Drive-In – was a charming place, but this was Easter Sunday and it was closed. In Britain it would have been open, but they take the Christian thing more seriously in these parts. Outside the diner, lined up along a wall, stood those three fibreglass, slightly larger-than-life-size effigies. There was space for one more, which I later discovered had been occupied by Marilyn Monroe, with her white dress billowing in the classic pose from *The Seven-Year Itch*. I had some fun with Elvis and Betty. I cleaned up her skirt and posed and jived around in front of them, making a fool of myself, before moving on down the road.

After just two miles I came to Godley, a tiny place with a population of less than six hundred but a racy history. Not so much a town as a single street with a collection of buildings on either side, Godley has a geographic quirk that shaped its destiny. The left side of the main street, which crosses Route 66, is in one county and the right side is in another. You might think that's nothing special, but in the 1930s, when the Illinois coal mines and stone quarries were in full swing, it made Godley the hottest destination for miles around on a Friday night. Loaded up with their end-of-week pay, the miners and quarrymen would head for Godley, knowing there was a brothel there that had a unique way of evading the law. Some enterprising resident had turned a railway carriage into the brothel and parked it on the line. The lads would turn up and get down to drinking and shagging their earnings away. If word came down that there was going to be a raid, a shout would go up and all the lads would interrupt their activities to push the carriage into the neighbouring county. Once across the county line, neither police force could do anything about it. The crime had been perpetrated in one county, but they were now in the neighbouring county, so unless they got down to business again, they were back to being law-abiding citizens.

Driving through Godley, I could barely concentrate on the road, I was laughing so much at the mental image of all those bare-arsed men diving out of bed to push the carriage into the next county while the hookers looked on and the two counties' police forces scratched their heads, unable to do anything about it. The thought of a bunch of mad-shagging train-pushers made my heart sing. There's something wonderful – and very pragmatic, in that typically American, no-nonsense way – about a brothel on wheels. And to think the little village was called Godley. It should have been called Godless.

At first glance, Pontiac is just an ordinary town, like hundreds, maybe even thousands, of others in the Midwest of America. Located smack bang on Route 66 and built around a town square with a county courthouse on one side, it's like so many small towns portrayed in so many Hollywood movies. It was even used as the setting for *Grandview, USA*, a 1980s romantic comedy starring Jamie Lee Curtis, Patrick Swayze and John Cusack. *Time* magazine called it one of the best small towns in

America. You can imagine the kind of place – there are shops and restaurants around the square, and the courthouse has a clock tower, just like the one in *Back to the Future*.

It's the kind of place where you can picture that whole American Dream thing happening – people setting up in Pontiac and making successes of their lives in a modest, wholesome way. Those sitcoms of the fifties and sixties suddenly come alive when you're in Pontiac; you realise they were based on real life. Then, in June 2009, the town's local government did an amazing thing. It invited 160 artists to paint nineteen murals in the town in just four days. The council put up the artists, fed them and gave them booze, and the whole thing turned into a huge party. And, if you ask me, it was a huge success.

The murals were painted by a group of artists called Walldogs, which is what the commercial painters of old were often nicknamed. The group's members came from all over the world, and their paintings aren't anything like those ghastly murals that look half like graffiti and always give me the pip. These murals are handsome replicas of the advertisements that used to be painted on the sides of businesses at the turn of the twentieth century. They are very detailed figurative paintings, beautifully executed, and they make the town look smashing.

Residents of Pontiac stumbled on the idea of having their lovely town bedecked in murals after they had commissioned a Route 66 mural for the centre of the town. It was a simple image – the Route 66 highway shield – but it immediately drew visitors to the town. The nineteen murals painted in 2009 have been even more successful, doubling tourist numbers. I'm not surprised.

I went for a walk round Pontiac to have a good look at the murals. They were all a delight, but I was most tickled by the one for the Allen Candy Company. It appeared to have been painted by several artists (the signatures read: 'Roy, Noah, Brad, Teddy and Jackie'), and apparently one of them had owned a dog that died the week before the mural was painted. So the artist had the dog cremated and mixed its ashes in with the paint. Now the dog is part of the mural. I loved that.

There's more to Pontiac than the murals. They've also had funky wee cars inspired by Route 66 – each about the size of a kiddie's pedal car – placed around the town. With the cars dotted all over the place and bolted to the ground, I had to watch my step, particularly on street corners. On the steps of the courthouse there's a particularly weird car with a windswept Abraham Lincoln sitting in the back seat. Long before he became President, Lincoln had tried his first case as a lawyer in Pontiac. It was a strange thing to imagine as I strode around the town, dodging the wee cars and other artworks and admiring the murals.

Some of the cars were painted in rainbow colours. One, a wee beauty called 'Pussy Footin' around Downtown', had a leopard-skin pattern. Another, with big sunglasses and a cheesy smile, was called 'InCARgnito'. Then there was a brightly coloured van called 'Vincent "I'm not a Van" Gogh' that had a reproduction of one of Van Gogh's paintings on it.

There are also pyramids and all sorts of nonsense, such as a pair of man-sized footprints in the concrete pavement next to a set of doggie paw-prints, so that it looks like some guy was just there, walking his dog. It's terrific that a town will go to such lengths to cheer itself up. When you see so many towns falling into the abyss with pound shops and charity stores everywhere, it's lovely to see one making the effort to tart itself up a bit.

Before I give the impression that Pontiac is a wee bit of heaven on earth, I ought to get something off my chest that bothered me right from the start of the trip. It's not something unique to Pontiac, but by the time I reached the town it had become really hard to ignore. If this book inspires you to travel along Route 66 and you're hoping to eat well, think again. There's not much decent or wholesome – or even particularly healthy – food to be found along the Mother Road. There are plenty of pancakes and burgers and shakes and fries, but after a while it becomes a very monotonous diet.

The night before I toured Pontiac, I visited a restaurant and ordered the broasted chicken. I only had it to see what *broasted* was. I soon discovered it meant broiled and roasted, or what most people would call burned. Maybe I should have known better when I saw the menu. It had pictures of the food, which is always a dead giveaway (unless you're in Japan, where the food is invariably fantastic, even though the restaurants often have wax replicas of their dishes in the window). If you're on Route 66 and you stop at a place where the menu has pictures of the grub, you'd be well advised to carry on until you find somewhere better. Unfortunately, along Route 66, there aren't too many better places. I know it sounds deeply snobbish, and I probably shouldn't say it, but the amount of fat and sugar and junk eaten in Middle America is scary. That's why everyone's getting obese.

However, there's a silver lining to every cloud. In this case, we have the inventor of one of the staples of unhealthy fast-food cuisine – the Cozy Dog – to thank for also creating one of the greatest artists associated with Route 66 – Robert Waldmire. Route 66 attracted a lot of poets, writers, painters, wanderers and all sorts of scallywags who were just in love with the road and made it their whole life. Bob was one of them. He was due to paint a mural in Pontiac in 2009, but he died before he could carry out the commission. Now a bunch of artists are going to get together and paint one in his memory.

Bob grew up watching the Route 66 traffic pass by his parents' restaurant in Springfield, Illinois (which was where his father, Ed, came up with the Cozy Dog, of which more later). In 1962 Ed took the whole family on a road trip along the 66 to California. Bob, who was already an accomplished artist at school, was hugely inspired by what he saw and fell in love with everything to do with the Mother Road – the motels, diners and truck stops, and particularly the Arizona and New Mexico deserts. He decided he wanted to spend his time travelling the route, but first he went off to university, where he spotted a fellow student's illustration of the local town. Wishing to do something similar for his hometown, Bob had a brainwave: he would get local merchants to pay him to include their businesses in his poster.

Bob appears to have been completely different from his father. He was a hippy type, a big, bearded vegetarian who ate 'not dogs' rather than hot dogs. His illustrations are very like those of Robert Crumb, very intricate and detailed, with little buildings in the plan of a town, all seen from above. He'd include all the details, like telegraph poles and street signs. They're very, very good.

His first poster was a great success, both critically and commercially. Bob made even more money from selling it to local residents than he'd made from getting the businesses to pay up front to be included in it, so he set off to visit college towns, repeating the formula as he travelled. This one idea changed his life for ever. Provided he lived relatively cheaply, he could travel back and forth across America supported entirely by his illustrations. Best of all, it meant that Bob, who hated the cold, could spend winters in his beloved desert, drawing the buildings, towns and landmarks of Route 66. These drawings became famous icons of the road themselves, as did the orange 1972 VW campervan in which he travelled. When Pixar made *Cars*, they based Fillmore, the VW bus character, loosely on Bob Waldmire.

Some of Bob's best work was his set of four large and highly intricate state posters of Route 66 winding through California, Illinois, New Mexico and Arizona. Filled with hundreds of drawings of scenic vistas, sketches of the wildlife and historical attractions, they also contained short philosophical comments, quotes from literature and pleas for peace, non-violence and sound ecological practices, many of them quietly rebellious. 'It is estimated that Lake Mead and Lake Powell [two massive reservoirs created by the damming of the Colorado River] evaporate more water per year than the multi-billion-dollar central Arizona project will provide annually,' it said on the Arizona poster. And on his New Mexico poster: 'The state has a cradle to grave affair with nuclear technology – the atom bomb was born here, nuclear wastes are buried here.'

But, personally, I think Bob did his best work when he turned his pen on hunters and really went to town. 'The campaign to "control" the coyote is more like a war of extermination,' he wrote in small print on his poster of Silver City, Arizona. 'The

Steel Jaw-Leghold Trap . . . Scourge of the Earth.' However, a hunting shop spotted the comments and threatened to sue Waldmire. Fortunately, he managed to get the law on his side and avoid court.

While I was in Pontiac, they were displaying Bob's old converted bus in which he used to spend the winter travelling through the southwestern states. It's one of those yellow American school buses with corrugated sides, but Bob added solar panels, rainwater collectors, a solar oven, a sauna and solar shower, and all sorts of gizmos so that he could live off-grid when he was in the desert. From the outside, it looks a bit ramshackle, but it's an absolute dream machine. It's even got a veranda and an observation deck on the back. I was so jealous.

It was a bit of a squeeze to get in the bus, but well worth the effort. With his old shoes still lying near the steering wheel by the front door, and all his bits and pieces dotted about on shelves and tables and walls, it's the cosiest place. All of Waldmire's wee favourite things are still in there – ornaments, pictures, photographs of Mahatma Gandhi and Martin Luther King, key rings and things that other people would consider junk – so it's like stepping into Bob's dream world. I don't know what would have happened in an emergency stop in this bus. Everything would have ended up beside him on the floor, I imagine.

All in all, the bus is an amazing thing. A great way for an artist to live, going away for four or five months every winter, a real free man. Before visiting it, I was kind of reluctant to go and see it. I wondered what the hell I'd have to say about a school bus in which a guy buggered off to New Mexico every winter. It seemed a limited subject. But when I got there I was delighted. It made me wish I'd known Bob Waldmire personally. He seemed like an amazing fella. And Pontiac is all the better for having his bus parked there.

Outside the town, there's another Route 66 landmark that's worth a look if you're passing. In 1926 Joe and Victor 'Babe' Seloti built a diner and petrol station on the road that would become Route 66 in a couple of months' time. They named it the Log Cabin Inn. Close to the railway line and built of cedar telephone poles, it seated forty-five customers. The interior still has the original knotty pine walls. After the war, Route 66 was widened to four lanes and moved to the west side of the Log Cabin, which left the back of the restaurant facing the road, so Joe and Victor took a wonderfully pragmatic approach to their problem. First they jacked up the building. Then, using a team of horses, they turned it round to face the new road and dropped it back on to the ground. Business continued as usual.

Pushing on from Pontiac, past Normal, through Shirley and McLean (neatly separated by Funks Grove, famous for its maple 'sirup', made since the 1820s by successive generations of Funks), I arrived in Atlanta. This is another lovely town, the highlight of which is a slightly strange story that makes the Seloti brothers' ingenuity seem like child's play.

It reminded me of an old joke from Scotland about a railway station in the Highlands where people got off the train with their suitcases only to discover there's nothing there. The village was away down the road, so they walked and walked with their cases until they finally reached it, exhausted.

One of them asked a local, 'How come the station isn't closer to the village?'

And the local said, 'Well, we thought it would be much handier if the station was closer to the railway line.'

That's an old music-hall joke, but – believe it or not – life imitated comedy in Atlanta. The town began its existence as Newcastle in 1854 and was happily minding its own business until a year later, when the railway came to town. Or rather the railway *didn't* come to town – for some reason, they laid the tracks more than a mile away from Newcastle. That worried the residents, who thought they'd miss out on all the passing trade, so they uprooted the whole town, lock, stock and barrel, and hoiked it up to the railway line. When they'd finished, they renamed it Atlanta. I find this an absolutely wonderful, inspiring story. It's a very American, let's-get-up-and-do-it kind of thing.

A lot of old Atlanta is no longer standing, but it still has its outstanding 36-foot-tall clock tower, which dates back to 1908 and is one of the few in America that continues to be wound by hand. I met a guy called Bill Thomas, the owner of a café called the Palm Grove. Like a lot of places on Route 66, the Palm Grove had crumbled after the interstate bypassed Atlanta, but Bill had brought it back to life, partly through his championship-winning pie-making skills. He'd promised me a piece of his award-winning pie, but first I had to wind up his wee clock. I'm not belittling the Atlanta clock when I call it wee. It's just that I've wound up Big Ben, and when you've done that, every other clock in the world is wee.

Bill fixed a crank to the mechanism and let me at it. 'How many cranks will it take?' I asked.

'About fifty-three total. And Billy, see what you're doing? Right up here.' He pointed to a weight on a wire. '*That*'s what you're actually lifting.'

'It's exactly the same method as Big Ben, although it's smaller scale.'

'And see this? You want to stop.' A white mark on the apparatus had reached a bar. 'Stop. You've done it.'

'Oh, glory be.'

Then, because I'd wound the mechanism correctly, he declared me an honorary 'Keeper of the Clock'. I even got a certificate.

'Lucky me!' I said.

'It might help with the police or in a bar or something.'

'And you've spelled my name right and everything. Thank you very much. Now, to the pies.'

I'd really enjoyed it. And my new status as an official clock-winder of Atlanta has improved my CV no end. I'm sure I'll pick up loads of work in that field as I wind my way through life from now on.

Bill's café was a delight. He had worked very hard to make it look like it might have done in the 1930s. I had the last piece of peach pie. I nearly went for the apple, but I thought: Oh come on, be original. My super-duper favourite is key lime pie, especially from diners on the road. I also like coconut cream and banana cream, but Bill recommended the peach. As soon as I took a bite, I could appreciate why he'd won awards. It was delicious. The crew wolfed down blackberry, strawberry, apple and all sorts of other pies. A wonderful time was had by all.

Over the road from Bill's café stood another Route 66 giant – exactly the same size as the Launching Pad's spaceman, but this time holding a big hot dog in place of the rocket. In the time since I'd seen the Gemini Giant, I'd found out a bit more about these massive figurines. Most of them were made in the 1960s by International Fiberglass, a company based in Venice, California. The first, designed to hold an axe, was made for the

Paul Bunyan Café on Route 66. Most similar statues along the road came from exactly the same mould, albeit without the axe, which explained why they all had their hands held out in front of them. The one with the huge hot dog had spent thirty-eight years outside a restaurant in Cicero, Illinois. Then, in 2003, someone from Atlanta spotted it for sale on eBay and cheekily asked the seller if he could have it for nothing.

'Fine,' said the seller. 'Come and get him.'

So the giant with the big hot dog arrived on permanent loan in Atlanta, Illinois. And the seller, whoever he is, booked his place in heaven.

I'd already had a great time in Atlanta, then things got even better. Having broken the banjo badge I usually wear on my lapel, I went into a shop to buy a new one. It was a funky wee shop, full of esoterica and built with Route 66 travellers in mind. The owner, Gene, who was a really friendly guy, had heard I was on a bike and asked me about it.

'Actually, I'm on a trike,' I said.

'Can I see it?'

I let Gene sit on the trike – because he asked me nicely – then he invited me to his home. He said I could visit any time I liked and that he'd take me up in his aeroplane. I'm very tempted to return to Atlanta just for that. We returned to his store and I bumped into a woman from York. She'd been following me around because her sister was a huge fan, and she asked for an autograph. When I'd finished writing a wee note and signing it, she thanked me, then dug something out of her bag.

'Here's some decent tea,' she said, holding out four Yorkshire teabags. 'You'll have trouble getting a decent cup of tea as you go along Route 66.'

I don't recall ever meeting so many nice people in such a short space of time. Atlanta was an absolute joy.

My next stop was Springfield, where Abraham Lincoln lived before going to Washington, DC as the sixteenth President of the United States. For the first time since leaving Chicago, I was back on an interstate. Riding in torrential rain, it was quite heart-stopping at times, especially when passing trucks. With the spray and the shit flying everywhere, it was tough going. And as I've said, I'm a poser, so I don't believe in riding in the rain. I don't want to be wringing out my underwear every time I stop. I've seen some guys who are even prepared to ride in the snow, but that's a different trip. That's pure sado-masochism. I like the fun of bikes. And this was no fun.

But I made it to Springfield. It was a totally crap night by the time I reached the hotel, but I told myself that something good would come of it. I'm a great believer in carrying on and not stopping just because it's raining.

Ahead of me, less than a hundred miles down Route 66, a tornado had struck Missouri. Watching the television news in my hotel room that night, I saw a bus sitting on top of the airport building in St Louis. Outside the room, thick branches were flying past the window. I couldn't foresee any kind of lush day hanging out in the sun, covered in suntan oil, coming up any time soon. Ever since we'd arrived in Chicago, the weather had taken a turn for the weird, but I was determined to make a go of my Route 66 trip. It *will* be good, I kept telling myself. It *will* be fun.

5

Travel My Way, Take the Highway

I'd stopped in Springfield to see Lincoln's home and tomb, but to be honest I wasn't looking forward to visiting either of them. In America, Lincoln is often portrayed as a leading opponent of slavery, but having recently read about him, I'd started to doubt how much liberty he was really willing to grant the slaves. Everyone assumes he wanted total freedom, but I wasn't so sure. Although he was anti-slavery, I suspected he wasn't too keen on former slaves and other black Americans having the vote. So I was in two minds about one of America's most revered statesmen, frequently referred to as the greatest President in American history.

Going to Lincoln's house, a charming and handsome – but still quite modest – painted-frame building in a shady residential neighbourhood with wood-plank pavements, started to change my mind. It might sound ridiculous to describe it this way, but Lincoln's house was a really human home. He came over as a father, a man who had been a good dad to his children and a good husband to his wife, quite apart from being the President of America and leading his country through one of the bloodiest civil wars in history.

Lincoln was born in poverty to a Kentucky farming family. With illiterate parents and only a year's formal education, he had few prospects, but while working as a storekeeper and postmaster he developed a love of reading and a keen interest in politics. In 1834 he was elected to the Illinois State Legislature, and two years later he passed his bar exams to become a lawyer. Seeking work in his new profession, in 1837 he arrived in Springfield, the state capital of Illinois. A wee while later, he met Mary Todd, and they married in 1842. The next year, the couple's first son, Robert, was born, and in 1844 they bought a little house, painted white with green shutters, from the Reverend Charles Dresser, who had performed their marriage ceremony. Over the years, the Lincolns enlarged the house to a full two-storey Greek Revival-style home for their growing family. By 1853, the couple had four sons, although only Robert reached adulthood, married and had children of his own. The others died of pneumonia, tuberculosis or yellow fever, spread by flies from the Washington swamps.

The Lincoln home has been declared a national historic site and forms part of a small national park dedicated to the President. Four blocks of a section of Springfield that used to be quite rundown and occasionally dangerous have been restored to something approaching their mid-nineteenth-century prime. Lincoln's house is the centrepiece, and you can walk right through it. You can even inspect his outside loo. Around the house, several other buildings have been equally well restored. Most of them were once occupied by friends of the Lincoln family.

It's always very strange to visit a place where a great person used to live. When they're dead and gone, it's hard to imagine them inhabiting the space. And yet you can touch things that they've touched. Lincoln's house is particularly peculiar in that way because it's such a historically important place. In 1860 the Republican Committee arrived in his front room and offered him their nomination for President. I stood on the exact spot where Lincoln stood, all six feet four of him, when they made the offer. He pondered what to do, saying, 'Well, I don't know.' At the time, he was on the court circuit and still a member of the State Legislature, so I suppose he was quite comfortable with that. I like the fact that he clearly wasn't one of those hell-driven careerists. That's probably what made him such an outstanding leader of his country. He knew that accepting the presidential nomination would launch him from the relative anonymity of Illinois to national fame. Of course, we all know what happened to him in the end, though.

Walking around the house, I started to feel great warmth for the man. There were little bits of paper on the desk where he worked. And the dining room where the family used to have their meals still had the stand on which Mary, who did most of the cooking, placed the cakes she made for them. I'd imagined a huge dining room to entertain great dignitaries, but, like everything about the man, it was very modest and homely. Upstairs, the bedrooms were just as interesting. I especially loved the wallpaper, an intricately patterned design that was possibly made by a French company. It said so much about Lincoln and his wife. I bet they were a really modern couple for their time.

But the kitchen was my favourite room in the house. With a wood-burning stove – a bit like an Aga – it must have been like hell in there, with smoke and flames everywhere. When they moved to Washington, Mary wanted to take the stove with her, but someone put their foot down and said, 'No, come on, behave yourself.' But I could see why she wanted to take it with her: it's absolutely beautiful.

The more I learned about Abraham Lincoln, the more I liked him. In the parlour, where the family spent a lot of their time, the kids would roll around and play on the floor, and Abe would either read or roll around on the floor with them, while Mary would do a bit of sewing and stitching. Apparently Lincoln was very fond of his children and liked to spoil them. One of his kids once had a birthday party and Lincoln invited sixty children, so the place must have been in uproar. He was often seen pulling his kids along the street in a cart, something that was considered very unmanly and feminine in those days. I liked the sound of that because I remembered pushing my own son around in a pushchair in Glasgow. It was the delight of my life at the time, but even then people responded to me strangely and often looked at me as if I was a bit of an odd hippy. They'd say, 'Aren't you embarrassed? That's a woman's thing to do.' So I could only imagine how the residents of Springfield must have reacted to Lincoln in the nineteenth century.

Another thing I like about him is that he lived in a sort of suburbia, a modest neighbourhood. He was born in a log cabin, so the Springfield house must have been a huge move up for him, and it was the only house he ever owned. He moved straight from Springfield to the White House in February 1861. Four years later, it was *boom*, goodnight Vienna, when John Wilkes Booth, a Confederate sympathiser, shot him in the back of the head.

Lincoln was a giant and I came away from his old home in

great admiration of the man. And I'll retain that admiration, I think.

Clearly, I'm not the only one to hold Lincoln in such high regard. For evidence, you only need to look at his tomb, built in Springfield after that stumer shot him. ('Stumer' is a Scottish word that really appeals to me. I don't know where it comes from, but I like to think of it as a cross between 'stupid' and 'tumour'. It means you're no good for anything.) The centrepiece of Oak Ridge Cemetery, Lincoln's final resting place is surrounded by towering oak trees in a gently rolling landscape. His 117-foot-tall granite tomb also contains the bodies of Mary and three of their four sons – Edward, William and Thomas.

Although relatively modest by the standards of presidential tombs, this is one of the most revered places in America – and rightly so. It's worth a visit just to see the sculptures of Lincoln, both inside and outside the tomb, the most impressive of which is a large bronze bust of the President at the entrance. A facsimile of a marble bust that stands in the US Capitol in Washington, DC, the bronze was created by Gutzon Borglum, who also sculpted the vast Lincoln figurehead at Mount Rushmore. Many visitors rub the nose of the Springfield bust for good luck. It's not encouraged, but I've never done what's encouraged, so I gave it a rub.

Inside the building, other bronze statues portray Lincoln in various stages of his life. Some include excerpts from his most famous speeches. Walking down a circular hallway to a marble burial chamber, I was confronted by the sombre words that Edwin Stanton, Lincoln's Secretary of War, uttered at his death: 'Now he belongs to the ages.' Stanton's next words after the assassination – 'There lies the most perfect ruler of men the world has ever seen' – aren't displayed in the tomb, but I think they would have been quite appropriate. Standing in the chamber, there's a very real sense of the terrible human cost of the American Civil War, almost as if Lincoln died yesterday.

A red marble marker stands above the underground vault where Lincoln's coffin lies. People have twice tried to steal the body, so the vault has now been reinforced with concrete and steel to foil grave robbers. God only knows why anyone might want to steal it. What would they do with it? Put it on eBay?

One of the things that sums up Lincoln for me is that he spoke for less than three minutes at the dedication of the Soldiers' National Cemetery in Gettysburg, Pennsylvania, where four and a half months earlier, the Union armies had decisively defeated those of the Confederacy. Before the President's concise, powerful and deeply moving speech, Edward Everett, a former Secretary of State, had talked for two solid hours. Everett's seldom-read, 13,607-word oration was slated to be the main event of the day, but Lincoln's 'few appropriate remarks', which summarised the war in just ten sentences, is now recognised by everyone in America as *the* Gettysburg Address.

He began the speech with a reference to the American Revolution of 1776: 'Four score and seven years ago our fathers brought forth on this continent a new nation, conceived in liberty, and dedicated to the proposition that all men are created equal.' Then he invoked the principles laid out in the Declaration of Independence and redefined the Civil War not merely as a struggle for the Union but as 'a new birth of freedom', which would bring true equality to all of America's citizens, ensure that democracy remained a viable form of government, and create a unified nation.

Now one of the best-known speeches in American history, Lincoln's Gettysburg Address was greeted first by a stunned silence and then by wild, prolonged applause for the man who was guiding the nation through the Civil War and preserving the Union. He was a fantastic guy and a true lover of freedom. His assassination did nobody any good. John Wilkes Booth simply killed a very good man.

As I mentioned at the start of this chapter, I had arrived in Springfield swithering, as we say in Scotland, between whether Lincoln was a truly great guy or just an ordinary guy made to look great by history. By the time I left, I was in no doubt. To abolish slavery and to keep the Union of America intact were two extraordinary achievements. I ended the day wishing I'd had the chance to meet Lincoln. I think he would have been a friend of mine. I reckon I would have liked him and I hope he would have liked me.

In a few hours I'd completely changed my opinion of the man. And I kinda like that. I'm not locked closed on everything.

Moving from the sublime to the ridiculous, I climbed on to my trike, headed out of the cemetery, passed the Illinois State Capitol Building (built from Romeoville limestone) and arrived at the home of the Cozy Dog, one of the birthplaces of fast food.

This was the place where Bob Waldmire, that fabulous artist who lived on a bus, grew up watching the traffic on Route 66. His father, Ed, invented the Cozy Dog after visiting Oklahoma and eating a speciality of the state – a corn dog – which is a sausage baked in cornbread. Ed liked it, but thought it took far too long to prepare. He mentioned it to a pal, but then the Second World War intervened and he thought no more of it.

A few years later, when Ed was stationed in Amarillo, Texas, with the US Air Force, his pal wrote to say that he had developed a batter that would stick to frankfurter sausages, allowing them to be deep-fried. He sent some of the batter to Ed, who tested it in the air force kitchens, creating a thickly battered hot dog on a stick. Ed called them 'crusty curs'.

These meat lollipops became hugely popular on the air force base and around town, so when Ed was discharged in 1946, he decided to set up a restaurant to sell his creation. But his wife thought 'crusty cur' was a terrible name and suggested Cozy Dog instead, possibly because it was like a hot dog in a blanket. Their Cozy Dog restaurant in Springfield was the first fast-food joint on Route 66. For the first time in history, big groups of people were driving long distances and they needed places to grab a quick bite to eat. Cozy Dogs could be prepared in advance, so the customers could grab one and then just keep driving.

Incidentally, did you know that it took a wee while for anyone to come up with the idea of putting a frankfurter in a bun to make a hot dog? The story goes that a Bavarian sausage seller called Anton Ludwig Feuchtwanger had been selling frankfurters with a pair of white gloves so that his customers could eat the hot sausages in comfort. But when the customers started keeping the gloves as souvenirs, Feuchtwanger responded by serving his sausages in rolls. Nobody seems to know for sure whether he first tried this at the 1893 World's Fair: Columbian Exposition in Chicago or the 1904 Louisiana Purchase Exposition in St Louis. Whichever it was, Feuchtwanger is credited with inventing the hot dog, although I can't believe that nobody thought to put a frankfurter in a bread roll between the thirteenth century – when the sausages were invented in Germany – and 1893. By the way, if you've ever wondered why a hot dog tastes the way it does – with that unique flavour that no other sausage or meat has – well, the answer is coriander. That's the secret ingredient. Tell your friends. And tell them who told you.

The people at Cozy Dogs were terrific and the souvenirs were great, but something was not sitting well with me. Then I realised what was bothering me. In 1996 they'd moved from their original location. I knew the building didn't look like the kind of restaurant that would have been built in the 1940s or 1950s, the kind of roadside eatery that a young Bob Waldmire would have sat outside, watching the world drive past. It fed into my irritation about parts of America rejecting Americana. They used to build roadside diners and restaurants that were very funky, but now they've stopped doing that. Instead, they build plain little brick sheds that all look like public toilets. The Cozy Dogs had a plainness about it that I found kind of sad. What a shame.

As for the Cozy Dog itself? Well, I guess it's an acquired taste. But the chips are to die for, and the decor inside the restaurant is brilliant, so it's still well worth a wee look. I just wish they sold vegetarian 'not dogs'. Considering the restaurant's association with Bob Waldmire, they really ought to have them on the menu. They've got his artwork up on the walls, so they should sell his favourite snack.

Leaving Springfield, the weather immediately improved. The sun came out for a wee while for the first time since I started my journey. The rain had been belting down non-stop and I was getting a bit bored with it. I don't mind weather if it changes all the time, but constant rain and greyness really get to me. And I'm speaking as someone who comes from Scotland. So I know of what I speak.

I was making my first detour off Route 66 since leaving Chicago, and rode for what seemed like thousands of miles across vast empty plains of wheat, corn, soya bean and potato fields. Known as the Prairie State, Illinois has some of the most fertile soil in the world. The cold winters allow it to replenish itself, while the long, warm summers and reliable rainfall produce ideal growing conditions. The state produces enough soya beans each year to fill the Empire State Building more than fifteen times.

My destination was the largest Amish community in Illinois. As I approached Arthur, about ninety miles due east of Springfield, it soon became obvious that I was entering a religious community where the way of life had changed little since the current residents' ancestors had settled there some 150 years ago. About ten miles from town, there was a road sign I'd never seen before: a black silhouette of a horse and buggy on a yellow background. The sign warned that the local people lived and farmed in a unique way, one firmly based on centuries-old traditions and practices. Then I rode past a field in which the soil was being ploughed by horse.

About four thousand Amish people live in Arthur, where they humbly follow their community's strict but simple rules. Each family traditionally owns around eighty acres of farmland, which is used to feed the family and the wider community. They use only horse-drawn machines with metal wheels, and their main crops are wheat, oats, clover and corn. However, this pastoral way of life is changing for the Amish, who are struggling with ever-increasing land prices and decreased demand for home-grown, non-mass-produced food. In response, some members of this resourceful community are turning their hands to other skills, such as furniture- and machine-making, in order to supplement their agricultural income. Tourism is also becoming an important part of the Amish existence, as the cottage industries and country shops continue to thrive.

That's why I found myself pulling up outside a large, plain wooden shed and offices that served as the workshop of Mervin, the Amish furniture-maker I mentioned at the start of the book. I liked Mervin from the first moment I met him. He has an easy smile and a gentle manner, as well as that fantastic pudding-bowl haircut. Dressed in a plain shirt, dark trousers and button braces, Mervin was very welcoming and offered to show me around his workshop. He answered every question honestly, such as when I asked how he took orders from customers, given that the Amish weren't meant to use modern appliances like telephones.

'We've got a phone that we use to take orders,' he said. 'We're not allowed to have phones for ourselves, but they're all on the outside of the building.' He indicated something that looked like a payphone, bolted to the side of his office. As an Amish businessman, he can receive calls from people who have no other way to contact him, but he can't phone out, except in an emergency. 'More and more of them have their own phones,' said Mervin, referring to the other Amish residents of Arthur, 'since more of them run businesses in the area.'

In my ignorance, I'd always thought that Amish communities didn't extend any further than Pennsylvania, but Mervin explained that they had spread across large parts of the United States. Originating in Switzerland, the Amish are a Christian group who migrated to America in the early eighteenth century in search of freedom to practise their religion as they pleased. Although I was right in thinking that they initially settled in Pennsylvania, which is still home to one of the largest Amish communities in the world, some families eventually travelled further west in search of more land.

For years, the Amish lived very enclosed lives, almost entirely self-sufficient and spurning contact with the outside world. But times have changed, and Amish furniture-makers, renowned for their old-fashioned, high-quality woodworking skills, now sell their goods outside the community in order to survive. Mervin showed me how his team of cabinetmakers made every piece by hand in a large joinery workshop that he'd set up in 1996 after working for another Amish carpenter. Surprised to see some power tools in the workshop, I asked Mervin whether the Amish way of life allowed him to use electrical machinery.

'No, all the tools in the shop are run off hydraulics and air,' he said. For instance, Mervin's saws and sanders were hydraulic, rather than electric. 'We've got some electric lights and appliances. We're allowed to have some electrical power, but we run it off diesel generators. We're not allowed to have it come off the line, so we produce it ourselves.'

'Why's that?' I asked. 'Because it would connect you to the outside world?'

'Not just that,' he said. 'Mostly it's to stay away from as much modern stuff as we can.'

'It seems to be working well for you. You seem to be managing pretty well without it.'

'Yeah.'

Mervin asked if I would like to have a go at putting a cabinet together, but I turned down his kind offer. 'I'm too clumsy,' I said. 'I don't want to waste one.'

The wood is mostly imported from Canada, although a small amount comes from the northeastern US states and the South. Mervin said the most important member of the team was the man who cut the wood. 'If he doesn't get it right,' he said, 'then it's real difficult for the guys who put it all together.' Clearly, the man who cut the wood was doing his job extremely well, because the finished products were all beautiful, with an astonishingly smooth finish. Such well-made pieces of furniture are surely destined to become the antiques of tomorrow.

In his showroom, Mervin showed me an entire kitchen that had been constructed in his workshop. With excellent craftsmanship and fantastic attention to detail, it was splendid, top-of-the-line stuff – the kind of furniture you buy only once, because it lasts a lifetime. I'd dearly love to have something like it in my house.

Mervin had a charming, very practical, down-to-earth attitude to making furniture. 'Who designed this?' I asked, pointing at one of the kitchen cabinets.

'We see it,' he said, 'and then we just make it.'

It was at this point that Mervin suggested we should go for a ride in his horse-drawn buggy, something I'd always wanted to do. He showed me out to the yard, then directed me into the stable so that I could bring out the horse. As I explained earlier, I'm a wee bit wary of horses, but Mervin helped me lead out a lovely chestnut. Very gently, Mervin attached some tackle to the horse while I continued to pepper him with curious questions.

'As we were driving here I noticed that many Amish were waving at us from their buggies. Is that normal?'

'Oh yes,' said Mervin. 'We think that if you don't wave, you're stuck up.'

'Really?'

Mervin laughed. 'That's the way a lot of people feel. It's like: try to be friendly to everybody.'

'That's wonderful.'

Mervin then attached the horse to a black buggy, which, like Mervin's furniture, was a beautiful example of skilled craftsmanship. It had two sliding panels on each side, so the passengers could travel either entirely enclosed and protected or with the sides open.

'She's a little worked up today,' Mervin warned as he adjusted the horse's reins.

'Why's that?' I asked, even though the horse seemed perfectly calm to me.

'A few strangers about. She's not so used to them.'

As he fixed the horse, he told me that most Amish families owned a buggy or two, all of them made by local craftsmen. A larger model typically costs around seven thousand dollars. We set off and Mervin explained that he learned how to control a buggy as a kid. Then he showed me the ropes.

'It's not hard at all,' he said, as I took the reins.

'Not with you here, it isn't,' I replied.

We pootled along for a little while, chatting idly.

'You know what I find very impressive, Mervin? You keep

talking about the rules for this, the rules for that, and the rules for the other. You seem very comfortable with it.'

'It's something you get used to, you know.'

'From the outside, people think it's kind of fanatical. But up close you seem very happy with what you're doing.'

'It's nice to keep your family together and just kind of do your own thing.' We plodded on a bit further in silence, then he said: 'I guess, as far as the rules and stuff go, it's . . . '

'Do you find comfort in it?'

'Oh yeah, oh yeah.'

'You certainly seem to,' I said. 'You seem to be a very happy man.'

'Yes.'

'Another thing. On the way here we stopped at an Amish restaurant, and when we were among Amish people there, I thought they would keep themselves separate, but they made a point of saying "hello" and "good morning".'

'Oh yeah.' Mervin nodded, then turned to me. 'So, you got any children, Billy?'

'Four girls and a boy.'

'How old are they?'

'The youngest one's twenty-two and the oldest is forty-one.'

'All still living with you?'

'Well, two of them still live with me.'

'I see.'

'The rest are out working in different places.'

Mervin interrupted our conversation to explain that if I wanted the horse to go a little faster, I should give her a gentle tap and click my tongue. 'There you go,' he said, showing me how.

'How many children have you got?' I asked.

'Five. We had six but the youngest one passed on,' said Mervin. He hesitated before continuing. 'We had an accident when he was fourteen months old.'

'Oh, fourteen months. That must have broken your heart.'

'It was kind of a sad situation. I was out in the barn and I was using the skip-loader to move a hay-bale and I backed over him.'

'*Oh no*.'

'Yeah, and . . . so it was kind of sad.'

I looked at Mervin. He was telling me about this tragedy in such a quiet, calm, matter-of-fact way that it broke *my* heart. He'd simply accepted that it had been God's way. Whether I agreed with that was a different story, but he accepted it and that was the whole cheese.

'It's been twenty . . . The second of April. It was twenty years ago, so it was kinda . . . '

The anniversary had just passed, a couple of weeks before. 'Oh, my goodness me,' I said.

'You know, it's still tough.'

I nodded. 'That must have taken a bit of getting over.'

'Yeah. We still think about it a lot.'

'I bet you do.'

'But, you know, life goes on and . . . you've just got to make the best of it sometimes.'

'Of course you do.'

'It's one of those things.'

'Yeah.'

We sat in silence for a few moments, watching the countryside slowly slide past and listening to the clip-clop of the horse's hooves.

'We had a lot of rain lately,' said Mervin, 'and we got water across the road here.' He explained how you get the horse to cross a deep puddle. 'If she runs, that's fine; but if she wants to walk, let her walk.' It seemed like a good approach and the horse took us through the water.

Next we took a spin around the fields, a vast, flat landscape with little protection from the elements. Winters here are long and hard, but Mervin said they were bearable and I could understand why. Sitting behind a horse clip-clopping down the road was a lovely way to travel, and I seemed to have got the hang of it.

'It's not hard at all,' repeated Mervin.

'It's very nice. I would love to go into town like this.'

We both cackled.

'And when you're young and single,' I said, 'is this how you go out with your young lady?'

'Yeah, we can. They get those gatherings and then they'll sometimes end up taking the lady home and getting acquainted and so forth.'

'Is that allowed? Are you allowed to be alone with your girlfriend? Or do you need a chaperone?'

'It's allowed.'

'And do you do that thing here where you ... Is it called *rumspringa*?'

'Yeah, they call it *rumspringa*.'

Rumspringa literally means 'running around', which is an apt description. It's the period between the ages of sixteen and eighteen when adolescent Amish kids decide between being baptised and officially joining the Amish Church or leaving the community. It's also when they look for a spouse. It's a rite of passage, and maybe a time for sowing a few wild oats. Some Amish communities allow their young men to purchase small 'courting buggies', while some families paint their yard gate blue to indicate that a daughter of marriageable age lives there.

It seems a very sensible system to me. By recognising that adolescents need to rebel and defy their parents, it allows a degree of misbehaviour to be tolerated. Some of the kids turn their backs on Amish practices, wearing non-traditional clothing and styling their hair differently (they call it 'dressing English'), driving vehicles, drinking or taking drugs and engaging in pre-marital sex. Up to half of them may temporarily leave the community or eschew the traditional practices, but almost all eventually return and choose to join the Church.

I told Mervin I thought the *rumspringa* was a very sane thing to do.

'Yeah, but there's some things that go on that I don't really like or . . . '

'That you don't approve of?'

'Some of the kids get carried away.'

'Of course.'

'And people's people, you know? People's people.'

'Do people get disappointed if the youngsters don't come back?'

'Some do. That varies from family to family. It might be more disappointing to one person than it is to another.'

'It all seems very basic and understandable to me.'

'Well, we just try to be simple, you know? A lot of them get it out of their system and then . . . '

'Settle down?'

'Yeah. We're all humans, just like the rest of them.'

I like that attitude. There's something very accepting – and very Scottish – about it.

I was intrigued how Mervin met his own wife, so asked: 'How would an Amish guy find an Amish wife?'

'Well, a lot of them have activities going on. Or, like what I did, I met her, my wife, at a certain place and got acquainted. Then we started dating each other. I'd take her places.'

'Did you meet in a sort of community thing, a dance or a get-together or something like that?'

'I was probably where I shouldn't have been.'

That made me laugh.

Mervin told me that the various Amish communities across America all have the same basic rules, but with some variations, according to geography. 'You know, because you live in a certain circumstance, a certain rule doesn't work.' A few are allowed to have mobile phones or to fly on aeroplanes because they are considered necessities. Occasionally, Mervin will take a train into Chicago for business purposes, but in his community aeroplanes are still forbidden. I'd love to have seen him with his hat and beard striding through the Windy City.

'In this area we don't fly,' he said. 'But it's one of those things – maybe one community needs something where another one doesn't. When I was younger, I asked one of the bishops how we should decide what's appropriate and he said it's important that everybody agrees to whatever we're doing.'

'That seems to bind everything you do. With the Amish, everybody has to agree.'

Mervin nodded. 'You know, it varies. It's not all one hundred per cent. Just everybody tries to do their part. It makes it easier for everybody.'

'I like the way you combine resources. If someone's got cancer and the treatment is expensive, you all take part in paying for it. I think that's a wonderful thing.'

'I really appreciate that, too. Helping each other binds people together. It's kind of the key thing.'

'Visitation' is another big thing among the Amish. It's all about maintaining their community. They'll gather at each other's homes to drink coffee and eat popcorn. Alcohol is not permitted, but Mervin said the youngsters often have a drink anyway. 'They go through that age when it's an attractive thing, even though it's not allowed.' Weekends and holidays are spent dropping in on friends and relatives. 'If someone needs visiting, maybe they're sick or they need company, we go see them.'

In their spare time, many of the Amish folk fish for bass or sing in choirs, particularly on Sunday evenings, when all the generations congregate together. They go to church at least every fortnight, often visiting other churches in the district, although communion is only ever taken in their local church.

Mervin and I kept talking until, about half an hour later, we arrived at the family farm and he invited me into his parents' house. Mervin himself lived next door.

'Your stomach getting empty?' he asked. 'Are you ready for lunch?'

'Absolutely.'

After several days of eating rubbish on the road, it was a delight to sit down to some proper home-cooked food, prepared by Mervin's wife and mother. They were both dressed in long, plain dresses, pinafores and bonnets. Near by, a small girl, no more than two years old, wandered around, also dressed in traditional Amish dress and bonnet, a dummy in her mouth. I listened as the family chatted in what sounded like a combination of English and High German.

Mervin invited the director, the producer and the rest of the crew to join us as we sat down to a huge spread, including chicken, ham, pie, salad, vegetables, potatoes, noodles, corn and bread. It all tasted wonderful.

After dinner, Mervin showed me how the gas lighting in his parents' house worked. It gave out a lovely glow. Then he asked where I was going next.

'St Louis. It'll take about two and a half hours.' I told Mervin that the throttle on the bike was a bit tight and made my thumb sore. 'So it'll be a little painful by the time we get to St Louis, but all in all it will be good fun . . . if the rain stays away.'

As we prepared to leave, I told Mervin that this had been one of the nicest days of my life.

He just laughed.

'Going around with you in the buggy was delightful. I'd like to thank you very, very much. It's been such a pleasure meeting you.'

'You're welcome. Appreciate you stopping in.'

'I'm very happy. You've made me very happy.'

I rode away from Arthur thinking it had been the best day's filming I'd done in a long, long time. Mervin is a lovely man. A complete man. He knows exactly who and what he is, and what he does. He makes beautiful things, and he makes them extremely well.

It's lovely to know that there are still people in the world who are making wonderful things. I'd thought that when it came to furniture-making, maybe the best days were over. But they're not. There are still guys like Mervin making fantastic things that will be handed down in families from generation to generation. It fills my heart with joy.

And Mervin is not just a master craftsman – he laughs easily and can take a joke. At one point I'd asked him to put on his Amish hat. I'm sure plenty of guys would have refused, not wanting to conform to some outsider's stereotype. But Mervin immediately agreed and plonked his hat on his head with a big smile.

I still know very little about the Amish way of life, but it seems very humane to me. I don't know of any other religion that has that. The fact that most of them choose to come back and live that way after the *rumspringa* says a lot. And there's a wonderful social side to it. For instance, I really liked the way that Mervin and many of the other Amish guys grew beards but not moustaches, just because they all wanted to look the same as each other. Like, for instance, when I asked Mervin, 'Why no moustache, why just the beard?'

'Nobody else has moustaches,' he said, 'and we like to all be the same.' That's a lovely sharing concept which really appeals to me, and it's not phony.

Being Amish is not for me, because I'm too long in the tooth and set in my ways, but if I could have my time again, I'd be proud to be Amish. I think I would have made a pretty cool Amish guy, with my hat and bib and brace overalls, making beautiful furniture. I would have settled for that.

My day in Arthur left me with a similar feeling to when I'd visited Quinn Chapel. It's nice to see people happy in the knowledge of who and what they are.

The weather was still crap – there were even reports of more tornadoes in St Louis – but I was content now. It was what it was, and as much a part of the journey as the road and the people I'd meet along it. Everything doesn't always have to be in primary colours. But I must admit, I could have done without the permanently wet crotch.

6

Go through St Louis; Joplin, Missouri

I arrived in St Louis to find I was staying in the Moonrise Hotel's Buddy Ebsen Suite, which was strangely appropriate, as Buddy was the reason why I was on the journey. A movie star in 1930s Hollywood, Buddy later played the dad in *The Beverly Hillbillies*, one of the most successful sitcoms of all time. I used to watch it at home in Glasgow in the 1960s and delight in its bluegrass banjo theme song. It made me rush out and buy a banjo, thereby kick-starting the whole long story that took me out of the shipyards, into playing in folk bands and from there to comedy, movies and ultimately a television series about riding a trike along good old Route 66.

If it hadn't been for Buddy Ebsen and the other guys in *The Beverly Hillbillies* – and Earl Scruggs, who played that theme song – I would never have written this book. So it was kind of nice to be in Buddy's suite. It put a big smile on my face when I went into the room and saw pictures of him all over the place.

The journey to St Louis had been longer and harder than I'd anticipated when I left Mervin's place in Arthur. The rain battered down, drenching me until I was freezing wet and shivering. Then, mercifully, Mike, the director, offered to take over on the bike. He rode twice the distance that I did and was nearly drowned by the spray of passing trucks. It was terrifying. Driving along on a three-wheeler with your arse eighteen inches off the floor as forty-ton trucks come whooshing past is not fun. It's not a game for children at all. But Mike did it, and we all arrived in St Louis to tell the tale, so I was a happy boy. It felt like a good day's hard work.

We had arrived in St Louis by crossing the Mississippi on Poplar Street Bridge, the route since 1966. In the 1920s Route 66 took the McKinley Bridge, a three-arch structure, across the river, but in the 1930s, Route 66 was diverted on to the Chain of Rocks Bridge, allowing travellers to bypass St Louis. It soon became a well-known landmark on the road west, so I decided to take a look at it. But good intentions can result in tricky outcomes, and when I arrived at the bridge with the film crew my first thought was: What am I going to say about *this*? It was just a wee bridge over a wee river. How would I entertain the great British public with that? Some of them would have bigger bridges in their back gardens.

Then the crew took a run up the road to investigate and discovered we were at the wrong bridge. A big, proper bridge was just around the corner. Relief all round.

Straddling the border between Illinois and Missouri, the Chain of Rocks Bridge follows a line of large rocks, which at one time could be seen stretching across the Mississippi like a giant's stepping stones. But the rocks created rapids, making that particular stretch of the Mississippi extremely dangerous to navigate, so in the 1960s a low-water dam was built across the river to raise the water level. Now you can see all the rocks only during extreme low-water conditions. On the day I visited the river was very high, so we couldn't see any of them – not that it detracted from the fabulous bridge.

Standing in front of the bridge, you can see why it has become an icon of Route 66. It has eleven truss sections that look like they're made out of giant Meccano pieces, and it bends by twenty-four degrees about halfway across the river. The construction company had purchased land on each side of the river, but the parcels were not directly opposite each other. Initially they planned to build the whole bridge on a diagonal, but the US Army Corps of Engineers objected to that plan on safety grounds. So they built the first section, which crosses the major navigation channel, straight across the river from the Illinois shore. Then the remaining part was built at an angle to meet up with the Missouri shore.

Now decommissioned and out of use for motor vehicles, the Chain of Rocks Bridge takes only bicycles and pedestrians these days, but we had secured special permission to drive my trike across it. Built in 1929 as a toll bridge, at first it wasn't very successful, mainly because it didn't connect easily to downtown St Louis. Soon after opening the bridge, the company that built and operated it went bankrupt, so it was handed over to Madison, Illinois, the city at its eastern end. In 1936 it was included in Route 66, and traffic numbers soared. By the time it was closed in 1970, the city had made seven million dollars profit from it. Not bad, eh?

For years a wee mystery surrounded the bridge. Every year a huge bouquet of flowers would appear on it. Nobody knew what these signified until 1959, when someone noticed an envelope attached to the flowers. Inside, they found a tragic wee note dedicated to Todd Costin, who had worked on the bridge and had fallen off in 1929, just before it was completed. Engineers had predicted that there would be ten fatalities during construction, but only Todd was killed. He was dragged to the bottom of the Mississippi by the weight of his tools.

In the mid-1970s Madison City wanted to demolish the bridge, but a recession put paid to that when the market price for scrap iron collapsed. At the time, the cost of demolishing the bridge would have been several million dollars more than its scrap value. So the bridge was left to rust, largely forgotten until a local bicycle group rediscovered and renovated it to create what might well be the longest pedestrian and bicycle bridge in the world.

The bridge is still in a pretty rusty state, but I like it. It has a rural, funky, southern feel to it. And it was lovely rumping along it on my bike, with the metal rattling and the noise of the engine echoing all around me. At the far end of the bridge, I arrived in *Missoura*. Did you notice how I went all local there? We know it as Missouri, but all the locals say *Missoura*. And it's St *Lewis*, not St *Louie* – you have to pronounce it that way if you don't want them thinking you're a square.

From the bridge, I had a good run of a few miles down the road with a helicopter following me, which is always a gas. I feel like such a star whenever I do that, like Ray Liotta in *Goodfellas*. I was scared to look around for the helicopter, so I just leaned back on my trike and posed. I was being moody and bikey and overtaken by trucks, and it was a jolly day – the kind of day when I feel like I'm being successful at what I do. Usually I don't actually know what I'm doing. It's the same on stage – I do what feels good, but I don't know how it looks. I don't practise in front of mirrors and I don't look at rushes. Instead, I rely totally on how it feels . . . and as long as it feels good, that's fine by me.

It can be weird, because people tell me that my movement on stage is getting funnier and better, but I've still got no idea what I'm doing. All I know is that they're laughing while I'm poncing around. And I don't go and look at other people, in case I inadvertently steal their moves, so I've not even got anything to compare it to. I also avoid watching other comedians, because I know I'll just absorb their material and then think it's mine later.

A lot of comedians who are accused of stealing stuff don't intentionally nick it. They just become a sort of comedy black hole, sucking in material. They see and hear so many funny things when they go to clubs, performing with other guys, and everything they hear goes straight into their mental filing system. Months or even years later, it'll pop out and they'll swear it's their own idea. But actually they heard it ages ago in some obscure club in Chicago or wherever. Then the guy who actually did come up with it gets mad – and quite rightly so. But we all pick things up by mental osmosis, and comedians are no different to anyone else.

To avoid this problem, I go completely by feel – a bit like reading Braille – whenever I'm on stage or making a television show. It's a weird and frightening process because I never know how I'm doing. And making the series about Route 66 was no different. I was sure the director and half of the crew thought I was fishing for compliments because I kept asking them how it was going, but I genuinely didn't know.

So it was a gamble, but quite an exciting one. I knew it could backfire. I could have spent these seven weeks doing a live tour, where thousands of people would have paid good money to see me and would have given me a warm welcome. But one night of television would reach *millions* of people. Which meant I had to be good, even though I hadn't scripted a single word beforehand. So, before arriving at each location, I immersed myself in my research notes and just hoped it would all come out in the correct order. As on stage, whenever I remembered something interesting, it would just plop out. There was no preconceived plan. But it seemed to work, and it always gave me a boost when I saw the crew laughing. That was my quality-assurance test.

St Louis is a rather beautiful city, with lovely people. In fact, every town I'd passed through up to this point had been beautiful, clean and tidy. America really is a country of small towns, most of which are handsome and well kept, although some are stultifying in their dullness. Driving through them, the streets are often empty, with nobody walking along, something I've never encountered in Britain. Whenever I stopped to eat or have a pee, I'd meet charming people in the shops and restaurants, but on the street the towns and villages were invariably completely dead. It lent a sadness to these places – like the locals had all given up their streets to the car.

Before riding back into the centre of St Louis, I visited an area that one of those tornadoes I'd seen on the news had torn apart only a few days earlier. Riding towards it, there was no sign of anything out of the ordinary, but then we turned a corner and arrived in the district of Bridgeton. *God Almighty.* With wind speeds up to 200 m.p.h., the tornado had cut a swath half a mile wide and twenty-one miles long through several counties in and around the city. Within that zone – total devastation. Three feet outside the zone – everything perfect and orderly. From a distance, it looked like a big machine had cut a valley clean through the town. Houses had been decimated, leaving only the foundations and enormous mounds of crap. Huge trees had been uprooted, just pulled right out of the ground, showing the awesome power that the tornado must have possessed. Officially, it had been designated an EF4, the second-worst type of tornado. I couldn't imagine what the worst type must be like. We sometimes get wind speeds of about 100 m.p.h. in Scotland, but when you're talking double that, well, that's just fantasy land for me. It must be so terrifying to have your house turned to scrap around you.

The first thing I noticed in Bridgeton was the amazing silence. There was an awe and drama about the place. Churches were missing their roofs. At the Ferguson Christian Church, they'd been watching Mel Gibson's *The Passion of the Christ* when the storm showed up. As the congregation watched Jesus being whipped, the roof was ripped off, frightening the bejesus out of them. They must have thought they'd been sent for. Meanwhile, the house next door and a big Buddhist temple further down the road were left untouched. I didn't think for a moment that it meant anything significant, but it still amused me a lot.

The second thing that struck me was the cheeriness of everyone. The police, the fire service, the victims – they were all in a good mood. I visited a house in which only the concrete basement, where the family had hidden from the worst of the storm, was intact. A friend was helping them sort through the detritus, looking for valuables and anything of sentimental value. I introduced myself and asked a few questions about the house, or what was left of it.

The friend pointed at a pile of wood and rubbish. 'This was the deck and the pool.'

'*This* was the deck and the pool?' It was a complete mess.

'Yes,' she said. 'They were down in the basement.'

I looked. 'This was their basement?'

'Yes. Where the refrigerator is lying.'

'They were down there? And they came up to see *this*?' I pointed at the devastation.

'Actually, I think he stuck his head out of that stairwell right there and just kind of looked around and said, "Our house has gone."'

As we were chatting, Bridget, the daughter of the house, turned up. She was in great shape, just pleased that she and her family had survived unhurt.

'Were you here when it happened?' I said.

'No. I had just recently moved out of the house, about three weeks ago.'

'Good timing!'

'Well, I left about half my stuff here. I hadn't completely made it out of the house, so ... good timing for me, but bad timing for my stuff!'

She was incredibly jolly. And yet, all around us, it was total chaos, as if vast garbage dumpsters had been turned upside down either on the houses or beside them.

'I can't imagine how it must have felt,' I said. 'What was the noise like?'

'My dad said it sounded like a freight train was going right through the house. He said that the instant his ears popped, he knew it was coming. It was the pressure of the tornado.'

'Is that when he was still up here?' I pointed to where the deck had been.

'As he was going down the steps. He made it down just before it hit.'

'Oh my God!'

'My dad was standing at the top of the steps, watching the news, looking out the window. My mum was already in the basement. My uncle called and said, "There's a tornado that landed in Bridgeton. You guys need to be downstairs!" No sooner had he gotten down the steps than it hit.'

Her father sounded just like me – the type who ignores advice until the last possible moment. As soon as he locked the basement door behind him, it started to shake. Looking up the stairs, he could see debris flying everywhere.

Then Bridget told me that her father had recently been diagnosed with colon cancer, and he was recovering from surgery. On the day that the tornado hit, he was on a portable chemotherapy pump.

'Oh my God!' I said again.

'It makes him feel pretty sick, but he's been out here digging and doing his thing.'

Bridget explained that they had a couple of days to sift through the wreckage before everything would be bulldozed away and the clean-up operation would start.

'So you're just going through all this rubble, hoping to find precious things?' I said.

'Yes. We've found a couple of very, very valuable things, like my engagement ring. It was at my parents' house, sitting on my night stand, and she found it in the rubble.' Bridget pointed towards her friend. 'When she found it, we all cried. Everybody did.'

'Oh my God!' Of course I hadn't known she was engaged. What an amazing story. 'I'm going to touch it for luck.'

'It had travelled about seventy-five feet, so it's definitely one of the luckiest pieces of jewellery I know. And my wedding dress survived, too. It has a little bit of mud on it, and a small hole in one of the seams on the side, but all that can be fixed before I get married.'

I told Bridget that I thought her community's optimism was extraordinary.

'In the first few days my parents were very upset. But now my mum's talking about wanting a new big front porch. She's already designing the new place. This was just a one-storey home and they're discussing whether to make it taller instead of having it so long. They might go for a two-storey home.' Apparently, she was also planning a whole new deck area and a veranda.

'You're all insured, aren't you?' I asked.

'We had full coverage on the house.'

'I love thinking about your mother redesigning.' It made me laugh.

'The first thing she said was "I want that big front porch." She likes the big country style.'

'I know what she means. I'm married to a woman like that.'

It's such an American thing to be so pragmatic and optimistic, always looking at what the future might bring, rather than reflecting on what has been lost in the past.

'This was our party place for all our friends,' said Bridget.

'There was a pool and a hot tub in the yard, and a trampoline. So they're planning somewhere to continue having parties.'

Remarkably, no one was killed by the tornado. In fact, not so much as a pet had been reported missing. But I wondered what it must be like to live in a place where tornadoes are a permanent threat.

'Have you had tornadoes here before?' I said.

'Not anything like this,' said Bridget.

'About 1967 was the last one that was equal to this,' added Bridget's friend. 'And it was two miles down the road. I was a kid and I remember that one; it was on my fifth birthday. I spent it in the basement waiting for a tornado to pass.'

'You wouldn't need to blow your own candles out that time!' I said.

'No, I didn't even have a cake that day. And people died in that one. It was really severe.'

She told me that they got lots of tornadoes, but their routes were unpredictable, so the outcome was always a bit of a lottery. In fact, St Louis is one of the most active urban areas for tornadoes in the United States. Every April, on average, 163 tornadoes will strike America, most of them in Tornado Alley. In this zone cold, dry air from Canada and the Rocky Mountains meets warm, moist air from the Gulf of Mexico and hot, dry air from the Sonoran Desert. When they collide, the air streams create rotations, like the swirl of cream being stirred into coffee. In storms, when the air streams are fast and powerful, the rotations can turn into tornados. Tornado alley stretches from the Eastern Plain of Colorado and the Texas Panhandle, through Oklahoma, Kansas and Missouri, and up to Nebraska and South Dakota. But this year, by 25 April, they had already experienced 292 tornadoes. And everyone was nervous, because May usually has twice as many as April.

They were right to be worried. A fortnight after I'd visited Bridgeton, one of the worst tornadoes in American history, a mile-wide whirlwind, struck Joplin, Missouri, killing 138 people. At the same time, Arizonans were fighting some of the largest wildfires they had ever known; and the greatest flood in US history was spreading down the Missouri River. Meanwhile, Texas was suffering its eighth year of 'exceptional' drought in the past twelve years. Something very weird was happening to the weather.

The next day, we took the trike to a garage to get the throttle fixed. It was now so stiff that it made my thumb and forefinger ache. It was all I could think about when I was riding along, and that was dangerous. My mind ought to have been on the road, not my throbbing thumb, when I was flying up an interstate or bumping along Route 66. With the bike out of action for the day, I took a taxi down to the Gateway Arch.

The world's tallest man-made monument (they really like superlatives in America), the arch is America's symbolic gateway to the West. Four million people visit it each year. They just want to touch it or gawp at it or be near it.

According to those who know about these things, it's an inverted catenary curve – the kind of organic shape that forms naturally when you hang a piece of string between two points. The designer, Eero Saarinen, also designed the Tulip chair and the TWA Terminal at JFK Airport in New York (that's the funky, space-age one). He came up with the design of the Gateway Arch by dangling a twenty-one-inch length of string between

Mike Reilly

The Gemini Giant (or welder), in Wilmington, Illinois.

Tim Pollard

Striking a pose at the Polk-a-Dot Drive-In with my new friends Elvis, James and Betty.

Mike Reilly

Artist Bob Waldmire's bus in Pontiac, Illinois.

Tim Pollard

The bronze bust of Abraham Lincoln at Springfield, Illinois. With my finger up his nose.

My friend Mervin, a lovely, complete man whose company I'll remember for ever. The picture was taken from behind out of respect for his Amish beliefs.

Tim Pollard

Maverick Television

My buggy-riding lesson.

Maverick Television

Heading across the Chain of Rocks Bridge, St Louis, Missouri.

Maverick Television

The Gateway Arch, St Louis, Missouri.

Maverick Television

Getting to know the 'soldiers' at the Civil War re-enactment at Jefferson Barracks, Missouri.

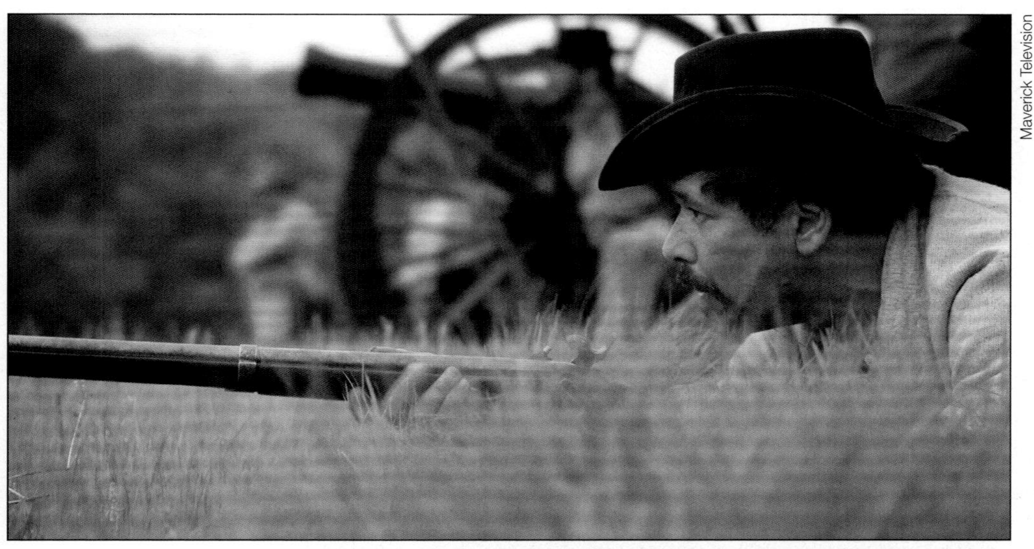

Maverick Television

Maverick Television

My, Grandma, what big teeth you have! Despite appearances these wolves at the wolf sanctuary in Eureka, Missouri, proved that they're far more scared of us than we are of them.

Maverick Television

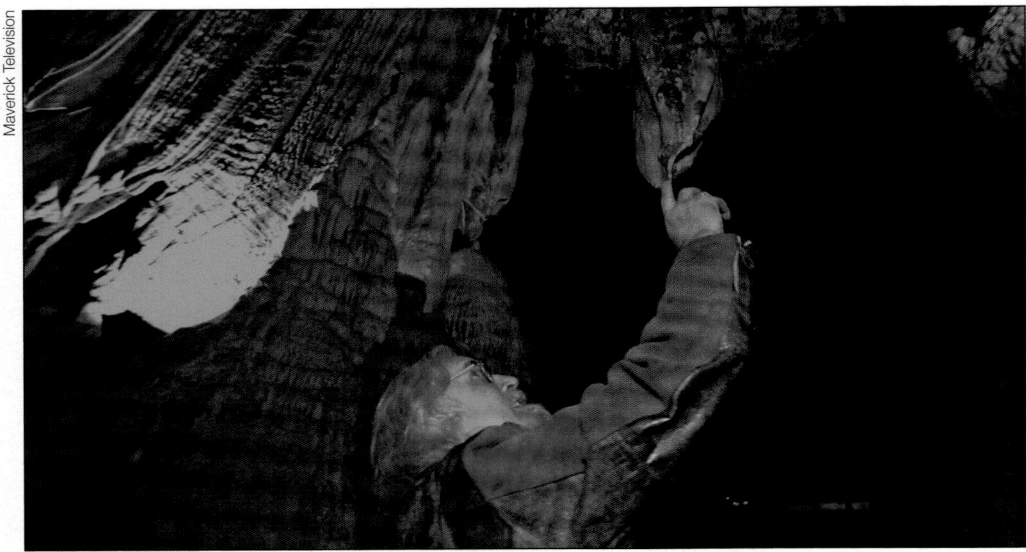

The light show at the Meramec Caverns – I couldn't quite understand why something as staggeringly beautiful as a cave would need a light show to improve it.

Tim Pollard

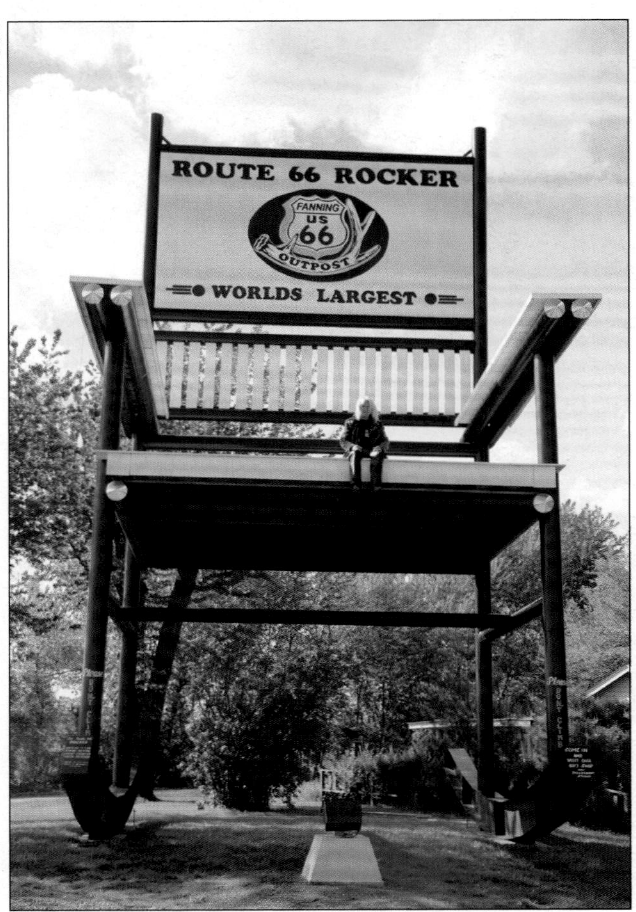

Taking a load off on the 'World's Largest' rocking chair, Fanning, Missouri.

Maverick Television

Bubbly jock, bubbly jock . . . Getting kitted out for the turkey hunt at Fanning, Missouri.

Tim Pollard

With twins Carolyn and Cheri.

Mike Reilly

Rob Lurvey and his astonishing collection of instruments.

Maverick Television

The Oklahoma City National Memorial.

Mike Reilly

The National Stock Yards in Oklahoma City, where up to 12,000 cattle are traded in a single day.

his fingers, held seven inches apart, and scaling it up from there. Saarinen said he chose the shape of a dangling necklace in tribute to the great explorers, hunters and trappers of the West. As most people know, those pioneers always wore a wee single-strand pearl necklace and a twinset underneath all their rawhide gear, just in case they were ever invited to a tea dance in the outback. (Okay, I made that up. But they did always make sure they had a wee black dress in their saddlebag in case of emergencies.)

A lot of people rave about Saarinen's Tulip chair, but the Gateway Arch is surely his finest piece. I'd seen it maybe half a dozen times before, but always from a distance, between buildings. It's a bit like Paris and the Eiffel Tower – you keep seeing it from unexpected angles. But when you get to see it properly, it's a thing of amazing beauty. My only slight disappointment was that I'd always thought that it straddles the Missouri River, but in fact it stands alone, on the west bank of the Missouri. But that doesn't detract from how magnificent it looks.

The 630-foot arch was gleaming in the sun when I arrived. There were nine hundred tons of stainless steel standing in front of me, the most used in any single project in history. It fascinated me that they did the surveying during construction overnight, when it was cooler, so that expansion of the metal would be minimised. They built the arch as two separate legs, and then joined them together at the top. And do you know what the margin of error was for the base of each leg at ground level? One sixty-fourth of an inch. *One sixty-fourth of a bloody inch.* Any more than that, and the two legs would not have met at the top. It made me imagine the builders finishing the two legs to find that they'd built them perfectly, but a foot apart. Can you picture it? 'Excuse me, mate, you wouldn't happen to have a twelve-inch piece of stainless steel on you? We're a bit short up here.'

I descended into the basement to take a lift all the way to the top. When I say lift, I mean a strange little pillbox that goes sideways as well as up and down, which of course it has to do as the top of the Gateway Arch is not directly above the base. Designing it presented a unique challenge for some of civil engineering's finest minds, who knew that no conventional lift would be able to carry passengers all the way to the planned observation deck at the pinnacle of the arch. They suggested that two or more lifts would be needed, with passengers hopping from one to the next on their journey to the top. Nobody wanted that – it had to be a single-lift design. But after a lot of scratching of heads, the Harvard- and Yale-educated engineers drew a blank. No one could work out how to put a single lift into a structure that didn't rise in a pin-straight line.

Then a young man came forward. A lift repairman by trade, his only qualification was a high school diploma, but he reckoned he had designed a lift that could ascend the whole parabolic structure. When he'd finished explaining his idea to a room of architects and engineers, he asked if there were any questions.

'Yes,' said one of the audience. 'Who are you?'

'I'm thirty-four,' he said. And left it at that.

A few years later, the mysterious lift repairman's design was adopted and installed in each leg of the arch.

It's a very curious lift. Officially, it's called a cantilever railway. I climbed into a tiny cabin, almost bending double to get through the door. Four adults can just about fit into one cabin, which at first goes up diagonally in one direction. Then there is a lot of clanking and grinding of gears and the little wagon rises in the opposite diagonal direction. It was kind of weird, a bit like being on an underground train, except moving in a different direction. I couldn't see much, aside for some rivets and girders, but I quite enjoyed that. As I've said before, I like engineering. I like things that are built to be beautiful and to show off the skill of the human race.

The trip took about four minutes, near the end of which the little pod appeared to go straight up for a short time before resuming its strange zigzag movement and arriving at the top.

I'd been in a few other monuments in my time, like the Atomium in Brussels and the Walter Scott Memorial in Edinburgh. And I'd always wanted to go inside the Statue of Liberty, but never managed it, although I can tell you a story that will make you jealous. Once, on Elton John's birthday, he took me on a trip around Manhattan in a helicopter and we flew around the statue. Then we hovered right in front of her face and had a good look. Are you jealous yet?

Anyway, back to the arch. At the top, there's a small observation capsule with a great view. I've always loved being up high, so it was fantastic to gaze down at the State Capitol Building and the riverboats far below on the Mississippi. I was a bit disappointed that no one asked me how to spell Mississippi, because it was one of those words that they tested us on again and again at school. Back in those days, I'd never have dreamed that one day I would be at the top of a huge monument looking down on it. Isn't life the strangest thing?

Just as I'd done from the top of the Sears Tower in Chicago,

I gazed west, contemplating where Route 66 would take me next. Whereas Chicago had been the central distribution point for goods coming from and going to the West, St Louis was often the starting point for people moving westwards. This was made possible when President Thomas Jefferson bought fifteen US states and two Canadian provinces from the French in 1803. Doubling the size of the United States, the Louisiana Purchase included all of present-day Arkansas, Missouri, Iowa, Oklahoma, Kansas and Nebraska, as well as parts of Minnesota that were west of the Mississippi River, most of North Dakota, nearly all of South Dakota, northeastern New Mexico, northern Texas, the portions of Montana, Wyoming and Colorado that lie east of the Continental Divide, and Louisiana west of the Mississippi, including the city of New Orleans. In addition, it contained small portions of land that would eventually become part of the Canadian provinces of Alberta and Saskatchewan.

Jefferson commissioned two Virginia-born veterans of the Indian wars in the Ohio valley, Meriwether Lewis and William Clark, to survey all the rivers and land west of St Louis. Accompanied by a fifteen-year-old Shoshone Indian girl called Sacagawea, they crossed the Rocky Mountains and reached the Pacific Ocean in present-day Oregon, claiming all the territory that lay beyond the nation's new boundaries for the United States. This led to the biggest migration in history, as people from all over the world first arrived on America's East Coast, then moved west.

While up in the observation deck, I met a nice family from Newfoundland. I've never met a Newfie I didn't like – they are fabulous people from a breathtakingly beautiful part of the world – and these Newfies didn't disappoint. They even knew who I was, which made a pleasant change from being mistaken for John Cleese.

From the Gateway Arch, I headed to St Louis station, to see its own famous arch. I took a taxi again, but a huge parade was blocking off several streets, so I was forced to continue on foot. On the way, I passed a park known as the Citygarden, which was chock-a-block with some fabulous sculptures. I was fascinated and went to have a closer look. Some girls were trying to squeeze inside one of the sculptures, a giant man's head lying sideways on the ground. It would have been great to film them as they messed around, but by the time we'd set up the camera, they'd moved on. Not to worry – before long, some other children were climbing all over it.

This art was so alive. Most towns have statues of dowdy characters with big moustaches, dressed in frock coats and covered in pigeon shit. They're the great and the good of the town, but nobody gives a toss about them. People swan straight past, even if they're Robbie Burns or Robert Tannahill, rather than some general or lord mayor. Abstract and modern sculptures are so much more accessible. People are drawn to them and like to touch them. I love the fact that abstract art can do that for people, entitle them to go up and touch it. To me, it gives the art a life of its own. If I was the artist, I would be absolutely over the moon if I saw those kids reacting to my work in that way.

As I walked through the park, I saw another bunch of kids treating a big red abstract sculpture like a slide, whizzing down it on their bellies. Another statue had water squirting out of the ground and the kids were running through it, getting soaked. It made me so happy. It was such a joy to see these inert statues brought vividly to life.

I spotted a sign as I was leaving. It warned that playing in or near the water and sculptures was inherently dangerous, but it didn't say, 'Keep Off!' It just asked visitors to exercise some caution and common sense when they let children loose on them: 'Treat it and one another with respect, thereby maintaining an atmosphere which provides enjoyment for all.' It was that easy to get people to behave responsibly. Much better than the usual threats of 'Clear off or we'll call the police, you scoundrel.' What a wonderful place. A public garden with spectacular landscaping and internationally renowned sculpture in a completely open, accessible setting – what more could anyone want?

After that delightful, unplanned detour to the Citygarden, I must admit I was dreading my planned trip to the railway station. I was on my way to see its 'whispering archway', but I was wondering what on earth I could say about a station, no matter how beautiful. Even Grand Central Station in New York is difficult. You say it's stunning. Then what?

However, I was very moved by some of the details of this station, such as that two million soldiers passed through it every month in 1943. I wondered how many of them returned home after being shipped over to Europe and Asia. All those goodbyes and cheerios and tidings of 'good luck' and 'look after yourself'. And the arch turned out to be quite interesting, too. Most whispering galleries work on the horizontal inside a dome. For instance, at St Paul's Cathedral in London, you whisper against the wall and the sound goes round horizontally. But this one goes up the wall, across the ceiling and down the opposite wall in a channel. Apparently no one realised it carried whispers until a workman hit himself with a hammer and swore. One of the other workmen on the other side of the arch heard the expletive distinctly. Now some guys say to their girlfriends, 'Stand there. There's something I want to tell you. I want you to hear this.' Then they shoot over to the other side of the arch and whisper: 'Will you marry me?' Lovely.

I tried it out and it works perfectly. But I had nothing more to say about it, so we packed up the camera and went for lunch.

Entering a Japanese restaurant, I looked up at the television to see *The Last Samurai*. It stars Tom Cruise, Timothy Spall . . . and me. We asked the manager to rewind to the beginning and then we all watched it, something I've never done before. Usually I don't even go to the premiere of a film in which I've appeared. If can get away with it, I'll sneak away. But enough time had passed since I'd filmed this one, so it was fun to watch. All in all a rather jolly time was had in St Louis.

The next day, we collected the repaired bike and I was itching to get back on the road. But first I wanted to stop off at a soul food restaurant run by a remarkable woman.

Robbie Montgomery used to be one of the backing singers for Ike and Tina Turner – an Ikette – shaking her tail feathers and singing fabulous soul songs such as 'River Deep, Mountain High'. That meant she'd got to know everybody. She'd sung with Mick Jagger and lots of other sixties and seventies stars like Dr John, Stevie Wonder, Barbra Streisand, Elton John, Pink Floyd, Rod Stewart and Joe Cocker. When she'd been starting out, restaurants on the road would often refuse to serve black performers, so Robbie and others in the band would cook dinner in an electric skillet in their motel rooms. Eventually forced to quit singing because of a lung disorder, Robbie turned to her second love, cooking soul food. She opened a restaurant, and after many years and a lot of hard work, she now owns two fantastic restaurants called Sweetie Pie's, one of which is in South St Louis.

It was a real privilege to meet a woman I'd previously admired in a soul revue. Now seventy years old, she is still very beautiful, with a shock of white hair tied back under a chef's hat.

'I never thought I'd stand this close to you,' I said. 'The only time I ever saw you before, you were . . . '

'Shaking my tail feathers?'

We both laughed.

'That was my favourite,' I said. 'Shaking the tail feathers!'

'Really? Well, the tail feathers broke. I can't shake it any more. I've gotten too old for that now.'

It was very easy to laugh with Robbie.

'Well, welcome. Are you going to come on in?' she said.

'I hear I have to stand in line like everybody else. That's democratic. I don't need special treatment. I don't seek it, I don't need it.'

'Oh, good.'

Robbie's dishes, learned at her mother's hip, are best described as from-scratch cooking. The menu features recipes like baked chicken, ox tails, candied yams, macaroni cheese and peach cobbler made in the traditional way.

'White people call it home cooking,' she said. 'Black people call it soul. We call it comfort food. Or we call it Mississippi-style cooking, because these are all my mom's recipes and she was born in Mississippi, like me, and she taught me to cook.'

I was really looking forward to my first taste of soul food, but

I was nervous about sitting there – the only white guy in the restaurant. It was nothing to do with race. I just didn't like being the only guy who didn't understand what was on the menu. But Robbie guided me, and it was just darling.

'It's Sunday,' she said, 'so most people have collard greens and candied yams; and if you like meatloaf, that's your choice.'

'I like meatloaf,' I said. 'And I haven't had it in such a long time.' I'd never had candied yams or collard greens. I'd only read about them in William Faulkner books. They were fantastically good, but the experience was made so much better by being able to sit and talk to the woman who had sung such sensational songs. We talked a lot about music, food and life in general, and Robbie was the best company. It was a great start to the day.

So far on Route 66, my meetings with black people – from Preston Jackson in Bronzeville and the Quinn Chapel congregation to Robbie here in St Louis – had been a joy and a constant surprise to me. If I was black in America, I think I'd be angry at the way black people have been treated over the years. And I'm not just talking about slavery. From the Civil War through to Vietnam and Iraq, black people have fought for America, then returned home to bloody shoddy treatment. Yet they seem unfazed by it. Their experiences haven't broken their niceness. On this trip I was constantly amazed and pleased by their attitude. I know that sounds hellish – like I was a fucking explorer – but I'd expected them to be angry, and they just weren't. There was a quality to black people in America that I found unbelievably impressive, especially when I was talking to Robbie. I was glad to meet her, and I was even gladder that I ate her food. It was unbelievable.

All that said, though, my macaroni cheese would smash Robbie's out of the park. But my macaroni cheese would smash *anybody*'s out of the park. I'll take on anyone. And I do a mean fishy pie, too.

7

You Haven't Seen the Country 'til You've Seen the Country by Car

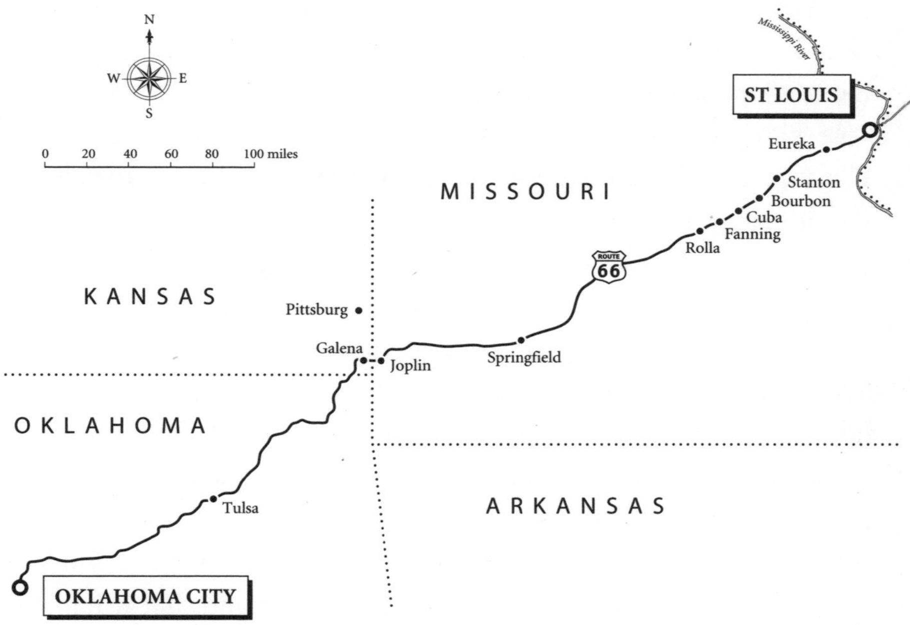

Leaving St Louis, I stopped off at Jefferson Barracks, the oldest operational military base west of the Mississippi River. Established in 1826 on land obtained as part of the Louisiana Purchase, these barracks assisted and supported the westward expansion of white settlers by keeping hostile Indian groups at bay.

Exactly 150 years before I visited, Missouri was torn apart by the Civil War, an appalling event that left 625,000 Americans dead, more than perished in the two world wars combined. Missouri endured more than a thousand battles and engagements between 1861 and 1865. On the day that I passed through, a Civil War re-enactment group was recreating the Camp Jackson Affair, which set Missouri on the violent, turbulent path to war between the opposing Confederate and Union armies. On 10 May 1861, Union forces clashed with civilians on the streets of St Louis – at least twenty-eight people were killed and another hundred injured. The incident polarised the border state of Missouri, leading some citizens to advocate secession with the Confederacy and others to support the Union, thereby setting the stage for sustained violence between the opposing factions.

Eleven southern Confederate states fought twenty-five northern Union states, but even today nobody can be certain *why* they went to war. This very complex issue sells millions of books in America every year, and thousands of academics dedicate their lives to studying it. To Abraham Lincoln, the President at the time, the conflict was entirely about slavery; but a recent poll in America found that two-thirds of people think it was actually about issues to do with how much power the federal government had over individual states and that it had nothing to do with slavery at all.

Whatever the true cause, I was enjoying the smell of cordite at the re-enactment. Held over two days in a green, rolling Missouri field, it involved several hundred participants in grey and blue coats watched by several thousand spectators. Like some other scheduled stops on the trip, I must admit that I hadn't been looking forward to this one. I didn't expect to have a good time with people who re-enacted battles during their weekends. But I was proved wrong yet again. The re-enactment was beautifully executed, although it was hampered by one fatal flaw: none of the re-enactors wanted to die, because that meant lying on the battlefield for hours on end until the entire shooting match was over. I spotted only one dead guy. He was lying face up and was so still that I wondered if he might actually be asleep. There were far more wounded guys, limping off the field. The bastard that I am, I watched them closely to make sure they kept playing their part right to the end, but I didn't spot any who gave up hobbling when they thought no one was looking.

It was all very impressive, but I still didn't have a clue what to say to the camera crew about it. I made a few comments, and an American guy standing next to me started to laugh, so I felt reassured that I'd not overstepped the mark by making fun of the Civil War. He seemed like a good guy, so I asked him to explain exactly what was going on.

'This battle kept St Louis in the Union,' he said. 'So the Unionists are supposed to win, I guess.'

'Well, they have to in the end, don't they?'

'The bit about America losing 625,000 Americans, that's the tragedy. I heard you talking about it.'

'That's right. And we keep doing it. We keep sending people to war. Young, healthy, bright people.'

'In England you send them on honeymoons, right?'

This guy had a sense of humour. A couple of days earlier, Prince William had married Kate Middleton and now everyone was talking about where they might be going on honeymoon.

You couldn't escape it – even in the middle of America. 'I don't know why you're so interested in it all,' I said. 'Didn't you have a war to get rid of them?'

He laughed, then nodded at the re-enactment. 'This is the first time I've ever done this.'

'Me too.' One of the re-enactors suddenly put his hands in the air. 'Oh look, he's surrendering and he's a bluecoat!'

The bluecoats were Unionists, whereas the Confederates traditionally wore grey. Not the easiest of colours to tell apart at the best of times, but what made it even worse was that the Confederate Army struggled to find grey material, so some of their soldiers wore dark blue. Unsurprisingly, this led to considerable confusion. For instance, during the Battle of Shiloh, some of the Confederate forces fired at their own soldiers. As if that wasn't crazy enough, the Union then ran out dark blue cloth, some of their old uniforms faded to grey as the dye washed out, and many Unionist troops were given grey jackets to wear over their blue shirts. No wonder so many soldiers died.

After a few hours, the re-enactment ended with no sign of who had won. Several of the participants recognised me and wandered over for a chat. They told me they'd all made their uniforms themselves and had been very accurate about the details, to the point where one of them had a period pipe that he kept smoking, staying in character throughout. They were great fun. I couldn't have asked for better company.

From the re-enactment, I drove directly to Jefferson Barracks National Cemetery, a military graveyard on the banks of the Mississippi. More than 220 generals from the Civil War spent time at Jefferson Barracks and many of them were laid to rest in the cemetery, which covers more than 330 acres. Established after the Civil War, it contained nearly 160,000 graves by 2005. Since then, several thousand more have been added.

There wasn't much I could say about this place. The sight of all the graves said it all, really. Every grave was identical – each one a uniform size in an indistinguishable serried rank. Tombstones in civilian graveyards are often engraved with poems and little one-liners, but there's none of that in military graveyards. Just the bare details: name, regiment, date of birth and date of death. Occasionally, the tombstone would have a few additional words, such as 'Loving Father' or 'Dear Brother', but more often it was just the basic facts in row upon row of tombstones, rolling over hill and dale.

To me, it seemed a wee bit obscene to make something so horrible look so neat and tidy. I know that's a very cruel thing to say, because I'm sure the people who designed the cemetery did it with the very best intentions, but it reminded me of the National Memorial Arboretum in Staffordshire – a monument to all the British forces killed on duty or as a result of terrorism since the end of the Second World War. When it was opened, a commentator on television explained that some of the walls listing the dead had been left blank. Apparently, there was space for about ten thousand more names to be added. When I heard that, I thought: Does this bastard know something I don't?

What horrifies me most about war memorials is that no anti-war sentiments are ever displayed. It's as if war is fun or noble, when actually it's all about shit and snot and blood and guts and soldiers' stomachs hanging out and people with their faces blown off. But they never showed that side of it. Perhaps, if they did, there'd be less of it. I remember seeing a picture of a soldier in Vietnam who was sitting, waiting to die, with his jaw missing. His head now started at his top row of teeth; everything beneath that was gone. They didn't put that on the recruitment posters, did they? But that's what war is to me. And I don't care who we're fighting, I don't hate them enough to do something like that to them.

Maybe all of this hit me particularly hard at the Jefferson Barracks National Cemetery because I visited it shortly after Osama bin Laden was nailed and America was rejoicing in a huge wave of triumphalism. I found all of that rather horrifying – that delight in death and that attitude of 'Why don't we just kill the bastard?' We have to move beyond that kind of thinking or we're doomed as a species.

Fortunately, my mood, which had got more than a bit dark at the cemetery, immediately lightened as I rode west from St Louis and Route 66 entered some of the most pleasant, verdant country along its entire length. Scenic wooded drives through hills and valleys, far from the superslab of Interstate 44, gave a tantalising impression of what riding the road must have been like in its heyday. But the weather was still remarkably turgid and *dreich* (a Scottish word for dreary) as I pulled up at my next stop, a wolf sanctuary in Eureka, Missouri.

I've always had great respect for wolves. Many years ago, when I was a boy, I read that the wolf's fierce reputation was the creation of writers who had never even seen one. Sitting in London, Birmingham or Manchester, they wrote about the call of the wild with little or no experience of it. If they'd seen these magnificent creatures, they would have realised immediately that they're terrified of humans. Absolutely terrified. There's no chance at all of that cartoon image of them sneaking up behind you and tearing out your throat with their vicious teeth. The wolves I saw at the sanctuary couldn't get far enough away from us.

Tucked away in a wooded area, the Endangered Wolf Center is home to forty animals from five different species, including the two most endangered species of wolf – the Mexican grey and the red, which used to be native to Missouri. Only around a hundred red wolves exist in the wild and they're all in North Carolina. As for the Mexican grey, there are only about fifty left anywhere outside captivity.

A lovely young lady called Regina showed me around, explaining that their mission was to breed wolves in captivity and then release them into the wild. 'We're unique in that aspect,' she said. 'We don't pat the animals, we don't talk to 'em, we don't play with 'em. We want them to keep that fear of humans, so when they go into the wild, they stay away from people.'

They had already released some Mexican grey wolves in the New Mexico–Arizona border area – the only spot where they can still be found in the wild. Some red wolves had been released in the Alligator River National Wildlife Refuge in North Carolina.

'Sarah Palin likes to shoot wolves from helicopters,' I said.

'Yeah. In Alaska and a few other areas, that's their practice.'

'It's ridiculous, isn't it?'

'It's different management styles. These guys, you definitely don't do that with them' – she pointed at one of the red wolves – 'because there are so few left. They're the most endangered mammal in North America, so they're very protected.' We both watched the wolf, which was bright red with big ears and exceptionally long legs that made it walk funny, like it was wearing high heels.

In addition to the wolves, the sanctuary houses some brilliantly coloured African wild dogs – all yellow, white, grey and brown. Fucking great, they are. Superb hunters and killers with massive strength in their jaws, second only to the hyena, they're also hugely social animals. When they wake up in the morning, they all greet each other like they've never seen each other before. Then, in the afternoon, they have a wee kip, wake up, and do it all over again. They really seem to love each other.

The final two species in the sanctuary are maned wolves from South America, which have manes of black hair, like horses, and swift foxes from North America. All of them are kept for education, research and breeding purposes.

'Swift foxes?' I said. I'd not heard of them before.

'They are,' she said. 'Their name kind of gives away what they do.'

I laughed.

'They are the fastest animal we have here. About forty miles per hour.'

'Really?'

'They're pretty fast. So whenever we have to give them their vaccines and catch 'em, it's a challenge.'

I told her that I'd always liked wolves.

'Yes. They're a creature that really touches your heart. One of my favourite things about working here is that I get to work with species that are going to be released into the wild.'

'They've been lied about for so long, you know. Fiction writers have written such nonsense about them for years.'

'That's true. Kids grow up listening to *Little Red Riding*

Hood and *The Three Little Pigs* and stories about werewolves and they become scared of wolves. But the old cliché – that they're more scared of you than you are of them – is true.'

Then she asked if I'd like to help feed a deer to one of the wolf packs. I could see several wolves lurking among the trees in the distance, looking very nervous. The dead deer had been donated by the Missouri Department of Transportation after it was hit by a car. Instead of going to waste, it would give the wolves a welcome taste of their natural prey.

The warden handed me a long stick. 'It's your protection stick,' she said. 'The wolves won't come up to you, but if you feel threatened, you can wave it. But like I said, they're gonna be at the back of the enclosure.'

A protection stick. I liked that. 'I'm sure wolves are terrified of white sticks,' I said.

'You'd be surprised.'

There were six animals in the pack – an alpha male, a female and their cubs. As well as an occasional deer, the wolves were fed a dry mix made specifically for them and they could hunt raccoons, possums and even any turkeys that wandered into their enclosure.

'Do those animals just stray in not knowing?' I asked.

'Yep, they don't know there are wolves in there, so it's quite a shock. And these guys get to practise their hunting skills.'

The deer was frozen stiff. 'Will they be able to eat this?' I said.

'Oh, yes. Think of the wolves in Yellowstone. They come across deer that have been killed by the winter cold. They're still able to get in there and break apart the carcass and get the healthy, nutritious stuff.'

After dropping the deer in the enclosure, I watched from a distance as the wolves approached it very warily. The alpha male took the first bites, eating the best meat; then the female tucked in. Finally, they let the cubs come in and eat, too.

'In the wild,' said the warden, 'the entire pack helps take down a deer or an elk, and they all have their roles. One of the cubs distracts the deer or the elk and then the alphas come in and take down the deer from the rear, by the neck. Then the rest of the pack helps bring 'em down. You'll actually see 'em kind of take roles when they're chasing. One will chase for a little bit and then take a break, then the next one'll chase until they get 'em down. And they all help. So when they say it's a family pack, they really mean that every animal works to get the dinner.'

When wolves hunt, they're successful only about 10 per cent of the time. A well-placed kick from an elk can break a wolf's leg or jaw. And there are no vets in the wild. It would be like us going to the supermarket and being chased out with a baseball bat nine times before we were able to buy any food. And the one time that we managed to buy anything, the food would be kicking and fighting us the whole time.

I looked up to where one of the wolves was watching me, the warden and the camera crew. 'Look at that one – on top of the shed.'

'He's checking you out. We think we're being quiet, but these guys have amazing hearing. They can hear from several miles away. One of the ways they communicate is by howling, which they can hear up to ten miles away, depending on the wind speed. So even though we're quiet, they can hear us. They can smell us, too. When you're out there hiking, they can hear you coming before you even know and they'll take off running.'

'They're really wishing we weren't here, aren't they?'

'They are. They're ready to go for dinner and we're making 'em nervous.'

'You can see them coming round and saying, "Oh God, they're still there."'

'They're very shy. And that makes them tough to study out in the wild. You want to observe their behaviour and learn about them, but they know you're there before you even know you're there, so they run away. But being shy helps them survive.'

We watched the female wolf circle the deer cautiously. Tall and weighing about forty-five pounds, she was very light on her feet. All legs, like a supermodel, she backed off the deer when she sensed that the alpha male was returning for another wee snack. Then he peed on the deer, marking it as his own.

Wolves have the most awful reputation for crowding and circling hikers, pulling them down, tearing out their throats and killing them in a fevered bloodbath. Well, it's all a load of bollocks. There's no recorded instance of wolves attacking humans in history. They're the most delightful, tender creatures, and the people working with them at the sanctuary are lovely. They've dedicated their lives to looking after these beautiful animals and I'm full of admiration for them.

I also think we could learn a little about social interaction from those African wild dogs. The French have learned it already: they all shake hands in the morning, as if they are being introduced for the first time. I really like that, and was inspired to try it myself. So, at breakfast the next morning, I shook hands with one of the crew. Maybe he was surprised, but I can be quite human when I try.

My journey continued through green farmland, across little bridges over creeks and past red-brick and wood farmsteads, for about thirty-five miles to Stanton, site of one of the best-known and most hyped attractions on Route 66: the Meramec Caverns. So far, I'd travelled nearly four hundred miles along Route 66, and most of that distance had been regularly punctuated by large billboards advertising these limestone caverns, often accompanied by a painting of the outlaw Jesse James. The bill-boards draw over 150,000 visitors each year to the caves, so they're clearly doing something right.

The Meramec Caverns are a weird combination of phenomen-ally beautiful and utterly awful. They're a wee bit showbiz, with neon signs, souvenir shops and a moonshiner's cabin outside, all of which I thought was pretty unnecessary. They were first opened up in 1722, when a French miner met an Indian who told him the caverns contained seams of gold. The miner found no gold, but he discovered lots of saltpetre, an essential component of gunpowder. During the Civil War, the Union Army used the caves as a saltpetre plant, but it was discovered and destroyed by Confederate guerrillas, among them Jesse James. Years later, Jesse and his brother and partner in crime, Frank, reportedly used the caves as their hideout. One legend claims that a sheriff staked out the caves, waiting for Jesse and his gang to emerge, but they found another exit and sneaked out that way.

By the early twentieth century, hundreds of tons of saltpetre had been extracted, creating vast underground chambers. In the

1920s the locals started to hold dances down there. One of the largest caves was named 'the ballroom' and it still has a tiled floor and a stage. Bands and their audiences would drive their cars right into the caves and dance the night away. Later, the likes of Dolly Parton played concerts there. The sheer size of the place is quite breathtaking. It's so high that I didn't even feel like I was underground. There's no sense of claustrophobia at all, and it has a kind of magnificence.

In the 1930s a guy with big ideas called Lester B. Dill set about tarnishing that magnificence. He bought the caves, explored the full extent of the underground system, and claimed to have found artefacts belonging to the James boys. It's entirely possible that Dill added more than a wee bit to local legends about the caves being the James Gang's hideout, and he certainly knew a good marketing opportunity when he stumbled across one. But in my opinion he didn't need to push the James angle, because the caves would be much more remarkable without all the hype. For instance, in one of the caves there's something that looks like an art student's attempt to sculpt a vast Scottish clootie dumpling. In fact, it's the world's largest stalagmite, and it's very impressive and beautiful.

But Dill just couldn't stop himself when it came to promoting his investment. While sightseers were in the caves, looking at the stalagmites, stalactites and supposed Jesse James relics – as well as genuine Pre-Columbian Native American artefacts that were found later – Dill hired wee boys to tie adverts on to the visitors' car bumpers. In one fell swoop, he had invented the bumper sticker, so you know who to blame the next time you're stuck behind a particularly offensive one on the motorway.

I loved the stalagmites and stalactites, and I particularly liked the huge pendulum in the main cave. It was supposed to rotate in concert with the spinning of the earth, but the ball at its end was the wrong weight – it should have been a thousand pounds heavier – so it didn't work. To compensate, someone would just give it a shove every now and then to get it going. Fantastic – the idea of a wee guy whose job it is to slink along when nobody's looking and give it a big push.

However, the climax of any visit to the caves is a light show that has to be seen to be believed. To the accompaniment of a musical soundtrack that culminates in 'The Star Spangled Banner', a fella flicks switches on a board to light up various stalagmite and stalactite sections in garish colours, ending with the American flag superimposed on one section of rock. I couldn't understand why people thought something as staggeringly beautiful as a cave needed a light show to improve it.

Sometimes there's a tackiness about Route 66 that out-tacks any tackiness I've ever seen anywhere else. And the Meramec Caverns are the pinnacle of that tack.

Relieved to be moving on, I rode through the village of Bourbon, where the huge water tower, built in 1853 and labelled with the small village's name, has delighted countless tourists and passers-by over the years. (Bourbon called itself a city, but with just over 1,300 residents and occupying little more than one square mile, and no cathedral or university, it's a village in my book.) A few miles further, I arrived in Cuba, Missouri, where I spent the night.

I woke the next morning feeling depressed and fed up. I didn't think I could take another shitty, grey, rainy day, freezing my bollocks off on the bike. Route 66 wasn't meant to be like this.

Then I opened the blinds and let out a big 'Oh yes!' The sun belted into the room. It was a glorious, warm, bright day. My mood immediately changed. I was even upbeat about the itinerary for the morning: a visit to the world's biggest rocking chair. Another bit of tack, I thought. But it might be a laugh.

The rocking chair is in the town of Fanning, right alongside Route 66. And would you believe it, it's the most beautifully made, smashing piece of (giant) furniture. It was the brainchild of a funny, big man called Danny Sanazaro, and it really is vast: forty-two feet tall with thirty-one-foot rockers, each of which weighs a ton. Standing beside it would make anyone feel like they'd woken up in one of those 1950s B-movies like *The Incredible Shrinking Man*. In the grand Route 66 tradition, Danny commissioned it to persuade drivers and riders to stop at his store. It was designed by a local acquaintance with no formal engineering training, and built by the owner of a local welding company. The designer's plans were off by only a fraction of an inch, Danny told me. The chair was formally unveiled on April Fool's Day, 2008 – a particularly nice touch.

Unfortunately for Danny, apparently there's a sixty-foot chair somewhere in Italy. But when I visited, the back of his rocker still boasted 'World's Largest', not 'America's Largest', so I guess that news of the Italian titan hasn't reached Fanning yet.

Danny let me climb up on a ladder to sit on the seat so that the camera crew could film me saying that I was going to stay up there until someone made the biggest coffee table in the world and brought me a cup of tea. It had been a long time since a piece of furniture had made me so happy. I spotted one great failing, though: it didn't actually rock.

After climbing down, I had a pootle around Danny's store,

which also included a taxidermy place and an archery range. He invited me to have a wee arch and showed me how to fire an arrow. I scored rather well, although that worried me a bit. You start off shooting at targets, like the ones they use in the army with a soldier running towards you with his gun blazing. Then, after about a hundred shots, you think: I wonder how it would be with a real guy who shoots back? I've never done it, but it crossed my mind.

When I'd finished firing arrows, Danny and his wife, Carolyn, invited the whole crew back to their house and gave us the best barbecue I've ever had. Standing on their raised deck in golden evening sunlight, looking out over the treetops in the valley below, they cooked the most tasty, juicy fish from the river, which they called suckers. We'd been joined by their son Laine, who did all the cooking, and Carolyn's twin sister, Cheri. The twins were identical blondes and really stunning.

'Did you have fun growing up identical?' I said.

They both nodded.

'I used to be in a band with a guy who had an identical twin,' I said. 'It was almost spooky.'

'We had a lot of fun with it,' said Carolyn.

'Oh, I bet you did. Did you have fun with guys?'

'Yeah,' she said. 'We still mess with Danny. He'll grab her ass' – Carolyn gestured at Cheri – 'and she'll go along with it.'

She said that they often catch suckers, which look similar to trout, by spearing them in the river at night. The boat is fitted with a big light on the front to attract the fish. 'It's fun,' she continued. 'It's just a big party. You light a big fire down there and you kill 'em and then you clean and you eat 'em right there on the river.'

'That sounds amazing,' I said. 'God, what a lovely place.'

Below us, the woods seemed to be teeming with wildlife.

'I was just watching a deer over here.' Cheri pointed into the woods. 'It's gone now, but we see turkeys and deer and coyotes, all kinds of stuff out here.'

'Most people don't know the turkey's an American animal,' I said. 'They nearly chose it to be the national bird. Somebody insisted on the bald eagle and they went for it, but it could have been a turkey. Of course, you never think of a turkey as being a beautiful thing because it's got that kind of Christmassy, overfed look about it, but the wild one is a thing of beauty, isn't it?'

'Oh, it is,' said Carolyn. 'It's nothing like the white, tame turkey. No, the wild ones, they're pretty.'

'And all the Christmas ones, they never have sex. They can't; they're the wrong shape. Fancy living without sex and then you die at Christmas. What a party.'

Carolyn and Cheri offered to take me out on a hunting trip the next morning. They pointed at a ridge where they said there were many wild turkeys. They'd been hunting since they were little girls, when their father had made them a turkey call – a piece of wood that they would strike to attract the birds.

'I was with a woman, away up in the Arctic,' I said, 'and she was hunting for moose with a bow. The guy with her had a sort of megaphone and he would go *whoaaa*. And you could hear the moose answering, *whoaaa*. It was the most thrilling thing. It got nearer and the *whoaaa* got louder. But I won't tell you how the story ends. It was a disaster. You would hate it.'

'Did she get it?' asked Cheri.

'No, she didn't. One of the crew did a terrible thing.'

'Oh?'

'The director farted . . . '

'What did you say when he did that?'

'Well . . . there was no more *whoaaa*, you know.'

Danny, the twins, his son and all the crew cracked up with laughter.

'But the hunter made a living from manipulating people's bodies. She was a naturopath or something. And she cured the director. He had been sick for days, making these terrible noises and running to the bathroom every five minutes with that funny run. You know the one, with the knees together.'

'Squeezing it in, yeah.' Carolyn was giggling again.

'She did all sorts of things with him. She knew things about the body I'd never seen in my life, you know? Asian opposition muscle stuff. And she messed around with him and made him better. She told him what not to eat, what definitely to eat, and what to eat less of . . . '

'Lay off the beans, huh?'

'Yeah.'

'God, I hope that don't happen in the morning,' said Cheri.

'I'm in show business, so I've never farted. When you're in show business, you have a de-farting operation. Some people get a new nose at the same time. You can have the wrinkles taken away and be de-farted all on the same day.'

There was little danger that the barbecue would cause any problems. As well as the sensational fish, Laine cooked the best mushrooms I've ever tasted in my damn life. Actually, they were the only barbecued mushrooms I've ever tasted, but that didn't make them any less stunning. The previous night, I'd eaten in a barbecue restaurant – oh fuck, what a disappointment that had been. Again I'd seen just how dodgy the food could be in the middle of America. On the whole, it was edible, but eating fast food almost every day was really taking its toll. I'd begun to think there was something wrong with me, like I'd left a bit of my body behind . . . or added a bit. Fast food is okay once or twice a week; but it's a fucking disaster for your digestion if you eat it every day. So it was doubly delightful to share a proper barbecue with Danny and his family.

Up before dawn the next morning, I found myself crashing through woods before I'd even had breakfast. In semi-darkness – with lights, cameras and a non-farting director in tow – I was following Carolyn and Cheri on a turkey hunt. I reckoned I could hear the turkeys running away. There was a turkey noise – *buck-buck-buck-buck-buck-buck* – that I think translated roughly as: 'Let's get the fuck out of here, boys. There's a crowd of people with cameras and sound equipment coming.'

After stumbling through the woods for a while, we reached a turkey blind. A camouflaged canvas tent, it was large enough for three of us to fit inside. We peered through a netted slit, watching for wild birds. It was freezing and we sat there for an hour or two while one or other of the twins wandered around with the turkey call. Whenever she stopped, all I could hear was the sound of real turkeys getting further and further away, which delighted me, as I don't know how I would have reacted if we'd killed one. I like eating them, but I'm not in the killing business. Even when I go fishing, I don't use barbs on my hooks, so I know that the fish will be unharmed when I release it. I'm fine about people who go fishing and eat whatever they catch, but to catch something, kill it and not eat it is a very bad thing. I'm not a fishmonger, I'm an angler, and I don't like to kill things. And I think that hunting with guns fitted with telescopic sights gives the human a deeply unfair advantage over the animal. When you're hunting with a bow and arrow or a crossbow, at least you're really at the sharp end. You have to be very good to hit anything, and you have to get in close, which demands a bit of cleverness.

Going turkey hunting reminds me of a joke that my daughter Kara claims I told her years ago, although I can't remember doing so.

'How do you keep a turkey in suspense?'

'I don't know.'

'I'll tell you tomorrow.'

I wish it was my joke – it's quite a good one – but I think Kara must have confused me with someone else.

Incidentally, do you know what the Scots call turkeys? Bubbly jocks – because that's the noise they make when they're chatting away. *Bubbly jock, bubbly jock*. We've got some great names for other animals, too. Frogs are puddocks, sparrows are speugs, owls are hoolits and a linnet is a lintie, which is lovely, I think.

'Oh, have you heard Margaret's big lassie?'

'Aye, she's a lovely big lassie.'

'Have you heard her singing? Sings like a lintie.' That always pleased me: sings like a lintie.

After the turkey hunt had thankfully ended in abject failure, I left Fanning and the gorgeous twins and had a lovely run on the proper Route 66, away from the interstate. As I've said, much of the original route has now disappeared. Some stretches of it hit dead ends while others simply run out of tarmac. And, of course, many miles have been widened, paved over and turned into interstates, leaving no choice but to travel on the freeway.

So, with the sun shining properly at last, it was terrific to bump along the real Mother Road, with railway tracks to my right and the interstate on my left. Rolling agricultural country stretched far into the distance as I entered the foothills of the Ozark Mountains. Above me, jet planes were playing noughts and crosses with their vapour trails in the sky. I passed a field dotted with bunches of flowers. It was a graveyard, but all the gravestones had been laid flat on the ground, so, from a distance, the commemorative flowers looked like a really peculiar crop.

A train passed me, so I waved. I think we all have a duty to wave at trains. This doesn't apply to planes or cars, but trains always get a wee wave from me, partly because I love those huge American locomotives, but mainly because I always hope to see a hobo looking out of one of the carriages. Apparently there are still loads of them around, catching goods trains across America, although I've never seen one.

This was God-fearing country, the buckle of the Bible Belt. At one crossroads, I stopped to wait for the traffic lights to turn green and spotted churches on three of the four corners. I passed a big billboard that featured a single word – 'Jesus', it said. This got me wondering why certain areas tend to be more evangelistic than others. I reckon it might be the lack of choice of things to do in small towns and agricultural communities. Churches don't loom quite so large in the sights of people living in Manhattan, Los Angeles or Chicago.

The previous day, I'd lain on my bed and watched a woman on television saying she had ascended into heaven and fought demons. According to her, the demons were red and black dragons, and God had given her a sword to slay them. The icing on the cake came when she told the viewers that she could teach them how to slay demons, too. All they had to do was buy her CD for twenty-five dollars. It sounded fanciful. And what a bunch of ninnies who fork out twenty-five dollars. Do you know what always strikes me as ironic? Jesus was such a pleasant person and he had some intelligent, earth-shaking views. So why are so many of his followers such ninnies? There seemed to be a church every five yards in Missouri, and some of them were monstrously huge. I didn't get it. Everyone I'd met in this state had been bright and likeable, but clearly a lot of them are gullible, too.

I stopped for a lunchtime pizza in an ordinary wee place. A woman was sitting in the restaurant with two boys, and one of them asked, 'Are you Billy Connolly?'

'Yeah.'

'I saw you in *The Last Samurai*. Could I have a picture taken with you?'

'Sure.'

'Is that your trike?' He pointed out of the window.

'Yeah.'

'It's a beauty.'

'Come on out and have a look at it.'

I showed him around the bike, then he said, 'That's my pick-up over there.'

It was a lovely green truck, old and very beautiful, so I complimented him on it.

'Yeah, I love it.' Then he pointed across the street. 'And that's my church, over there.'

It was one of those gigantic Midwestern churches, the type where a TV evangelist fraud might preach. God, you're so nice – and you seemed smarter than that, I thought. That might sound arrogant, but I've watched those preachers for years on American television. Almost to a man, they're frauds. They've got that politician look about them – two haircuts a day, whitened teeth, all that crap – and they talk a load of bloody nonsense. They're very selective about the Bible. None of the bits that hammer slavery ever get mentioned, but they're very keen on quoting the bits that hammer homosexuality. Oh yes.

Riding on, I was confronted by a typical example of why Route 66 was dying. Half a mile to my left, Interstate 44 surged through the landscape, sucking all the businesses towards it, like iron fillings to a magnet. On 66, lying in the shadow of the freeway, every business seemed to be crumbling. I could sense the local communities trying different things to attract any passing trade, but it was no good. The choice for the motorist was between whooshing along, seeing very little and contributing nothing to the local economies, or creeping along, seeing lots and keeping the local communities alive. A lot of people were still trying to keep the Mother Road alive, with murals and other tourist attractions, but almost every driver was in a hurry to get where they were going. You needed a lot of time on your hands to take Route 66. So it was collapsing. It was a shame, but it was a fact. I'd already seen hundreds of closed shops and decrepit businesses, and we were still only in Missouri.

Following what was left of Route 66 wasn't easy. The roads chopped and changed, and eventually I got lost, so I stopped at an old store, the Mule Trading Post, to ask directions. That was a stroke of luck, because it was run by a nice old fella and was full of bits and pieces of junk and memorabilia. It also turned out to be a bona fide Route 66 landmark, so I was closer to the Mother Road than I'd thought. I bought some badges and key rings from the old boy and we chatted about fly fishing. I really liked him, but I couldn't stay for long. Ahead of me were Springfield, Missouri, and Tulsa, Oklahoma, which always made me think of that Eric Clapton song, 'Living on Tulsa Time', and, of course, Gene Pitney or Dusty Springfield singing 'Twenty-Four Hours from Tulsa'.

The relentless road beckoned.

8

Springfield, Illinois . . . Springfield, Missouri too

Rolling on, I passed Rolla – which modestly calls itself 'The Middle of Everywhere' – and a string of places with evocative names – Doolittle, Hooker Cut, Devils Elbow, Buckhorn and Laquey – until I arrived in Springfield, Missouri, widely regarded in the folklore of Route 66 as the road's birthplace.

The Mother Road didn't get its snappy name by accident. In 1925 highway officials in Washington came up with a plan for assigning names to the 96,000-mile network of interstate highways that was being constructed and linked across America. Those running east to west would be given even numbers, while odd numbers would be assigned to the north–south routes. The longest east–west routes, stretching from coast to coast, would all end in a zero. But they decided to make one exception – Route 60 – which would head diagonally from Chicago to Los Angeles, crossing Routes 20, 30, 40 and 50.

Maps were printed and signs painted for the proposed Route 60, running from Illinois to Missouri, Oklahoma, Texas, New Mexico, Arizona and California. But then the influential William J. Fields, Governor of Kentucky, kicked up a fuss.

Upset that none of the prestigious routes ending in a zero would run through his state, he persuaded the authorities in Washington to assign Route 60 to a road from the Atlantic coast in Virginia, through various states – including Kentucky – to Springfield, Missouri. As a result, the road from Chicago to Los Angeles would now have to be relabelled Route 62.

Meanwhile, the owner of a restaurant and service station outside Tulsa, Oklahoma, was following all of this with a great deal of interest. Cyrus Avery was acutely aware of the impact of a busy road on business. As chairman of the Oklahoma Department of Highways, he had already successfully lobbied to ensure that the Chicago to Los Angeles road would not follow the old Santa Fe Trail, which bypassed Oklahoma. Instead, thanks to Avery, it would follow a lesser-known trail from the California Gold Rush era that ran straight through his hometown of Tulsa. Now, faced with the humiliation of losing the prestigious Route 60 designation, Avery joined forces with a counterpart in Missouri – A.H. Piepmeier. Telegrams flew between Springfield, Tulsa and Washington, but Avery and Piepmeier couldn't manage to convince the federal bureaucrats to reverse their decision to award Route 60 to the road running through Kentucky.

Then, during a meeting with Piepmeier in Springfield, Avery noticed that the catchy number 66 had not yet been assigned to any road. He swiftly fired off another telegram to Washington and this time the bureaucrats were happy to comply with his suggestion. As the first reference to Route 66 was made in that meeting in Springfield, the town has since claimed to be the road's birthplace. A few months later, the US Highway 66 Association was founded. At its inaugural meeting, Avery coined the name 'The Main Street of America' for the route, and the mythologising began.

Springfield is an attractive little city, the third largest in Missouri, and for the first time I felt that I was bordering the Deep South of America. Towards Springfield's centre, there are long avenues of large Victorian homes. With wicker porch swings on covered verandas, some of them look like southern plantation houses. It's a relaxed, calm kind of place. But if you're a cowboy at heart, which I am, it's also a hugely significant place.

In 1865 a guy called James Butler Hickok was living in Springfield. Tall, lean and muscular, with long blond hair falling to his shoulders and two pistols shoved into his belt, Hickok looked like a Western hero straight out of central casting, particularly with the lawman's badge pinned to his chest. We know him better as Wild Bill Hickok, although quite how they got that from James Butler, I don't know. Nevertheless, in July 1865, Wild Bill did something that set a trend for decades to come.

The final shot of the Civil War had been fired only a month earlier when Wild Bill, who had fought on the Union side, came face to face with his arch enemy, a Confederate veteran called Davis Tutt. Even though they'd fought on opposite sides in the war, they'd originally been gambling buddies, but had fallen out over a woman called Susanna Moore. There were also suggestions that Hickok had dallied with Tutt's sister, possibly fathering her illegitimate child. Whatever the cause, they now hated the sight of each other.

On 20 July, Hickok was playing poker when Tutt walked into Springfield's Lyon House Hotel. Wild Bill was doing well, so

Tutt started loaning money to the other gamblers and offering hints on how to beat him. It made no difference – Hickok's winning streak continued and he had soon amassed more than two hundred dollars (several thousand dollars in today's money), much of it straight from Tutt's pocket. Remembering that Hickok owed him forty dollars for a horse trade, Tutt insisted that he repay it there and then. Hickok shrugged and handed over the money. Then Tutt demanded another thirty-five bucks, for a gambling debt. This time Hickok disputed the figure, saying he owed only twenty-five. A furious Tutt grabbed Hickok's watch, which was lying on the table, pocketed it, and announced that he was keeping it as collateral. Faced with a room full of Tutt's allies, Hickok reluctantly agreed, as long as Tutt didn't wear the watch in public. That would have been a public humiliation, and retribution would have to be sought.

'I intend wearing it first thing in the morning,' said Tutt, with a sneer.

'If you do, I'll shoot you,' Wild Bill replied calmly. 'I'm warning you here and now not to come across that town square with it on.'

The following day Wild Bill came round the corner into Springfield's town square to find Tutt swanning around, asking people if they wanted to know the time. Flaunt, flaunt, flaunt.

Wild Bill warned Tutt to cut it out, but Tutt ignored him. They attempted to reach an agreement over the outstanding debt, but failed. After a drink, they parted.

Later that day, shortly before 6 p.m., Hickok returned to the square, this time with a pistol in his hand. Onlookers scattered, leaving Tutt standing on his own in the far corner of the square.

'Dave, here I am,' shouted Hickok from a distance of about

seventy-five yards. 'Don't you come across here with that watch.'

Hickok had cocked his pistol and returned it to his hip holster. Tutt stood his ground with a hand on his own pistol, silent. For a few seconds, the two men faced each other down. Then Tutt pulled his pistol from its holster. Hickok drew his gun too, steadied it on his forearm and fired at exactly the same moment as Tutt. Wild Bill's bullet hit Tutt in the ribs, sending him staggering back on to the steps of the courthouse, where he gasped, 'Boys, I'm killed.' He was dead right. Meanwhile, Wild Bill escaped without a scratch. He span on his heels, levelled his gun towards a crowd of Tutt's supporters, and, cool as an alligator, warned them not to interfere.

'Aren't yer satisfied, gentlemen? Put up your shootin' irons or there'll be more dead men here,' he said.

They took the hint.

This was the first recorded example of one of those face-to-face, in-the-street, Hollywood-style gunfights – the quick-draw duels that are so familiar from the movies. However, they were not as common as the Westerns would have us believe. In fact, this was one of very few occasions when such a gunfight happened. More often, cowboys shot each other in the back. But Wild Bill's story was quickly seized upon and exaggerated by the dime novels of the time. He even went on to act in a Buffalo Bill production – the forerunner of the Western movie.

Nowadays, a couple of brass markers in Springfield's town square show where Hickok and Tutt stood during the face-off. On the day I visited, there was a huge building site in the middle of the square, obscuring the line of sight between the two markers. But they were so far apart that I started to grow suspicious about the whole story. I reckon that Wild Bill must have arranged for a sniper on the roof of one of the buildings, because it's almost impossible to hit anything from seventy-five yards with a handgun, especially the pistols they had in those days. That's why so many people were shot in the back, from point-blank range.

Hickok was arrested for the murder of Tutt, then charged with manslaughter, but he was acquitted at trial. As Tutt had initiated the fight, been the first to display overt aggression and, according to two witness reports, reached for his pistol first, Hickok was absolved of guilt. He was even praised for giving Tutt several chances to avoid the confrontation, rather than simply shooting him the moment he felt disrespected – which was how matters of honour were usually resolved in the Old West.

Hickok went on to become the law in various other Western towns. Often his reputation alone was sufficient to persuade dusty cowboys to think twice about disrupting the peace, but his fame was a double-edged sword. To some reprobates, killing a man of such high repute was a trophy worth pursuing. During the afternoon of 2 August 1876, Wild Bill was playing cards in the No. 10 Saloon in Deadwood, Dakota Territory. For once, he'd abandoned his usual precaution of sitting with his back to the wall, and somebody shot him in the back of the head. Crack – straight through the skull. None of that quick-draw nonsense. *Boof.* Dead. Bill was holding two pairs – aces and eights – a decent poker hand. Ever since that day, it's been known as the 'dead man's hand'.

Back in Springfield, the square is now radically different from how it was in 1865. When I visited, it appeared to have become a place where people with nothing much to do hang out. I saw one poor guy being moved along by the police. All he was doing was having a little snooze on the pavement. I always find something like that sad, but here it struck me as peculiar, too, because I'd met unparalleled kindness since arriving in the city. The people had been unbelievably friendly and helpful.

Earlier in the day, I'd been standing at a cash machine in a garage. A very pretty black girl, probably only fourteen or fifteen years old, was being served at the next counter.

'Excuse me,' she said.

'Yes?' I replied.

'Your shoes are beautiful,' she said. 'Have a nice day.' Then she simply left the garage.

Isn't that lovely? My shoes *were* beautiful – black and white with tassels – but how often would somebody take the time to compliment you on something like that? And everyone I met in Springfield was exactly the same. Exceptionally friendly, those Springfielders and Missourians – or Ozarkians, as they call themselves, because of the Ozark Mountains.

I can't tell you precisely where I went next, because it's kind of a secret. I'm not joking. I was off to meet a man called Rob Lurvey, a self-confessed recluse who hasn't received a letter addressed to his house in more than forty years.

Rob has collected things all his life. As a boy, he started with stamps, like everyone else, but then he diversified. He now has one of the largest personal collections of guitars in the world, including more than five thousand historical pieces. And he had an entire room dedicated to the trusty banjo, with some dating back to the 1800s. Rob's collection wasn't for sale or auction, and he didn't want anyone knowing where he kept it. So we weren't allowed to film the approach or the exterior of his warehouse. I thought that was fair enough, and I couldn't wait to see the collection.

Inside a nondescript warehouse, I met Rob, a man in his fifties with a big, beaming smile. 'You must be Billy,' he said.

'And you must be Rob. Lovely to meet you.'

'You look just like yourself.'

That immediately broke the ice and we both laughed.

It was soon obvious that the stringed instruments were only a small part of Rob's collection. He also collected all kinds of memorabilia, and especially anything to do with 3D – like stereoscopes and Viewmasters and holograms. But I was primarily interested in the instruments, so he took me to them.

Guitars, ukuleles, banjos, harps, zither banjos and mandolins – he had them all. The first thing I saw was a long row of zithers – those alpine instruments most of us know from the soundtrack of *The Third Man* – hanging on a wall. Most of them were made between 1865 and 1905 by a company called Schwarzer that had been based in Washington, Missouri. The company folded around the time of the First World War because of anti-German sentiment in America. Rob told me he was one of the few zither collectors anywhere in the world. 'I don't know anybody else who's crazy enough to buy them,' he said.

I love the zither, though. 'I've got a friend in Amsterdam who comes to my stand-up shows and he can play one,' I said.

Rob's collection was so extensive that he even had consecutively numbered zithers with their shipping records from the manufacturer. He bought one in 2002 and the other in

2003, reuniting them after 113 years apart. Some of them were real beauties, like a Smithsonian zither that had taken more than a year to make. It had more than five thousand inlaid pieces of wood, carved ivory and gold plating.

'Do you have people look for stuff for you or do you do it all yourself?' I asked.

'I have people.'

'Spies?'

'Not really spies, but I've been going to shows since 1985, so most everybody knows what I buy, and there's people out there looking for me all the time.'

At one time, Rob had twenty guys searching for a Gibson toy guitar that was missing from his collection. He couldn't even know for sure that it existed – having seen it only in rough illustrations in books – yet he'd spent more than two decades looking for it.

'I was on my way to a national sports collectors' convention in Cleveland – I collect baseball cards too . . . ' he said.

'Of course you do.'

'And we stopped at the Heart of America antique mall in Springfield, Ohio. [Yes, there's yet *another* Springfield.] It's the largest antique mall in America. I was with a friend who doesn't care about collecting and we got there when it opened at nine-thirty in the morning. I started going through the mall and my friend was checking with me every two hours to see if I was done yet, but I wasn't.'

Rob's eyes were sparkling with excitement as he continued to tell the story.

'I was getting ready to go down to the last wing and in a showcase was this toy. I knew immediately what it was and so

I immediately rang the buzzer to get somebody there. Nobody would come. They were all busy, I guess. But I wouldn't leave. I didn't want to take a chance of missing this toy. They finally got to me about twenty minutes later and I didn't care what it cost. But I saw it was a hundred and ninety-five dollars, so I asked if they'd take a discount. You gotta ask, you know?'

'Oh yes,' I said. 'Part of the gig, isn't it?'

'So they gave me ten per cent. I got it for one-seven-five. I'd been looking for one of these for twenty-four years and I started to shake. It's like the Holy Grail. I just couldn't stand it. It was one of the real thrills of my life to finally find one. Other guitar people, they'd all known about it, but nobody had ever seen one. They were all just amazed.'

The variety in Rob's collection was astounding – the first double-neck electric guitars, dozens of twelve-string guitars, obscure stencil guitars. It was fabulous to see so many fantastically good instruments, rooms and rooms and rooms of them, one after the other. I'd never seen a music shop with that many guitars. It was absolutely amazing.

'I've never met anyone like you before,' I said.

'Oh, I'm out there. When people ask who I am, I say: "Well, I'm an obsessive, compulsive, manic depressive, eccentric eclectic or eclectic eccentric" – it depends on what day it is.'

Some parts of his collection were especially astonishing – like dozens of almost identical versions of the same guitar, each with some obscure, minute difference that only an obsessive fanatic like Rob would notice.

To my great delight, Rob had something that he hadn't identified yet, but which I knew well. With only one string, it looked a bit like a banjo and a bit like a ukulele, and it had a wee funny bridge. 'It's a one-string fiddle,' I told him proudly. Rob's example was a toy version. 'It's played with a bow vertically. They used to be popular in Victorian times. You held it between your knees, there was a metal board going down and a horn at the bottom, and you played it like a cello, but it just had one string.' It was wonderful to tell Rob, a man with such a vast knowledge of stringed instruments, something he didn't know already.

The fiddle produced a pleasant sound that I remembered from childhood, because a busker used to play one in Byres Road in Glasgow. He had fought in the Battle of Hill 60 on the Western Front in the First World War, and I used to like watching him.

As I continued to look around the vast collection, something intrigued me. 'What'll happen to all this, Rob, when you disappear?' I said. 'When you leave this mortal coil?'

'It's kinda set up right now to where my nephew gets everything I have. I've got it set up to where he can keep it, he can sell it, or he can donate it to one of several museums. One is the National Music Museum in Vermillion, South Dakota. It's a really cool collection. Or the Ralph Foster Museum, which is down in the College of the Ozarks – it's called the Smithsonian of the Ozarks. That collection down there belonged to a guy named Ike Martin. When I first moved to Springfield, I was in the cub scouts and we'd go down to Ike Martin's music store. In the basement he had this museum. And he'd collected everything. He was really a big influence on my life. He collected arrowheads, he collected guns, he collected just anything you can think of. He was kind of the impetus for getting me started. I mean, I always collected stuff. I've been collecting baseball cards all my life and coins and stuff like that.'

Rob's collection is truly unique and I really liked the guy. But that's nothing new – I tend to like people who collect things. I once met a woman who collected ice-cream cones, and a guy in Scotland who collected space guns. And I heard about someone who collected matches with something wrong with them – like the Siamese-twin matches with two legs and one head that sometimes pop up in matchboxes. Over the years, he had apparently collected enough to fill a frame. Something like a paperclip might be completely ordinary, but if you meet someone who collects paperclips, and they proudly show you their collection, it takes on a kind of majesty.

When I was a kid, I had a friend who used to collect bus tickets – each one of which had a five-figure number running along the top. But he didn't collect just any old ticket – the five numbers always had to add up to twenty-one. If they didn't, he wasn't interested. He had a load of them in a shoe box. I think that's the oddest hobby I've ever known.

Personally, I used to collect snow globes. I've still got hundreds of them at home. In fact, if anybody has been inspired by this and wants to start collecting something, I'd be happy to give you my snow globes to get you started. Although, now that I think about it, one of my daughters – Scarlet – would probably kill me if I did. I think she's got her eye on them.

Having collected the snow globes for years, I just decided to stop one day. I do that kind of thing sometimes. I kept a diary for eight and a half years and then suddenly stopped. My wife says it's possibly the most boring thing she's ever read in her life. 'Oh God, rain again today. Hope it clears up tomorrow.'

Riveting stuff. I started to ask myself why I was writing it. Was I hoping that somebody would read it when I was dead? Or was I hoping to publish it so that people could see how windswept and interesting I was? Then I decided I would rather have a big book with random writings and collections of theatre tickets and bus tickets and things I had done that day. So, if it was a boring day, I wouldn't write anything. I finished only one page of that before I got bored shitless and didn't do it any more.

After Springfield, I headed towards the Kansas state line, riding on Route 66 out of sight of the interstate through rolling wooded hills and wide-open green prairies. It was perfect country for leaning back, enjoying the road and singing its fantastic signature tune to myself.

Although most of us associate 'Route 66' with Chuck Berry, or maybe Nat King Cole, or the Rolling Stones, it was actually written by a former marine called Bobby Troup. He'd made a bit of money writing a few tunes for Frank Sinatra, Tommy Dorsey and Sammy Kaye, so he bought himself a second-hand Buick and set off with his wife for America's entertainment capital, Los Angeles. According to Troup, they stopped for a bite to eat in a restaurant and his wife suggested he should write a song about travelling west by car. At the time, they were on Route 40 east of Chicago, and Troup didn't feel at all inspired, but the idea intrigued him.

A few days later, having joined Route 66, Bobby's wife tapped him on the shoulder and said, 'Get your kicks on Route 66.'

'God, that's a marvellous idea for a song,' replied Bobby.

He wrote half of the lyrics in the car, but then got stuck. A while later, Bobby was working with Nat King Cole and played him the sections he'd written. Nat immediately urged Bobby to finish the song. More in frustration than anything else, Troup simply used the names of some of the towns and cities he'd driven through during his trip: St Louis, Joplin, Oklahoma City, Amarillo, Gallup, Flagstaff, Winona, Kingman, Barstow and San Bernardino. (Winona is the only one out of sequence, as it was included to rhyme with 'Flagstaff, Arizona'.) Somehow that list of places managed to encompass the allure, sense of freedom and romanticism of the open road.

Nat King Cole recorded the song and it was a big hit, earning Troup, who went on to write many more songs and star in movies and television series, more than four million dollars in royalties. Over the years, dozens of artists have recorded it, although they often change the lyrics. In most cases they use a shortened version of the song that omits a couple of verses and doesn't mention a string of towns that appeared in Nat's original version – Tulsa, Albuquerque, Tucumcari, Needles, Essex, Amboy and Azusa. All of these places still lay ahead of me.

Approaching the Missouri–Kansas state border, my eye was caught by a sign for a place called Precious Moments. Then, outside Carthage, a town near Joplin, huge billboards started to loom up on both sides of the road. They all featured pokey wee characters similar to those 'Love Is' cartoons that used to appear in the British press. The wee figures on the billboards would always be saying holy things to one another under a 'Precious Moments' banner. My curiosity had been well and truly piqued by the time I came to a sign for the Precious Moments exhibition, so I pulled off Route 66 and went to have a look. What I found, in my opinion, was absolutely horrific.

Riding through double gates, I entered a landscaped park with hedge-lined drives that led me to a car park in front of a pink and peach building. Inside was a gift shop the size of bloody Selfridges, and scenes from the Bible depicted by the same little cartoon characters I'd seen on the billboards. Each one conformed to that gooey, soppy, syrupy idea that some Americans have of something good. I wanted to scream.

Leaving the hideous building, I followed more hedge-lined paths that weaved through the little cartoon characters – this time modelled in stone and blowing trumpets, as if they were welcoming us to heaven. Before long, I was walking towards a pink and orange chapel. Clearly inspired by Michelangelo's Sistine Chapel in Rome, it was highly decorated inside, with the same little dinky-poo characters acting out scenes from the Bible. Moses, for instance, had a wee roundy face and a tear in his eye. It was nightmarish. The climax of the thing was a whole wall, supposedly heaven, featuring hundreds of little boys and girls in togas – all playing basketball or spinning hula hoops. Above, it said: 'No more tears'.

I was close to vomiting. But some people – usually fat adults in T-shirts – were busy proclaiming how much they loved Jesus, so I kept my mouth shut. The camera crew and Mike, the director, were standing beside me, waiting to shoot something, but I just couldn't bring myself to do it. I'm not in the business of taking the mickey out of people, and I've got no time for television shows that try to entertain by making fools out of people. I've never liked it, and I wasn't going to start indulging in it now. Far be it from me to kick a person's faith away from them, no matter how sick it made me.

The funny thing was that Mike and I had entered the place

feeling quite jolly, laughing and smiling. But we exited in silence, like we'd been to a funeral. It was very odd. Seeing the extent to which people will twist religion was very weird and kind of scary. It was a side of the Bible Belt that I just didn't understand. The way they seemed to have removed all of the dignity from religion was really quite creepy.

It would have been all too easy to stick the boot in. But then little grannies and aunties, people who take their religion very seriously and practise it with quiet dignity, would be wounded by someone like me clumsily tearing into their faith. I admit that part of me was desperate to get in there with my big swinging boot, but I was quite proud of myself and the crew for just walking away that day.

After the bizarreness of Precious Moments, I needed something to jerk me into a different mood. A few miles further down Route 66, a sign announced that I was leaving Missouri and entering Kansas. Galena lay ahead, then Tulsa – less than a day away if I rode straight through. But with plenty of places to stop, it was going to take me significantly longer than twenty-four hours.

The Mother Road only clipped the southeastern corner of the Sunflower State. Blink and you'd be in Oklahoma, as the Kansas stretch lasted a mere thirteen miles. However, every mile of it was genuine, historical Route 66 hardtop because Interstate 44 completely bypassed the state of Dorothy and Toto, leaving a perfectly intact section of the old Mother Road.

There isn't much to say about Galena, a perfectly nice but unremarkable former mining town with an air of its best days being long behind it. Like so many American small towns, nobody was in the street. Not a soul. Riding down Main Street,

I spotted the obligatory church and, directly opposite it, a poker house offering Texas hold'em. Apparently Galena had all the bases covered for anyone hoping for redemption from the pressures of the world.

Whereas 'Missouri' comes from a Sioux word, *ouemessourita*, meaning 'those who have dugout canoes', and 'Oklahoma' is Indian for 'red people', the origin of 'Kansas' is an Indian word that means 'people of the wind'. It's a sadly appropriate name for this part of the world, as it lies in the heart of Tornado Alley.

As I continued to ride through the Sunflower State, I became slightly despondent. I'd been assured that although Route 66's passage through Kansas was short, it boasted a surprisingly large number of fried chicken shacks – fourteen in just thirteen miles – and all of them teeming with customers buying up to five thousand chicken dinners a day. I'd even been promised a Scottish connection, because fried chicken was allegedly a traditional Scottish dish. This was news to me, so I was determined to investigate. But do you know what? There was nothing but a great big hole where I was expecting hustle, bustle and the sweet smell of chicken fat.

Making a television travelogue can occasionally turn into a crap shoot. And I hate it when that happens. I arrived at Chicken Annie's in Pittsburg, Kansas – a slight detour off Route 66, but I'm prepared to suffer for my art – expecting to find hundreds of people wolfing down their dinner. Instead, there were about four cars in the car park, and inside it looked like the dining room in an old folks' home. I'd schlepped all the way over there only to discover it was the dullest fucking place on earth. I'd been promised a string of chicken businesses, all jostling with each other for trade, but when I stood outside Chicken Annie's,

I couldn't see any sign of a single shack. There was one other chicken shop, but it was way behind some trees. There was no fucking competition whatsoever.

I had this weird feeling, like I was spiralling downwards. I couldn't think of anything to say about the place, and I started to doubt everything. Kansas was turning into a big disappointment. I'd not been there before, and I doubted I'd return. As for the suggestion that fried chicken was a traditional Scottish dish ... that was bullshit, too. I've never known a single Scot who makes a fuss over chicken. And I've never seen a single Scottish cookbook that features recipes for fried chicken. It was a non-story and it left me feeling a bit like the centre of a doughnut. Empty.

The combination of Precious Moments and the chicken shack fiasco meant I finished the day in a foul mood. But sometimes I find a kind of comfort in being grumpy. There's a feeling of righteousness, a sense of being the great misunderstood, which is probably bollocks, but comforting all the same. At least I knew it would pass, and that something else would show up. Something interesting would stick its head up, and I'd be intrigued by it. That's the glory of Route 66 – there's always something new around the corner.

It would have been great to end the day with a feeling of a job well done. If I'd achieved anything, I could have nipped upstairs to my room, lain back on my bed and watched *Ghost Finders* on the telly before falling asleep with a sense of satisfaction. I didn't see that happening tonight. But then I remembered Rob and his crazy collection. It seemed so long ago that I'd met him, but it had only been that morning. I'd had a good chat with him. I'd known my stuff and he'd certainly known his. Maybe the day hadn't been so bad after all. In fact, as long as I thought about Rob surrounded by all his instruments in his anonymous warehouse in the middle of nowhere, I felt pretty good.

9

Oklahoma City Looks Oh So Pretty

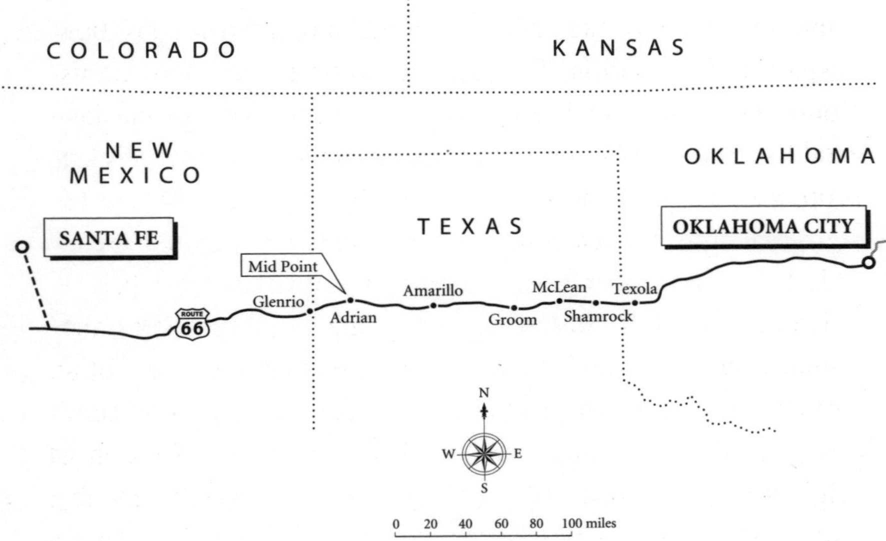

A sign by the side of the road, then a slight thud under the wheels as one section of tarmac ended and another began. Those were the only indications that I'd slipped out of Kansas. 'You Are Now Entering Oklahoma On Historic Route 66', said the sign.

In many ways, Oklahoma is the heart and soul of Route 66.

Although Springfield was the birthplace of the road's moniker, Oklahoma was the home state of Cyrus Avery, the man who chose that name. And it boasts more miles of original Route 66 than any other state. Somewhat ironically, it was also the first state to bypass the Mother Road, dealing an early death blow in 1953 when it opened the Turner Turnpike (later part of the oppressive Interstate 44), which replaced more than a hundred miles of America's Main Street. Oklahoma is also the state from which the characters fled in *The Grapes of Wrath*, in which John Steinbeck coined 'The Mother Road' to describe Route 66, immortalising it as 'the path of a people in flight' from dust bowl despair and starvation. It was also the first state to recognise Route 66's historical and social significance. Enthusiasts established the Oklahoma Route 66 Association to preserve and promote the road, and they designed the 'Historic Route 66' signs that now punctuate the landscape all the way from Chicago to Los Angeles, having been adopted by most other states.

Route 66's first miles in Oklahoma pass through fairly nondescript towns and villages. First there's Quapaw, another former mining town, followed by Commerce, now semi-deserted, then Miami, from which a magnificent section of original 1926–37 Route 66 – bumpy, gravelly and only nine feet wide – stretches for two miles. A little while earlier, having passed through a wee ghost town, I'd spotted a handwritten sign by the side of the road: 'Swamp Sale', it said. Let's have a look, I thought. You never know your luck. I'm one of those guys who sees a sign for a car-boot sale and thinks he's bound to find a great guitar for twenty bucks. Maybe watching all those auction shows on television has done it. Whatever the reason, I was curious, so I pulled over and went for a wander.

Near the entrance, dressed in dungarees and lounging on a plastic garden chair, was a character straight out of *The Grapes of Wrath*. Shading himself from the sun under the raised rear door of a people carrier and some low trees, Vernon Willoughby looked kind of poor, but happy. A well-worn blue vest barely held in an impressive belly, and a greying beard framed his ruddy face. Around him, his family lazed in the sun, waiting for someone to take a look at their wares.

'Are you selling those chickens and all?' I pointed at some birds in a cage.

'Yeah.' Vernon had a twangy Oklahoma accent.

'How much does a chicken cost?'

'A lot of people sell 'em for fifteen dollars a piece when they're grown, laying eggs.'

'Yeah? And you?'

'Anywhere from eight dollars to fifteen dollars.'

'Eight to fifteen?'

'Yeah.' Vernon spoke very slowly and deliberately.

'And how much is a duck?'

'That's for five. Because they grow quicker than chickens do.'

'But the duck eggs are delicious, aren't they?'

'Yeah.'

'Where do you come from yourself?'

'A little town called Quapaw over here in Oklahoma.'

'Oh yeah?'

'66 runs right through it.'

I nodded. 'I'm going to Tulsa and then Oklahoma City.'

'That's a good ride on that 66.'

'Yeah?'

'Long one, though.'

'They're all long. It's too big, this country.'

As well as fully grown chickens, Vernon was selling some guinea fowl and those wee yellow fluffy chicks. On another table there were various ornaments and bits and pieces, presumably from his house, nice items of Americana, a well-crafted wooden box, a ceramic buffalo with the ubiquitous 'Made in China' imprinted on its base, and an elephant-shaped incense holder. It all looked a bit desperate. A duck for five dollars seemed like a bargain – they lay eggs for ever – but of course I couldn't buy one.

Further up the lane, another half-dozen stallholders were displaying their wares. The first I came to shouted, 'Whoa, no, no, no! Get the camera away!' He was a nice fella, but he was selling guns and knives and didn't want to be filmed. I was happy to respect his wishes. I'm not one of those people who thinks everything about guns is bad. Not everyone who's interested in them is a potential murderer or a militia man – just some of them. Many of them are simply into hunting and collecting knives. The working knife is a big thing in America.

The next stallholder was similarly reluctant to be filmed. 'No problem whatsoever,' I said. 'I understand.'

So I moved on to another stall, where a large man called Olen Robbins, dressed all in black and wearing black shades was standing in front of a large black pick-up truck.

'Yeah, go right ahead,' Olen said when I asked if we could film him. 'Where are you folks from?'

'I'm from Scotland.'

'Really? Well, welcome to the United States.'

'Oh, I live in New York, but I'm from Scotland.'

'You'll find a variety of interesting stuff along old Route 66 and quite a bit of history here.'

While I perused the items on his stall, Olen chatted away, recommending a visit to Baxter Springs, back across the state border in Kansas.

'What's a boot hunter knife?' I asked, holding up a knife in a box.

'It's styled after the old riverboat gambler knives. It's still mint in the box. The gamblers carried that style of knife as they played cards on the riverboats along the Mississippi.'

'What's that?' I pointed at a black dagger with a Gothic inscription.

'That is an old German piece. I acquired a small collection of German military memorabilia from an elderly gentleman in Joplin, who brought them back from Germany during the war. This is a type of fraternal piece. We haven't identified it exactly yet.'

'Can I see?'

'Absolutely.'

Picking up the dagger, I shuddered as I noticed a Nazi flag draped over the front of the man's stall.

'And this old banner was from the same gentleman.' Olen held up an eighteen-inch pendant. It looked like some kind of fraternal medallion on a ribbon. About the size of the palm of a hand, it had enamel inserts with various signs and insignia. The stallholder turned it over and there was a swastika on the back.

'Oh my God.'

'He liberated this banner from a building in Germany during World War Two. I've had some difficulty translating it, but loosely translated it was something that was presented to the government by this particular guard corps that protected a castle in Germany, and it celebrates the hundredth anniversary of that military unit.'

'Yeah.' I was starting to recoil from the items on Olen's stall.

'I don't . . . I don't really keep this kind of stuff,' he said. 'I do buy and sell and trade it when I find it, but I'm not really a big fan of it.'

'No, I'm not a fan of it myself.'

'Due to the history behind it. But I've always picked up anything unusual or unique. Of course, you may not wanna film that particular bumper sticker.'

I looked at the sticker and read it out loud: 'Obama Sucks'. Then I looked at Olen.

'It does kind of express the sentiments of a good deal of the people in this country at this time,' he said.

There was another bumper sticker on the stall: 'Speak To Me In English', it said. Now I knew exactly where he was coming from, but I didn't react to it.

'I like Obama,' I said. 'I think he's great.'

'Well, I know a lot of people from other countries think he's absolutely wonderful.'

'What about the killing of Osama bin Laden?'

'He's taking full credit for that, but one thing that a lot of folks don't realise is that the interrogation techniques that they started using under the previous President were responsible for gaining the intelligence that led to his ultimate capture. And Obama wanted to abolish those techniques, calling them harsh and cruel.'

'What? Torture? You think torture's okay?'

'Well, no, I don't agree that torture's okay, but if someone's gonna kill a large group of people, I think you get the information out of 'em however you have to in order to prevent the death of many.'

I wasn't convinced.

'He's not greatly liked at this point, but his popularity did take a bump for Osama. We'll see.'

'I think you're jealous. I think if the Republicans had done it, you'd be dancing in the street.'

'Absolutely not. I'm an independent. I don't follow the Republican agenda.'

'Were you a George W kinda guy?'

'No, no.'

'Are you a libertarian?'

'Yes. I would say you'd have to lock me into the libertarian category.'

'Small government and no taxes?'

'Or low taxes, at least. I don't think we can get by without taxes, because we definitely need the services, but we're taxed too much.'

'Yeah. Everybody's taxed too much.'

'I would have to agree.'

'Well, thanks for your time. Thanks for allowing me to rumble through your stuff.'

'I don't know if you've noticed the silver and gold market in the country since you've been here?'

'It's rocketing, isn't it?'

'It plummeted last week.'

'Did it? Last week?'

'Do you know who George Soros is?'

'Yes.'

'He sold one of the largest hoards of silver, to my understanding, in the country. It crashed the market.'

'Why would he do a thing like that?'

'That goes back to why a lot of people don't like this guy.' Olen pointed at the 'Obama Sucks' bumper sticker. 'They're pals.'

I laughed. It was all I could do in the face of such unshakeable beliefs. The Nazi banner said more to me than I felt he would have liked it to say.

It always amazes me that, in the most religious corners of this country, you often find little dark patches. You'd think that people who like Jesus would be pulled to the left politically – they should be attracted to the sharing aspect of society. But they usually seem to be deeply suspicious of it, whether it's socialist or Amish. Instead of cooperation and sharing, they want small government, small taxes and business to be left in charge of the country. They want business to tell the government what to do, not the other way round.

Ultimately, as far as I was concerned Olen was just a fat little fascist to me, so fuck him. He said he was a libertarian, but then they all say that. A lot of weird crap hides under the banners of nationalism and libertarianism. I'm not saying that nationalism is necessarily fascist – that would be ridiculous – but fascists like to hide in that independent-minded corner of things. And they do that corner a real disservice.

I moved along to some of the other stalls, which were reassuringly closer to what anyone would expect to find at a car-boot sale in Britain: people selling second-hand clothes, children's pyjamas, unwanted exercise gadgets, CDs by obscure musicians, DVDs, badges, toys, tools and rusty garden equipment. Carol and Dave Archer, a charming retired couple who spent their time travelling in a huge motor home between their various children in Florida, Massachusetts and Kansas, were selling seashell wind chimes and funky tie-dyed T-shirts. It was a pleasure to meet that kind of American. They weren't rich – they were just sauntering along, getting by. I had the time of my life chatting to them.

Mostly it was an absolute pleasure bumbling around the market, stopping to chat to people. But one guy caught me having a pee behind a tree and gave me a hard time. I wasn't going to kill the tree – I'm a healthy guy – but he insisted: 'There's bathrooms over there.' So I ambled over to two horrible portaloos. Have you ever looked in the hole in a portaloo? It's like gazing into the depths of hell. I couldn't help thinking that those portaloos were liable to do much more harm to the environment than me having a quick pee behind a tree.

Moving off again, riding on through the Oklahoma countryside, I caught a glimpse of the annual *Cinco de Mayo* celebrations. For reasons that nobody seems able to explain, this victory of the Mexicans over the French is a national holiday in America. Even more bizarrely, this year they were celebrating it on 7 May. I stopped for a chicken–pork pie. God, I loved it! I don't get enough chances to eat chicken–pork pie.

About a hundred miles further down Route 66, as the road widened into four lanes, crossed two huge steel bridges over the Verdigris River and approached Tulsa, a blue whale hoved into view. Given that we were more than a thousand miles from either coast, that might sound strange, but this was no ordinary blue whale. For a start, it was made out of concrete. Smiling from its pond of water, it was the creation of a man who simply wanted to bring a little joy and happiness to his son and his son's friends.

Hugh Davis was a zoologist who had travelled in Africa before settling with his wife Zelta in Catoosa, on the outskirts of Tulsa. There they opened a little zoo and reptile house beside a swimming hole on the roadside of Route 66. The local kids used to splash around quite happily in the swimming hole, but Hugh's son, Blaine, kept bugging him to build something they could dive off, because there were no rocks or trees around the pool.

In typical dad fashion, Hugh said, 'Sure, sure, I'll get round to it, I'll get round to it,' and did nothing for years.

But then, in 1972, when Blaine was drafted into the army and sent to Vietnam, Hugh finally fulfilled his promise. He had a friend who was a welder – the first giveaway that he might be a lunatic and could embark on something seriously stupid. (I'm a welder; I know these things.) As the welder set to work on a large steel framework, everybody's first thought was that Hugh must be building an aeroplane. But then Hugh started to cover the frame with concrete. He mixed 126 sacks of the stuff and pushed it into place with his hands. Once it had set, he painted it all light blue.

On their wedding anniversary, Hugh unveiled his concrete creation to Zelta. His lavish gift was a blue whale. In total it had cost him nearly two thousand dollars, a lot of money in the early 1970s.

When I first drew up beside the concrete cetacean, I have to admit I was a bit disappointed. Some kids were happily fishing off it, but the whole place looked a bit forlorn. This is just a park with a blue whale made of concrete, I thought. Who the hell cares? There was a wee cash desk in a wee log cabin, and a bloke came out to explain what it was all about. That happened quite often on Route 66: as soon as I stopped anywhere, someone would turn up, say hello and start chatting. They were usually very friendly, and this man was no exception. Dressed in a straw hat, Hawaiian shirt, gold watch and big glasses, he introduced himself as Blaine Davis – the fella whose badgering had prompted his dad to build the whale nearly forty years earlier.

Now about sixty years old, Blaine gave me a charming guided tour of the whale. We walked across a lawn towards the water's edge. Then, like Jonah, I entered the beast through its mouth. Inside, there was a ladder up to a space in the top of the whale's head – a huge room with a wooden floor where children could play and meet and scheme in the way that kids love to do. It was the best kids' gang hut I'd ever seen. Obviously, Blaine himself didn't play in it when he came back from Vietnam, but I'm sure the local kids had a whale of a time in it. (Sorry about that, but I couldn't resist!) Hugh also rigged up some plumbing which allowed the kids to be squirted down a slide and into the pool. And there were some diving boards – one on the side of the whale, a high one off its tail, and three more dotted around the lake.

Hugh and Zelta opened the whale to the public, and for a couple of decades it was a popular local spot. Over the years, thousands of people visited it and had a grand old time. It was so successful that they eventually closed the zoo. But by the late 1980s, when litigation culture was starting to get a grip on America, their accident insurance premiums became

Mark Atkinson

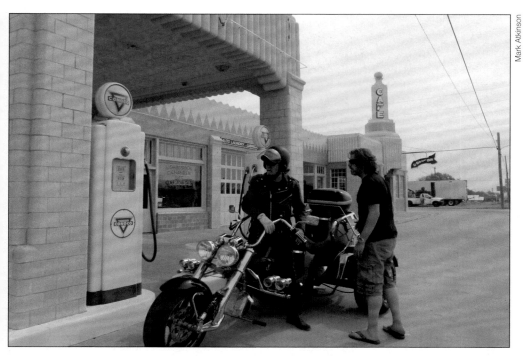

The U-Drop Inn petrol station in Shamrock, Texas – a stark contrast to the rest of the town.

Tim Pollard

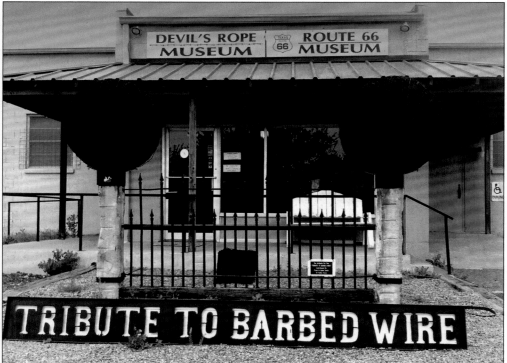

The barbed wire museum in McClean. I never knew the 'Devil's Rope' came in so many different shapes and sizes.

Mike Reilly

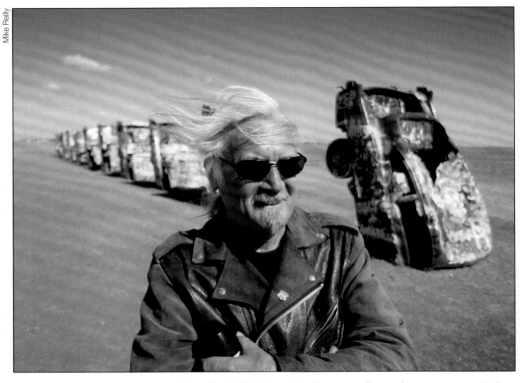

Cadillac Ranch on the outskirts of Amarillo. I fell in love with this extraordinary place – a representation of the American love of automobiles, and an unexpected shrine to me!

Mark Atkinson

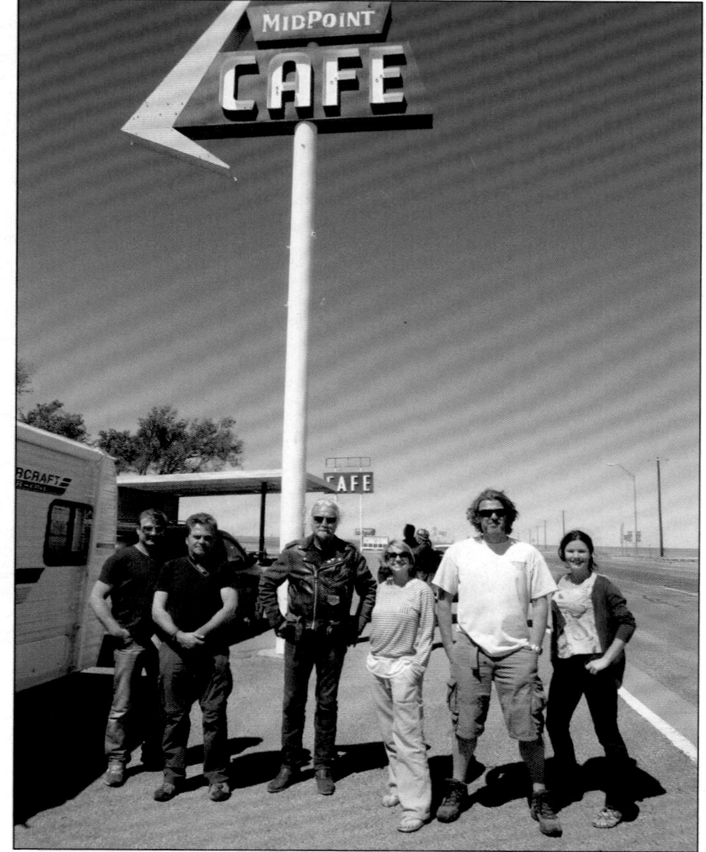

Nicky Taylor

At the Midpoint Café with the crew, from left – Mark Atkinson (Soundman), Tim Pollard (Director of Photography), Me, Nicky Taylor (Series Producer), Mike Reilly (Series Director), Jane Nowak (Production Manager).

Jane Nowak

The sign says it all – I felt a real sense of achievement having made it this far.

Tim Pollard

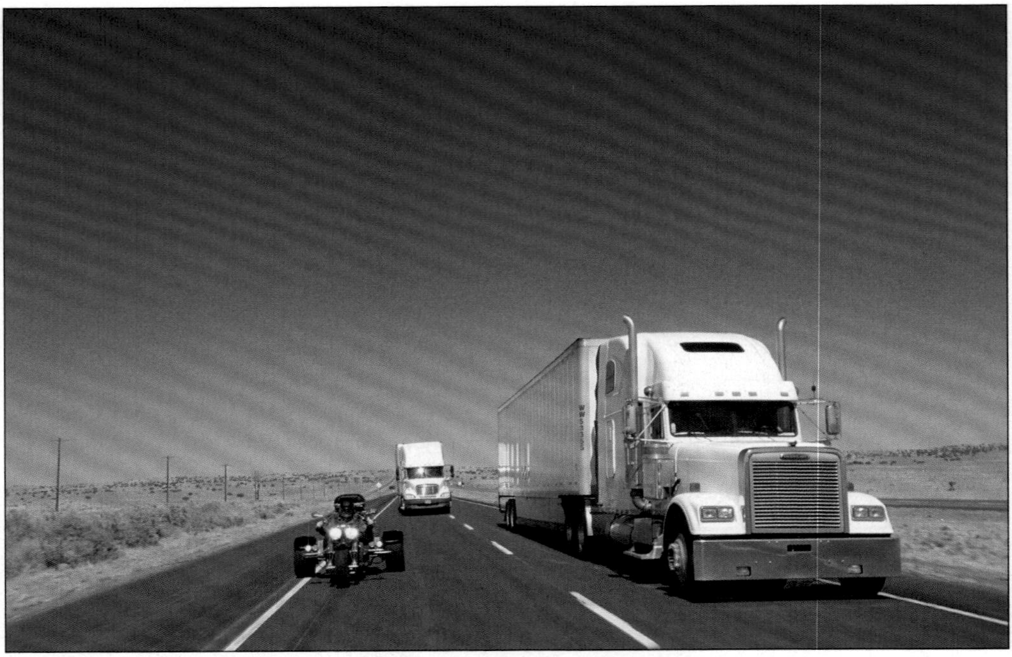

Trucks – sometimes a welcome shield from the side winds, sometimes a lethal hazard.

PhotoQuest/Getty Images

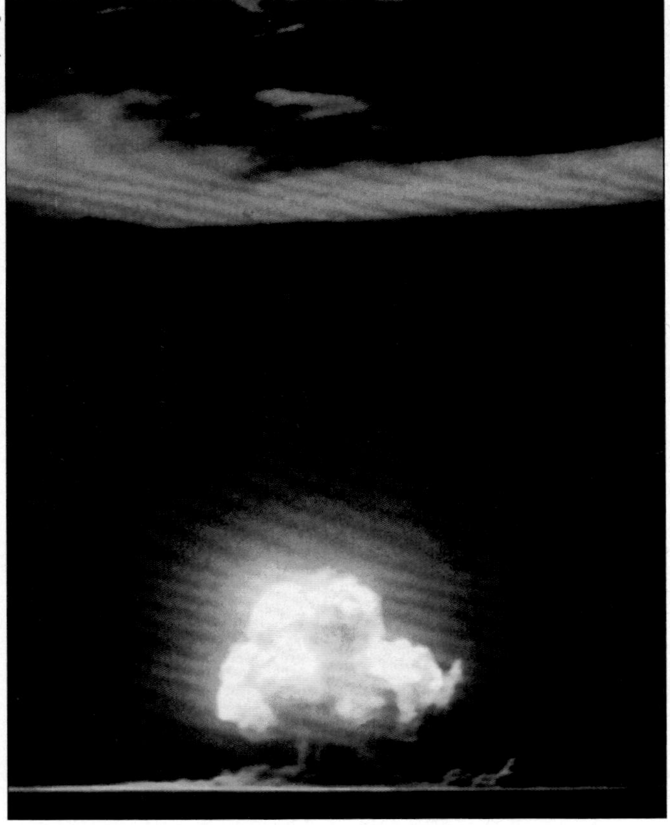

The world-famous photo of the first atom bomb test at White Sands, Albuquerque – facing the wrong way.

Maverick Television

The world's oldest continuous rodeo in Payson, Arizona.

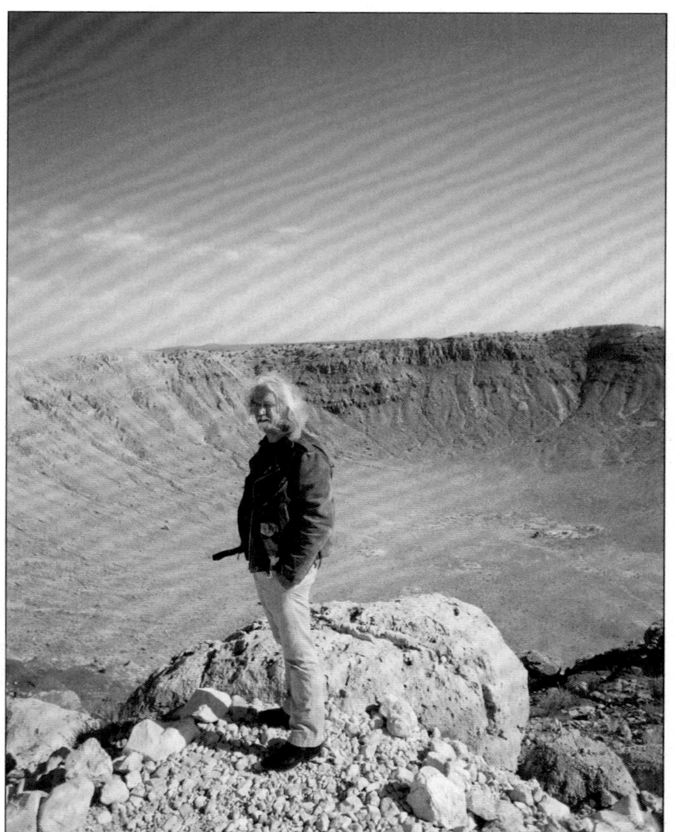

Mike Reilly

Meteor Crater, Arizona – it'll fascinate you or bore you to tears, depending on your gender . . .

Mark Atkinson

The medicine man who attempted to cure my sore leg and aching rib – I felt very privileged to have the experience.

Mike Reilly

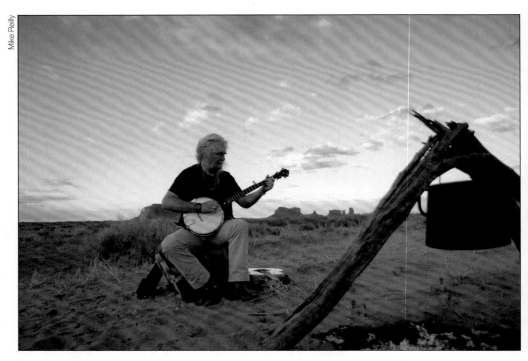

Strumming my banjo in Monument Valley – an incredible place (see facing page), filled with vistas I'd ridden through in my imagination as a child.

Nicky Taylor

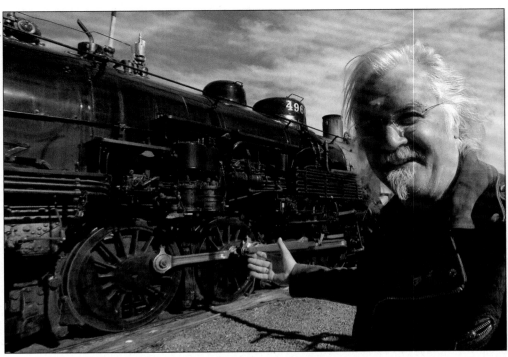

Nicky Taylor

I've always loved steam trains and this one, which took me to the Grand Canyon, was no exception – although the vegetable oil it was powered by gave off a rather different whiff to the sulphurous smells I was used to from my childhood.

Mike Reilly

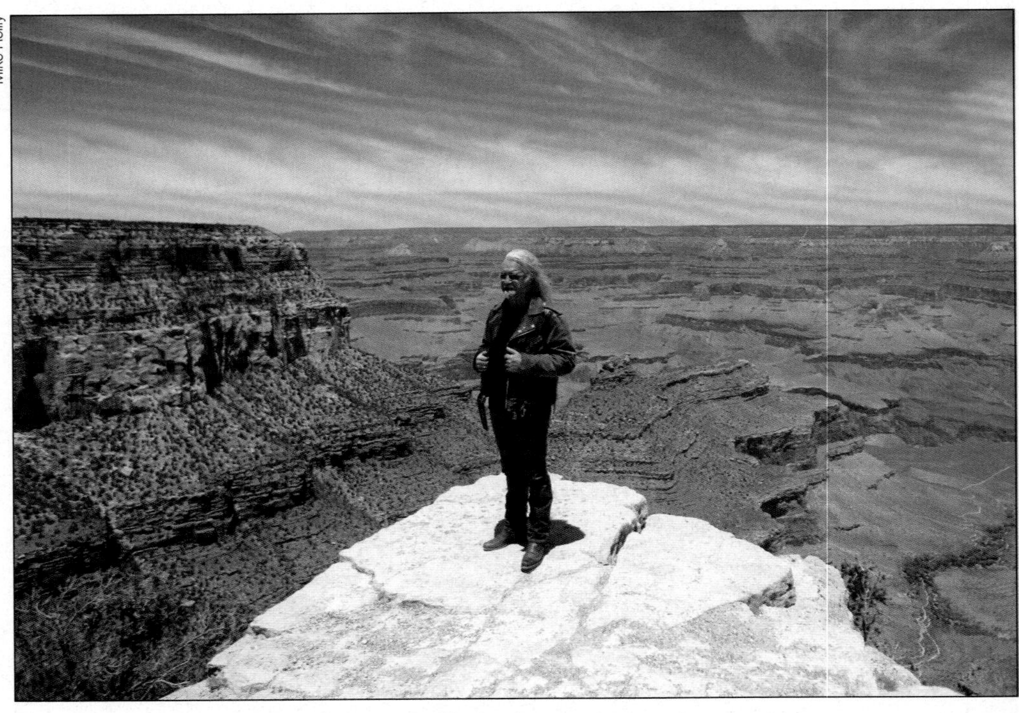

The Grand Canyon. Much more than I'd imagined, and quite unlike anything I'd ever seen in my life.

prohibitive and they were forced to shut the whale, too. By then, a lot of locals had swimming pools in their backyards anyway, so they no longer wanted to come to the swimming hole.

The blue whale and the park around it fell into disrepair. Nature took over, and for a while it looked like the Catoosa Blue Whale would crumble to dust. But then some locals, people who had fond childhood memories of jumping, diving and sliding off the whale, got in touch with Blaine and asked if they could form a group to preserve it. They drummed up sponsorship from a chain of hotels on Route 66 and set to work. Nowadays, the whale even has its own Facebook page.

'We had a big sit-down dinner here last Thursday night,' said Blaine. 'First time we've ever had one of those. Tables, chairs, steak cooked right here on the site and everything. We had over a hundred people here.'

I think it's terrific that the whale has once again become a focus and asset for the community.

'That's wonderful,' I said.

'We had live music, a string quartet and everything, down here playing music.'

'Really?'

'Yeah, yeah. We invited wine vendors from four different vineyards to bring their wares out here and to treat people to wine and free food. It was great.'

I love the idea of millions of people driving down Route 66 over the years, glancing across at the park, and saying, 'What the heck? Was that a whale?' And I was thrilled that the whale was probably having the same effect on today's passers-by, all thanks to the efforts and energy of a group of community-minded locals. The whale is nothing but a whole bunch of fun, which is what's so great about it.

But that's not what tickled me most about this wee park. Hugh also made a toilet block to serve his customers. With no architectural training, he based his design on some tribal huts he'd seen in Africa. But instead of making the toilet block from mud, he fashioned it from concrete. And, boy, has it stood the test of time. The building looks just like an African village hut, but it's as solid as a rock. Blaine told me that whenever tornadoes rip through this part of Oklahoma, which they do throughout April and May, he locks up his caravan beside the lake and barricades himself in the toilet. It's the only tornado-proof loo I've ever seen. I love the idea that Blaine shelters in there while the tornado passes by. What a tribute to his dad's skill. I was terribly impressed by it.

Incidentally, the section of Route 66 that runs through Catoosa is called the Will Rogers Memorial Highway. I'm a huge fan of Will Rogers – a cowboy, comedian, social commentator, vaudeville performer and actor who was born to a Cherokee family in Oklahoma and became known as Oklahoma's favourite son – so I was tickled that the road had adopted his name. He was a phenomenal talent, first appearing in vaudeville shortly before the First World War. I've seen films of him doing his lasso act from around that period and it's quite breathtaking. But he was also a philosopher, the type that I'd call country-wise rather than street-wise. He travelled around the world three times, made seventy-one movies (silent and talkies), wrote more than four thousand nationally syndicated newspaper columns, and became a world-famous figure. By the mid-1930s, the American public adored him. He was considered the leading political wit of the age and was the top-paid Hollywood movie star.

After the First World War, there had been plans to march the returning troops past the White House in Washington. Rows of planked seating (called bleachers in America) were erected, which sparked huge arguments over who should get the best seats for the victory parade. Someone asked Will what he thought of all the fuss about the seating arrangements.

'If you really appreciate what the soldiers did, let them sit in the seats and we'll march past,' he said.

What a guy, eh? Wasn't that a splendid idea? That was Will Rogers all over. I once went to his house in Los Angeles and was really impressed. He made good use of his fame, serving as a goodwill ambassador to Mexico and briefly as Mayor of Beverly Hills. In print and on radio he poked fun at gangsters, prohibition, politicians, government policies and various other controversial topics but in a folksy, down-to-earth way that was readily appreciated and offended no one. 'Lord, the money we spend on government,' he said of Franklin Roosevelt's administration, of which he was a fervent supporter. 'And it's not one bit better than the government we got for one-third of the money twenty years ago.'

That kind of thinking was born in Oklahoma, and I can only urge you to come and experience this part of the world for yourself. I've not known friendliness and hospitality like it anywhere else, and I guarantee you'll experience it, too.

From Catoosa, I had a long ride ahead of me, and another storm was brewing. The weather had been sensational for the previous few days, and I'd hoped to be wearing fewer clothes as I continued to head southwest. But I wasn't so sure as I set off down the road towards Oklahoma City.

Before the state capital, though, I had one more stop to make. I was going to meet an oil baron.

Now, whenever I think about oil, what comes to mind is Libya, Iraq, Saudi Arabia, Texas or big plumes of flame burning on North Sea oil rigs. I've never thought of Oklahoma as an oil state. But here's the thing – less than a hundred years ago, Tulsa was the oil capital of the world. In 1859 a driller seeking salt water struck oil, and fortune-seekers immediately invaded the local Indian territory. Then, in 1901, prospectors discovered vast oil deposits at Red Fork in southwest Tulsa. Investors swarmed to the city, which in a matter of months went from a cow town to a boomtown. Four years later, an even larger oil deposit was struck and Tulsa's population grew to almost a hundred thousand people. Four hundred oil companies were based in the city. Propelling Oklahoma at breakneck speed into the twentieth century, the black gold brought two daily newspapers, four telegraph companies, more than 10,000 telephones, seven banks, 200 lawyers and more than 150 doctors, as well as numerous other businesses, to Tulsa.

Nowadays, Tulsa's big industry is gas. However, oil still has a presence, albeit in a less obvious way. It's more like a cottage industry, with 'mom-and-pop' oil companies producing just two or three barrels a day.

White-haired and dressed in a light blue Lacoste polo shirt and jeans, Wiley Cox (what a great name) is a very unlikely looking oil baron. He described himself as 'just about the smallest end of the oil industry you're going to get' and had agreed to show me around his oilfield. Anyone who has been to Los Angeles or some parts of Texas will have seen those nodding metal donkeys at the side of the road, steadily pumping oil out of the ground. They look like the kind of thing boys made with their Meccano sets in the fifties. Wiley had four or five of them and, with the recent escalation in oil prices, was making quite a decent living out of them.

Wiley's a perfectly pleasant man and he gave me the full guided tour, but I couldn't summon up much interest. In fact, as I listened to him talking about oil and the process of getting it out of the ground, I almost lost the will to live. That might seem ironic, given that there would be no Route 66 without oil, but it just held no fascination for me.

So I said goodbye to him, got back on my bike, and headed for Oklahoma City, which was still about ninety miles away. It was a harsh ride: long, straight roads pointing all the way to the horizon. Whenever I crested a hill, the road would stretch out in front of me again, as long and as straight as the previous stretch. The monotony and emptiness were quite extraordinary, and by the time I reached Oklahoma City I was ready for dinner, bed and a long sleep.

The next day started with the promise of a big, fat, juicy steak. It's one of those things that horrifies almost any British person – the idea of steak for breakfast – particularly if eaten the American way, which is with a Coca-Cola on the side. A *steak*? For *breakfast*? What kind of people are they? What kind of savages eat a hunk of meat dripping with blood for their first meal of the day? But actually it's fabulous. Steak and eggs set you up for the day, especially when you're going to spend that day astride a trike, and possibly even more so when you've not eaten steak for forty or fifty years.

I gave up red meat decades ago because I thought that was the healthy way to go. But in the last year I'd started eating it again. My daughter advised me to tuck in after reading a book that advocated matching your diet to your blood type. Both of us are Type 'O', rhesus-negative. According to the book, red meat is good for us. So, since the beginning of the year, I'd been eating a bit of steak and quite enjoying it. Now I was really looking forward to my steak breakfast at the Cattlemen's Steakhouse. But I'd forgotten it was Mothering Sunday, and the place was jammed. There was a huge queue, so I went elsewhere and had a hamburger instead. I was disappointed to miss out on the steak, but it was a cracking good hamburger, and it set me up for the long ride out to Stan Mannshreck's cattle ranch.

Stan is a smashing guy and a really good laugh. I watched as he and his hands rounded up twenty head of cattle under the golden morning sun and drove them on to a huge trailer. Then, sitting in the cab beside Stan as we drove the cattle to market, I felt like a proper cowboy. The boys could have herded the cattle in the traditional manner all the way to the market at the edge of Oklahoma City, but Stan didn't want to do that. Oklahoma had suffered a drought for most of the last fifteen years, so his cattle were already underweight, and they would have lost even more pounds on a long drive. But there was a silver lining to this particular cloud: because of the drought, far fewer cattle were being sent to market, so each animal fetched a much higher price than a similar steer would have ten or fifteen years ago.

Travelling in Stan's big trailer with the cattle in the back, occasionally the smell wafted into the cabin. *Holy Mother of Jesus!* It was something else.

Approaching the toll gate near the end of the interstate, Stan turned to me and smiled. 'Watch this girl. She's been here a while,' he said. 'She'll notice I've got cattle on the back. Just watch the speed with which she shuts the window as soon as she gets the money.'

We pulled up at the toll booth and Stan handed over the cash.

'See you, Stan.' *Va-voom*, the window shot across.

Stan told me that on a previous trip into town, one of the cattle had peed and shat itself during the stop at the toll booth and it had squirted straight through her window. After that, she wasn't taking any chances.

We dropped off the cattle at the Oklahoma City National Stock Yards, the largest feeder cattle market (dealing only in young, male calves) in the world. Twelve thousand cattle might be sold there in single a day. Since its inception, more than 102 million head of livestock had passed through the iron gates.

The National Stock Yards form part of Stockyard City, a neighbourhood of Oklahoma City that's more like a self-contained town. A bit like the Vatican, it rules itself, and it answers to the county, not the city, which dearly wants to get rid of it because of the smell and the effluent, the noise and the traffic. But it's not going anywhere. Many of the businesses in the area date back to 1910, when the Oklahoma National Stock Yards Company began its public livestock market. At its height, in the 1950s, Stockyard City's meat-packing operations employed about 10 per cent of the city's workforce. When I visited, though, it almost felt like a theme park. The fronts of many of the stores – which catered exclusively to cattlemen, selling Western clothing – were wooden and lit by gas. It was a lovely piece of period history.

Noisy and smelly, Stockyard City and the National Stock Yards are well worth a visit. I loved all the mooing and seeing the cowboys riding up and down. Anyone who went into the stockyards could see the cattle arriving and being herded into pens. Poor things, they didn't know they were destined to be hamburgers or steaks soon, although they seemed to sense that something sinister awaited them. But at least the huge abattoirs that used to be right next door to the market area had been relocated. Nowadays the cattle were transported by truck to the slaughterhouses once they'd been sold.

The stockyards hold auctions only on Mondays and Tuesdays, so I had to wait until the next day to see the auctioneer in action. In the meantime, I decided to visit the place that, tragically, most of us now associate with Oklahoma City.

On 19 April 1995, twenty-six-year-old Timothy McVeigh parked a Ryder rental truck packed with nearly three tons of ammonium nitrate fertiliser, nitromethane and diesel fuel outside the nine-storey Alfred Murrah Building. McVeigh had built a cage inside the truck so that the explosive mixture would blow towards the front of the building – he really put a lot of thought into it – and shortly after nine o'clock in the morning he detonated the bomb. The explosion decimated the building, killing 168 people and injuring another 800.

About ninety minutes later, an Oklahoma state trooper stopped McVeigh for driving without a licence plate. The trooper arrested him for that offence and for unlawful possession of a weapon. However, within days, McVeigh's old army friend Terry Nichols was arrested, and both men were charged with the bombing. McVeigh, a Gulf War veteran with extreme right-wing views, was seriously screwed up about the federal government and was a member of a militia movement. I saw him interviewed after his trial and he expressed no regret about what he'd done. He'd timed the bomb to coincide with the second anniversary of the Waco siege, in which seventy-six people (including twenty-four Brits) died when the headquarters of the Branch Davidians, a weird Protestant sect, went up in flames. That tragedy, and an earlier incident at Ruby Ridge, Idaho, in which the FBI had besieged the home of another religious fanatic called Randy Weaver, had motivated McVeigh to seek revenge. He was executed by lethal injection on 11 June 2001. Nichols was sentenced to life in prison for acting as his accomplice.

The entire front was blown off the Alfred Murrah Building, which contained the offices of the Bureau of Alcohol, Tobacco and Firearms – the body that had conducted the siege in Waco – as well as various other government departments, such as Social Security. In the aftermath of the attack, it was decided to demolish the building and replace it with a memorial to the victims. It's now a simple, quiet and understated place, which makes it all the more moving. At its centre is a large reflection pool of shallow water on black granite, at either end of which are two large bronze gates. It's quite beautiful. I spotted a bird standing in the pool and the water hardly came up to its ankles. At one end, the eastern gate is inscribed with '9:01', which represents innocence – the last moments of peace before the bomb exploded a minute later. At the other end, the western gate is inscribed with '9:03' to symbolise the first moments of recovery after the outrage.

It really is an extraordinarily powerful memorial to the 168 victims. The authorities encourage children to dip their hands in the water and then pat one of the gates to leave a handprint on the bronze. Eventually, the handprint will turn green and last for ever. I think that's a very touching idea.

To the side of the reflecting pool, 168 empty chairs, handcrafted in bronze, glass and stone, represent each of the dead. The nine rows of chairs, each inscribed with the name of a victim, represent the nine floors of the building. They're laid out to correspond with where the victims were found, with the greatest number clustered in the most heavily damaged portion of the building. Nineteen of the chairs are smaller than the rest, representing the children who were killed in the bombing. Three unborn children also died; they are listed on their mothers' chairs, beneath their mothers' names. At the western edge of the field of chairs is a small column of five chairs representing the five people who died outside the building. At night, each chair's glass name plate illuminates the darkness. This creates a kind of life for the victims that will never go out. Like the Vietnam Memorial in Washington, the abstract nature of the memorial seems to attract people, maybe because it allows them to distance themselves from the physical image of those who suffered and to concentrate instead on their memory.

I had seen pictures of the Oklahoma City National Memorial in a magazine and had been terribly moved by it, but of course it's even more moving when you're standing within it. I was struck by how quiet all the other visitors were. It was a very hushed place. Everyone lowered their voice when they had a conversation and took the time to take it all in. When they first opened it, there was a railing along the side of the field of empty chairs, but people were constantly stepping over it in order to place things on the chairs, in the same way as they leave messages and flowers at the Vietnam Memorial and on countless war memorials in Britain. Eventually, the authorities decided to remove a section of the railing, thereby encouraging visitors to leave even more tributes. This means that everyone is now free to walk among the chairs, so I had a wander between them, reading the names and the short biographies as I went. Names like Katherine Louise Cregan, who was sixty years old and died in the Social Security offices on the first floor. Or, on one of the smaller chairs, Ashley Megan Eckles, who was only four years old. She also died on the first floor. Walking between the chairs was a deeply moving experience. It had a kind of Stonehenge feel to it. I wondered who these people were – Mary Anne Fritzler, Laura Jane Garrison, and Gabreon D.L. Bruce, who was only three months old. What lives they might have led if it hadn't been for that lunatic McVeigh.

On the north side of the memorial stands one of the most extraordinary things about the whole place. In an orchard, one tree is much older than all the others. This American elm, now known as the Survivor Tree, was the only tree that threw any shade across the parking lot outside the Alfred Murrah Building. Commuters would arrive early to secure one of the prime parking spots shaded by its branches, but otherwise it was largely taken for granted. When the bomb exploded, the tree, which is now about a hundred years old, was one of the few things left standing. However, it was heavily damaged by the bomb, with most of the branches ripped off the central trunk. Later, it was nearly chopped down as investigators recovered evidence hanging from its few remaining branches and embedded in its bark. The trunk itself was heavily scarred and blackened by the heat of the blazing cars that had been parked beneath it. Few thought it would survive.

But then, a year after the bombing, when victims' relatives, survivors and rescue workers gathered for a memorial ceremony by the tree, they noticed it was starting to bloom. The Survivor Tree became a symbol of defiance against the fools who perpetrate acts of extreme violence against society, and it is thriving again. The authorities now go to great lengths to protect it. For instance, when they were constructing the memorial and needed to build a wall close to the tree, one of its roots was placed inside a large pipe so that it could reach the soil beyond the wall without being damaged. They've even dug an underground space beneath it so that workers can monitor its health and maintain its very deep roots. On a wall around the Survivor Tree, an inscription reads, 'The spirit of this city and this nation will not be defeated; our deeply rooted faith sustains us.'

That tree was a lone witness to what happened on the morning of 19 April 1995, and I found it particularly moving. Every year, hundreds of its seeds are incubated, and the resultant saplings are distributed around the country and planted on the anniversary of the bombing, so there are now thousands of Survivor Trees growing all over America.

I found the memorial even more powerful than I thought it would be. It provided another example of people at their best – creating something wonderful out of something really horrific and terrible. For some reason, I felt particularly sorry for the five victims who were outside the Alfred Murrah Building that morning. There was an awful feeling of really bad luck – of just being in the wrong place at the wrong time. The other victims had no choice – they were in the building because that's where their jobs required them to be – but the five outside would have evaded the blast if they'd arrived five minutes later or left five minutes earlier.

Beside the memorial there is a small museum. One of its most extraordinary exhibits is a tape of a meeting that was taking place in a nearby building when the explosion occurred. You could listen to people doing business, then *whoomph* – the bomb went off. But I couldn't bring myself to listen to it. I didn't want to experience that.

I was very glad I made the effort to visit the memorial. I almost didn't go, because storms were forecast for that afternoon. But as soon as I arrived, the skies turned very calm. That seemed strangely appropriate.

The next morning I returned to the National Stock Yards to see Stan's cattle being auctioned. Keeping my fingers crossed that Stan's beasts would achieve the target price of about a thousand dollars apiece, I took a seat at the edge of the auction ring. Surrounded by farmers, cowboys, cattlemen and dealers in jeans, plaid shirts, boots and stetsons, I waited for the action to begin while everyone else gabbled on mobile phones to their bosses and clients.

Having been to a cattle auction in British Columbia a few years before, I wasn't particularly looking forward to repeating an experience I'd already had, but this one was brilliant. Physically, it wasn't that different from the Canadian auction. In Canada the cattle were herded behind the auctioneer's booth by cowgirls, who were extremely good at their job. In Oklahoma a couple of cowboys did the same job. But here the auctioneers' patter was something else. It was like listening to bluegrass banjo music. I've seen and heard a lot of auctioneers in the flesh and on film, but none of them could hold a candle to the Oklahoma boys. It was as if they were speaking in tongues or in some strange cow language. I couldn't understand a word, but it was absolutely smashing. The auctioneer would relate information about the cattle at such a rapid pace, yet so lyrically, that I felt I could listen to him all day.

'One twenty-six Western, one twenty-five, one twenty-six Western, one twenty-five,' I thought he said, but I wouldn't have bet on it. Maybe that's what I sounded like to English audiences when I first came down from Scotland?

My only concern was that I could lose a lot of money just by twitching at the wrong moment, so after a while I left and got back on the trike.

Driving along the interstate for a short stretch, I had to pull over because I was getting scared. The wind was blowing me towards the hard shoulder and I didn't like it one little bit. So when I saw some billboards advertising the Cherokee Trading Post, I seized the opportunity to get off the road and investigate.

I mention everything that follows as a warning. If you decide to travel along Route 66, and you find yourself passing signs urging you to visit the buffalo at the Cherokee Trading Post, please take my advice. *Don't do it.* By all means fill up with their petrol or buy something from the gift shop. I bought some key rings and badges for my grandchildren, and if that's the sort of thing you're after, it's the place. But the buffalo will break your heart. And the campsite beside it will just make you feel like poor white trash.

I'd seen buffalo before and they were majestic, amazing animals with the most extraordinary eyes in huge, magnificent heads. But the pen at the Cherokee Trading Post was like a concentration camp for two miserable beasts that wandered around in their own shit, moth-eaten and ill behind double lines of barbed wire. Near the pen was a plastic buffalo with 'In God We Trust' painted on the side of it. To the side were a couple of the worst totem poles I'd ever seen. I hate it when people do that kind of thing in the name of 'culture'. When they commercialise culture just to make a quick buck. It happens in Scotland, too, and this made me just as angry as when I see cartoons of Highlanders with kilts that are too short and big red noses. Where's the pride in that?

Buffalo are magnificent creatures, genuine Indian culture is a splendid thing, and both of them deserve much better than what was on offer at the Cherokee Trading Post. Buy your petrol there, and maybe even a key ring, but then get straight back in your car or on your bike and head on down Route 66 without a backward glance.

I wish I'd done that.

Now, though, the end of Oklahoma was in sight. And ahead lay the mighty high plains of Texas.

10

You'll See Amarillo . . .

Within a few miles of reaching the Lone Star State, the landscape started to look like Texas. I'd been rolling through the verdant hills and pastures of Oklahoma for hundreds of miles. Then, as I approached Texola – the last place in Oklahoma – the land flattened, the soil became scrubby, and I crossed the Texas state line into a lonely, empty, dusty nothingness.

Common wisdom has it that the 178 miles of Route 66 that run across the Texas Panhandle – that square block of land jutting up from the northwest corner of the state – is the most boring drive on the entire journey, if not the planet. There's some truth in that. Texas isn't a place that tolerates any deviation, and the road is as flat as a pancake and almost uniformly straight right through the state. Water towers, windmills, grain elevators, deserted towns and the whistling wind provided the only relief from the thrum of tyres on the road.

Distances between places stretched out as if Route 66 had been squeezed through a mangle, emerging flattened and with fewer interruptions. Sixteen miles into the state, I pulled into its first town, Shamrock.

Now, I always hesitate to criticise any town, as I grew up in one that most people would describe as a slum. But Shamrock, Texas, is a horrible place. Although it allegedly has a population of a couple of thousand people, it was like a ghost town when I visited. And, God help me, the hotel I stayed in was possibly the worst part of the whole place. Lying on my bed that night, I gave my current situation some thought. I didn't want to give anyone the impression that Route 66 was a glorious place where they could always get their kicks, because that patently wasn't true. The road was dying. Nevertheless, some wonderful people were trying to keep it alive, and in some places they were succeeding. In others, like Shamrock, they most certainly were not.

The next morning, I asked the waitress if I could have two fried eggs over easy and some bacon. It seemed a fairly modest request, but she just shrugged and said I could only have what was on the menu. The choice was between some soggy old thing that looked like an omelette or some wee shrivelled sausages – or both – served on a polystyrene plate with white plastic knives and forks and a polystyrene cup of coffee. Anyone who travels Route 66 needs to prepare themselves for a bit of that on the road. And if, like me, they're a bit spoiled, it gets hellish.

After breakfast, I went to look at a rather beautiful art deco building that had been restored. The U-Drop Inn – originally a restaurant and a petrol station – was one of the icons of the road. Built in the early 1930s from a design scratched in the dirt beside a nearby motel, it had a tall tower over the petrol station and a beautifully detailed café that was called 'the swankiest of the swank eating places'. It was also the only café for a hundred miles, so it was highly successful in its day. But like many of the establishments along Route 66, it sank into disrepair with the demise of the road. Thankfully, though, it was eventually recognised as architecturally significant and restored with the help of a local bank.

Apparently the U-Drop was best viewed at night, illuminated by its neon strips, but even in the day it was an impressive building from the outside. But it was no longer a petrol station or a restaurant. It wasn't even a museum. They had tarted it up, then shut it to the public, which confused the hell out of me.

I have a bit of a problem with art deco buildings in general. They're interesting when you drive past, but that tends to be the end of the story. Take the Hoover Building in West London. Everybody raves about it, but how many of them have been within five feet of it? They've all seen it from a car, but then *whoom*, they're past it. That's fine – no one needs to go up and lick it to like it. But art deco lovers get on my tits. They're the kind of people who read *Lord of the Rings* and like movies about little ginky punkies attacking wanky wonkies. I wouldn't let my corpse be taken to a movie like that. And I feel pretty much the same about art deco. It's for dead people. You'd be amazed at the number of funeral parlours that are art deco. That's all I have to say on the subject.

Moving on from Shamrock, I rejoined Route 66, which for most of its distance through Texas runs beside the interstate as a service road. The landscape, as flat and featureless as ever, rolled on. But the wind – *Holy Mother of Jesus* – was something else. Several times I thought I was going to be killed when side winds hit me, blowing me off course like a big hand sweeping me across the road. I was really frightened a couple of times, but after about half an hour we arrived in McLean under a very hot, blazing sun.

McLean was my mother's name, and although she had no claim on McLean, Texas, I wondered if there might be a connection. Pulling into the small town, I asked an old man in a truck if he knew where the name stemmed from, but he didn't have a clue.

'I have lived here for fifty-three years,' he said. 'It used to be a good town but it's pretty dead now.'

I later discovered more than the old fella had learned over the previous half-century. Until 1901, the area where McLean now stands was nothing more than an unnamed cattle loading station on the Chicago Rock Island and Pacific Railroad (nicknamed the Cry and Pee, because of its initials). Then an English rancher, Alfred Row, donated some land near the loading station, thinking it might make a good site for a town. He was right – it grew quickly and within two years it had several banks, a post office, a newspaper, a wind-powered water pump, various stores and stables. By 1909, it was well established as a busy loading point for the railway, handling crops as well as animals, and requiring four telegraph operators to deal with commercial communications. Three years later, Alfred Row visited his relatives back home in England. For the return voyage, he booked a passage on a ship making its maiden voyage. That ship was the *Titanic*, and Alfred was last seen on an ice floe, frozen to death, hugging his briefcase.

McLean continued to prosper after his death, profiting from the oil boom in the 1920s and 1930s, and serving as the site of a camp for German prisoners-of-war in the 1940s. Any escapees were easily recaptured and were usually quite pleased to return after a few days on the bare plains of the Panhandle.

In 1984 McLean was the last Texan town to be bypassed by the interstate, and its sad decline began. Interstate 40 is about a mile away, but it seems like another world. Much of the town is now deserted. According to the mayor, who runs the Cactus Inn Motel, a marvellous old place, the population is significantly less than the official figure of eight hundred, although she was fully in favour of young people leaving the town to improve their prospects.

Nowadays, many of the buildings in McLean are abandoned. Petrol stations no longer pump gas, restaurants haven't served food for years, and plenty of houses have boarded-up windows and doors. On one tumbledown shop – above a fading mural featuring Elvis, a Chevy and a waitress on roller skates – a banner still proclaims McLean 'the Heart of Old Route 66'. I could imagine those days when the town was booming, when solid lines of cars streamed in from New Mexico to the west and Oklahoma to the east and the local petrol stations and diners were open around the clock to cater to travellers and tourists. Now it's a very different story. The main street is littered with the wreckage of the past and the concrete landscape is slowly being reclaimed by weeds. For photographers, it's a treasure trove of atmospheric pictures of urban decay, but I couldn't imagine what it must be like to live there.

Nevertheless, McLean still has several places that make it worth a visit. Next to the Cactus Inn Motel, the Red River Steakhouse serves steaks that are so juicy and tasty that many of its clientele regularly drive the hundred-mile round trip from

Amarillo to eat there. It also has charming waitresses and a fantastic atmosphere, so it takes some beating. Inexpensive and mind-blowingly good, it proves that you can find good food on Route 66, even though it can be a long search sometimes.

McLean also has a lovely old art deco cinema, the Avalon, which has been restored by a Route 66 association. (Sadly, though, just like the U-Drop, it was closed when I visited.) And on Route 66 itself, McLean boasts the first Phillips 66 petrol station to be opened in Texas. Built in 1929, it served the town for more than fifty years, and it's now been beautifully restored by the Old Texas Route 66 Association. The bright colours of its freshly painted pumps were a stark contrast to the faded splendour of most of the rest of the town. It is apparently the most photographed petrol station on Route 66. It no longer pumps gas, though.

In what remains of the centre of town, McLean's main attraction is housed in a former bra factory that once gained the town the fantastic nickname 'Uplift City'. But it no longer specialises in lingerie; now it's a museum dedicated to barbed wire. That might sound daft, but barbed wire – or the devil's rope, as they call it – is a very important thing in Texas. I've always thought of the Colt and the Winchester as the tamers of the Wild West, but apparently barbed wire was much more important in bringing order to the wilderness.

Invented by a man called Samuel Glidden, who made millions when he became the Henry Ford of the 'thorny fence', it was highly controversial at first. To the settlers of the American West, it provided security and stopped cattle barons from driving their herds across the settlers' land. But many others wished Glidden dead because his invention ended the era of free grazing on the range – which led to absolute misery out there.

This was the land of huge drovers' trails hundreds of miles in length. I'd passed a famous one the previous day, the Chisholm Trail, which led right across Texas and Oklahoma. There was also the Goodnight-Loving Trail, named after the cattlemen who used it to move longhorns from Texas all the way to Wyoming. For years, anyone could move cattle along these trails. But then people got selfish and started demanding fees, like tolls, to pass through their land. When that happened, all hell broke loose, and people started shooting each other. Anyone who put up a barbed-wire fence could stop herds in their tracks and charge for the water. This prompted countless feuds, many of which escalated into range wars, such as the Lincoln County War, which culminated in a gunfight at Blazer's Mill, a shootout that turned a young cattle guard called William McCarty into a fugitive better known as Billy the Kid.

With vigilante justice reigning supreme, much blood was shed and many communities were torn apart by the range wars. Eventually the lawmen settled the disputes, but by then the devil's rope had changed the nature of the West. So barbed wire already had a very unsavoury history, even before pictures of a corpse hanging over barbed wire and concentration camp inmates clutching barbed wire became symbols of the First and Second World Wars.

Within years of its invention, Glidden's wire spanned the nation from the Great Lakes to California, following a line very similar to that later taken by Route 66. Although Glidden ruthlessly sued anyone who infringed his patent, hundreds of rival designs were patented and many of them are now on display in McLean's museum. I'd never realised there were more than two thousand types of barbed wire, and that they even make barbed-wire jewellery and barbed-wire cocktail stirrers in Texas. The names of the different types are intriguing: Half McGlynn, Braided, Pitney, Evans, Elsie, Kitter and Ford. I'd always thought all barbed wire was the same – a series of double twists of wire around a long length of wire, seemingly designed to cut an L-shaped gash in your shorts when you were escaping from the orchard with your jumper full of apples and the farmer shouting, 'Come back here yer bunch of bastards.' But in the museum there were all sorts of designs on the walls, in cases and in cabinets. And people actually collect the stuff, too. They even have their own magazine, imaginatively titled *Barbed Wire Collector*.

There were lots of other novelties in the museum, like a hairy-arsed road runner with barbed wire for a tail, and a wee covered wagon made of spurred, rolled barbed wire by Sunny Mills of Amarillo. Looking at the First World War barbed wire reminded me of a song whose lyrics go something like, 'If you want to see the captain, I know where he is'. Then it continues for a few more lines of 'I know where he is' before the refrain comes in: 'He's hanging on the old barbed wire'. Each verse follows the same pattern, except the person changes – 'If you want to see the colonel', and so on. It's a bit of a boring song, but imagine singing it in the trenches when your friend was hanging upside down on the barbed wire. Grim times.

But by the time I'd scouted right around the museum, I had to admit it was a rather limited subject. All anyone really needs to know about barbed wire is that it can tear the arse out of your trousers, give a cow a good fright, entangle a Yorkshire terrier for life, and is nasty stuff made by greedy men.

Returning to the road and continuing my journey across the Texas Panhandle, at least there was no chance of getting lost. Route 66 closely follows the interstate, occasionally joining the freeway for a few miles at a time, and there were no other roads around to confuse me, which made a change. Quite how anyone riding solo on a motorbike through Missouri or Oklahoma manages to follow the road without getting lost is a mystery to me. In some parts, the path of Route 66 chops and changes so much that I frequently found myself lost, even with four of the production crew in a nearby car, all consulting satnavs, maps, books and all sorts of crap. Now, in the vast emptiness of Texas, at last I could relax and just follow the road.

Riding on, I passed several notable Route 66 landmarks. East of Groom, I spotted a leaning water tower that was one of the most photographed sights along the whole road – Texas's version of the Leaning Tower of Pisa. However, the Groom tower was purposely set at an angle by the owner of a local truck stop who had bought it to attract trade, so it was just another example of Route 66 tack in my book.

A mile or so further down the road stood a 190-foot-tall white crucifix that could be seen from up to twenty miles away on a good day. For a while, the crucifix, which was surrounded by life-sized statues of the Stations of the Cross, laid claim to being the tallest cross in the western hemisphere. However, the residents of Effingham, Illinois – which I'd passed nearly a thousand miles previously – put paid to Groom's boasting by erecting a cross that was eight feet taller. (Although, in the typical style of American superlatives, neither was as tall as the cross at the Valle de los Caidos in Spain, also in the western hemisphere the last time I checked.)

After about an hour, I reached Amarillo, appropriately known as 'Cow Town'. Near by, I passed a cattle ranch that has a larger population of cows than most towns have people in this part of America. Running alongside the road for several miles and stretching far into the distance, it is home to 28,000 beasts. The impact of the smell matched the scale of the operation, providing a succinct olfactory answer to the question: is this the way to Amarillo?

Those steers' ultimate fate was laid bare in Amarillo's temple to gluttony, the Big Texan Steak Ranch, a Western-style saloon restaurant with a twenty-five-foot neon cowboy standing by the side of the interstate. Here, the steak is free provided the diner eats it with a baked potato, salad, dinner roll and shrimp cocktail in less than sixty minutes. The catch is that the sirloin steak weighs in at seventy-two ounces, about the same as nine regular steak dinners, and you have to eat it on a raised platform under the gaze of the rest of the restaurant . . . and the world, via a live webcam. A few people, such as Klondike Bill, a professional wrestler, have managed *two* of the steak dinners in an hour. But since the Big Texan initiated its challenge, fewer than eight thousand of the fifty thousand who have attempted the single dinner have succeeded. So it's hardly surprising that the restaurant will ship in anyone wishing to accept the challenge – a small fleet of white stretch limos with longhorns on their bonnets wait outside to collect contenders free of charge from any hotel in Amarillo.

It was immediately obvious that Amarillo was in a much

better state than many of the Texan towns I'd passed through earlier. It's a rather beautiful place, with a lot of impressive buildings and successful-looking people in nice shiny cars, so I reckoned it was a good place to stop.

The next day, riding through the west side of town, as Route 66 headed back into the wilds, I pulled over to have a quick look at what some people call Route 66's version of Stonehenge. Smack in the middle of miles of empty flatland, on a giant, windswept wheat farm, stands a line of ten Cadillacs that look like they have plunged from high in the sky into the earth. For reasons best known to the artist, each of the semi-submerged Caddies is arranged at a slant on an angle exactly the same as the Great Pyramid of Giza. It might sound bizarre, but I think it's an outstanding piece of art.

The site belongs to a local wheat farmer, artist and philanthropist called Stanley Marsh 3 (that's the way he writes it), who enlisted some mates who were part of an art collective called Ant Farm to build Cadillac Ranch. Stan created it in the 1970s to represent the American love of automobiles and freedom, and it has to be seen to be believed. I had seen it in many books and brochures, but when I saw the real thing with the sun shining on it, my heart missed a beat. I fell in love with it.

What's really great about Cadillac Ranch is that Stan encourages people to graffiti on it, so it changes every day. Every now and then, Stan resprays the Cadillacs in plain paint to create a blank canvas, allowing the public to start again from scratch, drawing and writing whatever they like on it. I came prepared with a spray can of black gloss, but I was quite nervous. Having seen so many pictures of it, it felt odd to be walking towards it. The closer I got, the more I thought it was a cracking thing. It's a fairly simple work of art – just a row of ten cars poking out of the ground – but it changes shape in really interesting ways, depending on how you look at it.

What really appeals to me about Cadillac Ranch is that it's a big two-fingered salute to the kind of people I really don't like – the beige-ists of the world, the kind of people who get all upset about artwork that they can't buy, hang on their walls or give to their Auntie Jeanie for Christmas. When they see something like Cadillac Ranch, they don't know what to do with it. It brings out things in them that they find disturbing. I like disturbing people like that. I grew old without growing up and I'm very proud of it. I don't give a toss what anybody thinks.

I'm so full of admiration for Stan and his creation. It was one thing to have an idea like Cadillac Ranch, but quite another to go ahead and build it.

But then, as I got within striking distance of the line of lovely, multicoloured cars, their patches and streaks of paint gleaming in the sun, I spotted something that made my eyes stick out on stalks.

'To make love to me, I know it will never be Billy Connolly,' it said.

What?

I read it again: 'To make love to me, I know it will never be Billy Connolly.'

How in the name of God had that ended up on the side of a Cadillac? I thought that Stan himself must have done it. Then, looking down the line of Caddies, I saw my name repeated again and again.

'Billy + Amarillo.'

'Billy C.'

'Billy, see you Billy.'

'Billy Dilly.'

'BC.'

'Welcome to the windy city, Billy C.'

It was freakish. I wanted to look at them sideways, see them from different angles, just to get my head around them. That entire fantastic artwork had been prepared specially for me. What a lucky chap I was. And, God, this guy was good.

Cadillac Ranch had turned out to be the last thing on Earth I had thought it would be: a shrine to me. Well . . . I was all pleased with myself. How many people had an artwork on the Texan plains customised for their benefit? Holy Moly. It left me speechless. It wasn't just fabulous. It was amazing.

With my spray can of black paint, I added a few touches of my own. Just an exclamation mark on one set of initials and a few other bits and pieces. It was great fun, but I soon discovered that I wasn't a very good graffiti artist. It's not as easy as it looks. Ending up with dirty black fingers covered in paint, I didn't make too good a job of it.

From Cadillac Ranch, I rode round to Ant Farm's studio, where some of the artists were working on projects that Stan would later install in various parts of Amarillo. One of the wonderful things that they do is make road signs that are meaningless. They have slogans such as 'I have known a slut', with the idea being that people should just stumble upon them when they're driving along or hanging out in a public place. They call this the Dynamite Museum – the 'only museum in the world without walls'.

When I arrived, an artist called Drew showed me around and suggested I should paint one of their rogue signs.

'What do you want to paint?' he said.

'I have no real idea,' I said. 'I had a thought last night and the one I came up with was, "She kissed me once but it melted".'

'For your sign? That *is* good.' He smiled. 'Are you going to draw a picture or are you just going to do words?'

'I can't really draw.'

'I can't either.'

'You can't?'

'So what inspired you to do the Route 66?'

'I think it was just rock'n'roll. It seems to mean more to Europeans than it does to Americans. It seems to have more sort of . . . magic.'

'I think you're right. I think it's one of those things we just take for granted. To Europeans, it is what they associate America with – wide-open spaces and hitting the road. In America, it is our lifestyle, but we don't really appreciate it.'

In the end, I painted a cartoon of my face. Beneath it, I wrote, 'I have got biscuits'. It meant nothing at all, but then I started to worry that I'd done what I mentioned earlier – unwittingly absorbed another comic's material. I was so concerned that I phoned my daughter, who works in a New York art gallery. I asked her if she'd once shown me some T-shirts, one of which might have said, 'I have got donuts at home'. Maybe that had been floating around in the ether and I'd just adapted it a bit. But my daughter assured me that 'I have got biscuits' meant nothing to her. Then I met the woman in whose garden my road sign would be placed and she seemed delighted, so I was very pleased.

I think the rogue road signs are wonderful and ought to be expanded worldwide. My original idea had been to paint a sign that said, 'Beware of Route 666'. I'm glad I didn't do that – it's kind of dark and strange. But I do wish I'd gone with 'She kissed me once but it melted'. I don't know what it means, but I like it.

As I said to Drew, I was nervous about drawing, although I am an artist. I'll say that again: I am an artist. Once you admit that, you get good. I admitted it a long time ago, and I got good. I had noticed some rappers calling themselves artists – the kind of rappers who sold stuff on the street in New York, just regular guys. They would ask, 'Would you like to buy my art?' I thought that was a good stance to take. Gerry Rafferty tried to instil the same sort of thing into me when we were in the Humblebums – that what we did was art. Everyone else did junk, he used to say, but we did art. And I believed that attitude was true.

I also really believe Lenny Bruce's theory that a comedian is a man who thinks funny things and says them, while an actor is a man who learns funny things and says them. They're as funny as each other, but only one of them is a comedian. Going to bars and learning other people's jokes then telling them in other bars does not make you a comedian – it makes you an actor ... or a thief. It's just being a rip-off artist. But if someone thinks funny things and is brave enough to say them on stage, then they have entered the world of art. Whatever that might be.

I was mulling over all of this in the Ant Farm's studio, but I have to admit that I was starting to tie myself up in knots. I had entered that realm that we Scots call *wunnert*. 'Aye, he's a wee bit *wunnert*,' we say. It means lost and wondering, and it was old Uncle Willy who got wunnert: 'Aye, you'll get used to him, but he's a wee bit *wunnert*, you know? He might take a piss in a frying pan, but don't worry about him. He means well.'

It was clearly time to change the subject, and luckily I had the perfect thing. Somebody had told me the funniest joke a few days earlier: 'Why do they give old men in old folks' homes Viagra? To stop them rolling out of bed.' I thought that was the funniest thing ever!

After another fifty miles through the mind-numbingly flat and plain landscape of this flattest and plainest part of Texas, I pulled up outside a café in the town of Adrian. I had reached a point in the journey that anyone who was fascinated by facts, figures and statistics – which I'm not at all – would regard as highly significant.

A sign by the side of the road said it all: 'Los Angeles 1139 miles – Chicago 1139 miles'. I'd arrived at the exact midpoint of Route 66. It was just like anywhere else along the journey, but at the same time it was a funny position to be in. I'd been on the road for longer than I had left to run. It had taken me four weeks to reach the midpoint, and I had less than three weeks remaining. Arriving at the halfway point made sense of the road and gave me a feeling of achievement.

The café – called the Midpoint Café, of course – is famous for its ugly pies. Personally, I thought they should be far uglier than they were – all big and lumpy and burned. Like a lot of things on Route 66, there was a lot of talk, a lot of bragging, but not much when you got there. Compared to many pies I'd eaten in Scotland over the years, these were very good-looking pies. I had a cup of tea and a peach cobbler, and was a wee bit disappointed that its ugliness didn't come up to scratch. Maybe they used to be properly ugly and now they were concentrating on making them nice. That would be a mistake. I was starting to like the shabby side to Route 66. Once I accepted that the road's best days were well behind it, it was much easier to accept its limitations and get on with having a good time.

My next stop was the last town in Texas and the first in New Mexico – it straddles the border. This was a particularly poignant destination because, in its heyday, Glenrio was a thriving and hectic pit stop on Route 66. Some of the scenes in John Ford's film version of *The Grapes of Wrath* were shot there, but it has never been a highly populated place. At its peak in the 1940s, it had a population of just thirty. But its famous motel had a big neon sign that proclaimed either, 'First Motel in Texas' or 'Last Motel in Texas', depending on how you looked at it. And the busy post office straddled the state line, with the depot receiving mail in Texas and the office distributing it in New Mexico.

Then, one day in September 1973, Interstate 40 opened. That day, Glenrio died. The stream of tourists who had flowed through the town along Route 66 en route to California or from the Pacific coast towards the American heartland dwindled to a trickle, then stopped altogether.

By 1985, that post office was the only business left open. It served a population of two. Today, among a string of dead or dying towns along hundreds of miles of the old road, Glenrio is the deadest of all. It now has just one resident, a softly spoken mother of two, who lives among the critters and the tumbleweed.

Roxann Travis told me she was in Glenrio on the day the highway opened. Her father's petrol station became an immediate casualty. Now in her sixties, she is happy to live there alone in the house in which she was born, and she has no desire to move on.

'My dad moved house here when I was a baby and built the station and the diner,' she told me. 'Every summer all the traffic would be lined up the highway, both directions. It was very, very busy. He would have us go wash the windshields and check the oil so they would be ready to pump the gas and keep them moving through.'

Her mum and dad used to keep horses across the road from one of their two petrol stations, but it was hard to get to them because there were so many cars. A few years later, when Roxann was raising her own kids, they could play ball on the road. Nowadays, you could take a nap on it. You'd only be disturbed when occasional tourists, like me, stopped by to gawp at the ghost town.

'It must seem very strange to you,' I said, 'because you must see your dad and your siblings when you look at this place.'

'I do, yes. And it's real sad to watch it crumble.'

'So, how long did it take for the town to die with the coming of the interstate?'

'Four or five years, I guess. The Texas Longhorn – a café, station and motel down there – was the last to go.'

For a while, Roxann lived in Glenrio with her husband, Larry, who commuted to their business in Adrian – another petrol station. But in 1976 the gas station was raided and Larry was forced to his knees and shot through the back of his head. The killer went on to murder a second man the same day at another petrol station in the Texas Panhandle.

'How does it feel to live here all alone?' I said.

'I'm used to it. I'm fine with it. I like the peace and quiet.'

Roxann has six dogs to keep her company, but they make the noise of twelve.

'Do you get visitors? Do any of the old people who used to live here ever come back?'

'Not really, no, because some are scattered out in the country. There was another house next door and they moved to Lubbock and they never looked back.'

'So, where do you get your groceries?'

'I usually go to Amarillo, but for a short trip, if I don't have that much time, I'll go to Tucumcari. That's forty miles.'

'Well, I really admire you. I really admire your guts. I don't know if I could do it.'

Roxann showed me some pictures of Glenrio in its heyday. With a barbecue restaurant, various diners, a hamburger joint, several petrol stations and motels, it was a buzzing, vibrant place.

'They're all sitting having their dinner and they look like they're laughing,' I said, looking at one of the snaps. 'They all look so happy sitting eating their hamburgers. Little did they know what was going to happen. It just happened in a flash really, didn't it?'

'It went downhill fast.'

'What made you decide to stay?'

'It's home!'

We both laughed at the absurdity of it. Roxann is a lovely woman, who doesn't feel at all blighted by her situation.

'But don't you need other people round you to make it a home?'

'My daughter comes every chance she gets. My son drives for a trucking company and he stops by pretty often. And I like to read, do my garden and sew and mess with the animals.' Her daughter-in-law couldn't understand how she could live in Glenrio and wanted her to move to a town, which she thought would be safer. But Roxann said, 'I don't think town is safe. I feel safer out here. With my dogs, no one's walked in that yard in a while without me knowing.'

'Well, you certainly seem very happy.'

'I like it here. I plan to stay as long as I'm able.'

'Why not? You could be the mayor as well, if you like.'

'People tease me about that. I'm the mayor, the sheriff and everything else.'

'Postmistress ... and, of course, you're the entire police force as well.'

For a while, Roxann shared the town with a young cowboy, who was living in a deserted building, but he didn't last long. Now the only regular visitor was a cow that had broken out of a nearby ranch and was harmlessly roaming the streets.

I thought she was a wonderful, brave woman with a brilliant attitude. I'd found another friend.

As she said, this was her home. What more could anyone want?

11

Albuquerque and Tucumcari, Make New Mexico Extraordinary

Glenrio took me into New Mexico, the sixth of eight states I would pass through on Route 66. Extremely beautiful and more than a little mystical, New Mexico is where Route 66's origin in the cattle tracks and wagon trails of the Wild West becomes obvious. Here, Route 66 looks more like a ribbon suspended from the vast, deep-blue sky than a road built on the ground.

Now the distances were truly vast, the destinations remote and the rides long, hot and hard.

Almost perfectly square in shape, New Mexico has more history than any other state along Route 66, with Native American Pueblo dwellings dotted along the road. But it also has its fair share of the bizarre, outlandish and freaky often found along the Mother Road. South of Albuquerque, for instance, there's a town named after a 1950s radio quiz show. The programme's producers offered to rock up and record the next episode anywhere that was prepared to change its name to the title of the show. That's why some seven thousand people now live in a town called Truth or Consequences rather than Hot Springs.

From Glenrio, I rode straight through to Santa Fe, a distance of nearly 250 miles. Once again, I was buffeted by a side wind that was beyond belief. It blew me all over the damn place. Sharing the road with big rigs when there were side winds was a double-edged sword. Sometimes I thought the wind would sweep me under one of them and I'd be squashed into the tarmac. At other times, a truck would come along and shield me from the wind. But this was a finely judged thing – if a gust slipped under the truck, or between the truck and its trailer, my shield would become a lethal hazard. I had to keep my wits about me all the time.

Arriving in Santa Fe, I was booked into a hotel in which my wife and I had stayed some years previously. It hadn't changed a bit. Santa Fe is a beautiful town. It's full of tourist traps, but I don't mind that. The stores sell turquoise jewellery and all sorts of beaded things, some of them outstandingly fabulous and very expensive, but that doesn't detract from the fact that it's a lovely, relaxed and relaxing place. And the food is great – a blessed relief after all the crap I'd been eating for weeks.

Strictly speaking, Santa Fe wasn't even on Route 66 during the road's heyday. When the route was first designated in 1926, everyone expected it to go straight through the town because it was the capital of New Mexico and where the Pecos and Santa Fe trails met. And indeed, for the first eleven years of Route 66, it turned northwest at Santa Rosa, headed up to Santa Fe, then turned back down south to Albuquerque.

However, in 1937, A.T. Hannett, the Governor of New Mexico, was not re-elected and he blamed a ring of powerful lawyers and influential landowners based in Santa Fe. As an act of defiance against this cabal, he re-routed Route 66 directly to Albuquerque, bypassing Santa Fe altogether. With just a few months to go before the new governor was inaugurated, Hannett forced the road builders to work seven days a week, including Christmas, to construct a new highway through virgin landscape. The road cut across public and private land, showing complete disregard for ownership rights. By the time the new governor was installed, it was too late for him to do anything about it. Drivers welcomed the change, which shaved more than ninety miles off Route 66 between Santa Rosa and Albuquerque, but in the end Santa Fe benefited, too. The city grew on its own merits, without relying on Route 66 traffic, so when the road was decommissioned Santa Fe was unaffected, unlike most places along the route. Its isolation also meant it developed in a unique way. It's a beautiful city of adobe buildings, with none taller than three storeys. I'd strongly advise you to make the detour off Route 66 and have a look.

I'd come to Santa Fe to experience a miracle. At least, that's what I'd been told. I don't believe in miracles or the supernatural, but I don't have a problem with anyone who does. So I was quite looking forward to my visit to the Loretto Chapel, a charming former Roman Catholic church in the shadow of St Francis Cathedral on the fringes of the downtown area. The oddest thing about the chapel is that it has no priests. Introduced to someone who was described as the owner, my immediate thought was: What do you mean, 'the owner'?

It turned out that the Loretto Chapel had been decommissioned – it's now a business that charges an entrance fee. But anyone can still get married there, if they hire a priest, which seems kind of odd to me. Anyway, it's a very pretty place, built in the 1870s in the Gothic revival style for an order of nuns called the Sisters of Loretto. At the top of the church is a choir loft, a very nice and large one. But when the building was finished and the nuns looked up at the loft, they noticed a quite serious problem with it: there was no staircase, so they had no way to get up there. Apparently, the architect had died suddenly when drafting the blueprint for the building, and then the builders hadn't noticed that the staircase was missing from the plans.

Faced with a bit of a dilemma, the nuns prayed day and night for nine days. On the tenth day, a guy showed up at the chapel. Riding a donkey, he had long hair and a beard, and he offered to do the job for them. In what seemed a ridiculously short amount of time – just three months – he built a spiral staircase that led up to the choir loft. He then promptly disappeared before anyone could determine his identity or even pay him for his work. Mysterious, eh?

The staircase is certainly very beautiful. I had a close look and couldn't see a single nail mark or any trace of glue. And I found it difficult even to find any joints (that is, the carpentry kind of joint: I don't want to suggest that the carpenter was smoking dope while he was making the staircase). Apparently it's all held together with dowels, but it's still a remarkable feat of construction. Unlike most spiral staircases, it has no central support and it isn't attached to a wall. That said, the owners of the church very rarely let anyone use it, so I had to wonder if it was as strong and stable as it looked.

The Catholic Church eventually declared that the creation of this staircase was a miracle, purely because some people reckoned the bearded guy was St Joseph. It was also claimed that he used only a small number of primitive tools, such as a square, a saw and some warm water – although how anyone knew that when he supposedly worked entirely alone and behind closed doors might be a miracle in itself. It's also alleged that the staircase is constructed entirely from non-native wood, yet no one saw any lumber delivered during the three months that the carpenter was in the chapel. These mysteries had kept 250,000 pilgrims a year guessing, and the entrance-fee dollars pouring into the tills. The church was so geared up for tourists it was almost silly.

As with many 'miracles', there are rational explanations for several of the staircase's apparent mysteries. For instance, experts have pointed out that plenty of other spiral staircases don't have a central support; and anyway, the Loretto Chapel's staircase seems to have a concealed support that acts like a central pole. Also, its double-helix shape, like a DNA molecule, will lend it some strength – although this design probably makes it bounce like a giant spring, which might explain why the owners don't let people walk up and down it.

Even supposing that the legend is true and St Joseph did build the spiral staircase, I still have one big unanswered question: how did the builders construct the choir loft? It's a big, high platform, so how did they build it without a staircase to get up there? Did they hang upside down from the roof? That's what I wanted to know.

Seeing the crowds inside the church made me think that some people seem to be desperate for miracles. They really long for them to be true. Personally, I like Thomas Jefferson's attitude that miracles spoil religion because they are obviously tosh and go against nature. Jefferson even went to the trouble of writing an alternative Bible with no miracles or other supernatural events in it.

I left Santa Fe and headed even further away from Route 66, northwest into the mountains, through a landscape that looked like it had been built by giants. The freeway up to Los Alamos, some 7,320 feet above sea level, was one of the most extraordinary roads I'd ever seen. If European road builders were faced with a similar challenge, they would cut the road into the side of the mountain, making it wind up the incline in a series of hairpin bends. Not so in New Mexico, where they unashamedly and pragmatically built the six-lane Los Alamos Highway straight up and through the valley.

For many years, Los Alamos was a secret town that didn't officially exist. The locals carried driving licences that had no names, addresses or signatures on them, just always the same occupation – engineer – which indicated to the police that the holder was conducting secret government work. Cut off from the outside world, this small town in the mountains was home to the Manhattan Project – America's top-secret effort, with participation from Britain and Canada, to develop the first atomic bomb during the Second World War.

When I arrived in Los Alamos, I was flabbergasted to find it was a beautiful country town – clean, well laid out, with fantastic facilities and crystal-clear mountain air. It also has the highest concentration of residents with Ph.D.s anywhere in the world, and consequently the highest per capita income of any American city (and the highest house prices).

It was a beautiful day, the kind you dream about, as I rode into the centre of town, where a string of handsome wood and stone lodges make up the Los Alamos Historical Museum. In 1942 these mountain lodges were requisitioned by the military from Los Alamos Ranch School, a private boarding school. The site was chosen for the Manhattan Project because of its isolation, access to water, and location on a table mountain that allowed all entrances to be secured. Originally referred to only as Site Y, it later became the Los Alamos Scientific Laboratory and, after the war, the Los Alamos National Laboratory. In a strip of buildings known as Bathtub Row – because they were the only houses in Los Alamos with baths – stood the school's Fuller Lodge and Big House. Both were social gathering places for Manhattan Project personnel, while other nearby buildings were used for housing.

At one of the historic lodges I met Jack Aeby, who used to be a driver for the project's scientists, many of whom had codenames in this no-questions-asked town. Sitting beside him was Frank Osvath, a machinist on the project. Both men are now in their eighties. I asked Frank what he did exactly.

'Can't you tell by looking at me?' he said. 'I glow in the dark. I machined uranium for thirty-nine years.'

'You did not!' I was amazed.

'I did.'

'Is that a safe thing to do?'

'It was mostly depleted uranium. Enriched uranium – I just did a little bit of that.'

'How did you feel about being part of manufacturing an atomic bomb? Did you know that's what you were doing?'

'They came looking for machinists at the Ford Motor Company in Detroit and about a dozen of us came out here. They told us we would build something that might end the war, but we didn't know for sure what it was.'

'Really? Well, it certainly did that.'

'They said they couldn't tell us how long we would be here. We would be restricted from travelling and our letters would be censored, so it was quite a restriction to come out here. Our names were changed; they gave us false names. My folks, who lived in Detroit, used to write me letters and they were censored coming in and going out. My folks came from Hungary and I wrote them in Hungarian. Those letters couldn't be censored here, so they sent them to Washington, DC, then back here, and then they delivered them to my folks. So it took a very long time.'

I turned to Jack. 'And you were a driver?'

'I would get the people who were coming up here,' he said, 'take them to 109 East Paulos, which was the headquarters in Santa Fe, and they would be met by military personnel for their induction to work up here.'

'Were you allowed to speak to them about the project?'

'They all arrived with assumed names, like everybody else that worked here, and they never remembered their names, but

I'd taken physics long enough to know who they really were and I'd even remind them what their codename was when I put them in the car and brought them up.'

It must have been a most interesting time. I was especially fascinated by the museum's pictures of people having parties, wearing funny hats and holding drinks in their hands, and presumably falling in love in the evenings, while by day they were building the first atom bomb.

'We weren't allowed to travel, so we had to have our parties here,' said Frank. 'We ate our lunch here in this room. One time I came down and six men sitting around that table started to sing the Hungarian national anthem. So I joined in and sang with them. When we got through singing I went over to talk to some of those fellows and one of them said his name was Edward Teller. He was the father of the hydrogen bomb. He played that piano over there several times to entertain us.'

I found that kind of strange. There was no reason on earth why these people shouldn't have played the piano or held parties or fallen in love or got drunk, but it still seemed incongruous.

Jack took the picture of the first atom bomb test explosion at the Trinity test site, White Sands, south of Albuquerque, on 16 July 1945. It's one of the ten most published photographs in the world and I've always thought it's extraordinary – the mushroom cloud billowing in the desert – but Jack told me there's something wrong with it. He pointed to a print of the famous picture on the wall. 'It's facing the wrong way. It was taken on a slide and whoever made that picture turned it over.' Then he pointed at a whisp of smoke on the right of the picture. 'That little plume', he said, 'should be on the left. It belongs on the other side.'

'It doesn't matter much, does it?' said Frank.

'I was back at base camp when I took it,' said Jack, 'on the south side of everything. So everybody thought that any good picture must have come from the technical staff at the bunker on the north. I'm strictly an amateur; I didn't have any technical knowledge.'

The night before the explosion, Frank and a group of friends climbed a mountain called South Baldy, the highest peak of the Magdalena Mountains in central New Mexico, and slept at an altitude of ten thousand feet to ensure they would get a good view of the detonation the next morning, but when the appointed hour arrived, they thought the bomb had failed to detonate.

'We thought it didn't work,' said Frank. 'We knew what time it was supposed to go off in the morning and it didn't go off. They delayed it because of the weather. So all of my friends crawled back into their sleeping bags, but I was sitting up, watching the sun come up from the other direction. All of a sudden a flash went off and then I heard the sound come in later. All the others woke up and watched it; it was quite an exciting experiment. We looked down at it from above and saw the mushroom building up below us.'

Their stories were extraordinary. What a privilege to have been present at such a momentous event in history, even if there was something quite horrific about it. 'How did you feel?' I said. 'Did it fill you with fear or joy or horror? You must be one of the few people on earth who have watched an atomic explosion for pleasure.'

'Right,' said Frank. 'And unofficially – from a high place.'

'As a matter of fact,' said Jack, 'there was a lottery going and people bet on the yield that it was going to give. I guessed at about twelve kilotons, which was pretty close, and it was estimated all the way from zero to infinity. There were those who thought it would set the atmosphere on fire and melt the earth.'

I wondered how that person felt when the explosion took place. He probably ran off to hide under his bed somewhere.

'After the explosion, we came down the mountain to have breakfast in Socorro,' said Frank. 'The newspaper already had the headlines out: "Accidental Explosion". They thought it was an ammunition dump. We knew it was a lie, but they had to publish something because everybody around there heard that explosion and saw the big flash.'

'Were they aware of radiation and fallout?' I said. 'Or did it take them by surprise?'

'They knew there were going to be fission products and that they had to go someplace. The wind was blowing, so they could trace it across the country, and they interviewed people who were in that path. There were cattle that died and some people got mild exposures, but nothing serious.'

Frank and Jack both looked in very good health, especially considering all their years of work on the project. A few weeks after the explosion, Jack was part of a group that dug up some of the radioactive remnants at the test site in search of new elements. In the debris they discovered a few new isotopes, including plutonium.

Then Frank told me something astonishing. 'A friend of mine is the only person in the world who saw the first three atomic bombs. He not only went to Trinity, he also flew on the airplanes that dropped the bombs on Hiroshima and Nagasaki.

He invented the trigger for the bomb so he was asked to go along in the airplanes to set it up when they got close. And then he dropped it. When he came back, I asked him, "How did you feel, killing so many people?" He said at first it was a very bad feeling, but then he prayed a lot about it and realised that many of our soldiers wouldn't have to go there to continue fighting the Japanese. The war would end, so he saved a lot of lives. He was satisfied with what he did.'

'Was anybody troubled with guilt?'

'A large number were,' said Jack. 'They circulated a petition not to use the bomb aggressively but to demonstrate its power at a deserted island someplace. There were literally hundreds of signatures on that petition, but it never reached Roosevelt. Secretary Byrnes [James F. Byrnes, the US Secretary of State in 1945] blocked it. He didn't want Roosevelt to see that.'

'Really?' I was amazed.

'He had already decided with the military and all,' said Jack. 'They may have been correct, I'm not questioning that. But, yes, there was guilt. A lot of it.'

I was very glad to hear that. Not glad that people felt guilty exactly, but it would have been deeply disturbing if no one had even cared about it.

One of the lodges had been the home of Robert Oppenheimer, who led the Manhattan Project and is widely regarded as the architect of the bomb. He apparently served the best dirty martinis in town, but he never came to terms with being the person who unleashed the horrific power of the atom bomb. Immediately after the test, he admitted that he had 'become the destroyer of worlds'.

Nevertheless, Jack said there 'were a lot of fun sides to the pre-explosion bit. Working here was fun, a great deal of pleasure in finding things out. It was exciting looking for something very new. That question of how might it work and could we build one? And then: "Wow, we did it!" That kind of thing. But it wasn't anybody's idea to blow up people with it. They wanted to end the war, no question about that. Certainly a demonstration would have been possible, inviting everybody in, but that suggestion didn't work. Nobody accepted that outside of the people who were concerned.'

Personally, I wish the ones who drew up the petition had won. America has been left in a very weak position because it has used an atomic weapon in anger. 'How could America say to Iran, "You mustn't do it" when they've done it twice?' I asked.

'Absolutely right,' said Jack. 'And it's worse than that. We will not sign a non-first-use treaty with anybody.'

That made me shiver.

Frank and Jack clearly had misgivings about where the world had been led by the Manhattan Project. They'd both also been involved in the development of the hydrogen bomb. Frank was sent to New York State, where they assembled the outside steel case of the new, much bigger bomb, but it was so large that it wouldn't fit under some of America's railway bridges, so it was sent by ship to the Pacific. Frank wasn't present at the detonation, but Jack took a picture of it.

'I was in a health physics group that kept people from hurting themselves with all that radiation around,' said Jack. 'I happened to be there at Operation Bravo. It destroyed an island completely. It's gone.'

Eventually, Frank joined an outfit that cleaned up thirty-two

FUAES – Formerly Utilized Atomic Energy Sites. 'The big first hydrogen bomb left a great big hole in the ocean,' he said. 'Water filled it up right quick, but the hole was still there. All the debris from years of testing on Enewetak Atoll was dumped down that hole and covered over with concrete. I worked on that job for years. I was the garbage man.'

Both Frank and Jack were intensely interested in the outcome of the latest Strategic Arms Limitation Talks that were going on at the time. 'I think there are some level-headed people that realise that we've got a gadget we cannot use,' said Jack. 'That's what we need to realise.'

Even though I didn't know much about the subject, it seemed kind of incongruous to have weapons that would wipe us all out if they were ever used.

'You use it, you're dead,' said Jack. 'That's why there's just no point in it.'

It was fascinating to meet these two men in Los Alamos, and they were an absolute delight. I had expected them to be totally atomic, all for the atom bomb, so I was very pleasantly surprised to discover that they weren't. I had one last question: 'When you were living here in the war, was there any sneaking out going on?'

'It was easy enough to do,' said Jack. 'Our travel outside was monitored and restricted to visits to Santa Fe. However, I had a girlfriend in Phoenix, who I managed to meet at least once. They knew about it down there because the bomb went off and she wrote me a letter and said, "Aha, a little bigger than you thought, eh?" The censors read that and I didn't have an answer.'

*

The next day I rode to Albuquerque, a short hop down the pre-1937 Route 66 route from Sante Fe. Again, a lot of the buildings are low-rise adobe structures, but Albuquerque lacks Santa Fe's charm. At first I thought it was a nothing kind of town, just a one-street joint with some dodgy stores, but then I visited the Rattlesnake Museum. A lot of good things were happening in the square outside the museum, and the place seemed to be buzzing, with live music and busy restaurants.

The museum itself is owned and run by Bob Myers, a self-confessed rattler fanatic. I'm not that fond of snakes myself, so I quite like the idea of one that warns you it's there. That rattling noise, which sounds like a high-pitched footballer's rattle, is a very succinct way of saying, 'I'm scared! Don't come any nearer. Get lost.' And, of course, it's never a good idea to go near scared animals. The old prospectors who roamed the Wild West and played guitar around camp fires at night used to keep rattlesnake tails inside their guitars. If a thief lifted the guitar, he'd hear the *tikka-tikka-tikka* of the tail, think there was a snake inside, and drop it.

Stacked to the rafters with tanks containing rattlesnakes, the museum is fascinating. Bob had a stick with which he prodded some of the snakes to make them rattle properly. There's no other noise quite like it, and anyone would recognise it instantly. If you hear it, you should stop dead in your tracks, then slowly back up the way you came and get the hell out of there. As Bob told me, rattlesnakes are not aggressive and they're much more scared of us than vice versa, but if they're cornered and unable to escape to safety, they will invariably retaliate.

Many of the snakes were beautifully camouflaged and almost

impossible to spot against the rocks and sand. I was very impressed. The canebrake rattlesnake reminded me of Tom Waits, the only person I've ever known to talk about them. Then there was the mottled rock rattlesnake, the black tailed rattler, a southwestern speckled rattlesnake and a panamint rattler, which was the most difficult to spot of all. Most of them gave me the willies.

Once, in an earlier TV show, a python was placed around my neck. She was very nice, and kept whispering in my ear. I told the keeper that I thought his snake must fancy me, and he said, 'It's a boy.' It didn't seem quite the same once I knew it was a gay snake. And in the movie of *Lemony Snicket's A Series of Unfortunate Events* I had a snake wrapped round my wrist as I played a musical instrument. At one point in the film, I said goodbye to the snake and it kissed me. It was a magical moment, but I wasn't inclined to repeat it with any of those rattlers, just in case one of them tried to bite my face off.

Approaching the New Mexico–Arizona state line, I crossed the continental divide, the line that splits where America's rivers flow – either to the Pacific or to the Gulf of Mexico and the Atlantic. Then I spent a night at the El Rancho Hotel in Gallup, where stars from Hollywood's golden age like John Wayne, Katharine Hepburn and Spencer Tracy stayed while making cowboy movies in the nearby mountains.

Moving on the next morning, a sign caught my eye. 'Indian Ruins', it said. Hmm, I thought, that might be interesting. But, as so often on Route 66, the sign promised much more than the place delivered. Pulling in, I discovered the ruins had long since gone. Flooded or possibly blown away, only a few markings remained in the dirt. There was a trinket shop, but it had nothing different from all of the other Indian gift shops along this stretch of the road. So I got back on the trike and resumed the relentless journey west, hoping to reach Holbrook, Arizona, before too long.

Winona – which, like Gallup, is name-checked in the song – lay just beyond Holbrook and everything seemed to be going well. Then, all of a sudden, we ran out of Route 66. In itself, this was nothing new: Route 66 had stopped or disappeared plenty of times before. One moment there would be tarmac; then there would be gravel and scree, or a dead end. The crew and I would consult our maps, fire up the satnav, have a wee discussion, then go in search of Route 66. Usually this entailed doing a U-turn, retracing our steps for a few miles and then taking a different road. It happened a lot.

But this time it was different.

Carefully edging the bike around – avoiding the side of the road, which disappeared into nothingness – the revs suddenly shot up and the bike went crazy. My hand was stuck. The throttle wouldn't respond. I tried to calm the engine, but everything was moving too fast. Even now, I don't know exactly what happened.

Fighting the jammed throttle, I spun out of control. The bike wheeled around, somersaulted, then bounced off me. The big rear wheels went right over the top of me and something slammed into my ribs. My knee thumped hard into the road – a crunch of bone and flesh on tarmac. Then I was lying on my back, staring at the sky. As I lay there, I wondered just how much damage I'd done to myself.

Desperate to stand up and just get on with it – because, of course, I'm a man of steel, a real hero – I was immediately told not to move, to stay absolutely still. Mike, the director, insisted that I must continue to lie down. He wouldn't even loosen my bloody helmet, the bastard.

While I waited for an ambulance to arrive, the crew looked after me brilliantly. Then the paramedics arrived. If there's one thing at which Americans excel, it's being the good guys in a time of crisis. Three of the four ambulance crew were motorcyclists themselves, and they knew exactly what to do – and not just in terms of medical attention. They instinctively knew that they could do whatever they wanted with my T-shirt – cut it to ribbons, for all I cared – but they had to tread very carefully with my jacket. Working with painstaking precision, they sliced the jacket along the seams, cutting up the sides and around the back, and removed it in one big flappy – but easily repaired – piece.

Slipping some metal plates underneath me, they eventually lifted me on to a weird folding stretcher, then carried me off to a helicopter for one of the worst flights of my life. Clear-air turbulence and chest straps were not a pleasant combination for sore, badly bruised ribs. I was absolutely stiff and couldn't move, immobilised in case my neck had been broken in the crash. But every judder and jolt of the helicopter, every sudden drop because of the turbulence, shot like a thunderbolt through my body. With the back of my head pressed against that bloody stretcher, I gritted my teeth throughout the hour-long flight to Flagstaff.

Once inside the hospital, the doctors examined me thoroughly. After several X-rays and some tests, the verdict was that I had one broken rib and lacerations to my knee. It could have been much worse. The pain was hellish, but I was more concerned about my jacket. Someone in the crew offered to take it to a seamstress, who pronounced that the damage wasn't terminal. My jacket could be saved. Twenty-four hours later, I had it back. Both my jacket and my leather waistcoat had been magnificently reassembled. I was left marvelling at the thoughtfulness and care of the ambulance crew. That's one thing I love about America – they think about little things like that.

Unfortunately, getting my body back into shape wasn't as easy as repairing my clothes. A broken rib might sound like nothing, but there's nothing anyone can do to help the healing process. It can't be bandaged and there are no fancy creams to apply. So I just had to rest and leave the bloody thing as it was.

Back at the hotel, easing myself into bed, I coughed. *Christ!* I thought I'd been hit by a bolt of lightning. And when I sneezed, it felt like someone had dropped a Volkswagen on my chest. The pain was excruciating. I couldn't laugh, either. And getting in and out of bed was a nightmare. Just hellish pain.

I was prescribed some serious painkillers, but they were so strong that I was a bit scared of them and soon decided they probably weren't the best idea. I was feeling too good on them. Opiates can creep up on you like that. Opting to give the serious stuff a wide berth, I settled on some simple anti-inflammatories and had a good rest. Meanwhile, the crew and everybody else who helped me were very kind, even though I was turning into a grumpy whinge-bag. Eventually,

I had to sit down and have a word with myself about my behaviour. This was real. It wasn't a game. It wasn't an act. People really were that nice, kind and pleasant. They accepted that I'd been through the mill. I'd really been kicked on Route 66.

12

Flagstaff, Arizona, Don't Forget Winona

After four days' recuperation, I had to face the fact that I'd have to get back on the bike the next day. My rib was still tender, my knee was still bandaged and covered in weeping scabs, but I needed to continue the journey. To be honest, I didn't give it too much thought. Like getting back on a horse, it just had to be done. Hanging around until everything had healed was not part of the deal.

The bike itself held no fear for me, but I was a wee bit apprehensive about going over bumps – simply moving around on my bed still sent sharp shocks of pain through my rib. I told myself I'd be okay. After all, the bike was a relatively comfortable vehicle with a relaxed riding position, so I ought to be fine. My main problem was that I'd now reached the part of the journey where every destination was a very long way from the previous stop. This was the big country with big distances and big, big drives.

Thanks to my emergency helicopter trip to the hospital in Flagstaff, I'd ended up further down Route 66 than I'd planned to be, so I double-backed to Payson, Arizona, where it was rodeo time. I'd never seen a rodeo in the flesh before, but I'd watched it on television and quite liked it. It was like skateboarding or BMX biking; I hadn't realised it was a proper sport until I'd seen it on TV, but then I'd learned about it and become interested. And I'd worn cowboy boots for many years, so that had to count for something.

I was most fascinated by the clowns. For ages, I'd thought they were kind of useless, some of the worst clowns I'd ever seen. Then I discovered they aren't there to make the crowd laugh. Their real function is to protect the guy riding the horse or the bull by acting as a human decoy. I really wanted to meet one, so I turned up with high expectations in Payson, which claimed to hold the world's oldest continuous rodeo. That meant wall-to-wall ridin', ropin' and dancin' fun, and a chance for me to meet some real-life cowboys and cowgirls.

First held in August 1884, when some ranchers and cowboys got together to test their roping and riding skills and the speed of their horses, Payson's rodeo, like all the others, is based on traditional cattle-herding practices. It involves a number of sports, including racing horses around barrels, lassoing, roping and tying down various animals, but the highlight is bareback riding of horses (called broncos) and bulls. And that's when the clowns are an essential part of the action. They live their lives in terrible danger. They're not just dafties doing tricks; they distract the bull from a guy that it wants to kill. And the only way they can defend themselves is by jumping into a barrel in the arena. They wear shirts and jeans that are stitched together, teamed with stripy stockings and boots, and look absolutely ridiculous. But I suppose that's the idea – to catch the eye of the bull.

I was introduced to Rob Smeets, who told me that he and his mates didn't call themselves clowns. The guys clutching on to the backs of the bulls called themselves bull riders, so the clowns called themselves bull fighters.

'You know, I used to fight bulls,' he said.

'Really?'

'Yeah, I used to fight bulls for twenty years. Three broken necks later, I had to quit. I then became a rodeo clown bull fighter. These days I just get the bulls away from the riders.'

'I broke my rib last week,' I said. 'Now, when I think of all the people with broken ribs, there must be a high percentage among you guys.'

'You bet. Especially pre-1989, when we lost Lane Frost, one of our world champion bull riders, at Cheyenne.'

Frost, a professional bull rider, died in the arena as a result of injuries sustained on a bull called Takin' Care of Business. Since then, a lot of rodeo participants had worn Teflon vests.

'The vest doesn't make you Superman,' said Rob, 'but it does absorb a lot of the hit. So the safety factor has gotten better in the last twenty-plus years.'

'And these are Braymer bulls?'

'These are all Braymer or Braymer cross. Our sport in the last twenty-plus years has really gotten into genetics, just like for years they've bred good dogs. They all of a sudden said, "Boy, I've got a daughter out of this great bucking bull, let's cross it with this one," and now we've got some super high-bred bucking bulls.'

Next, Rob explained what happens during a competition: 'When they give a marking at a rodeo, the judges mark out of twenty-five points on how well the rider performs, and it's also out of twenty-five points on how well the animal performs.' So, between them, two judges will award up to a hundred points for each ride – with half the points being earned by the bull, not the rider.

'How long do you have to stay on?' I asked.

'Eight seconds, one hand. And during that eight seconds, you can't reach and slap the animal. That one arm has got to stay up as a free arm.'

Unlike in the horse-riding events, bull riders are not required to shuffle their feet or spur the animal. They just have to maintain control. What amazed me was that the bulls, some of which weighed more than a ton, could arch, flex and twist like cats when they had a cowboy on their back. As I talked to Rob, though, they seemed quite docile. 'How do you get them from this quiet state to that wild state?' I asked.

'It's just there. It's like pro-soccer players lying around in the locker room and then they go out there and can run and do the things that they do. The bulls are professional athletes.'

'They know when it's show time.'

'Exactly. When that music starts rocking'n'rolling and the noise starts going, everybody's adrenaline starts pounding, they know.'

'What makes a guy want to be a bull rider?'

'The cowboy lifestyle, the mystique, being your own boss.'

'It's rock'n'roll, isn't it?'

'It's man against beast. Can I ride him or am I going to get thrown off? And being able to say that I'm entered in Payson, Arizona, tonight, I'm in Reading, California, tomorrow and I'm in Hayward, California, after that. It's the road life.'

'You say you fight bulls. What does that mean?'

'When those cowboys hit the ground, I step in and get that bull's attention and make him come to me.'

'You do the most impressive job.'

'They have what we call a freestyle contest, a lot like your Mexican matadors. They turn out a bull without a rider and they judge how well we manoeuvre around the bull.'

'Just using the barrel?'

'Just my hands. No weapons, no cape.'

'No barrel for protection?'

'Mainly they judge me on how well I run around him and the tricks that I perform. If I run up the fence, I lose points. If he runs me over, I lose points. I won the World Championship five times.'

'*Woah*.'

'Yes, sir.'

'I thought your entire job was to protect the bull rider.'

'It is. But back in the day, for twenty years, Wrangler Jeans put on the Freestyle Bull Fighting Contest and they turned a bull out for seventy seconds. You were judged on how well you could manoeuvre around him, if you could jump over him, the tricks that you could do.'

I thought it was extraordinary. I'd never seen anything like that. Then Rob told me something that surprised me even more.

'There's a reason in Mexico they kill those bulls the first time they fight them. They're not a dumb animal; they get very smart. After a while, if he fights you, he's seen all the tricks and it's like climbing in the ring with Muhammad Ali. They get real smart.'

Rob showed me a couple of his moves. The main challenge,

he said, was that 'four legs are going to outrun two legs all day long'. Completely outclassed by the bull for strength, power and speed, the key to surviving was to stay close to the bull's shoulder, so that he had to turn in a tight circle in order to attack. 'The closer and tighter you can keep to him, the better. Hopefully, his head is right in your hip pocket and you're able to just keep circling tight and making good tight rounds. The further he pushes you out, the more he isn't bent down, then the more room he has to come and gather you. That's when they knock you as high as a telephone pole.'

Speaking to Rob was a joy, but I didn't enjoy the rodeo half as much. It went on far too long and was too commercial, with a constant string of interruptions by the announcers plugging 'our good friends who'll supply you with all your plumbing needs' and suchlike. 'I don't have any plumbing needs,' I wanted to yell. 'Just get on with it. I want to see somebody being flung off a bull.'

The comedy was crap, too. Seriously crap. And I know this might sound ridiculous, but I'd never previously equated rodeos with cruelty to animals. I was horrified by the shabby treatment of the animals and especially by the crowd's lackadaisical disinterest in their welfare. The bulls and horses were heaved and pulled and thrown to the ground, tied up and kicked and harassed. Nobody else seemed to mind, but I didn't like it at all.

Worst of all were the mutton busters. These are children who are too small to ride bulls. So, instead, they ride sheep. They wear crash helmets, jump on the backs of the sheep, then hang on for grim death. A lot of them were crying and limping once they'd finished their rides. It reminded me of fox hunters blooding the children after a kill. In the rodeo culture, maybe it all makes perfect sense. But, to me, it was grotesque – with the kids as well as the sheep being mistreated by the adults who arranged the whole thing. Everyone at the rodeo had been really kind to me, so I felt uneasy about criticising their way of life, but my honest opinion was that a lot of it was cruel and unnecessary.

The rodeo was an overly long, cold, unpleasant experience. By halfway through, I knew I would never attend another one in my life. But towards the end, as if I needed any more convincing that I shouldn't be there, they enacted the most embarrassing patriotic gesture. Some old soldiers and sailors marched shambolically into the arena, carrying flags that signified the army, the navy, the air force, the coast guard, the marines and soldiers who were missing in action. The whole thing was a shabby, redneck affair. Very low rent. I felt embarrassed and started to get the distinct impression that I wasn't among friends. These people were the exact opposite of me politically. Then it got even colder, so I headed back to the hotel.

With the centres of population and civilisation now much further apart, I was having to get used to travelling longer distances each day. But after leaving Payson, I soon arrived at something I suspected would divide households across Britain. I suspected that every man would say, 'Oh, interesting,' while every woman would lose the will to live and say, 'So what? It's just a hole in the ground.'

I have met thousands of men – possibly millions – and I'm sure that every single one of them has, at some point in his life, taken a stick, sat on the ground and dug a hole between his legs for no reason whatsoever. Meanwhile, I've never met a single woman who has done the same thing. So, my theory is that a fascination with holes is what truly separates men from women. And now I was visiting a really interesting – some might say spectacular – hole.

It's 570 feet deep and 4,000 feet across (I also know that every man will be desperate to have these details), and those people who are good with calculators say it could hold twenty football stadiums and seat two million people if it were an arena. Quite why anyone would want to work out such meaningless statistics is a mystery to me, but at least they give an indication that this is a really vast hole in the ground. What makes it even more interesting, though, is that it was made by something really extraordinary – namely, a meteorite.

About fifty thousand years ago, a meteorite with a diameter of about 160 feet, made of nickel and iron, came flying out of the sky and belted into the Arizona desert – although in those days it was neither Arizona nor a desert, but probably open grassland dotted with woods and inhabited by woolly mammoths. Flying at a speed of maybe 45,000 m.p.h., the 300,000-ton rock hit the ground with as much force as ten million tons of TNT. That's about the same as 650 Hiroshimas. *Bosh!* Of course, it flattened everything for many miles around. The surrounding landscape is still as flat as a pancake until you come to a range of mountains in the far distance, so the shockwave must have travelled a very long way before something stopped it.

Midway between Winona and Winslow, it's at a place appropriately called Meteor Crater and the way in which it was formed plays a large part in making this such a fantastically atmospheric place. What's so great about it is that you can't see into it until the very last moment. You approach up the side and then – *boof* – there it is, revealed in front of you. Standing on the edge of the crater is like being in some kind of weird experiment. It has a magnificence and a grandeur. It's very windswept, too, which apparently has something to do with the crater's shape, the altitude and the flat environment all around it.

Before the moon landing in 1969, American astronauts trained in the crater because it was thought to resemble the lunar surface. On one of these practice sessions, one of the astronauts tore his suit as he was clambering around near the rim. If he'd done that on the moon, he would have been a dead man. So they strengthened the material and, of course, Neil Armstrong's first steps on the moon took place without incident.

Although I couldn't find much to say about the crater for the TV show, it was certainly one of my highlights of Route 66. It's well worth paying a visit . . . but only if you're a bloke. If you're a woman, there's a nice wee shop in the visitors' centre.

My rib was still agony, and the bandages on my leg needed changing twice a day, but I had to push on if I wanted to see everything before the end of Route 66 at Santa Monica. My God, sometimes it's hard being a star.

That afternoon I arrived back in Flagstaff, but this time on the trike rather than strapped to a stretcher in a helicopter. It's a lovely city that has the feel of a frontier town combined with a ski resort, mainly because that's pretty much what it is. At nearly seven thousand feet above sea level, it's a popular area

Tim Pollard

Angel Delgadillo – an extraordinary man whose guardianship of Route 66 has ensured the survival of much of it.

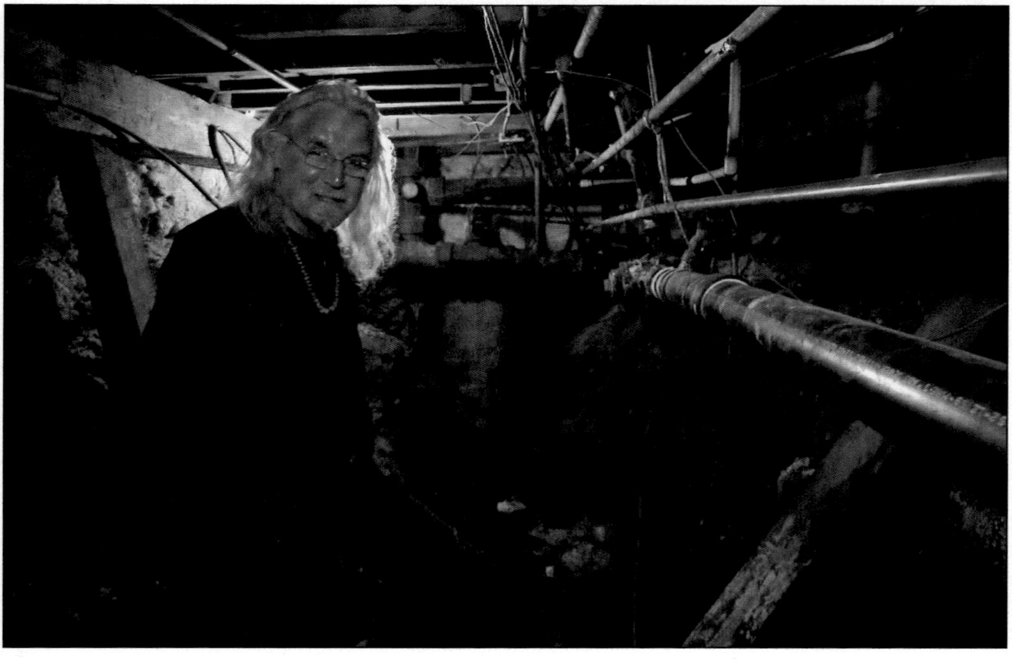

Maverick Television

The network of tunnels beneath Williams, Arizona.

Mark Atkinson

One of the extraordinary custom-made trikes I encountered in Seligman, Arizona.

Tim Pollard

Heading through the desert and onto the home stretch of my journey.

Nicky Taylor

Me and Mike, the director, with the lions from the Keepers of the Wild refuge in Valentine, Arizona. The whole crew fell in love with Anthony, the wee lion cub.

Nicky Taylor

Mike Reilly

FLOODED

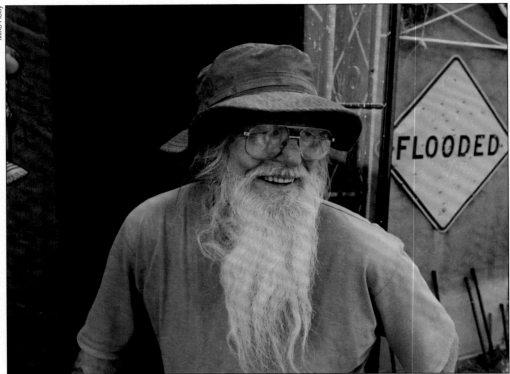

Elmer Long and his bottle orchard outside Helendale, California – my favourite find of the trip.

Mike Reilly

Coca-Cola

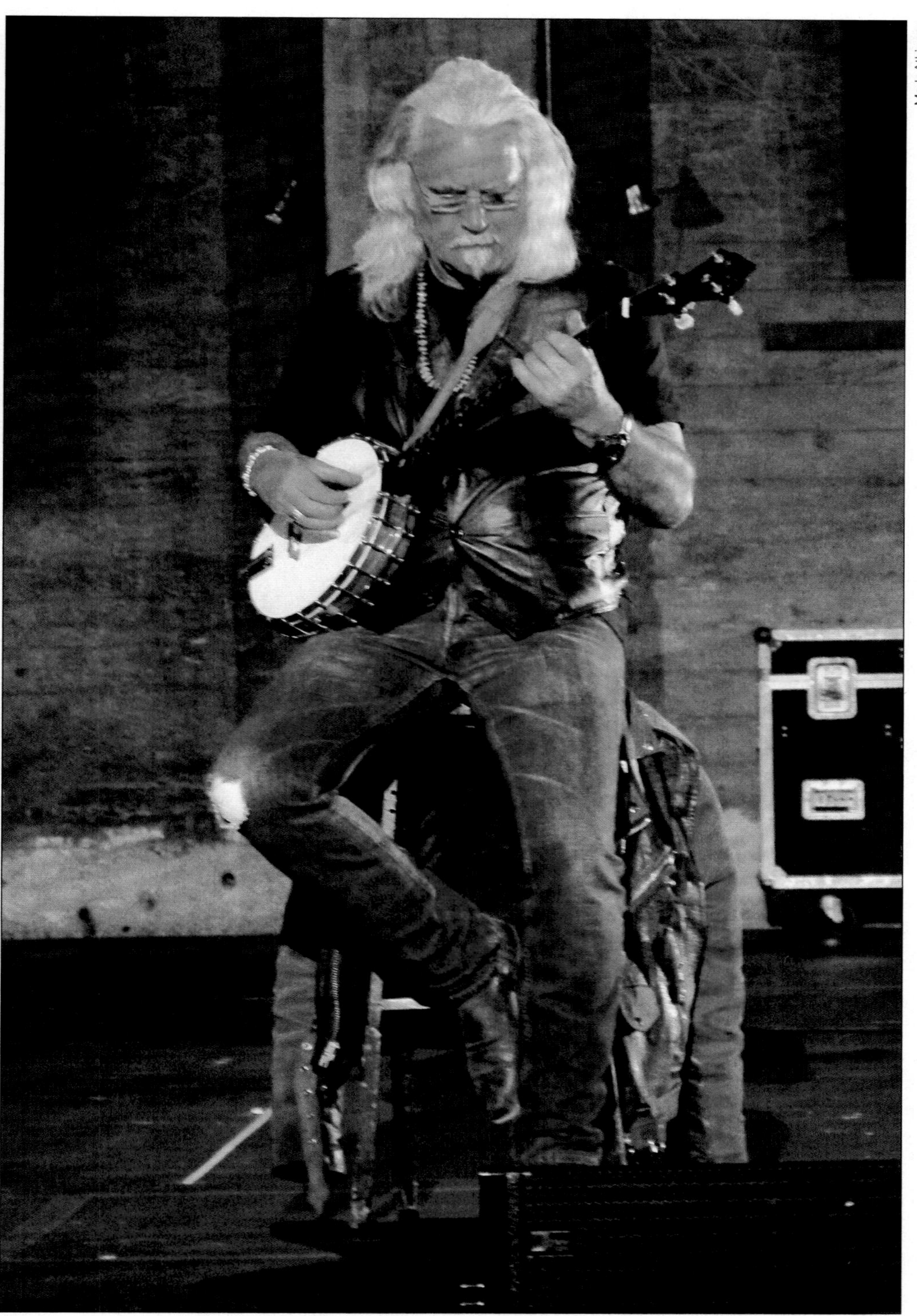

Mark Atkinson

Offering my own take on 'Over the Rainbow' at the California Theatre, San Bernadino.

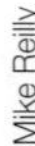

Mike Reilly

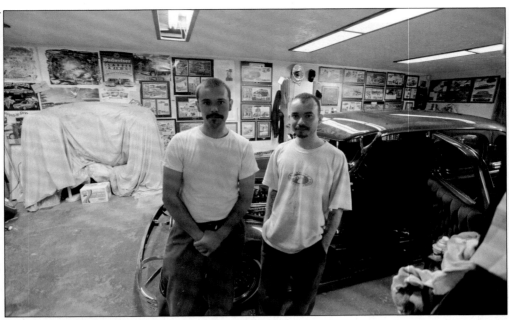

The De Alba boys in front of one of their incredible low riders.

Tim Pollard

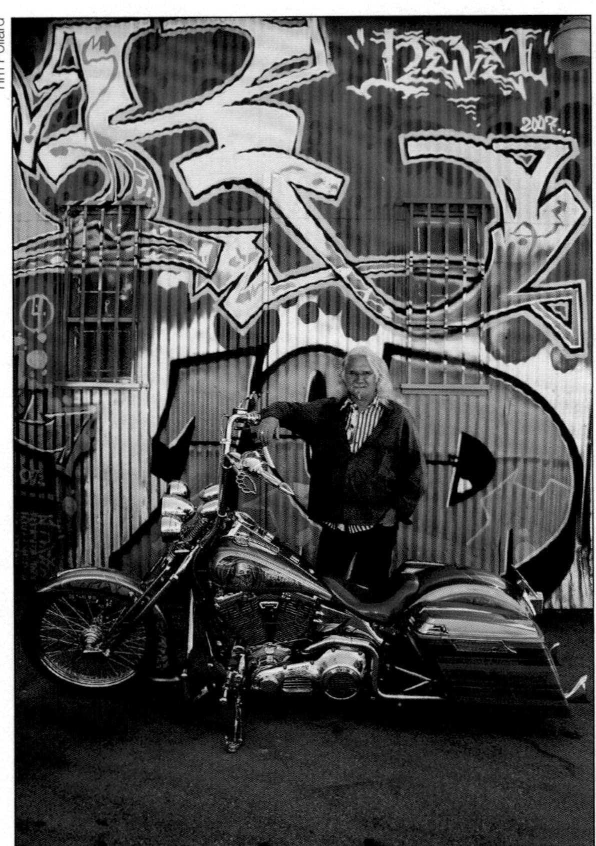

Outside the De Alba garage with a breathtakingly impressive customised Harley.

Tim Pollard

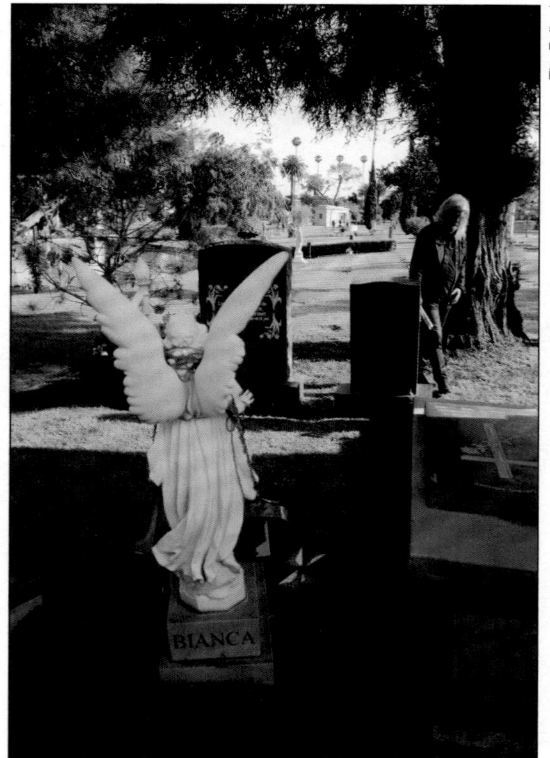

Forever Hollywood – a cemetery that could only exist in this part of the world.

Tim Pollard

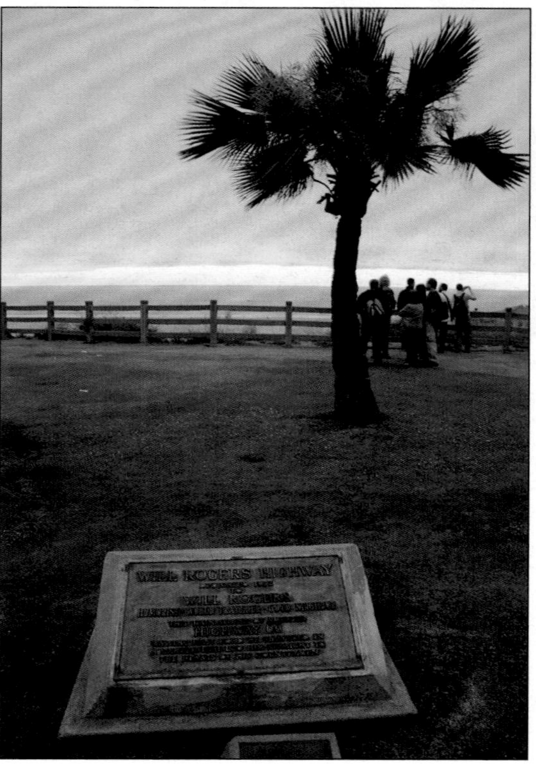

The Will Rogers Highway marker in Palisades Park.

Mike Reilly

Santa Monica Pier and the Pacific Ocean beyond – the end of the road, and a chance to reflect upon my extraordinary journey.

for winter sports – the Arizona Snowbowl is just fifteen miles north of the city and the 12,633-foot Humphrey's Peak is even closer.

That evening, I rode up to the top of a mountain on the edge of Flagstaff. From the top, the city looked like a wee village and it was hard to believe it has a population of more than 65,000 people. In particular, it seemed very dimly lit. But there's a reason for that.

Since 1894, when Percival Lowell, an astronomer from Massachusetts, chose Flagstaff as the location for his observatory because of its high elevation, the city has been a world centre for stargazing. In the 1930s they discovered Pluto at the Lowell Observatory, which really put the place on the celestial map. People came from all over the world, and they still do to this day. When I was visiting there was a flood of anoraks in the city. There are now several other observatories, in addition to the Lowell, including a military one and a university one. To aid the astronomers, the local authorities passed laws to minimise light pollution and allow the boffins a really clear view of the night sky. Special low-intensity sodium street lights helped to make Flagstaff the world's first 'dark sky' city. And it's one of the few places in America where you're not assaulted by neon signs on every block. I think this is all a rather good thing. For an amateur stargazer like me, it was almost as good as being in the far north of Scotland – where there's no artificial light at all.

I think there's something fundamental to our existence about looking at the stars, wondering what they are and what it all means. Back in the Dark Ages, they thought the black part of the sky was solid and the stars were wee holes that let through rain and the light of heaven. I've spent a lot of time looking heavenwards and wondering what it's all about, but I've never understood how the constellations got their names. Take the Great Bear – if you take away the drawing of the bear, it's just a cluster of stars that look nothing like a bear. So, as a schoolboy, I named them myself and compiled my own drawings of the night sky, creating constellations that suited my designs. I had the Great Bicycle and Uncle Harry's Ear. Have a go yourself. I can guarantee it always works.

Then, when I'd finished devising my map of the stars, I moved on to the planets, which led to my own grand unified theory of the universe – the Cup of Tea Theory.

If you look at the sun and the planets – like Mars, Venus and Jupiter – they resemble a basic atomic structure – with a nucleus and electrons spinning around it. In a way, they're almost exactly the same thing. So, I thought we'd made a big mistake over the years thinking we were the big shots in the universe. We aren't huge. In fact, we're teeny weeny – the smallest things imaginable – but we're parts of something huge, like atoms are parts of something relatively huge, like this page, or a T-shirt, or a little finger. We're all made of atoms, and the whole cosmos is like an atomic structure, so we're all part of something enormous. Our planet is like a tiny bit of gravel flying around in this gigantic thing called space that's far too big for us even to see, let alone understand, in the same way that a trout has no idea that we exist. So what is out there that we don't know about? What is so huge that we are unable to realise we are only a wee part of it? In the end, I came to the conclusion that we are swimming around in an unimaginably enormous cup of tea. That's why I loved being in Flagstaff,

Arizona – it let me gaze into the heavens and think about my Cup of Tea Theory.

Standing on that hillside above the town on that very dark night, I pronounced my theory to the camera. I hope to have legions of devoted followers chanting my name before too long, with cups of tea tattooed on their chests, and wearing wee gold cups of tea around their necks, in much the same way as Christians wear crucifixes. For many years, my wife has been pushing me to publicise my Cup of Tea Theory. So I took great pleasure in writing to her to tell her that I had finally brought it into the public domain and that she should expect our first disciples to start turning up imminently.

Leaving Flagstaff the next morning, I was in the best of spirits. The mood up on the hillside had been just right, and all the crew thought we'd done a great job. And we felt proud of Flagstaff. So few places on earth would be prepared to reduce their lighting to suit the wishes of a group of astronomers. The only stain on our stay in the town had come when I'd disappeared into the bushes for a pee. It was only when I finished that I realised I'd peed right in front of a couple who were using it as a lovers' lane. Oops.

We had a long day ahead of us, so Mike rode the trike for a couple of hours while I hitched a lift in the crew's truck. I took over once we reached an easy stretch, and the painkillers dulled the twinges I was still feeling in my leg and rib. After stopping at a dodgy gas station for an equally dodgy burrito, we arrived at Monument Valley, 175 miles northeast of Flagstaff. At that point I forgot all about my injuries.

Monument Valley took my breath away. Eerie and haunting, it's hugely significant for anyone who grew up watching

Westerns and John Wayne – who called this remote region the place 'where God put the West'. Its majestic landscape of vast, vivid-red sandstone buttes that rise to heights of up to a thousand feet is one of the most extraordinary, magnificent things I've ever seen.

Most of us have seen at least one of the seven Westerns that John Ford shot in Monument Valley, so the shadow they cast on our culture is long and pervasive. Movies like *Stagecoach*, *Fort Apache* and *The Searchers* created the image of the heroic, romantic West. I spent my childhood Saturday mornings at the local flicks watching those films, then running down the street in a cowboy suit with a gun holstered on my hip, so it was an absolute joy to see the place for myself. I just stood there, a tiny dot in that massive vista, trying to soak it all in and really appreciate it.

The place is almost impossible to describe in words. Awestruck by the red, pink and orange rocks, I immediately took pictures on my phone and emailed them to the whole family. Within minutes, the replies came flooding in, all of them saying they wanted to swap lives with me. But pictures cannot do it justice. You have to stand within it to understand it and feel its full force. Suddenly, in my head, I could hear some typical Western movie music – the sort that surges to a crescendo as a line of Indians appears in silhouette on the skyline – which only added to the drama of the place. Because of its prominent place in our cultural history and its uniqueness on our planet, I think Monument Valley is something we all own. We had better look after it well.

Shortly after arriving in the valley, I met Larry, an extremely friendly Navajo man who would guide us through the entire area the next day. Monument Valley is very sacred to the Navajo, so no one is allowed to go barging through it in their four-wheel drive with the radio blaring. There's a certain protocol, and Larry was going to lead us through it. He also offered to introduce me to a medicine man, which sounded like a wonderful idea. I hoped he'd be able to sort out my sore leg and aching rib.

The medicine man was dressed in a plaid shirt and grey slacks when I met him, which didn't really fit the image I had in my head. But at least his thick, coiled turquoise necklace and silver bracelets looked authentic. He told me I looked like Kit Carson, the American frontiersman and comic-book hero. It must have been the beard and the long hair, because I wasn't wearing a fringed jacket and I've never hunted buffalo in my life. I told him about my ribs and my knee, then showed him on a map exactly where the accident had happened. He listened intently before taking me into a building called a hogan. From the outside, it looked like a large garden shed crossed with a mud hut; but once inside I could see it was actually a really sophisticated wooden building. Made from long juniper branches arranged like a wigwam, then covered with mud, it was apparently strong enough to withstand a tornado.

Sitting beside me along the wall of the hogan were the medicine man and his assistant – a kind of roadie who looked after him on his travels. They lit a little fire by removing some coals from a stove and adding some wood. Then the medicine man opened some leather and hide wallets to reveal 'male' and 'female' arrowheads (the females had a kind of waist; the males were a traditional diamond shape), sacred stones he'd collected over the years and crystals. Laying the arrowheads, stones and crystals on a mat, he next unpacked fragments of beech ash and threw them on the fire to make smoke. Then he prayed, blew a small whistle, and held a cup of water and some feathers in his hands. There was a lot of praying, meditating and bowing to the four points of the compass, most of which we were not allowed to film. At times, the praying intensified, becoming repetitive, like a mantra, and I found myself quite caught up in it. I'd had the same feeling listening to Tibetan and Hindu chants, and even Catholic recitations of the Psalms.

Next the medicine man consulted the map to see where I had come off my bike. He had to cool the earth where I'd landed. Muttering another prayer and fluttering the feathers, he brought peace to the earth, resettling it back to how it had been before it experienced such violence from me and the bike at the time of the crash. Having realigned the planet, he turned his attention to me. It was time for a cosmic x-ray. While I clenched a wee crystal, about the size of a cigar, in my hand, the medicine man rubbed my rib with a feather and gazed into a much larger, clear crystal – about the size of a clenched fist.

'There's a fracture in it and it's lightning shaped,' he said. 'It's gone along the rib in a lightning shape.'

Then he picked up some hot coals from the fire with a pair of pincers, blew on them and held them near my rib, chanting all the while and waving his feather.

I loved all that stuff. It wasn't a question of whether I believed it or gave myself over to it. As far as I was concerned, it was all about being in the company of people who *did* believe it. That was the whole cheese for me, and I felt very privileged to be part of it. When I spoke to Larry afterwards, he was very open minded about it and told me he used both Navajo and

Western medicine when he was sick. I thought that was a very healthy attitude.

Midway through the healing ceremony, a drummer arrived. He was a fireman, and had been delayed by a plane crash. Fortunately no one had died, he told us, although the pilot had been in a bit of a state afterwards. No kidding, I thought. Pulling out the most extraordinary drum I've ever seen, the fireman got to work, banging out a beat. His drum was actually a wee dumpy iron cooking pot with three wee legs and a skin stretched over the top. Some beads and rattles were arranged on the skin, and the pot was about a third full of water. When the drummer hit it, the beads and rattles moved and the water made the sound resonate. It was extraordinary. He said the sound would carry for several miles.

In the midst of all the chanting, singing and drumming, the medicine man's mobile phone rang ... and he answered it. I thought that was brilliant – the clash (or possibly the merging) of the modern world of the United States and the spiritual world of the Navajo. I'd already seen an example of it when I'd handed over some money to pay for the ceremony. I was fine with that – you have to pay the doctor – and his reaction to the money had been fascinating. He'd taken the notes, straightened them out, made sure all of the heads of Thomas Jefferson on the stack of twenty-dollar bills were pointing in the same direction, then aligned all of his arrowheads and other bits and pieces in the same way.

Shortly after the phone call, the ceremony came to an end. It had all been done with a sincerity that I think is missing in Western religions, and I'm really glad I took part in it. But my rib felt no different the next day. Then again – who knows –

maybe it would have felt worse if the medicine man hadn't intervened? I didn't really care either way, because he was great company. The last time I saw him, he was sitting on my trike, laughing and enjoying having his picture taken.

Larry took us back into Monument Valley just before dawn the following morning, but this time into the sacred part that the Navajo owned and controlled. They are deeply attached to the environment, and don't allow anyone to climb the buttes and mesas here. Because of their care, it's in wonderful shape – a truly moving and magnificent place.

At one point, a big beetle came over to me. I was just about to nudge it when Larry said it was a stink beetle that squirted a kind of urine if it was irritated. Apparently it's very smelly stuff, but it's used by the Navajo to treat mouth diseases in babies. Larry also told me about the huge tarantulas that come to Monument Valley from the plains each year to mate. I would have loved to see that.

His next story was about the Navajo code talkers, a band of young men recruited by the US Marine Corps in the Second World War to transmit secret messages. At a time when America's best cryptographers were searching for ways to keep ahead of the Japanese code breakers, these modest Navajo farmers and herdsmen constructed the most successful code in military history. Even now, it hasn't been broken. With a complex grammar and no written form, Navajo is the most complicated of all Native American languages, and it is spoken only on the Navajo territories in New Mexico and Arizona. In 1941, when America entered the war, fewer than thirty non-Navajos were thought to be able to understand the intricate syntax, tonal qualities and dialects of the language. So it was the perfect foundation for a code.

However, there were few Navajo equivalents for many modern military terms, so the code talkers had to be inventive. For instance, the Navajo word for tortoise was used to mean tank, and the Navajo for potato signified a grenade. Equipped with their mental dictionary of terms, the code talkers joined the marines on the battlefield and were able to encode, transmit and decode messages at lightning speed. They could pass on a three-line communiqué in just twenty seconds, while conventional coding methods took more than half an hour. Their importance was highlighted when the commanding officer of the marines' signals division at the crucial Battle of Iwo Jima said that the island would not have been taken without the Navajo's efforts.

The code talkers were also used in Korea and Vietnam, but then knowledge of the code started to die out and now many Americans are unaware of the vital role the Navajo played in so much of their country's recent history. Partly this is because the US government kept the Navajo's work secret for many years, just in case their unique abilities might be needed again. And partly it's because the Navajo are very modest, quiet, unassuming people.

Bumping around Monument Valley with Larry, I listened to more of his stories – such as how John Ford came to film in the Navajo's sacred place. Larry said it was all due to a rancher called Harry Goulding, who had been living in a tent in Monument Valley since the 1920s. In the late 1930s Goulding heard that Ford was making a big new Western called *Stagecoach*. Convinced that Monument Valley would be ideal for the film, he enlisted a photographer to take some pictures. Then this uneducated man of the wilderness packed up his bedroll, his coffee pot and some grub and made his way to California.

Arriving in Hollywood, he hoped to talk to Ford in person, to try to convince him to come and film in Monument Valley. While his wife waited, knitting in their car, Goulding approached the receptionist at United Artists, where Ford was preparing to shoot his new film. Of course, he was told he couldn't see anybody without an appointment – because that's the way they work in Hollywood – so he just said, 'Well, I'll make myself comfortable,' and took out his bedroll. The staff at United Artists had never met anyone quite like Goulding, and eventually they realised they'd have to do something about this bloke who seemed to be setting up camp in the lobby. So they called the locations manager, who arrived with every intention of sending this lunatic packing. But as soon as he saw the photographs, he was convinced. Goulding was introduced to Ford, who thought the rancher was a great guy, and the rest is history.

Larry took me to an outlook called John Ford Point, which features in *The Searchers* – it's where John Wayne, looking for a girl who has been captured by Indians, rides out on to a spit of rock and sees the Indian village beneath him. It was one of Ford's favourite places, and I could almost smell the Duke as I looked at it. While I was standing there, soaking in the atmosphere, a red truck with a water tank on its back bounced past, a tiny speck in the distance. Larry explained that most of the Navajo people who lived in Monument Valley were elders who preferred to live in the old, traditional way. They didn't want water piped in or electricity. I thought that was kind of appealing, but it meant their water had to be delivered by truck. In a funny way, I wanted them to live in the old way, too, because that meant the place would be kept intact.

Driving around with Larry, time and again I saw vistas which

I'd ridden through in my imagination when I was a child. I'd come out of the cinema and ride home on my imaginary horse, smacking my backside as I harried up Highlands Street, which was transformed into Monument Valley in my little fantasy world.

I love Monument Valley, and I felt very privileged to be standing within it. But when we were filming, part of me wanted to tell the viewers not to visit it themselves – just take my word for its beauty. Selfish, I know, but I don't want it spoiled. If anyone does come, I hope they don't come on big tourist buses with loads of other people. The way to see it is to get up early and watch the sun rise, before all the buses arrive. Of course, this is a very snobbish, elitist way of looking at things, but for a wee while now I've been saying that if anyone wants to do the world a real favour, they shouldn't come to any of the places I film for TV shows. They should just read about them or watch the programmes, and leave it at that.

After our day exploring Monument Valley, Larry helped me build a fire and prepare to sleep under the stars. He explained the problems that exist in modern Navajo families whose children get involved in drugs and alcohol. An outreach social worker, he organises *Brat Camp*-style four-day treks for Navajo teens to help them understand their sacred land, the sky and nature. An inspiring, knowledgeable and passionate character, Larry is a very gentle man whose real passion is to help the next generation. Listening to him in such a fascinating place, I hoped he succeeded in educating the young Navajo in their culture. He deals with problems that parents and social workers face around the world, but it was still strange to hear him talking about issues that are very familiar to anyone living in Govan. Crystal meth, heroin and all that other poison are being peddled everywhere, and Larry is trying to keep Navajo youngsters away from it by making them aware of their culture. He knows it's a big step back from hard drugs to the indigenous culture, but I had to wish him the best. And I'm optimistic about what he might achieve, because he's a very inspiring man.

That night, as the sky darkened and I strummed my banjo by the camp fire, my thoughts turned to what lay ahead. For weeks now, my daily existence had been determined by the need to keep moving west. But now the end of the journey was starting to loom ahead. The next day I was due to leave for Williams, Arizona. From there, I'd go to the Grand Canyon. There were a few more destinations in Arizona to visit after that, but soon I'd be in California. And then the Pacific Ocean would be right in front of me and my great adventure would be over.

I started to wish there was more Route 66. Two and a half thousand miles suddenly didn't seem quite enough. Because one thing I had learned on this trip was that Route 66 was cut up into bits and pieces – some of it tragic, some of it inspiring, most of it fascinating and all of it interesting. All along the Mother Road, I'd found people working very hard to bring it back to life. Something as simple as painting a few murals or making delicious pies could wind the clock back a bit. But despite all of their efforts, Route 66 didn't officially exist any more, so anyone who went in search of it had to find the fragments and piece them together to make their own Route 66. That was one of the things that made it so special.

13

You'll Wanna Own a Piece of Arizona

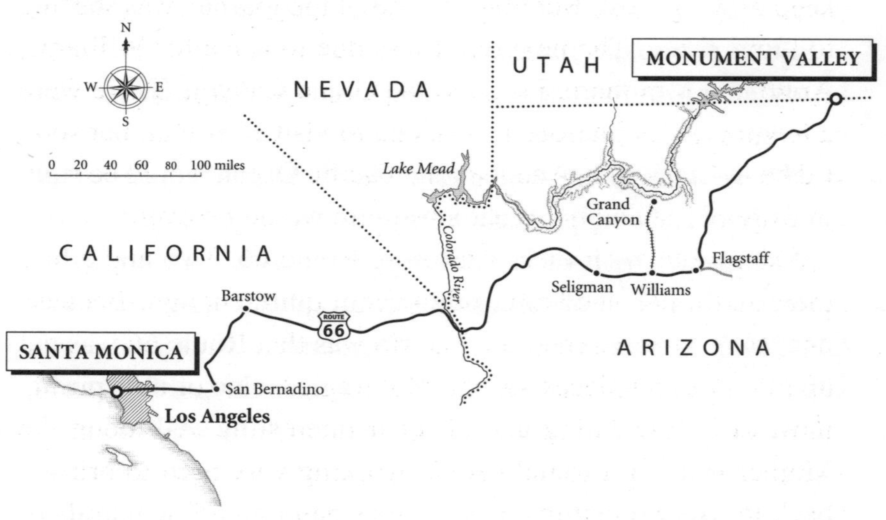

I had a great start to the week in Williams. A further two hundred miles down the road towards California and the coast, this was the last place on Route 66 to be bypassed. On 13 October 1984, the final stretch of Interstate 40 opened, but Williams didn't go down without a fight. It held an official day of mourning when the freeway took over. The next day newspapers in America reported the demise of Route 66; and a year later the road was officially decommissioned.

A lovely wee rural community, Williams was named after Bill Williams, a trapper and hunter. Although it was nice to name a town after a trapper, I'd hoped it was named after Hank Williams – but then I'm disappointed quite a lot. I'd come to Williams to catch a steam train to the Grand Canyon. As you can imagine, I couldn't wait to see the world's biggest hole in the ground, but I was equally excited about the steam train because there's nothing I like more than a wee choo-choo.

Bores of my age have never stopped going on about how lovely steam trains used to be back in the day, and I'm no different. They have played such an important part in my life that I have nothing but fond memories of them. Everything that I remember as being great about my childhood involves a steam train. Some of the loveliest holidays I had as a kid were spent in Rothesay, and all of them started with a steam train ride from Glasgow's Central Station. I can remember it as if it were yesterday – passing through the barrier from the public area to the ticketed platform, the engine right there in front of us, a lovely olive-green colour, hissing away. My sister, brother and I would walk with our cases, our wee bags and all our things along the platform until we came to the bit where the engineer, with his shiny cap and a blue cotton suit, was hanging out of the window, saying hello to the passengers. He had black marks on his hands and on his sweaty face, and behind him the engine was warming up with a cacophony of *whissshes*. As we passed, we would hear the fireman shovelling coal. It was magical.

Taking our places in the carriage, we'd be beside ourselves with excitement, waiting for the steam engine to start its countdown to our holiday. Like an orchestra tuning up, there would be a steady increase in random noises, culminating in a whistle, and then the engine would start pumping – *shooosh, shooosh, shooosh* – as it struggled to push the carriages out of the station. It was like a countdown from ten to one. By the time we reached one, the *shooosh, shooosh, shooosh* had become *shussssh, shussssh, shussssh* and the wheels had started to go *dickety-da dickety-dee, dickety-da dickety-dee* on the rails. We could soon see Glasgow disappearing underneath us with a *shoossssh*. Then the River Clyde: *shoossssh, shoossssh.*

We were heading west, to the seaside, miles away. The train would take us to Wemyss Bay, down on the coast in the Firth of Clyde. *Shoossssh.* On the train, there was very little to do. No connecting carriages, no tea trolley. You had to bring your own sandwiches. My dad would urge us to be quiet and not fidget while he read the paper and we'd look out of the window, getting cinders in our eyes from the smoke of the engine. Every year it was the same: 'Argh, there's something in my eye!' But I couldn't resist looking out, getting a face full of smoke and steam while watching it flying across the fields of corn like a ghost, disappearing as if it were being sucked in by the crops. It was one of the loveliest things. The smoke had a funny charcoal, sulphurous smell, but to me it was eau de Cologne. I thought it was absolutely fabulous.

At Wemyss Bay, we disembarked on to paddle steamers. The first one I was ever on was the *Marchioness of Brid Albion*, which I thought was a kind of posh name. There was also a *Queen Mary II*, the *Caledonia*, the *St Columbus* and the *Waverley* (which is still operating – the last ocean-going paddle steamer in the world). Linked by a quayside bridge to the train, there was always a magical engine-room mixture of diesel and coal smoke and steam and fumes as we boarded the boat. It was fantastic.

So when – in Williams, Arizona – Mike asked me if I liked steam engines, I thought: Do birds sing in the morning?

From 1901, steam trains had carried passengers and supplies from Williams to the south rim of the Grand Canyon, which had become a tourist destination in the 1880s. Although hugely popular, by the 1960s most of the traffic had switched to the roads and the last train, which ran on 30 June 1968, carried only three people. That should have been the end of the Grand Canyon Railroad, but the train refused to die. Enthusiasts clubbed together and started to renovate the sixty-five miles of track, the stations and the depots, and the old locomotives and carriages. In 1989 the powerful pull of the steam engine returned to the track, exactly eighty-eight years to the day since the first train had run. Since then, they've carried more than two and a half million people to the Grand Canyon.

Unlike the steam trains of my childhood, the big locomotive I met in Williams was powered by vegetable oil – like a gigantic fish supper – which was towed in a stainless-steel tanker behind it. Donated by all the restaurants and fast-food joints in Williams, the smell of the oil was something else. One moment there might be a whiff of fish, then it was kind of meaty, then veggie. But it was always a million times better than diesel.

Looking just like Casey Jones, the train's engineer was a big man with a striped hat, overalls and gloves sticking out of his back pocket. His assistant, a thin man with glasses and a bowler hat, welcomed us on to the boiler plate of the engine and we all clambered aboard – the camera man, the sound man, Mike and me. Squashed beside the assistant, I winced as we reversed out of the station. Something seemed to be missing. Then I realised what it was: the shovelling. No *whist, whist* as the coal was shovelled and no *kerchang* as the little door to the furnace was clanked shut. Instead, there was just a wee hole with a shining flame behind it. That's progress, I suppose.

After *chuff, chuff, chuffing* out of the station, we linked up with a diesel that was hooked on to the other end of the train. Maybe a steam engine powered by vegetable oil couldn't pull such a big train on its own? I transferred to a very fancy carriage at the rear of the train, the kind of thing I'd expect the Queen to roll around in – all plush blue furniture, cinnamon rolls, cups of tea, and an open bar. Chuffing along, it took nearly two hours to reach the Grand Canyon. All the way, I couldn't help thinking about Jesse James riding through that rolling countryside. The James Gang were the first criminals ever to rob a train, so I pictured them in their dust coats with their guns out, ready to jump aboard. This was perfect terrain for an ambush – prime baddie country.

I'd never visited the Grand Canyon before, so I used the journey to try to get my head round some of the statistics. Two hundred and seventy-seven miles long (I'd thought it was about five), eighteen miles across at its widest point, more than a mile deep, and all created by the Colorado River taking four million years to cut its way through layers of rock, exposing two billion years of the earth's geological history. Unless, of course, you're a religious nut, in which case all of that erosion never happened and the fossils were placed in the ground by God, and none of the geological history counted for anything – it all just magically appeared one day about six thousand years ago.

We finally arrived at a little siding and I set off to walk up to the canyon. One of the many great things about the Grand Canyon is that it has a similar element of surprise to the one I'd experienced at Meteor Crater: you can't see it until the last few seconds before arriving at its rim. My guide – a lovely woman wearing a kind of boy scout's cap and the olive-green uniform of a National Park ranger – walked with me up about forty stairs, then steered me towards a little promontory. She promised I'd get a good view when I reached the top. I walked along a path and then got my first glimpse. I almost stopped dead in my tracks; I certainly slowed my pace. Oh my God, I thought. It was magnificent. Stunning. But then I realised I was only looking at the hills in the distance. I'd been bowled over by the beauty and grandeur of them, and I hadn't even seen the main attraction yet. I walked further forward and caught my first glimpse of the actual canyon. Of course, I'd known there was drama lurking just around the corner, but I hadn't appreciated the sheer scale of that drama until the moment when I stood at its edge. I felt the same as the first time I saw the Himalayas. But, if anything, the Grand Canyon is even better.

It's like a thousand temples of rock painted in a vast palette of colours. Sandy, pale yellows merge with cool or warm pinks and dozens of shades of red and orange. There are greens and blues, pale greys, like ash, darker blue–greys and black. It's truly awesome and almost impossible to describe – its grandeur and magnificence are just too grand and too magnificent. All I could think to say on camera was that it was so much more than I had imagined and quite unlike anything I'd ever seen in my life.

Standing back a wee bit because there was a sense of being blown by a wind whooshing up and out of the canyon, I suddenly got the frights. In the short time that I had been staring open-mouthed at it, the canyon had already changed. Even relatively small movements of the sun had quite profound effects, simply because it's so vast. There are canyons within canyons within canyons. And there are probably canyons within those canyons, but I couldn't see that far into its depths. Like an inverted mountain range, vastly more was hidden than could be seen.

With a kind of creepy silence to it, the canyon has a lovely eeriness that overwhelms and hushes the voices of all the tourists. I'm reluctant to say it has some of that old hippy 'a certain kind of energy' stuff, but it does. Like the Arctic, it has a presence, a dominance, a weird kind of silencing effect that's impossible to explain to anyone who hasn't stood at its edge. It has to be seen and heard to be believed, so when you stand on the edge, it's a matter of just shutting up and sucking in the experience. As I'm sure you can tell, I loved it.

As I said earlier, I've recently started telling people not to visit the places I film for television shows. I've become concerned that these often remote, empty places will be spoiled if people rush to see them. 'Go and see a good film of it,' I say, 'and leave the bloody thing alone.' But I'm prepared to make an exception in the case of the Grand Canyon. I would urge everyone to go and see it. But, as President Teddy Roosevelt said, 'Leave it as it is. You cannot improve on it. The ages have been at work on it, and man can only mar it.' God bless his wee bum. What a wise guy.

*

Back in Williams, having returned from the canyon, I was getting ready to move on to the next destination when I heard something that piqued my interest. As one of the stops on the Chicago–Los Angeles railroad line, Williams's history had been shaped by its position on the great east–west railway that transformed a transcontinental journey from six months by covered wagon to six days by train. The railway companies recruited thousands of people for this massive construction project. Some were Civil War veterans, others were Irish immigrants, but most famously the companies also imported ten thousand Chinese labourers, fifteen hundred of whom were killed on the job. Nitroglycerine had just been invented and it was incredibly unstable – it could hardly be moved without blowing up. So the company foremen assigned the task of blowing tunnels and cuttings through the bedrock and mountains to the Chinese labourers, whom they reckoned were used to handling gunpowder and fireworks. But, of course, they had no experience with nitroglycerine. On some of the lines, one Chinese labourer died for every mile of track laid. Not that this bothered the rail companies or the government, who had a very dismissive attitude to recent immigrants.

When the railway companies reached a town like Williams that was at the end of a line, the Chinese labourers, the Irish immigrants, freed slaves, low-lifes and the poorest of the poor often wanted to settle there. However, they would only ever be offered the worst land, on the other side of the railway from the locals. Hence the phrase 'on the wrong side of the tracks'. When I was a boy, the tramlines in Glasgow divided the city in exactly the same way: they separated the poor from the rich.

Of all the immigrants, the Chinese were often treated worst. There was no good reason for this, as they were hard and loyal workers. It was just racial prejudice and suspicion of people who were different. But the Chinese workers came up with an ingenious way to duck out of bad treatment. In the part of Williams that was very much on the wrong side of the tracks was a brothel called the Red Garter (although I had a funny feeling that it would have been on the right side of the tracks for me). Next to it were a series of other fun palaces – mainly bars. Whenever the boozed-up locals stumbled out into the street, looking for trouble, they would usually target the Chinese workers who lived near by. But the Chinese were too smart for them. They excavated a network of tunnels underneath that part of Williams so they could slip down trapdoors, scarper down their escape routes and reappear somewhere else entirely.

Eventually, though, the constant attacks got too much for them and they moved away. Thinking about the effort that must have gone into digging all those tunnels, I was struck by how threatened they must have felt. They had done the most incredible job of building the railway, blasting paths through mountains and losing their friends, only to be attacked and vilified when the job ended. It was a rotten, shameful thing. To me, it seemed to be yet another example of the tendency among immigrant communities to seek out and persecute anyone who is socially beneath them and make their life a misery. I've seen this around the world and I wish we could get rid of it. It must have been terrifying to run like hell through those tunnels, chased by those bastards, shooting left and right to lose them.

A large fire in the 1970s destroyed much of the tunnel network, but it was still extraordinary to see the remnants. I was shown to one of the entrances by a local bar manager called Jackie. Convinced that the ghosts of two Chinese guys guarded the tunnels under her bar, she had never ventured down there herself. As you know, I'm very sceptical about that type of thing, but she was welcome to her beliefs, and she was a great sport for letting me peer through the tunnels before continuing my journey west.

After another fifty miles of sun-baked Arizona desert, I arrived in Seligman, which was immortalised as a Route 66 town in a fabulous photograph taken in 1947 by Andreas Feininger that appeared on the cover of *Life* magazine. As so often on Route 66, Seligman was later bypassed by the interstate, but unlike many other places along the Mother Road, the small town (population 456) was not prepared to take its demise lying down.

The really sad fact about Route 66 is that so many towns have been unable to put up a similar fight. For instance, the journey from Williams to Seligman took me past at least ten derelict gas stations and umpteen shutdown motels, with the wind blowing through their vandalised remains. I was often told that Route 66 was dying, but in the most derelict parts it was already dead. Many people obviously gave up the struggle a long time ago.

And yet, amid the decline, the decay, the death and destruction, little pockets along Route 66 are still thriving. This is something anyone travelling the length of the road has to get used to. You can't expect it to be like the famous song – one long, glorious highway all the way to California. It's now in bits and pieces. One place will be doing just great, with big statues in the streets, bustling businesses, everything alive and healthy. Then, just ten miles down the road, there'll be nothing but derelict houses in a ghost town.

When I visited, Seligman was certainly one of the thriving, lively places. There was a lot of tourist tat, but it was keeping the small town alive. And that survival – not to mention much of the survival along the whole length of the road – is largely due to one extraordinary man: the owner of Seligman's barber shop, Angel Delgadillo.

Born in 1927 in a house directly on Route 66, Angel has witnessed the rise and fall of the road. When the interstate bypassed the town, Seligman started to die. To make matters worse, the authorities even removed the signpost that pointed to the town, so it became a secret destination. Businesses closed, people left, buildings decayed. In desperation, Angel and fifteen others called a town meeting. The result was the founding of the Historic Route 66 Association of Arizona. Elected president, Angel successfully appealed to the Arizona State Legislature to reinstate the sign. He then went on to fight in a thousand different ways to bring the town back to life. And lo and behold, his campaign worked. Next he lobbied other states to follow Arizona's lead and form their own Route 66 associations. Now, all eight states along the route have recognised the historical and social significance of the Mother Road. Eight international associations have also been formed.

Now in his eighties, Angel is Route 66's guardian angel – a role he was clearly still relishing when I visited him in his barber shop. He rarely cuts hair these days, but he continues to spend much of his time in the shop, watching the world go by on his beloved Route 66. He is a wonderfully warm, positive man, with a wicked sense of humour and a wisdom that comes from years of experience. I asked what it had been like to spend his entire life at the side of Route 66.

'I saw the dust bowl when the Okies came travelling through on Route 66, when the road was still dirt and they were going west for a better life. Then I saw all the service boys pass through during World War Two. And I saw the children of the same boys when they grew up, travelling to go see Grandma back in Oklahoma or Texas. I saw the automobile get better – from no heater and no refrigeration to heat and refrigeration. Then I saw the day that this town died for ten long years.'

'Was that when the interstate came?' I said.

'September 22, 1978, at about 3 p.m., the business community died. Just like that. The world forgot about us for ten long years. The travelling public took to I-40 like ducks take to water. They got their wish to just zoom. But after ten years I got angry.'

I laughed. 'Good on you.'

'When I found out that we didn't have any signing between here and Flagstaff, I got angry. I fought the state to get those signs up and I called a meeting in Seligman to tell everyone how I thought we could get the economy back. We formed the Historic Route 66 Association of Arizona. We had a big three-day celebration with a fun run, a pageant for Miss Route 66, and we invited Bobby Troup, the man that wrote the song. We fed six hundred people at the old gym, the town was filled with news media and they begun to tell the world Route 66 is not dead.'

In the summer of 1988, Angel's brother Juan, who managed

a hamburger restaurant that had served almost no customers for a decade, needed to hire extra staff to cope with all the tourists who were now flocking to Seligman. Since then, the number of visitors has increased every year. Angel told me he was on his fiftieth guest book, but he'd noticed one curious wee characteristic in those books: Europeans and Asians vastly outnumbered Americans. I asked him why he thought that was.

'The United States is like the new kid on the block. We're only two hundred and thirty years old. European countries, they're centuries old and they understand the value of history. They know where they come from. They know preservation. When they read about us and see that we, the people, helped to save a piece of history, they want to come.'

'That's wonderful,' I said.

'And we take it for granted. We live here, right?'

'Well, you've done a grand job, Angel.'

'It is beautiful to be here and witness the happy, happy people that come to travel Route 66. It's beautiful. That's a big pay for me. They don't have to spend a dime, but they are so happy that we have preserved.'

He told me lots more about his life – how he followed in the footsteps of his father, who bought the barber chair in which I was sitting on 10 April 1926 for $194. In those days, Angel's father's pool hall and barber shop business was one block further south – on the path that Route 66 took through Seligman from 1926 to 1933. When the road was moved north, to its current position, Angel's dad was bypassed and went bust. He seriously considered joining the stream of Okies heading west: 'We were all but loaded to go to California, a Model-T Ford pulling a trailer and eleven of us, but music stopped us,' said Angel.

His brother Juan played in the Hank Becker Orchestra in Seligman. Another brother, Joe, played banjo. They'd receive five dollars each to play at a dance. 'But ten dollars wasn't enough to feed eleven of us,' said Angel, 'so we were going to California to pick apples, pick whatever they let us.' However, when Hank Becker heard the family had loaded their belongings on to a trailer, he found jobs for Juan and Joe in Santa Fe, which allowed the rest of the family to stay in Seligman. Later, Juan started his own orchestra with Joe and ten other musicians. According to an unwritten family law, each of the nine Delgadillo children joined the band when they were old enough. 'I was the last one to audition and I played the drum from when I was twelve years old,' said Angel. Playing at local events such as high school graduations, the band eventually became the Delgadillo Orchestra. When his brothers Juan, Joe and Augustine went to war, Angel moved on to the trombone and tenor sax, supporting the rest of the family by keeping the band going.

The remaining members of the family still play together today, rehearsing every week. One of Angel's daughters, Myrna, manages a store in Seligman, and the other, Clarissa, works in the barber shop with her husband, Maurizio, and Angel's sister-in-law. It is a proper family business, a throwback to when Route 66 ran through the real America.

Angel is a remarkable man. With an impressive talent for remembering dates, his conversation is peppered with the precise times of every key event in his life. When I listened to the way he had held his town together, and looked after his family, I wanted to be his grandson – even though he's only twenty-odd years older than me. He was named Angel for a reason.

'Billy, we have so much fun here and we make a living. Both of those things matter,' he said. 'But you also want to understand that the world is not what it was fifty-six years ago. The world moves so fast, we have so many distractions. I'm not against McDonald's, I'm not against Wal-Mart. We need them. But there, you're a number. Here, we greet you: "Hello, how are you?" I guess what we're selling is service, and that is something that was lost years ago.'

I agreed wholeheartedly with him.

'I've had many, many tourists over the years and still they come in and say to me: "You people on Route 66 are like one big family. I started in Chicago, Illinois, and they all treat us so well."'

I knew exactly what he meant. 'That's what's happened to us,' I said. 'We were flabbergasted in Missouri, Oklahoma and other places by how nice people were to us.'

'And that is what we helped to preserve. Isn't that beautiful?'

'It's lovely. Small-town America is wonderful. I'm a big fan.'

'At first the travelling public that came here were mainly grown-ups. But when John Lasseter made *Cars* – I'm in it, incidentally: he interviewed me for about two hours for the extra disc with the DVD – he captured the imagination of the children, the generation that's going to inherit all of this. And now we have children coming here from all over the world, saying, "We saw you on the DVD."'

Angel exuded this sort of positivity throughout our conversation. It was one of those great days, and it got even better when I walked down Seligman's Main Street and bumped into a gang of leather-clad trikers.

Ever since I'd started my journey on Route 66, I'd noticed a lot of people riding next to me on hired Harleys. Frankly, I'd grown to dislike them. Big, chrome-covered monsters, to me they had begun to look more like tourist buses with every passing day. The people who rented them were okay. Many of them were early retirement guys in search of freedom and escape after decades of hard work. But I also had a sense that they were buying into that corporate image of Route 66 that I mentioned at the start of the book. They all seemed to think that it had to be ridden on a Harley or driven in a red convertible. And that sort of corporatisation was exactly what killed the Mother Road. It had transformed the drive from Chicago to Los Angeles from a cobbled-together passage through small towns with family businesses into a sanitised procession along freeways interspersed with strip malls, fast-food chains and plastic motels.

So it was a relief to meet a bunch of fellow trike riders. They had some extraordinary custom machines, some factory ones and some home-made ones with bits and pieces of cars and other odds and ends. Like me, most of the riders refused to call their bikes trikes. Many of them were older people and had moved on from bikes to trikes, which pleased me as patron of the British Disabled Trike Society. A lot of the guys had been injured in motorbike accidents and couldn't balance on two-wheelers any more, so they'd gone down the trike route. Anything to keep biking.

One of them had created his trike by sticking a wheel on either side of the rear wheel of his Honda motorbike (actually,

I suppose it was technically a quad, because it had four wheels). It was a splendid, neat-looking machine, still powered by the original rear wheel; the extra wheels simply acted as stabilisers.

'Why did you do it?' I asked. 'Why did you change your bike?'

'My left leg had given up the ghost,' he said. 'It would go to sleep, so I would stop at the traffic lights, put my feet down and the bike would collapse on top of my leg.' He'd come up with the perfect solution to keep biking.

Another wee man was there with his wee girlfriend, who had only one leg and one arm. She had a wee trike of her own, but had come on the back of his this time. They told me they still went everywhere together, and they were bursting with positive energy. Happy-go-lucky and delightful, they would be an inspiration to anyone.

Then there was Catfish Larry, the owner of a big, beautiful, yellow trike. He told me the hilarious story of how he got his nickname, but all I can say here is that the clues were to be found in a catfish and his big bushy moustache. It was not that clean. In fact, it was downright dirty and great fun, but not wanting to offend anyone of a delicate disposition, I'll leave the rest of you to use your imaginations. Anyway, Larry came from a wee town about ten miles down the road. It had died because the stone works had been operated by illegal immigrants and the government had deported them all. Broke and trying to sell his trike, he didn't have a bad word to say against the immigrants. He thought it was ridiculous to deport them, because the economy plummeted as soon as they were forced to leave. If they'd been allowed to stick around, they could have continued to work, generating money for the town, and eventually becoming legal citizens. I thought that was a rather good idea.

After the fun of Seligman, I spent the night in possibly the weirdest hotel room in the world. At Peach Springs, Arizona, the room was in the centre of a dry cavern, 220 feet deep and 65 million years old. One of the few dry caverns in the world, there was not a drop of water in it, which made it uniquely suitable for use as the world's deepest hotel room.

Until quite recently, the cavern was a tourist attraction. People would be winched down on ropes, through holes in the rock, holding a paraffin lamp. Promised the chance to explore what was billed as a 'dinosaur cave', those must have been the bravest tourists in the world, because I certainly wouldn't have done it that way. I took the newly built lift, which was scary enough, especially when I realised it was my only lifeline back to the surface.

As soon as I stepped through the lift door, I felt a huge rush of air surging up through the shaft. That air, I was told, came from the Grand Canyon, more than sixty-five miles away. It makes its way through a series of tunnels all the way to that cavern at Peach Springs. Then, in a way that nobody really understands, it escapes from the cavern, meaning it sort of breathes. Weird . . . and a little bit scary.

Having walked down a short corridor, I entered the most unbelievable cave. It consists of two enormous rooms, with a wooden platform in the middle of one of them – my quarters for the night. With two double beds, some nice Route 66 furniture, a couch, a television and an assortment of *National Geographic* magazines to remind me what the world upstairs looked like, it was a pleasant enough place to stay. There was also a wee shower and a toilet. It was pretty much the same as any other motel room I'd stayed in on Route 66 . . . aside from the fact that the roof was about seventy-five feet above my head and made entirely of solid rock that had been hollowed out over millions of years by an ancient waterfall. I started to wonder exactly what I thought I was doing down there.

In 1962 President Kennedy decided that the cave would make a good bomb shelter. At the height of the Cuban missile crisis, when Americans felt there was a very real possibility that Soviet missiles might be launched against them, JFK had the cavern filled with enough provisions to feed two thousand people for thirty days. I suppose it was a good idea in those very dark days, but the idea of two thousand people in that cave, fighting for the food – most of it sweeties and crackers – just boggles my mind. The smell, the dark and the crush of people would have been unbelievable. And how would they get two thousand people in and out of a cavern using a lift that could carry a maximum of a dozen people at a time? And what would they do if the food ran out? And would they really have wanted to return to the world up top, which presumably would have been full of people with two heads running about, eating anything that dared to show its face, human or otherwise?

Wandering through the cave, I struggled to come to terms with the sheer size of it, but then I always get freaked out by the size and age of things like that. Talking about squillions of years confuses me. I spotted some helictites – very rare crystals that baffle geologists, who still don't understand how they are formed. Neither do I, so I moved on and found JFK's store of food and other vital supplies. It didn't look very big. Some big black plastic drums contained water that had been stagnant for years, but the provisions also included purification tablets that would make it drinkable. It would taste rotten, but that would be the least of your worries if you were confined down there for a month.

It was properly dark – not like the dark you get in your living room and to which your eyes eventually become acclimatised. Down there, my eyes never acclimatised, because there was no source of light whatsoever.

Having investigated my surroundings, I returned to my tasty little bachelor pad. About 150 feet wide and 400 feet long, the cave was quite a desirable little number, even though it reminded me of one of those rooms in which some mad bastard would hole up and plan the destruction of the world. I could imagine him sitting on one of the beds, cackling to himself and saying, 'That'll show them. That'll teach them to fail me in my exams and make me a laughing stock. I'll give them something to remember.'

Few people have slept down there on their own. Most guests come with their partners, but Pamela was back at home, which most of the crew seemed to find quite funny. They just skittered off and left me down there on my own. Sitting on the sofa, looking at the rocks all around me, it was hard to think that it had been like that for sixty-five million years. The thought did cross my mind that if anything went wrong, like the whole thing dropping by ten feet, they would never be able to rescue me. I would have given up the ghost long before they'd managed to drill through 220 feet of granite – no matter how many crackers and sweeties I managed to find in JFK's stash. That was a dodgy moment, but pretty soon I started to relax. Before long, it was time to go to bed, so I slipped between the sheets. That's when the one true drawback of the place struck me: maybe I was not alone.

Back in the 1920s, when these caves were first opened, they found two human skeletons. I could just about cope with that. But they also found the bones of a fifteen-foot-tall four-toed sloth – a prehistoric creature that was the ancestor of the three-toed sloth, which is ugly enough. They showed me a picture of it before they left me alone for the night, and it was kind of terrifying, especially as it was so tall. Lying in my bed, I couldn't help peering around, staring down the dark wee tunnel to check if any big hairy monsters were coming to say hello.

Eventually I overcame my fears about monsters, and after reading my book for a while I turned out the bedside lamp and fell asleep. I slept wonderfully well. With no moisture, there were no creepy crawlies. Tarantulas, lizards and snakes that could have crept around in the middle of the night and given me a bite couldn't survive down there. With nothing to tug at my bedclothes and give me the jitters, I slept the sleep of the just.

I enjoyed it so much that I decided I must come back, but next time I would try to convince Pamela to spend the night down there with me.

Emerging into the bright Arizona desert glare, I bumbled eighteen miles down Route 66 to Valentine. This section followed the path of the old Beale Wagon Road through a dusty, sandy landscape. I was a long way from the interstate again, seeing Route 66 as it had been at its inception in 1926. Although the road was very rough in parts of Arizona, lots of terrific sections were still intact, particularly the infamous Oatman Highway, which crossed the 3,550-foot Sitgreaves Pass via a series of tight hairpin bends next to sheer drops. Regarded as one of the highlights of the entire 2,278 miles of Route 66, it lay an hour or so ahead and I couldn't wait to see it. But first I had an appointment at another wildlife sanctuary.

Keepers of the Wild is a refuge for abandoned pets and showbiz animals. The vast majority of the animals are seriously dangerous and had been donated by their terrified owners. Others had been seized from people who had abused them. Compared to what they'd been through, the animals were now in heaven. One of the sanctuary's jaguars used to roam around a notorious drug dealer's back garden and was seized by the Drug Enforcement Agency in a raid. Another former resident was a cougar that used to live freely in the Los Angeles home of Slash, the former guitarist with Guns N' Roses – until it attacked his wife.

The sanctuary was founded by Jonathan Kraft, who used to have his own big cat show – like Siegfried and Roy's in Las Vegas – before he saw the light and decided to work for the animals instead of having them work for him. Grey-haired, tanned and fit in his fifties, he looked more like a movie stuntman than a conservationist, but his stories were fascinating.

'Big cats are a huge business in the United States, a fifteen-billion-dollar illegal trade,' he said. 'There are more animals – fifteen thousand big cats – in private hands in the United States than there are in all habitats in the rest of the world put together. It's kind of crazy.'

Jonathan told me there were about seven thousand privately owned tigers in the United States, which meant there were more tigers in American back yards than there were in the whole of

India. I couldn't imagine what anyone who kept a tiger at home was thinking.

'We just rescued a little baby lion that was typical,' said Jonathan. 'Surplus in a zoo, he was sold to a wild animal auction and some girl out of Washington bought him for eighteen hundred dollars. She thought she could keep him, but she didn't have any licence or permit, so she tried to sell him to a guy in Canada. This animal was two and a half weeks old. Crazy. So we had to intervene and we took the animal from her. His name is Anthony and he's wonderful. He's ten weeks old now, a little rascal, and so darned cute. People think they stay that way but unfortunately they end up like this guy over here.'

Jonathan pointed at Sultan, an adult male lion with a huge mane of hair. Lying nonchalantly in his enclosure, Sultan was looking the other way, minding his own business, licking one of his paws, but when Jonathan called his name, he turned around, stood up and walked about four steps towards us. Then he saw the camera crew and stopped to have a think about it, until Jonathan encouraged him. With Sultan standing right in front of us, looking magnificent, Jonathan's partner, Tina, brought some meat and they threw it over the rail. This giant, beautiful animal looked straight at us, then wandered closer and started eating the meat.

'We rescued him along with a tiger and he is all right now,' said Jonathan. 'He's about ten years old, right in the middle of when male lions are very dangerous. They have a lot of testosterone. I used to go in and brush his mane. I don't do that any more. He'd be brushing mine, you know?'

'It just baffles me,' I said. 'I don't know how somebody could think they could keep a thing like that in the back yard.'

'Plenty of them do. I know people, private individuals, who've got thirty or forty cats in their back yards. Of course, most of them can't provide the right habitats for them, so you've got a cage situation. Next thing, the neighbour's kid comes over and does a little touchy–feely and the kid loses their arm or their fingers. And then it's the animal's fault. It happens all the time.'

Jonathan spent years interacting very closely with wild cats, but he stopped doing that because he thought it sent out the wrong message to anyone who might be watching. All food is now passed to the animals on the end of a long stick or chucked over the fence.

Jonathan pointed at a beautiful female jaguar. 'Her name is Hope. She's only a little jaguar, but jaguars pound for pound have more crushing power than any other cat. Compared to a leopard, she has a very short, fat body with stocky legs. Considered the wrestler of the cat family, the jaguar is very tenacious. They're the only cat that doesn't kill by a throat bite. They take their prey, bite it in the back of the head and crush its skull.'

Skull crushers. That sounded horrific. Yet people kept them as pets. 'What kind of thing would tick her off?' I asked.

'Food, for one. And other animals. Jaguars are solitary, so she gets annoyed with other animals. I have a separation between her and the leopards. If she were to be up against their cage, she would constantly fight with them.'

With about forty big cats, the sanctuary is extraordinarily expensive to run. It costs about half a million dollars a year just to keep the show on the road – not that surprising when you consider that the big cats gorge their way through four cows every week.

Quite a few of the tigers and lions had come to the sanctuary after unscrupulous photographers had abandoned them. Once they stopped being cute and fluffy at about six months old, they became surplus to requirements as far as the photographers were concerned.

'Most of them end up in a canned hunt,' said Jonathan, 'where you can shoot them for a fee. It's disgusting.' Others had formerly been in zoos, mostly private ones. 'That's the only thing I have against zoos. Why do they keep breeding these animals? We all know why: everybody wants to come and see the cubs. But what happens to the cubs when they are full grown? They end up in facilities like this. Or, worse, they go to a canned hunt where the big brave hunter can shoot one.'

'Where do they do that?'

'All over the country. There are more than three hundred canned hunts in this country. It's illegal, but they move from place to place. Sometimes they let hunters shoot them in the back of a horse trailer. It's ridiculous.'

'For the sheer joy of doing it? I just don't get that.'

'The trophy-hunting thing is just ridiculous. And there's a couple of places in this country that actually breed lions for human consumption, to make lion hamburgers. Now, why would you want to do that? And they have licences! I would love to shut them down. Lions are now on the endangered species list.'

'I've never seen it for sale.'

'Some of them here in Arizona sell lion burgers for twenty-seven dollars a burger. They mix it with cow meat, but why would you?'

We moved on through the park, which had a total of about

175 animals in around forty compounds and enclosures. Jonathan introduced me to a cougar called Bam Bam that was more tame than most. 'They're wonderful cats,' he said. 'Great survivors. This cat can take down a horse, big prey. He is a little bit shy, but if you get him one on one, he'll come and sit right in your lap. He's just a real sweetheart. I've got other cougars I wouldn't do that with, but this one is pretty safe.'

'It's astonishing that in America a thing like that' – I pointed at the cougar – 'is still roaming in the wild. There's something quite nice about that.'

'In Arizona there are about twenty-five thousand in the wild. In the southern part of Arizona there are some jaguars in the wild. They've spotted about six of them. They've come up from South America. People always wonder what they eat. I always tell them "slow natives".'

Later, Jonathan took me into an enclosure that housed a lioness. Standing a foot behind Jonathan, I was quaking as he tried to entice her to come out from behind a rock. Oh my God, I thought. This will be the one day when she loses the plot and rips off someone's face. But Jonathan got her out from her hiding place, put a leash on her – a *leash* – then sat her down and cuddled and kissed her.

'Come on over and see her,' he said.

Very gingerly, I approached. I sat down beside the lioness, as instructed by Jonathan, who was stroking her. When my heart had stopped beating out of my chest, I gave her a bit of a stroke. I'd never stroked a lion before. It was an amazing feeling.

We moved on to look at some beautiful wolves, then Jonathan showed me some of the ways in which people have mistreated the animals that are now in his care. One monkey couldn't keep its tongue in its mouth because some bastard had removed its incisor teeth. The tongue was just hanging out, and the poor little thing was slobbering.

I thought it was wonderful that a man who had made his living from lions and tigers by making them disappear on stage had turned completely the other way and now devoted his life to their welfare. Jonathan should be celebrated and congratulated. It had been a fantastic day and I came out feeling much better, rejoicing that people like Jonathan make the world a better place.

14

Get Hip to This Timely Tip, When You Make That California Trip

Crossing the Colorado River, I entered California, the Golden State, and my home for many years. Entering the eighth and final state I would have to pass through to complete the long journey from Chicago, I had mixed feelings about the approaching end – both disappointment and relief that it would all soon be over. Shouting the battle cry of generations of westbound travellers – 'California or bust!' – I eased back in my seat and pointed the bike in the direction of Barstow, some two hundred miles down the tarmac. However, when I arrived at the little town I found little worth exploring, so I just kept rolling, the miles passing easily under my tyres as I crossed the wide-open spaces of the Mojave Desert, en route to the fleshpots of Los Angeles. Then, shortly after passing through the village of Helendale, I spotted an oasis of colour in the sandy desert – an orchard made of bottles.

It was an astonishing sight. In the front yard of one of a strip of dusty properties stood row upon higgledy-piggledy row of trees constructed out of coloured bottles, most of them topped with metallic pieces of junk, like car wheels or watering cans or even a rusty old rifle. I had to meet the person who'd created this magical world of ironmongery and glass in the middle of the desert. At the back of the wonderful enchanted crystalline forest I found him – a man in a sun hat with a trailing white beard that was even longer than those sported by the guys in ZZ Top. He told me his name was Elmer Long.

Elmer is a genuine eccentric in the traditional English sense. In other words, he thinks he's completely normal; which, for my money, he is. He'd built the hundreds of trees in his front yard by welding rods on to poles bought from a scrap dealer and slipping the bottles on to the ends.

'I love it,' I said to Elmer. 'When did you start doing it?'

'In 2000.'

'As recently as that?' Judging by the extent and intricacy of his orchard, Elmer had been working very hard.

'Yes, eleven years. But I've always collected and some of the bottles my father collected. He was a bottle collector but he had no way of displaying it.'

'What was your father's idea when he collected the bottles? He just liked them?'

'He thought he was going to get rich. I mean, he found some good bottles. They're put away. But I've got photographs of him digging for his bottles. He would dig a hole in the ground maybe five foot deep and when he found an old one, he honestly thought he had a gold mine in his hand.'

'Sometimes you do.'

'Yes, well . . . it didn't work out that way. You've got to find someone who is willing to pay the price. You know what I found out, just by doing what I do? There's no money in it. It's all free. Yesterday, I had a couple of ladies from Mexico come here, a mother and a daughter. The daughter had an eight-year-old son with her, and before they left, the grandma gave me a hug and her daughter immediately gave me a hug. Now, if you were to compare going to a mine and excavating a vein of gold and taking it to the bank and getting rich, that's one thing. But little hugs like that coming from people from another country, that's pure gold. You don't put that in a bank, you put it in your heart, you know?'

'You've got it.'

'That's the key here. I have so much fun talking to and meeting people, you never know what you are going to run into.'

Just before Elmer's father died, he gave away all of his best bottles, but there were still thousands left. Around the same time, Elmer chopped down his fruit orchard. 'The birds were getting all the fruit anyway,' he said. 'So I just pulled the orchard down and I made this.'

All around us were piles of bottles, some of them sorted by colour or size, but most of them piled up randomly. 'Are these ready to go up?' I said, pointing at some bottles that looked quite old.

'I found a new dump. Well, not a new dump, it's an old dump. About 1950. Somebody reached in this pile the other day and found a 1942 beer bottle. These are all old. They're better-quality glass, thicker, a lot different than the new beer bottles. And I know where there are thousands of these now. The dump continued for miles and I just gathered enough to get me by for a while. It's an hour and a half from here.'

'When does the forest look at its best, in the evening or the morning?'

'It looks different every part of the day.'

I asked if Elmer had a favourite bottle or tree among his collection.

'The only thing that's favourite is the things I've had since I was a kid,' he said. 'I've got childhood items out here. I still have my teddy bears. I don't throw nothing away. This handmade rake right here' – he struck it – 'you hear this ring?'

'Oh yes.'

'I found that near the town of Boron in 1960. I was a freshman in high school. I've got photographs of the trip.'

'And you brought it home with you?'

'I bring everything home.'

'And do people think you're nuts?'

'No. Well, in a good kind of way.'

'I don't think you're nuts at all. I think you're the sanest man in the place.'

Elmer's glass orchard is spectacular. I enjoyed every second of going around it with him. He's a completely non-violent man, but he'd built all sorts of bullets and empty cartridge cases into his bottle-tree sculptures. He doesn't believe in guns and bullets, but he's happy to buy old broken guns and weld them into strange shapes. They look fantastic.

Most of the items in the forest were obtained for free by sifting through rubbish dumps. Claiming to know the whereabouts of dozens of dumps, Elmer talks about them like other people talk about old churches or ruined castles – 'I know where there's a beauty' – and he's marked several on his mental map that he wants to investigate in greater detail.

'I've got my eye on this rubbish dump,' he said. 'My wife comes with me and she sits in the car and I go and dig.'

For hours or days at a time, Elmer sifts through the dumps, digging up bottles and bits of metal. One time, he found a car door with a metal detector. Then he dug a bit further, 'And there was a whole car there and it's flat. So I've covered it up and I'm going back for it.'

In time, he hopes to put the car on top of one of his trees. God, I'd love to see that. When I visited, there were already metal parts from at least three military Jeeps, a Model-T Ford, several tractors, a swing, a trailer, a boxing-ring bell, a shotgun, an old train, a chicken feeder and dozens of other things – all of them welded on to the tops of his trees.

Elmer's home is equally eccentric. It's made from a Bailey bridge (those portable bridges that military engineers use to cross rivers), although you would never know to look at it. And it has no taps. Instead, the pipes have on–off switches like those used on commercial pipelines. There's no television or radio, just an aquarium full of fish, and only one bed. Elmer is worried that people might ask to stay if he gets a second one. That doesn't make him unfriendly or weird. He just knows what he likes and what he wants. He'd recently held a family reunion at his house, but all the relatives had stayed overnight in nearby hotels, which was better for everyone. Elmer is actually the friendliest of men, and he spared no effort or time in showing me everything and describing every inch of his garden. He was exactly the type of person I'd expected to meet in spades on Route 66. If only there had been more dreamers like Elmer over the previous two thousand miles.

Elmer Long was by far my favourite find on the 66. He embodied everything I imagined might be on the Mother Road. I wish I'd got to know him long before I did. I wish I could call him my friend.

At San Bernardino, a few miles on from Elmer's place, the great Los Angeles sprawl began and the traffic started to build up. After weeks of empty roads and wide-open vistas, it was quite a shock. The Los Angeles basin famously has some of the most dense and aggressive traffic anywhere in the world. To get a new perspective on it, I went up in a local traffic reporter helicopter with a pilot called Chuck.

From the air, the intersecting lanes of merging freeways make Spaghetti Junction in Birmingham look like a country lane. Tens of thousands of cars mingling, going round and up and down and back and forth. It looked like a tangled fishing net. And, of course, it all started with Route 66 bringing travellers from the East who were seeking fortune or fame in the West. Although the thud of the rotors made it difficult for us to talk in anything other than broken sentences, Chuck was a terrific guide. He did a lot of swooping around, with the rotors at right angles to the ground, which I loved.

Regarded as the gateway to metropolitan Los Angeles, San Bernardino used to greet Route 66 travellers with orange groves and vineyards. But those days are long gone. In the words of that great Joni Mitchell song, paradise has been paved over and replaced by a parking lot. Nowadays, San Bernardino is a long succession of strip malls, offices and housing. But right in the middle of all that is a stunning Spanish colonial-style building – the California Theatre.

In the early years of Hollywood, filmmakers would screen test their films at the California Theatre, which in those days was regarded as being sufficiently distant from Los Angeles to escape the influence of Tinseltown. Dozens of classics, such as *The Wizard of Oz* and *King Kong*, were first seen by the public in this magnificent 1,718-seat cinema. *The Wizard of Oz* was screen tested in June 1939 and the audience adored it. But the studio executives still felt uneasy about the final song, 'Over the Rainbow', and seriously discussed cutting it from the movie. They were worried that the ballad might end the film on a bit of a slow note. But Victor Fleming, the director, managed to persuade Louis B. Mayer to keep it in the final cut, and his faith was rewarded when it won an Oscar. Since then, the American Film Institute and many other polls have voted 'Over the Rainbow' the greatest movie song of all time.

In addition to screening films, the theatre has presented plays, ballets, concerts and musicals, as well as stand-up comedy. Over the years, hundreds of big stars have appeared there – including my hero, Will Rogers. So when Mike suggested I should give a banjo rendition of 'Over the Rainbow' on the California's stage, I knew I would be following in some very large footsteps. Slinking off to a dressing room, I sat down and had a bash at the song. I'd played it plenty of times on a guitar, but banjos are fickle wee things – some tunes just don't sound right on them. Fortunately, though, I came up with a nice, slightly melancholic arrangement – a little folky picking tune.

On the empty stage, lit by a single spotlight and with my jacket draped over a stool, I stood in front of a completely empty auditorium and had a go. I used to play the banjo in public a lot, but over the years I grew kind of nervous about it.

I started making a lot of mistakes whenever I played in front of people, so eventually I cut it out of the act. Very occasionally, I'll play at a charity show or for my pals in Glasgow, but that's about it. So I was as surprised as anyone when I did 'Over the Rainbow' as clean as a whistle four times with no shakes at all. Admittedly, I played a very simple version of the song, but I think it worked well. It was a bit of a breakthrough for me. Buoyed by that unexpected triumph, I got out my guitar and sang 'Waiting for a Train' by Jimmie Rodgers and 'We're Gonna Go Fishin'' by Hank Locklin.

Riding deeper into Los Angeles's metropolitan sprawl, after thirty miles I arrived in Pomona in the Hispanic–Latino side of town. This is probably the world capital for hot rods and low riders. To some people around here, these cars – which are fitted with amazingly complex hydraulic suspension systems so they can bob up and down – are almost a religion. Some of them are works of art, and I've always loved them. Even when I was a welder in Glasgow, I used to look at *Hot Rod* magazine and drool over the paint jobs. Now, I'd come to meet a bunch of guys who were among the best in the business.

The first thing I saw as I approached Mario De Alba's garage was a customised Harley-Davidson. It was breathtakingly impressive. As well as boasting every imaginable accessory – including knuckle-duster brakes and a skeleton side rest – it had a wonderful engraving of Benjamin Franklin on the engine block. The seat was covered in stingray leather, which was beautiful but not really to my taste. I usually prefer bikes that are stripped down rather than tarted up, but I couldn't deny that Mario had done a fantastic job.

The De Albas are a close-knit family, with Mario working alongside his three sons in the garage. They have real respect for each other's talents, and all three brothers are deeply grateful to their father for everything he's taught them. One of them – who specialises in bodywork – pointed out the artistry of his brother's paint jobs. In return, the second brother told me that the bodywork was really amazing.

'My brother's a genius,' he said, while his sibling stood just three feet away.

'Oh, I don't know about that,' the other brother said modestly.

It was a joy to see such love and pride within a family, especially as it was justified. They were just as talented as their siblings said they were. It was the attention to detail that really impressed me. They showed me an old Cadillac that was nice enough in itself, but then they lifted the bonnet. *Holy moly!* The firewall, between the engine and the passenger compartment – which in most cars is an oily, dirty, rusting plate of steel – had been high-gloss sprayed and lacquered. When I saw that, I thought: These guys really know what they're doing.

We went outside, where a four-wheel drive pick-up sat high above its own wheels, like a giant Tonka toy. It was amazing, but I was even more impressed by Mario's 1936 Chevrolet. A total dream car, it had red metal flake paint and an intricate pattern on the roof. Even the sun visor had been hand-painted in pinstripes. It was by far the best car I'd ever seen, which seemed fitting, as I was nearing the end of the longest road trip of my life. Inside, it was decked out like a high-class brothel, with red velvet overstuffed seats.

Mario was obviously immensely proud of it, yet he became very shy and matter of fact when I asked him about it. Standing in his overalls, he just shrugged when I praised his beautiful Chevy. Then he pulled out a photograph of a burned-out wreck and told me it was a picture of the car before he'd started to work on it. In total, the job had taken him nine years. Now it looked like a piece of fine jewellery. The paint job was so good that I had to stifle an urge to lick it.

'Show him how the hydraulics work,' one of the brothers said to Mario, before going round the back of the car and opening the boot. Inside were some huge cylinders, each about the size of a fire extinguisher, but highly chromed and beautifully engraved.

Climbing into the car, Mario pushed some buttons that made the Chevy go up and down, enjoying himself immensely as the car bounced around. Whenever he took it out on the open road, he would raise it up to drive, but then drop it down whenever he came to a stop. Sitting as close to the ground as possible is a big deal in low-rider circles.

On the way to the garage, I'd worried about what I might say to a group of guys who built low riders. I thought they'd just waffle on about carburettors and pistons, which I would have found stultifying boring. Nothing could have been further from the truth. They were charming people who loved what they did, and loved and respected their family. Like so many of my good experiences along Route 66, I'd stumbled across an unexpected delight in the most unlikely of places.

As I was leaving, I thanked them for a great day, then said that I thought customising cars and bikes was like an obsession for their family. 'There's no cure for you – you realise that?' I said. 'You're stuck with this for ever.'

'Yes,' said Mario. 'And I'll love to do it until I die. I guess it's special. I love to work on cars and so do my sons now. So I guess I passed it on to them.'

'Do you love it as much as he does?' I asked the three brothers.

'Oh yeah, definitely,' said Mario Junior, with the others nodding in agreement. 'As you said, there's no cure for our illness. But it's a good illness to have.'

'And I'm very happy that they learned all the skills,' said Mario. 'They started following me and doing everything. And they're doing it just the way I like to do it. They've got the same patience now. And I'm very, very happy that they went along with it. Because they are my good boys, my good sons.'

My last destination before the end of Route 66 was strangely appropriate, given that I'd started this journey reminiscing about an encounter at Mary Shelley's graveside in Dorset. I pulled off Santa Monica Boulevard into Forever Hollywood, a grand, sixty-two-acre cemetery that boasts both Renaissance villas and palm trees. Only in Hollywood, I thought.

As I've said, I'm a taphophile – a lover of graveyards. And with the graves and cenotaphs of Rudolph Valentino, John Huston, Jayne Mansfield and Dee Dee and Johnny Ramone, among many others, this particular graveyard was a real treasure trove for someone like me. For instance, I learned that Jayne Mansfield was only thirty-four when she died. And Douglas Fairbanks Junior's mausoleum looks like something that might have been built for the Tsar of Russia. It even has a lake in front of it. Then I saw a particularly interesting gravestone. The guy's name – DeVito – had been engraved on it, as had his date of birth – 1944. But there was no date of death. I thought he must still be alive, and had arranged his grave exactly how he wanted it while he still could. Next door was another tombstone, this time with a picture of a guy with a moustache. Again the year of birth was 1944 and again there was no year of death. I reckoned they were a couple who had seized the opportunity to invest in two prime plots in the cemetery, overlooking the lake.

Another interesting grave – belonging to a girl called Bianca – featured an angel with a broken guitar. The epitaph read: 'She lived to love, She loved to rock.' There was also a comment about the devil, so I guessed Bianca must have been a bit of a rocker. That pleased me.

Finally, I wandered over to the crematorium, where some big women were consoling a wee man. Everyone looked deeply sad, and it was a timely reminder of what graveyards are really all about.

Now I had to face the inevitable: it was time to bring this great, exciting, fascinating journey to an end. It was Bobby Troup's song that first prompted me to take a long ride down the Mother Road, but 'Route 66' had one crucial flaw. According to the song, the road runs from Chicago to LA, but the reality is ever so slightly different. Officially, Route 66 has always ended fifteen miles beyond the City of Los Angeles boundary, in Santa Monica, so if I was going to do this properly, that had to be my final destination.

For the very last time, I swung my leg over my trusty steed – the trike that had carried me more than two thousand miles from Chicago. Then I slipped into the traffic on Santa Monica Boulevard and rode towards the setting sun. I enjoyed every second, every yard of it, but I remained very vigilant because I didn't want a repetition of an incident that had occurred a few hours earlier, when I was nearly wiped out on the Pasadena Freeway. Out of nowhere, a lunatic had veered towards me from my right-hand side and missed my front wheel by inches. Any closer and he certainly would have killed me. No doubt about it. I would have been mincemeat.

I'd had a few other hairy moments on California's freeways, too. This state clearly needed a campaign to teach people how to drive properly. They needed to learn that giving way every once in a while didn't make you any less of a man. I think the way they drive is a manifestation of a rampant selfishness among some Californians. Certain types of people are attracted to the state, and they show their true colours on the freeway.

But now, cruising along Santa Monica Boulevard, through tree-lined Beverly Hills and West Los Angeles, I managed to forget all about my near-death experience with the maniac on the Pasadena Freeway. I was approaching the last few miles of Route 66. Ahead of me I could see the warm glow of a Pacific sunset. And then, suddenly, I was there, pulling up beside the Will Rogers Highway marker in Palisades Park at the junction of Santa Monica Boulevard and Ocean Boulevard. Only a vast beach and then the Pacific now lay in front of me.

Leaning on a barrier above the beach, gazing out at the ocean, I thought back over the trip. It felt very peculiar to have come to the end. It had been a long, long way from that little signpost on Adams Street in Chicago. Officially, it was 2,278 miles, but I had ridden at least a thousand miles more than that because of all the wrong turnings, the enforced detours and the visits to interesting destinations off the beaten track. I'd covered a lot of ground, and now the sun was sinking into the ocean. It couldn't have ended better.

Route 66 means many things to many people. Everyone who travels along it experiences it in their own unique way. For the dust bowl Okies, it was a road of escape and hope. For the beatniks, it was a road of self-discovery. For many millions, it was a road of new beginnings. For countless others, it was a road of romantic adventure.

I still wasn't quite sure what it was for me. It was too soon to assess such a long and varied journey. I needed time to take it all in, sift through my memories and work out just what Route 66 was really all about. But I already knew for sure that it had been quite different from the Route 66 I'd had in my head before starting my journey in Chicago. Some parts of it had been wonderfully alive; others had been alarmingly close to death; a few had already gone for ever.

Thinking back over the many miles I'd covered, the constantly shifting landscape had certainly made a deep impression. The deserts, the prairies, the hills and the canyons were all unforgettable. But it was the people I'd met along the way who I would carry in my heart for ever: Mervin the Amish carpenter, Elmer and his bottle trees, Angel the barber, Roxann in the ghost town of Glenrio, and defiant Preston in Bronzeville.

Somebody once said that Route 66 was not for everybody; that it wasn't for people in a hurry. But I think it's for anyone and everyone. It can be whatever you want it to be. On it, you'll find whatever you're seeking and plenty more. It's about America's past, its present and probably its future. Above all, Route 66 just *is*. And it always will be.

There was a spirit and a feeling unique to the Mother Road.

To understand it and to feel it, you need to drive it or ride it. So, if you're thinking of travelling from Chicago to LA – more than two thousand miles all the way – take mine and Bobby Troup's advice:

> *If any Joe tells you to go some other way,*
> *Say, 'Nix!' Get your kicks on Route 66.*

Appendix
Mileages from Chicago to Santa Monica

Exactly how long is Route 66? A simple question with a complicated answer.

Anyone who travels Route 66 will at times encounter several remnants of the road between any two points on the map. In some places, travellers are faced with the choice of following the path of the original 1926 Route 66, or a mid-1930s alignment of the road, or one of two or more post-war routes.

Sometimes, such as between Santa Rosa and Albuquerque in New Mexico, one path is more than 90 miles longer than another. Consequently, there is no definitive length for Route 66. Some people say it is nearly 2,700 miles. Others claim it is 2,448 miles. The Historic Route 66 Association of Arizona states the length as 2,278 miles and that's the distance that has been used throughout this book.

Illinois

Chicago	0
Springfield	200

Missouri

St Louise Green	296
Rolla	402

Springfield	511
Joplin	583

Oklahoma

Miami	605
Tulsa	691
Oklahoma City	800
Clinton	885
Elk City	910
Sayre	926

Texas

Shamrock	961
McLean	983
Amarillo	1056
Vega	1125
Adrian	1139

New Mexico

Tucumcari	1167
Newkirk	1199
Santa Rosa	1222
Albuquerque	1341
Grants	1416

Arizona

Flagstaff	1661
Williams	1695
Seligman	1737
Hackberry	1787

Kingman	1809
Needles	1870
Amboy	1943
Barstow	2107
Victorville	2157
Los Angeles	2248
Santa Monica	2278

(Distances according to the Historic Route 66 Association of Arizona)

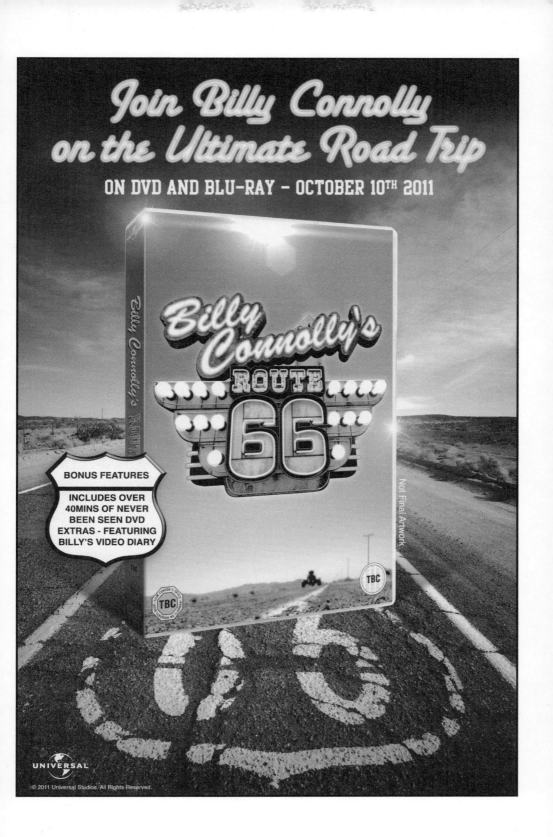

Hiding in Plain Sight

Also by Susan Lewis

Fiction

A Class Apart
Dance While You Can
Stolen Beginnings
Darkest Longings
Obsession
Vengeance
Summer Madness
Last Resort
Wildfire
Cruel Venus
Strange Allure
The Mill House
A French Affair
Missing
Out of the Shadows
Lost Innocence
The Choice
Forgotten
Stolen
No Turning Back
Losing You
The Truth About You
Never Say Goodbye

Too Close to Home
No Place to Hide

Books that run in sequence
Chasing Dreams
Taking Chances

No Child of Mine
Don't Let Me Go
You Said Forever

Series featuring Detective Andee Lawrence
Behind Closed Doors
The Girl Who Came Back
The Moment She Left
Hiding in Plain Sight

Series featuring Laurie Forbes and Elliott Russell
Silent Truths
Wicked Beauty
Intimate Strangers
The Hornbeam Tree

Memoir
Just One More Day
One Day at a Time

Susan Lewis

Hiding in Plain Sight

CENTURY

1 3 5 7 9 10 8 6 4 2

Century
20 Vauxhall Bridge Road
London SW1V 2SA

Century is part of the Penguin Random House group of companies whose addresses can be found at global.penguinrandomhouse.com.

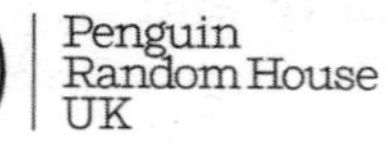

First published in Great Britain by Century in 2017

www.penguin.co.uk

A CIP catalogue record for this book is available from the British Library.

ISBN 9781780896069 (Hardback)
ISBN 9781780896076 (Trade Paperback)
ISBN 9781473537675 (ebook)

Typeset in 13/16.5 pt Palatino LT Std by Jouve (UK), Milton Keynes
Printed and bound by Clays Ltd, St Ives Plc

Penguin Random House is committed to a sustainable future for our business, our readers and our planet. This book is made from Forest Stewardship Council® certified paper.

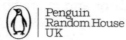

In memory of Georgina Hawtrey-Woore, a truly talented editor and cherished friend, already missed by many and loved by all

She'd dreamt about nothing else for years.

That was when she'd been able to dream.

Now here he was, standing in front of her, shaking so hard she'd surely have been able to hear his knees knocking if the wind weren't so fierce.

His once handsome, now dissolute face was a white, stricken moon in the dark night. His hair was tossing around like trapped straw in a gale. He'd have run if he could, but the men either side of him – nameless, faceless and handsomely paid – were preventing it.

They were watching her too. Neither of them spoke. They were silent, solid, knew why they were there, knew that after they must silently disappear.

A fleeting memory of little Michelle Cross on a busy street flashed into her mind and was gone. She'd been there one minute, gone the next – to the arms of the Virgin Mary.

The Virgin Mary.

She could see he was shouting, crying, begging, but

the wind was snatching his words away, hurling them like feathers into the stormy night.

The cliff edge was so close.

A hundred feet below the sea was a foaming, furious black mass, heaving colossal waves on to the slick, jagged rocks.

She wondered if he'd ever dreamt about her.

Had she troubled his mind at all since he'd last seen her?

She knew she must have. How had he felt?

Guilty? Afraid? Vulnerable?

Certainly not as terrified as he felt now.

He'd no doubt hoped he'd never see her again.

But here she was, standing before him on this deserted tourist spot at the edge of the world, and he knew why.

What he didn't know, yet, was whether she was going to let him live or die.

Chapter One

These meandering, cobbled streets in the heart of Provence, laced through with sleepy canals and narrow, filigree footbridges were known as the Venice of France. Surrounded by the River Sorgue, with glittering waterways, tree-lined banks and many splendid mossy mill wheels, the area was home to a whole host of pavement and waterfront cafés, along with antique shops of every period and description.

It was through one of the leafy arcades that Andrea – Andee – Lawrence was strolling, aware of the ghosts she couldn't see, but sense: children, old women, thieves, sociopaths, philanthropists, spurned lovers, victims of grisly murders. Their spirits were as light and intangible as the wispy clouds overhead; their stories embedded in a forgotten time.

Andee Lawrence wasn't French, but with her effortless elegance and dark, compelling looks she could easily have passed for a wealthy Parisienne, here to while away a few hours before other demands claimed her. In fact, she was a British ex-detective turned occasional freelance investigator, who'd lately developed an interest in – and talent for – interior design. She was also the mother of two, Luke aged twenty-one and Alayna nineteen; she was separated from her husband, Martin, and was now enjoying a new relationship with antique dealer and property developer Graeme Ogilvy, who'd brought her to France.

Other than her striking looks, there was nothing to set her apart from the other browsers who'd come to L'Isle-sur-la-Sorgue today – not a Sunday in the middle of summer, but a Wednesday in early June. Sundays were crazy days when hundreds, thousands, of stalls cluttered the streets and eager bargain-hunters, tourists and vendors outnumbered even the ghosts of former times.

No one, least of all Andee, was aware of fate trailing her today like a sinister bridesmaid. She was experiencing no sixth sense, no unease, nothing untoward at all, only the pleasure of wandering from one small emporium to another, as entranced by the treasures and oddities as she was by the nuances of possible stories.

She'd left Graeme a few minutes ago discussing delivery of a neglected *bergère* chair to the villa they were here to renovate and furnish for a wealthy Spanish client. Their instructions were clear. Nadia Abrego, the Catalonian beauty who could roll out several more surnames and possibly even titles if she so wished, had provided them with photographs of the Renaissance chateau she wanted copied as closely as possible. The villa was an inheritance, apparently, from a recently deceased great-aunt.

The day was warm, the sounds of traffic, haggling, laughter, music were drifting like charms through the still air, passing by lace tablecloths and sombre tapestries, brushing scabbards and teapots, tangling an invisible web around people and relics of the past. A Frenchman in a beret and red neckerchief was posing for photographs with tourists, while an accordionist on the corner of Quai Jean Jaures was pumping out jolly tunes and winking at his admirers as they tossed coins into his waiting cap. As Andee crossed the Pont de la Rivière with its intricate iron balustrades and worn wooden treads, the aroma of freshly baked baguettes floated its temptation out of a nearby *boulangerie*, while the clink of glasses from pavement cafés provided its own irresistible lure.

Taking out her phone she sent a text to Graeme.

Fancy a glass of rosé? Meet you at the cafe next to Hubert's Antiques.

Graeme knew the heart of this small town so well that he'd have no trouble finding her, especially as Hubert was a friend of long standing.

She didn't notice the car approaching as she prepared to cross the road, she only knew it was there when it came to a stop in front of her, blocking the way. She was about to go round it when the rear window descended to reveal a blonde, middle-aged woman wearing dark glasses and crimson lipstick.

'Are you lost?' Andee asked, in French.

The woman smiled and removed the glasses.

Long, strange seconds ticked by before the woman said softly, in English, 'Remember me?'

Shock was twisting Andee's heart into a terrible knot. It couldn't be. It simply wasn't possible. And yet those eyes, the colour and shape, the cheekbones, the retroussé nose . . .

Apparently satisfied that she'd been recognised, the woman tapped the driver's shoulder and the car moved on.

Andee watched it go, too stunned to move, even to think beyond the shock that had trapped her in an unworldly grip.

'Are you OK, madame?' a voice asked from behind her.

She turned to find a concerned man watching her.

'Would you like to sit down?' he offered, pulling up a shabbily upholstered parlour chair.

Andee meant to thank him and move on, but her legs had turned weak. All she could do was sink into his kindness.

'It is 'ot,' he observed in heavily accented English. 'I find you some water.'

As he disappeared inside his shop Andee stared along the street searching for the silver Mercedes, but like the figment of a dream, it had vanished into thin air. She should have run after it, and would now if she had any idea of the direction it had taken. She tried again to make herself think, but her mind remained locked into that brief, earth-shattering moment of recognition.

Remember me?

How could Andee forget? Even after all these years she'd have known the woman anywhere, yet . . . How could it be? It simply wasn't possible.

The woman in the car was dead, so how could she possibly be here?

Andee was with Graeme now, sitting beneath the parasols of a favourite canal-side café next to Hubert's Antiques. She was watching his shrewd dark eyes dilating with shock as he connected with what she'd just told him.

'Are you sure?' he asked, then apparently annoyed with himself, 'Sorry, of course you are, you wouldn't be saying it if you weren't.'

Feeling for him, Andee said, 'Don't worry, I keep asking myself the same question.' She glanced up as a waiter brought a *pichet* of rosé to the table with two glasses. She couldn't remember when she'd last been in such need of a drink.

'I guess you didn't catch the car's number plate?' he ventured.

She hadn't even thought to look. 'It happened so fast. I can't even tell you if it was French.'

'Left-hand drive?'

Andee thought about it. 'She was in the back. She had to reach over to tap the driver, so I'd say it was right-hand, but I – I can't be sure . . . I couldn't stop looking at her.' She finally understood now what it felt like to be a witness to something that happened so fast and unexpectedly that the memory could barely cope.

Clearly as bewildered and stunned as she was, though probably not as badly shaken, Graeme stared hard at the wine as he poured it.

'I don't know what to say,' she murmured after taking a sip. 'I don't even know what to think.' Her eyes were darting about the street, falling on random women, cars, empty windows behind lacy balconies where someone could be hiding, watching, waiting . . .

Why was she thinking that?

Because the car, the woman, had appeared out of nowhere?

How had she known where to find Andee – and at that precise time?

The questions rushing through her mind were as uncomfortable as they were impossible to answer. The woman must have been stalking her, but for how long, and why?

'How on earth did she know you were here?' Graeme demanded, echoing Andee's thoughts.

Their eyes met. His handsome face was taut with concern as he tried to make sense of what had happened.

'I'm already starting to doubt myself,' Andee confessed. 'It might not have been her.'

'So why would she ask if you remembered her?'

Andee drank more wine as though it might sort the craziness in her head.

'If she'd been a child, I mean a small child, two or three, when she disappeared,' Graeme continued, 'she'd have changed . . .'

'She knew I'd recognise her,' Andee cut across him. 'She stopped only for that, and then she drove on. Why did she drive on?'

Offering the only answer he could, Graeme said,

'Whatever the reason, she's decided she wants you to know she's alive.'

Andee's head started to spin. Almost thirty years had passed since her younger sister, Penny, had vanished from their lives. At the age of fourteen she'd left them with nothing more than a one-page letter, sent weeks after she'd gone. Everyone had long believed it to be a suicide note.

Dear Mum and Dad, I probably ought to say sorry for leaving the way I have, but maybe you already don't mind very much that I'm not around any more, so instead I'll say sorry for always being such a disappointment to you. I know Dad wanted a son when I was born, so I guess I've been a let-down to him from the start, and I don't blame him for always loving Andee the most because she's much nicer-looking than I am and likes sports, the same as him, and is really clever so it stands to reason that he'd be really proud of her. I know I shouldn't say this, but sometimes I hate her for being so much better than I am at everything. No one ever seems to notice me when she's in the room. It's like I become invisible and I know she wishes I would go away. So that's what I'm going to do.

I don't know what else to say, except sorry again. I expect you'll all be much happier without me. Please tell Andee she can have whatever she likes of mine, although I don't expect she'll want anything at all.

Your daughter, Penny

Although Penny hadn't actually said she was going to kill herself, it had certainly sounded that way.

However, because of the doubt and failure to find a body, Andee and her parents had never quite been able to give up the hope of one day finding her. It was the reason Andee had followed her father into the police force instead of going to uni, in the naïve belief that she might succeed in finding Penny where others had failed. By then Penny's disappearance had turned their father into a shadow of his former self. He'd never been able to get over it, and had died without ever knowing what had happened to his younger daughter.

Andee's mother was still alive, and Andee knew that she thought about Penny almost every day. Each case of a missing child that appeared on the news moved them both as deeply as if it were happening to them all over again. It was part of the reason Andee had finally given up her job as a detective. Every search she became involved in for a missing child drew her focus back to Penny, and dealing with other people's tragedies, finding bodies, uncovering murders, having so few happy endings, she'd come to realise, was keeping her own tragedy alive.

'What do you want to do?' Graeme asked gently, bringing her back to the present.

She looked at him, so lost for an answer that she almost laughed.

'We can lunch here, or go back to the villa,' he said.

Her gaze drifted along the street, as though lured there by the invisible Mercedes. 'The ridiculous thing is,' she said, 'I'm feeling afraid to leave in case she comes back.'

'Do you think she will?'

Andee shook her head; she had no idea.

He reached for her hand. 'Let's go,' he said. 'We need to talk this through and here's not the right place.'

An hour later they were on the vine-covered terrace of the villa they'd rented for the two months they were planning to be in Provence. It was just a few kilometres from the stunning medieval village of Gordes, surrounded by lavender fields and vineyards and partly sheltered from the warm mistral winds by the magnificent Mont Ventoux.

The villa's sprawling gardens were alive with the incessant scrape of cicadas. On the table in front of them were prawns, pâté, cheese, ham, beefy tomatoes, and succulent peaches collapsing from their skins. Graeme had opened more wine, but neither of them ate or drank. Andee's shock at seeing her sister hadn't lessened, and in fact was only increasing as disbelief, confusion and a horrible unease stole through her.

'Why did she do that?' she demanded in frustration. 'What was the point of showing herself to me, then simply driving off?'

'I still can't fathom how she even knew you were there?'

The fact that neither of them could answer these questions didn't matter, because it seemed clear that Penny *had* known; had indeed timed her return – if it could be called that – with the kind of precision that was as calculated as it was disturbing.

'What about your mother?' Graeme said, batting a

fly from the food. 'She's the only one I can think of who might have told Penny where to find you.'

Andee was already shaking her head. 'If my mother had heard from her she'd have called me straight away.' Her frown deepened as she said, 'Should I tell her about this?'

He reached for his wine glass as he thought. 'If she doesn't already know, then perhaps not yet,' he cautioned. 'Let's see if your sister approaches you again.'

Relieved that he didn't seem to doubt her, although she kept doubting herself, Andee checked her mobile. She had no idea if Penny knew her number, but she was ready to believe she might.

No messages of any sort.

To Graeme she said, 'Over the years I've imagined seeing her again in so many ways. The police bringing her to us; her turning up on the doorstep one night; randomly running into her on the street; seeing her on TV. I guess I've thought most of all about how we'd cope if her body was found. I never envisaged anything like what's just happened.' She shook her head in bewilderment. 'I keep asking myself why be so . . . *mysterious* about it? It's like she wants to tease, or even unnerve me. If that's true, she's succeeding.'

At the sound of a car passing along the shady lane beyond the villa's high stone walls, Graeme turned his head.

Andee listened, tense, half expecting the car to stop at the gates, but it didn't.

'Do you think we should contact the police?' he suggested carefully.

Her eyes went to his. 'I guess you mean the English police.'

'If she's no longer missing . . .'

'But what can we tell them? A random sighting in a foreign country of a woman who might, or might not be her.'

They both looked at his mobile as it rang.

Seeing it was Nadia, their demanding client, Andee said, 'You should take it. I'll clear these things away.'

As he clicked on and wandered through the olive trees towards the pool, Andee could hear him assuring, agreeing, advising while she continued to sit where she was, soft splashes of sunlight falling through the overhead vine to dapple her bronzing skin. The heady scents of honeysuckle and jasmine floated on the warm breeze, lending a potent sense of unreality to the strangeness she felt inside. She had no way of assessing or comparing it to anything, no idea how to articulate it, or even how to escape it. It was as though the world had carried on turning, leaving her at a standstill in the midst of a vortex that could so easily sweep her up again, though when or how, she had no way of knowing.

She tried casting her mind back to the time Penny had vanished, already knowing that the intervening years had blurred and buried the memories so deeply that their reality was all but impossible to reach. Of course they'd been different people back then, children, she sixteen, Penny fourteen. She recalled Penny as moody, insular, and erratic, but she could picture her laughing too, her funny fresh face with its freckles and rosy complexion, and her riotous giggle that had been so infectious. As a younger child she'd been mischievous and daring, they'd had fun, but Penny had frequently been sad or angry, spiteful even, and they'd fought often, the way sisters did. Andee had had no idea until the letter arrived that Penny had felt unwanted by her family, and worthless to the point that no life at all was better than a life with them.

But apparently she hadn't chosen no life at all.

Andee looked at her mobile again, and felt the need to talk to her mother, or one of her children, or even Martin, her ex, who hadn't known Penny, but had come into Andee's life soon after the disappearance. Her eyes drifted to where Graeme was seated on a lounger next to the pool. He was still talking to Nadia, the shock of the day no longer at the front of his mind. Andee didn't feel offended by that, only slightly cut off, as though this issue, this dilemma, this craziness, had her trapped in a place she could neither define nor escape.

Remember me?

The question echoed in her mind, softly spoken with a smile, and a kind of knowing that had seemed, she thought now, almost malicious. Maybe she was making that up. The eyes were the same blue-green as Andee's, their shape more oval than almond. Her face had barely altered, only aged, with prominent cheekbones and a determined jaw that might have appeared masculine were it not for the rosebud mouth and girlishly upturned nose. Her hair had been razored around the neck, like a boy's, with a thick blonde sweep on top that fell neatly over one eye. It wasn't the colour she'd been born with, but the change hadn't disguised her at all. The sighting had lasted for no more than a few seconds, yet Andee could still see her as clearly as if she were in front of her now.

Her sister was alive.

It was almost impossible to make herself believe it. She had no idea where Penny was, or even *who* she was now. She felt a desperate need to do something, but what? In the end, she had to accept that all she could do was wait and wonder if Penny was planning to show herself again.

Andee's mother rang just after eight that evening, while Andee and Graeme were in the kitchen listening to jazz on the radio and trying to focus on the plans for Nadia's villa.

As soon as she saw it was her mother, Andee's sixth sense kicked in with alarm and caution. She knew what the call was going to be about, but she kept her tone cheerful just in case she was wrong. 'Hi, how are you?' she asked.

With no preamble her mother said, 'I hope you're sitting down, because I've just had a call from . . . from someone who sounded just like you. She said . . . she said she was Penny. Can you believe that? I don't know whether to believe it. I thought it was you, but I know you'd never play such a horrible trick.'

Feeling for how shaken her mother clearly was, Andee held the phone so Graeme could hear and asked what else Penny had said.

'You're not sounding shocked,' Maureen accused, and Andee could almost see the uncertainty, perhaps even fear, clouding her mother's gentle blue eyes.

'I'll explain in a minute,' Andee told her. 'Just tell me what else she said.'

'She wants to see me. Oh dear God, do you think it's really her?'

Instead of answering, Andee said, 'Did she say where or when she wants to see you?'

'She's going to call again in the next few days to set up a time to come to the house.'

Surprised by that, Andee said, 'Does she know where you live?' Her parents had moved from Chiswick – Penny's childhood home – to Kesterly-on-Sea almost twenty-five years ago.

'I didn't ask. It all happened so fast. I could hardly believe I was having the conversation . . . Andee, I feel . . . I don't know how I feel, but you're not helping, because I'm sure you're holding something back from me.'

There was no point in lying. 'I saw her today, in L'Isle-sur-la-Sorgue,' Andee told her. 'Not to speak to, there wasn't time, she drove off as soon she was sure I'd recognised her.'

Maureen was silent, and Andee wished with all her heart that she could be with her mother now. She might be unflappable most of the time, able to deal with most things life threw at her, but this was too much for her to handle alone. 'What's happening?' Maureen asked shakily. 'I don't understand.'

'I don't either,' Andee responded. 'All I can tell you is that she pulled up in front of me, asked if I remembered her, and as soon as she was certain I did she drove off.'

'But . . . I don't . . . Why would she do that?'

Having no answer, Andee asked instead, 'Did she call your mobile or the house phone?'

'The house phone, and yes I rang 1471, but the caller's number had been withheld.'

Andee looked at the note Graeme had passed her and asked her mother the question. 'Have you told anyone else about the call?'

'No. I rang you straight away. If you're sure it's her . . . I mean . . . Do you think I should contact the police?'

Andee's eyes returned to Graeme's as she said, 'Probably, but we won't do it yet. We don't know anything for certain, so let's see what happens.' She grimaced regretfully at Graeme as she added, 'I'm coming back.'

'It's OK,' he mouthed.

Maureen was saying, 'I must admit, I'll feel happier if you're here when she comes. If she comes. Do you think she will? Are we even having this conversation?'

'It'll be OK,' Andee tried to reassure her. 'If you're feeling nervous you should go and stay with Carol until I get there.' Carol was Maureen's closest friend and Andee's 'ex' mother-in-law.

'Carol and the family are in Spain,' Maureen reminded her.

And Graeme's sisters Rowzee and Pamela, also good friends of Maureen's, were driving a camper van around Europe with Pamela's boyfriend, Bill, attempting to keep them on the road and out of trouble. 'Blake and Jenny must be around?' Andee queried, referring to Graeme's business partner and his wife, who had recently become Maureen's neighbours.

'Yes they are,' Maureen confirmed, 'but I don't want to bother them. I'll be fine. I mean, I can't imagine she intends us any harm, can you?'

'No, of course not. Why would you say that?'

Maureen hesitated. 'I don't know,' she murmured. 'I suppose it's the way . . . I keep thinking . . .'

'Thinking of what?' Andee pressed.

'Nothing. I guess I'm just . . . all shaken up. Finding it hard to get my head round things.'

Feeling the need to be with her, Andee said, 'I'll book myself on a flight into Bristol tomorrow. Can you meet me at the airport?'

'Of course. Just let me know what time to be there.'

After ringing off Andee turned into Graeme's embrace and rested her head on his shoulder. 'I'm sorry,' she whispered, 'but if my sister has come back . . .'

'There's nothing to be sorry about,' he assured her. 'You should be with your mother, and I can manage here – at least in a business sense.'

Andee pulled back to look at him, and felt the pleasure of being with him trying to insist that she stay. 'We were having such a good time,' she murmured.

With the dryness she loved he said, 'I'm taking it we will again.'

She looked at him, feeling a reassuring sense of closeness surrounding them. Though they'd known one another for several years, it was only in the last few months that their relationship had developed into the intimate and easy connection that made it so pleasurable for them to spend time together. During the past week, since arriving in Provence, they'd begun to explore the idea of her moving into his elegant town house in Kesterly-on-Sea when they returned home. It was something they both wanted, and neither of them saw any reason why it wouldn't work, given how much time she was already spending there.

Andee began to wonder if this sudden surprise from Penny might have an effect on that. Though she couldn't immediately see how, she realised Graeme could be asking himself the same question. Whatever was going through his mind, she knew he was concerned on her behalf about this sudden shock life had thrown her. He was a man of genuine compassion and sensitivity, combined with easy humour and the kind of generosity that made her heart swell with admiration when she saw his kindness towards those needing help. He could be fierce too, and very determined, especially in business, and he made a convincing show of tolerating no nonsense from his two much older sisters, who completely adored him, or from his sons. In their twenties, and independent as they liked to consider themselves, they rarely did anything without seeking their father's approval first.

Smiling, she reached for the wine and refilled their glasses. 'If this is really happening,' she said, 'then it's going to turn the world upside down. How can it not? Someone walks back into your life after almost three decades . . . And not just someone . . .' She sighed as she tried to gather some sense from the confusion. 'I wonder what she's like now. I mean what sort of person she is, and where she's been all this time.'

'You'll soon be able to ask her.'

Andee's eyes narrowed as she pictured the woman she'd seen earlier. 'She didn't look like someone who'd been taken from her family against her will; shut away, imprisoned, enslaved for years on end,' she said. 'That's what usually happens when someone, especially at the age she was back then, disappears without trace. They're taken and held captive, and only a few manage to escape alive.'

'Well she's alive, we know that much.'

Andee nodded. 'And presumably on her way to the UK, if she's planning to see my mother in the next few days.'

Chapter Two

By the time Maureen collected Andee from the airport the following afternoon she'd lived through the shock and strangely suppressed elation of hearing from her younger daughter for a second time.

'Apparently her name's Michelle now,' she informed Andee as they drove out to the A38. 'Michelle Cross. I feel I should know the name, but I can't think from where.'

It rang a vague bell for Andee too. She turned to her mother, not quite knowing what to say.

Maureen's eyes stayed on the road ahead. She looked as she always did, calm, composed, a supremely elegant woman who wore her seventy plus years as though they were a mere sixty. Her expression was hard to read, but Andee knew that behind the bright, watchful eyes and gently lined complexion her mother was in turmoil. How could she not be, considering the enormity of what was – or could be – happening?

'What else did she say?' Andee asked.

'She'd like to come on Thursday at three if it's convenient for us.'

'Us?' Andee echoed. 'Did you tell her I was going to be there?'

'No. I decided she presumed you would be.'

'Even though she knew I was in France?'

Maureen speeded up to overtake a tractor. 'I've no idea how to answer that,' she said. 'I only know I never imagined it happening like this.' Andee didn't miss the tremor in her voice, and noticed her hands tightening on the wheel. 'The truth is, I'd stopped imagining it happening at all,' Maureen admitted, wretchedly. 'I thought, if we ever saw her again . . . I thought it would be a body.'

Andee wondered how long ago they'd started thinking that way. But no matter how many years had passed, the Lawrences' hope of Penny's safe and happy return had never entirely gone away.

Was the joy of that hope burning again now, and Andee was failing to feel it? Naturally she wanted to see her sister, more than anything, but whoever she was now, Penny, Michelle, she was going to be a stranger. Her adult years weren't entwined with her family's; they were all hers, untouched by the Lawrences. She had a story, a history completely separate from the world she'd been born into. It was possible she had her own family now. Two, three or more children as old, maybe even older than Andee's. What about the father of her children, if they existed?

Considering how long it had been there were likely to be many stories.

Everyone's lives were like that, going from one major event, to a smaller maybe happier time, only for disaster or triumph to strike again. The years were like chapters, some long, some short, with new characters and old drawn into the dramas, and each tale superseding the last.

'I wonder if she knows that Daddy's dead?' Maureen said quietly.

Andee had been thinking about her father throughout the journey here, wishing with all her heart that he was still with them, that the trauma of losing a daughter hadn't sent him to an early grave. He'd always been their rock, the one they'd turned to in a time of crisis. There was nothing he couldn't do or fix, nothing he didn't understand, no one who wasn't a little in awe of him. As a detective chief superintendent with the Metropolitan Police he'd commanded a great deal of respect, but at the same time he'd been known for his fairness and compassion. He had been seen as a pillar of the community, until his younger daughter had disappeared and the rock had eventually began to crumble under the weight of helplessness and grief, until finally it had been eroded completely.

How was Penny going to feel when she found out?

Maybe she already knew.

It wasn't a good feeling to think of her sister watching them from the shadows, knowing what was happening to them yet never showing herself. It surely hadn't been like that? More likely someone had told her – taunted her even – with details of what her family was doing, holidays she could never enjoy, a father she'd never see again, a new home she'd never get to know . . . Except she had known the Kesterly home, because it had belonged to their grandparents before their parents had taken it on. It had been where she and Andee had often spent their summer breaks when they were small.

'Does she want us to call her Michelle?' Andee ventured.

'I'm not sure.'

'Do you think you'll be able to?'

Maureen hesitated. 'I guess it'll depend . . . I mean, after all this time, if she feels like a stranger then perhaps calling her Michelle won't be so hard.'

Andee regarded her mother carefully. 'You're managing to sound very philosophical,' she commented warily, 'but I know you.'

Maureen cast her a glance. 'I'm not sure how else to be,' she confessed. 'If I'm truthful I keep thinking it's going to turn out to be a hoax, or that I'll wake up in a minute and discover it's a dream. It can't be her, surely.'

It was how Andee felt, and yet here she was, back from France having already seen her sister, even if for a mere few seconds. It had been long enough for her to know.

After a while, Maureen said, 'Did Graeme mind you leaving?'

'He understood that I needed to be here.'

Maureen reached for her hand. 'Thank you for coming. I don't mind admitting I'd be finding it very difficult if I was on my own.'

Feeling a surge of love for her mother, and a deep sense of protectiveness, Andee lifted their joined hands to her cheek. They'd always been close, and should anyone ask her to name her best friend she knew her answer would probably be Maureen.

Second in line would be Rowzee, Graeme's older sister, who had sweetness, vitality, mischief and miracles all over her. She and her merry little dance with terminal cancer were a source of endless fascination for the medical profession, and sparked up so many emotions for those who loved her that the easiest refuge was in denial. It wasn't happening, Rowzee wasn't going to die, so now let's get on with life.

How blessed Graeme was in his sisters, whose far greater age had made them more like mothers while he was growing up; now they were getting to be like troublesome teenagers.

As though reading her mind, Maureen said, 'Do you know when Rowzee and Pamela are due home?'

'Not for a while yet,' Andee answered, checking her mobile as a text came through. It was Graeme wanting to know if she'd landed safely.

After messaging him back, Andee said, 'Have you told anyone about this since we spoke yesterday?'

Maureen shook her head. 'I know this is going to sound odd, but it's like I'm afraid to.'

Andee sort of understood.

'I'm afraid no one will believe me,' Maureen expanded. 'They'll think I'm getting delusional in my old age. I've even wondered it myself.'

Andee smiled.

'What does Graeme say?'

'He's as shocked and mystified by it as we are. He asked me to tell you that if you're worried about anything and you feel I'm not listening or responding appropriately, you're to call him any time of the day or night.'

Maureen's eyes lightened with humour. 'Did he really say that?'

'His exact words; give or take.'

'Then he knows you well.'

Andee regarded her sardonically. 'Because I'm given to responding inappropriately?'

'If we're putting it politely,' her mother countered.

Laughing, Andee checked her mobile again and seeing it was her daughter Alayna on the line, she quickly clicked on.

'Hey Mum!' Alayna cried in her sing-songy, I'm-a-supercool-student way. 'I just saw that a couple of the *Strictly* dancers are appearing at the Hippodrome, here in Bristol, at Christmas so I thought I'd get some tickets for Grandma's birthday treat. I'm checking with you first though to make sure you haven't already done it.'

'I haven't,' Andee confirmed.

'OK, so you'll come too, and drive her? We know she's not keen on driving at night. I can check out some Airbnb places for you, if you like. It'd be great if you stayed over so we can go for dinner and breakfast and do other stuff, like shopping so I can spend all your money.'

Wryly, Andee said, 'I'm fine thanks my darling. I hope you are too.'

'Yeah, dead cool, and you're very funny. How's Provence?'

'Actually, I'm in England.'

'I thought it wasn't a French ringtone. So why are

you back already? Weren't you supposed to be going for two months? Oh my God, don't tell me you've broken up with Graeme. I've only just got used to you being with him. Are you very upset?'

Rolling her eyes, Andee said, 'Graeme and I are still together, but there's some business I have to attend to back here, so Grandma just came to pick me up from the airport.'

'Are you saying you guys were in Bristol and you didn't come to see me? How am I supposed to get over that?'

'We assumed you'd be busy.'

'You should have rung, just in case. Anyway, don't mention the tickets if Grandma's there because I want it to be a surprise.'

'It's a lovely idea, and yes to everything.'

'You are so totally amazing, did I ever tell you that?'

'Not often enough.'

With a splutter of laughter, Alayna said, 'So what business have you got back here? Please don't tell me someone else has gone missing. You're supposed to have left the police because you didn't want to get involved in those searches any more, but everyone still keeps coming to you.'

Having already decided that now wasn't the time to tell Alayna what had really brought her back, Andee made up something about a client of Graeme's needing some special attention. She could always be truthful later, when she had a clearer idea of how things were going to progress with Penny. Michelle.

'OK, well if anyone's good at special attention it's

Grandma, so you should take her with you. Have you spoken to Luke, our man in Africa, lately?'

'Not since last weekend. Have you?'

'No, but he messaged me yesterday to say they had a run-in with poachers the night before last. Pretty scary stuff, if you ask me, but you know what he's like, I bet he loved it.'

Knowing for sure that her son was enjoying every minute of his time on a South African game reserve, Andee said, 'Did he say if the baby rhino's been born yet?'

'No, which means it hasn't or he'd have sent pictures. Dad's planning to go out there, did he tell you? We could go too if you felt like it?'

'I thought you were working all summer to earn some money.'

'Yep, I am totally doing that. Anyway, have to run, I'm already late for my next lecture. Only two weeks to go and summer officially starts. Yay! Love to Grandma, and to you. Kisses,' and she was gone.

'She makes me feel exhausted just to hear her jabbering,' Maureen commented, as they joined the M5. 'Is she all right?'

'I think we can rest easy.'

'And Luke? Has she heard from him?'

Deciding not to mention the poachers, Andee said, 'Apparently Martin's planning to go out there.'

'He's in Spain with his mother.'

'For now, but he was always intending to fly out and see Luke, so why don't you go and join Carol when he's gone?'

Maureen glanced at her. 'Are you trying to get rid of me?' she challenged.

'No, but I know you. You really wanted to go, but ended up deciding to stay behind in case one of the children changed their plans, so someone would be at home for them. They're twenty-one and nineteen, Mum. You don't have to arrange your life around them.'

'I know you're right, but it feels wrong for none of us to be in Kesterly. Anyway, given what's happening, it's a good job I did stay at home.'

Thinking again of Penny and how easy it would be for her to take over their mother's life from here on, maybe even Andee's too, Andee attempted to put herself in Maureen's shoes. It was one thing losing a sister, and God knew it had been bad, but losing a daughter . . . How would she feel if Alayna vanished without a trace and suddenly turned up so many years later? It would make her feel sick with shock and apprehension, riven with curiosity of course, and no doubt insanely relieved and excited; it might also cripple her with guilt. She'd feel ashamed of having moved on without her, and afraid of somehow letting her down again; or of not being good enough; of doing and saying the wrong things; of being unable to make things up to her.

Andee felt all these things herself, was becoming more stressed by them as time ticked on, so she could only guess at how much worse it was for her mother.

'I was wondering,' Andee said, when finally they approached Kesterly seafront where early summer visitors were braving a feisty downpour, 'if I ought to have a chat with Gould about things.'

As Maureen slowed behind the tourist train Andee sensed her tension. 'You mean your old boss, Detective Inspector Gould?' Maureen said evenly. 'I'm not sure either of us is ready for that yet, are we?'

'It would be off the record,' Andee assured her.

Maureen's gaze drifted across The Promenade to where spirited waves were flinging themselves against the bay's flanking rocks. Andee suspected she was thinking about all the press attention that was likely to erupt once the news was out. Her mother had lived through it all those years ago, and it had come close to giving her a breakdown. She wouldn't want to go through it again. 'He doesn't know anything about the case,' Maureen said. 'It wasn't handled here, besides he's far too young. He wouldn't even have been in the force at the time she disappeared.'

'I realise that, but he's a friend, someone who can advise us if we need it. Maybe advise Penny too.'

Maureen's face was growing paler. 'I think we should wait and find out from Penny what she wants to happen,' she replied.

Deciding not to press it, since she wasn't sure herself of the best course to take, Andee said no more as her mother drove them up on to the northerly headland and along the steep, winding roads towards home.

The random sprawl of quaint grey stone cottages brightened by flower baskets and rose-covered porches, along with the handful of newer red-brick bungalows that made up the residences of Bourne Hollow, were gleaming wetly in a sudden burst of sunshine as

Maureen and Andee drove into the hamlet. At its heart was a neatly mowed patch of green shaped vaguely like a kite with a children's play area and sandpit at one end, several carefully tended (by Maureen) flower beds at the other, and half a dozen or more memorial benches parked invitingly around the edges. The Smugglers' Arms, a centuries-old whitewashed inn, was on the north side of the hamlet with a garden full of picnic tables and parasols spilling out on to the street, while the Bourne Hollow convenience store-cum-café and newly opened gift shop nestled together on the western tip. The old smugglers' tunnels that laced through the heart of the headland had mostly been filled in by now, but two were still offering guided tours for those bold enough to make the descent – and confront the ghosts.

The Lawrence family home, Briar Lodge, rambled sedately along the eastern end of the green with tall brick chimneys at each end, several slate roofs at different levels and a low stone wall to mark the garden boundary. It had started life back in the eighteen hundreds as a hunting retreat for a wealthy merchant from Bristol, but these days, with its Victorian-style extensions and large sash windows, it was a much lighter, more homely version of its original incarnation.

After pulling up behind Andee's car in the drive at the side of the house Maureen continued to sit at the wheel, holding on to it as though unwilling to let go.

'Are you OK?' Andee asked gently.

Maureen nodded stiffly. 'I think so . . . I just . . .'

'Take a moment,' Andee advised. 'We don't have to rush anywhere.'

Maureen inhaled deeply and slowly let the breath go. 'It's going to be all right,' she whispered to herself.

Andee stroked the back of her mother's neck. 'Of course it is,' she assured her.

Maureen started to nod without seeming to realise she was doing it. She gave a slight twitch and put a hand to her head. 'I wish Daddy was here,' she said.

Andee did too, but he wasn't. Trying to be upbeat, she said, 'We have each other, and think what it's going to be like for Penny seeing us after all these years.'

Maureen's face was bleak and colourless as she turned to Andee. 'You're right,' she replied. 'It's going to be much harder for her.'

Though Andee had conflicting thoughts about that, all she said was, 'Let's go and make some tea.'

Maureen led the way through a side door into the large kitchen-cum-sitting room that never failed to exude the irresistible cosiness that made everyone, family and visitors alike, reluctant to leave.

To Andee the place seemed hauntingly empty as they went about putting on the kettle and taking out mugs. It was as though, she thought, something indefinable had shifted. The house no longer seemed entirely theirs, as if it was preparing for new chapters in its existence, and she supposed it was.

'I should feel ecstatic,' Maureen suddenly declared. 'I think I do. Somewhere inside me I'm sure I do, but I'm so nervous, Andee. Why did she want us to think she was dead? The note she sent . . . We all thought . . .'

'We all thought the same,' Andee comforted her, 'but in our hearts, with there never being a body . . .'

'We never gave up hope of this day. But now it's here . . . Do you think someone forced her to write the note?'

'It's possible. Even likely, now that we know she's alive.'

'What if she hates us for not being able to find her? What am I . . . ?'

'Mum, stop,' Andee interrupted gently. 'She's not going to hate us . . .'

'But where has she been all this time? What's been happening to her? How did she find us? Tell me, how did she look?'

'She looked like a normal woman in her early forties. There was nothing to set her apart.' Andee tried to sound reassuring.

Maureen clearly needed more.

'She was quite stylish, well groomed,' Andee expanded. 'Her hair is blonde now, but her features are just the same, only older.'

'And her eyes?'

'The same colour as mine.'

'Does she still have freckles?'

'I don't think so.'

'What sort of car was she in?'

'A silver Mercedes which was being driven by somebody else. I've no idea who because I didn't see them.'

'I don't understand why she just drove off.'

Andee shook her head. 'Nor do I, but I expect she'll explain when we see her.' Though she didn't feel exactly confident of that, she wasn't going to say so to her mother. The last thing Maureen needed now was to try and cope with her elder daughter's misgivings.

'The truth is,' Andee said to Graeme later on the phone while her mother was having a lie-down, 'I've got no idea how I feel about seeing her again, because it changes by the minute.'

'It would when you've no way of knowing what to expect,' he replied.

'It's more than thirty years since your father died,' she ran on, 'so imagine how you'd feel if you suddenly found out he was still alive and wanted to see you.'

'I've tried putting myself in that very place,' Graeme admitted, 'and I know I'd be as thrown and as anxious as you are, excited too, of course, because he was a great guy. But pretending to be dead, deliberately removing himself from our lives, which is what it would mean in his case . . . I don't know if I could forgive that. But if we're looking at it that way, we're suggesting your sister was instrumental in her own disappearance. Do you think that could be the case?'

'No, no, of course not. She was only fourteen and she was depressed at the time, something we should have paid more attention to. But that doesn't explain why she's waited all these years to come back to us now.'

'Teenagers and depression can be a lethal combination, that's for sure. Have you thought any more about contacting the police?'

'My mother thinks we should wait to find out what Penny wants to do. Incidentally, she calls herself Michelle now. Michelle Cross.'

'And you've already Googled the name?'

'Mainly because I thought I recognised it, but no one came up to jog my memory, nor was there anyone who could conceivably be her. I might try again later, or I might just wait until she comes.'

'The day after tomorrow?'

'It's going to feel like an eternity, and heaven only knows what I'll do with my mother for all that time. We've no way of contacting her to ask if it can be sooner, so looks like we have to do it her way, and you can probably imagine how I feel about having someone else pulling my strings.'

Drily, he said, 'I can, but you have to consider that this probably isn't easy for her either.'

Hearing a repeat of her own words, Andee found herself relaxing for a moment, but was soon bristling again. 'It was easy enough for her to approach me in L'Isle-sur-la-Sorgue and ask if I remembered her,' she reminded him.

'OK, point taken. So how *are* you going to fill the time between now and when she comes?'

Hearing her mother on the stairs, Andee said, 'I'm sure we'll think of something. Tell me now, how are things going your end?'

Taking his cue, he said, 'Not bad. I've managed to pin the builder down at last. He's meeting me at Nadia's place on Friday at ten. I'll be there for most of tomorrow and Thursday with the cornice restorers and roofers. When you have a minute can you text or email me the details of the mirror chap you found on Avenue des Quatre Otages?'

'Actually, I left his card in a tray by the front door so you should have it.'

'Andee,' Maureen said quietly.

Andee turned to find her mother staring down at her mobile. 'I have to go,' she told Graeme. 'I'll call you later,' and taking her mother's phone she read the text that had clearly shaken Maureen quite badly.

Hi Mum, hope you're well. Really looking forward to seeing you. Do you remember Smoky, the kitten? He was so sweet, wasn't he? I wonder what happened to him? So many memories, lots to talk about, can't wait to hear all your news. Andee's too. Love Michelle.

Andee looked at her mother. 'When did it arrive?' she asked.

'A few moments ago. The jingle woke me.'

Andee went through to the sender's number, stored it and returned to the message. 'Smoky the kitten?' she asked her mother.

'I'd forgotten all about him,' Maureen replied. 'We gave him to Penny for her birthday one year, do you remember? She must have been eight or nine. He disappeared a few weeks later . . .' Her voice trailed off as her eyes stared glassily into the past.

'Mum?' Andee prompted gently.

Maureen looked at her.

'Are you all right?' Andee asked.

'We searched and searched,' Maureen told her. 'In the end we decided someone must have taken him.'

Andee kind of remembered, and frowned as she looked at the message again. Why bring it up now? 'She hasn't mentioned wanting to hear Daddy's news,' she observed.

'So maybe she knows he's gone.'

Experiencing a sudden surge of frustration, Andee went to the fridge and took out a bottle of wine.

'A large one for me,' Maureen said, sinking down at the table.

'How did she get your mobile number?' Andee demanded. 'You say she called the house phone before.'

Maureen shook her head as Andee passed her a glass and sat down too.

Picking up her mother's mobile again Andee tried calling the number, and wasn't surprised to find herself greeted by an announcement stating the mailbox was full and unable to take any more messages. She was faintly relieved, since she hadn't considered what she was going to say. Returning to the text she tapped in a reply, speaking the words aloud. *I'm looking forward to seeing you too. Where are you staying?*

Putting the phone down between them, Andee sipped her wine and stared at the mobile as they waited for a response.

Long minutes ticked silently by.

'She's not going to answer,' Maureen predicted.

Andee messaged again. *Do you have my address? Shall I send it to you?*

Still no reply.

'Maybe she's turned her phone off,' Maureen ventured, 'or she's in a bad reception area.'

Since either was possible, Andee put the phone aside and refilled their glasses. 'Even though she looked the same,' she said, 'apart from the hair, I'm still finding it hard to connect the woman I saw in France with my timid little sister.'

'She wasn't timid,' Maureen said emphatically.

Andee was surprised by this. It was how she remembered Penny, for the most part, but maybe that was because she'd shut out everything else. Memory often did that to a missing or dead person; it rubbed away the faults and turned qualities into almost saintly distinctions.

'You're both different people now,' Maureen reminded her.

While conceding the point, Andee said, 'The woman I saw seemed very confident, very sure of herself. That wasn't Penny.'

Maureen stared into her glass as she sank into her own thoughts, leaving Andee to wonder what they were, if she would even share them. She was about to ask when Maureen said, 'I sometimes wonder how well you knew her.'

Taken aback and slightly affronted, Andee waited for her mother to continue, but Maureen only sighed and drank more wine.

Andee found herself remembering the part of Penny's letter that had haunted her with the harshest of guilt for all these years. *I know I shouldn't say this, but sometimes I hate her for being so much better than I am at everything. No one ever seems to notice me when she's in the room. It's like I become invisible and I know she wishes I would go away. So that's what I'm going to do.*

Which meant that whatever had happened to Penny had been Andee's fault, or so she'd believed for most of her life.

Perhaps her mother did too.

Did she still believe it?

'Why do you think I didn't know her?' Andee asked guardedly.

Maureen shook her head slowly. It was a while before she said, 'You were just very different.' *Not close the way sisters should be; you were never very interested in her.* Though Maureen didn't say the words Andee could hear them, and felt undone by how wretched, even resentful they made her feel.

'We had so little in common,' she said. 'I loved sports, she hated them; I didn't have much of a temper, hers was terrible; she laughed at things that weren't funny, at least not to me, and we were young. We had different friends, different interests. There was nothing unusual about that.' She wished she didn't sound so defensive.

'No, of course not,' Maureen agreed.

'Then what are you saying?'

Maureen sighed. 'I'm not sure,' she replied. 'I guess, her being in touch is making me remember a lot of things I haven't thought about in years. It must be happening for you too.'

Of course it was; however, the moody sister she'd loved and yelled at, played with and rejected, cuddled and slapped, was impossible to connect with the woman she'd seen in France. The fourteen-year-old girl had gone for ever, so there was no point thinking about who she'd been then. It was who Penny was now that mattered, and how they were going to go forward once she was back in their lives.

Chapter Three

The following morning, after speaking for some time with Graeme on the phone, Andee arrived downstairs to find a note from her mother saying she'd gone to her yoga class.

Why don't you meet me at the Seafront Café for coffee at eleven? she'd added in a PS. *Text to let me know. I'm on library duty between twelve and three.*

Relieved that Maureen was keeping busy, Andee messaged to say she'd be at the café, and realising she should find something to do as well she rang Blake, Graeme's business partner, to find out if he needed any help at the shop.

'How soon can you get here?' Blake replied eagerly. 'Jenny's due back around eleven, but I need to go out now to make a delivery I promised yesterday.'

'I'm on my way,' she assured him, and retrieving her keys from the dresser drawer, she grabbed an apple from the fruit bowl and locked up behind her.

To her surprise, as she started to reverse out of the drive she found a motorcyclist blocking the way. Giving a brief toot on the horn to alert him to her need to exit she watched him in the rear-view mirror, certain he'd move out of the way, but he didn't.

Assuming he hadn't heard her through his helmet she tooted more firmly, but all he did was rev his engine and stay put.

Wondering what his problem was, she was about to get out of the car when a group of hikers strolled out of nearby Sheep Lane and he suddenly took off around the green.

A few minutes later Andee was driving along the narrow country road that snaked and dipped across the headland towards the edge of town, when she realised the motorcyclist was behind her. She couldn't be sure if he was purposely following her, but she had a feeling he was. Then he was so close that she was afraid to brake in case he went into the back of her. She speeded up and only just managed to swerve into a passing space as another car came around a bend towards her.

Once the other car had gone she waited for the motorcyclist to overtake, but he simply sat on her tail apparently waiting for her to move first. She stayed where she was, watching him in the wing mirror, realising he was trying to intimidate her. That she couldn't see his face through the black visor of his helmet was as annoying to her as the fact that he was too close for her to get his registration number.

Making sure her doors were locked, she lowered the driver's window and waved him on.

He stayed where he was, and revved aggressively.

Andee's police instinct kicked in and, suspecting

that this might be a mugging, she put her car into reverse and waited for him to spot the lights. Though he must have seen them he still didn't move, so pressing a foot on the accelerator she began edging back. Only when her bumper connected with the front wheel of his bike did he suddenly swerve out into the road and race past with a deafening roar.

He might have thought he was too fast for her to get the number, but if he had, he was wrong.

After entering it into her phone she drove on, half expecting to find him waiting around the next bend, but ten minutes later she was driving into town still apparently free of him.

As soon as she was parked she rang Barry Britten at Kesterly police station. Since ending her days as a detective sergeant with the Dean Valley force she'd stayed in regular contact with her former colleagues, mainly thanks to the freelance investigations she'd been persuaded into by Helen Hall, one of the town's more prominent lawyers. Whether her old boss, DI Terence Gould, had instructed his team to help her where they could, or whether they were just happy to anyway, she had no idea. She guessed the former, since Gould was regularly on her case to come back into the fold.

That certainly wasn't a part of her plan these days. She was very happy working with Graeme – she'd even completed a six-week Introduction to Interior Design course at the local college, and was intending to return for further instruction after the summer break. No, searching for missing people, especially children, was definitely behind her.

What lay ahead, with her sister coming back, was another matter altogether.

After giving Barry the motorcycle's details, she walked through the busy arcade towards the cobbled square where Graeme's antiques shop was located. The thought of Penny and what might happen in the next few days was making her feel very strange inside, and now this business with the motorcycle was throwing her off even more.

She didn't really think the motorcyclist was anything to do with her sister, but for a moment during their standoff the suspicion of a connection had been there. Even now the thought was wheedling its way around her normally trusty common sense, as though trying to insist there was no such thing as coincidence, when she knew very well that there was.

But why on earth would Penny, or anyone else come to that, send a motorcyclist to try and intimidate her? It was ludicrous even to think it.

Taking out her phone as it rang, she saw it was Barry and clicked on.

'The bike was stolen,' he told her. 'We've had a spate of thefts in the area. Kids mostly. They use them to mug people stupid enough to get out of their cars to find out what's going on.'

Since that had been her first suspicion Andee relaxed, and after thanking Barry she rang off, chiding herself for the uncharacteristic paranoia that had attributed the incident to her sister. Just because Penny had made contact the way she had in France, and was behaving oddly over texts and phone calls, didn't mean the motorbike had anything to do with her. Penny might be a stranger, but she wouldn't be out to intimidate Andee in that way.

Maureen was sitting on a bench in the changing rooms of the Downley leisure centre, only distantly aware of the thump and whirr of the spinning class going on in the studio next door. Her combined yoga and Pilates session had started several minutes ago, but she had yet to change into her leotard and leggings, or even open her locker.

She was staring blindly towards the mirrors and dryers, none in use at the moment, no one there to distract her from seeing back through the years to their lives in Chiswick, before Penny had vanished. And as the stress and anxiety of those times emerged from the past, the despair, the love and confusion followed by horror and grief began to feel as real now as they had been then.

Do you remember Smoky, the kitten? He was so sweet, wasn't he?

Why had Penny brought him up now, and in the way she had? Yes, Maureen remembered him. How could she ever forget?

The questions, the sickening shock of what had happened to the kitten were all over her, pushing any sense of today aside. She could see the dear little creature as clear as day, curling up on Andee's bed, and Penny becoming incensed by the disloyalty, even though Andee hadn't been there.

'He's not hers, he's mine,' she'd shrieked, snatching him up.

Startled and frightened, the kitten had scratched her, and Maureen had never forgotten the look that had come into Penny's eyes.

Remembering that time, Maureen felt her throat turn dry.

Yesterday, having wondered how well Andee had known her sister, Maureen had to admit that there were times she'd doubted how well she herself had known Penny. She'd loved her, of course, with all her heart; there had never been any doubt about that, at least not in her mind, but in Penny's . . . Had she ever really known what was going on in Penny's mind? One day she would be like any other girl her age, the next she could be sulky and withdrawn, defensive or aggressive, even violent.

She and Andee had argued a lot, even fought physically at times. Andee had always been the first to make up, while Penny, appearing quick to forgive, had been unable to hide, at least from Maureen, the way she was still brooding inside. She'd been full of contradictions and self-doubt – and consumed by a longing to be more like her sister. She'd adored Andee, while resenting her deeply. As Andee had progressed through her teens she had become increasingly irritated by Penny's sulks and outbursts. She'd accuse her of self-pity, and tell her to get a life or she'd never have any friends.

Penny hadn't always been without friends, though it was true she'd never managed to keep them for long, even when she was small. However, Maureen could remember pre-teen sleepovers at their house when she'd hear Penny giggling along with the others, sharing secrets, trying out make-up and creeping downstairs to raid the fridge for a midnight feast. She'd seemed happy and carefree during those times, just like any other young girl her age. Maureen had listened to them chattering away about pop bands and boys and who they were going to marry when they were older. Penny's crush had usually been on someone Andee was interested in, another source of irritation for Andee that had often ended in tears.

Penny was thirteen the first time she'd taken off. She'd said she was going to stay with a new girl at school called Madeleine, but it had turned out that Madeleine didn't exist and for three days no one knew where Penny was. Maureen still didn't know for certain where she'd been during that time, but she was sure her husband, David, had found out. He'd brought Penny home and taken her into his study for a very serious talking-to. Penny had come out swollen-eyed, angry and determined not to be contrite. She'd apologised to her mother, clearly because she'd been told to, and no one had referred to it again until the next time it happened.

'You have to tell me where she's going,' Maureen had shouted at David after he'd brought Penny home again.

'The least said soonest mended,' he snapped. 'She's grounded for the next month and all privileges are to be taken away.'

Penny had been furious with her father, but he'd remained unmoved even after she'd calmed down and tried to apologise.

'She's crying out for attention,' Maureen had told him, 'can't you see that?'

'Well she won't get it if she runs away,' he pointed out. 'Please don't try to take her side, Maureen. I can assure you I'm not being unreasonable, and she knows it.'

Neither Andee's nor Maureen's efforts to persuade Penny to tell them where she'd been had ever worked. Penny remained as close-lipped about it as her father, while her eyes seemed to glitter with the power of knowing something they didn't. That was until the sense of triumph finally turned to tears, and a horrible, black depression swallowed her into a pit of mumbling despair.

'Maureen? Are you all right?'

Startled, Maureen looked up to find a younger, sweet-faced woman stooping over her, her gentle blue eyes showing concern. 'Sorry,' Maureen muttered, collecting up her bag. 'Miles away.'

'You look pale,' the woman persisted. 'Can I get you something?'

'No, no really, I'm fine.' She knew this woman, but what was her name? She looked around, and found herself unable to connect with where she was.

'Maureen? What is it?'

Maureen shook her head. 'I should go,' she said, and leaving the woman staring worriedly after her she rushed outside to find her car.

'Another coffee while you wait?'

Andee glanced at her watch and looked up at Fliss, the owner of the Seafront Café, whom she'd known for years and liked a lot. 'I guess I could,' she replied. 'I don't know what's keeping her. She definitely said eleven and it's half past already.'

'You've tried calling, obviously?'

'And left several messages. It's not like her to be late.'

'Well, the road's up over by the leisure centre, so she could be stuck in traffic.'

Andee smiled gratefully and pushed her mug across the table. 'Better make it decaff this time,' she said, realising that her appetite for a biscotti or even a muffin had been swallowed up by concern.

Considering how uptight and distracted her mother was feeling right now, the failure to turn up, or message to say she was on her way, was worrying Andee more and more as the minutes ticked by.

She rang Graeme, needing to talk to someone, but she was pushed through to voicemail and the same happened when she tried her mother again.

Alayna texted to say she had the tickets for the *Strictly* show, and a few minutes passed as they went back and forth with details. Next came a message from the lawyer, Helen Hall, asking if they could get together when Andee was back from France. It was quickly followed by a text from Graeme's sisters attaching a photograph of themselves waving to her from a gondola in Venice.

Remembering that Luke had emailed earlier asking if his pictures of the baby rhino had arrived, she replied saying she hadn't seen them yet but would open them as soon as she got back to her computer.

By now it was a quarter to twelve. She'd finished her

second coffee and anger at herself was climbing all over her concern. Why on earth hadn't she put Penny's number into her own phone as well as her mother's? What a stupid oversight for someone like her. Except what was she saying here, that Penny had come along and kidnapped their mother?

No, she wasn't thinking that at all. However, it was possible that Penny had been in touch again and the two of them had made an arrangement to meet.

Her mother would have let her know if that were the case.

Maybe Maureen had gone to Graeme's shop, though why on earth she'd do that when she had no idea that Andee had been helping out between nine and eleven, Andee had no idea.

'Blake,' she said into the phone, 'I don't suppose my mother's wandered over your way, has she?'

'I haven't seen her,' he replied. 'Should I be looking out for her? It's Andee,' she heard him tell someone with him. 'Have you seen Maureen this morning?' To Andee he said, 'Hang on, Jenny wants to speak to you.'

A moment later Blake's wife was saying, 'I saw your mother at the gym earlier. I'd just come out of my spin class and found her sitting on her own in the changing rooms.'

Feeling a twist in her heart, Andee said, 'Did you speak to her?'

'Yes, but to be honest she didn't seem . . . I'm not sure . . . Well, she didn't seem to know who I was.'

Getting to her feet, Andee said, 'Was she still there when you left?'

'No, she rushed off saying she had to go.'

'She was due to meet me at eleven and she hasn't shown up,' Andee told her.

'Oh no. Is there anything I can do? Maybe she went to the library. Isn't it her day? It's just around the corner, shall I pop and see if she's there?'

'If you wouldn't mind,' Andee replied, handing some money to Fliss. 'I'll head over to the shop and meet you there.'

By the time Andee got through the bustle of the Inner Courtyard to Graeme's shop, Jenny had already rung to let her know that Maureen was at the library.

'Did she seem all right?' Andee asked, relief flooding her.

'Better than earlier,' Jenny replied, 'but to be honest I don't think she remembered seeing me, because when I asked if she was feeling better now she seemed surprised, as though she wasn't sure what I was talking about.'

Andee's insides turned over as she once again considered the turmoil her mother was in, far worse than Andee's own.

'What is it?' Jenny asked, as Andee sank into a Queen Anne walnut wing chair on the visitor's side of Graeme's desk. 'Something's going on. Is there anything I can do?'

Andee gazed around the shop, seeing but hardly registering the myriad treasures that had found their way down the years to pause here before setting off on the next stage of their journeys. She wished with all her heart that Graeme would walk through the door now. She was very fond of Jenny, and she longed to confide in her, but she knew, because of what Jenny and Blake had been through, that it would be an incredibly selfish thing to do. The Leonards' daughter, Jessica, had disappeared without trace for over two years, so they knew very well what it was like to experience that kind of fear and heartache. It was only after they'd called on Andee to help find her that the truth had emerged, but not in time to save the girl. She'd died the very day she'd gone missing, not murdered by a monster, but as the victim of a tragic accident that hadn't been reported.

Terrible though it was, the Leonards had had their closure, and were now doing their best to move on. Hearing about Penny was unlikely to help them with that, no matter how genuine or willing they might be in their offers of support.

'Andee?' Jenny gently urged. 'You're looking a bit like your mother did this morning. I don't want to pry, but if something's wrong . . .'

'No, it isn't, really,' Andee assured her. 'It's just that I saw this woman in France . . .' What was she saying? Why were these words coming out when she hadn't intended them to? 'My mother received a call, and a text. It turns out my sister, Penny . . .'

Jenny frowned in confusion. 'What about her?' she prompted.

'She's alive,' Andee stated, unable to stop herself.

Jenny's kindly blue eyes dilated with shock.

'It was her,' Andee continued, 'the woman I saw. I was in no doubt of it.'

'But what happened?'

Andee explained about the car that had pulled up to block her way. 'Then later the same day my mother rang to say she'd heard from someone who sounded just like me. We know how sisters sound alike.'

Jenny dropped into Graeme's leather-padded chair, clearly lost for words. 'So this is why you came back early?' she finally managed.

Andee nodded. 'Please don't mention it to anyone, apart from Blake, of course. I guess everyone will know soon enough, but for the moment my mother and I feel it's best to see her without the complications of police or media pressure.'

'Of course. Do you have any idea where she's been all this time? Or when you're likely to see her next?'

'No to the former. She's coming to the house tomorrow at three.'

Though apparently still thrown, Jenny regarded her carefully. 'How do you feel about it?' she asked, clearly sensing that Andee was far more disturbed by the way things were unfolding than relieved or joyful.

Andee shook her head as she sighed. 'Not how I'd expected to if it ever happened,' she confided, 'and nor does my mother. It's thrown us completely, mostly because of the way Penny's going about it. It's like . . . I don't know what it's like: it just doesn't feel good.'

'Does that mean it has to be bad?'

Andee shrugged. 'I guess not, but I keep seeing the car driving off as soon as she was sure I'd recognised her. She didn't want to engage any further, that much was clear. It was like she'd put down a marker, or played some sort of tease. And yesterday, she sent my mother a text asking if she remembered a kitten she'd had when she was small that disappeared and was never found. Much like she disappeared when she was fourteen – and was never found.' Her bemused and troubled eyes went to Jenny's. 'I'm asking myself, why bring that up about the kitten? Of all the things that happened when we were young . . . Why pick on that?'

'Maybe it was an attempt to establish that she really is your sister?' Jenny suggested. 'A shared memory, something no one else is likely to know about.'

'That would make more sense if she thought I was in any doubt about who she was. She knows I recognised her . . .'

They both looked up as someone came in to enquire about a Stölzle green glass bowl in the window.

As Jenny admired it with the woman and gave her some history on it, Andee checked her phone for messages, and finding one from Graeme she sent a quick text back saying she'd ring later.

'What's really bothering me,' she said to Jenny when they were alone again, 'is how she knew where to find me. If she'd turned up here, in Kesterly, that would be one thing, but in France . . .'

A few minutes ticked by as they sat with the mystery of that. In the end, Jenny said, 'Are you saying you think she's having you watched?'

Andee sat back, a hand to her head. 'I've no idea what she's doing,' she declared, 'but she apparently knew where to call my mother – we moved from Chiswick over twenty years ago – and she even has my mother's mobile number. How did she get hold of that?'

Having no answer, Jenny simply looked at her.

'I guess,' Andee said evenly, 'I'll just have to ask her – if she turns up, that is. If she doesn't . . .'

'What will you do?'

'The truth? I've absolutely no idea.'

Chapter Four

The following afternoon Andee and Maureen, appearing calmer than Andee suspected she felt, were staring at each other across the kitchen table, where a home-made coconut cake – Penny's favourite when she was young – and the best china were neatly set out as a welcome. It was only ten minutes to three, but they'd been ready for over half an hour, and now they'd finally run out of words that hadn't already been spoken dozens of times that day.

First thing this morning Maureen had said, 'I texted her the address. She'll probably remember it was Granny and Grandpa's place when she sees it.'

Feeling certain Penny already knew where they were, Andee said, 'Did she ask for it?'

'No, but I thought I should send it anyway, just in case she thinks we're still in Chiswick.'

Deciding not to point out that the first call had come to this house in Kesterly-on-Sea, which didn't have a London number, Andee said, 'Did you get a reply to the text?'

Maureen shook her head.

Andee stayed silent, not trusting herself to say anything impartial. Her mother was already stressed enough, she didn't need her elder daughter's anger adding to it. But Andee couldn't understand why Penny seemed to be toying with them.

At ten o'clock they'd driven into Kesterly so Maureen could get the ingredients for the cake as well as pick up some things for dinner in case Penny decided to stay for the evening – maybe even the night.

'Do you think I should get a room ready for her?' Maureen had asked during the drive home.

Finding it hard to imagine the woman she'd seen in France settling into their chintzy little guest room, Andee said, 'Do you want to?'

Maureen didn't answer. She was distracted, anxious, and Andee understood that, so she let the matter drop and continued to gaze out at the bay where a score of small sailboats were bobbing about the waves like sprightly ballerinas.

Now Maureen said, 'Maybe I should find some old photographs of her and put them on the mantelpiece with the rest of the family. She might find it hurtful to see she's not there. Do you think it was terrible of us to take them down? It was just so painful seeing her never getting any older . . .'

Andee looked at the framed shots of herself and the children, her mother and father, her grandparents and Maureen's nieces and nephews. There always used to be one of Penny, aged about ten, grinning widely and looking adorably mischievous. It was, Andee realised, how she'd come to remember her sister, since it was the only way she'd seen her for the fifteen or so years that it had been on display. It was as though she'd frozen in time, not as the fourteen-year-old who'd featured in the shots the police had circulated during the search for her, but as a younger, cuter version of the moody teenager with mussed dark hair and shocked, staring eyes.

'Do you still have any photos of her?' Andee asked.

'Of course. They'll be in the attic with the family albums.'

'So shall we get them down?'

Maureen regarded her warily. 'I can tell you don't think it's a good idea.'

Andee didn't, but wasn't sure why. Perhaps she didn't want to be too eagerly welcoming with Penny, after all this time.

'Are you looking forward to seeing her?' Maureen asked after another pause. Without waiting for an answer, she said, 'I wonder how she's feeling right now. Do you think she has far to come?'

Since Andee had no idea, she got up from her seat at the table and pulled her mother into a tender embrace.

'I wish Daddy was here,' Maureen said, for what must have been the hundredth time. 'Or do I? I wouldn't want him getting cross with her the way he used to. Except he wouldn't. He'd be nothing but relieved to know she was safe, and it won't be her fault that she hasn't been in touch for all these years.'

Though ready to accept that there might well have

been a period when Penny hadn't been in charge of her own destiny, Andee simply couldn't feel convinced that it had continued for the entire time she'd been gone. Certainly the woman in the Mercedes hadn't shown any signs of being controlled by anyone but herself.

'What if she doesn't come?' Maureen said now, gazing at the cake.

'We'll call Blake and Jenny and have a party,' Andee quipped.

Maureen's eyes shot to hers, and at last she managed a smile.

Smiling too, Andee said, 'If she does come, I'm wondering how we should greet her. With a nice big hug for the long-lost daughter/sister? A polite handshake for a stranger? How about a salute?'

'Stop it,' Maureen chided.

'Do we say hello Penny or hello Michelle?'

'I think I shall call her darling, or nothing at all, until we can work that one out. I wonder if she'll call me Mum? She did when she rang.'

Andee tensed as the clock in the hall chimed the hour.

Maureen glanced at her watch. 'It's a couple of minutes fast,' she reminded Andee.

Andee picked up her mobile as a text arrived.

Sorry, running about ten behind. Be there soon. M aka P Xxx PS: I took something of yours when I left, I wonder if you know what it was ☺

Andee's first thought was, 'So she has my mobile number too.' Her second thought, 'Does she think this is a game?' She passed the phone to her mother and went to fill the kettle.

'Do you know what she took?' Maureen asked.

Andee shook her head. She was feeling angry again; the sense of being controlled, or played, was seriously getting to her. Why on earth wasn't this gearing up to be the joyous family reunion she'd always imagined if her sister came home, the way her mother deserved it to be?

'She's upset you,' Maureen declared.

Throwing out her hands, Andee said, 'I just wish I knew what was going on with her. First that bizarre episode in France, then the text about the kitten, now this . . . Why is she running ten minutes late? Is it deliberate, to show some sort of power over us?'

'Maybe she came by train and has to wait for a taxi. She should have rung, we could have picked her up.'

Andee looked at her mother and felt a sudden urge to tell her they were going out, that they wouldn't be here when, if, Penny decided to show, because they had other things to do. Of course Maureen would refuse if she tried, so she didn't even attempt it. 'What did you mean yesterday,' she challenged, 'when you said that I didn't know Penny?'

Maureen gave a jerky sort of shrug as she gazed at the cake. 'I just meant that you two were very different,' she mumbled.

Reluctant to press her mother, but doing it anyway, Andee said, 'I think you meant more than that, so is there something you're not telling me?'

Maureen's eyes came up to hers, showing how helpless and anxious she felt. 'Please don't be angry,' she implored. 'We don't want to be in bad moods when she gets here.'

'I'm not angry,' Andee lied, although frustrated might have been a better word.

'The trouble is you're used to being in charge,' Maureen pointed out, 'but sometimes, and this is one of them, you have to ease up and just go with the flow.'

Amused by the way they were taking turns to bolster one another, Andee returned to the table and looked at her phone again. 'I should be feeling excited,' she said frustratedly, 'I want to believe that everything's going to be just wonderful, but it's not happening.'

'You're like Daddy. You never automatically trust anyone or anything. It's a part of having been a police officer.'

'Are you saying that you trust what's happening here?' Andee demanded. 'That you believe it's going to be wonderful?'

'I'm trying to,' Maureen insisted. 'And it is wonderful that she's alive. You have to admit that.'

Knowing she wouldn't be ready to explore how she felt until after she'd seen her sister, Andee sat down and regarded her mother keenly as they continued to wait. The fact that Maureen had avoided her question about knowing more than she was letting on hadn't escaped Andee, but now wasn't the time to push it any further. However, if Maureen thought they wouldn't return to it she was gravely mistaken, particularly when Andee had always believed she knew everything there was to know about her sister's disappearance. She'd seen the police files, had even carried out an investigation herself some ten years after the initial, exhaustive search, so what else could there be to know? But her mother's comment yesterday had made Andee feel that there *was* something else. If so, it hardly made any sense for her mother to be holding it back, especially from Andee, but Maureen was nervous about something, that much was clear.

It was just after three fifteen when they heard a car pulling up outside.

Maureen's eyes shot to Andee's. Her face had paled.

With her insides knotting, Andee said, 'Do you want me to go?'

'We both should,' Maureen replied, and got to her feet.

Feeling strangely disconnected from what was about to happen, as though she was watching rather than participating, Andee led the way along the hall, past her father's paintings that decorated the cream-coloured walls, to the rarely used front door. He'd painted the landscapes during the worst of his grief, a form of therapy designed to distract him, and in a small way it had seemed to help.

Though Andee had no deep-rooted belief in the afterlife, she couldn't help wondering if he was watching them now, and if he was, what he was thinking. Did he feel, as she did, that it would be better if their meeting weren't happening like this, or was he quietly rejoicing that his girls were finally about to be reunited?

No one had rung the bell or knocked on the door, but someone was outside, Andee could see their shape through the frosted glass. She turned to her mother. Maureen's eyes were bright with emotion. Her hands were bunched at her throat. She looked older all of a sudden, and smaller. She gave Andee a weak smile of encouragement, and feeling as though she was going through the motions of a long-rehearsed scene from some dystopian play, Andee swung the door wide and found herself face to face with the woman she'd last seen in the back of a Mercedes.

She wasn't as tall as Andee had expected – though Penny had never been tall – or quite as composed as she'd seemed that day in France, but the blonde hair was as immaculate as the make-up, and the outfit as expensive as the leather bag over her arm. Her smile seemed hesitant, even slightly shy, while the curiosity and eagerness in her aqua eyes sent Andee spinning back through the years.

Different and unexpected as she was, any lingering doubt that this was her sister vanished along with whatever Andee had intended to say.

'I'm sorry I'm late,' Penny said, and Andee, disoriented by her own emotions, turned round as her mother sobbed.

'I can't believe it,' Maureen gulped, holding out her arms. 'Oh my goodness, my goodness,' and as she folded her younger daughter into the agonised tenderness of her embrace, Andee watched from inside a profound sense of unreality. She glanced outside and saw a silver Mercedes at the gate with a suited man in the driver's seat. Presumably the same car, the same driver that had been in France.

'Andee,' Penny murmured holding out an arm.

Realising she was being invited to join the hug, Andee stepped obediently into it.

'Mummy, my very own mummy,' Penny smiled through her tears as she clasped Maureen's hands to her chest. 'I can't tell you how good this feels, how I've dreamt about this moment . . . Is it really happening?'

'You look so . . . So . . . grown up,' Maureen spluttered with a laugh. 'In my mind I kept seeing you as a teenager, and now here you are . . .' She looked at Andee, and Andee remembered to smile.

'My beautiful big sister,' Penny enthused, gazing directly into Andee's eyes. There was something behind the tenderness in Penny's, a kind of wariness, or amusement, or an emotion too well masked for Andee to read. 'You've hardly changed,' Penny ran on, 'apart from to get even more beautiful. I always knew you would. And you're tall, just like Daddy.'

Was there resentment in her tone? Their difference in height had always been a sore point for Penny. There was none that Andee could detect.

Andee simply smiled again and closed the door.

'Is anyone else here?' Penny asked, glancing down the hall.

'No, we haven't told anyone,' Maureen replied. 'We weren't sure you'd want us to yet.'

Penny said, 'So no one's been here – ahead of me?'

Curious, Andee countered, 'Like who?'

Penny laughed. 'I've no idea, but I do think it's important for us to have this time to ourselves, don't you? There's so much catching up to do, and we really don't need all the distractions of the police and media. After all, this isn't anyone's business but ours.'

Andee didn't disagree, but she was preoccupied with wondering if Penny really thought the press and authorities were ahead of her, or if her question had been about someone or something else entirely.

With a playful twinkle Penny turned back to Maureen. 'There's so much I want to ask you, and tell you, the question is where to begin?'

In spite of having several suggestions for that, Andee gestured for everyone to go inside.

'We've got tea and coconut cake,' Maureen announced as they went into the kitchen, clearly waiting for Penny to comment on how wonderful it was that her mother had remembered.

Penny said, 'I'm sure I'm too excited to eat a thing.'

Hiding her disappointment, Maureen tried again. 'Maybe we should be having champagne. Oh my, I still can't believe . . . Is it really you? I know it is. Andee's right, you haven't changed . . .'

'Apart from to get older,' Penny said wryly. She was looking around the room, taking everything in. 'You've redecorated, and the furniture's different, but it's still taking me straight back to my childhood and all the school holidays we spent here with cousin Frank. How is he? Are you still in touch with him?'

'Of course,' Maureen assured her, starting towards

the family photos then apparently changing her mind. 'He's married now, and his children are all grown up, like Andee's.'

'You have children?' Penny directed at Andee, appearing delighted. 'Of course, I should have known you would. What're their names? How old are they?'

'Luke's twenty-one and Alayna's nineteen,' Maureen told her proudly. Andee remained silent, appraising Penny, and letting her mother do the talking.

'So have they left home?' enquired Penny.

'Oh yes, a while ago,' Maureen replied. 'But we still see them quite often and they're in touch all the time. Luke's currently in Africa helping to save rhinos, and Alayna's at Bristol Uni studying English and drama. She's planning to go off travelling for a year when she finishes.'

Penny's eyebrows rose with interest.

'She decided to take her gap year after she graduates,' Maureen explained. 'She's working and saving very hard to finance her trip.'

Deciding this was enough about her children, Andee said to Penny, 'What about you? Are you a mother?'

Penny laughed and rolled her eyes. 'I'll tell you all about it,' she promised, 'but first shall we sit down and have a cup of tea?'

Andee filled the teapot while Maureen fussed about with napkins, listening and chuckling as Penny fondly recalled how she and Andee, with their cousin Frank, used to ride their bicycles down to the caravan parks of Perryman's Cove, known locally as Paradise Cove, to make friends with kids from all over the world.

'The world?' Andee echoed, bringing the pot to the table.

'OK, the country,' Penny conceded, 'but there were a couple of kids from Germany once, as I recall, and you must remember that hilarious hippy family from Ireland.'

Actually, Andee did remember them, the Irish and the Germans, and she wondered if this was an attempt on Penny's part to prove she wasn't an impostor.

'You fell in love with one of the Irish boys,' Penny teased. 'He was completely gorgeous. All the girls fancied him, and we were devastated when his girlfriend turned up for the second week. What was his name?'

'Actually, it was a Welsh boy, Evan, whose girlfriend turned up for the second week,' Andee reminded her.

'Oh, that's right, but it was the same year, I'm sure of it. What was the Irish boy's name?'

'I can't remember.'

'Well, it was a long time ago, and we were falling in and out of love all over the place back then. How could we possibly remember them all?'

'I had no idea you were having so many romantic adventures,' Maureen commented wryly.

'Oh, it was all perfectly innocent,' Penny assured her, adding with a wink at Andee, 'until it wasn't.'

Wondering why she'd added that when it had never been anything but innocent, Andee poured the tea while blushing Maureen cut the cake.

'So fancy you living in Granny and Grandpa's house now,' Penny remarked, looking around again. 'I can't tell you how thrilled I was when I found out. It would be awful to think of strangers here.'

'Exactly when did you find out?' Andee enquired mildly.

Penny frowned as she thought. 'Quite recently,' she admitted. 'I guess it was in one of the first reports I received.'

Andee's eyes flicked to her mother.

Penny laughed. 'I'm sorry, I have to confess that I hired someone to find out all about you. I felt I had to before I got in touch so I could work out whether or not I'd be welcome. Of course as soon as I was told you'd been a detective, Andee, I knew you'd be sceptical, ready to pick apart anything I said, and I honestly don't blame you. I'm sure I'd be the same if the tables were turned. All these years and no contact, you must be asking yourself why suddenly now?'

Andee waited for her to answer the question.

'I've wanted to be in touch many times,' Penny told their mother. 'I've hated holding back, but it's taken until now for me to feel confident about approaching you.'

'But you're my daughter,' Maureen exclaimed, 'there was never any reason to hold back.'

Penny smiled and lowered her eyes to her plate. As she lifted a dainty fork to eat Andee noticed that her hands were covered to the base of her fingers by a glove-like extension to her silk sleeves. She was wearing an exquisite gold band studded with yellow sapphires or diamonds on the third finger of her left hand, and a more subtle assortment of rings on the other, but there was no disguising the cracked and flaking soreness of her skin. Penny had never suffered with eczema as a child, but she apparently did now. 'I needed to be in the right place, up here, to answer your questions,' she said softly, tapping her head.

'And you feel you are now?' Andee asked.

Penny nodded slowly, still not looking up. 'I think so. It won't be easy, for any of us, and I kept asking myself if it wouldn't be better just to let things go on as they were. You're used to me being gone. The space I left has long since filled up, and I've made a new life for myself . . . Why disrupt it?'

Why indeed, Andee was asking herself. 'But you decided to,' she said shortly, 'and now here you are.'

Apparently unfazed by Andee's manner, Penny sighed softly as she reached for her mother's hand. 'Yes, here I am,' she said. 'We've got so much time to make up for, so many stories to share.'

Though Maureen was smiling, her eyes were uncertain as they moved briefly to Andee's.

Understanding that her mother wanted her to continue asking the questions, Andee said, 'Naturally, the first story we'd love you to share is what happened to you all those years ago. Where did you go? Why could no one ever find you?'

'Mmm,' Penny murmured, nodding her head as she gazed absently down at her cake. Then quite suddenly she gasped. 'This always used to be my favourite. I can't believe you remembered. I haven't had it in years. Did you make it?' Her eyes were bright with surprise and affection as she looked at her mother.

'Yes, I did,' Maureen told her, flushing with pleasure. 'I'm not sure it's as good as I used to make it . . .'

'Oh, I'm sure it is,' and digging in with her fork Penny helped herself to a generous mouthful. 'Mmm, it's perfect,' she insisted, showering a few crumbs. 'Oh God, it's bringing back so many memories.'

Andee said, 'Such as where you went all those years ago, and why no one could find you?'

Maureen stared an admonishment as all the joy seemed to drain from Penny, and she put her fork down again.

'That was a strange time,' she said quietly, 'and it was so long ago that it feels now as though it happened to somebody else.'

But it didn't, it happened to you, Andee wanted to point out, *so now please tell us what we need to know.*

'It's not a good story,' Penny admitted, gazing into the distance, 'and definitely not one for us to start with. It'll bring us all down and I think today should be about celebrating our reunion, don't you?'

Andee would have pressed her, had Maureen not said, 'You're right, dear, it should be a celebration, and if it upsets you to dwell on those times . . .'

'It does,' Penny confessed, 'quite a lot, but I've had counselling, and fortunately for the most part I've managed to put it behind me. I'm afraid I still have nightmares from time to time, but I have such a lot to feel thankful for now.'

They waited for her to elaborate, but she didn't. Seconds ticked by, until Maureen said brightly, 'Well, you look marvellous.'

Penny smiled. 'Yes, my life is very different now to what it was when I first went away, but a lot of years have passed, and things always change.'

'So what do you do now?' Andee enquired.

Penny shrugged as if to say, where to begin? 'I have an import-export company that we run from London,' she replied. 'A real estate and property management company, also based in London. Two medical centres, one in Connecticut, the other in Houston. A travel agency that we run out of Stockholm,' her eyes danced playfully, 'and as of about a year ago we have a highly exclusive online dating agency.'

Maureen was clearly as stunned as she was impressed.

Andee said, 'We?'

'I have a number of partners,' Penny explained, taking out her phone as it rang. After checking who it was she said, 'Will you think me terribly rude? It's a call I've been waiting for and I really ought to take it. I'll be just a minute,' and clicking on she announced herself, 'Michelle,' as she got to her feet and began speaking in a language Andee couldn't even identify, much less understand.

'Nej, han har inte varit här.' (No, he hasn't been here.) *'Ja, jag är säker.'* (Yes, I'm sure.) *'Hur tror du det känns att vara tillbaka här?'* (How do you think it feels being back?)

Penny laughed in a vaguely bitter way. *'Allt är ett spel, det bara beror på hur man spelar det.'* (Everything's a game, it just depends how you play it.)

Andee watched her mother's eyes following Penny out of the back door on to the patio. They had no idea what had been said, or who Penny had been talking to.

The phone call, the incomprehensible language was emphasising more than ever what different worlds they inhabited.

Turning to Andee, Maureen murmured, 'She's obviously doing very well for herself.'

Andee said, archly, 'And managing not to tell us very much.'

Maureen's nod was slow, pensive.

'Especially about the time she disappeared. Do you have any idea why she's being so reticent?' Andee asked.

Hearing the challenge, Maureen looked at Penny again as she said, 'She just told us, she'd rather not talk about it, and if it was that bad who can blame her?'

'Mum,' Andee said darkly.

'Please don't be like that,' Maureen protested. 'She's hardly been here . . . Ssh, she's coming back.'

Andee watched her sister return, tucking away her phone and breaking into a smile. 'All sorted,' Penny declared, closing the door behind her, 'but I'm afraid time is running out and there are several more calls I need to make.'

'You can use the front room,' Maureen offered. 'You'll be nice and private in there.'

Penny tilted her head fondly. 'That's so kind of you, but I've booked myself into the Kesterly Royal for tonight. It'll be easier if I work from there. I was hoping we could meet again tomorrow before I go back to London?'

'Yes, yes of course,' Maureen agreed, glancing at Andee. 'We'd love that, but it's been so short today. Are you sure you can't stay any longer?'

'I wish I could, really I do, but I'm afraid my time isn't my own. Could we meet for lunch tomorrow? I hear the Royal has a very good restaurant overlooking the bay.'

'The Palme d'Or,' Maureen told her.

Penny came to hug her. 'I'll book a table for one o'clock. I hope you'll join us, Andee.'

'I wouldn't miss it,' Andee assured her, and after coolly returning her sister's embrace she remained in the kitchen while her mother went to the front door.

'She's got a chauffeur,' Maureen stated when she came back.

Andee raised an eyebrow as she slid Penny's teacup into a plastic bag. She might not doubt that the woman who'd drunk from it was her sister, but Detective Inspector Gould would almost certainly want to run a more scientific check.

Maureen was staring at the chair Penny had vacated. 'Did I just dream all that?' she murmured.

'Have some more tea,' Andee advised.

Sitting down, Maureen pushed her hands through her hair as Andee poured.

Andee allowed several minutes to pass before she spoke in a quiet, but steely voice. 'I really don't know what's going on with her,' she said, 'but why is she in touch with us now after allowing us to think she was dead for so many years? I think there's more to it than her being ready to reconnect.'

Maureen flicked a glance her way, but said nothing.

'Mum, please talk to me. I feel like you're keeping something back . . .'

Maureen shook her head.

Andee took a breath. 'As you said yourself, I never automatically trust anyone or anything, but you usually do. And the fact that you've been more nervous than excited about seeing Penny is telling. I'm getting the sense that you know more about her disappearance than you're letting on, and it's tearing you apart.'

'OK, OK, but it's not what you . . . Actually, I don't know what you think, but it's been so long since we talked about her, I mean really talked about her, and you've either forgotten, or chosen to forget what she could be like.'

Accepting that was at least partly true, Andee waited for her to continue.

'It's not unusual,' Maureen told her. 'When someone dies, or disappears the way she did, you only remember the good things. It's human nature; it's the same for everyone. You put all the other things out of your mind. I told myself she was just a child, that they had nothing to do with why she went, and I still don't know that they did.'

'What other things?' Andee asked.

'You really don't remember?'

'Why don't you just tell me?'

Maureen swallowed hard and ran her hands over her face. 'Well, there were times,' she began, 'that I felt your sister did things deliberately to make herself . . . to annoy or even to hurt people. She didn't seem . . .' She shook her head. 'She never really seemed sorry when she said it, or to care if she was punished. She'd put on a show of being upset . . . Sometimes I think the tears were real, but there were other times . . . I don't know, it was like she was behaving the way we thought she should rather than the way she felt.'

'Did you ever talk to Daddy about her – behaviour?' Andee asked.

'Actually, we talked about it endlessly before she went and after she'd gone. We never knew if the depressions were genuine, or if they were something she'd read about and decided to pretend were afflicting her. I mean, obviously something was wrong or she wouldn't have been the way she was, or run away as often as she did . . .'

'Did you ever find out where she went?'

Maureen shook her head. 'I think Daddy knew. He never told me, he thought it was best for me not to know . . .'

'But she's your daughter! How could it be best for you not to know?'

'Times were different back then and your father was very . . . protective.'

'How was holding information back from you protecting her?'

'It wasn't just her he was protecting, it was me, and you.'

'From what?'

'I didn't ask.'

'Not even when she didn't come back?'

'If your father had wanted me to know, if he'd felt it would help in some way to find her, he'd have told me.'

Stunned by such blind faith, and lack of maternal strength, Andee said, 'So where do you *think* she went all those times?'

Maureen sighed. 'I told myself she was with homeless people, and I think she was . . .' When she broke off, Andee used silence to demand more, but Maureen stayed silent too.

'Mum, you obviously believe something else, even if you never knew it for certain.'

Maureen's cheeks coloured. 'OK, I think he found her with men,' she admitted finally.

'What men?'

'I don't know.'

'I think you do.'

'I swear I don't.'

Andee was ready to scream. 'Why did you never tell the police what you suspected?' she cried. 'It wasn't in any of your statements . . .'

'Your father knew what I thought . . . what I was afraid of. Andee, please don't shout at me. If there had been . . .'

'Mum, Penny was thirteen the first time she disappeared, and only fourteen when she went for good. That makes her . . .'

'I know what you're going to say, but I'd rather not have it spelt out, thank you very much.'

Andee clutched her head. 'I can't believe you're only telling me this now . . .'

'We thought she was dead. Why would I try to make you think badly of her when it wasn't going to bring her back?'

'You know I investigated her disappearance. You could have told me then.'

'Maybe, but you didn't ask . . .'

'I most certainly did. We went over and over your statements . . .'

'OK, you did, but if there had been any men you can be sure your father would have found them. Now, if you don't mind, I'd like a very large glass of wine, and perhaps we can sit quietly for a few minutes while I try to gather my thoughts.'

They were still sitting at the table, silently reeling from the past few minutes, when Maureen's mobile rang. Seeing it was Carol, her closest friend and Andee's mother-in-law, calling from Spain, Maureen hesitated.

'Should I tell her about Penny?' she asked Andee.

Andee baulked at the very idea. Until she'd managed to straighten things out in her mind she didn't want anyone else's thoughts or reactions to cloud it, and certainly not her estranged husband's, who was currently in Spain with his mother. Carol would be bound to tell him. 'Let's see how tomorrow goes first,' she cautioned, and leaving her mother to it, she took herself up to her room to make some calls of her own.

The first was to the Kesterly Royal Hotel, who politely informed her that they had no one booked in for that night by the name of Michelle Cross, or Penny Lawrence. The second was to her old boss, DI Terence Gould, asking him to call back when he got her message. The third was to Graeme.

After filling him in on the details of Penny's visit and brushing over the scene she'd had afterwards with her mother, Andee said, 'So now, you tell me, why has Penny come back after all these years, when she appears to be doing very well, and has no apparent need of us? Because I certainly have no idea.'

Sounding as bemused as she did, Graeme ventured, 'Sentimental reasons? Even if she's doing well, maybe it doesn't mean anything if she has no family to share it with.'

'We don't know that she has no family. She didn't answer the question when I asked, which is odd, or certainly if she's a mother. Why not just say that she has children – or not?'

'So her return is something to do with conscience? She feels guilty about not letting you know she's alive, and now she's putting it to rights.'

'She's had a very long time to do that, and she's chosen not to. So I go back to my first question, why now? Incidentally, she admitted to hiring someone to find out about us ... And let me read you the text she sent before she got here earlier. *"I took something of yours when I left, I wonder if you know what it was."*'

'Do you?'

'No.'

'Did you ask her?'

'I didn't get the chance. She wasn't here more than twenty minutes, and during that time all we really managed to get out of her was how successful she is, but even that was vague.'

'Do you believe it?'

'She was carrying a Hermès bag, and wearing some expensive-looking jewellery. Oh, and she was driven here by a chauffeur. I'm pretty sure it was the same car that I saw in France.'

'Did she explain about that? Why she just drove off?'

'I'll make sure she does the next time we meet, which is supposed to be at the Palme d'Or tomorrow.' Making a mental note to check if there was a reservation, Andee said, 'I called the hotel just now and they don't have anyone staying there under the name of Michelle Cross or Penny Lawrence.'

'So you're thinking she might have another alias? Or she's staying somewhere else?'

'I guess anything's possible. I've left a message for Terence Gould to call me.'

Sounding surprised, he said, 'So you're going to involve the police?'

'Off the record, for the moment, because things are definitely not adding up for me. Why, for instance, did she seem to think that someone might have paid us a visit ahead of her?'

'Really? Like who?'

'I've no idea, but my gut is telling me it could be why she came.'

'Which leads us to what, exactly?'

'Good question; I'll let you know when I have an answer. Oh, and she pretended not to know that I had children, when it surely must have come up in one of her reports. I'd love to know how in-depth they are and how long they've been going on.'

'Indeed. What did you call her, by the way? Michelle or Penny?'

'I don't think we called her anything, but she called herself Michelle when she answered the phone. After that she spoke in another language and before you ask, I've no idea what it was. Definitely not French or Italian. Could have been Dutch. Actually, she mentioned having a business in Stockholm.'

'What sort of business?'

'A travel agency.'

'Called?'

'She didn't say. I wonder if she'll make it for lunch tomorrow? I have a feeling she won't.'

'Well, I guess you'll find out when you get there, presuming she's not in touch sooner. Don't forget to let me know if she is.'

Chapter Five

Maureen received a text at nine the following morning.

Hope you had a good night. Too excited to sleep much myself. Would it be possible to come and see you at eleven? Have to return to London earlier than expected and I don't want to leave without seeing you. There's still so much to catch up on. Love Penny/Michelle.

After reading it Andee handed the phone back to her mother. 'Interesting that she's asking to come when I won't be here,' she commented.

Maureen looked startled. 'But how on earth would she know that you're going to the shop this morning?'

Having no sensible answer for that, Andee said, 'Let's put it down to paranoia, and I'll change my plans.' The fact that she'd arranged to see DI Gould wasn't one she'd shared with her mother, and wouldn't until she'd heard what he had to say.

Clearly relieved not to have to deal with Penny alone, Maureen mumbled, 'Thank you,' and sat quietly staring at the table, blinking only when Andee put some toast in front of her. 'Are you going to ask her if she stayed at the Royal?' she ventured.

'If I get the chance, but there are other questions I'd like answers to first. I'm sure you would too?'

Maureen simply sighed. She was looking tired this morning and distracted, which was hardly surprising when her mind, her thoughts, were running around in jumbled and difficult circles.

'Would you like me to see her on my own?' Andee offered.

'No, no, I should be here. I *want* to be here.' Maureen's eyes came up, and her face seemed pinched and sallow as she said, 'If you can, I'd like you to find out where she went when she left all those years ago. I know she says it's painful for her, but it was painful for us too.'

'Of course,' Andee replied softly. 'Do you happen to have any theories you'd like to share with me before I go there?' she asked.

To her surprise Maureen said, 'Yes, I do, but I'd rather hear what she has to say first.'

Andee sat down slowly, keeping a hand on her mother's shoulder as she controlled her frustration. 'Let me get this straight,' she began, 'yesterday you said you thought there might be men involved, and now you're saying that you had an idea *where* she might have gone?'

Maureen looked so uncomfortable and apprehensive that Andee might have backed off if it weren't so important.

'Did Daddy know where she went?' Andee pressed.

Maureen shook her head.

Not sure if that was a no, or please don't ask, Andee

said, 'Did he know that you had suspicions of where she might be?'

Maureen stared down at her plate; her hand was shaking. 'Yes, he did,' she mumbled, 'but nothing ever came of it.'

'So he followed up on your suspicions?'

Maureen nodded.

'Where are we talking about?'

'I don't know. I mean, it wasn't . . . It was who . . . I was afraid of who she was with.'

Andee sat back in her chair, needing some time to assimilate the enormity of this. Probably the hardest part of it was the fact that nothing like this had shown up in the police files, which could only mean that her parents – her *father,* whose integrity she'd never doubted – had held things back from the investigation. 'So *who* are we talking about?' she asked carefully.

Her mother didn't answer.

'Pimps? Traffickers?'

'No, no, nothing like that.'

Unable to think of anything else, though realising that her mind was coloured by experiences in the force, Andee stared hard at her mother.

'I know that look,' Maureen told her, 'but I'm not going any further with this until after we've heard what Penny has to say. It could be I'm wrong, and if I am . . . Well, I'd rather . . . I'd rather not speak ill of the dead.'

Andee reeled. 'Are we talking about Daddy?' she demanded incredulously.

'No, of course not. It's just . . . Well, I think I've said enough. I'd like to have some breakfast now.'

Andee's eyes didn't let go of her mother's face. Were it anyone else in the world she'd never have backed down, not that she was doing so now, but she was reluctant to try and force answers out of her mother when she looked about ready to fall apart.

'What on earth does she mean she doesn't want to speak ill of the dead?' she cried down the line to Graeme, with the bathroom door closed and shower running to drown out her voice. 'Who the heck's she talking about? She says it's not my father, but I can't think of anyone else.'

'OK, this is a long shot,' Graeme replied after giving it some thought, 'but what about your grandparents? They're both dead, and died after Penny went . . .'

Andee was shaking her head. 'They were devastated when she disappeared. They never got over it. Grandpa even stopped speaking . . . It was awful, especially for my father. He'd lost his daughter, and then he was seeing his parents deteriorate in front of his eyes.'

'Were they living in Kesterly at the time?'

'In this very house, which is where Penny and I spent most of our school holidays until the time she vanished. I came the following year with my cousin Frank, and I think the year after that. It wasn't the same, obviously. We were miserable and scared and Granny and Grandpa didn't really know how to handle us. Then my parents sold up in Chiswick and moved here. No one was coping well and my father, who was probably more broken than any of us, wanted to try and hold us all together.'

Sighing, Graeme said, 'We saw what Blake and Jenny went through when their daughter disappeared, but eventually, thanks to you, they had an answer, or closure as some would call it. For your family . . . So many years . . .'

'But we know Penny's alive now, which should be all our prayers coming true, except it's starting to feel as though some kind of nightmare is just beginning.'

It was a little before eleven when the chauffeur-driven Mercedes pulled up outside Briar Lodge and Penny, looking spruce and elegant, got out of the back. She was wearing cream-coloured slacks and a matching shirt with long sleeves cut to cover her hands – she must have them made specially, Andee decided.

As Andee watched her glancing around the hamlet, taking in the scenery and sea air, she was thinking of the ghosts that could be watching too, her father, her paternal grandparents, and her mother's mother who'd suffered along with everyone else when her youngest grandchild had disappeared without trace.

Had her grandparents known more than they'd ever told?

'I hope the change of plan isn't a problem?' Penny grimaced playfully as she kissed Andee on both cheeks. She smelled of expensive perfume, and peppermints, and as she touched her hands to her cheeks Andee couldn't help wondering if it was a deliberate gesture to show she wasn't wearing any rings today.

Andee stood aside for her to go in, saying, 'Mum's in

the kitchen,' and after quickly clocking the registration number of the Mercedes she entered it into her phone and went to join them.

Finding them locked in a tearful embrace, Andee went to fetch the coffee pot and three mugs. As she poured she said to Penny, 'Do you take yours black or white?'

'Oh, I'm sorry, I don't drink coffee,' Penny apologised, 'but please don't mind me. I'll be very happy with water.'

'We can make tea,' her mother offered. 'It won't be any trouble.'

'Water's fine,' Penny assured her.

Filling a glass from the tap, Andee put it on the table and passed her mother a coffee.

'Lovely,' Penny declared after taking a sip of Kesterly's finest. Smiling at Andee she said, 'By the way, did you work out what I took of yours when I left?'

Andee hid her irritation as she shook her head. In truth she hadn't given it much thought, largely because she'd wanted to resist being pulled into some sort of mind game, presuming that was what it was.

Penny laughed. 'I really thought you'd have realised, but there again I don't suppose it was amongst your most treasured possessions.'

Maureen looked from one to the other. 'Are you going to tell us what it was?' she prompted Penny.

Penny seemed to consider it, then apparently decided against it as she said, 'I didn't stay at the Royal last night. I thought I'd try the Kingsmere opposite the marina instead. It was very comfortable, in fact quite respectable for a four star. I wouldn't have a problem recommending it to anyone coming this way.'

Not particularly interested in her TripAdvisor review, Andee said, 'Are we allowed to ask what's taking you back to London so soon?'

Appearing surprised, Penny said, 'You're allowed to ask anything, and the answer is business, of course.' She checked her phone even though it hadn't rung. 'A problem's come up that we didn't foresee,' she confided. She appeared slightly strained as she added, 'We'll get it sorted, of course.' At that moment her phone rang and she quickly clicked on. 'Yes?' she barked shortly. She listened, keeping her eyes down, until eventually she said, 'OK, stay on it . . . I should be there by four.'

As she rang off she looked as though she'd like to swear before her expression brightened and she was smiling again. 'Things rarely run smoothly, do they?' she commented wryly.

'Is there anything we can do?' Maureen offered.

Penny laughed as she said, 'I'm not entirely sure what to do myself, but don't let's think about it now. It's not . . .' She broke off as her phone rang again. 'Yes, I was informed last night,' she told the caller, 'and yes I'm coming back to London. This afternoon. *Nej, naturligtvis vet jag inte var de är. Då hade jag ju inte varit här. Jag måste gå nu.* (No, of course I don't know where they are. I wouldn't be here if I did. I have to go now),' and she abruptly ended the call. 'I'm sorry,' she grimaced, 'I'll turn it off or this will keep happening.'

'It sounds serious,' Andee commented.

Penny hesitated, seemed on the brink of saying something, then appeared to change her mind. 'It could become so, if we don't get ahead of it,' she declared, 'but please let's forget it for now and use what time we have to carry on getting to know one another.' She gave an amused, incredulous shake of her head, using the moment, Andee felt, to refocus herself. 'My mother and my sister. I have family. Of course, I've always known it, but being here, seeing you again after all these years . . . I should have come sooner. I wish I had, but I was so afraid you wouldn't want to see me.'

'We've always wanted to know what happened to you,' Maureen assured her, clearly distressed that she could think otherwise. 'It's dominated our lives.'

Penny looked from her mother to Andee and back again. 'Well, I can believe you were probably upset and even worried at first, after all I was only fourteen, but as time went on . . .'

'Upset? Worried?' Maureen cut in incredulously. 'We were beside ourselves. We thought you were dead. The note you sent . . .'

Penny frowned.

Andee's senses were suddenly alert.

Maureen said, 'The note that turned up after you disappeared. The things you said . . .'

Penny waved a dismissive hand and sighed. 'I remember it now,' she said, 'and it wasn't my idea. I just went along with it because it seemed like the right thing to do at the time. If you thought I was dead you might stop looking.'

Clearly appalled, as much by the tone as the words, Maureen could only stare at her.

Just as shocked, Andee kept her tone even as she said, 'So you send a note, intending to make us think you were dead . . .' She was finding this hard to take in. Who did something like that?

Appearing contrite and even managing to sound it in spite of her words, Penny said, 'I'm sorry to say I'd had enough of being in this family. You were the golden girl, I was the burden, the difficult one; the one who just wouldn't conform – at least not to the way *Daddy* wanted things. He might have been happier if I'd been born a boy, I couldn't have got into so much trouble – or that's what he told himself, I'm sure.'

'Your father loved you,' Maureen insisted hoarsely.

Penny's eyebrows arched. 'I think we both know that's not true,' she argued with an oddly disconcerting smile.

'It was losing you, never knowing what had happened to you,' Andee informed her, 'that took him to an early grave.'

At that Penny lowered her eyes and allowed several moments to pass before she said, 'I'm sorry that you think that.'

Momentarily lost for words of her own, Andee waited for her to elaborate on what the hell she was meaning, but Maureen was the next to speak.

'Penny, where did you go when you left?'

Penny's eyes rose to her mother's. For what seemed like an eternity she simply regarded Maureen as she dealt with whatever thoughts were behind her intense, unreadable eyes. 'Do you really want me to answer that?' she asked finally.

Maureen visibly blanched.

'Just tell us,' Andee snapped.

Penny's gaze flicked to her, and returned to her mother. 'It's up to you,' she said. 'If you want to know . . .'

'Your father checked,' Maureen broke in shakily. 'The police, everyone . . . It's not where you were.'

'They looked in the wrong places, but Daddy found me, once. He stared right at me, then he turned around and walked away.'

'No!' Maureen cried. 'He'd never have done that.'

Penny didn't argue.

'What is going on?' Andee demanded of them both. 'Where were you, Penny? Who hid you? Someone, others, had to have been involved . . .'

'Oh, someone was,' Penny confirmed. 'His name was John.'

Maureen flinched, and clasped her hands to her face.

'John who?' Andee pressed.

Getting to her feet, Penny said, 'I'll leave Mum to tell you. Oh look,' she exclaimed, gazing out of the window, 'you have a cat. How lovely.'

'It belongs to next door,' Andee informed her.

Penny nodded. 'That makes sense. I don't suppose you'd ever want another after what happened to Smoky.'

Maureen looked as though she'd been struck. 'Where are you going?' she asked desperately. 'I thought . . . I've made some lunch.'

'I need to go,' Penny told her. 'You two have things

to discuss. I'll be in touch,' and moments later the door closed behind her.

Andee regarded her mother's ashen face. The air in the room seemed to have contracted, as though Penny had somehow taken it with her. 'So who is John?' Andee demanded, trying to keep her voice even.

'I can't do this now,' Maureen replied, clearly deeply upset as she got to her feet. 'I need to think. Please don't press me, Andee. It won't help.'

'Then what will?' Andee shouted. 'You're going to have to tell me at some point . . .'

'Just not now!' her mother snapped, and leaving Andee staring after her she ran upstairs and shut herself in her room.

She didn't come out for lunch, or accept a cup of tea. When Andee called out, all she would say was, 'I'll be fine. Please just leave me alone.'

Andee was so angry she wanted to beat the door down, but knowing it would only stress her mother more to be terrorised she kept herself in check and waited.

Eventually, still pale and visibly shaken, Maureen appeared downstairs and announced she had to hurry or she'd be late for one of her regular WI teas at Kesterly town hall.

'And you think that's more important than what's going on here?' Andee queried tersely.

'I'm not arguing about it,' Maureen replied, picking up her keys and handbag.

'So when will you be back?'

'In time for dinner, but I won't want much. There's some fresh pasta in the fridge if you'd like that.'

More worried now than frustrated, Andee said, 'Mum, I'm not sure you should go anywhere while . . .'

'Don't fuss, Andee. I need to get out of the house and do something . . . normal. So please let me be.'

'Then let me drive you.'

'I'm not an invalid. I'm capable of driving myself.'

If it had been possible, Andee would have stopped her, but without getting physical there was nothing she could do. Nor was she able to go and see DI Gould, for he'd texted to say he was at a conference somewhere in Devon this afternoon, not due back until tomorrow.

Deciding to call Penny, Andee found herself bumped through to voicemail. Abruptly she said, 'I don't know what you were hoping to achieve this morning, but Mum's very upset and I need to know what's going on. Call me when you get this.'

Two hours passed with no response.

In the end, in need of some air, Andee took herself over to the pub where she sat at an outside table with a shandy, barely aware of the world going by as she tried to deal with the unsettling, even alarming turn events were taking. Her past, and all the perceptions she'd had of people and things that had happened, the beliefs in those she loved, the guilt that had weighted her for years over Penny, the longing she'd felt for a sister she'd wanted so desperately to share things with, none of it seemed rooted in reality any more. And why was her mother so reluctant to talk to her, when it was clear that she needed to lean on her now more than she ever had? For some reason Maureen wasn't allowing herself to do that.

Becoming vaguely aware of a car slowing as it passed, Andee watched it absently, registering a young couple in the front who seemed to be staring at her. Were they friends of Luke's or Alayna's? She didn't recognise them, and when they didn't wave she simply assumed they were tourists and tracked the red Corsa round to the other side of the green, where it came to a stop a few yards from the entrance to the Smugglers' Cave. No one got out, and Brigand Bob, all kitted out in his usual scary smuggler's gear, was too busy seeing in a tour group to move the car on. Bob was very strict about parking, and the area around the green, especially outside the cave, was strictly off limits to anyone, except the disabled.

Maybe there was a badge in the car that she hadn't seen.

'Fancy another one of those?'

Shading her eyes, she looked up to find Graeme's partner, Blake Leonard, standing over her, and felt a rush of gladness to see him. If it couldn't be Graeme himself appearing out of nowhere, then Blake was an excellent second best.

'No more shandy,' she replied, 'but I'd love a glass of Sauvignon.'

'Coming up. Crisps, nuts, scratchings?'

Realising how hungry she was, she said, 'Nuts would be good. Thanks. You're home early.'

'I had to go and see a client over on Temple Rise, so I

decided to call it a day rather than go back to the shop. Have you spoken to Graeme today?'

'Briefly this morning. Everything seems to be going well in France.'

'Will you be surprised to hear that he's asked me to keep an eye on you?'

Andee smiled wryly. 'I guess not, but please tell him I'm fine, and he shouldn't worry.'

With a dubious arch of an eyebrow, he said, 'Right, wine and nuts it is. Don't go anywhere, I'll be right back.'

Admiring how upbeat he managed to seem when inside she knew he was still grieving deeply for the loss of his daughter, Andee gazed across the green again. The red Corsa was still there, and the young driver was standing beside it talking to Bob. Next thing, the two men were shaking hands before the younger one returned to the car, while the smuggler ambled back to the cave.

In spite of feeling surprised that Bob was allowing the Corsa to stay where it was, Andee soon dismissed the thought as Blake returned with their drinks and settled down opposite her.

'OK, do you want to do small talk, business talk, or some other kind of talk that might explain why you're looking so worried?' Blake offered after taking the top off his Guinness. He was a remarkably good-looking man with sandy brown hair, clean-cut features and eyes that were as kind as they were knowing. 'I can also do no talk at all,' he added generously, 'but that doesn't seem like much fun.'

Knowing from his tone that Jenny had told him what

was going on, Andee said, 'My sister visited again this morning.'

Blake didn't look surprised. 'Jenny saw the Mercedes on her way out,' he told her. 'So how did it go?'

Heaving a deep, uncertain sigh, Andee said, 'I hardly know where to begin, apart from with the fact that my family has apparently been hiding something from me for years. And I don't just mean something, I mean information that I should have been told, that probably should have been in the police files, but never was.'

Frowning, he said, 'Do you know what it is now?'

She shook her head. 'My mother still won't tell me, and Penny isn't returning my calls.'

Clearly understanding how upsetting this was for her, he sat back in his chair and regarded her steadily. 'So do you have any theories?' he prompted.

'Not really. Penny mentioned someone called John. How many Johns do you think there are . . .' She broke off suddenly and stared at Blake. 'My mother had a brother called John,' she stated, only just remembering. 'We never really knew him, he was a bit of a black sheep, so no one ever talked about him, at least not in front of us children. I don't recall him coming to visit more than a handful of times. He was into gambling, I think, or drugs, maybe both . . . He had a dreadful row with my father once. I don't remember what was said, only that there was a lot of shouting and my father ended up throwing him out of the house.'

'Did you ever ask your father about it?'

'No, I was quite young at the time, maybe thirteen or fourteen, so I was probably afraid he'd tell me off for eavesdropping. But my mother told me later ... that's right... that he'd wanted Daddy to lend him some money, and he'd started threatening him when Daddy refused.'

'A gambling debt?'

'Possibly.'

'So do you know where this villainous uncle is now?'

She shook her head. 'As far as I know no one's heard from him ... Hang on. He died. Quite a long time ago. I must have still been in my twenties and there was something ...' Her eyes sharpened as they went to Blake's. 'They found his body off the coast of Carmarthen, I think it was.'

Blake's eyebrows shot up. 'Well, the first question that comes to mind, is did he jump, or was he pushed?'

'I don't know. There must have been an investigation ... Maybe I need to look into it.' She was watching the red Corsa again. It was pulling away, heading out of the hamlet. 'Given my mother's reaction to the name John being mentioned this morning,' she said, 'I'm going to guess that her *brother* was somehow involved in Penny's disappearance.'

Blake said nothing, only watched her as she continued trying to pull things together. It was like attempting to complete a jigsaw in a fog with no idea if she even had the right, never mind all the pieces.

'Maybe she just assumed my father checked out her brother,' she said, 'but in reality it never happened. I know it sounds odd, but from some of the things she's said lately, there didn't seem to be a lot of proper communication going on between them at the time Penny went missing.'

'It doesn't sound odd to me,' Blake responded. 'Jenny and I all but dried up when Jessica disappeared. It's like you're afraid to talk in case something you say will raise hope where there is none, or stir up guilt, or blame . . . It's like navigating a minefield with something blowing up in your face every other step.'

Feeling for how desperate it must have been for the Leonards during those two agonising years of not knowing, Andee said, 'Well, whatever did or didn't happen with my uncle, we know that Penny was never found. Except she claimed this morning that she was. She said that my father saw her once, but he left her wherever she was and walked away.'

Blake blinked in shock. 'Do you believe that?' he asked.

Andee shook her head. Her father had been an unflinchingly honourable man who, more than anything in the world, had wanted to find his daughter and bring her home.

'So why would she lie?'

'Because she's messing with us,' Andee declared, certain it was true. 'Don't ask me why, maybe she's getting a kick out of it, but she definitely wound Mum up this morning, and I think it was intentional. In fact, I'm sure it was. The big question, though, is what is she really up to?'

Maureen couldn't think how this had happened. One minute she'd been driving home from the WI tea, the next she'd found herself here, on the wrong side of the headland with the car hopelessly stuck in a ditch.

She obviously hadn't been paying attention when she'd reached the fork at Pollard's farm, and had somehow managed to veer to the right instead of driving straight on towards Bourne Hollow.

There was nowhere to go from here, apart from over the cliff into the rampantly foaming sea below. Thankfully there was a barrier in place to stop such plunges from happening, or she might have done just that. Instead she'd tried to turn around on this narrow, rutted track and her back wheels had dropped into a gully, so were now spinning uselessly in thin air.

Her eyes scanned the mountainous landscape around her dotted with sheep and cattle, dissected by trees and hedgerows. Beyond there was only sky and sea, a vast swathe of perfect blue with the speck of a ship in the far distance on its way to the docks in Bristol. Seagulls screeched and dived through the air, and she could see, but not hear the merry lights of Paradise Cove curled into the hook of the bay. No matter how loudly she shouted or heartily she waved, no one there would be able to see or hear her.

What was she to do? There was no mobile phone reception here, and Pollard's farm was at least three miles back.

She gazed along the track, feeling hopelessly daunted by the prospect of such a long walk, too exhausted to do anything more than sink on to the grassy bank beside the car and drop her head in her hands.

Everything was crowding in on her, and she just knew that the next thing she was going to learn were gruesome details of all that her daughter had suffered at the hands of her brother and his cronies. She didn't want to go there. She simply couldn't bear it.

How had he hidden her?

Why had the police been unable to prove that he had her?

She knew so little of what had happened during that terrible time; she'd left it to David, knowing he'd had every available resource assigned to the search, that he'd have given his life to save his girl . . .

Daddy found me, once. He stared right at me, then he turned around and walked away.

It wasn't true; David would never have done that.

So why had Penny said it?

Maureen could only despise herself now for how weak she'd been back then. How could she, a mother, have allowed things to happen without asking more questions, insisting on more answers? It was no excuse that her husband had been far better placed than she was to understand, even oversee, the investigation. She shouldn't have been so trusting, should have forced them to let her be more involved, or at the very least more informed.

She was sure David had appointed a special team to interrogate John, for she could remember the relief she'd felt when she was told that her brother wasn't involved in Penny's disappearance. It wasn't that she'd ever been close to John, or cared about him enough to want him to stay in their lives, she'd simply needed to know that he hadn't carried out the veiled threat he'd once made to David.

Keep playing things my way, David, and I'll make sure everyone stays safe.

Oh Andee, Andee, she wailed desperately inside. She so badly needed to reach out to her elder daughter, and she would, because she had to, even though she knew Andee would never understand her mother's weakness, because Andee simply wasn't the sort of woman Maureen had been all those years ago. She was someone who took control, who wasn't afraid to stand up for herself and those she loved. If she wanted answers she'd get them, and Maureen was in no doubt that Andee would be expecting them now.

'Hello. Are you all right? Is there anything I can do?'

Maureen looked up, and her heart gave a twist of shock as her mouth opened and closed. 'Penny, what are you doing here?' she asked hoarsely. She wanted to pull away from the hand on her shoulder, but her limbs were like liquid, the world seemed to be spinning. 'Did you follow me? Why did you follow me?' she asked.

Penny looked confused and concerned. 'Have you had some sort of accident?' she said.

'It's proper stuck,' someone grunted from behind her. There was a man, with a beard and long hair inspecting the car.

'How did you know I was here?' Maureen asked Penny. 'I thought you were going to London.'

'Have you hit your head?' Penny enquired, coming down to her level.

Maureen drew back. 'Why did you go with him?' she asked. 'Did he force you?'

'We need to get help,' the man decided. 'Stay with her, I'll go and rustle some up.'

Maureen watched him start down the track, then

turned back to the woman beside her. She could see now that it wasn't Penny, and felt a surge of bile rush to her throat.

'I'm sorry,' she mumbled, trying to dab away her tears. 'I'm not . . . I got confused.'

'It's OK,' the woman soothed. 'It seems like you've had a bit of a shock. It's lucky we were passing, you could have been stranded here for hours. What happened? Did you get lost?'

'I took a wrong turn,' Maureen told her. 'Silly, because I live up this way, in Bourne Hollow, with my daughter, Andee. I should call her. She'll be worried.'

'Give me her number and I'll run after Simon. He can ring as soon as he's able. Will you be all right for a minute if I leave you alone?'

'Yes,' Maureen assured her, and after giving the woman Andee's number she lay down on the bank and closed her eyes.

Never, in all the years since Penny had disappeared, had she imagined herself one day wishing that she'd never come back, but it seemed that day had arrived, and she couldn't have felt more racked with guilt and remorse if she'd tried.

'Mum, wake up,' Andee urged gently.

Maureen's eyelids flickered as she rose slowly from the depths of a strangely dark sleep back to the sunlit world. 'Andee?' she said faintly, seeing Andee's face swimming about before her.

Easing her up, Andee said, 'Come on, let's get you home.'

Maureen looked around. 'Where are we?' she asked.

'Bearing Drop. You took a wrong turn and managed to get stuck.'

It was coming back to Maureen now, in slow, horrible waves. John, Penny, the search, the suicide note that hadn't been a suicide note at all, just a way of trying to get away from them all . . .

'We'll leave them to it,' Andee said, referring to Blake and the others who were helping him to bounce the Punto out of the ditch. 'Blake will drive your car back. I don't think there's any damage.'

Minutes later, as they were navigating the bumpy track back to the main road, Maureen mumbled, 'Why did she come? I don't understand it. After all these years . . . Why has it taken her so long?'

'Only she knows the answer to that,' Andee replied, 'but I intend to find out what it is, whether she's willing to tell us or not. Have you heard any more from her today?'

Maureen shook her head. 'Have you?'

'No, I tried calling, but she hasn't responded.'

Maureen gazed out at the passing hedgerows and hidden gates. 'We need to talk,' she stated, as Andee turned on to the road home.

'Yes, we do,' Andee agreed. 'And I need you to be honest and hold nothing back. Can you do that?'

Maureen nodded. 'Yes, I can,' she promised. 'We'll start as soon as we get home. And then I think we should go to the police.'

Chapter Six

An hour later Andee sat down at the table and raised her glass to her mother. 'To us,' she declared, putting both energy and affection into her tone.

With a tender smile Maureen clinked her glass and drank. There was more colour in her cheeks now, her eyes shone clearly; the ordeals of the day no longer seemed to be taking such a destabilising toll. If anything she appeared more together than Andee had seen her since Penny had returned to their lives. It was the relief, Andee realised, of having decided to let go of whatever she was holding back – had clearly been holding back for years.

At last, sounding slightly exasperated with herself, Maureen said, 'I keep trying to think of where to begin, but after so long it's become very jumbled.'

'Why don't you tell me if the John Penny referred to is John Victor, your brother?' Andee asked gently.

The light in Maureen's eyes dimmed.

Stepping through the partially open door, Andee said, 'And you suspected at the time that he might be involved?'

Maureen nodded. 'I was afraid he might be, because of something he once said to your father.' She paused as her mind swam with dark memories, secrets she'd kept buried for too many years. 'It was a horrible time,' she said quietly. 'John had been staying with my mother, Granny Victor . . . Do you remember, she used to live around the corner from us in Chiswick? Yes, of course you do. He hadn't seen her in almost five years. He hadn't been in touch either, not even for her birthday or Christmas. Then he turned up unannounced one day, and we soon found out that he was hiding from someone he owed money to. Granny wasn't in a position to help him and he knew it, but he told me that he'd ask her for it, even make her sell her flat, if I didn't give it to him myself. Of course I told Daddy – all the money I had belonged to both of us. He wasn't someone who'd give in to blackmail; he was very angry about it, but we knew, and so did John, how much it would upset my mother to discover that her beloved boy was in trouble, and she wasn't strong enough to deal with it. We'd already been told that she didn't have much longer to live, and because Daddy cared for her deeply, and was afraid of what desperation might make John do to speed up his inheritance, he agreed to let him come to the house so we could discuss things.

'They had a terrible fight, truly terrible, but Daddy ended up paying off the debt. He knew far better than I did the type of people John was involved with, the things they were capable of, and though his main concern was Granny, of course, he didn't want John's punishment or early demise on his conscience either.

When he handed the cheque over he told John that it would never happen again, and that after Granny's funeral he'd be on his own.

'John didn't seem in the least bit put out. If anything, he found it amusing. He said things like, "You know you can't resist me, and I'll come whenever I like . . ."' Maureen shook her head, as though still appalled and shamed by the scene. 'It was as he was leaving that he said to Daddy, "You know you really ought to watch out for those girls of yours, they're growing up fast, and that Penny's already a . . ." I can't remember the exact words he used, but there was no mistaking what he meant. He said, "Keep playing things my way, David, and I'll make sure she stays safe."'

Maureen sighed shakily, clearly as horrified by the threat now as she'd been at the time. That her own brother, the boy she'd played with growing up, who'd had the same parents as her, the same love and care, could threaten her teenage daughter that way . . . It was so beyond her comprehension that Andee could see how bitterly she still struggled with it.

Maureen forced herself to continue. 'Your father pushed him out of the door and slammed it hard in his face, letting him know that it would never be opened to him again. But by then Penny was already going off the rails; she'd started staying away from home, lying about where she was going and who she was with. The first time your father found her was probably the third or fourth that she'd taken herself off, but it was definitely the longest. Do you remember she told us she was staying with a friend called Madeleine? It turned out she was at Granny's and so was John. I don't know the exact details of what happened, Daddy didn't want to discuss it, but Granny told me later that she'd called Daddy herself because of the way Penny was behaving with John. It wasn't decent, she said, and she was afraid of where it would lead.'

Appalled, Andee said, 'What on earth did Granny mean? You don't think she thought Penny was sleeping with him?'

Maureen flinched. 'If not with him then with others he'd set her up with, possibly to help pay off his debts.'

Andee's eyes closed. It wasn't so much Penny she felt for as her mother, and the desperate, ravaging fear that her thirteen-year-old daughter was sleeping with anyone at such a tender age.

'It was what she wanted,' Maureen stumbled on, 'to go with men. She told Daddy that, but whether she meant it, or whether she said it to hurt him . . .' Her voice shook with emotions new and old, harsh and merciless. 'She was out of control. We didn't know what to do with her. When she asked to go on the pill I let her, because I didn't want the situation to get any worse than it already was. Daddy was furious when he found out, he told her she was grounded until she was sixteen, eighteen, I can't remember now. I only know that it wasn't long after that that she disappeared for good and I was always afraid that John had helped her in some way. And then the note came . . .'

Ashamed of how wrapped up in her teenage self she must have been not to have noticed any of this, Andee said, 'Well, we know now that he did help her.'

Maureen nodded awkwardly.

'What I don't understand,' Andee said, 'is why there's no record of him being questioned.'

'I can't explain that,' Maureen replied. 'Only Daddy could tell you, and obviously that's not possible.'

'Ah, but what is possible,' DI Terence Gould pointed out the following morning, after Andee had filled him in on everything so far, 'is that one or more of the officers working the case is still around to have a chat with. Can you give me any names?'

Andee's relief was so profound it was physical. 'So you'll help me?' she said, only realising now how much she'd been counting on it.

'Were you really in any doubt?' he countered, his large head tilted to one side as he regarded her with bright, steely eyes. He wasn't a man to be messed with, or taken for granted – or one who'd ever shied away from bending the rules in order to get to the truth. 'I'm guessing you want to keep it below the radar for the time being,' he went on. 'I'm good with that, but just run it by me again why you're so convinced this person is your sister.'

'She just is,' Andee said simply. 'She looks the same, sounds the same – my mother mistook her for me the first time she rang . . . Look at photos of yourself at fourteen, you'll find you haven't changed that much either.'

'Bit weightier, and greyer,' he grunted, 'but I take your point. And your mother's equally convinced?'

'She is. She was going to come with me today, but

decided at the last minute that she wasn't up to it. She's willing to talk to you any time if you think she can be helpful.'

'Lovely woman, your mother,' Gould commented. 'Reminds me a bit of my own, but with more class.'

Amused, Andee said, 'I wouldn't let your mother hear you say that if I were you.'

'She says it about herself. Anyway, your sister's motive for being in touch after all this time? You're obviously convinced it's not about happy reunions, so any theories?'

Andee blew out a breath as she shook her head. 'At first I thought she might be wanting to show off how successful she's become, but there's definitely more to it.'

'Go on.'

'OK, the first time she came she wanted to know if anyone had visited ahead of her. When I asked like who, she just shrugged it off. The second time she had a good look round the hamlet before coming into the house, trying to make it seem as though she was soaking it all in, but my gut told me she was at least half expecting to spot someone.'

He nodded thoughtfully. 'OK, I've had experience of your hunches, or instincts as you'd rather call them, so I'm willing to run with it. I can see it's unlikely her motive is money related, since you say she seems to have a lot of it. So we can put that aside and return to it if it becomes relevant. Passion is always a big motivator, but I'm not sure it's fitting with this. You're definitely not persuaded by the family ties?'

Andee shook her head. 'She's putting on a show to try and convince us of that, but it's not ringing true for me, or my mother. In fact I'm pretty sure she's playing with us – for kicks or for some other reason, I've no idea. I told you about the kitten – that keeps coming up – and apparently she took something of mine when she left that she wants me to try and remember.'

'But you don't?'

Andee shook her head.

'So she's manipulative? Calculating? Sly?'

'Possibly all of the above, with a veneer of friendliness that's good, but not Oscar-winning.'

'Did you believe her when she said your uncle was involved in her disappearance?'

'We both did. I think he had to be, given what my mother told me last night, but there's nothing about him in the police files.'

'Which is indeed odd, because there should be. Did you ever talk to your father about revisiting the case?' Gould asked.

'I tried, but it wasn't easy for him. He was already going downhill by then, and I could see that reliving it was causing him problems.'

'Because he knew there were some irregularities and he didn't want you to find them?'

'The thought never crossed my mind at the time. Maybe it should have, but we're talking about my *father*. I knew how hard Penny's disappearance had been for him, and I'd never had any reason to doubt him – over that, or anything else.'

He nodded, clearly understanding a daughter's trust,

even if they were both now questioning it. 'What's that?' he asked as she put a plastic bag on the table.

'It's the teacup she used the first time she came to the house. I'm not in any doubt, but I brought it just in case anyone wanted to run a check.'

'If we do it now we'll alert the Met to the fact that she might have turned up, and I thought you didn't want that.'

'Just in case you have any doubts . . .'

'If you don't, I don't,' he retorted, airing a confidence that made her wonder if she ought to be back on his team, if only to repay him for his trust in her.

'I realise I'm asking a lot,' she admitted, 'and that this could all backfire horribly . . .'

'. . . on me.'

'On you,' she conceded, 'but I think we're agreed that it's important, at least for the time being, to find out why now, and what she's hoping to gain.'

His eyebrows rose in agreement. After a while he started to shake his head as the enormity of it coursed through him again. 'Twenty-seven years,' he murmured, reaching for his phone as it rang. 'I've never come across anything like this before – unless it's a dead body.' Clicking on, he said, 'Gould speaking.'

Feeling dreadful for thinking that a dead body might have been less traumatic for her mother, Andee glanced out of the partition window to where a number of her ex-colleagues were busy at their desks. She'd stopped to greet Leo Johnson and Jemma Payne on her way in, the DCs she'd worked most closely with during her time in CID. The new detective sergeant, Lydia

Mitchell, who'd replaced her, hadn't seemed especially thrilled to meet her, although from the grimness of her features she didn't seem especially thrilled by life.

'OK, so going back to your sister's presumed ulterior motive,' Gould continued after ending his call. 'We don't think it's money, so that's parked for now. Passion we've dealt with. When are you next seeing her?'

'We have no arrangement, and she's not returning my calls, but I'm sure she'll be in touch at some point.'

Seeming as certain, he said, 'How much have you found out about her business life?'

'I only have access to Google these days, and it's not offering me a Michelle Cross that matches the kind of profile she's given me.'

'Remind me again what her businesses are.'

'Import-export . . .'

'Which could mean anything, unless she said what she's importing and exporting? No, of course she didn't. Go on.'

'Apparently there's a property management company, based in London. Two medical centres in the States. A travel agency in Stockholm, and an online dating service. And before you ask, I've no idea if any of it's true.'

'If it is, it's pretty diverse. Did she happen to mention the names of any of these companies?'

Andee shook her head. 'The only name she's mentioned so far is John Victor who we know met his untimely end twenty years ago.'

He wrote it down and stared at it, as though an epiphany of some sort might emerge.

'I've checked and the verdict on his death was open,' she told him.

'How long after your sister disappeared did he go off the cliff?'

'Eleven years.'

'Where did it happen?'

'Apparently at a remote spot off the coast of West Wales. No suicide note. I need to get hold of a copy of the inquest.'

He nodded, clearly processing it all as he continued to stare at Victor's name. 'He didn't have a wife or kids, no other family?' he asked.

'None that I know of.'

'What about Penny? When you spoke to her did she mention a husband or children?'

'We asked about children, and she avoided answering. As for her marital status, all I can tell you is that she turned up the first time wearing what could have been a wedding ring, but the second time there was no jewellery at all.'

Gould's eyebrows rose. 'So I'm guessing your next step is to find an address for her or one of her companies. How are you going to do that?'

'I have the registration number of her car, which I was hoping to leave with you.'

'No problem. I'll bring Leo Johnson up to speed about everything when you've gone and let him do the necessary. Shouldn't take long. Meantime, I'll get on to the Met and find out who worked the case with your father. Any names you remember?'

'Gerry Trowbridge was always close to my dad.

I spoke to him at the time I revisited the case, but his daughter and grandson had just been killed in a skiing accident so I didn't push very hard. Anyway, I didn't have any reason to when I presumed it was all on file. I've no idea where he is now. He'll be retired, obviously. Alive and compos mentis, we can always hope.'

'If he isn't, he won't have been the only member of the team, but I'll put him first on the list. You realise I won't be able to come with you?'

She did, though she regretted it.

'OK, now fascinating as this is, and much as I'd like to sit here all day discussing it, I have to be somewhere.'

'But you'll speak to Leo before you go?'

'No, when I get back, but there's no harm in letting him have the reg number now. Oh, and should you happen to hear from your sister before we're next in touch, be sure to let me know.'

Andee was driving back to Bourne Hollow, her mind so full of the conversation with Gould that it took her a moment to realise her mobile was ringing. Seeing it was Martin, her estranged husband, she was tempted to let it go to messages. However, she dutifully clicked on and delivered a cheery hello.

'Hi, everything OK your end?' he asked, trying to sound upbeat and managing resentful.

'Everything's fine my end,' she confirmed. 'Are you having a lovely time in Spain?'

'It's relaxing and hot. My mother's worried about

your mother. She says she's not sounded herself the last couple of times she's rung.'

'Really? Well you can tell her that Maureen's fine, no cause for concern. And I have to wonder,' she continued, turning at the end of the busy promenade to head towards home, 'why your mother isn't calling me herself.'

'I needed to speak to you anyway. Alayna tells me you're back from France. Is everything all right with you and Graeme?'

Since Martin was still bitter over their break-up, and would love nothing more than to hear that her relationship with Graeme had failed, she had to bite down hard on her annoyance. 'Yes it is, thank you. I just had a few things to do here.'

'So you won't be staying long?'

'I don't want to be rude, Martin, but how is this any of your business?'

Ignoring the question, he said, 'I've told Alayna that I'm happy to make up her loss in wages if she'd like to come to Africa with me to see Luke. I think she'd be more inclined to accept my offer if you came too.'

Silencing a weary sigh, Andee said, 'You know very well that she's determined to finance her gap year herself. I think you should feel proud of that instead of trying to tempt her out of it.'

'She needs a holiday.'

'Why don't you let her decide? She's not a child any more. When are you flying out?'

'Next Tuesday. It's a fascinating and worthwhile

project he's working on that I might be interested in supporting.'

Deciding not to remind him of how negligent he'd been of his children's projects during the time he'd walked out of their lives to go and find himself, she said, 'Well, I hope you have a lovely time.'

'Why *don't* you come along? You're an animal lover . . .'

'Martin, just stop. It isn't going to happen and you're making it harder for everyone, the way you keep trying to use the children to bring us together.'

'It's what they want.'

'No it isn't, and anyway, it's not about them, it's about me and what I want, which is for you to understand that I'm in another relationship now, and that's the way it's going to stay.'

Chapter Seven

Early the next morning DC Leo Johnson rang Andee with the information she had requested about the Mercedes.

'I don't know how helpful this is,' he told her, 'but the vehicle's registered to a chauffeur-drive company in Knightsbridge. I'll text the address and phone number when we finish this call. I've also taken the liberty of looking into the company's ownership. It's a couple of blokes with the same family name, Balodis, so I'm guessing they're brothers, or father and son, something along those lines.'

'It doesn't sound English.'

'Your guess is as good as mine. I'll text the correct spelling with the other details when we finish the call.'

'Thanks. I take it Gould has already filled you in on things?'

'Some, and it's just about blowing my mind. I guess it must be having the same effect on you, times ten.'

'Something like that. Can I ask another favour while you're on?'

'Sure, shoot.'

'Can you get hold of a copy of the inquest report on John Victor?'

'Your uncle?'

'That's him. I'll text the dates and details I know. In addition to that, can you find out if he had any kind of police record, where he lived at the time of his death, what he did for a job, who his friends or associates were. Anything you can dig up that may or may not seem relevant.'

'I'll get back to you as soon as I have something.'

By ten thirty Andee was on a train to London, knowing that to get the kind of information she was after from Exclusive Chauffeur Drive she'd stand a far better chance if she turned up in person than if she tried to do it on the phone. Even so, it probably wouldn't be easy, since it was highly likely Penny had guessed she'd have the Mercedes traced, and had briefed the company to expect her. Had she needed to do that? There was simply no way of knowing.

A quick Google search had told her that the name Balodis was Latvian, which might have been the language Penny had used during her first visit. Since Andee knew not a single word of it herself, she had no way of recognising it.

It was after midday by the time the train pulled into Paddington, spilling fast-moving wheelie bags and important owners on to the platform to begin a race for the Tube, taxis and buses. As she moved with the crowd Andee was remembering what a thrill it gave her as a small child to come to this station; she'd always felt sure she'd spot her favourite bear if she looked hard enough.

She and Penny had had Paddingtons when they were young; she remembered them swapping bears because Penny had decided Andee's was bigger, or cuter, or more cuddly, or something that had made it better than hers.

'She's just a baby,' their mother had said when Andee had tried to hang on to hers. Penny had been two or three at the time. 'You don't mind swapping really.'

Strange the things that came to mind that had never seemed to have much significance before. She wasn't sure this memory did now, apart from the fact that it was an early example of Penny coveting what was hers, this time viewed in a different light thanks to recent events.

Since she was wearing flat shoes and carrying a light bag she decided the sunshine was too good to miss, so she set out on foot for Knightsbridge. On reaching Hyde Park she started across the grass, weaving amongst sunbathers and strollers, while trying, not very hopefully, to get hold of Penny.

To her amazement she got an answer on the third attempt.

'Andee! What a lovely surprise. How are you?'

Adjusting rapidly, Andee said, 'I'm fine. Actually, I'm in London, and I was hoping we could meet.'

Seamlessly, Penny said, 'Gosh, that would have been lovely, but even as we speak I'm on my way to Heathrow.'

'I see.' Why wasn't she surprised? 'Where are you going?'

'To the States. I'm afraid we have some clients who are in a bit of a state and it's my job to go and calm them down. But I should be back in a couple of days. If you're still around I'd love to see you.'

'I'm just here for the day. I was wondering when you were going to be in touch with Mum again.'

'Soon. Very soon. I just need to get this problem sorted first. It's such a pity you're going home today. I'd have offered you my apartment if you were going to stay longer, except it's having a makeover at the moment. However, I have a suite at a very nice hotel on Buckingham Palace Road. You're more than welcome to use it if you change your mind and decide to hang out in town for a while.'

'That's kind of you, but not this time, thanks.' During the awkward pause that followed Andee's gaze fell on a stray cat, wending its way through the bushes at the edge of the park. 'Tell me something, do you know what happened to Smoky the kitten?'

With a sad-sounding sigh, Penny said, 'Oh dear. Poor Smoky.'

Since that wasn't an answer, Andee waited.

'It was your fault, of course,' Penny told her. 'You shouldn't have tried to take him away from me.'

Andee's insides knotted. She had no memory of that, could barely remember the cat at all. 'So what did you do?' she asked, certain she didn't want to know the answer.

Without sounding in the least perturbed, Penny said, 'I broke his neck.'

Andee was sitting on a bench in the shade of a towering horse chestnut, still shaken by Penny's admission and needing to try and deal with it somehow. 'Mum, it's me,' she said when her mother answered the phone.

'Hello darling, are you there yet?' Maureen asked.

'Yes, I'm in Hyde Park. I've just spoken to Penny.'

Her mother's voice lost its buoyancy. 'Did she ring you?' she said.

'No, I rang her and this time she answered. Apparently she's on her way to the States, but that's not the reason I'm calling. I asked her about the kitten and she said . . . Did I try to take it away from her?'

'No, but the kitten seemed to prefer you and I suppose . . .'

When her mother didn't continue Andee said, 'She told me she broke its neck.'

When Maureen remained silent Andee's eyes closed at the gruesome, stomach-turning picture of a nine-year-old girl, her own sister, ending a kitten's life with her bare hands. 'How could she have done it?' she whispered incredulously.

'I don't know,' Maureen replied. 'It was very upsetting, a horrible, horrible shock when I found it.'

'Did you ever talk to her about it?'

'No, because I didn't want to accuse her in case she hadn't done it.'

'But you felt sure she had?'

'I kept trying not to believe it.'

Andee took a breath. 'Did she ever do anything else like that?'

'I don't know. I . . . There were things . . . She was always jealous of you, kept convincing herself that people preferred you to her.'

. . . sometimes I hate her for being so much better than I am at everything. No one ever seems to notice me when she's in the room. It's like I become invisible . . .

Andee felt her head starting to spin. 'How come I never realised any of this?' she asked bleakly.

'I think you did on one level, but you were older, more confident, and I guess you treated it more as an irritant than anything to be taken too seriously.'

Which would only have made it worse for Penny.

So was she responsible for Penny abandoning her family and putting her parents through utter hell?

No, only Penny could be responsible for that. She, Andee, wasn't going to fall into the trap of blaming herself, or of allowing Penny to get to her, however hard she tried.

A few minutes after ringing off from her mother she was updating Graeme. 'When I met with Gould yesterday,' she said, 'he suggested a couple of motives for why people do things, the first being money, the second passion. There are others, of course, including revenge, and I'm wondering if that might be what's behind Penny's return.'

The possibility of it silenced him.

Hearing herself say it silenced her, too.

'But for what?' he protested.

'I don't know. Imagined wrongs . . . The way her

mind works, it's . . . well, it's different . . . I just can't get a handle on what might be going on with her.'

'But to have held a grudge for so long? You know, I'm really not liking the sound of this. You need to speak to Gould again.'

'Perhaps she decided to punish us by staying away. Punish us for what, I'm still not sure. I'm not sure about any of this to be honest, but right now I'm going to see what I can find out at this chauffeur company.'

Exclusive Chauffeur Drive was at the end of a smart cobbled mews close to Belgrave Square, with vivacious begonias spilling from pots each side of its front door, and a small brass plaque bearing its name in elegant script above the bell. The opaque bay window to the right of the door glowed like cloudy silver in the afternoon sun, while what had once been an old-fashioned carriage entrance was now an olive green, square-panelled up and over garage door. It was closed, so it wasn't possible to see what vehicle, if any, was inside, but the garage didn't appear big enough to hold much more than a Smart and a motorbike.

Andee pressed the bell and glanced up and down the exclusive, quaintly crooked street. No one was around; it was as quiet as a rural idyll, right here in the middle of town. So quiet that she almost jumped as a voice came from a hidden intercom inviting her in.

Spotting a surveillance camera tucked under the guttering two floors up, she stepped into a postage-stamp lobby with a door to the right marked Private, another to the left signalling the garage, and a staircase straight ahead with a sign directing visitors up to reception.

'Hello,' a cheery female voice shouted down, 'have you been here before? If not, we're upstairs; if you have you know the way.'

The first level, with its surprisingly high ceiling and pale carpeted floors, turned out to be mostly open-plan, with a chic leather-fronted welcome desk, three arty sofas arranged around a glass and steel coffee table, a small bar with tall stools, and a large cardboard cut-out of an S class Mercedes.

'Hi, welcome to Exclusive, it'll be a pleasure to serve you in any way we can,' the beautiful, sparkly-eyed receptionist gushed. From her Slavic features and marked accent Andee guessed her to be Polish, and in spite of the sober dove-grey suit over a white silk shirt, she gave off the air of a mischievously happy life-lover. 'My name is Martyna,' she declared. 'Is it permitted to ask yours?'

Andee gave her name as Jenny Leonard, waited as Martyna repeated it, and was about to say more when a door behind the reception desk opened and a portly man with slicked-back hair, narrow eyes and a gold-glinting smile came out to greet her.

'Oto Balodis, at your service,' he told her, holding out a hand to shake. His grip was firm and cool, his smile was warm. 'Please tell us how we may best assist you, Ms Leonard.'

Deciding she wouldn't want to meet him on a dark night, Andee said, 'Actually, I'm hoping you can help me to find someone.'

He appeared surprised and intrigued. 'Please, take a seat,' he offered, directing her to the sofas. 'Martyna will bring us some refreshment.'

'Thank you,' Andee said as she sat down. 'Water will be fine for me.'

After nodding in Martyna's direction, Balodis said, 'So who is it you're looking for? Of course we will do our best to help.'

So gracious, and yet Andee could sense a certain wariness gathering. 'Well, it's the strangest thing,' she said chattily, 'but I was in the South of France recently, L'Isle-sur-la-Sorgue to be precise, when I saw an old friend of mine in the back of a Mercedes. She saw me too, but the traffic was crazy that day so she couldn't stop. Fortunately I managed to get the registration number of the car, and an old colleague of mine at the DVLA did me the favour of giving me your address. I hope you don't mind.'

Balodin's narrow eyes turned to slits. 'No, of course not. As I said, we are happy to help.' Funny, but he wasn't sounding all that happy.

'Here's the number,' Andee said, handing him a piece of paper. 'And the date I saw the car. My friend and I go back a long way. It's a real shame that we lost touch, our families were very close, but you know how these things happen. Time goes on, people get busy . . .'

Balodin was passing the registration number to Martyna.

Taking it, Martyna began entering it into the computer.

All charm again, Balodin said, 'I'm sure you understand that we can't give out our clients' details. It would be highly unethical and against all our principles. It is a very *exclusive* service that we operate here.'

Andee mimicked crestfallen. 'I was afraid you'd say that, it's just that I have something of hers that I'd really like to return.'

'Perhaps you can leave it with us and we'll pass it on. This is presuming the registration belongs to one of our cars, of course.'

Certain he already knew that it did, Andee grimaced. 'I don't have it with me, I'm afraid, and I'd really rather do it myself.'

Martyna said, 'According to our records, that car was in London on the date you've given me.'

'Oh, I see,' Andee said dolefully. However, since learning there was a chauffeur service involved, it had already occurred to her that the car she'd seen outside Briar Lodge might not be the same one Penny had used in France. 'Well, my friend's name is Michelle Cross . . .'

Balodin was getting to his feet. 'I'm afraid we do not have any clients by that name,' he interrupted.

'Perhaps the booking was in a company name,' Andee suggested.

Balodin said, 'Forgive me for repeating myself, but we are not in a position to discuss our clients.'

Intrigued by the brush-off, Andee stood up too. 'I guess she must be a client if she was in one of your cars . . .'

'But the car wasn't in France that day,' he reminded her, 'so you must be mistaken. Now, if you'll excuse me, I am due at a meeting in a few minutes. It was a pleasure making your acquaintance, and I'm very sorry that we haven't been able to help.'

Finding herself already on the stairs, Andee reassured him again that she understood his situation, and after thanking him for his time she took out one of Jenny's business cards. 'When you next speak to Michelle,' she said, 'would you mind giving her this?'

'As I said, we have no clients by that name.'

She watched him look at the card.

'Interior design?' he queried.

Andee smiled. He'd obviously been no more convinced by her claim to an old friendship than she had by him apparently running an everyday chauffeur service. However, the card had momentarily thrown him. 'If you're ever looking for anyone,' she offered.

He nodded distractedly and after asking Martyna to see 'our guest' out, he returned to his office.

'I probably shouldn't tell you this,' Martyna whispered as they stepped outside the front door, 'but it *was* one of our cars you saw in France, just not that one.'

Smiling her appreciation, while feeling certain the girl had been instructed to pass on the information, Andee said, 'And the client inside was Michelle Cross?'

Martyna shook her head. 'Not according to the file.'

Intrigued, Andee said, 'So who was it?'

Martyna glanced over her shoulder. 'I really shouldn't tell you . . .'

Going along with what she felt sure was a charade, Andee said, 'I'm just an old friend attempting to renew contact. I promise, I'm not out to cause trouble.'

Martyna dropped her voice again. 'She's a regular client of ours. Her name is Andrea Lawrence, so you see it couldn't have been your friend.'

Andee stared at her hard. Penny was using *her* name to . . . To what? And did this girl know that *she* aka Jenny Leonard was the real Andrea Lawrence? 'Well, whoever Andrea Lawrence is,' Andee said, managing to sound no more than chatty, 'she looked very like my friend.'

'I'm sorry if you've had a wasted journey,' Martyna said, seeming to mean it.

'Oh it hasn't been,' Andee assured her. 'It was lovely meeting you. Have you worked here long?'

'Almost seven years. Actually, it was Mrs Lawrence who helped me to get my job. It's fantastic what she does. She helps so many people. I would not be where I am if it weren't for her. None of us would, including my bosses.'

Deciding to be fascinated, Andee said, 'So what does she do, Mrs Lawrence?'

'As I said, she helps people. Ssh, I'd better go back inside, but I wanted you to know that you were mistaken about your friend. Such a pity, I do hope you find her.'

Andee thanked her and set off back to the station.

'I have to admit,' she told Graeme on the phone, 'finding out that she's using my name really blindsided me. That's if she is. I'm pretty certain the receptionist was briefed to say what she did should I happen to turn up.'

'To what end?'

'I've no idea. The boss certainly didn't want to discuss Michelle Cross. I'm guessing, when I mentioned the name, that was the moment he realised I was the person he'd been tipped off about.'

'Whereupon he left it to the receptionist to deliver the bombshell that Andrea Lawrence was the client in the car?'

'Apparently. I'm intrigued by the do-gooder who helps people get jobs.'

'Do you believe it?'

'I've no idea what to believe, but right now I'm interested to see how long it takes for Penny to contact me, because I'm sure she'll have been told about my visit the minute I left the office.'

Maureen had just reversed from the drive at the side of Briar Lodge when a young lad around her grandson Luke's age suddenly appeared out of nowhere and held up a hand for her to stop.

Winding down the driver's window, she said, 'Are you looking for Luke?'

He shook his head. 'No, I . . .'

'Are you lost?'

'I don't think so. I'm sorry to interrupt you.' His voice was surprisingly soft and sounded quite cultured, maybe accented, and even at a distance she could see that he was extremely good-looking. 'I'm looking for Andee Lawrence,' he told her.

'She's my daughter,' Maureen replied. 'Is there something I can help with?'

He glanced over his shoulder to a red car that was

parked close by. 'If you're her mother,' he said, turning back to her, 'then you must be my grandmother.'

Maureen's eyes dilated as her heart gave a slow, strange contraction. 'You're . . . You're Penny's son?' she asked, in a whisper.

He nodded briefly and glanced at the car again. 'I need to talk to Andee,' he told her. 'She's a detective, isn't she?'

'She was,' Maureen managed to confirm. This boy, this stranger with his beautiful voice and shock of fair hair, was her grandson? 'I'm just going to pick her up,' she ran on, hardly aware of what she was saying. 'She's been in London today.' She started to get out of the car. She needed to hug him, or invite him in, or do something other than just sit there, but he stopped her with raised hands. He was looking at a white van coming around the green towards them. 'You're being watched,' he muttered.

Maureen blinked.

'I have to go,' he gasped, and before she could utter another word he ran back to the car, jumped in and drove around the green at speed.

Maureen gazed after him, too thrown to do anything more. She barely even registered Blake as he drew up outside his own house in the white van.

'Is everything OK?' he asked, coming to find out why she was standing next to her car with it parked half in, half out of her drive.

'I'm not sure,' she replied, still staring after the red car that had vanished over the brow of the hill. 'I've just had . . . The car that just drove off . . . Did you see it?'

He nodded. 'Was it someone you know?'

'The lad driving it just told me he's my grandson.'

Blake blinked with shock. 'You mean, Penny's son?'

'That's what he said.'

Blake looked across the green to where the hamlet entrance was quietly empty and shaded by a wind-blown holm oak. 'What else did he say?' he asked.

'That he needed to speak to Andee, then he saw your van and seemed to take fright.'

Clearly as baffled as she was, he glanced back across the hamlet as he said, 'Did you happen to get a number for the car?'

She shook her head.

'And he didn't tell you his name?'

'I'm afraid we didn't get that far.' She checked the time. 'I should go, Andee's train is due in at half past.'

Opening her car's passenger door he said, 'Come on, I'll drive,' and going round to the other side he got in and started towards town.

Andee was at Fruit of the Vine wine bar in the old town with her mother and Blake, feeling as stunned and baffled as they were by the mysterious visit from the lad claiming to be Penny's son. 'And he didn't say what he wanted to talk to me about?' she asked. 'Or give you a number for me to reach him?'

'There wasn't time,' Maureen replied. 'It all happened so fast. A van appeared, which was Blake's. He said something about me being watched and the next minute he was in his car and gone.'

To Blake Andee said, 'It was definitely a red Corsa?'

'It was,' he confirmed, sitting back as their drinks arrived.

'Did you notice a red Corsa parked on the green, close to the Smugglers' Cave, when we were at the pub the other evening?'

Grimacing, he said, 'I can't say I did, but I'm surprised Brigand Bob didn't try to move him on, you know . . .'

'He might have,' Andee interrupted. 'He certainly spoke to him, and then ended up allowing him to carry on parking there. Which means we have to speak to Bob to find out *why* he didn't move him on. The cave will be closed by now. Does anyone know where Bob lives?'

No one did.

Taking out her phone Andee pressed in Leo Johnson's number. As she waited for him to answer, she said, 'Did you notice if there was a girl in the car?'

Both Maureen and Blake looked perplexed.

'I thought I saw a girl with him on the green,' Andee explained, and put up a hand as she was connected to Leo's voicemail. 'Hi, it's Andee,' she announced. 'I need an address for Brigand Bob who helps run the Smugglers' Cave at Bourne Hollow. Call me when you can. If it's not this evening, don't worry, he'll be at the cave by nine tomorrow so I'll see him then.' As she rang off, she said to her mother, 'So did this boy happen to resemble Penny at all?'

'I didn't get that good a look,' Maureen replied doubtfully. 'His hair was fair, and hers was always dark when she was young, like yours. But of course he could take after his father.'

'Whoever that might be,' Andee muttered. 'What sort of age would you put him at?'

'Not much older than Luke, maybe twenty-three or four.'

After messaging Gould requesting another meeting in the morning, Andee was about to speak again when her mobile rang. Not bothering to hide her surprise, she said, 'This should be interesting. It's Penny.'

Chapter Eight

'Andee, I hope this is a good time,' Penny cried cheerfully.

'As good as any,' Andee replied smoothly. She hadn't yet told her mother about Penny calling herself Andrea Lawrence, and wasn't keen to if she could avoid it. Maureen was finding it hard enough to cope with things as it was, the prospect of any further mind games would only make matters worse. 'How are you?' she asked. 'I take it your flight's arrived wherever it was going.'

'Houston. Texas. We got in about an hour ago. I'm currently on my way into the city. So, how was your day in London? Are you still there?'

'No, I'm back in Kesterly. It was . . . productive.'

'You didn't tell me why you were there.'

'I was looking up an old friend.'

'And you found her? Him?'

'Kind of.'

'I have a lot of resources at my fingertips, if there's anything I can help with.'

'That's very kind of you. I'll remember that.' She

waited, wondering what the point of this call really was, for Balodis, or Martyna, had almost certainly informed her of the visit to their office, so what was she hoping to find out now?

To her surprise Penny said, 'Well, I should probably ring off. We've just arrived at the hotel. You have my number if you need me.'

'And you have mine.'

After Andee had ended the call, her mother said, 'What was that about?'

Andee sipped her wine and shook her head slowly, thoughtfully. 'A good question,' she replied.

'Does she know you went to the chauffeur-drive office?' Blake asked.

'I'm sure she does, but she didn't mention it. I used Jenny's business card, by the way.' Catching the expression on her mother's face, she wished she hadn't mentioned it. 'I told you this morning,' she said, 'that I was afraid if I gave my own name I might not get in the door. Penny will have been expecting me to trace the car, so there was a chance she had the people at the chauffeur-drive company on some kind of alert.'

Maureen either didn't remember or she simply didn't understand. 'Why would she do that?' she asked.

'Why is she doing anything?' Andee countered.

'You didn't ask about her son,' Blake pointed out.

'I wanted to see if she mentioned him first.'

'But she didn't?'

Andee shook her head again and refilled her glass. 'We've no idea what's going on here,' she sighed, 'but if he is who he says he is and wants to speak to me . . .

I'd like to give him the chance before . . .' Before what? 'Before I jump to any conclusions,' she decided.

'And if he turns out to be an impostor, someone sent by Penny to . . .' Blake broke off as Andee kicked him under the table.

Maureen was looking more bemused than ever. 'He came across as a nice enough lad,' she mumbled, 'but you can never be sure these days, can you?'

The following morning Andee was waiting outside the Smugglers' Cave when Brigand Bob, looking for all the world like an ageing Jack Sparrow in his tricorne cap, black frock coat and fancy breeches, came swashbuckling along the street ready to start the day.

Their chat lasted only a few minutes, during which Andee learned that the boy in the Corsa had asked if he and his girlfriend could park up for a while as his girlfriend was pregnant and feeling faint.

'Proper pale, she was,' Bob told her. 'And just a slip of a thing, with this great big belly . . .'

'I don't suppose,' Andee ventured, 'you happened to ask their names?'

Clearly astonished, he said, 'Why on earth would I do that?' Then, apparently remembering that she used to be police, he added, 'Should I have?'

'No, no,' she assured him. 'It's just that they came back here yesterday . . . Did you see them?'

'No, can't say I did. Why, what are they supposed to have done?'

'Nothing as far as I know, but he told my mother he wanted to speak to me. If you happen to see him again, could you try to get his name and maybe even a number?'

'I'll do my best. I could give him yours if you didn't mind me passing it on.'

After texting him the number Andee left him to his first tourists of the day, already straggling up the hill from the coach park, and went to get into her car.

As she drove into Kesterly her mind was darting about all over the place, though she was aware of how lack of sleep could alter perspective and even create a sense of paranoia. Heaven knew she'd been there during the night, when she'd become increasingly bothered by Penny's use of her name. What on earth was that about, and how often had she done it? Did she actually have documents such as a passport and driver's licence in the name of Andrea Lawrence? Apart from the chauffeur company, who had very possibly been instructed to give her name as a part of some warped little game directed by Penny, who knew her as that?

Then there was the mysterious appearance of a boy claiming to be Penny's son, with a pregnant girlfriend. What would he have done, or said, if he'd found Andee at home yesterday? Had he seen her the other evening at the pub? Maybe he didn't know what she looked like, although, given how frequently she'd appeared in the media, it wouldn't have been hard for him to find out.

So the boy either hadn't wanted to approach her the other evening, or he'd been waiting for instructions from Penny before making his next move.

After leaving her car in the underground car park on

Victoria Square, Andee splashed through the puddles of a sudden downpour over to Kesterly police station. Leo Johnson, looking as cute as ever with his mop of carroty hair and rash of cornflake freckles, was waiting to take her up to a fourth-floor conference room. Someone, probably Leo, had thought to order a Thermos of coffee, and when Gould joined them a couple of minutes later he tossed a greasy bag of pastries on to the table with an instruction for them to help themselves.

Gould and Johnson listened quietly as Andee updated them on the past twenty-four hours. Occasionally one or other of them made a note, or nodded, but mostly they scowled with concentration.

'OK,' Gould announced when she'd finished. He leaned back in his chair to retrieve the coffee pot from the buffet behind him. 'Leo has a copy of the inquest report you asked for, which contains some interesting background on the deceased Uncle John. We'll let you read that at your leisure, because I can't see how it'll impact what we're trying to find out now, which is why your sister has decided to return to the fold, if that's how we want to term it, and how frequently she's used your name.'

'Could it cause me a problem?' Andee wanted to know.

'On the face of it, it shouldn't. If she's committed any kind of crime while using it you'll presumably have an alibi, or sufficient grounds for denial, so I can't see anything to worry about. It's more a question of why she's using it. Leo, over to you.'

'After I got your email yesterday,' the young DC began, 'I made some preliminary searches and it turns out that your name appears as a director of Exclusive Chauffeur Drive. It's down as A.G. Laurence, with a "u", but it's as near as damn it.'

'Andrea Greta,' Gould stated, as if she didn't know.

'My maternal grandmother,' she informed them.

'Going further into the company documents,' Leo continued, 'it shows that A.G. Laurence provided the firm's start-up funding back in 2007.'

'Which is kind of what the receptionist told you,' Gould pointed out, 'that she helped her bosses get the company going.'

Andee looked at them, hoping they could come up with some suggestions of how this information might serve them, but apparently they were as lost for an explanation of anything as she was.

Moving them along, Gould said, 'Your nephew, her son, or whoever he is. As we have nothing to go on right now we'll just have to wait to see if he gets in touch again. If he does, I'd caution you to be careful, for the simple reason that we have no idea who he actually is, or what he wants.'

Worriedly, Andee said, 'Do you think my mother's vulnerable in the house when I'm not there?'

'I've been thinking about that,' Gould replied, 'and if there is somewhere you can take her that's a little less remote then it might not be a bad idea.' He took a sip of his coffee and referred to a printout in front of him. 'I'll email this to you,' he told her, 'but, in brief, I've heard back from the Met about your father's old colleague, Gerry Trowbridge. He was a DCS himself by the time he retired, nineteen years ago, but as you're no doubt aware he was a detective inspector at the time of the search for Penny. The good news is he's alive, the bad news is he lives in Wales.'

Confused, Andee said, 'Why is that bad news?'

'I've never got on with the Welsh,' Gould grunted.

Amused, she cast a glance at Leo, who was hiding his own mirth. 'Which is relevant how?' she challenged.

'It's not,' Gould conceded, 'but it's likely to mean you have to go there if you want to speak to him.'

'Well, it's hardly the other side of the world, and I happen to love Wales and the Welsh.'

Casting her a pitying look, he said, 'I tried calling him myself when I got the email, but so far I haven't managed to get hold of him so I can't tell you how willing he might be to talk to you.' He waited as she checked an incoming text.

As she read it her heart skipped a beat moments before her blood ran cold.

Good morning from Houston. Thought you might like to know that the young man who visited our mother yesterday is indeed my son, her grandson. His name is John Victor Jr.

Andee felt suddenly sick. She kept staring at the words, knowing what Penny wanted her to think and trying desperately not to think it. Was she doing this to be spiteful, to hurt her mother in some way, or was it the truth?

Taking the phone Gould read the message, swore under his breath, and passed it to Leo.

'My mother can't know about this,' Andee told them.

'Under no circumstances should she be told, whether it's true or not.'

Neither of them argued.

As Leo returned the phone, Gould said, 'I really don't like what's happening here. In fact, I don't like it at all.'

Andee was so shaken by the text that she couldn't face returning home right away. She needed to be alone to think and try to make sense of what was happening, if there *was* any sense, so switching off her phone she drove along the coast road, turning at Hope Cove to climb the hill to where Graeme's sisters lived, before driving on to the moor.

The weather wasn't at its best as she strolled away from the car, a low gloomy sky stretching out over the bay turning the sea a drab slate-grey and preventing the sun from showing the cliffs and heathland in their natural vivid colours. As she headed towards a deserted bench at a lonely lookout point, she found herself wondering if she was being watched. There was certainly no sign of this, but that was the whole point of surveillance, not to be seen or even sensed by the target. However, it would be hard for a watcher to blend into the landscape here, given that it wasn't possible to reach the spot without a car, and no one had known she was coming, or had been driving behind her for at least the last three miles.

With the breeze tossing her hair and the scent of salty sea mixing with pungent damp earth, she sat quietly staring at the distant choppy waves, picturing Penny as a child, trying to work out what had gone wrong, and why she, as the older sister, hadn't noticed things about her that perhaps she should have done.

What kind of person just walks away from a decent, loving home, no matter what problems there might be, and never comes back?

Not a normal one, that was for sure.

So her sister wasn't normal, at least not in a conventional way, but did that make her bad or crazy, or something much worse?

In her mind's eye she could see Penny during their holidays in Kesterly, laughing excitedly at some mischief they were up to, scampering about the beach in her blue cotton shorts and stripy top, climbing the rocks, foraging for crabs or seashells or whatever booty the tide had delivered. Andee could only remember her sister being happy here. She had scant recollection of their quarrels, though they'd happened, of course, but she had no memory of anything worse than the usual sibling tensions, and certainly not of Penny building a towering resentment that would drive her to inflict cruelty on innocent creatures.

However, there were times when *she,* Andee, had been cruel to Penny, either not wanting to share something with her, or take her to wherever she was going, or help her to look pretty. Teenage behaviour that she was ashamed of now.

'I want to look just like you,' Penny used to beg, 'then everyone will like me too.'

'Don't be ridiculous,' Andee had snapped. 'It's not

about looks, it's about personality and you just don't have one.'

The dreadful things she'd said to her, and she couldn't remember now how Penny had reacted, but she must have been hurt, who wouldn't be when spoken to like that?

'Will you teach me to dance the way you do?' Penny had asked.

'I don't have time, now get out of my way.'

'Have you kissed a boy yet?'

'It's none of your business.'

'I have.'

'Don't lie, you're only thirteen.'

'What's that got to do with it?'

Andee couldn't think why that particular conversation had come back to her now; she had no recall of being especially intrigued at the time. It was the kind of thing Penny used to say to make herself seem more interesting or mysterious without, Andee had assumed, a shred of reality behind it.

Yet according to their mother Penny had actually been sleeping with men at that age. It was what she'd wanted, Maureen had claimed.

Closing her eyes, Andee held her face up to the feathery rain, feeling the dampness in her hair, seeping between her toes and covering her hands. Was it loneliness that had driven Penny to be the way she was, a terrible certainty that her older sister was the favourite and that she wasn't wanted at all?

It didn't excuse what she'd done to their parents; nothing would ever excuse that.

'I've found something out that you don't know,' she'd told Andee not long before she'd disappeared.

'Good for you.'

'Don't you want to know what it is?'

'No.'

'It's about Mum's brother, Uncle John.'

'Sorry, couldn't care less.'

She'd assumed at the time that Penny was about to make something up, or maybe she'd been through their mother's letters and found some old scandal. Whatever, Andee genuinely hadn't been interested. Was that, insignificant as it had seemed at the time, what had finally prompted Penny to go?

She'd said it was her decision.

And what then?

Had she wanted to come back at any time but John Victor had refused to let her? Or had she been happy to stay with him?

John Victor Jr.

Andee's insides churned at the unthinkable suggestion.

With all her heart she wished she could speak to her father right now.

What had really happened back then?

Had he found Penny and walked away?

What clues was she, Andee, missing now?

What did Penny want?

The only person who could answer her questions was Penny, but with the way things were Andee felt no confidence in receiving straight, or even truthful answers. Penny simply wasn't the kind of woman Andee had imagined her growing into; she wasn't someone Andee could feel any sort of affinity with at all. It would appear that, behind the sophisticated, friendly front she so effortlessly put on there was something deeply disturbed and malicious about her sister. Why else would she have reminded their mother about the fate of Smoky the kitten? What had been the point of that? What was she getting from it? And why make her decision to leave, and all the heartbreak she'd caused, sound as though it wasn't something that had remotely worried her? She must have known how hurtful that would be for her mother, though it didn't come close to how Maureen would feel were she to be told who'd fathered her grandson.

'Talk about being careful of what you wish for,' she said to Graeme as she drove back into town. 'All these years I used to dream about how wonderful it would be if she came back into our lives, and now here she is and I can't help wishing . . .' She didn't finish the sentence, he knew what she was saying.

'What have you decided to tell your mother about John Victor Jr?' he asked carefully.

'Nothing at the moment, but I guess I'll have to at some point, or there's a good chance Penny will. Do you think she's done it this way to set me the challenge of telling Mum?'

'If it's true, then given how she's operated so far, I'd say it's possible she wants you to do it for her.'

'Because it would churn my stomach, and once I've told my mother Penny's as likely to deny it, or say I misunderstood, or he isn't her son at all, meaning she'll have caused a lot of stress and upset for no good reason other than to give herself some sort of perverse pleasure.'

But what if she wasn't lying, and she really had had a son with her own uncle?

Slowing as she descended the hill to pass Hope Cove and the Mermaid pub, she said, 'I want to tell her not to bother us any more, that we're not interested in playing her games or finding out any more about her, but even if I did I can't imagine she's going to give up until she's achieved whatever she's come back for.'

'Which frankly is causing me some concern,' he said darkly. 'What are you doing now?'

'I'm on my way home. When I get there I'll contact Gerry Trowbridge to set up a time to go and see him, then I'm going to read the inquest report on John Victor.' Checking to see who was calling, she said, 'I have to ring off now, but I'll call again later if you're going to be around.'

'Dinner with Nadia,' he replied, sounding fed up about it, 'so I'll call you when I get back to the villa.'

Sorely wishing she was still in Provence with him, Andee clicked on to the incoming call saying, 'Hi darling, how're things?'

'Hey Mum. I'm cool,' Alayna replied. 'Did you see the baby rhino? She's soooo sweet. Oh my God, I wish we could adopt her. I think we should.'

'I'm sure it can be arranged.'

'Let's do it. Anyway, you need to check your phone because apart from Hermione – that's what we're calling the rhino – you'll find pictures of me in three different outfits. I so need you to tell me which I look the best in.'

'Is it for something special?'

'I've only got a date with this guy who's the hottest, most ripped, most amazing, coolest dude in town. I'm so excited, but I can't make up my mind what to wear. Sophie says it should be the white lacy top with peppermint jeans; Sanako reckons I look best in the yellow dress with daisies all over and Tamsin's going for the kind of grungy-looking string thingy over the red slip with the Roman sandals you got me the last time you were here. Can you look at them now?'

'I'm driving, but I will as soon as I get home. Actually, if you have the time you could do me a favour.'

'I never have time, but shoot.'

'I'm trying to find someone who we believe is staying at a hotel on Buckingham Palace Road in London. If you can get me names of all the hotels with that address, and their phone numbers, that would be great.'

'I can do better than that if you give me the name of the person we're looking for.'

Loving how she'd immediately jumped on board, while aware that she couldn't give Alayna her own name or Penny's, Andee said, 'She has several aliases, but let's start with Michelle Cross.'

'Got it. When do you need it by?'

'Before you go on your date?'

'No probs. Got to go now, love you,' and she was gone.

By the following morning Andee had read through the inquest report on John Victor's death and left a message for Gerry Trowbridge to call her back as soon as he could. She'd also received an email from Penny, using the name Michelle Cross, asking if she'd met John Jr yet.

Andee hadn't replied.

Let Penny think she'd been spammed, or ignored, either would do. A discussion about the boy and all it could entail wasn't one to have via email. She wasn't even going to bother wondering how Penny had got her email address.

She looked across at her mother as Maureen put aside the inquest report.

'Did it tell you anything you didn't already know?' Andee asked.

Maureen shook her head. 'Not really.'

Having expected as much, Andee said, 'For me one of the most interesting parts is the statement from the neighbour, Alison Brown. Did you know he was living in Shepherd Market up until the time he died?'

'We found out after. Until then we didn't know where he was.'

Andee reached for the report and turned to the part that had caught her attention. '"He was really upset about something during the weeks before he disappeared,"' she read aloud. '"He wouldn't tell me what it was . . . I assumed he'd got into some sort of trouble over money again – he was always owing money to someone – but he said that for once it wasn't that. He was definitely on edge. He kept checking to see if anyone was outside. He thought someone was watching him, and a couple of times he said, 'I saw her, I know she's out there.' Then he said, 'She wanted me to see her. She's doing this to freak me out.'

'"Did he ever say who this person was?"

'"No, but it was definitely a she."

'"And you personally have no idea who 'she' was or what she might want?"

'"He said once, 'It's about the kids.'"

'"Kids?"

'"That's all he said. I asked him what he meant, but he wouldn't tell me. He said, 'It's best you don't know or you'll be involved too and you really don't want that.'"

'"Did anything else happen during that time to concern you?"

'"Well, he kind of stopped going out and there was one time when he said, 'If anything happens to me, tell them it wasn't my fault.'"

'"What did you understand from that?"

'"I didn't know what he was talking about, but I guess he might have meant the people he owed money to, or someone he'd hurt in some way. For all I know he could have been talking about the police."'

Andee lowered the report and looked at her mother.

Maureen's face showed the strain she was feeling.

'So who was "she"?' Andee asked. 'This person he thought was stalking him.'

Hoarsely, Maureen said, 'You're thinking it was Penny.'

'It's possible. And who are the kids he mentioned?' Since neither of them could answer that, she went back to the report. 'The last time Alison Brown saw him was about a week before his body was found. She says he was getting into a car outside their building with a man who looked to be around fifty. He was tall, distinguished-looking, with white hair and wearing a long dark coat and round glasses. She didn't think JV was being forced, and she didn't see any sign of a woman.'

After a while, Maureen said, 'So what does that tell us?'

'Nothing on the face of it, but it'll be one reason why the verdict was open, because the man has never been traced. The other reason is that no one has been able to say why John Victor was in West Wales or give any insight into how he got there.' She read again. 'The police searched the clifftops for signs of a struggle, but with so much foot traffic in the area and bad weather at the time the findings were inconclusive.'

Maureen swallowed dryly. 'Do you think he was murdered?'

'Well, given that there was no suicide note or any evidence of him being suicidal at that time . . .' She broke off as Maureen's hands clenched tightly shut and opened again. Her breathing was unsteady; Andee could almost feel her stress building as she got to her feet and went to the window. 'Do you really think she's having us watched?' she asked, peering out at the back garden.

'If she is, it's unlikely that anyone's out there,' Andee replied. 'But I do think Gould's right, that we should move down into the town for a while. We can stay at Graeme's . . .'

'But what on earth do you think is going to happen? This isn't making any sense, Andee. Whatever you think is going on, she's my *daughter* . . .'

'That's who she used to be,' Andee came in gently. 'She's another person now, you've seen that for yourself, and until we know . . .'

'I'm not being pushed out of my own home. Blake and Jenny are just across the way, and the Villiers are right next door. I know he's deaf, but Susan's always in and out of the house. If anyone was behaving strangely around here, she'd be sure to spot them and let us know.'

Thinking of how the most effective form of surveillance was to blend with the environment, Andee said, 'Well will you at least go and stay with Blake and Jenny if I manage to get a meeting with Gerry Trowbridge?'

Maureen looked worried. 'Maybe I should go with you. I don't like to think of you all alone if you're being followed.'

'I'll be fine, I promise. I'm far more worried about how badly this is affecting you.'

Maureen seemed suddenly annoyed. 'I need to pull myself together,' she declared, straightening her back. 'I don't know why I'm letting it get to me, and I certainly don't need to go and hide myself away.'

Deciding not to argue any more for now, Andee went to give her a hug. 'Just don't agree to see Penny without me, OK?' she said, mindful of how shocking the news about Penny's son would be should Penny decide to drop in and break it while Andee wasn't around. 'Or anyone else come to that,' she added teasingly.

'You mean no talking to strangers.'

'That's exactly what I mean,' and going to check who was calling her mobile she saw it was Alayna and clicked on.

'Sorry I didn't get back before,' Alayna stated, 'bit of a late night last night.'

'How was the date?'

'That's not until Friday. So you definitely think the third outfit?'

'The grungy thing over a red whatsit with the Greek sandals,' Andee confirmed.

'Roman, but hey! Brilliant, that's what I thought too. But that's not why I'm calling. I've just emailed you a list of the hotels on Buckingham Palace Road. There are a bunch of them, but it turns out that someone called Michelle Cross is staying at the Forty One. It looks dead posh, so she must be a bit minted. What's she supposed to have done?'

'I'm not sure yet,' Andee hedged. 'You've done brilliantly, thank you. Grandma's here, have a quick chat with her while I go and see who's at the door.'

Thrusting the phone at her mother, and bracing herself for the unexpected caller, Andee closed the hall door behind her and went to answer a second ring on the bell.

To her amazement a deliveryman was brandishing an enormous bouquet of white flowers, mostly lilies and roses. 'Someone's birthday?' he smiled, handing it over.

'Are you sure these are for us?' Andee asked, searching for a card.

'Right there,' he said, pointing. 'And this is Briar Lodge? Mrs Maureen Lawrence?'

'OK, you're in the right place. Thanks very much. Do I need to sign?'

'No, you're good to go,' and with a cheery wave he returned to his van.

After closing the door Andee put the flowers on the stairs and tore open the card.

Dear Mum, I shall be visiting again very soon. Meantime, I hope you like these. Watch out for the roses, we don't want any blood shed now do we. With love, xxx

Fighting back a surge of anger, Andee quickly pocketed the note, and would have binned the flowers had there been a way to get them out of the house before her mother saw them. What the hell was Penny doing? Just what kind of message was this? It was intimidating, full of spite, like venom wrapped up in candy. And how were they supposed to react? It was as though they were in some sort of twisted game that only Penny knew the rules to, and only she derived any satisfaction from.

'Oh my goodness,' Maureen exclaimed, as Andee carried the bouquet into the kitchen. 'They're beautiful. Are they from Graeme?'

'I don't think so. There doesn't seem to be a card.'

Perplexed, Maureen searched amongst the blooms, and finding the cane that had supported the card she said, 'It must have fallen off in the delivery van. We should call to find out who's been so generous. Are you sure they had the right address?'

Without answering Andee plonked the bouquet in the sink and went in search of a vase.

'Oh, they're from Penny,' Maureen declared, reading from her phone. '*Hi Mum, hope you got the surprise I sent. Sorry haven't been in touch for last few days, but will get there very soon. PS: Watch out for those thorns.*' Maureen looked at Andee, clearly not sure how to react.

Covering her anger with a shrug, Andee left her mother to sort the flowers while she went upstairs to photograph the card. After texting it to Gould and Leo Johnson, she added the message, *What do you think?*

Within minutes she had a reply from Leo. *Blood shed? Sorry, but your sister's starting to creep me out.*

Just after came a text from Gould. *I read the inquest report last night. Do you think she might have been involved in death of JV?*

I do, she texted back in spite of having no grounds to go on.

Have you contacted Gerry Trowbridge yet?

Waiting for a call back. Why?

I've been hearing things.

What sort of things?

Too soon to clarify, but something's up. Just watch your step.

'OK, that does it, I'm on the next plane back,' Graeme declared when she updated him later.

Startled, Andee cried, 'No, no, you don't have to do that . . .'

'Oh, I do. I've got no idea – *you've* got no idea – what the hell is going on over there, and I'm not prepared to let you go and see this Gerry Trowbridge alone when Gould himself is telling you to watch your step. What's that about? To me it's smacking of some sort of cover-up that might be nearly three decades old, but someone still doesn't want it out there. Have you set a time with Trowbridge yet?'

'Yes, he rang me back just before I called you. He's in the Lake District for the next couple of days, taking a break with his brother and sister-in-law, but he'll be home on Thursday. He's asked if I can go on Friday.'

'OK, what time?'

'After ten in the morning. Apparently his wife has Alzheimer's and she goes to a group therapy session at nine thirty. He's recommended a place for me to stay the night before. The Bell at Skenfrith.'

'I know it. Is that where he lives? Skenfrith?'

'Apparently, yes.'

'Did you tell him Penny was back?'

'I did. He went silent on me. I thought he'd rung off, but then he said, "Yes, come and see me. It's time we had a talk."'

Chapter Nine

She could see Penny ripping into dolls with a knife, stabbing, tearing, gouging out eyes, slicing off fingers, amputating toes. The dolls were Andee's, no longer played with, passed on with love to her sister and destroyed by the inner demons that had powered Penny's growing jealousy. The violence of the dream was still so intense that the very air seemed to crackle and vibrate with it. Maureen was shaking, sitting up in bed, trying to breathe, to shut out the grotesque images that had no place in reality.

Or did they? Had it happened, or was it a figment of her tormented imagination?

It was the suspicion of Penny being involved in John Victor's death that had stirred up the terrible dream, Maureen was certain of that, but thankfully the images were beginning to fade.

Tears continued to run down her cheeks as she lay in the darkness with no sounds to disturb or distract her. Life had never been easy for Penny. She'd forever been losing friends, making new ones only to lose them too. Teachers found her helpful one day, distant and dismissive the next, and Maureen had always known they didn't like her. Other parents never seemed thrilled to see her, the way they often were with Andee, and Maureen had seen how hurt Penny had been by that. It had made her feel more protective of her youngest, but she'd clearly never done a good enough job.

Knowing she wouldn't sleep again for a while, she took herself downstairs to make some tea. She was still feeling shaky, inundated and disoriented. Having shut out so much for so long, it was as though it was all suddenly trying to come back at once, in her waking moments and in her dreams. Her poor mind was struggling to separate fact from fear, to sort dates and times, to know what had really been said and what hadn't, where blame lay and guilt had a rightful home.

Memory wasn't infallible, especially at her age. It had ways of colouring, distorting events that might not even be real.

'Are you OK?'

Maureen started and turned to find Blake in the doorway, looking sleepy and concerned. Remembering that he and Jenny had come to stay while Andee was in Wales, she felt glad he was there. 'Had a bit of a dream,' she confessed. 'I'm sorry if I woke you.'

Dismissing it, Blake said, 'Would you rather be alone?'

'No. I mean, please don't stay up on my account . . .'

'I'd like some tea, if you're making it.'

A few minutes later they were sitting at the table, gazing into their mugs with the early-morning seconds ticking by and the sound of a brisk wind whistling in the chimney.

'They were very different,' Maureen stated after a while. 'Andee was so easy whereas Penny . . .' With a catch in her voice she said, 'I loved her just as much, but I don't think I showed it or told her often enough.' Her tired eyes flickered briefly to Blake and away again. 'I couldn't reach her the way I could Andee. Sometimes she was like an adult before her time. She would look at me in a way that just didn't seem right for a girl her age. And yet she could be such a child, needy, insecure, and she'd put on baby voices . . . Her father hated it when she did that. He'd get cross with her, and she'd do it even more, either to annoy him, or because she couldn't help herself. I've never been sure.'

'She was obviously a complex child,' Blake said softly.

Maureen nodded, thinking that complex was putting it mildly, kindly. 'She'd lie and steal,' she confessed, 'mock people who were worse off than herself, and yet at the same time she could be the kindest, most generous person in the world. She'd come up with ways to make money for good causes, dance-a-thons, cake bakes, fancy-dress walks . . . Everyone used to flock to her then, wanting to be part of the fun. They were full of praise . . . I think she wanted it from her father most of all, but he wasn't good at expressing his feelings. He was proud of what she did, of course, but I don't think she could see it. All she saw was how proud he was of Andee.' Her eyes went back to Blake's as a cold dread ran through her. It wasn't the first time this random fear had come back to her, but this time it was so clear and persistent that she couldn't move past it.

Apparently sensing some sort of change, Blake remained silent, allowing her to decide whether or not she wanted to carry on.

Eventually, in a voice that was barely audible, Maureen said, 'I never met the child. She was in the same class as Penny, and everyone said what a lovely girl she was. They were on a school trip to Canterbury Cathedral and there was . . . there was a terrible accident . . . One of the girls tripped and fell off a pavement into an oncoming bus.'

Blake's breathing had all but stopped.

'Why,' Maureen asked helplessly, 'would Penny choose, all these years later, to use that poor little girl's name?'

Blake took a breath. 'Are you talking about Michelle Cross?' he asked quietly.

Maureen blinked and looked away. 'Yes,' she replied. 'Yes I am.'

Andee and Graeme had just returned from an early-morning hike along Offa's Dyke and were now slumped at each end of a cosy sofa in front of the inglenook fireplace at the Bell in Skenfrith. It was a welcoming old coaching inn at the edge of the village, where castle ruins imposed their grandeur from behind a derelict mill and the River Monnow flowed and gushed and meandered its way south to join the Wye.

Their reunion last night, after not quite two weeks, in one of the pub's luxurious guest rooms, had taken precedence over everything else, and during their walk this morning Andee had encouraged Graeme to share his memories of bringing his sons to the area, to fish, or canoe, or climb Coedanghred Hill, otherwise known as Heart Attack Hill. There would be time enough later to focus on her issues, she'd decided, and she was enjoying learning more about him.

She was also intrigued, as was he, by the young guy in leathers who'd arrived on a motorbike just after they had last night. He'd appeared for dinner with an iPod plugged into his jug ears and a phone never far from his fingertips. He'd barely acknowledged them, in spite of Graeme's cheery hello.

There was no sign of him now, nor of anyone else, as coffee was served along with a delicious assortment of pastries and a menu for more if required.

'Do you think it's safe to talk?' Graeme asked, clearly enjoying the cloak and dagger of it all.

Smiling, Andee said, 'We've got nothing to hide, so why not? What's on your mind?'

With twinkling eyes he said, 'I confess I'm intrigued to know what you're going to find out today. Did you tell Trowbridge I'd be with you?'

'I did and he's fine with it. He sounded very together, as a matter of fact; he didn't even seem to have a problem hearing, and he must be close to ninety by now.'

'What's important is how clear his memory is, and from the response you've got so far I think we can assume it's pretty well intact. Are you nervous?'

'A little.' She checked her phone as it rang. 'It's Blake,' she said, surprise turning quickly to concern. 'He and

Jenny stayed with Mum last night,' she explained, clicking on. 'Hi, is everything OK?'

'It's fine,' Blake assured her. 'Maureen's sleeping in. She had a broken night . . .'

'Did she hear from Penny?'

'No, it was a dream, but she asked me to let you know that she's remembered why the name Michelle Cross was familiar to her.'

As Andee listened to the explanation her insides turned to liquid. Of course. Why hadn't it come to her before? She might have been at another school when it happened, but she remembered the tragedy, she just hadn't remembered the child's name. Then, realising what her mother was really thinking, her head started to spin. 'Did anyone ever say that it might not have been an accident?' she finally asked.

'Your mother doesn't think so,' Blake replied, 'but apparently Penny had fallen out with the girl over something, Maureen can't recall what. She thinks it might have had something to do with Christmas.'

An hour later, aware of their fellow guest in leathers rambling at a distance behind them like a fascinated tourist, Andee and Graeme strolled through Skenfrith village where sweet peas tumbled over drystone walls, and the medieval church of St Bridget's with its dovecote belfry and red sandstone walls watched over its visitors and residents with a benevolent air. The cottages were small and quaint; the sky overhead was blue, while the hills cradling the community's hollow were towering and green.

'I wonder if he knows Penny as Michelle Cross?' Andee murmured as the pale-haired man with apple cheeks and a bow-legged gait stopped to consult a map. Why on earth had Penny chosen that name when she, of all people, would remember what had happened? It wasn't good, in fact it was downright horrible.

'Shall we ask him?' Graeme suggested mischievously.

Though tempted, if only to let Penny know that her tracker had been rumbled, Andee shook her head and slipped her hand into his. She was so glad to have him here, and so moved by how close they'd been last night, and even now simply walking side by side, that she suspected she was falling quite deeply in love with him. And what a wonderful place it was to be.

After only a few minutes they reached the gate to the last small white house on the right. 'Not the bigger, smart-looking place that's next door,' Gerry Trowbridge had told her. 'I'm afraid ours is a bit run-down these days, but you'll recognise it from the birdhouse in the front garden, and the glorious bundles of buddleia that seem to be trying to take us over.'

As Graeme pushed open the gate Andee glanced back down the street to where their shadow appeared to be reading something in the parish hall window. When he looked her way she gave him a little wave and stepped in behind Graeme as a formally dressed, rangy man with wispy tufts of grey hair clinging to a balding scalp, droopy red cheeks and watery brown eyes came down the path to greet them. Were it not for his stoop he'd probably have been as tall as Graeme, but as it was he was closer to Andee's height, and seemed as fragile, yet durable as the cane assisting his progress.

'Andee,' he said warmly as Graeme moved aside to let her through. 'It's been so many years.' He clasped his arthritic hands around hers, and smiled into her eyes. 'I remember you well, my dear. Your father was always so proud of you.'

'Hello, Gerry,' she said, hoping it was all right to be informal. 'It's good to see you. You're looking . . .'

'Old,' he interrupted with a chuckle, 'because I am. I'll be ninety in a couple of years, if I make it till then. And you must be Graeme. Welcome, I'm very glad to meet you. Any friend of Andee's is a friend of mine.'

'Are you going to keep them standing around out there?' a voice called from inside.

'We're on our way,' he responded, adding so only Andee and Graeme could hear, 'My daughter-in-law. She insisted on coming to make sure you had uncracked cups to drink from and well-plumped cushions to sit on.'

'I'm Meryl,' a cheery-faced, chubby little woman with a melodic Welsh accent and pink-rimmed glasses informed them, as Trowbridge ushered them into what he called the best room. 'I live over by Abergavenny, so not far away,' she chatted on. 'I generally call in here a couple of times a week to make sure they're still breathing. It's a bit doubtful sometimes, but today's a good one. I won't stay, because I haven't been invited to, but there's a nice pot of tea on the table there, and I baked the biscuits myself.'

'She thinks they're delicious,' Trowbridge declared, 'and none of us have the heart to enlighten her.'

'You haven't got a heart,' she countered cheerily. 'Now, don't go overdoing things, I don't want to be calling an ambulance, they've got better things to be doing with their time than fussing about with you.'

Amused by the banter, Andee and Graeme said a reluctant farewell to the twinkling Meryl. Andee set about pouring the tea after Meryl had popped back to warn them not to let her father-in-law near the pot, unless they wanted to drink out of their laps.

'She's a cruel woman,' Trowbridge sighed as the door closed behind her, 'and I don't know where any of us would be without her. She's a saint with my wife, and I can tell you it needs a saint to be dealing with her at times. Terrible business, Alzheimer's, but I can't put her in a home. Not yet, anyway.'

'How long has she been ill?' Graeme asked.

'She was diagnosed six years ago.' With a shaking hand he brought a dainty cup to his mouth and flinched as the hot tea scalded his lip. 'But you didn't come here to discuss my problems,' he said, putting the cup down again, 'so I shall wade right in, if I may, and ask if you're sure it's Penny.'

'As sure as I can be,' Andee replied. Then added, 'Yes, it's her.'

'And where has she been for all this time?'

Having half hoped he'd be able to tell her that, Andee hid her disappointment as she said, 'You don't seem to doubt my word.'

'I don't,' he confirmed. 'Is this the first time she's made contact in all these years?'

Andee glanced at Graeme. 'It is,' she confirmed, adding, 'You sound as though you knew she was alive when the suspicion, or the general belief, was that she'd killed herself.'

'Mm,' he murmured thoughtfully. 'I was never convinced by that suicide note, any more than your father was. Of course, we couldn't discount it, it was definitely written by her, but there were other circumstances . . .' His rheumy eyes moved to Graeme and back to Andee. 'I'm sure you remember your uncle, John Victor,' he said.

Andee tensed as she nodded.

Trowbridge gave a grunt of dislike. 'I met a lot of worthless individuals during my time on the force, it goes with the job . . . He was right up there with the worst of them.'

'So she was with him when she left?' Andee prompted.

'Him and others.'

'How did you know?' Astonished that the police had known where Penny was, Andee bit her tongue, determined to hear the rest of the story first.

Sitting back in his chair, he steepled his gnarly fingers as he let his mind travel across the years to those distant days. 'The first time she went,' he began, 'she was only thirteen. I believe she'd told your parents she was going to stay with a friend, but when she didn't come back after a couple of days they found out the friend didn't exist. We, the police, were already organising a search when your grandmother rang your father to say that Penny was at her place. That was only good news until your grandmother told your father who else was there and what was going on. It was very upsetting for the poor dear, I remember how she tried to blame herself, as if anything like that could possibly be her fault. When we got there there was no sign of Victor, he'd taken off as soon as he found out his mother had called us, but Penny was still there. She told us she didn't want to leave. She was enjoying herself, she said, as if we ought to be pleased for her in some way.' Trowbridge shook his ancient head in dismay. 'Such attitude she had, and she was still so young. She kicked up badly when your father and I grabbed her and carried her out to the car.'

He sighed unsteadily and leaned forward to take another sip of his tea. 'I'm not sure how long it was before she disappeared again,' he continued, 'but the next time we knew where to look. Not her grandmother's, she didn't go there, but she was with Victor all right, at a big house in Chelsea, and I mean big. It belonged to some Russian, I forget his name; it was a long time ago.

'He'd rented the place for his people, we were told, and by people no one was meaning family. Don't ask me where Victor fitted into the picture, I guess he was some sort of drone, you know, one of those types that the very rich and crooked usually surround themselves with . . . A court jester, a facilitator – who knew what his role was? He must have had one, because he was clearly at home there, and didn't seem in the least bit upset that we'd found him. I guess, when you're surrounded by thugs and hitmen and they're on your side, you can afford to be cocky.

'We didn't have to tell him why we were there, he told us. He even took us to Penny. There she was, lying on the bed, drugged or drunk, we didn't know which, and not wearing very much. She was just about conscious, enough to tell us to get the hell out, not using those words exactly, far more colourful. Thirteen years old and she was behaving like a . . .' He caught himself. 'She was like a woman twice her age, and she was clearly learning from the girls she was mixing with.'

'Who were they?' Andee asked.

'A lot were foreign. In fact, I think they all were, or the ones we met, and of course none of them could speak English, or so they claimed. We didn't press it, not then, we just wanted to get her out as fast as we could. She didn't come without a fight, but we got her home eventually and your father tried just about every way he could think of to deal with her. Nothing worked, because she just kept on going back. We always found her in the same place, and because the "people" didn't want any trouble they usually took us right to her and even helped us to get her out to the car. It damned near broke your father's heart, I can tell you. Well, it did in the end. We know that.'

'But if you found her all those times, how come you didn't the last time?' Andee asked.

'Because she wasn't at the house when we got there, and everyone swore they hadn't seen her. I've got no idea where she went, all I can tell you is what happened during our interviews with John Victor.'

'So there were interviews? Why aren't they on record?'

'Because your father and I decided to deal with him ourselves, in the hope that if we guaranteed to keep him and his friends out of it he could be persuaded to tell us where she was. He swore he didn't know, but we could tell he was lying. He knew all right, but we didn't even manage to get the cuffs on him before he said that if we even attempted to implicate him he would expose the sexual abuse she'd been suffering for years at home.'

Andee drew back in shock. She hadn't heard right, surely. Somehow she'd misunderstood, but she could see from the expression on Trowbridge's face that she hadn't. 'It isn't true,' she told him.

'I never thought it was, but we could see Victor was serious. She'd told him, or so he said, that her father and grandfather had been molesting and raping her since she was six years old. I'm sure I don't have to describe how that affected your father . . . I can tell you this much, Victor was lucky to come out of that interview alive.'

Andee sat back in her chair, so appalled she hardly knew what to say.

'Did you see her at that time?' Graeme stepped in. 'She claimed recently that her father saw her once and turned around and walked away.'

Trowbridge shook his head. 'I don't remember that,' he replied. 'As far as I'm aware, after the last time she disappeared none of us ever saw her again.'

'So how did you know that she'd back Victor in his claims?'

'Because she called your father and told him she would. I didn't hear the conversation; I only know that he didn't doubt she meant it. If he made her come home she'd tell the world what he'd been doing to her.'

'Jesus Christ,' Andee murmured, unable to imagine just how devastated and afraid her father must have felt at that time.

'You know what it would have done to your father's career,' Trowbridge went on, 'never mind to your family, if even a whisper of an accusation like that came out. You'll have seen it plenty of times. Innocent men's lives ruined by false accusations of child abuse. Even if he could prove himself innocent you'd always be the daughter of the child-molester cop, because that sort of mud sticks. People would look at you and wonder if you'd been molested too. He couldn't even be certain that you and your mother would believe in his innocence. Penny didn't want to be a part of the family any more, she'd given that as the reason, so maybe in your hearts you'd always wonder . . .'

'We never would have,' Andee told him forcefully. 'Not my father, or my grandfather . . .'

'I believe you, but it was hard to convince your father, especially when we still had no idea where Penny was or what she was doing. We couldn't even be sure, after the phone call, that she was still alive. And I guess he wasn't thinking too straight; the stress, the fear was tearing him apart . . . I tried to advise him, but I barely knew what to do myself.'

Andee tried to imagine what she'd have done faced

with such a harrowing dilemma, but there were no easy answers.

'A lot of rules were broken after that,' Trowbridge admitted. 'The higher-ups knew what was happening, we had to tell them and I'm glad we did, because it turned out they were no keener for one of their senior officers to be embroiled in a child abuse scandal than your father was to be at the centre of one. So he was given time to carry on playing things his way with Victor. Then the note turned up, and he decided it would be easier on you, and your mother in particular, to believe in the possibility of suicide rather than to have to deal with what he'd learned about Penny.'

Stunned, Andee cried, 'It was the wrong decision.'

Trowbridge didn't argue.

'So you stopped looking?' Graeme prompted.

'No, of course not, but in the backs of our minds there was always the fear that the letter was for real. There were never any sightings of her, and surveillance on Victor never got us anywhere apart from up a garden path. So perhaps she was dead. We know now that she wasn't, but where she went and what she's been doing for all these years, I'm afraid only she can tell you.'

Andee looked at Graeme, knowing there was more she needed to ask, but for the moment she seemed unable to unravel her thoughts or emotions.

Apparently understanding, Graeme said to Trowbridge, 'I take it you know John Victor's dead?'

Trowbridge nodded.

'Can you tell us anything about that? Do you think Penny might have been involved?'

Trowbridge's eyes remained focused on the middle distance as he said, 'It happened a long time after she disappeared, but anything's possible, and I certainly don't think his death was an accident. No one did.'

'Did you go to the inquest?' Andee asked.

'Yes, because your father asked me to. He'd retired by then, as you know, and taken you and your mother to Kesterly . . . In fact, you must have been in the force yourself by that time . . .'

'I was at detective school,' she confirmed. 'I remember the death. I didn't go to the funeral, or the inquest, but I've read the report. The neighbour, girlfriend, Alison Brown had an interesting story to tell.'

Trowbridge agreed. 'I expect you're wondering if the woman Alison Brown referred to, the one Victor kept seeing, or feeling was stalking him, was your sister. I wondered the same, so I spoke to Alison after the hearing but she was certain he'd never mentioned a name.'

'She said he mentioned children. Kids.'

'Yes, but I'm afraid I can't tell you anything about that.'

Andee said, 'My mother's been approached by a young man claiming to be Penny's son. Apparently his name is John Victor Jr.'

Trowbridge's eyes closed. He seemed to be struggling mentally with something deeply unpleasant. 'Have you spoken to him?' he asked in the end.

'No, but he says he wants to speak to me. I just don't know how to get hold of him.'

Seeming more upset than he had throughout the entire time they'd been talking, Trowbridge said, 'I wish I could be of more help to you, but I suppose the question of whether or not Penny's alive is no longer in doubt. Maybe that's something.'

'Maybe,' Andee murmured.

Graeme went to help as Trowbridge rose unsteadily to his feet.

'See if you can track down Alison Brown,' Trowbridge advised as he walked ahead of them to the front door. 'As I recall she found something in Victor's apartment that didn't get mentioned at the inquest, probably because no importance was attached to it. When she showed it to me . . . I remember it rang some bells. It was like something I'd read before, or heard someone say . . . I'm sorry, I can't remember the words now, but maybe she does, and you never know, they might mean something to you.'

Andee and Graeme were back at the Bell, sitting at a table in the bar with drinks and lunch menus between them. There was so much to think about, to try to understand and know how to process, that neither of them gave a thought to the fact that their stalker seemed to have disappeared.

'It's hard to imagine the kind of hell my father went through,' Andee said, staring into her wine. 'I don't blame him for making some wrong decisions. When you're in the thick of something like that, especially where family's concerned, it's impossible to know what to do for the best. I just wish he'd trusted us.'

'I don't think it was a question of trust,' Graeme responded. 'It was the burden you and your mother would have to carry that clearly worried him the most. The scandal, the heartache, the unforgiving memories some people have . . . You know how these things work. The world never seems to forget the sordid details of other people's tragedies, even if those details turn out to be lies.'

Yes, Andee did know, particularly where accusations of child abuse were concerned. She'd seen too many lives ruined by the malicious claims of others who had no care for anyone but themselves – no conscience or morals.

'And let's not forget,' Graeme continued, 'he would have been trying to protect Penny so that she wouldn't have to live with what she'd done, if she'd carried out the threat. She was very young, he would've believed her capable of change. He probably even expected it.'

Sighing sadly as she considered her father's terrible dilemma, Andee said, 'All those years we spent turning her into a saint in our minds, deliberately forgetting the bad things, only focusing on happy times, wishing she was still with us to share in a world that should have been hers. We had no idea she'd completely and deliberately rejected it. How is it possible for someone to be so cruel to her own family? Of course, people can, I know that, but I'm having a hard time accepting that it's happened to mine.'

Graeme was reading a text on his mobile, but looked up when she stopped speaking.

'Are you going to call her?' he asked, indicating to the waiter that they needed more time.

'Not yet, but I will, unless she calls me first.'

'And what are you going to tell your mother?'

'I'm still undecided about that, but I think it probably has to be the truth. It'll be too hard trying to hide it.'

Glancing at his phone as it rang, he grimaced an apology. 'Nadia. She's just texted so she's clearly keen to get hold of me . . .'

'Don't mind me,' Andee insisted, and reaching for the menu as he left the table she tried to concentrate on the appetising choices on offer, while her mind continued to whirl with everything she'd learned from Trowbridge that morning.

I've found something out that you don't know, she recalled the teenage Penny boasting all those years ago. *Don't you want to know what it is? It's about Mum's brother, Uncle John.*

What would Penny have told her if she'd bothered to listen, and if she had would it have made a difference?

Hearing Graeme laugh, she came back to the present.

'Don't worry, don't worry, it'll all be done,' he was telling Nadia. 'Yes, I promise. I'm not exactly sure when I'll be back, but everything's running to schedule . . . OK, ciao, ciao. Mm, same to you.'

As he rang off Andee almost asked what the 'same to you' meant, but managed not to. It was true that Nadia was an exceptionally beautiful woman, not to mention rich, charming and flirtatious, but now definitely wasn't the time to start feeling worried when Graeme was here, with her, lending every bit of support he could to this bizarre and unnerving crisis that was consuming her world.

Had her father expected Penny to return one day? Had he even seen her before he died and never told anyone?

Chapter Ten

It was just after five that evening when Andee and Graeme drew up outside Briar Lodge, where they had to wait for a chauffeur-driven silver Mercedes to clear the drive so they could get in.

'Why didn't my mother let me know she was coming?' Andee demanded, sounding angrier than she actually felt.

'Maybe she turned up unexpectedly,' Graeme suggested.

Accepting that could be true, Andee got out of the car, still annoyed because this was not how she'd wanted the next encounter with her sister to happen. She'd rather have seen her alone first, or at least have had a chance to speak to her mother so she could prepare her, but that clearly wasn't going to be possible. 'I think the way to handle this,' she said as Graeme joined her, 'is to let Penny do all the talking and see where it gets us.'

Agreeing, Graeme pushed open the kitchen door for her to go ahead, and almost collided with her as Penny's greeting brought her to an abrupt stop.

'Speak of the devil, and here she is,' Penny gushed, arms wide as she came to Andee. 'Tell me, how was dear old Gerry Trowbridge? As informative as you'd hoped? Or has the poor soul lost his marbles by now?'

Andee's eyes shot to her mother, but the way Maureen quickly shook her head told her that Penny hadn't got her information here. So this was a blatant admission that she'd had Andee followed. Coolly accepting the embrace, Andee said, 'This is a surprise. Had you said you were coming?' Again she looked at her mother.

'I was in the garden,' Maureen told her. 'I didn't even hear the door. She only just got here, less than ten minutes ago.'

Realising her mother was both flustered and relieved that she was no longer having to handle Penny alone, Andee briefly softened her expression before saying to Penny, 'So when did you get back from Houston?'

With an airy wave Penny said, 'This morning. Panic allayed, or at least delayed. I only wish I could say the same for here, but that's another story. I'm going to guess that you're Graeme,' she said, treating him to an appreciative once-over as she reached for his hand.

'It's good to meet you,' he told her.

'Likewise. I hope we're going to get to know one another much better.'

Was she flirting, Andee wondered with no little ire?

Appearing oblivious to it if she was, Graeme offered to make tea while Andee followed her mother and Penny to the sofas where they'd been before she came in.

'So,' Penny prompted chattily, 'are you going to tell us how you got along with Gerry Trowbridge?'

Determined not to be rattled, or led, Andee said, 'I'd rather hear about why you chose to come now, when you apparently knew I wasn't here.'

Penny looked amazed. 'I'm sorry, I didn't realise I needed to check with you first, but I promise I'll be sure to do so next time. I hope I haven't caused a problem.'

Since she didn't appear to have done so, Andee let it drop and instead indulged in some wrong-footing of her own. 'Why did you use my name when you booked a chauffeur to take you to France?'

Penny looked startled, then laughed. 'Well, I suppose I was feeling ironic at the time,' she countered with a playful glance towards Maureen.

Andee waited for more, but no more came. 'That's not an answer,' she pointed out.

'Isn't it? I thought it was. Is it not permissible to feel ironic?'

'Are we going to have a sensible conversation,' Andee challenged, 'or are you here to waste our time?'

'Andee,' her mother scolded.

'It's all right,' Penny assured her. 'I can see Andee's cross with me, and I suppose I don't blame her. It's probably quite upsetting to discover that someone has been using your name, but it's not as if it was identity theft, or anything serious like that. It's just a little thing I do from time to time to keep us close.'

To keep us close! What the heck was that supposed to mean?

'Do you have documents in my name?' Andee demanded.

'No.'

Hoping it was true, Andee continued. 'And what about Michelle Cross? Is using her name something you do to keep yourself feeling close to her?'

Penny's expression turned mournful as she said, 'Poor, sweet Michelle. It was so tragic what happened to her. Losing her life before it had even properly begun. Yes, I use her name as a reminder, as a tribute almost, kind of letting her share in a life she missed out on. And before you ask, yes I do have documents in her name. She didn't need it any more, and when I required a new one hers was the first that came to mind.'

Faintly repulsed by that, Andee looked at her mother as Maureen asked, 'Why did you need a new name?'

Penny regarded her in a way that said *surely you know the answer to that.* To be clear, she replied, 'Everyone was looking for Penny Lawrence. It was the only thing we could think of to help me hang on to my new-found freedom.'

'Freedom?' Maureen echoed faintly.

'From all of you,' Penny explained. 'No one seemed to understand that I didn't want to come back. I was happy, for the first time in my life. I was living in John's world, doing things I loved with people I loved and who loved me.' Twinkling, she added to Andee, 'I expect Gerry Trowbridge has already told you all about it.'

Wishing this wasn't happening in front of her mother,

Andee said, 'Maybe you'd like to tell us yourself, in case he got it wrong.'

'Oh, I don't suppose he did.'

Maureen was watching them carefully, apparently trying to keep up.

'I'm presuming you don't want to spell it out in front of Mum,' Andee stated, 'so shall we . . .'

'I will if you want me to,' Penny interrupted.

Too stubborn to back off, Andee said, 'Then perhaps you can begin by telling us how you made your initial connection with John Victor.'

Maureen flinched as Penny threw out her hands in amazement.

'He was our uncle. You knew him as well as I did.'

Since that was patently untrue on the second count, Andee stared at her hard.

Apparently enjoying the silent treatment, Penny let it run for a while, before saying, 'It was quite simple, really. I knew he was the black sheep of the family, which was exactly how I felt, so I found his number in Mum's phone book and called to ask if I could go to see him. He said yes, we got along . . . Would you like the details of that particular part of it?'

Certain her mother wouldn't, and nor did she, Andee said, 'Whose idea was it for you to stay with him?'

'Mine. And his. Actually, everyone's. I fitted in. We were a happy-go-lucky commune living life to the full in a house on Glebe Place, in Chelsea. Do you know it?' She was looking at Graeme.

'The street,' he confirmed. 'Probably not the house.'

'But I'm sure you've been there.'

'I'm sure I haven't.'

Penny's eyebrows arched as she turned back to Andee.

Wondering what she was up to, Andee said, 'How long did you stay in that house?'

Penny frowned as she thought. 'Well, I was back and forth quite a lot between various countries and so on, and I was almost seventeen when I got sold, so that would make it close to three years.'

'Sold?' Maureen echoed in disbelief. 'What are you talking about?'

Penny's tragic look struck Andee as a tad overdone as she said, 'I'm afraid your brother ran into some financial difficulties, and selling me was how he solved them.'

Maureen looked at Andee, so aghast she had no idea what to say.

Unable to tell if Penny was being truthful, Andee said, 'Who did he *sell* you to?'

'Ah, well there begins a part of my life story that I'd really rather forget, but I understand that you need to know so I'll do my best. You see, I was already working as an escort – sorry, Mum, but you must have guessed.'

Maureen didn't deny it.

'The difference was, at the house on Glebe Place we girls were treated like princesses. We had everything we could ever want, money, clothes, jewellery, holidays . . . Men would fly us in private jets to their yachts, or their gorgeous villas in exotic places and lavish us with everything our hearts desired. We could even say no if we weren't in the mood . . . It was a magical time. I really felt as though I belonged, and I was quite popular as well, being as young as I was.'

Seeing that her mother was shrinking inside, Andee said to her, 'Do you want to hear any more of this? If you don't I'm sure Graeme will take you over to the pub.'

'No, I want to hear it,' Maureen assured her, sounding hardier than she looked. To Penny she said, 'Was my brother acting as your pimp during that time?'

Penny frowned. 'That's a harsh word,' she chided. 'The way I'd put it is that he was very good at introducing me to people he thought would enjoy my company, and whose company I would also enjoy. He was very attentive to my needs. He even organised private dance lessons for me so I could expand my entertaining talents. I'm afraid I'm nowhere near as limber these days, but we are talking some time ago.'

Knowing precisely what sort of dancing she was referring to, Andee let her mother continue to study Penny's expressions and tone.

'So the entire time we were going out of our minds with fear and worry,' Maureen declared incredulously, 'you were right there, in Chelsea?'

Penny grimaced. 'Well, not then,' she admitted. 'It was all getting a bit fraught around the time I decided to take off for good, so John's boss Val, short for Valentin, flew me to his home on the Black Sea. You should see it, it's as grand as Buckingham Palace, or it was. I've no idea if it's still there, but . . .'

Cutting her off, Maureen said, 'So you knew what

you were putting us through, but it didn't matter to you?'

Sounding apologetic, Penny said, 'To be honest I didn't think you cared.'

'But if you saw the news, heard me making an appeal . . .'

'Actually, I stayed away from the news because it always brought me down. I find it very depressing, even now. Oh lovely,' she smiled as Graeme set a tray on the table. 'I'm getting quite thirsty doing all this talking.'

After waiting for their cups to be filled and for Graeme to settle into the chair her father had always used, Andee said, 'So you were sold. To whom?'

Penny's eyes went down, and the way she seemed to hunch into herself made her appear surprisingly fragile.

Was this an act, Andee wondered.

Maureen said, 'You don't have to tell us . . .'

'I was sold to some very bad people,' Penny murmured, not looking at them. 'Very bad indeed. I expect you came across their type, Andee, when you were in the police. Traffickers. They're the kind no decent people ever want to meet, and no one in their right mind would ever want to mess with. They didn't take care of us girls at all. The places they kept us . . .' She swallowed dryly and put a partly-gloved hand to her head. 'One mattress between three girls, paper peeling off damp walls, windows cracked and broken to let in the freezing air, bare floorboards, the kind of toilet facilities that made you gag to go near them. Sometimes we were lucky to get fed more than once a day, and the men they made us work for were animals.'

Andee could see her mother's colour draining.

'They gave us drugs, of course,' Penny went on. 'Hard drugs and often cut with something bad. Anything to keep us quiet and submissive.' Putting down her cup, she peeled back the gloved end of one sleeve to reveal her eczema-ravaged hand, and rolled it up further to show the scars she still bore from those days. Though faint now, there was no mistaking the old puncture wounds and purplish withering of the skin. 'My neck and feet don't make pretty pictures either,' she told them. 'Most of my hair fell out during that time, and several teeth – one was knocked out by someone who tried to stab me. It was its own kind of hell. I wanted to come home then, when I was lucid enough to remember I had a home. When I was sober I felt so sick and afraid that I wanted to die. We all did. We tried to escape, but we never could and the punishment when we were caught was terrible. Our handlers were brutal beyond anything I even knew existed. I can still remember some of their names, Rafal, Edouard, Mohammed . . .'

'Where were they holding you?' Andee asked, trying to break what might have been a rehearsed story, although the scars and even the tone were certainly convincing.

Penny didn't appear thrown. 'They moved us around so we never really knew where we were, north, south, England, Wales. I don't think we ever went overseas, but I can't say for sure. They used to pile us into the back of a van that had no windows, no air, and drive us for hours to the next place and keep us there until they decided it was time to move us on again.'

'Were there never any police raids? Someone at some stage must have been suspicious, even if they didn't realise exactly what was happening?'

'The only police that came weren't there to rescue us.'

The meaning of that was so clear that Andee almost regretted asking the question.

'In better moments I used to try and teach the other girls to speak English,' Penny continued. 'Most of them had been brought from other countries, lured in with promises of a better life and money enough to send back to their families. It was tragic and hopeless. We were so young, all of us. I knew they'd need to speak English if we ever managed to get away, even if it was only to ask for help. I remember one girl who was only twelve and so tiny she looked closer to ten. Her name was Helena. She'd left home with her sister, but no one knew where the sister was. I never found out where she was from; the first rape she suffered was so vicious it killed her before I could get that far. I've no idea what they did with her body, or any of the bodies they ended up with, because it wasn't unusual for someone to die. There were never any questions asked, no one even knew they were in the country.'

Knowing very well how those types operated, Andee said, 'How did you manage to survive it?'

Penny shrugged. 'I've no idea, but there were plenty of times I thought I wouldn't.'

'How long were you there?' Maureen asked.

'Four, nearly five years. And do you want to know how I got out? Now here's an irony for you, the man who put me there, who sold me to save his own skin, was the same man who brokered the deal to get me out. In fact, if I were feeling generous I could say he rescued me, but actually it wasn't really John Victor who did that, it was Sven and his wife Ana. They changed my life. I have them to thank for everything.'

Though keen to know more about these angels of mercy, if they existed, Andee was more interested right now to hear the vital part of the story that Penny had blithely missed out. 'Where was your son all this time?' she asked softly.

Penny's demeanour changed; her eyes sharpened with a wariness that hadn't been there a moment ago.

'If he's the age we think he is,' Andee continued, 'you must have had him when you were sixteen or seventeen.'

Penny's face was taut. 'My son is my business, no one else's.'

'But he's my grandson,' Maureen pointed out. 'That alone makes him my business. The fact that he came here . . .'

'Was an act of foolishness on his part and he knows it.'

'Foolish to want to meet his family?' Andee countered.

Penny didn't answer, and when it became clear no one else was going to speak, Graeme said, 'Where was he during the time you were . . . imprisoned?'

Minutes ticked by. The air was awful, tense and full of resentment. In the end Penny spoke as if the question hadn't been asked. 'Did Gerry Trowbridge tell you about the time Daddy saw me and turned around and walked away?'

Stiffening along with her mother, Andee said, 'He says it never happened.'

Penny didn't appear surprised or troubled. 'I was still in Glebe Place,' she said, 'and I admit it probably wasn't the best way to see your daughter. I was high and not alone. The man I was with actually invited Daddy to join in.' She smirked sourly. 'He didn't know who the stranger at the door was, of course.'

Trying to blot the scene from her mind, Andee said, 'Did you speak to him?'

'I don't think so. I can't remember now. He was there one minute, gone the next.'

'If he knew where you were,' Maureen stated, 'he'd have brought you straight home. Or he'd have sent other officers in to get you.'

'He couldn't do that.'

'Why? I don't understand.'

'Mum,' Andee tried to interrupt.

'Please listen,' Maureen admonished.

Penny looked directly at Andee. 'Trowbridge told you.'

'Would you have carried out the threats?' Andee challenged.

'Of course.'

'What threats?' Maureen wanted to know.

Penny said, 'I told him I'd tell the world what he and his father had been doing to me for years.'

Maureen's jaw dropped; a moment later she was looking desperately at Andee.

'It's not true, Mum,' Andee assured her. To Penny she said, 'Why would you lie like that?'

'They abused me,' Penny declared, 'and our mother allowed it to happen.'

Stunned, Andee watched Maureen turn white as she got to her feet. With a shaking hand pointing towards the door, she said, 'Get out of my house. Get out right now and don't ever come back.'

Penny's eyes darkened with something terrible as she stood up. 'If you think this is over . . .'

'Get out!' Maureen screamed. 'You are no daughter of mine.'

Graeme rose quickly to steady her as Andee, not yet finished, followed Penny outside. 'Why are you telling these lies?' she hissed, spinning Penny back as she closed the door behind her.

'Lies?' Penny echoed smoothly.

'We both know that Daddy would never have laid a finger on you that way . . .'

'You tell yourself what you want to.' She was looking at her phone as it rang.

Grabbing it before she could answer, Andee said, 'Tell me this, does your son know who his father is?'

Penny's eyebrows arched, almost as though she was enjoying the challenge. 'Are you saying you'd tell him?' she asked. 'I don't believe you would, but you won't get the chance, because he knows what'll happen if he tries to come near you again.'

Having no idea what that meant, Andee glanced round as the door opened behind her.

'Ah, Graeme,' Penny smiled sweetly. 'Tell me, how's Nadia?'

'You know her?' Graeme responded, startled.

'Not as well as you do,' she replied, and taking her phone from Andee she went to get into her car.

'None of it's true,' Maureen insisted as soon as Andee returned. 'Why is she saying these things? Neither your father, nor his father, would ever . . .'

'I know, I know,' Andee interrupted, going to calm her. 'Nobody believes it, but according to Gerry Trowbridge Daddy was afraid people would and if they did he was even more fearful of what it would do to us, you and me . . .'

'But if he knew where she was . . .'

'She didn't want to come back. That was the whole point. She just told us, she was happy where she was. At least while she was in Chelsea.'

'But what happened after . . .'

'He wouldn't have known where she was then.'

'Oh, Andee. This is terrible. I wish . . . I don't want to say it, but I'm starting to wish she'd never come back.'

'Me too, but she's done it for a reason, and I'm damned sure that it's connected to her son.'

'Which means we have to find out more about John Victor,' Graeme stated, pulling the cork from a bottle of wine. 'She must have had the baby before he used her to pay off his debts. A child would never have survived what she went through, and the thugs who bought her wouldn't have wanted it around anyway.'

'So what happened to him?' Andee murmured, afraid that she might already know the answer.

Not until she and Graeme were alone did Andee voice her suspicions. 'Did John Victor keep the baby,' she wondered, 'or, God forbid, did he sell him too?' Taking out her phone she connected to Gould, and took a few minutes to update him on what she'd learned over the last couple of days. 'If you can spare Leo,' she said, 'I need him to find out everything he can about this Val or Valentin who owned the house on Glebe Place, and anyone else living there at the time in question. I'd also like to know the whereabouts of Alison Brown.'

'Remind me,' he prompted.

'She's the woman who gave evidence at the inquest.'

Chapter Eleven

Thanks to a shooting on the notorious Temple Fields estate, followed by a chaotic hunt for the gunman, it was over a week before Andee received any news from Leo. During that time neither she nor her mother heard anything from Penny, or her son. All that seemed to be happening, to Andee's annoyance, was that she was becoming ever more aware of how often Graeme spoke to Nadia on the phone. In spite of knowing that this was exactly what Penny had intended – plant a seed of doubt and let insecurity or paranoia or simple imagination take it from there – she was in danger of falling for it.

But the calls were frequent, the tone was usually fond and Nadia was clearly quite gifted when it came to making him laugh.

'It's a huge job, and she's paying him a fortune,' Andee informed her mother, as they waited for Graeme to finish yet another call before they wandered over to the pub for lunch.

'She's probably one of those needy types,' Maureen

commented, 'can't do or think anything without getting someone's approval first.'

Although this wasn't the Nadia Andee had met, she decided to let the subject drop rather than allow Penny's manipulation to occupy any more of her thoughts.

'I'll need to go back in a day or two,' Graeme informed them as they meandered across the green. 'The builders should be ready to move on to the next phase by the end of the week, so I ought to be there to supervise.'

'Have you asked Nadia if she knows my sister?' Andee wondered, as they settled down at one of the outdoor tables.

'No, I haven't. For one thing I wouldn't know which name to use for your sister, and for another it would make me feel I was dancing to her tune.'

Surprised and impressed by that, Andee said, 'So you thought the same as I did, that she was trying to get to me?'

'Of course, I *know* she is trying to get to you. And I'm glad to see it hasn't worked. Now, Maureen, what will it be? A glass of Picpoul?'

As he went into the pub Andee began texting Alayna, wanting to know how her second date with the ripped and amazing coolest dude in town had gone, when Graeme's phone vibrated. Glancing at it, she saw the message was from Nadia and had read it before she could stop herself. *Don't worry about the hotel. I'll see to it. Bisous chéri.*

As the screen darkened Andee looked at her mother, who had also read the text.

'It doesn't have to mean anything,' Maureen said carefully.

'I'm sure it doesn't.'

'He's a good man.'

'I know that.' Andee was trying to be patient.

'But she's rich and beautiful . . .'

'Says who?'

'You, but money won't sway Graeme any more than looks. For someone like him it's personality, character that counts.'

'Well, she's blessed in that area too,' Andee commented, waving out to Brigand Bob who'd just emerged from the Smugglers' Cave.

'I asked Bob yesterday,' Maureen said, 'if he'd seen the boy in the red Corsa again, but he hasn't.'

Andee had been thinking a lot about her nephew too.

'I wonder where he is, what he's doing,' Maureen sighed.

Andee said, 'If you're serious about not wanting Penny back here . . .'

Maureen's jaw tightened. 'Of course I'm serious. I'll never forgive her for what she said about your father, and to claim that I stood by and let it happen . . . What kind of person is she?' She raised a hand as Andee made to interrupt. 'I don't know and I don't care who she is,' she declared, 'but I do know that we don't need her in our lives.'

Although she was aware of how much it was hurting her mother to say that, Andee didn't argue. What she said was, 'But her son might need us, that's what you keep thinking?'

Maureen didn't deny it. 'Don't you?' she asked.

'Of course, and I'll find him, but to do that I'll either need to see Penny again or make some sort of breakthrough where John Victor is concerned, possibly both.' She checked her phone as it rang. Seeing it was Leo Johnson she clicked on. 'Leo,' she declared, relieved to get a call at last. 'Do you have any news on Valentin of Glebe Place, or John Victor?'

'OK, we know JV bought it going over a cliff. In Valentin's case it was cancer and he was back in Moscow by then. The Chelsea house was sold in '99 to some advertising type who's still there throwing his own lifestyle parties, but I don't think they fall into quite the same category as those of Valentin's day. Tracking anyone who lived in the house around the time your sister was there is going to be near impossible, given that there are no records to assist us. However, I've had a bit more luck where Alison Brown of inquest fame is concerned. It wasn't easy; she's Ally Jackson these days and is a very respectable solicitor for a firm based in Kensington. She, her husband and two kids live in Hammersmith, not far from the River Café she told me, as if I'd know where that is.'

'You've spoken to her?'

'I took the liberty of using my position with the force to ask if she'd be willing to talk about John Victor, and she said she'd be happy to, but she doesn't know any more than she told the inquest.'

'People always know more than they think,' Andee murmured. 'You're a star, Leo. Thanks very much. Will you text me her number and the address?'

'Sure. On its way. I told her you're a relative of Victor's, by the way.'

Andee couldn't object to the truth, much as she disliked it. She waited for Ally Jackson's address and phone number to come through and called right away. 'Hello,' she said to a voicemail, 'this is Andee Lawrence. I believe Leo Johnson told you I'd be calling. I'd be grateful if you could get back to me so we can set up a time to meet.'

As she was ringing off Graeme's phone vibrated again. Not a text, a call from Nadia. Andee's eyes went to her mother. She couldn't answer it, she had no right to. All she could do was wait to see how long it took Graeme to get back to her, which turned out to be almost immediately after he brought the drinks.

'I'll just be a minute,' he said, and taking the phone out of earshot he left Andee and Maureen wondering why he always seemed to have to speak to Nadia in private.

Whatever the reason, it was plain when he returned that he was worried or upset, possibly even angry. 'Apparently half the tradesmen have walked off the job,' he informed them.

'Why?' Maureen asked, confused.

'Nadia is not a project manager,' he replied, meaning, Andee suspected, that Nadia had managed to upset them all. 'I'll have to go back, or heaven only knows what sort of mess it'll end up in.'

Andee said, 'You should be able to get a flight in the morning. I'll drive you to the airport if you like.'

'Thanks. I'm sorry, but right now I think I'm needed a lot more there than I am here.'

Andee didn't correct him. How could she, when it appeared to be true?

It turned out that Ally Jackson's home was indeed close to Hammersmith's River Café, and since she'd told Andee there would be somewhere for her to park Andee had driven straight there after dropping Graeme at the airport.

'You're not letting me down,' she'd assured him as he got out of the car. 'It's just that your priorities are different right now, and I understand that. You can't put this project into any further jeopardy.'

It was true, he couldn't, and because she knew he wasn't deceitful or in anyway uncaring of what was happening in her world, she really did believe there were problems in France. She only wished she'd been able to go with him to help sort them out. Their first big project together and she was the one letting him down.

Pulling into the small forecourt that had once been a garden at the address Ally Jackson had given her, she closed the sunroof and turned off the engine. It was a humid, overcast day, the kind of weather that sapped energy and made everything seem flat and lifeless. However, the hanging basket next to the house number was as lively as an artist's palette, and the front door itself was a cheery cobalt blue.

'You must be Andee Lawrence,' a slender, middle-aged

woman greeted her warmly on answering Andee's knock. 'You found it all right. I'm Ally, please come in.'

Andee followed her along a beige-carpeted hallway, past a post and bar staircase cluttered with shoes and toys, and into a large, airy kitchen with three skylights in the ceiling, a set of bifold doors opening on to a small square garden, and a range of wall and base units that were clearly as expensive as they were artfully designed.

'I've made coffee,' Ally told her, her large, dimpled face and cat's-eye glasses making her appear both maternal and lawyerly, 'but have you had any lunch? I can easily set up a cold plate. We've plenty of ham and cheese.'

'I'm fine,' Andee told her, 'but thank you. And thanks for agreeing to see me.'

'I'm happy to help in any way I can,' Ally assured her, waving her to a leather and stainless steel chair at a matching table, where her computer and a stack of files were taking up most of the space. 'I'm working from home today,' she explained, quickly pushing everything to one side, 'and the kids are with my sister in Kew, so we shouldn't be disturbed. Having said that, I'm afraid I didn't know your uncle all that well, and it was quite a long time ago. Do you take milk and sugar?'

'Just milk, thank you. You were his neighbour, I believe?'

'For about a year. We were across the landing from each other, but we kept quite different hours. If you're wondering how I managed to afford to live in Shepherd

Market, my place was a tiny studio that my parents paid the rent on while I finished my studies.' Bringing the coffee to the table, she sat down too. 'His flat was much bigger; two bedrooms, might even have been three, but he was hardly ever there. Weeks on end would go by without any sign of him. I've no idea where he went, he never said and I didn't feel it was my place to ask.'

'Did he have any visitors when he was there? Or even when he wasn't?'

Ally shook her head. 'Not that I can remember.'

'Do the names Penny or Michelle ring any bells for you?'

Again Ally shook her head.

'OK, at the inquest you talked about how edgy and anxious he seemed during the weeks before he died. So presumably he was spending more time at the flat then?'

'Yes, he was.'

'Alone?'

'As far as I knew.'

'Did he ever tell you why he was worried?'

'No, but he definitely was. I told him, you can't keep coming over here banging on about how someone's out to get you and not tell me who. It was like he was turning paranoid, he kept saying things like I saw her, I know it was her, or, she's doing this to freak me out.'

'It was always "she"?'

Ally frowned. 'I'm pretty sure it was.'

'Did you ever see anyone yourself?'

'No. The street was always empty when I looked out. Or empty of anyone who seemed interested in him.'

'He mentioned children? Or kids.'

'More than once, but that was it. "It's about the kids," he'd say. Obviously, I asked him what kids, but it was like he didn't even hear me. He was in another world, another zone.'

'The last time you saw him . . .'

'He was getting into a car right below his apartment. The man with him was tall, white hair, glasses, but it was dark so I didn't get a very good look.'

'Was he forced into the car?'

'It didn't look like it. In fact, I forgot all about it until the call came a week or so later to say his body had been found. It really threw me, I can tell you. I liked him. I had no reason not to.' Her eyes drifted to the garden, and after a while she said, 'There's something I told the police after the inquest. It only came back to me then. I don't know if they did anything about it. To be honest, I'm not sure if there was anything they could do, it was so vague.'

Andee waited.

'I remembered that a couple of days before he went off in the car, he said he'd heard from . . . I think he said Sven, but I can't be certain, which is probably why the police ignored it.'

Sven. It was the name of the man Penny claimed had rescued her.

Allowing a moment to pass, Andee said, 'I met with someone the other day, a detective who was at the inquest. Gerry Trowbridge? Do you remember him?'

'Yes, kind of. He came to see me a couple of weeks after. He wanted to know if John had ever talked about someone called . . . Penny? You just mentioned that name. Who is she?'

'Someone John Victor used to know,' Andee replied blandly. 'Gerry Trowbridge said you showed him something . . .'

'Oh yes, I did. It was odd, or I thought it was. A bit creepy actually, considering what it said. I found it when I packed up John's stuff. No one else came to do it so the landlord asked me to clear the place so he could rerent it. Anyway, an envelope fell out of one of the books . . . I still have it, in fact I can show you.'

Amazed, and quietly intrigued, Andee said, 'That would be lovely.'

A few minutes later Ally was back from upstairs carrying an old box file from which she produced a heap of wedding invitations, funeral service leaflets, photographs, ticket stubs, newspaper cuttings – all obviously things from over the years that she'd decided to keep and didn't know what else to do with. Eventually she pulled out a worn white envelope with John Victor's name and a Shepherd Market address on the front, and a London postmark dated, Andee noted, about a fortnight before John Victor's body had been found.

'That's all that was in there,' Ally said as Andee took out a single yellowing page and unfolded it. 'Whether it came with a letter, or something else . . .'

Andee read the typeset lines, several of which had been underlined in ink. She frowned. She knew these words . . . She couldn't say from where at this moment, but it would come to her . . .

'It looks like a page from a book,' Ally commented.

Andee swallowed dryly. It was indeed, and as she realised which book, her heart started to pound. 'Can I . . . Is it possible to take a copy?' she asked.

'Of course. Or you can have it if you like. I've no idea what I'm going to do with it.'

Putting the page back into the envelope, Andee got to her feet. 'Thank you,' she said, 'you've been incredibly helpful.'

Appearing doubtful, Ally walked with her to the door. 'If you think I can be of any more help feel free to call,' she insisted, as Andee got into her car.

With a wave of further thanks Andee reversed out of the forecourt and turned towards the Hammersmith roundabout. Once there she took the A4 in the direction of central London and called Penny on her hands-free. The ringtone was British, telling her that Penny was at least in the country.

'Well, here's a surprise,' Penny drawled as she answered.

'I know what you took of mine when you left,' Andee told her.

Penny laughed.

'Are you in London?' Andee asked.

'I am.'

'I'll meet you at the Forty One hotel in an hour.'

Maureen had no idea that she was being followed around Waitrose, no sense at all of someone watching what she was putting into her trolley, or examining and replacing on a shelf. If the truth were told she was barely aware of where she was or what she was doing. She'd forgotten to bring her shopping list so she was picking goods at random, the kind of things she usually got, and some she'd never bought before.

She was thinking about Penny, seeing her not as she'd been during that terrible scene just over a week ago, with that awful look in her eyes, but as a small child, toddling along in front of the trolley, turning now and again to make sure her mother was still behind her.

Once she'd thought she was lost and Maureen and Andee had watched her looking around slowly, until she'd spotted another woman with a small girl and a trolley and had gone to join them.

How they'd laughed about it with the woman, and later with David.

Penny had done it again the next time they were out, and the next and the next. She'd just go off and join other families, looking for all the world as though she'd be happy to stay with them.

It was as if, Maureen was thinking now, she'd been testing her mother, wanting to find out if she would always come and get her.

When Penny was older she'd started telling stories of how she'd got lost, aged three, and the police had found her just as a creepy man was trying to force her into his car.

It had never happened.

Nor had Penny been one of twins, the other having apparently died at birth.

She'd never appeared on TV, or fallen overboard when they were on a ferry to France, or been made to stay in her room for a whole week without anything to eat or drink.

They used to call them Penny's tall tales.

This wasn't how Maureen could describe the monstrous lies Penny had told about her father and grandfather. Those vile accusations were nothing short of evil. And to say that she, Maureen, had stood by and let it happen . . . It was so shocking and so cruel that Maureen was still reeling from the horror of it.

What was the matter with Penny? She knew she was lying, and she knew that her mother knew it, so what was making her want to cause so much terrible pain?

She was in the car park by now, taking out her phone to read a text from Andee while loading her shopping into the back of the car.

Will call later to update you on things, but am now in central London waiting to talk to P. Did you find your glasses? Ax

Maureen's heart sank at the reminder. She'd searched high and low for her glasses earlier and still had no idea where she'd put them. It was just as well she had a backup pair, which she'd had no trouble tracking down in the drawer next to her bed, or she wouldn't have been able to leave the house.

She texted back, *I've invited Blake and Jenny for supper. What time should we expect you?*

Receiving no immediate reply, she popped the phone

back in her pocket and was about to close the boot when she became aware of someone standing beside her.

With a jolt of alarm she quickly stepped back, ready to hand over her purse, or her shopping, whatever he wanted.

'It's OK, I'm not going to hurt you,' he said softly.

Maureen stared at him. His eyes were a summer-sky blue, his features handsome and intense . . . It was the boy who'd claimed to be Penny's son. She felt a rush of panicked emotion. 'What do you want?' she asked shakily.

'Please don't be scared,' he said. 'I just need Andee to call this number.' He was handing her a slip of paper.

Maureen barely glanced at it. 'Why don't you call her?' she demanded. 'I can give you her mobile . . .'

'Please, just ask her to be in touch with this person. He'll explain everything.'

'Who is it? You need to tell me who it is?'

'His name is Sven. Tell her not to mention anything about this to Mich—Penny.'

As he hurried away Maureen called after him, 'Please wait.'

A blue Mini paused for him to get in and drove out of the car park. To Maureen's astonishment another car went after it, at speed, and both vehicles disappeared over the Kester bridge with horns blaring furiously all round them.

Maureen tried to pull herself together. There must be more she could do. She'd noticed a girl was driving the Mini, and that the registration number ended in VRT. She needed to write that down. She could remember nothing about the other car, apart from the fact it was white.

Quickly slamming shut the boot of her own car, she got into the driver's seat and rummaged around in her handbag for a pen. Not finding one, she decided to text what she could remember to Andee.

Girl. Blue Mini. VRT.

After giving herself a minute, she began driving slowly out of the car park, knowing there was something else she should do, but unable to think what it was. Her thoughts were all over the place, fragmenting and reforming into images and words that seemed almost meaningless.

For a moment she forgot where she was. She recognised nothing around her and had no idea where she was going.

Fear blossomed like a flame.

Her mind cleared and she drove on towards home, aware that her heart was racing and a cool sweat was breaking on her skin. How had the boy known where to find her? Why wouldn't he call Andee himself? What on earth was going on between him and his mother?

How could Penny have said those terrible things about her father?

Sickened all over again by the wickedness of the words, Maureen forced them from her mind and kept going.

On reaching home she took the shopping inside and set about making a cup of tea. She was focusing on the scene in the car park, and realising the boy had an unusual accent. It was American, but there was something else too. French, maybe? Or Italian?

Had the other car caught up with him?

Someone was texting her. Taking out her phone she saw it was Andee.

This could take a while. Will let you know asap.

What could take a while?

Realising she must tell Andee what had happened at Waitrose, she was about to text her back when she remembered the boy had given her a number for Andee to call.

Where was it?

What had she done with the slip of paper?

She rapidly checked her pockets, her handbag and purse, the shopping bags, the floor in case she'd dropped it on the way in.

No sign of it.

Rushing out to the car she searched the front seats, back seats and boot.

'Oh no,' she gasped wretchedly. She must have dropped it in the car park. How on earth was she ever going to find it?

Chapter Twelve

Andee might have guessed that Penny would keep her waiting, but two and a half hours with no text, no call, nothing at all to excuse or explain the delay, or even to confirm that she was on her way?

Maybe she wasn't coming.

It was clearly a power trip to show who was in charge, which might have irritated Andee had she not been filling the time so usefully – and in such luxury.

Her sister certainly knew how to pick her hotels. This, at Forty One Buckingham Palace Road, was about as exclusive as they came. With Her Majesty as a very close neighbour, it was for residents only. No passing members of the public were encouraged to enter, indeed there was no way of getting past the concierge unless you were expected. Penny, it seemed, had given instructions for her sister to be allowed in. She'd then been escorted to the Executive Lounge on the fifth floor, welcomed with the offer of a glass of expensive champagne, which she'd politely declined, served tea, given the Wi-Fi code and was now seated in a cosy niche in front of a grand fireplace in what could almost be a private sitting room.

Did all the residents' guests find themselves treated so well? Or did the name Michelle Cross conjure that extra magic?

By now Andee had used her phone to photograph the page Ally Jackson had given her and sent it to Gould, asking him to let her know when he'd read it and she'd explain. Not that she fully understood its relevance, but she certainly knew where the words had come from.

She'd also explored the Exclusive Chauffeur Drive website where she'd found Martyna's full name – Martyna Jez – before switching to Facebook to try and track her down there. It didn't take long. The girl was Polish, aged twenty-nine and from a place called Sanok close to the Ukraine and Slovakian borders. She was in a relationship with Todd Rushton, and had one hundred and fourteen 'friends'. There were no details on education or how long she'd been in the UK, nor was anyone listed under family.

A quick read through the latest postings told Andee that her initial assessment had been correct – Martyna was a party girl, very fond of cocktails and taking selfies with Todd at various bars and nightclubs.

A more detailed scan of older exchanges proved far more interesting. Several were with Polish friends, to be expected, while the rest were with girls from various other parts of Europe and beyond. The most intriguing aspect was the number of exchanges thanking Martyna for being the best thing that had ever happened to them.

So happy now. Loving this life. Could have been so different. Love you Martyna Jez.

Never dreamt I'd live anywhere like this. Love everything about it. So glad I signed up. Friend for life, Martyna.

I was so scared when I left, but I know now I didn't need to be. I hope anyone else who reads this and is feeling scared will take heart. Definitely nothing to worry about.

Thanks for asking about my mother. Treatment going well, hoping for more good news soon. Couldn't have done it without you.

There were many more comments in Polish, or other languages, making them impenetrable for Andee, but with all the emoticons and kisses attached they were almost certainly along the same lines.

So how, if this rash of postings was to be taken at face value, was the office manager of a chauffeur-drive company having such a positive effect on so many people's lives?

Though Andee found no mention of anyone who could conceivably have been Penny, she was mindful of what Martyna had said the day she, Andee, had gone to ECD. 'It's fantastic what she does. She helps so many people. I would not be where I am if it weren't for her. None of us would.'

Andee looked up as one of the receptionists came to speak to her.

'I'm sorry,' the girl said sweetly, 'we have just received a call from Ms Cross's office to inform us that she is unable to come and meet you.'

Having expected it, Andee said, 'Thank you. I'll give

her a call. Would you mind if I continued to work from here for a few more minutes?'

'No, you are very welcome. There is a business area up on the mezzanine, if that is helpful.'

Andee glanced up to where a highly polished railing was closing off an area of desks and computers beneath an exquisitely vaulted skylight.

'But if you prefer to stay here,' the receptionist hastily added, 'there is no problem. Can I bring you any more refreshment?'

'I'm fine thanks,' Andee assured her. Her mind was already going into overdrive, certain that Penny was messing with her again. Let her, it wasn't particularly intimidating, only annoying.

She'd talk to the receptionist again when she went to settle up for her tea, meantime she needed to speak to Martyna, preferably away from the ECD offices, and some official backup could be useful for that. Since she was within a stone's throw of Scotland Yard, she thought immediately of her old friend and colleague Tim Perroll. They'd attended detective school together and he'd worked with her during the time she'd revisited the search for Penny. She'd heard from his wife, in a recent Christmas card, that he was with SO15 these days, Counter Terrorism Command, so this was going to be a big ask. If she could even get hold of him.

Eventually, after being put through to several different extensions she found herself talking to a familiar voice that wasn't Tim's, but turned out to be Jan Shell, another old friend and colleague.

'It's great to hear you, Andee,' Jan cried warmly. 'It's been too long. We must get together.'

'Absolutely,' Andee agreed. 'I just need to get up to London more often. Or if you're ever in the West Country . . .'

'I'm sure it can be arranged. Anyhow, I hear you're looking for Tim. He's not around at the moment. In fact, he could be on leave . . . Hang on, I'll check.' A few moments later she said, 'I'm being told that he's in Portugal this week.'

Damn!

'I'll give you his mobile number, it'll be easier to get hold of him with that.'

After jotting it down Andee decided not to ask when he was back; she'd call and ask him instead.

A few minutes later, with the surprise of hearing from her and the reason for her call out of the way, Tim Perroll was saying, 'OK, still getting my head round the fact that she's turned up after all these years, but you can fill me in more when I see you.'

'So where are you? I was told you were in Portugal, but the ringtone was home-grown.'

'We should be on holiday, but Karen's mother had a fall so she's gone to York and I'm left here doing all the jobs I never get round to. Now, what is it exactly that you need me to do?'

Wishing she could hug him, Andee said, 'I want you to be my official escort when I go to interview someone, so I can say we're from the police, but actually it's going to be unofficial.'

'OK,' he said, drawing it out. 'Is this person dangerous?'

'Nothing I've come across so far would suggest it. She's female, by the way.'

'Ah, the deadlier of the species. So, tell me when and where I can be of assistance.'

Andee glanced at her watch. Almost four thirty. What time did Martyna finish work? 'Would this evening be too soon?' she asked.

'Fine by me.'

'You're my hero. I need to make a call first and I'll get right back to you.' After ringing off she connected to Exclusive Chauffeur Drive, and learned from Martyna, without letting on who she was, that the office closed at six.

'Can you get to Knightsbridge for five thirty?' she asked Tim when she rang back.

'I'll do my best, but it's rush hour. Where do we meet?'

'I'll text you the address.'

Realising she was unlikely to make it back to Kesterly until late that night, Andee rang her mother. 'Hi, are you OK?' she asked when Maureen answered.

'Yes, I . . . Um . . .'

Not liking the hesitation, Andee said, 'What's happened?'

'Nothing. I just . . . What time will you be home?'

'I won't make dinner. Are Blake and Jenny still coming over?'

'Yes. I . . . Andee, I have an awful confession to make. Please don't be cross. I'm still looking for it, I've even been back to the car park . . .'

'Mum, what are you talking about?'

'The boy,' Maureen answered. 'He came up to me outside Waitrose and asked me to give you a number to call, but I can't find the piece of paper he'd written it on.'

Realising who she was talking about, Andee's eyes closed in frustration. 'Did he say anything else?' she asked.

'He said it was a number for Sven . . . I remember the name because Penny mentioned it. He said not to tell her anything about it.'

And her mother had managed to lose the number. Aaaagh!

'I texted you,' Maureen told her. 'There was a girl driving the car he went off in, and the registration . . .'

'Oh, that's what that was about,' Andee cut in, having put it down to one of her mother's funny five minutes. 'You didn't get the entire number plate?'

'No, I'm afraid not. I'm obviously not as quick as I used to be.'

Understanding how wretched she felt, Andee said, 'There's been a lot to deal with lately. We've both been thrown off course . . . But if you do find that number, call me straight away. I'll let you know when I'm on my way home.'

As she ended the call Gould rang.

'What the hell is this?' he demanded when she answered. 'Satan, saints, all good, all bad? I don't get it.'

'It's a quote from John Steinbeck,' Andee explained. 'It's what he said about his character Cathy Ames in *East of Eden*, which is basically that if you believe saints are completely good, then you have to believe that someone can be completely bad.'

'Yeah, I got that much. And your sister sent this to John Victor?'

'I'm presuming it was her, and here's why I think it was. I was studying the book for GCSE at the time she disappeared. It never occurred to me that she'd taken it. She was never that interested in literature, and anyway losing it was hardly at the front of my mind. I just remember searching for it and giving up without really caring where it might be. Fast forward to a couple of weeks ago when you might remember she asked me if I'd worked out what she'd taken of mine when she went. I think this quote from Steinbeck is giving me the answer.'

Sounding bewildered, he said, 'OK, so what are we supposed to read into it?'

'Maybe that she considers herself to be like Cathy Ames, bad through and through?'

'And that's supposed to what? Intimidate you?'

'Not me, John Victor. He's who she sent it to, and the postmark on the envelope shows that it arrived ten days before he died. Of course there's nothing to say it was from her, and I doubt after all this time that forensics could do much with the page that's clearly been torn from a book, but I'll hang on to it anyway.'

'Right, so tell me more about this Cathy Ames character.'

'Well, from what I remember, she was very sexually advanced for her age, getting boys into trouble rather than the other way round. She burned her parents' house down, killing them both, and took off with all their money. She then went to work as a whore for a character called Edwards, I think – it's been a long time since I read it. He fell in love with her, but ended up beating her so badly he almost killed her. She was rescued by one of the Trask brothers who took her in and married her, but she got pregnant by the other brother. She tried to give herself an abortion and failed. I'm picking things at random here, I'd have to read it again to be more accurate. Anyway, after her twin sons were born she abandoned them and went to work in another whorehouse where she became the madame's favourite. She ended up poisoning said madame and inheriting the brothel, which she turned into a seriously sordid den of iniquity.'

Astonished, he said, 'And you were reading that aged sixteen?'

Andee had to smile.

'So how does it end?'

'Her sons find her. One of them is disgusted by her, the other . . . I can't remember exactly, but I'm sure she made the one who hated her the sole beneficiary of her will before she committed suicide.'

As Gould stayed silent Andee felt the words resonating inside her, while watching a couple come into the lounge and go to sit by the window. She wondered if they'd been sent by Penny to keep an eye on her. Presumably the receptionist had been doing that up to now.

'My mother's had another visit from John Victor Jr,' she informed Gould.

'Your sister's son. Do you think he has a twin brother?'

'I've no idea. You're looking for parallels.'

'Aren't you?'

'Yes and no. She didn't burn our house down and kill our parents, but she did, of her own volition, go to work as an escort, as she prefers to call it. I'm asking myself was John Victor the Edwards character, falling in love with her, then selling her on to get himself out of a fix?'

'I thought you said Edwards beat this Cathy up,' Gould put in.

'Beating up, selling . . . Either way, it's abuse.'

'And she, Penny, came back to make Victor pay?'

'It's possible,' Andee agreed.

'Which doesn't quite chime with the book.'

'Does it have to? Anyway, what I'm asking myself is did John Victor keep her son?'

'Do you think it's likely he'd want to, considering his lifestyle?'

'No, I don't, but there's a good chance he knew where the boy was. Penny was around twenty-one when she claims she was rescued from a life of virtual slavery by someone called Sven. She was twenty-five when John Victor went over a cliff. So where had she been for the intervening four years, and was this Sven the same person Ally Jackson saw Victor getting into a car with just before he died? I should return here to my mother's visit from JV Jr. Apparently he gave her a number for me to call. He said it was for Sven and that he doesn't want me to mention anything to his mother.'

'Well, that's interesting. So have you rung the number?'

'My mother's lost it.'

'You're kidding me, right? So how are you going to get hold of this guy?'

'At this moment in time I've absolutely no idea, but I'm working on it.'

Before leaving the hotel Andee paid her bill and at the same time managed to get an address for Michelle Cross.

'She just emailed asking me to meet her at her office,' Andee told the receptionist. 'The trouble is, I can't remember exactly where it is.'

'It's no problem,' she was assured, and a moment later she was handed a printout giving the name of the company, K.T. Holdings, and where it was located.

Belgravia! Addresses didn't come any fancier than that.

Since Andee was more or less in the neighbourhood she decided to make a brief detour on her way to meet Tim, going past the small park on Lower Grosvenor Place, right at Eaton Square and into Upper Belgrave Street. The imposing white Georgian terraces with their supremely elegant porticoes and numerous blue plaques – Alfred Lord Tennyson being the only name she recognised – were quite clearly homes to the unimaginably rich. She could find scant evidence of any businesses located here, although Google Maps was telling her that several embassies and high-commissions were located nearby.

When Andee reached the correct house number, she searched for a sign announcing K.T. Holdings, but there was none. The main entrance, with its shiny ebony front door and topiaried trees, didn't appear to have an entryphone, or even a knocker, which she found odd – how did anyone make contact with someone inside?

Presumably they weren't supposed to.

Wondering if Penny was watching from within, Andee took a long slow look over the tall sash windows up to the roof and blue sky beyond. She had no problem with Penny knowing that she'd discovered the name and location of K.T. Holdings, and once she'd passed the details to Leo she was hopeful of knowing a lot more.

Several minutes later she was at the other end of Belgravia approaching the mews where she'd asked Tim to meet her, and seeing his impressive six foot six frame packed out with bulging muscles and far too much testosterone already stationed on the corner looking for all the world like a drug dealer, she felt a rush of pleasure. She'd missed him, she realised. She'd always felt safe when he was around, as though nothing could possibly go wrong, although it had, plenty of times, but somehow he'd managed to make any disaster feel less problematic than it was. He'd been a friend, a brother, a partner . . . He'd been a very big part of her life.

'You're looking good,' he chuckled, his husky baritone as familiar as the swamping feel of his embrace. 'And I hear you're kind of available again these days.'

'I was,' she countered, thinking of Graeme and the fact that he hadn't called or texted since she'd dropped him at the airport earlier. She hadn't called him either so she was hardly in a position to make a big deal of that.

'OK bring me into the picture,' Tim prompted as she glanced along the mews towards Exclusive Chauffeur Drive. 'Why here? Who are we looking for? And what do we need to get from them?'

After explaining that her sister was apparently behind the chauffeur-drive company, effectively making her Martyna's boss, and showing him some of the posts on Martyna's Facebook page, Andee said, 'The girl should be finishing work any minute, and I want to have the kind of chat with her that makes it clear she ought to be helping me.'

'So what exactly are you suspecting her of?'

'There's some kind of cover-up going on, I'm certain of it, but of what and of whom . . . That's what I'm trying to find out.'

'Which is where I come in?'

'Exactly. You don't have to say anything, unless you think it's relevant, I just want to see how the girl reacts when she realises you're a police officer. What we need right now is somewhere to take her for a quiet chat.'

Perroll looked around, and spotting a restaurant awning about fifty yards down on the right, he said, 'I'm sure they'll be able to accommodate us.'

Knowing that his imposing physique coupled with the flash of his badge would indeed get them what they wanted, Andee smiled and checked her watch. All she had to hope for now was that Martyna finished on time and left the office alone.

It happened exactly that way.

At a couple of minutes after six Martyna, looking her executive best in a beige skirt suit and matching low heels, exited the office, locked the door and started along the mews towards them. She was so focused on her phone that she didn't even realise anyone was there until Andee said, 'Hello Martyna.'

The girl stopped, shocked and clearly becoming afraid as she looked at Andee, at Tim and back again.

'Remember me?' Andee asked, hearing the echo of her sister's words on that strange day in France.

Apparently Martyna did, for her colour deepened and her eyes showed unease as she said, 'Of course. You came to see us . . . Your name . . .'

'Is Andrea Lawrence.'

Martyna stared at her.

'I believe it's the name used by one of your directors,' Andee said kindly.

Martyna glanced worriedly at Tim. 'What . . . What can I do for you?' she asked. 'The office is closed now.'

'I just need to have a little chat with you,' Andee explained. 'It won't take long . . .'

'But I'm in a hurry. I have to meet someone.'

'No, you really do want to talk to us,' Tim assured her, 'and as Andee just said, it won't take long.'

Paling at the sight of his badge, Martyna turned back to Andee. 'I can't tell you anything,' she exclaimed. 'I swear . . .'

Stopping her with a raised hand, Andee said, 'How do you know you can't tell me anything without even knowing what I'm going to ask? Come on, we're just going to have a friendly few minutes in the bar down the road and before you know it you'll be on your way to wherever you're going.'

On entering the bar they were told that a private party was expected at seven, but once Tim showed his badge, they were assured of the place to themselves until the guests arrived. After choosing a cosy banquette away from the window Andee and Tim sat on one side, with Martyna opposite and a highly polished brown table with a Tiffany-style lamp between them.

'I have to confess,' Andee began, 'I've been reading your Facebook page.'

Martyna's eyes widened with a mix of what seemed to be confusion and wariness. 'I don't understand. Why would you do that?'

'I wanted to find out more about you, and the messages I read told me that you're a very good friend to have. You seem to have helped a lot of people.'

Martyna glanced at Tim. 'Is there any law against that?' she asked carefully.

'Well, I suppose that depends on what you're doing to help,' Andee replied.

Martyna swallowed. 'I help them to get jobs, and to find somewhere to live,' she said.

'But you work at a car-hire company, so how are you giving assistance in these other areas?'

A hot colour was spreading over Martyna's neck. 'I am not responsible for people who post on my page.'

'Are you saying you don't know who they are?'

'Yes, no. I mean . . . I don't *know* them. I just . . .'

'If you don't know them,' Andee said, 'how come

they're calling you by name and thanking you with such . . . ?'

'I have never met them, but they are not doing anything wrong. No one forces them to do anything they don't want to.'

Andee's eyebrows rose. Maybe now they were getting somewhere. 'Would you care to elaborate on that?' she invited.

Martyna was starting to look scared. 'I cannot tell you any more,' she cried. 'This is all I know, I swear it.'

'But you haven't told us anything.'

'Because I don't know anything.'

'But you do know that there's more than a chauffeur-drive business being run out of your offices, and you're a part of it.'

'I just . . . do what I am told. But it is not bad. There is nothing bad, only good.'

'So tell me what it is.'

Martyna stared at her with wide teary eyes.

Feeling sorry for her, and suspecting she wasn't fully aware of what she was involved in, Andee decided to come at things another way. 'How did you meet Michelle Cross?' she asked. 'AKA Andrea Lawrence.'

Martyna's mouth trembled. 'My sister introduced us.'

'Does your sister also work for her?'

'No, not any more.'

'What did your sister do when she did work for her?'

'She – she was . . . She did the same as me. She work at ECD.'

'And where is your sister now?'

A tear fell on to Martyna's cheek. 'I don't . . . I am not supposed to say.'

'You can tell me,' Andee said gently.

'No. It is . . . She is at home in Poland.'

'Are you sure?'

Martyna nodded. 'I can give you her number. I write it for you here. You can call if you like, but please don't tell her that I give you the number.' She tore a page from a small notebook.

Taking it, Andee said, 'What are you afraid of, Martyna?'

'I am not afraid. You don't understand . . .'

'Then make me understand.'

'It is a wonderful thing that she does. It helps everybody. It can change their life in so many ways.'

'So explain it to me.'

'No, I cannot. It is not for me to do this. You are not being kind. I wish to go now.'

'If it's legal,' Andee said, 'then where's the problem?'

Martyna regarded her helplessly, clearly having no idea what to say next.

Stepping in, Tim said, 'Do you want our colleagues in Immigration to start investigating you and your Facebook friends? You know what things are like here since Brexit . . .'

Andee almost winced. He'd never been subtle, but she had to admit it had provoked an interesting reaction. Martyna's face was white.

'They are not illegal immigrants,' she insisted. 'I swear it. They are all here . . . It is allowed for them to be here.'

'*All?*' he repeated mildly.

She looked panicky and started to get up. 'Please, you must let me go now,' she implored. 'I do not want to be rude, but . . .'

'Martyna,' Andee interrupted in a calming voice.

'No,' Martyna cried shakily, 'I cannot help you. I am sorry, but it is not a good thing you are trying to do to me.'

'Tell me something before you leave,' Andee said. 'Do you know someone called Sven?'

Martyna appeared genuinely puzzled. 'No. Who is this person?'

Andee ignored the question. 'And what about John Victor? Does that name mean anything?'

Though she shook her head, she didn't seem certain.

Since she was too new on the scene to have been around at the time of JV senior, it had to be JV Jr. 'Do you know how I can get hold of him?' Andee asked.

Martyna's eyes filled with more panic as they flitted to Tim. 'He is . . . No one knows where he is,' she replied. 'Everyone is looking for him.'

'Why?' Andee pressed.

'Because he is doing a terrible thing. He will ruin everything if we do not find him,' and before they could say any more she darted across the bar and out into the street.

'Do you want me to go after her?' Tim asked.

Andee shook her head.

After a while he said, 'So how much of that was useful?'

Andee was still assimilating. 'Tell me what you made of it,' she prompted.

'Well, she's scared, that much is certain, but of what and *why*, when she's claiming everything is good, is beyond me. Who's Sven, by the way?'

'That's something I need to find out.'

'So what's your next move?'

Good question. 'I'm waiting to learn more about K.T. Holdings,' she remembered. 'I found out earlier that it's the name of Penny's company.'

'What's the K.T. stand for?'

'This is a wild guess, but Cathy Ames in *East of Eden* was also known as Kate Trask.'

He shook his head as though to clear it. 'OK, you're losing me now. Where does this come in?'

After explaining about the book, she said, 'What's not chiming with the story at all are the claims that Penny, Michelle, whatever we want to call her, is a good person doing good things. To begin with it's definitely not the way she's behaving with us, her family, and it's not something that could ever be said about Cathy Ames, aka Kate Trask. In Steinbeck's words Cathy was a "psychotic monster with a malformed soul".'

Tim's eyes widened. 'And your sister's modelling herself on her?'

Andee sure as hell hoped not. She checked her mobile as it rang, and seeing it was Blake she took it.

'Hi Andee,' he said gravely. 'Everything's fine and she's home again now, but I'm afraid Maureen had a bit of a turn earlier . . .'

'What does that mean?' Andee demanded, gesturing for Tim to follow her outside.

'They said at the hospital that it might have been caused by stress . . .'

'Hospital? Oh my God! What happened?'

'She seemed to lose a sense of things,' he replied. 'It didn't last long, but we decided she needed to be checked out so we took her to A & E.'

'Thank you. Thank you. Where is she now?'

'Asleep, in bed. She asked me not to tell you . . .'

'You did the right thing. I'm still in London, but I'll be back tonight. Can you stay with her until I get there?'

'Of course. She's going to be fine, honestly. She was her old self again by the time we brought her home.'

Though relieved to hear it, Andee was still worried, for her mother hadn't been her old self since Penny had come back into their lives.

'Before you go,' Blake said, 'have you spoken to Graeme today?'

'No. Have you?'

'I've left messages, but he still hasn't got back to me. Must be busy. I'll try him again tomorrow. Drive safely now,' and he was gone.

'I'm taking it that was some kind of emergency,' Tim commented, as they started towards Knightsbridge.

'My mother,' Andee replied. 'Apparently she's all right now, but I should go home. Damn, I was hoping to find a cheap hotel, if such a thing exists around here, and spend tomorrow staking out K.T. Holdings.'

'Where is it?'

'Upper Belgrave Street. No, please don't offer to do it for me, I can't use up your holiday that way, Karen would never forgive me, and besides, I need to speak to Penny myself.'

During the drive home Andee tried several times to contact Penny, but her calls kept going to voicemail. In the end she left a message saying, 'You're clearly avoiding me, so I have to ask what you're afraid of? If I'm right about what I think it is, then you should be afraid.'

As she rang off she was frowning hard. The fact that she had no idea what her sister might be afraid of was neither here nor there. What mattered was that Penny needed to think Andee was getting close to the truth. It undoubtedly had something to do with John Victor Jr, who was apparently doing his very best to avoid his mother, and everyone else.

'No, he hasn't been in touch again,' Maureen admitted dolefully when Andee got home. 'I'm so sorry. I feel such a fool . . .'

'It's OK,' Andee soothed. 'And you shouldn't have waited up. Blake told me you were in bed. It's gone midnight . . .'

'I was awake anyway, and when I heard you come in I thought you might be hungry. There's a pasta salad in the fridge.'

In fact Andee was ravenous, so grabbing the salad and a fork, she sat down at the table while Maureen made some tea. 'Where are Blake and Jenny?' Andee asked through a mouthful of food.

'In the guest room. I told them they didn't have to stay . . .'

'They did. This is really getting to you, Mum, and I'm worried.'

Sighing, Maureen brought two mugs to the table and set them down. 'Is there any other way to find a number for this Sven person?' she asked.

'There might be,' Andee replied, more to try and comfort her mother than because she felt confident there was. 'I think I've figured out what Penny took from me when she left.'

Maureen's eyes showed interest.

'My copy of *East of Eden*.'

Maureen frowned. 'Why would she take that?'

Andree shrugged. 'To be a nuisance; to have something of mine. I've no idea what was going through her mind back then, any more than I have now. However, I learned something today that was interesting. Apparently everyone's looking for her son. I was told that he's doing a terrible thing and will ruin everything if he isn't found.'

Maureen stared at her in alarm. 'What on earth does that mean?' she asked.

Andee shook her head, realising too late that tiredness had prompted her to confide in her mother when she probably shouldn't have done.

'If I could find that note,' Maureen mumbled, looking around as though it was hiding somewhere nearby. 'He's coming to you for help, I'm sure of it, and now I've gone and . . .'

'We don't know why he's trying to contact me,'

Andee interrupted, 'but whatever the reason he'll very likely try again when he realises I'm not going to ring the number he gave you.' Even to her own ears this logic sounded feeble, and it clearly hadn't done anything to assuage her mother's fears.

'What if Penny finds him first?' Maureen asked.

Chapter Thirteen

The following morning, at her mother's insistence, Andee was on her way back to London, this time by train.

'I'm fine, I'm fine,' Maureen had promised as Andee hesitated over leaving. 'You don't need to fuss. I'll be with Jenny most of the day anyway.'

Since that was true, Andee was now able to focus on her reasons for going, and after texting Tim Perroll to set up another meeting she rang Leo to find out if he'd made any progress with KT Holdings.

'Have you tried Googling them?' he asked.

'Of course, but I didn't get anything.'

'Same here, and I haven't had time to delve any deeper. As soon as I have I'll get back to you.'

Deciding that nine thirty wasn't too early to contact Alayna, Andee pressed to connect, and only realised she'd used FaceTime when Alayna's sleepy young face and copious blonde waves filled the screen. No matter what was going on in the world, or her life, the sight of one of her children never failed to lift Andee's spirits.

'Hey Mum, what's up?' Alayna yawned, apparently jostling with someone behind her.

'Can you talk?' Andee asked carefully.

'Hang on.' Alayna turned away, said something Andee didn't catch to someone Andee couldn't see, and a moment later she was back. 'Sorry about that. He's always in here, it drives me nuts, or it would if I didn't love him so much.'

'Who are we talking about?' Andee wondered casually.

'Tartie Bartie. You remember him. He's forever having boyfriend trouble and he seems to think yours truly can sort it all out. Like as if. Anyway, I expect what you really want to know is how things are going with Jaylan.'

Jaylan? Of course, the new boyfriend. 'Tell me,' Andee encouraged.

'Oh, Mum, he is so amazing. I really like him. Actually, I think it might be love.'

Spotting the mischief in her daughter's eyes, Andee laughed. 'Remind me what he's studying,' she said.

'Law. And he's only got a room in a flat two streets from here, isn't that amazing?'

'I'm blown away,' Andee assured her. 'So how many times have you seen him now?'

'Last night was the third. We went to the Albion, a whole gang of us, and got totally smashed. I expect you really want to hear that. His mum's coming down from London the weekend after next, and he's dead keen for me to meet her. I can't wait to show him off to you and Grandma . . . How is she, by the way? I tried calling her yesterday but couldn't get an answer.'

'She's OK. Missing Grandma Carol and Graeme's sisters, but she'll survive. Try her again today, she'd love to hear from you. Now, there's something I'd like you to do for me if you have the time.'

'Hit me with it, Sherlock.'

'Sorry?'

'I'm Watson, you're . . . Never mind. Name it.'

'OK, so using Facebook, or any other social media sites you think might be relevant, I want you to do some research on someone called Martyna Jez, I'll text you the spelling. Make a list of all her friends detailing where they're from, if the info's there, where they live now, what they do as jobs, anything about them you think might be useful. I'm particularly keen to know if you think they're real.'

Blinking, Alayna asked, 'What, are you saying it could be some kind of showcase page?'

'It's possible. Do they exist?'

'I've no idea. I'll try to find out. So, am I allowed to ask why this Martyna's of interest?'

'She works for Michelle Cross whose name you'll remember . . .'

'The one who stays in swanky hotels.'

'That's her. I want you to see if you can find any mention of her on the pages you turn up. Or of someone called Sven, I don't have a surname. Another name that's important is John Victor, senior or junior.'

'OK, got it. Can't wait to hear what all this is about. How soon do you need it?'

'As soon as you can.'

'OK, I'll make a start this morning, I don't have to be anywhere until two. Are you on a train?'

'I'm on my way to London. How are you managing for money?'

'Fine, and you're sounding like Dad. Well, not fine, because I'm missing out on a week in Ibiza with Tamsin and Sanako, but if I take the time off I'll lose my job and I definitely can't afford to do that now I'm saving for my gap year. And before you offer to make good until I find another, the answer's thanks, but no thanks. Anyway, Jay's also staying in Bristol for the summer, he's got a job at Bordeaux Quay on the Harbourside, so I don't mind so much about not going to . . . Hey, listen, I have to go, he's trying to get through,' and the screen went blank.

Minutes later Leo rang.

'OK, I don't have long, but here's what I have so far on KT Holdings,' he told her, 'which actually isn't anything we don't already know, apart from the fact that there's no record of it at Companies House. So, whatever it is, it's not registered here. Could be offshore, in fact it probably is. However, something that is at that address, is a property management outfit called UBS – Upper Belgrave Street? – and they have a website. Correction, a web page with a fancy logo and mobile numbers for Martyna Jez and Todd Rushton.'

Intrigued, Andee said, 'According to Martyna's relationship status, those two are an item.'

'I know, so I tried calling his number, but all I got was "Hi, I'm Todd, good to hear from you, leave a message and I'll get right back." Same sort of thing on the girl's. From there I had a quick look at Todd Rushton's social media activities to see if there was any mention of the businesses. I drew a blank, I'm afraid, but if you ask me it's all so non-specific that it has to be shady.'

Since Andee was already convinced of that, she simply said, 'I don't suppose you came across the name Sven anywhere?'

'Not that I recall. Is he significant?'

'I think so. And no mention of my sister?'

'None that I could find, but I'll keep looking, trouble is my workload's piling up here, so I'm not sure when I can give it any more time.'

'You've done brilliantly already, Leo. Thanks. I'll keep on it myself and let you know what I find.'

'Well, I think Mr Todd Rushton is our first port of call,' Tim declared confidently after Andee had shared her latest information. 'Did your guy in Kesterly send you the number?' She nodded.

Reading from her screen he connected to Rushton's mobile and told the voicemail, 'Hi, the name's Tim Perroll. I hear you can help with investments, so if you could call me back that would be great.'

As they walked on towards Upper Belgrave Street Andee said, 'So knowing what we do now, which admittedly isn't much, what do you think it's all about? What's your hunch?'

He took a while to think. 'Still too vague,' he decided, 'but if I had to hazard something . . . When you first told me about it you mentioned a couple of clinics in the US. If we put that together with Martyna's claims that her boss is doing wonderful things, helping many people . . . OK, I'm going right out on a limb now, but it could be some kind of organ trade.'

Andee baulked. That hadn't occurred to her at all. Amazing how differently men and women thought.

'What's your gut telling you?' he asked.

'Not that,' she admitted, 'but now you say it . . . I guess it could fit. Small fortunes change hands for healthy organs.'

'And from what we've seen so far, the young people posting on Martyna's page would definitely fit into the category of healthy. Plus they seem to have hit some sort of jackpot, "loving this life", "so scared when I left, but didn't need to be", "treatment going well". I'm just saying, it's a possible.'

Since she couldn't match it with any rational theories of her own, Andee didn't argue.

'OK, so here we are,' he announced as they reached the address on Upper Belgrave Street. 'As you said, no entryphone, and no knocker, telling us the people inside are not interested in getting to know the people outside.' Taking out his phone he left Rushton another message.

'Hi, Tim Perroll again. I forgot to mention that I'm with the Metropolitan Police. We're outside KT Holdings on Upper Belgrave Street. It would be a good idea to let us in, or to call me back on the number you'll now have. We'll wait five minutes.'

As he rang off Andee said, 'What are we going to do after five minutes?'

'I'm sure you have a plan.'

Choking on a laugh, she said, 'I feel like I've been here before with you.'

He grinned and glanced at his phone as it rang. 'My brother,' he said, 'I'll call him back.'

Going to sit beside him on the front steps leading up to the porch, Andee said, 'I think in your next message you should say that we have reason to believe that illegal activities are being conducted from these premises. If no one lets us in we'll be forced to obtain a warrant and if there is still no cooperation the door will be broken down.'

'I like it. There's one thing we haven't tried yet, of course,' and getting up he mounted the rest of the steps and hammered his fist against the solid bastion of a front door.

'Now why didn't I think of that?' Andee commented drily.

Receiving no response, he returned to the pavement and looked up at the silent, unblinking house. 'It's impossible to tell whether anyone's inside. I wonder if there's a way in – or out – round the back?'

As he started off down the street Andee received a text and immediately called him back.

It was from Penny.

You don't know what you're doing. You need to stop.

After showing it to Tim, Andee texted back. *Tell me why.*

Several minutes ticked by. In the end Andee texted again. *Why are you afraid to see me?*

The response came quickly. *I am not in the country. Please stop hounding my staff. They can't help you.*

Andee gave herself a moment before messaging

again. *I don't believe that and we won't stop until we've got some answers. Tell me about Sven?*

You'll never find him so do yourself a favour and stop trying.

'Ask if her son's with her,' Tim prompted.

'Why?'

He shrugged. 'Why not?'

Andee did, and no answer came back. How quickly the balance had shifted. It had been Penny who had sought out Andee, and now she was trying to push Andee away. Clearly Penny hadn't contacted her and her mother to rekindle their relationship. It had always been about something else, something bigger.

Andee tried texting again, but still no response. 'I think we can deduce from the way the boy's approaching me through my mother that he doesn't want to talk to me himself,' she said. 'Is that because he's afraid his mother is having me watched – and we know that she is – so I'd lead her right to him? Or is he part of whatever twisted game she's playing?'

'Do you think he is?'

'No, actually I don't, but I guess we can't rule it out.'

'Why doesn't he just contact you by phone or email?'

Andee shrugged. 'You'll have to ask him that.'

Tim was looking up and down the street, trying to spot anyone in a car or on foot who might conceivably be tracking them. There didn't appear to be anyone. Taking out his phone he called Todd Rushton again. 'OK, your five minutes is up. We're heading round to your gaff – yeah, we know where you live – while we wait for backup to join us here in Belgravia. If you're in put the kettle on, there's a good lad. Dying for a cuppa.'

'Where does he live?' Andee asked, falling into step with him.

'No idea, but keep walking in case someone's watching.'

Apparently someone was, for as they reached Belgrave Square a silver Mercedes drew up alongside them, and a middle-aged man with greying slicked-back hair and horn-rimmed glasses lowered the rear window. 'I'm Peter Graze-Jessop, lawyer for KT Holdings,' he informed them. 'Is there anything I can help you with?'

Thinking fast and hoping for the best, Andee said, 'We're trying to find John Victor Jr.'

Graze-Jessop appeared amused. '*John* Victor Jr,' he repeated, as though enjoying the name. 'Yes, a lot of people are trying to find that young man. I take it you haven't seen him.'

Before Andee could reply, Tim said, 'Why are you looking for him?'

Graze-Jessop pondered the question. 'Let's just say he has something that doesn't belong to him and he really needs to give it back.'

'And that would be?' Andee prompted.

'He knows what it is. He also knows that no good will come out of what he's trying to do. Nor are you helping anyone by harassing Martyna and Todd. I believe,' he continued, 'your sister has already cautioned you to stop. You'd be wise to heed her words.'

Astonished and annoyed, Andee said, 'Please tell

my sister that I don't appreciate being threatened by her lackeys.'

Graze-Jessop glided right over the insult. 'You must make your own decisions,' he said, 'but please don't say you weren't warned,' and before she could respond he instructed the chauffeur to drive on. However, Tim was too fast for them. He was in front of the car before it had moved an inch, holding up his badge and instructing Graze-Jessop to step out on to the street.

Appearing vaguely ruffled Graze-Jessop complied, his hands ludicrously raised as though someone was threatening him with a gun.

'I don't know what your game is,' Tim growled into his face, 'but I do know this. Nothing legal needs the sort of cover-up you're involved in here. So despite your threats, we're going to find out what it is, and *please don't say you weren't warned.*'

Still not looking as shaken as Andee would have liked, Graze-Jessop returned to the Mercedes, spoke to the driver again and minutes later they were turning off the square in the direction of Knightsbridge. 'That was subtle,' she told Tim.

'I do a good line in it,' he quipped. 'Bastard's so smooth you can practically see the trail he leaves behind.'

Andee turned to look back down the street, wondering if anyone inside the house had witnessed the last few minutes. 'Where do you suppose she is?' she pondered. Taking out her phone she connected to Penny's number, and the ringtone confirmed that she was indeed out of the country. Deciding not to leave a message, she ended the call just as another came in. Seeing it was her mother she clicked on.

'Are you OK?' she asked.

'I've seen him again,' Maureen replied breathlessly. 'He was waiting outside reception when I left the gym. He seemed very upset that you hadn't rung the number yet, so I told him it was my fault. I said I was sorry. He was very nice about it and wrote it down again. He really wants you to call this Sven. I promised you would, so you must . . .'

'I will,' Andee cut in, 'but you need to give me the number.'

'Yes, of course. Here it is. I've got it right here.'

After taking it down and double-checking she had it right, she said, 'Was anyone else with him?'

'Not that I saw. He seemed very worried. He said I should tell you that time was running out and he really needs your help.'

'With what?'

'He didn't say, and he'd gone before I could ask.'

'Are you all right?'

'I'm fine. Jenny's with me. She saw him too. I looked out for the car but he cut into the woods, so I've no idea where he went from here.'

After assuring her mother she'd call back as soon as she had some news, Andee rang off and relayed the information to Tim. 'The number begins 0046. Do you know where that is?'

Googling it, he said, 'Sweden. With a name like Sven we should have guessed.'

Wasting no more time Andee pressed in the number,

and felt her heart starting to beat a little faster as she waited for a reply. Where on earth was all this going to take her?

When the ringtone stopped it was followed by silence, so she said, 'Hello? My name's Andee Lawrence. I was told to call this number.'

'Yes, Ms Lawrence, we've been expecting to hear from you,' a quiet female voice responded. Her English sounded perfect, spoken as it was with a Swedish accent. 'I'm afraid it is not convenient for Mr Sylvander to take your call at the moment. Is it possible for him to ring back on this number in half an hour?'

Seeing no point in arguing Andee said, 'Yes, that'll be fine.'

Having walked round to the Rubens Hotel to have coffee while they waited for the call back, Andee and Tim chose seats at the streetside window overlooking the Royal Mews, watching crowds of tourists coming and going.

As Tim spoke to his brother on the phone, Andee poured them coffee from a cafetière and returned to an email from Leo detailing the information he'd given her earlier. Two companies without websites or registered addresses, neither of them offering services that could be accessed, other than by calling Todd Rushton or Martyna Jez, and no mention at all of any US-based medical centres.

'Do you have any helpful contacts in the States?' she asked Tim as he finished his call.

'I've been thinking about that,' he replied, picking up

his coffee, 'but there's no one I'd feel comfortable trading favours with at this stage. We need more to go on.'

Having expected that answer, Andee checked her phone as it rang, and seeing it was Graeme she felt unsure about answering. Now wouldn't be a good time while she was waiting for Sven to call back; on the other hand they hadn't spoken for what seemed too long.

'Hi, how are you?' she asked, clicking on.

'I'm fine,' he replied, his tone slightly querulous and distracted.

'How are things going over there?'

'I wish I could say also fine, but the problems seem to be piling up. What about with you?'

So much had happened since they'd last spoken that she couldn't think where to begin, or why he'd be interested when he was so challenged by events over there. 'It's still quite complicated,' she replied. 'No sign of Penny, but we're working on it. Listen, I'm waiting for a call that I have to take. Can I ring . . .'

'It's OK. I'll try again later,' and before she could draw breath the line had gone dead.

Tim regarded her curiously.

Not sure whether she was offended or worried, Andee simply shook her head and returned to her phone, this time to read an email she'd just received from Alayna.

Hey, made a start and thought I'd send this through. Out of first twenty friends on MJ's FB page five are Polish, two Estonian, six Latvian, three Slovakian, and four Hungarian. All living in UK. Can't find what they do for work, or where they live, but all sounding very grateful to

Martyna. Are they for real? No way of knowing. If you scroll on down from these posts you'll find more, mostly from guys in their twenties, definitely not older, and saying more or less the same thing. Again, no idea if they're real. More soon as I can. Xxx

Andee showed it to Tim, and was about to comment when a call came in. Seeing the Swedish number she quickly clicked on.

'Ms Lawrence, Sven Sylvander here. I'm sorry to have kept you.' The voice was low, gravelly and very slightly fractured. 'I am presuming that Jonathan gave you this number. Do you know where he is?'

Jonathan? 'No. Do you?'

'I'm afraid not, but it's very important that we find him. Can you come to Stockholm?'

Andee blinked in astonishment.

'I'm afraid my health won't allow me to make the trip to London,' he explained, 'but we need to talk. I will arrange the air travel from this end and someone will be at the airport to meet you. Is tomorrow too soon?'

Andee looked at Tim as she said, 'That sounds fine.'

'Thank you. If you will be kind enough to give me your email address I'll have my assistant send you details of flight times. I shall look forward to meeting you.'

Chapter Fourteen

The following morning, feeling as though everything was taking a truly surreal turn, Andee was settled into a business class seat on the 7.40 flight to Stockholm from Heathrow. Given the short notice of the trip, she'd paid a quick visit to Oxford Street yesterday to gather up enough essentials to last for three days, though no one had told her she'd be away for that long. In fact, there had been no mention of a return flight at all, and the ticket she had was only one-way.

'Don't worry,' she'd told Tim when he'd pointed this out. 'I'm sure no one's planning to kidnap me, and I can always buy myself a ticket to get home if need be.'

He still didn't look happy. 'You don't feel you might be walking into some sort of trap?' he challenged.

It hadn't crossed her mind until he'd suggested it. However, now, as the plane soared off into the blue beyond, she was asking herself if she was crazy to be following a stranger's instructions to fly to a country she'd never visited before, as though this were some sort of game for which she knew the rules – which she patently didn't.

There was no point trying to second-guess things; she had absolutely no idea what to expect when she got to Stockholm, apart from a meeting with Sven Sylvander, and after that, presuming it happened, she'd just have to wait and see.

In an effort to distract herself from the continued taunt of misgivings she tried to focus on her mother, whose concern about this trip to Stockholm hadn't been so very different to Tim's.

'I wish Graeme was around to go with you,' Maureen had commented with a sigh. 'It doesn't seem right you having to go there when I'm sure this man could just as easily come here.'

'It'll be fine,' Andee had assured her. 'I just want you to stop worrying and let me know immediately if either Penny or her son get in touch again.'

Having wondered earlier if this trip was some sort of ruse to get her mother on her own, Andee had already texted Blake to ask him and Jenny not to let Maureen out of their sight. She'd also alerted Gould and Johnson of her movements and of course Tim knew, and would have come with her had his wife not been returning from York today.

Remembering that Alayna had emailed her a further update last night, she scrolled to it and felt her curiosity growing, along with confusion and unease, as she tried to make sense of it.

OK, girls first. Seems like seven of those I checked yesterday are living in London. No actual addresses, but that's not unusual, only a moron would give that sort of information on social media. They're still active on various sites, but nothing unusual about their posts since those a couple of months ago, apart from the fact that they no longer seem to be in contact with Martyna. I went back a bit further on a couple of pages and found some interesting entries about someone called 'Polina' who 'didn't want to go through with it'. Have attached a screen shot. See where someone says, 'Oh my God, that's terrible. No one will ever find her.' The responses are all weepy emoticons, apart from a couple saying that she had a choice so it's her own fault. Couldn't find anything to explain what it meant. The next weird, or interesting thing, is a post from someone called Inga reminding them that they should be using their private chat room.

Sorry, got to go now, Jay's waiting. No idea what any of this means, or how real it is. Will try to check.

Love you, A xxx

(PS – Will focus on the guys next.)

Making a mental note to forward this to Leo when she landed, Andee refused a second coffee and croissant from the steward and closed her eyes. Although none of this confirmed Tim's theory, it wasn't ruling it out either; in fact it was making her increasingly uneasy. But organ-trafficking? Really?

Feeling faintly queasy, she turned to gaze at the clouds. Nothing was making sense to her, from Alayna's social media report, to Martyna's comments about Penny, to John Victor Jr's – *Jonathan's?* – need for help.

After an easy pass through immigration Andee wheeled her new overnight bag through to Arrivals, where a portly, well-groomed woman of around fifty was displaying a board with her name on it. Going to her, Andee found herself responding to the warmth of the woman's smile with some enthusiasm of her own.

'I'm guessing you're Selma,' Andee said, as they shook hands.

'Indeed I am,' Selma replied, her gentle voice confirming her as the woman Andee had spoken to on the phone. She was also the 'assistant' who'd sent the email containing flight details. 'I am very happy to meet you. Please come this way. The car is not far.'

With the pleasing anticipation of being in a country she'd never visited before mixing with some apprehension, Andee took in her surroundings as she walked alongside Selma to a large black Mercedes, where a chauffeur was already holding open a rear door.

'Is this your first visit to Stockholm?' Selma asked, as they merged with the traffic heading towards the city.

'It is,' Andee confirmed. 'I read something recently about Sweden being in the top ten best places to live.'

Selma's smile was full of pride. 'It is a beautiful country, and Stockholm, as you will see, is a very special city. Maybe you already know that it is made up of many islands which are linked by, I think, forty-two bridges. This is why we call ourselves the Venice of the North. Our waterways are much wider, and very blue at this time of year. Plus, we have many quaintly cobbled streets, historic buildings and a magnificent palace in Gamla Stan, which is the old town. Of course there are also many boats and cafés on the waterfronts, and also some of the best restaurants in Scandinavia, possibly the world. And then there is the coffee.'

Andee's eyes twinkled.

'I am reading your mind,' Selma told her mischievously, 'which is why our first stop will be at a very special place which is not far from your hotel.'

Interested to hear that she would be in a hotel, Andee said, 'When will I meet with Sven?'

Selma grimaced an apology and glanced at her watch. 'I am afraid it cannot be today. I will explain over coffee, meantime, if you will forgive me there are some urgent calls I must make.'

Deciding now wasn't the time to object to being kept waiting, Andee simply gazed out of the window, having no more success in reading the passing signs than in understanding whatever Selma was saying on the phone. She truly was in a foreign country, excluded by the language and possibly even the culture; however, she wasn't feeling too anxious yet, only curious and even vaguely excited.

Checking her own phone as it rang, she saw it was Graeme and gladly clicked on. 'Hi, how are you?' she asked quietly.

'I'm fine. Where are you? That wasn't a British ringtone.'

'I'm in Stockholm.'

'*Stockholm?* Why?'

'It's a long story. I'll tell you later. Have you ever been here?'

'Yes, a few times. I used to go with a client to buy art at the Auktionsverket. How long are you going to be there?'

'I'm not sure yet.'

'I'm guessing it's something to do with Penny?'

'It is.'

'Are you alone?'

'Yes and no. I was invited by Sven Sylvander, who I haven't met yet. He's someone Penny's son wants me to be in touch with.' If Selma was listening she showed no sign of it.

'Is Penny going to be at this meeting?'

'I've no idea, but I don't think so. Are you managing to get things back on track at your end?'

With a sigh he said, 'Don't get me started.'

'Oh dear. How's Nadia behaving?'

'The way she usually behaves, passionately.'

Not sure she liked the answer, Andee said, 'Is she with you?'

'Yes. I mean, not at this moment, but she's at the villa every day now and I really wish she'd go back to Spain for a while.'

Liking that answer much more, Andee fell silent for a moment, not sure what else she wanted to say, but not wanting to ring off either.

'I miss you,' he said softly.

Swamped by feeling, she said, 'I miss you too.'

'I'd like to be the one to show you Stockholm. It's one of my favourite cities.'

'If you can get here . . .'

'If I could I'd be on the next flight.'

Forty minutes later, having journeyed along a motorway surrounded by more glorious pine forests than she'd ever seen in her life, to be greeted in the city by the most entrancing baroque architecture on just about every street corner, Andee was sitting outside a famous café in the Gamla Stan being invited to name her bean type, grind size and froth style.

The coffee shop was on a quaint, cobbled street adjacent to a waterfront with towering and colourful old houses soaring skywards, and a tantalising glimpse of the royal palace glistening in the bright midday sun.

When eventually their bespoke brews arrived Selma raised her cup and said, proudly, '*Valkommen till* Stockholm.'

'*Tack,*' Andee smiled, using the only Swedish word she'd managed to pick up from watching every episode of *The Bridge.*

'When we are finished I will take you to your hotel,' Selma told her. 'It is not so far from here, in the area known as Ostermalm, which is like your Kensington or Knightsbridge in London. You will probably enjoy to freshen up a little before we begin our tour.'

Andee blinked. *Tour?* 'Oh no, I really don't want to put you to any trouble,' she protested. 'I'm quite . . .'

'It is no trouble. I am happy to do it,' Selma assured her, 'and Sven insists that you should see something of our beautiful city before you leave. I'm afraid it isn't possible for him to see you today, because he is very sick. He has – how do you say *leukemi* . . . ?'

'Leukaemia?' Andee ventured, hoping she was wrong. Who'd wish it on anyone?

'This is correct,' Selma confirmed. 'Yesterday he was receiving chemotherapy. He insisted he would be strong enough to see you today, but of course it is not true. He needs another day to regain some strength.'

'Oh, goodness,' Andee murmured. 'I'm so sorry.'

'We are all sorry, because we love him very much and sadly he is not going to recover. The doctors are keeping him with us for as long as they can, but not so long that his life becomes unbearable.'

Andee couldn't think what to say as Selma sipped her coffee and waved to someone she knew. In the end she said, 'Have you worked for Sven for long?'

Selma smiled. 'Since I was twenty. He is a very good man to work for, which is why he is so much loved.'

Andee weighed up her next question, and decided simply to go for it. 'Do you know my sister?' she asked.

'Oh yes, very well,' Selma replied, clearly unfazed. 'We call her Kate, which is what she prefers. Others know her as Michelle, and of course to you she is Penny.'

Andee had got stuck at Kate – the evil Kate Trask from *East of Eden*? – until the mention of Penny. 'So you know who she really is?' she asked incredulously.

Selma simply added more sugar to her coffee.

'Is she here?' Andee wanted to know.

'No, we have not seen her since Jonathan disappeared.'

'Jonathan? Her son?'

'That's right. He has been in touch with you?'

'With my mother. He wanted me to contact Sven. Penny calls him John. John Victor.'

Selma's eyebrows rose.

Hoping for more of a response, Andee waited, but none was forthcoming. 'What did you mean when you said he's disappeared?' she asked.

'He is not in contact with Kate or Sven.'

'Why?'

'It is Sven who must answer this question. I am here to keep you company for today and make sure that you have everything you need.'

Realising that Selma would have her instructions and that nothing she, Andee, could say would make her sway from them, Andee decided to resign herself to the wait and simply enjoy her tour.

By seven that evening she had crossed so many bridges, admired so much stunning architecture and gasped at such an abundance of picture-postcard views, many from Heaven, a rooftop bar in the Sodermalm district, that she couldn't imagine why she'd never been here before. The city was far more fascinating – and friendly – than she'd expected, and she couldn't help wishing Graeme was with her so she could enjoy his stories of previous visits.

Since she was eager to talk to him, she waited no longer than it took to get to her hotel room and pour herself a large glass of wine before connecting to his number. To her frustration she went through to voicemail, so after leaving a message for him to call as soon as he could, she sank into a plush armchair and opened her emails.

No more from Alayna, nor from Leo; however there was a curt note from Penny that immediately infuriated her.

For all these years I've left you alone, never digging into your life or trying to interfere with what you're doing. It would be to your credit if you would afford me the same courtesy.

'I can't believe the nerve of her,' she exploded to her mother when she got through. 'It's like she's completely forgotten that *she* got in touch with *us*. And how dare she say she's never dug into my life when she's so blatantly been having me watched. I don't suppose you've seen the boy again?'

'I'd have told you if I had. I keep thinking about him though, and wondering why he said time was running out. What on earth do you think he means?'

'I've no idea, Mum, but hopefully by this time tomorrow I'll be able to give you an answer.'

The following morning Andee was already waiting in the hotel lobby when Selma and the chauffeur arrived to take her to meet Sven. Having consulted a guidebook she was aware that the area they were travelling through – Ostermalm – was home to some of Stockholm's wealthiest residents, and this was very evident. The baroque and Renaissance buildings, immaculate in their upkeep and made glorious by ornate turrets, spires and onion domes, were as opulent and elegant as anything she'd seen in Paris or London, maybe even more so. She tried to imagine Penny moving around the area, speaking the language, meeting friends, shopping in the stylish boutiques, enjoying the history and charm. It wasn't easy, but given how little she knew of her sister's life that was hardly surprising.

Eventually they turned off a wide, busy boulevard with a tree-lined walkway down the centre of it into a quiet, triangular construct of exclusive mansion blocks. They came to a stop outside an ivory-coloured building with black wrought-iron balconies rising up over several floors, and a set of heavy black doors to mark the entrance.

'Sven also has a home at Djursholm, overlooking the sea,' Selma informed her as she put in a security code to enter the block. 'It is where he prefers to be, but his treatment means he must spend most of his time in town.'

Concerned for how sick he actually was, Andee said, 'Are you sure he's up to seeing me today?'

'Oh yes, he is looking forward to it.' Selma nodded her thanks to a security guard who was showing them into an elevator.

At the fifth floor the doors opened and they were greeted by a slightly bent old man with a complexion like tree bark and an expression that appeared half happy, half tragic, the result, Andee suspected, of a stroke. 'Thank you, Erik,' Selma said gently. 'You can tell Freja that we are here and will take coffee in the *lilla salongen* when she has it ready.'

'Of course. It will be my pleasure,' Erik responded with an awkward little bow.

Moved by the politeness of them speaking English, presumably for her benefit, Andee looked around the extraordinary circular entrance hall with its elaborate mid-European decor and wide marble staircase that curved up to the next level. There were statues and paintings everywhere, fresh flowers in large oriental urns and a rack filled with so many styles of walking cane that Sven – or someone in the household – must surely be a collector.

'Through here,' Selma invited, pushing open a large oak door with iron-studded hinges and, incongruously, but sweetly, a child's drawing of a house pinned to the front. Underneath the drawing were the words *Pappa's Den.*

'We found it the other day while going through some things,' Selma explained, 'and we decided to put it up again.'

The *lilla salongen* turned out to be a cosy, oak-panelled room with tall sash windows along one wall offering views over dense green treetops, a black and gold marble fireplace with a gilt-framed mirror over the chimney breast, and three matching sofas in mahogany leather forming an intimate square around a circular glass table.

'Sven will be with us shortly,' Selma told her. 'He favours this room above the others. It is less formal, he says.'

Andee was by now so riveted by the photographs on just about every surface that she was barely listening. Penny was in so many of them, staring out with watchful, almost solemn eyes, or seemingly trying to avoid the lens altogether. In some she was smiling, but only a few, and in others she was much slimmer and younger than she was now. Andee presumed the older man who often featured alongside her was Sven, and the young boy was surely John – Jonathan – at various ages. Selma also appeared, but the woman who really caught Andee's attention, apart from Penny, was a truly striking beauty. There was so much gaiety radiating from her in just about every shot that Andee felt a strong desire to meet her.

'Sven's wife, Ana,' Selma said softly, seeing Andee transfixed by the woman's appearance.

Before Andee could respond, a door beside the fireplace opened and the man from the photographs came to life. For a bizarre moment Andee felt thrown, for as strikingly similar as he was to his captured images, there was also an enormous change. The shock of white hair had gone, as had the swarthy complexion. His age-spotted head was completely bald, and the skin on his face was waxen and crusted. He was painfully thin and stooped, but his eyes, behind their frameless spectacles, were such a deep and arresting blue it felt almost as hard to look at them as it was to look away.

'Andee? May I call you Andee?' he asked, holding out an unsteady hand to shake. This was the voice she'd heard on the phone, low and gravelly and slightly hypnotic.

'Yes, of course,' she replied, feeling the knotted bones of his fingers as her own closed around them.

'Thank you for coming to Stockholm,' he said, holding her gaze in a way that felt authoritative yet reassuring. 'I am sure Selma has explained why it is not possible – or let us say it is not *easy* – for me to travel these days.'

'Yes, she has,' Andee replied, 'and I'm very sorry to hear what you're going through.'

He dismissed it with a wave of his hand, which he turned into a gesture for her to sit down. 'Ah, here is

Freja with our refreshments. I hope you'll forgive me for not taking anything myself – doctor's orders – but please enjoy the coffee, and Freja makes the most excellent *kladdkaka*, which I expect you know is a Swedish version of chocolate cake.'

Andee hadn't known it, but she was happy to try it, along with the coffee, which turned out to be excellent. As for the patisserie . . . She wondered how she was going to limit herself to only one slice.

'Selma will stay with us,' Sven informed her, as Freja set a bottle of mineral water and a glass on the table next to him. 'I don't think I'm going to collapse or die in the next hour or so, but just in case, it would be awkward for you to deal with it alone.'

The merriment in his eyes was so infectious that Andee had to smile.

'Now, I think we should come straight to the point of why you're here, don't you?' he said. 'Jonathan gave you my number, yes? Have you seen him?'

Startled by the suddenness of the question, Andee said, 'No, but my mother has. He gave her your number to pass to me.' She wondered whether to bring up the issue of the name, but decided to leave it for now. 'Why doesn't he approach me himself?' she asked.

Batting the air, as though there might be a fly near him, he said, 'Because he suspects his mother is having you watched, and I am sure he is correct about that.'

Andee's eyes widened. Apparently he didn't find anything inappropriate about this, or if he did he wasn't showing it. 'But there is always email, and the phone,' she pointed out.

'He believes his mother to be capable of monitoring all things.'

Andee held his gaze, an unspoken request for him to expand. When he didn't, she said, 'Is she?'

He smiled. 'I really have no idea, but I can tell you that she is very resourceful.'

'So what is going on? Why am I here?'

'To answer that I must tell you that I have not spoken to Jonathan in several weeks, but I imagine he has put us in touch because he wants me to ask you to help him.'

Andee's eyebrows rose. 'Why does he need help?'

Sven shifted uncomfortably, but waved Selma back to her chair as she made to get up. After sipping some water, he said, 'He has got himself into a situation that does not please his mother. It could end up causing her some . . . difficulties and she is very keen to avoid that. I'm afraid he can be as stubborn as she is.'

Realising she needed to back up slightly, Andee said, 'How did he even know about me?'

'Ah, yes. This is a good question. He knows because I told him, and once his mother realised I had done this she guessed he would go to you if things should go wrong between them. I confess this was my intention, although the current circumstances – I refer to the reason for his disappearance – were not in existence at the time I told him he had another family. I did it as a form of insurance. Once my cancer was diagnosed I needed to be sure someone would be there for him should things ever become . . . complicated, as they are apt to do with his mother.' He paused as Selma refilled his glass and passed it to him. 'He has come to you now,' he said, after taking a sip, 'because he feels that his situation is . . . It is becoming urgent. He should let me help, but he won't because of my health, and to be frank, I'm not sure he fully trusts me. This makes me sad, of course, but I understand it.'

Andee said, 'If you want me to help him, then you'll need to be more specific.'

Sven smiled and nodded. 'Of course, and I will be, but to explain properly means that first I must tell you about your sister.' He gave a ponderous shake of his head, suggesting dismay, even sadness. 'It still surprises me to think of her as part of another family, but of course, I've always known that she is.'

'If you've always known it then why didn't you . . . ?'

He raised a hand to stop her. 'I will tell you everything, from the beginning, and hopefully this will answer your questions.'

She regarded him carefully as, for several moments, he appeared to sink into his thoughts, until eventually his mesmerising eyes returned to hers. 'Kate came to us,' he began, 'Kate is what we call her. I hope that is not difficult for you?'

Andee shook her head, and wondered if he knew why Penny had chosen that name, if she'd even chosen it for the reason Andee suspected.

'Kate came to us when she was twenty-one,' he said. 'We found her . . . I should say we were told where to find her, by John Victor, who I know to be your uncle. He is also the man who sold us her twin sons four years before.'

Andee inwardly reeled. John Victor had *sold* Penny's *twin* sons. So there were two, just like in *East of Eden.*

'I realise you will think it a terrible thing that we bought two children,' Sven continued, 'but my wife was unable to have any of her own, and she so desperately wanted them. We could have adopted, of course, but it can take so much time and we weren't getting any younger. So we decided on a different route. It wasn't easy to find the right people to help us, but then I was introduced to John Victor . . .'

He paused and drank more water, and used a folded handkerchief to dry his lips. 'We were introduced, your uncle and I,' he continued, 'by a mutual friend whom I trusted and who assured me that Victor could help us. It turned out to be true, at least in one sense. At our second meeting Victor told me about a young girl who would willingly carry my child, so I paid him a great deal of money to keep the pregnancy and birth under the radar until it was time to bring the newborn – we didn't realise at the time there would be twins – by private jet, to our home in Connecticut. By receiving the child there and not returning to Stockholm for a while, it would be easier for us to pass the baby off as our own. So Ana faked her pregnancy, and one day we got a call from Victor to let us know that the girl had given birth to twins. It didn't matter. There was never any hesitation. We wanted them both. So Victor brought them to us, and Ana and I remained in America for the next two years, moving around quite a lot to avoid becoming too close to people, and of course to avoid awkward questions. After obtaining birth certificates and passports for the boys we brought them to our home in Djursholm.'

Andee was so stunned she hardly knew what to say. To think of two tiny babies, her own nephews, as the victims of such exploitation and bartering was so shocking and unacceptable that she simply couldn't deal with it right now.

'They thought, believed,' Sven went on, 'that we were their parents. Their birth certificates say that we are . . .'

Unable to stop herself, Andee said, 'Why would you call one of them after John Victor?'

Sven nodded soberly, apparently considering this a reasonable question. 'At the time he brought them to us he was our saviour. We felt very much in his debt, even though we had paid him a great deal of money. It was his wish that one of them should be named after him, so that is what we did, altering it slightly to Jonathan. We had no idea at the time what Victor was really like, although you would say that we should have, as no normal person would have been able to pull off what he had. I guess we only wanted to think about the boys and how blessed we felt, and how blessed they were too to have parents who wanted them so much, when their own mother had only given birth to them for financial gain.'

'Did you know that for certain?' Andee challenged.

Apparently chastened, he said, 'We took Victor at his word, and got on with our lives.' He stopped, took a shaky breath and drank some more water.

'The boys were four years old when Ana, my wife,

was seriously injured in a car accident and Alexander, Jonathan's twin, was killed.'

Andee felt the blow, and could see how deeply affected Sven still was by the tragedy.

Seconds ticked by. He was staring at nothing as he eventually said, 'When it became clear that Ana wouldn't walk again, that she'd be unable to do many things for herself . . . This was when she started to believe that we'd been punished for taking the boys the way we had. She became convinced that their mother hadn't wanted to part with them; even if she had, she might have changed her mind by now. She decided that we must try to find her, that she should be given the chance to be a mother to her son. I think she believed that only by doing this would she ever be able to forgive herself for the death of Alexander.

'So I contacted John Victor and for another considerable sum he told me where the mother could be found.

'It was appalling. The conditions she was being kept in were the worst I'd ever seen; I didn't even know that people lived like that. She wasn't alone; there were a number of girls there, and boys, barely existing in the kind of squalor I hope never to see again. She was so emaciated and sick that her captors were glad to be rid of her, but of course they made me pay. I didn't mind, I'd have given them twice as much, ten times as much, to get her out of there. She had no idea who I was; she was in no state to know anything. She just did as she was told, collected up the few possessions she had: a hairbrush that was clearly rarely used, a ragged selection of clothing; only one pair of shoes; a toothbrush and a book.'

A book.

'*East of Eden*?' Andee asked quietly.

He nodded, though he didn't appear to find her accurate guess either surprising or relevant. 'I brought her here, to this apartment,' he continued. 'Ana and Jonathan were still in Djursholm. I didn't want them to see Kate, as we came to know her, until she was well. It took a long time to get her well. I hired a nurse to help take care of her. She had the best medical and psychiatric attention, but it was still more than a year before she was able to converse without forgetting her words, or eat without vomiting, or even walk down the street without thinking someone was coming to get her. The psychological effects of her ordeal were profound.

'Eventually, when the doctors declared her well enough, I took her to Djursholm to meet Ana and Jonathan. By then she'd chosen her new name and we decided that she should also have ours, so she became Kate Sylvander. We did everything we could to get her started in a new life, and she did everything she could to help care for Ana.' He paused to take a breath. 'We could see right away that she was finding it difficult to bond with her son,' he said, 'and she showed no outward signs of upset when she was told about Alex. We understood that she had been forced to internalise her emotions for so long that she was still afraid to show them, so we simply continued as we were. Jonathan called Ana Mamma and me Pappa and that was the way it stayed.'

His luminous eyes came to hers, and seemed to leave his own thoughts behind to penetrate hers. 'You are wondering,' he stated, 'how much we knew of Kate's background when we brought her here.'

He was right, she was asking herself that, along with many other things.

'The truth is, we knew everything, because John Victor had told us before we entered into our agreement. He would not get his money unless he provided us with a full history of the mother. There could have been medical or psychiatric issues, and we needed to know what sort of legal complications we might face if she ever found the boys and wanted them back.

'In the event it was never a problem. After we took her in she was happy to stay with us. She felt safe, she said, as though she belonged. She and Ana became close, and I knew it would break Ana's heart to lose her, so there was never any question of her leaving and returning to you. It was her choice, never forced on her by us.'

His eyes remained on Andee's, slightly defiantly, showing that he'd known then, and knew now that he'd done wrong, but he wasn't sorry.

'You are wondering,' he said, reading her mind again, 'if she ever asked about you and your parents. The answer is no, she didn't. That isn't to say she didn't use the Internet to read about her disappearance, because she did, and she frequently Googled your name during the time you were with the police to find out what you were doing. But she never talked about you, at least not to me or Ana. We tried to encourage her, told her that we'd understand if she wanted to be in touch with you, but she insisted that she didn't. By then she'd begun working with me, helping to manage our properties here in Sweden, also those in London and the United States. She was very adept; a quick learner and as it soon turned out, a shrewd business-woman. I promoted her through the ranks of the company with far greater speed than I had with any-one else, which didn't make her popular, but she never seemed to mind about that. She wasn't in it to be liked, she would tell me, she was in it to repay me and Ana for our kindness, and to do whatever it took to help girls, or boys, who, through no fault of their own, found themselves in the same position as I'd found her.'

Andee sat quietly as he drank more water. She had the sense that he was moving forward too quickly, glossing over things to try and show his Kate in a good light, but there were shadows, far too much obfusca-tion for her to let it go that easily. However, for now she'd let him speak and if he didn't mention John Vic-tor again, she'd come back to it.

'Of course I couldn't help but admire her ambition,' Sven continued, putting his glass down, 'and I was more than ready to support her personal project, which she'd been working on quietly and diligently almost since her health had been restored. It was unusual, to say the least, but I was soon persuaded. Ana, on the other hand, was not. In fact she was very much opposed to it. We tried hard to persuade her to see things our way, but she never did, and I wasn't prepared to back it without her blessing.

'In the end it went ahead, but not until after Ana died.' He swallowed hard, and so did Andee. Ana had objected to Penny's idea, and now Ana was dead. Kate Trask had removed the madame from the path of her ambitions in *East of Eden* and had gone on to achieve them all, foul and depraved as they were. So how had Ana died?

'The project was not without its dangers,' Sven was saying, 'and this was a big concern to me, which is why, when we decided that we would press ahead, I wouldn't allow Kate to undertake it alone. We sought expert advice and hired people to escort her to various parts of this great continent to meet with the traffickers.' His eyes were boring into Andee's, gauging her response.

Traffickers. Her mouth turned dry, her heart began a heavy, dull thud. 'What were they trafficking?' she asked, matching his even tone.

'People,' he replied.

Again he showed no emotion, while she was finding it hard to stop herself reeling.

'Her project became very successful very quickly,' he continued. 'She gained a reputation for paying well and in cash, and she never divulged the whereabouts of the traffickers to the authorities.'

And this was a good thing? What kind of world was this man living in?

'Her operations have become more refined over the years, but they are still . . .'

Forcing a calm she was far from feeling, Andee

said, 'What kind of deal is she doing with these traffickers?'

He nodded, clearly ready to come on to that. 'She selects, she *buys*, the prettiest girls – and boys – the traffickers can offer and takes them under her wing. Everything is explained to them ahead of their departure, so if any of them don't want to go they are free to stay where they are. Of course, once they find out what Kate – or Michelle as she is for her business – is offering, they always want to come. She turns their lives around in a way that would never have happened if they'd stayed in their homelands, or with those who'd promised them a better life. This is not the only way she finds people. These days she now has many scouts and intermediaries working for her in several parts of the world. I do not get closely involved myself; she doesn't need my help, and now I am in no position to give it even if she did.'

Andee started as he waved a hand towards the open window, and Selma quickly went to close it.

'Do you need a blanket?' Selma offered, clearly concerned. 'Maybe you should take a break for a while?'

He shook his head and gestured for her to sit down again.

'You must be wondering,' he said to Andee, 'what Kate is offering these young people that is so irresistible to them. It would be easy to say a way out of poverty, a means of helping their families, we all know that is why most people leave their countries and those they love, to seek a new life. With Kate, instead of being cheated and lied to, beaten, raped, sold on to other traffickers and forced into prostitution and slavery, they are brought to Stockholm or Paris or London and installed in the various apartments we own around these cities. They are taught how to present themselves in the best way possible, so their hair is cut into sophisticated styles, their skin is given help if it needs it, they visit dentists, doctors, personal trainers, and then they are videotaped talking about themselves. They say their names and ages, where they are from, what sort of hobbies and ambitions they have, all sorts of things. These videos are then shown to couples in America, the Middle East, Asia, wherever they happen to be, to see if the girl is suitable for them. The girl's task is to carry a child for people who are unable to have children of their own. If they like the look of the girl Kate has selected for them – and they almost always do as she is very good at putting people together – then everyone meets. If they are still sure about going through with it, the necessary papers are drawn up and so it begins. Sometimes the husband will donate his sperm, or even have relations with the girl, I am told, but where that isn't possible a suitable donor is found. The fertilising process is carried out at one of the medical centres Kate owns in America. Surrogacy is legal in many states over there, as I'm sure you know.'

Whether Andee did or didn't hardly began to rate on the scale of issues being raised.

'There are so many people in the same sad position Ana and I once found ourselves in,' he continued, 'eager, desperate to have children but denied by nature.

They are prepared to pay very handsomely for someone – a healthy and beautiful young girl – to carry a child for them. If a sperm donor is being used then he too is very carefully selected. From conception the child belongs to the couple the surrogate mother has entered into an agreement with, and when she is safely delivered the infant is handed over to the happy parents.'

Instinctively knowing it couldn't be that simple, or as perfect as he was trying to paint it, Andee said, 'And the surrogate mothers? What happens to them?'

He smiled fondly. 'They are free to go home, if this is what they wish to do, or they can help another couple to have a baby, which many of them do. Or Kate and her team will help them to find jobs and places to live until they are ready to return to their families, if they have one. Sadly, some don't.'

'What sort of jobs?' Andee asked, wondering if she already knew the answer.

He held up a hand to stop her. 'This is not important,' he declared, 'and I'm afraid I am getting tired, so we really need to talk about Jonathan and why he needs your help.'

Andee gestured for him to continue.

'For some time,' he said hoarsely, 'Jonathan has been working with his mother, mainly in an administrative role, but they rarely see eye to eye. It is odd, given what she does to help others, how Kate seems to have very little maternal instinct of her own. She is not comfortable with her son, or with strong feelings, I have always known that. She is very focused on her work, which she finds much easier than many people would. Over the years I have heard her described as anything from a psychopath to a narcissist to a sadist, but I have heard many good things about her too, and it is on them that I prefer to dwell. She has brought us a lot of happiness, not least through her boys, especially Jonathan, who is the gentlest, sweetest soul you could wish to meet. It's hard sometimes to believe they are related. I think the fact that he isn't more like her is what frustrates Kate the most about him. She considers him weak, which is not the truth at all. He is as determined and strong-minded as she is, but over different issues, which is why she is rarely kind to him. I doubt she has ever told him she loves him, and this could be because she doesn't. To be honest, I don't know how capable she is of love in the way we know it.'

Certain that she wasn't, Andee said, 'Does he know who his biological father is?'

Sven's eyes narrowed as they came to hers. 'Do you?' he countered.

She could feel herself tensing as she said, 'Is it John Victor?'

He shook his head.

Experiencing an unsteadying relief, she continued to regard him, meeting his unflinching gaze with one of her own. 'Then it's you?' she said quietly.

He didn't deny it.

Andee looked at Selma.

'We never told Ana,' Sven said. 'It felt like a betrayal, to sleep with a girl I didn't know, to be able to produce a child when Ana couldn't . . . I wanted her to feel that we were equal parents. And when Kate came to join us . . . It would have been too hard for Ana if she'd known the truth. She was confined to a wheelchair, she was so helpless and we were unable to be close, in a physical sense, any more. She would have looked at Kate, and me, in a different way. Please believe me when I tell you that apart from the time the twins were conceived there has never been anything of that nature between Kate and me. She is like a daughter to me.'

Putting aside thoughts of her own parents, Andee said, 'Does Jonathan know how you came to be his father?'

'He does now.'

Since there was no more to be gained from exploring that, Andee said, 'Going back to John Victor. Do you know what happened to him? I mean how he died?'

From the way Sven looked at her she could tell that he did.

'Were you the man the neighbour saw getting into a car with him, just before he disappeared?' she asked.

'Yes, that was me.'

'Was Kate involved?'

Once again he simply looked at her. It was answer enough.

Andee turned to Selma, but Selma was looking at no one.

'Jonathan,' Sven stated, bringing them back to the reason they were there, 'is protecting one of the girls from his mother. The girl, Juliette, is pregnant, and the baby has already been signed away to a couple from

Texas. The trouble is, she has decided she wants to keep it and Jonathan is trying to help her to do this. I am not sure when the birth is due to happen . . .'

'In two weeks,' Selma put in quietly.

Sven nodded. 'She should already be in the States, at one of the clinics, but as far as I am aware she is still in England, or perhaps Jonathan has taken her somewhere else by now for her protection. I think not, or he would be more likely to face his mother, or to approach you himself. The fact that he won't means the girl must still be with him.'

Andee could hardly begin to work out the implications of it all, legal, moral or emotional.

Sven waved a hand towards Selma, her cue apparently to continue.

'If the girl goes into labour,' Selma said, 'which of course she will at any time now, Jonathan will have to get her to a doctor or a hospital, which will make it easier for Kate to find them.'

'But what can she do?' Andee protested.

'She will take the baby.'

'She can't just walk out of a hospital with a baby that isn't hers.'

Selma didn't argue, nor did Sven, who was looking at her again. The answer was clear in their eyes: Kate would find a way to do it because Kate was Kate.

'You have to help him,' Sven said. 'You see, the baby is also his.'

Andee's eyes closed in shocked dismay. How much worse could this get? 'What do you want me to do?' she asked.

'That will be for you to decide after you've spoken to him. I imagine he is hoping your law enforcement connections will be helpful.'

'And how do you propose I do that when he won't come near me?'

'We'll make it happen,' Sven assured her. 'We just have to know for certain that you're on his side.'

Chapter Fifteen

'How do you know you can trust this Sven?' Maureen asked after Andee had finished telling her about one of the most gruelling hours she'd experienced in a very long time.

'I don't, I suppose,' Andee replied, gazing at the fountain in front of her where the water was gushing and loud, but seemed oddly far away. She was sitting on a bench in the Karlaplan, an impressive and picturesque setting for yet more luxury apartment blocks that overlooked a circle of soaring oaks and this giant water feature, and where a market, or art exhibition, was currently being set up on the boundary. On leaving Sven's home she'd insisted on walking back to her hotel, needing the time to clear her head, to assimilate what she'd been told and what she needed to do next.

'Do you feel inclined to trust him?' her mother prompted.

Maureen seemed to be dealing with this much better than Andee was; however, Andee had been careful not to mention John Victor, or the unthinkable suspicion that Penny might have been in some way involved in the death of Ana Sylvander.

Kate Trask had used poison on Faye.

How had Ana died?

'Are you still there?' Maureen asked.

'Yes, I'm here, and yes I feel inclined to trust him,' Andee told her. 'Most of what he said makes sense, even if it wasn't the entire picture. I don't think he lied as much as omitted things.'

'If the baby is Jonathan's,' Maureen said, 'that makes it my great-grandchild, and your great-nephew, so we have to do something.'

Almost smiling at her mother's ready loyalty, Andee said, 'We'll talk about it some more when I'm back. For now, if you see him again, tell him . . .'

What should she tell him?

The question went from her mind as a message arrived and she saw it was from Penny. 'I'll call you back,' she said to her mother, and going through to the text she turned cold to her core as she saw what it was.

Pretty girl.

The picture was of Alayna's beautiful, smiling young face gazing cheekily, provocatively into the lens.

Starting to shake, Andee texted back, *What the hell are you playing at?*

Who's playing? Enjoy Stockholm, but try not to believe everything Sven tells you.

By the time Andee returned to her hotel she'd already been in touch with Alayna.

'In a casting,' Alayna had whispered down the line. 'Up next. Will call later.'

So it seemed her daughter was where she was supposed to be, and now that Andee was calmer she realised that the photograph Penny had sent was from Alayna's Facebook profile. So it was quite probable that she hadn't actually been near Alayna. Nevertheless, there was a warning in the text that Andee knew she'd be a fool to ignore. Penny would know by now, if she hadn't before, that Alayna was at Bristol Uni, and there was no telling what she might do with that information.

Determined to stop spooking herself, she went downstairs to the bar and ordered a beer. Not her usual drink of choice, but since it was in keeping with where she was she decided to give it a go.

A few minutes later, to her immense relief, as her tension was mounting again, Graeme rang.

'Do you have time to talk?' she asked as soon as she answered. 'I mean a lot of time?'

'If you need it,' he replied. 'What's up?'

Taking the phone and her drink out to the pretty courtyard, she chose a discreet table beneath a cherry tree, and spent the next half an hour bringing him up to speed with everything that was happening.

'Wow,' he murmured when she'd finished. 'I've sure been out of the loop.'

'But you're in it now and I desperately need to know what to do.'

'Well, as I see it, I'm not sure you can do anything until they put you in touch with your nephew. Any thoughts on when that might be?'

'No, but given the imminent birth it'll presumably be soon.'

'And you're still in Stockholm? Do you know where he is?'

'Probably England somewhere. I'm flying back tomorrow . . .'

'Oh hell, I don't believe this,' Graeme groaned angrily. 'Nadia's just turned up.'

'And you can't make a phone call when she's around?' Andee snapped.

'Please. This is difficult enough . . .'

'Forget it,' Andee cut in, and before he could say any more she rang off.

Minutes later she was regretting the overreaction, so after texting an apology, she decided to check her emails.

Finding one from Alayna that had apparently arrived while she was with Sven she immediately clicked on.

Boys

Interesting, but weird. The ones I checked out are mainly living in London or Paris, but they seem to travel quite a bit, and there's a kind of competition going on between some of them. They post things like: Bingo! Got it in one! Beat that. Or, Second attempt, wish me luck. Never needed more, unlike some. I've included a screen shot of some posts about 'Harry' who they seem worried about.

I'm going to say that at least half of them are gay judging by the photographs on their pages, but I don't know that for certain. No one seems to be 'in a relationship'.

How are things in Stockholm?

Love you Axxx

Andee was about to send a reply when her phone rang. 'Selma,' she said as she answered.

'Andee. I hope you are OK. I think this morning was probably quite difficult for you.'

'I'm surviving,' Andee assured her. 'How's Sven?'

'Sleeping. He was very tired by the time you left. I think it was too much for him, but as you saw, he can be very determined. Have you received details for your flight back tomorrow?'

'Yes, they've come through, thank you.'

'The driver will pick you up at eight. At the same time he will give you a mobile telephone with a number to call. I realise this must seem a little espionage-like, but Jonathan is insisting we do it this way. He wants you to call him, but he has it fixed in his head that his mother is able to monitor your calls.'

'Does this mean you've spoken to him?'

'A few minutes ago. He tells me Juliette is with him, but he won't give me an address. Hopefully he will give it to you when you call him, or at least arrange to meet you. Please tell me you are still willing to help?'

'If I can, I will,' Andee promised, 'but it's hard to know what I can do.'

'I am sure he has something worked out. He is a very smart, but impulsive young man, who is often too kind and too romantic for his own good.' She added gently, 'He means a great deal to Sven; to all of us.'

Remembering the child's drawing on the door to the den, and feeling for the boy – after all, he was her nephew – Andee said, 'Would you like me to be in touch once I've spoken to him?'

'We would appreciate that very much, thank you. And please let us know if there is anything we can do. Sven wants me to tell you that we are at your disposal in any way we can be.'

After ringing off Andee sat thinking about the call for a long time. She couldn't say why she was having so many trust issues, especially when helping the boy seemed to have no downside – or none that she could figure. Maybe it was Sven's description of Penny's career, his attempt to make it seem like some kind of charity . . . For sure, helping childless couples to achieve their dreams was a good thing, provided it was happening legally, which according to him it was. However, the fact that Penny was dealing with some of the most corrupt and dangerous individuals on God's earth in order to groom and exploit vulnerable young people wasn't sitting well with Andee at all.

'But if the girls are willing,' Graeme pointed out when they spoke again later, 'then it can't, as you seem to think, be forced prostitution. And if we're going to believe what Sven told you, then she's actually saving these kids from a far worse fate.'

'I realise that,' Andee replied, putting down her fork and knowing she'd never try smoked herring again in her life, 'but it doesn't stop there. What I want to know is what happens to these girls – and boys – after they've served their purpose?'

'I'm guessing your nephew can answer that.'

Certain he could, Andee said, 'This must have happened before, a girl not wanting to give up the baby. What I'm asking myself is how does Penny deal with it? And is it the reason her son won't go near her? He must know better than most the kind of lengths she'll go to to make sure things happen her way.' She was thinking about little Michelle Cross, John Victor, Ana Sylvander . . .

Graeme said, 'You know what's bothering me quite a lot? It's that the deeper into this you go, the more she's going to view you as a threat, and that's not feeling good. In fact, it's feeling a very long way from good.'

As arranged a chauffeur came to collect Andee the following morning to take her to Arlanda airport. Although she hadn't slept well she was feeling more apprehensive than tired, not sure what to expect when she returned to England, nor satisfied that she had completed her business in Stockholm. There was so much more she'd like to ask Sven, or Selma, but neither of them had been in touch since Selma had called to tell her about the chauffeur and mobile phone. As promised, when she'd got into the car she'd been given a small package which contained a phone with pre-paid credit and a folded sheet of paper with a number that was definitely British.

'Yes, I rang it about half an hour ago,' Selma had told her, 'but there was no reply. My belief is that he will only answer when he feels sure that it is you at the end of the line. I have texted him details of the pre-paid phone which he asked me to do.'

Though that sounded reasonable, it wasn't quite enough. 'I don't understand why he'd trust you to get a pre-paid phone for him, and yet he won't speak to you.'

'He is just being extra cautious. Are you having second thoughts about helping him?'

'No, but that could change once I've met him.'

She'd needed to say that, even though she wasn't sure she meant it. She simply didn't want Sven or Selma to think she was some sort of pawn they could use in a game she hadn't yet fathomed.

Thanks to the change in the hour it was still late morning by the time Andee boarded a train for Kesterly – and she wasn't far into the journey when the pre-paid mobile rang.

Digging it out of her bag she saw the caller's number was blocked, but clicked on anyway.

'Hello?' the voice at the other end said hesitantly. 'Is that Andee Lawrence?'

'Yes. Who's this?'

'It's Jonathan Sylvander. I've been waiting for you to call.' Before she could respond, he said, 'I'm sorry. I shouldn't have spoken to you like that. I'm just very eager to see you.'

'Where are you?'

'You spoke to Sven.'

'Yes.'

'So will you help us? Me and Juliette?'

'In so far as I can, but I'm not sure what you want me to do.'

'Juliette needs to give birth safely. Please can you help us to arrange that?'

'She has to go to a hospital . . .'

'Yes, but . . .' His voice dropped out as they went through a tunnel. '. . . is having you followed,' he was saying as the line came back again.

'I lost you for a moment,' she told him.

'Do you know if my mother is having you followed?' he asked. 'I'm sure that she is, because she is hoping you will lead her to Juliette so she can take the baby. Or to me in the hope of finding Juliette. Is someone following you now?'

Andee glanced around the carriage. 'It's hard to say,' she replied. 'I haven't been looking out for anyone.' Until now she hadn't felt concerned about anyone knowing where she was; if anything, she was happy to make herself an easy target.

'Do you think you can meet me without her spies knowing where you are?' he asked.

'Probably. When and where are you suggesting?'

'Is today too soon? I can text you our address.'

'I'm on a train still two hours from Kesterly. Where exactly are you?'

'About an hour south of Kesterly, by car. I'm not sure how you get here by rail.'

'Send me the address and I'll try to be there sometime late this afternoon.'

Since her car was in the driveway at Bourne Hollow, Andee took a taxi from the station and stayed at home long enough to unpack her bag and make a few discreet viewings of the green outside to see if there was anyone trying not to be noticed. There didn't appear to be, but maybe this one was smarter than the rest. It didn't matter, she had nothing to hide, and after leaving a note for her mother, who was at the library, she drove to Kesterly police station.

'Let me get this straight,' Gould said after she'd explained why she was there. 'You want to leave your car on the Quadrant outside and take mine to wherever you're going? And I would agree to this because?'

'Because you want to help me be sure I'm not followed.'

'Am I allowed to ask where you're going, and when I might get it back?'

'I'm going to meet my nephew and I'm hoping to be back before eight.'

'This evening, or tomorrow morning?'

'This evening.'

'And if I need my car before that?'

'You are welcome to use mine.'

He didn't look impressed. 'OK. So where is your nephew? What happened in Stockholm? And do we need to start making this official?'

'Please, bear with me for the rest of today at least,' Andee urged, holding up the mobile so he could see the address of where she was going. 'As soon as I've seen my nephew I'll come straight back here with your car and tell you everything I know.'

Sighing, he reached into his drawer and pulled out the car keys. 'It's in the DCI's space,' he told her.

She blinked.

'I won it for a week at poker,' he admitted.

'You boys and the things you get up to,' she chided, handing him her own keys.

Minutes later she was driving his BMW out of the underground car park, exiting at the back of the station into a one-way street, and after taking a zigzag route through to the main road she headed for the moor, certain no one was following her.

It was close to three thirty by the time Andee drove into the caravan park the satnav had brought her to. It was garishly resplendent in its colourful spread across its few acres of the West Devon coast, and seemed to have everything a holidaymaker could want, from fish and chip shops, to Costcutter supermarkets, to a heated indoor swimming pool, to a choice of bingo halls and a loudly musical amusement arcade. There was probably much more to entertain the tourists who were swarming about all over the place, but her focus was on searching out number 68 Seaview Way.

It turned out to be one of half a dozen or so rather smart log cabins – chalets she guessed they were called – at the far end of the park, with a small wooded area separating them from a sandy beach and the sea.

As she pulled up outside a face appeared briefly at a window, and a moment later a tall, muscular young man with dark blond hair came out on to the veranda to greet her. He reminded her of Luke, not in appearance for her son was much darker, but his demeanour, his age and slight awkwardness were similar. Could that be why she felt instinctively that she cared about this person she didn't actually know?

'Andee?' he said tentatively.

'And you're Jonathan,' she responded, going to shake his hand. How like his father he was, the same almost Slavic features and arresting blue eyes.

'Thanks for coming,' he said. He spoke with an accent that was slightly American and slightly Swedish. 'I realise I shouldn't be trying to put this burden on you, but I didn't know who else to turn to. Pappa – Sven – is very sick. I don't want this to make him worse.'

'Jonathan,' a female voice called from inside.

'Coming,' he replied, and standing aside he gestured for Andee to go in first.

It was a surprisingly spacious cabin, with an overwhelming scent of pine filling the air. A large picture window looked on to the woods and sea beyond, a kitchenette took up one corner, a staircase led to a mezzanine floor, and large sloppy armchairs and a sofa were grouped around an empty wood-burner. Standing in front of the burner was a slight, nervous-looking girl with dark curly hair and violet eyes; she was so heavily pregnant that Andee had an alarming vision of playing midwife in the next few minutes.

'I am Juliette,' she said, coming forward to shake Andee's hand. She seemed so delicate, too petite to be carrying with any sort of ease. 'I am Italian. My English is not so good, but Jonathan teach me every day.' She looked at him so adoringly that Andee couldn't help feeling moved. 'Thank you for coming,' she went on. 'I hope we are not a problem for you, but we want keep our baby very much. Please will you help us?'

Slipping an arm around her, Jonathan pressed a kiss to her forehead and settled her gently into an armchair. 'Can I get you something to drink?' he offered Andee. 'We don't have anything alcoholic I'm afraid, but I can make tea . . .'

'Water will be fine,' Andee assured him, dropping her bag on the arm of a chair and sitting down next to it. In fact, now she came to think of it she was ravenous, having not eaten since breakfast, and how odd it felt to realise that meal had been in Sweden. Now here she was on the edge of Devon in a remote wooden chalet, with the sound of waves wafting in through the open window and the distant screams of playing children seeming slightly surreal.

'How long have you been here?' she asked as Jonathan brought her a glass of mineral water.

'Almost a week,' he replied. 'We are moving around and changing cars. It feels safer that way.'

Andee frowned in concern, and slight scepticism. 'Do you really have so much to fear from your mother?' she asked. 'Surely if you explain . . .'

He was shaking his head. 'Forgive me, I know she is your sister, but you don't understand what she's like. She doesn't listen to explanations, only to what she wants to hear, and with us all she wants is for us to give up our baby. If she finds us she will make Juliette go to the States . . .'

'She can't force her,' Andee protested. 'And no airline will take her at this stage of pregnancy.'

'Kate would hire a private jet and people who would make Juliette do as she wants. As far as she is concerned Juliette must give birth in the States. That way we will have no control over what happens to our baby. The law in Texas says that it already belongs to the people who entered into the contract with my mother.'

'Which you and Juliette also signed?'

He nodded dismally.

Andee swallowed more water to give herself some time. She had no idea how the law in England would view a surrogacy agreement that had been drawn up in America, and Juliette wasn't British . . . However, she was European, which for the time being might protect her, if anything could. 'I'll have to speak to a lawyer to get some advice,' she told them, 'but one thing I do know,' she said directly to Juliette, 'is that Penny – Kate – will absolutely not be able to force you to go anywhere while you're in this condition.'

Glancing at Juliette, Jonathan said, 'Some of the people who work for her are not . . . They are not good people.'

Realising he was alluding to the violence that could be involved, that could extend to the kind of scenes Andee would prefer not to imagine, she became aware of her protective instincts rising. 'So what exactly are you hoping I can do?' she asked him.

'I want you to help me to keep Juliette safe while she gives birth. I know she must go to a hospital, but someone must be with her and the baby at all times to make sure that no one can steal the baby away. We're afraid that the hospital won't allow this, so we want you to use your influence to persuade them that they must.'

Knowing she could probably do that, particularly if it was known that the baby was at risk, Andee said, 'And after the baby comes and it's time to leave the hospital?'

'The baby will be British,' he reminded her.

'But will your mother pay any attention to that?'

'She will have to.'

Moved by his resolve, Andee said, 'We need to speak to her . . .'

'No, she will not listen. I have tried, but she is determined to honour the agreement she has made. She always is. You don't know what happens to those who go against her.'

Remembering the Facebook pages Alayna had found that had talked about people disappearing, Andee's eyes flicked to Juliette. The girl's face had turned worryingly pale. 'Tell me what happens to them,' Andee said quietly.

Clasping Juliette's hand, he replied, 'The babies are taken anyway, and the mothers . . . We don't see them again. No one does.'

Andee's throat tightened. 'What are you saying?'

'I am saying that people who cross my mother always live to regret it.'

'Be more specific.'

'OK. She sells them back to the traffickers, or to pimps and gangsters willing to pay. This is what she does with those who do not want to carry on working for her.'

Since Andee knew as well as any detective just how rife this sort of crime was throughout the sink estates and run-down areas of Britain, indeed the whole of Europe, areas that many people only heard about on the news one day, and forgot about the next, she said, 'And those who do carry on?'

'You can do this by being a surrogate again, or by becoming an escort, as she calls it. Of course it is prostitution, but not the same as for those who go to the Serbian or Latvian gangs. Those she has no more to do with. She will not take them back, even if they beg. The ones who choose to stay she takes care of. They live in nice apartments in Ostermalm and Belgravia, she selects their clients for them – men and women – and she keeps videos and dossiers of the most powerful ones to use if she needs to.'

'You mean for blackmail?'

He shrugged. 'I suppose so, but I have never known her to do this. I think it is a kind of insurance.'

Kate Trask's modus operandi almost to the letter. Although somewhat reassured that Penny's surrogacy project meant she hadn't followed her morbid fascination with Trask in every respect, Andee's head was starting to spin.

After a while she said, 'Do all the young people come through traffickers?'

He shook his head. 'No. Some of them are from poor families in remote regions who are recruited directly by her outreach workers – this is what she calls her scouts. Deals are done with the parents or guardians and they are taken away to live the kind of life they are promised, but only on her terms. Some are students, Juliette was one, looking to make enough money to pay their fees. My mother has a very large network of scouts looking out for vulnerable young people with beautiful faces and good health.'

'How many people are we talking about?'

'Twenty, maybe up to fifty a year.'

'Are they all used for surrogacy?'

'Most, but if they turn out not to be fertile they are given the choice of becoming an escort or going back to their families.'

'And do any of them make it back to their families?'

'I don't know. Maybe some.'

Andee looked at Juliette again and wondered how much of the English she understood. Presumably she knew the story, which was why she was so afraid.

'We have thought,' Jonathan told her, 'of letting this baby go and having another, but we made it together and we already love it, and we will always know that it is out there somewhere. Giving away a child that's yours is just not possible – unless of course you are *my mother*.'

The bitterness dug into Andee's heart, along with sadness and a desire to embrace him. He wouldn't welcome it, and it would embarrass them both, so she didn't attempt it, she simply said, 'I'm sorry.'

He looked away, clearly wishing he hadn't shown his feelings.

'Tell me,' she said, 'until you knew the truth, who did you think Kate was?'

He shrugged. 'Just someone who worked with Pappa and who also lived with us.'

'You had no particular relationship with her?'

'No, because she didn't want one with me. She doesn't like children, and she never pretended to.'

'So you thought Ana was your mother?'

He nodded.

Sensing how devastating it had been for him when he'd found out the truth, she said, 'How old were you when Ana died?'

'Eleven.'

Her heart ached with pity. 'But your father didn't tell you until many years later who your real mother was?'

'He told me when he became ill. By then I had already finished university and I was working with Kate, not recruiting, but I knew most of what was going on. At first I thought it was all a good thing, but then I realised what was really happening and I told Pappa I wanted out. This was at the time he was informed by the doctors that his cancer was terminal. He felt then that he must tell me everything he knew about my other family, how my mother had disappeared from your lives when she was in her teens, how she had given us to him after he'd paid her . . . Ana never knew that he was our real father. I don't know why he didn't tell her . . . I think because he didn't want her to know that he was involved in supplying surrogate mothers for childless people.'

'So he started the business?' Andee asked, having already guessed as much.

Jonathan nodded. 'He helped Kate to, and she is the one who has turned it into what it is now with a specialised travel company, the clinics, the apartments mostly in London where the young people stay before and after they have done their duty.'

Andee was thinking of the terrible grief he had suffered in his short life, to lose his twin brother when he was only four, then the woman he'd always believed was his mother seven years later. Now here he was, faced with the fear of losing his child. 'I'm glad Sven told you about me,' she said softly.

His eyes became desperate. 'Does that mean you'll help us?' he asked. 'We'll do anything to keep our baby, and we're afraid that if we turn to the police . . . We can't turn to them. There is a contract to say this baby belongs to somebody else, and my mother's lawyers . . .'

'I'll do my best,' Andee promised, not at all sure what her best might be.

It was as she was leaving and they were outside on the veranda that she asked, gently, 'How did Ana die?'

'She had a fall,' he replied. 'It happened at our home in Djursholm.'

'I thought she couldn't walk.'

'She couldn't. She was in a wheelchair. There is a lift at the house. One day she reversed herself into it, but it wasn't there so she fell and . . .'

Andee's eyes closed as her heart tightened. She wanted to ask if Kate had been around at the time, but she wasn't sure she was willing to hear the answer.

As Andee made the drive back to Kesterly she called Gould to assure him she'd be there within the hour, then her mother to let her know she'd be home soon.

Why on earth, she was asking herself, as she started across the wilds of Exmoor, had Penny tried to make her believe that Jonathan was the child of incest? What sort of twisted mind did she have even to suggest such a thing? The sort of mind, Andee had to accept, that could accuse her own father of abuse that had never happened.

Thinking of all she'd learned about Penny in the past few weeks, Andee decided her sister must be full of hatred or revenge for sins only she could perceive. Aside from those emotions, Penny was empty – devoid of basic human kindness, understanding and compassion that came naturally to most. Her conscience clearly didn't react the way other consciences did. Hers was unreachable, had no power over her thoughts or actions.

It wasn't hard to see why some had dubbed her a narcissist or a sociopath, for she exhibited all the signs, which meant that trying to reason with her would be like trying to reason with someone who didn't speak the same language. It wasn't possible to stir a heart that had no feeling, any more than it was possible to turn back time and hope to start again.

Andee wasn't aware of the tears on her cheeks as she took a turn towards the Burlingford estate, she only knew that there was a horrible ache in her heart as it tried to hold on to how she had felt about Penny during the years she was missing. She desperately didn't want her sister to be the person she was showing herself to be, nor did she want her mother to go through the pain of losing her daughter all over again. But it would happen; it had to, because Penny didn't want them in her life any more now than she ever had. She'd only come back because of Jonathan's attempts to turn to Andee in his time of need. If it weren't for the baby that she probably didn't even view as her own flesh and blood, she'd never have come back at all.

Quietly devastated, as much for Jonathan as for her mother, Andee returned Gould's car and drove her own back to Bourne Hollow. She'd talk to Gould in the morning; now she needed to be with her mother so they could decide together what they were going to do next.

Chapter Sixteen

Andee watched her mother going through a range of harsh emotions as she listened to what Andee had learned over the past few days, including how Penny had tried to make her believe that Jonathan was John Victor's son. It was plain from the way Maureen's eyes closed at that point that she'd lost all ability to understand what had made her younger daughter the person she was.

Andee continued gently trying to avoid distressing her mother any further, particularly when it came to confirming that Penny hadn't been lying when she'd told them she hadn't wanted to come back to them, not even after the horrific time she'd spent at the mercy of gangs.

'Does that mean she never cared about us at all?' Maureen said, seeming hardly able to believe it.

'I don't know,' Andee replied softly, trying her best to lessen her mother's feelings of rejection, failure, guilt and whatever other torturous emotions were assailing her. 'She obviously formed some sort of attachment to Sven and his wife, but how real that was . . .' Nothing would induce her to reveal her fears about Ana's death right now; she didn't even want to think about it herself.

'Do you think she cares anything for what her accusations did to Daddy?' Maureen asked. 'Oh God, if I'd known what he was going through. Why didn't he tell us?'

Her mother's pain and anguish were even harder to watch than Andee had feared. She kept trying to imagine how she'd feel if Alayna turned on her in the same way, and knew it would be devastating beyond bearing.

'Why did she hate him so much?' Maureen murmured. 'Why did she hate any of us? We were never cruel or neglectful; we were a normal, decent family . . .' She put her hands to her face. 'It has to be my fault, I must have done something, or maybe it's what I didn't do . . .'

'Ssh,' Andee soothed. 'I think we have to tell ourselves that she's just wired differently to us. We knew she was unpredictable, unusual, even before she left, and given what she went through during the time she worked for the gangs . . . The drugs alone will have had a disastrous, and lasting, effect on her, not only physically, but mentally.'

Maureen was clearly still having a hard time absorbing it all. 'How could this have happened?' she whispered. 'I just don't understand it.'

Giving the only answer she could, Andee said, 'I think for now we have to put ourselves and our feelings to one side, and consider how determined she is to get the baby away from Juliette.'

At that Maureen's eyes hardened. 'We can't let her,' she growled. 'It's not her child to take. Where are the youngsters now?'

Understanding she meant Jonathan and Juliette, Andee said, 'Not far away, and they're safe for the time being, but we need to bring them to Kesterly so we can be nearby when she gives birth.'

Maureen nodded. 'Of course. Yes, we must do that.'

'I'm going to ask Blake to collect them tomorrow,' Andee continued, 'and provided Graeme and his sisters agree, they'll stay at Rowzee and Pamela's coach house up by the moor until it's time.'

'Oh, I'm sure they'll agree. You know how soft-hearted Rowzee is, Pamela too.'

'But they mustn't know there's any sort of problem,' Andee cautioned. 'They'll only want to come rushing back from their holiday to try and help. It'll be best for everyone if they merely think that a relative of ours needs a place for a couple of weeks before his girlfriend gives birth.'

'Which is the truth.'

Andee nodded.

Maureen's eyes were suddenly bright with tears. 'To think of that dear boy and all that he's been through,' she whispered shakily, 'and now this. We have to make sure he knows we care, that we welcome him as a part of our family, because he is. Just as much as Luke and Alayna.'

Going to hug her, Andee said, 'I'm afraid the birth will only be the first hurdle. We have to work out what to do when Juliette and the baby leave the hospital.'

'They should come here. We've got room.'

'I'm talking more about the legal situation than where they'll live, but you're right, that needs to be sorted too. What we don't want is for the baby to be made a ward of the court and taken into care.'

Horrified, Maureen said, 'Is that possible?'

'It could be. I need to seek some advice.' Her eyes followed her mother's along the hall as someone knocked on the front door.

'Who on earth can it be at this time of night?' Maureen murmured, turning back to Andee.

Since it was only just after nine it wasn't that late; nevertheless their neighbours usually came round to the back door.

'I'll go,' Andee said, getting to her feet. 'You wait there. If I don't come straight back call 999.'

'You're not funny,' her mother scolded.

Still smiling past the unease that had flared with the knock, Andee went to see who it was.

'You wanted to talk,' Penny stated as Andee opened the door.

Andee stared at her hard, then standing aside she gestured for her to come in.

Maureen rose to her feet as Penny entered the kitchen. Her eyes were sharp and wary. She uttered no words of welcome, didn't even try to muster a smile.

Apparently mindful of being ordered out the last time she was there, Penny said, 'If you have any objections I can leave.' Though her tone wasn't hostile, it conveyed no contrition or sense of caring one way or another what the decision might be.

Maureen's eyes went to Andee.

Andee went to press a hand on her mother's arm, a gesture of reassurance and instruction to sit down again. After waving Penny to a chair at the other side of the table she decided against offering her a drink, and sat down too.

'So, have you seen him?' Penny asked bluntly.

'You mean Sven?' Andee countered.

'You know who I mean.'

'Yes, I've seen him.'

Penny's eyes flicked to her mother and back again. 'I suppose I'd be wasting my breath if I asked you to tell me where he is.'

'You would,' Andee confirmed.

Sitting back in her chair, Penny rearranged the gloved ends of her sleeves. 'I hope you understand,' she said, 'that obstructing me on this will serve no one, least of all them.'

Andee's eyebrows rose. 'Actually, I don't understand that. Maybe you could explain it.'

Impatiently Penny took out her phone as it rang and turned it off. 'I told you, when you went to see Sven, not to believe everything he said. The same goes for Jonathan.'

'So what should I believe?' Andee challenged.

Penny's eyes went to her mother again. It was impossible to know what she was thinking, or feeling, completely masked as she was by the steeliness of her expression. 'Tell me something,' she said to Andee while still looking at Maureen, 'have you given any consideration at all to the other people involved in this? The couple who entered the agreement in good faith? The couple who are beside themselves with fear and grief that their dream might not be about to come true?'

Andee had to admit, if only privately, that she hadn't allowed herself to dwell too much on that.

'Jonathan and Juliette knew what they were doing when they signed the contract,' Penny continued. 'They did it freely, willingly, knowing very well that they were giving the couple concerned a world of hope where before there had only been disappointment and heartbreak. They understood that these people trusted them and believed that, thanks to them, they would soon be parents.'

Her eyes remained harsh, but her tone was reasonable and calm. 'They have corresponded throughout the pregnancy,' she continued. 'Juliette has sent copies of her scans and all her medical reports. They Skyped regularly so Juliette could give them accounts of how she was feeling and show them how her bump was growing. The couple have been as involved as it was possible to be, given there is half a continent and an entire ocean between them. They have been expecting Juliette to return to the States for the birth, because that was what was agreed. They have rented two apartments next door to each other in Houston so they can be sure of Juliette's comfort in the final stages, and as close to her as possible until the baby comes. Can you imagine how they are feeling right now?' The challenge burned in her eyes.

In truth Andee couldn't imagine it, but she was more than ready to concede that it had to be terrible.

'The law in Texas,' Penny continued, 'states that the intended parents, not the birth mother, are the legal parents of that child.'

'But they're not in Texas,' Andee pointed out. 'They're here and they want to keep the child. I think British law will support their case . . .'

'I don't give a damn about British law. Juliette was paid a great deal of money to carry this baby, and there is more to come when she hands it over.'

'I don't think she's interested in the money . . .'

'She's already taken it.'

'Then she must be persuaded to give it back.'

Penny's scaly hands hit the table. 'They don't want it back; they want their baby and I am going to make sure they get it.'

Andee's eyebrows shot up. 'And exactly how are you going to do that?' she enquired.

Penny got to her feet. 'Don't cross me on this, Andee,' she warned.

'Maybe it's you who shouldn't cross me,' Andee countered darkly.

Penny regarded her with an icy contempt. 'You have my number,' she said. 'I want to know where they are by midday tomorrow.'

'It's not going to happen,' Andee assured her.

Penny walked to the door. As she opened it, Andee said, 'Doesn't it mean anything at all to you that this baby is your grandson?'

Penny turned back. 'You're a fool,' she said quietly.

'You have no idea what you're doing,' and continuing down the hall she let herself out to her waiting Mercedes.

'So where is she now?' Gould asked the following morning when he, Leo and Andee met in his office.

'I've no idea,' Andee replied, helping herself to more coffee.

'Why midday?' Leo wanted to know.

Andee simply shrugged.

'It's a bluff,' Gould stated. 'I mean, what the hell can she do? She doesn't know where they are. If she did she'd have . . . Where are they, by the way?'

Andee glanced at the time. 'Blake should be collecting them round about now to take them to Rowzee Cayne's place on the edge of the moor.'

Gould sat back in his chair, scraping a hand across his stubbled chin. 'You're right about needing to protect the young mother,' he said. 'We can't have anyone trying to force her into giving up her child, either before or after she's had it.'

'But what if . . .' Leo began.

Gould's hand went up. 'I don't care about any contract,' he declared harshly. 'We'll put the hospital on a high security alert, and I'll have someone keep an eye on Rowzee's place while the kids are there. Meantime, it's what happens to these surrogates after the births that's bothering me. Do you think it's real?' he asked Andee.

'I don't know about real,' she replied, 'but it's possible, given the contacts Penny's supposed to have.'

'In which case we need to contact the National Crime Agency, because if she's in any way involved in trafficking it's one for them, not us.'

As conflicted as Andee felt about that she didn't disagree. 'The problem is,' she said, 'we have no evidence of it. All we have is what Alayna found on Facebook, which is pretty inconclusive as it stands, and what I've been told by Sven and Jonathan. Right now wouldn't be a good time to ask Jonathan to provide us with a detailed description of what he knows. After the baby comes, hopefully he'll be ready to cooperate.' She couldn't admit either to herself or to Gould just how hard she was finding it, in spite of everything, to think of investigating and exposing her sister's activities. Given the choice, she'd find a way to force Penny to stop what she was doing and with any luck avoid all the harrowing publicity of an arrest and the revelation of who she actually was. However, it wasn't going to be in her hands, and in truth she was glad of it, for simply thinking about any young girl having to spend even one day in the kind of hellholes they were kept in made her sick to her soul.

Why wasn't it the same for Penny who'd actually experienced those hellholes?

Gould was saying, 'We found two brothels – and believe me that's talking them up – on the Temple Fields estate only last week, thanks to a neighbour coming forward. The girls are being taken care of in a rehab centre in Bristol now, and the toerags holding them are in custody here, but we didn't get them all.'

Puzzled, Andee said, 'Do you think they had anything to do with my sister?'

'I've no idea, but if she's been pushing the kids on to anyone who'll take them ... We know how much they get moved around, so it could be worth asking the girls if they know her, or have heard of her.'

'I'll get on to it,' Leo said, making a note.

Andee checked the time again. It was a quarter to twelve; fifteen minutes to the deadline Penny had set. Of course it was a bluff, but she couldn't help feeling uneasy.

Glancing at her phone as it rang, she saw it was Blake and clicked on. 'Is everything OK?' she asked worriedly.

'Yes and no. Her waters have broken.'

'Oh hell,' Andee groaned. 'Where are you?'

'On the moor, with about forty-five minutes to go before we get to Kesterly.'

Thinking fast, she relayed the information to Gould, and said to Blake, 'You need to keep coming in this direction . . .' She let the phone go as Gould reached for it.

'Stay on the main arterial road and we'll get the paramedics to meet you. Have you ever delivered a baby?'

'You're kidding me, right?'

'OK, if need be we'll have someone call to talk you through it until help gets there. Is she all right at the moment?'

'Calm. Being brave.'

Grabbing the phone back, Andee said, 'Can you put Jonathan on?'

Sounding hectic, Jonathan said, 'It's not supposed to happen yet.'

'It'll be all right,' Andee assured him. 'Help is on the way and we'll have briefed the hospital by the time you get there. The important thing is not to panic. Births can take a long time, so the baby's not likely to come for a while yet.'

'Will you be there, at the hospital?' Jonathan asked. 'We want you to be there.'

'Yes, of course,' Andee promised. 'My mother will want to come too. Is that OK?'

'Yes, we'd like that. Can you call Juliette's family?'

'Of course. Text me the number and I'll do it right away. Do they speak English?'

'No.'

'Don't worry. I'll find someone who speaks Italian.'

Alayna was sitting outside Carluccio's on the Cabot Circus plaza, trying to distract herself by working out her finances on her iPhone while waiting for Jay and his mother to join her for lunch. She was buzzing with excitement and nerves, and so eager to make a good impression that she felt sure she'd more likely end up making a prize fool of herself.

'Don't worry, she's cool,' Jay had promised when they'd FaceTimed that morning. 'Five minutes together and you guys will be best mates. She's like that. She's known for putting people at their ease – and you're like it too. So chill. You've definitely got the afternoon off?'

'Deff. I finish at twelve, so I'll get there early to grab a table outside.'

Given the time of day there were a gazillion people milling around, mostly shoppers and local workers, but loads of tourists too. Alayna was in love with Bristol; it was a really happening city, especially for the young. She'd love to come back after her gap year, but that would depend on finding a job, and there wasn't enough film and theatre work here to make that a realistic possibility.

She was just wondering if there was time to call her mum to share some of her nerves when a shadow fell over her, and she quickly looked up. With the sun streaming straight into her eyes it wasn't possible to see who it was, though it was clearly a woman, so had to be Jay's mother.

'Alayna?' The woman stood to one side, using her shadow to help Alayna to see her.

Alayna sprang to her feet. 'Yes, it's me,' she gushed, grabbing the woman's hand. 'It's lovely to meet you. Jay should be here any minute.'

The woman's smile was so friendly as she pulled out a chair to sit down that Alayna's spirits soared to a whole new high. 'I guess you recognised me from all the pictures Jay posts on Instagram,' she laughed. 'He takes so many.'

'He certainly does. But lovely as you are in them, they really don't do you justice.' She laughed softly as Alayna blushed. 'How long did you say he was going to be?' she asked, glancing at her watch.

'Oh, probably not long now.'

'Well, let's hope he takes his time so we can use it getting to know one another.'

* * *

It was just after four in the afternoon.

Andee and Maureen were at a corner table in the Starbucks coffee shop on the busy ground floor of Kesterly Infirmary. Upstairs in the maternity ward Juliette was resting through a lull in proceedings, with Jonathan at her side and a security guard at the ward entrance.

For several minutes, after bringing two lattes to the table, Andee had quietly watched her mother, knowing she was agonising over something and not sure she could guess what it was. 'So, does it feel strange to think you're about to become a great-grandmother?' she prompted gently.

Maureen continued to stare at her coffee, almost as though she hadn't heard. After a while she said, 'Everything about this feels strange.' She looked up. Her eyes were bright, almost harsh, yet Andee could sense how anguished she was. 'I don't feel like that woman's mother,' she stated bluntly. '*That woman.* This is how I'm describing my own daughter. But she's nothing like the child I lost, or the person I imagined her growing into . . . The daughter I lost . . . I failed her in ways I've never had the courage to confront.'

'Mum . . .'

'I didn't love her enough,' Maureen pressed on determinedly. 'I tried, I truly did, and it wasn't that I didn't love her at all because I did, very much, it just wasn't the same as the way I felt about you.'

'Mum, you have to . . .'

'She must have sensed it. In fact I knew she did, but I didn't know how to change how I felt. I kept trying, but . . .'

'Mum, you don't have to do this to yourself. You're not to blame.'

'Oh but I am. I'm her mother every bit as much as I'm yours, and look how different she is . . .'

'Not because of you . . .'

'Losing her felt like the punishment I deserved for not trying to understand her better.'

'But you did try.'

'Of course, but I was always so busy. I'd tell myself she didn't want to be fussed, and she didn't, she hated it. Her school reports were always erratic; I could never be entirely sure how well she was doing. Her teachers never seemed to know how interested she was; sometimes she'd try, other times she didn't engage at all. She could never keep a friend; it was as though they were all afraid of her, or just couldn't connect with her.' Her eyes returned to Andee's. 'After she'd gone I used to try and make a pact with God, *bring her back and I swear I'll be a better mother*. I'd give up work, focus entirely on her, build a relationship with her that was as special and easy as the one I had with you. But she never came back, and in my heart I think I always knew that she wouldn't. Of course, I thought she was dead, but if she wasn't . . . like you I always hoped she wasn't . . .' She shook her head impatiently. 'I'm losing what I'm trying to say, but what I mean is that if it weren't for the baby being born upstairs we'd probably never have seen her again.'

Unable to dispute that, Andee covered her mother's hand with her own and squeezed.

'I didn't have a breakdown after she'd gone,' Maureen

ran on. 'I didn't lose my way or become an alcoholic or keep going through her things day after day after day . . . That's what happens to some mothers. Well, you know that, you've dealt with enough of them. I've always despised myself for being able to cope. I mean, it wasn't easy. I was terrified. I dreamt about her all the time, I never stopped thinking about her, longing for her, jumping every time the phone rang, certain it was her, or news of her, but in the end I didn't fall apart. I coped. Daddy couldn't, but we know why now.' She fell silent for a moment, then sounding suddenly angry she said, 'Will she be able to take the baby away? I mean legally, through the courts.'

'I don't know,' Andee answered honestly. 'I'm still waiting to hear from Helen Hall.'

'The lawyer? Will she know?'

'If she doesn't she'll find out.'

After a while Maureen said, 'From what you've told me about him Jonathan seems very kind and caring. We don't really know him, of course, but he doesn't strike me as being at all like his mother.'

'I think, in his heart, he still considers Ana to be that,' Andee told her.

'And the other little boy. I wonder what he'd have been like if he'd lived. Do you know if he looked like Jonathan?'

Andee shook her head. 'Sven didn't talk about him much.'

'Twins,' Maureen murmured, almost to herself. 'I don't think we've ever had them in our family, so it must be from Sven's side.' She pressed her palms to her cheeks then pushed her hands back through her hair, leaving her skin looking taut and drained. 'Cathy Ames – or Kate Trask – had twins,' she stated, looking at Andee.

'But they both lived,' Andee reminded her.

Maureen nodded. 'One was like his mother, the other kind and gentle like his father. Is Jonathan like Sven?'

'I think he is, in so far as we know either of them.'

Seeming satisfied with that, Maureen said, 'I don't recall how the book ends, and I have to admit I'm almost afraid to find out.'

Remembering it only too well, Andee deflected by saying, 'There aren't so many parallels between the two stories, so there's no reason to think this will end the way the book did.'

Maureen nodded, apparently agreeing with that. 'Why, of all things to take did she choose that book?' she wondered.

Andee shrugged. 'To be a nuisance? She knew I was studying it.'

Her mother didn't appear to be listening. 'It wasn't a good ending, was it?' She was staring bleakly into the empty space her memory should be filling. 'You can tell me.'

'It depends how you look at it.'

Maureen swallowed dryly. In the end she said, 'Is it possible for someone to be rotten through and through, the way Cathy Ames was?'

Not knowing what else to say, Andee countered with, 'Cathy Ames was a fictional character.'

'Maybe Penny considers herself to be fictional, with all her different names.'

Andee reached for her phone as a text arrived. She was so certain it would be from Jonathan that it took her a moment to understand fully what it said.

'Jesus Christ,' she murmured, her heart turning inside out. 'Oh my God, this *can't be happening*.'

Chapter Seventeen

Abandoning her car on double yellow lines at the marina, Andee ran through the traffic towards the Grand hotel, answering a call from Gould as she went.

'Apparently Alayna left Carluccio's about one thirty,' he told her. 'She was with a middle-aged woman and young man. This allows just about enough time to get to Kesterly, if this is where she is. Still nothing to support that, unless you tell me differently.'

'I can't. Was there anything unusual about the way they left,' Andee demanded, almost colliding with a cyclist, 'something suggesting she didn't want to go?'

'Not that I've been told. No descriptions yet either. Are you at the Grand?'

'Just arrived.'

'OK. I'm a couple of minutes away. Are you sure you want to see her on your own?'

'Absolutely. If she's here.'

It would be just like the Penny she was getting to know to send her on a wild goose chase, either to give herself more time, or simply for the perverse pleasure of it.

* * *

Minutes later Andee was in the dimly lit hallway of the hotel's tenth floor, knocking at Suite Six, having been told it was where she'd find Michelle Cross who was expecting her.

If that were the case, why wasn't Penny answering the door?

She knocked again, praying with all her might that she was going to find Alayna inside and unharmed. She shuddered as she remembered the text: *Your daughter for my son.*

What the hell would Penny do to her? What was there to gain from hurting an innocent young girl – her own niece – whom she was apparently using as a bargaining chip?

Niece? Family meant nothing to Penny. She'd proved that definitively enough thirty years ago, and had carried on proving it the entire time she'd stayed away. Then there was her apparent disinterest, even contempt, for her own son, Jonathan. So why would she care about a niece?

Was it possible the other twin was still alive?

If he was then something far more threatening, even terrifying was happening than Andee could begin to imagine.

Why didn't Penny answer the bloody door?

She began to knock again just as the door opened.

'Sorry, I was on the phone,' Penny apologised, standing aside for Andee to come in. 'You're here sooner than I expected.'

'Where is she?' Andee demanded, infuriated and alarmed to find no sign of Alayna.

When Penny didn't reply Andee swung round, ready to shout at her again, but hesitated when she caught her gazing into thin air, as if she'd already forgotten Andee was in the room. Her hair wasn't in its usual neat style, but hanging loosely about her face, uncombed; Andee hadn't realised it was so . . . sparse. It made her seem oddly vulnerable, and the haunted, distant look in her eyes was baffling too. This wasn't a Penny she'd seen before. Instinctively she said, 'Are you all right?'

Penny's eyes came to hers. It was plain she hadn't heard anything Andee had said since she'd come into the room.

'I asked where Alayna is,' Andee repeated.

Penny's expression changed, showing a fleeting glimpse of surprise, even anger, before her manner dipped into coolness, as if she were perfectly in control and hosting nothing more bizarre than a tea party. 'I guess we're talking about your daughter,' she stated frostily.

Inflamed, Andee cried, 'Don't do this. I want to know . . .'

'I'm not doing anything. I've no idea where she is.'

'Then speak to whoever does know and tell them . . .'

'Andee, watch my lips. *I don't know where your daughter is.*'

'You had lunch with her today, in Bristol. You and . . . Who's the boy?'

Penny blinked, then to Andee's amazement she laughed. 'I've been here all morning, on the phone,' she insisted. 'I haven't left the room once.' As if to confirm this she held up her mobile, her knuckles showing white with the force of her grip.

Andee regarded her fiercely, still too worked up to know whether she believed her or not.

Penny turned away and went to sit on a sofa, gesturing for Andee to make herself comfortable too. She stared at her phone and fiddled with it.

Andee remained where she was.

'I have to understand from all this,' Penny said, 'that you don't know where your daughter is. Presumably she isn't answering her phone, or she hasn't turned up for a date she was supposed to make . . .'

'You sent a text,' Andee reminded her. '*Your daughter for my son.* It was a blatant threat . . .'

'Indeed! I was pointing out what it could come to if you don't tell me where Jonathan is hiding Juliette.'

Andee felt as though she was sinking, struggling, unable to get a grip on reality. 'So you were threatening to take my daughter . . .'

With an irritated sigh, Penny said, 'Wherever she is now, whomever she's with and whatever she's doing has nothing to do with me.'

So why wasn't Alayna answering her phone?

'I can see you're finding it hard to believe me,' Penny continued, glancing at her mobile again. She was clearly waiting for a call or message from someone that was setting her badly on edge. 'I don't blame you,' she continued, looking up again, 'because I am very capable of lying. In fact, I do it rather well, but in this instance I can assure you I am telling the truth.'

She was like a changeable sky, going from bright to

clouded in less than an instant. Guarded and restless, nervous, irritable and now she appeared so sure of herself, so contained and . . . smug that Andee was starting to feel wrong-footed at every turn.

'Who's the young man?' Andee demanded, feeling ridiculous, but she needed to know. At least she hadn't asked if it was Penny's supposedly dead son.

Penny said, 'I have absolutely no idea what young man you're talking about. Doesn't she have boyfriends?'

Andee's eyes turned hard, her mind was spinning as her phone suddenly rang, and without checking who it was she clicked on.

'Mum, what the f?' Alayna cried. 'Why's everyone calling me? Even the police have been in touch and your messages are freaking me out.'

Swallowing hard on her relief, Andee asked, abruptly, 'Where are you?'

'With Jay and his mum who're totally weirded out too. What's going on?'

'It's OK, nothing to worry about.'

'I need more,' Alayna insisted.

Andee said, 'It's just when you didn't answer your phone . . . Why didn't you?'

'I turned it off while we went for a walk around the Harbourside. Why are the police calling me? I feel such a schmuck, like my family is completely wacko . . .'

'I'm sorry. I'll explain everything when I see you. Please apologise to Jay and his mother, and call Grandma to let her know you're OK. I have to go now, we'll speak later.' After ringing off she ignored Penny's self-satisfied smirk and quickly texted Gould to let him know that Alayna was safe.

'So, panic over?' Penny asked with mock concern as Andee sank down on the chair behind her.

'You shouldn't have sent that text,' Andee told her. 'What the hell was I supposed to think . . .'

'The worst of me, of course. Isn't that a comfortable place for you?'

Their eyes locked and for a bewildering moment Andee felt her senses slipping, spiralling back into the past to who they used to be. This was her sister, the child she'd grown up with, the teenager whose disappearance had turned their world inside out . . . It seemed like only days ago that she'd vanished from their lives yet here she was, a woman in her forties with more self-possession and arrogance than seemed reasonable or right. But there was something about her today that was giving Andee pause. Somewhere beneath the harsh veneer of indifference and superiority that had never shown a single crack before, she seemed almost helpless, frightened even – but of what?

'Why are you staring at me?' Penny snapped.

'What's wrong with you?' Andee asked. 'Something's happened . . . Or you're . . .'

'There's nothing wrong with me. So shall we get down to the reason you're here. You currently have your daughter *and* my son. As far as I'm concerned you can keep both, but the baby has to come with me.'

Andee shook her head.

'I'm not asking, I'm telling you,' Penny stated. 'The

contract he and Juliette signed stipulates very clearly that . . .'

'I don't care what the contract says. If need be we'll put it to a judge, here in Britain.'

Penny got abruptly to her feet and went to fix herself a drink. It was obvious that she was still badly rattled over something that could have been about the baby, but Andee felt it was more. She hadn't put her mobile down once, and kept looking at it as though willing it to ring. Or maybe she was desperate for it not to.

'Do you want one?' she asked Andee, holding up a bottle of Perrier.

'No thank you.'

The silence as Penny filled a glass seemed to have a life of its own, drawing in sounds from the bay that had no place in this oddly functioning reality. By the time she sat down again she'd received a text, sent one in return and her manner seemed less irascible.

Eyeing Andee with a curiosity bordering on disdain, she said, 'You think you know everything, don't you?'

Since it was such a stupid remark Andee didn't bother to answer.

'In fact, you know nothing at all.'

Sounding as exasperated as she felt, Andee said, 'Is this a conversation worth getting into?'

Penny arched an eyebrow and took a sip of her drink. 'Have you ever imagined us having any sort of conversation?' she asked. 'I mean, over the years, have you ever found yourself talking to me in your mind?'

'Of course, many times. Needless to say it was never like this.'

'What was it like?'

'Does it matter?'

'I'm not sure. It might.'

Andee gave herself a moment to think, to decide whether to be truthful instead of defensive. 'OK, I used to imagine how happy and relieved we'd feel to see one another again. I thought there would be lots of tears and hugging as you told us what had been happening to you . . .'

'So I was always a victim?'

'It was hard to see you any other way, when I had no idea you'd *chosen* to leave us.'

'But mostly you thought I was dead?'

'Isn't that what we were supposed to think? The note you sent didn't leave much room for doubt.'

'Oh, yes, I keep forgetting about that. Selective memory, I suppose. Were you very upset when you thought I'd killed myself?'

'What a ridiculous question! You were my sister, I loved you . . .'

Penny's laugh was more scorn than disbelief. 'That's what you've been telling yourself?'

'It was the truth!'

'You did a good job of hiding it.' She appeared more amused than angry, which irritated Andee even further.

'We had some good times as children,' Andee pointed out heatedly. 'We laughed a lot, spent wonderful summers here in Kesterly . . .' Penny rolled her eyes. 'It wasn't all bad,' Andee almost shouted. 'In fact most of it wasn't.'

'Not for you, but you weren't me, and you had no interest in being me, or understanding what it was like to be the one who should have been a boy, who was never pretty enough or clever enough or sporty enough. The attention was always on you and you lapped it up. I might just as well have not existed.'

'And you're bringing this up now? Haven't you got over it yet? Even if it were true, and it wasn't . . .'

'Oh, it was.'

'If that's what you want to believe, then I'm afraid I can't do anything about how you perceived yourself, or the rest of us, while you were growing up. But I can tell you that in spite of what you've apparently convinced yourself, you were loved, deeply, and your leaving totally devastated our family. It was a cruel and insanely selfish thing to do to people whose only crime was to care for you . . .'

'You're not listening to me, Andee. You didn't care for me, none of you did.'

Andee wished she wasn't hearing her mother confessing to not caring enough, only an hour ago.

'You pretended sometimes,' Penny told her, 'you went through the motions, but it never rang true. I knew I was the oddball, the black sheep, the embarrassment, the one that was different and not in a good way. But it's OK, don't beat yourself up about it, because I finally discovered that I didn't mind being different. In fact, I loved it, because it was real, and because I realised I didn't care for any of you either. I really didn't. So that's why I went. I was in the wrong place with the wrong family, and when it became clear that *Uncle* John was going to make it possible for me to go, I leapt at it. He gave me a sense of myself that I'd never had before. I meant something – not to him, I've no idea what he thought about anything, but I meant something to me. There wasn't a moment, during those first years I was in Glebe Place, that I regretted taking my life into my own hands, because I was living with people like me, people who cared . . .'

Andee was aghast. 'You were a child prostitute,' she stated bluntly. 'Those people didn't care about you.'

Penny simply shrugged. 'I was doing what I wanted to with no one criticising me, or making me feel like I was a mistake or a waste of space. We were a family in Glebe Place; we looked out for each other, we had fun, we didn't need other people's approval or understanding, because we didn't belong to your rigor-mortised world. We never hurt anyone, all we did was entertain and be entertained in a way that I don't expect you to understand, because it would never have been the right life for you. You were always the one to conform. It never even occurred to you not to. You're not a rebel, a free spirit, a radical, or even an imaginative thinker. You see things through the eyes of a society that is ridiculously caught up in morals that it can't live up to. Standards that are forgotten when they're not convenient. Judgements that almost never see the other side of an argument.'

Andee was more intrigued than offended. 'Well that's a fancy little tale you've been telling yourself,' she commented. 'A very convenient fudging of what's right and wrong to make yourself into the heroine of the piece.'

Penny appeared to like the response. She chuckled, sipped more water and gave an odd sort of twitch as she checked her phone again. 'There you go, proving my point,' she said. 'You look at me and judge me by your own standards that may or may not chime with mine. You see, I know that what goes on inside me is different to what drives you. I don't share your mundane sensitivities or need to be seen to be doing what you call the right thing. I am who I am, which is nothing like you and who you are.'

Unimpressed, Andee said, 'You've got no idea who you really are.'

Penny's eyes narrowed.

'You're scared of something,' Andee told her, 'maybe even terrified. What is it?'

Penny seemed to find that funny. 'There you are, doing it again,' she accused. 'Presuming you know all about me, assessing me in a way that will never get you to the truth.'

'Then tell me the truth.'

Penny's eyes remained on hers.

Andee waited, but Penny didn't speak. 'OK, then tell me this,' Andee said. 'Do you consider accusing Daddy of child molestation was a good or right thing to do?'

Apparently rattled by the question, Penny sipped her water again as she gave it some thought. 'I told you before,' she finally replied, 'I did what I needed to in order to keep my freedom.'

'So in spite of knowing what those lies could do to him, you threatened them anyway, because you and your *freedom* mattered more?'

Penny tilted her head. 'Mm, I guess that about sums it up,' she agreed.

Outraged by how matter-of-fact she sounded, Andee said, 'You hurt him so deeply that it ended up killing him. Do you have any kind of conscience about that?'

'The way he chose to deal with what I said was down to him,' Penny snapped. 'I didn't force him to keep it to himself, to internalise it like a cancer. Now you tell me this, why do you think he was so afraid of it coming out?'

Andee's eyes widened with horror as nausea churned inside her. 'If you're about to say because it was the truth . . .'

'I'm just posing the question.'

'You know very well that that kind of slur destroys careers and families, even if it isn't true. That was why he kept it to himself. He didn't want Mum to know that you'd do something so despicable; he didn't want even the slightest shadow of suspicion to fall over him, not to save himself, to save us. Even you, in case you decided to come back.'

Penny was staring out of the window, but it was clear when she looked back that she'd heard every word. 'That's an interesting assessment of what was going on his mind,' she declared, 'coming from someone who never had the discussion with him.'

'He was my father. I knew him and I know that's what he did.'

'Do you mean you *knew* him the way you *knew* me?'

'I mean he was a decent, honourable man who would never have done what you accused him of. Why don't you just admit that you lied? You have your freedom now, your life, your family, your *business.* What's the point in holding on to the lie? It doesn't serve you any more.'

'You're right, it doesn't, so I'm OK with letting it go. I lied. Are you happy now?'

Happy? For God's sake. 'Aren't you sorry for what you did?'

'If I were, would it help you to like me a bit better?'

Startled by that, Andee said, 'Only if it were genuine, and why is it important for me to like you?'

'Believe me, it isn't.'

Not quite sure where to go with that, Andee read the text that had arrived on her phone a few minutes ago. It was from her mother, letting her know that Alayna had been in touch.

Her eyes returned to Penny. To her surprise Penny had a hand to her head as though soothing an ache, or trying to shut out where she was. When she looked up her face was even paler than before, and strands of hair were sticking to her perspiring neck. Before Andee could speak Penny said, 'So you worked out what I took from you when I left?'

Deciding to go with it, Andee said, 'It was my copy of *East of Eden*?'

Penny smiled.

'Why that?'

Penny appeared thoughtful, as though she'd never

considered the reason. However, she surprised Andee when she said, 'I guess initially, it was to annoy you . . . You kept going on about the book, how shocking and fantastic it was, how you felt so many different emotions when you were reading it . . . You and Dad talked about it for hours and hours . . . It got so much on my nerves that I thought I'd burn it, or tear it up, or just throw it away. Then I decided to take it with me when I left so I could think of you searching for it, getting angry because you couldn't find it and eventually giving up and getting a new one. A bit like you'd be while looking for me. You'd give up eventually, and one of your hundreds of friends would become your new sister.'

Andee could have told her then that since her real sister had vanished she'd never had a best friend again, but Penny was still speaking.

'I didn't read it,' she was saying, 'not while I was at Glebe Place, but I was glad to have it during that fucking awful time . . . It was the only book I had, my only means of escape, I guess. It was like the characters became friends, family even. Of course I was always with other girls, we were never allowed any privacy, but most of them didn't speak English and the book kind of spoke to me . . . It had your notes in the margins. I probably read them more often than I read the book. It brought you to life for me, made me feel close to you. It was as though you were helping me to escape from that hell, even if it was only in my mind. We were sharing the book. Your notes were my thoughts, because I wasn't capable of forming many of my own; you're not, when you're in the state I was usually in. You're looking surprised.'

Andee was more than surprised. This wasn't what she'd expected to hear at all. 'I thought I meant nothing to you,' she said, and immediately wished she hadn't. There were many other things she could have said that were less mocking or accusatory or cold.

'My perspective,' Penny went on, 'along with just about everything else, changed during that time. Like the others I was desperate to get away. That was when I was sober enough to feel desperate, to feel anything at all. I used to fantasise about you climbing out of the book to come and get me, bringing Daddy with you. Even when he decided to give up on me, he must have kept a check on where I was, but he never came so I knew that I'd been right all along, he didn't care.'

Though Andee had no way of challenging her father, she knew beyond any doubt that he'd lost track of Penny as soon as John Victor sold her to traffickers, for he'd never have left her to rot in the squalid conditions used for girls forced into prostitution. It was doubtful that Penny would accept this, even if Andee tried to speak up; she'd reached her conclusions a long time ago. They were undoubtedly a very big part of why she was so badly screwed up now, and she certainly was, Andee was seeing more and more of it as the days went by.

'I don't suppose you've ever taken drugs?' Penny asked suddenly. 'Of any kind? No, don't bother to answer that, it hardly matters whether you have or haven't. You'll have dealt with plenty who have during your time with the police. You know what they do to people, how they're used like chains to keep whores in check, make them do as they're told, suffer the kind of abuse and humiliation you wouldn't inflict on an animal. Which isn't to say real chains aren't used, because they are, locked around a wrist or an ankle, sometimes even around the neck. I'm still not telling you anything you don't know? But you didn't know about the book and how much it came to mean to me, how it unlocked the chains in my mind and took me to you.'

'No, I didn't,' Andee said softly.

Penny smiled and got up to pour herself another drink.

Accepting a glass of water this time, Andee said, 'Was it because of the twins that you began to identify with the character of Cathy Ames?'

Penny's eyebrows rose. 'I suppose you could have a point there, although I have to be honest, I didn't think about them much during those terrible years. If I did, it was only to hope that John had honoured the deal and taken them to Sven. I sure as hell wouldn't have wanted them with me. If you saw what happened to babies in those places . . . Well, I guess you have. Thank God I never got pregnant again, is all I can say.'

'Did it ever occur to you,' Andee said carefully, 'that Sven might have been part of a plan to get rid of you once you'd given birth?'

'Yes, it did, plenty of times, until he came to find me. He did everything he could to make me well again. He and Ana took me into their family, not to keep, I was free to go any time I wanted, but I didn't want to leave them. For a long time I was afraid to, but eventually I got over that too. I loved being in Sweden, learning the language, getting to know the people, rising up through Sven's business.' Her eyes seemed to glaze for a moment, as her mind drifted to only she knew where. When they returned to Andee they were guarded, restless, as though she wasn't entirely sure what had been said. 'I used to read about you on the Internet,' she stated. 'When stories came up that you were involved in I'd find them and wonder what your life was like. So it's not as if I wasn't interested in you, but life had moved on, we had different families now and I didn't want the complication of becoming Penny Lawrence, the missing child. It would only set me back, disrupt my life, and yours, and what was the point in that?'

To end the not knowing? To try and heal their mother's broken heart and shattered conscience? What Andee said was, 'So you chose to become Kate Trask?'

'Kate Sylvander,' she corrected, 'but yes, Kate from *East of Eden*. I felt we were similar in some ways. Not all, but in those that had significance for me. She didn't waste time on sentimentalities. Her children were never going to be a burden to her, she didn't want any, and nor did I. I only entered into the agreement with Sven to get John Victor out of trouble. And you know how he repaid me.'

Andee didn't hold back. 'So you killed him?'

Penny's eyes bored into hers. 'Yes, I had him killed.'

More shaken than she should have been, Andee said,

'What about Michelle Cross? Why did you use her name?'

Penny sighed, and as her eyes dropped to her phone Andee felt a loosening of the tension between them. 'I told you before, it was a kind of tribute,' she said bleakly. 'She hadn't been able to live her life, so it was a way of including her.'

'Did you push her under the bus?'

Penny looked up, apparently amazed and even slightly amused. 'Wow, you really do think the worst of me, don't you? Actually, she tripped and fell. That's how it happened.'

'And you went on to be cast as the Virgin Mary in the school nativity play? A role you'd already been cast in until one of the teachers took pity on Michelle.'

'You remember that?' Penny seemed impressed. 'It was such a long time ago, but yes, I did get to play the part. She was a foster child, did you know that? She didn't have any parents, or brothers and sisters, so I don't suppose it was too hard on anyone when she went.'

Shocked, sickened, Andee didn't bother to hide it. 'Are you saying you thought it was all right to push that little girl under a bus because she didn't have a family?' she asked.

'I didn't push her under a bus. I told you, it was an accident.'

Wanting suddenly to get out of there, Andee put her drink down and picked up her phone.

'You're judging me again,' Penny told her, 'and now you're running away. We can't all be like you, Andee.

Imagine how dull the world would be if we all had the same personalities, principles, beliefs.'

'But yours are deplorable, disgusting . . .'

'Says you, because you've told yourself I helped a little girl to go and join her parents in the next life. Well, if it makes you feel any better I really didn't push her. She tripped and fell, but for all I know she did it on purpose. She hated the foster home she was in, the social workers, the teasing at school. She was miserable and to be truthful, I felt sorry for her. I knew what it was like to be in a family where you felt you didn't belong.'

Andee was shaking her head incredulously. 'You're right about one thing,' she said, 'I really don't know you and I don't think I want to.'

Penny laughed, but it was a hollow nervous sound that had no humour. 'Believe me, no one is going to force you,' she promised. 'You obviously know you'd never have heard from me again if it weren't for Sven telling Jonathan about you . . .'

'Which he did to protect him from you. His own mother.'

Penny nodded. 'Yes, that's true, but I wouldn't harm him, after all he *is* my son. We don't often agree on things, but in this instance he's got to be made to see them my way. He knows what's at stake, what will happen if he and Juliette don't honour their agreement. I'm trying to save them from that.'

'You mean from the fate that you yourself suffered at the hands of men who abused and tormented you for over four years?'

'That's right,' Penny confirmed.

'But how could you? I don't understand when you've been there, you've . . .'

'No, of course you don't understand, because you don't think like me. You hear the words, see a picture and you believe it without going into the meaning, the depth, the reality of what's actually there.'

'Then tell me what's there.'

Instead of answering Penny fumbled with her phone, checking for texts or emails. In the end she said, 'You know, I quite like the fact that you always think the worst of me. It's reassuring, makes me realise that I was right to leave when I did and not come back.'

Andee said, 'So now you're blaming me for your disappearance?'

'No, I'm not blaming you. I'm just trying to make you see how little what you think of me matters to me.'

'So why are you bothering to talk to me?'

Penny said, 'Because I'm hoping you'll end up telling me where to find Jonathan and Juliette.'

'Why on earth would I do that when you've done nothing but warn me against it.'

'Ah, reverse psychology. Is that what you call it? I'm saying one thing when I actually mean the opposite. In other words, my subconscious is crying out for you to save those foolish young people from the wicked woman who means them only harm?'

'Why don't you give me an opportunity to see you in a different light?' Andee suggested.

'Why would I do that?'

'Because you're not being truthful either to me, or to

yourself. There's a hard shell around you that's almost impossible to penetrate, or it was until it started coming apart. I don't know why, what's making it happen, but I can see it, and I just know that buried deep inside you there is a human heart that's as capable of compassion and love as mine.'

Penny's eyebrows shot up. 'Are you forgetting about Kate Trask?' she challenged. 'She was evil through and through.'

'She wasn't real.'

'She was to me.'

Refusing to go any further with that, Andee sat watching her, waiting for her to speak again. When it became apparent she wasn't going to, Andee said, 'In France, when you stopped your car to ask me if I remembered you? Why did you do it that way?'

It seemed to take a moment for Penny to recollect the incident. When she did she smiled, almost mischievously. 'I suppose it was because it appealed to me to tease you a little.'

Knowing she'd never understand the sort of mind that would see a return from the dead as a tease, Andee said, 'How did you even know I was there?'

Frowning, Penny said, 'I thought I'd explained that before. I was having you followed in case Jonathan got in touch with you. When you and your boyfriend flew to France, I felt convinced it was to see him. Apparently I was wrong. How long have you and . . . is it Graeme, been together?'

'We've known one another for a few years, but together in the sense you mean it, just a few months.'

'And you trust him?'

Annoyed, Andee said, 'Don't do that again. You tried it once before . . .'

''Her name's Nadia. He's redesigning, remodelling a house for her.'

'And?'

'I have photographs of them together. You can see for yourself how close they are.'

With a burning anger masking how shaken she felt, Andee said, 'Why are you having him watched?'

'I'm not. It just happened. When you disappeared airside at Heathrow, on your way to Stockholm, as it turned out, I thought you were returning to France. So I had someone fly over to find out.' Her eyes seemed almost soft, even sad as she said, 'I'm sorry he's not who you think he is.'

Wanting nothing more than to get off the subject, Andee said, 'You told me just now that Jonathan and Juliette know what's at stake if they don't honour the contract.'

'That's correct, they do.'

'Well?'

Penny started as her phone finally rang, and almost dropped it as she checked who it was. She didn't answer, just let it go to messages.

'What's going on?' Andee asked. 'Something's really getting to you . . .'

'It's the couple waiting for this baby,' Penny shouted. 'Their lawyers are ringing, threatening me . . .' She broke off abruptly. 'You asked what's at stake?' she said more evenly. 'And you think, probably because

Jonathan told you, that any girl who defies me ends up in forced prostitution, the way I did thanks to John Victor.'

'Is it true?'

Penny tossed her head irritably.

'He says girls have disappeared because they defied you.'

'It's true, they have. In fact, I could tell you where to find them, if I were of a mind to, but I really won't be until I have that baby out of here and on its way to Texas.'

Andee eyed her coldly. 'It's not up for negotiation. If the baby is born here it will be a British citizen registered into the British system, and there will be nothing you can do to get it out of here.'

'If necessary the lawyers will take care of it, but we can save all that if you would just take a break from the moral high ground and think of the parents waiting for that baby. Use your naturally bleeding heart to feel compassion and kindness for them. The child doesn't belong exclusively to Jonathan and Juliette. In fact, none of it belongs to them, because they've led these people on, taken their money, destroyed their dream . . .'

'Now isn't the time to get into the ethics of what you do,' Andee interrupted shortly. 'I just need you to understand that even if I were able to see it your way, I still wouldn't take you to them.'

'Because you're afraid of what's going to happen to Juliette after we've handed the baby over?'

'Amongst other things. She'll obviously never work for you again, and as we know what that means . . .'

'Do we? Do we know for a certainty that I sell these girls to the highest bidder? That's what you've been told, isn't it? It's what I tell them, that's for sure, but do we actually know that I do it?'

'If the girls aren't seen again . . .'

'They're not seen because they're returned to their families. I know you don't want to believe that, it won't fit with your disgustingly low opinion of me . . .'

'If you didn't behave the way you do . . .'

'Let me tell you this one more time,' Penny raged, 'I don't give a damn what anyone thinks of me. It's not important. What is, is finding girls who are about to make the biggest mistake of their lives, *before* they make it. Girls who are desperate to help their families, or to escape abuse, or to better themselves in some way . . . Girls who are more vulnerable to traffickers than they'll ever know. I make it my business to get to them first, to save them from themselves so that they'll never end up in the kind of nightmare I was stuck in for almost five years. I offer them the chance to help someone else, to carry babies for those who aren't able to do it for themselves. Jonathan will have told you that I do deals with traffickers, that I sell the girls back when they're no longer of any use to me, but it isn't true. There are no traffickers, or not that I deal with. He thinks there are because it's what I want him and everyone else to think, that I'm evil, not a person to cross. If they weren't afraid of me I'd have no power. They'd feel free to defy me, to break their contracts, to trash people's dreams, and I can't let that happen.'

Quietly stunned as she absorbed this bizarre, twisted

version of charity, it was a while before Andee could find her words. 'What about the young people acting as escorts?' she asked.

'What about them?'

'Are they doing it of their own free will?'

'Of course they are. If they didn't want to do it they'd be in other jobs, jobs that I'd help to find if necessary, or they'd be back in their own countries. They might even be working at one of three centres I've opened in Latvia, Lithuania and Belarus to provide refuge for vulnerable young people. The only condition I put on those who don't want to continue with me is that they don't ever contact anyone who stays. I don't want to destroy the image I've created of myself. They need to be afraid or they won't understand that they could ruin everything. So tell me, is this helping your troubled sensibilities? Are you feeling better about me now that I've confessed I'm not as evil as Kate Trask?'

Andee could only look at her. Her way of thinking, reasoning, even feeling was so tortured, so completely beyond fathoming that Andee knew it would be pointless even to try.

'Someone just texted you,' Penny told her.

Andee read the message from her mother and got to her feet. 'Before I leave,' she said, 'I have one more question for you. What happened to Sven's wife, Ana?'

Penny blinked in surprise, then standing up too, she said accusingly, 'You think I caused the accident that killed her.'

'Did you?'

'What if I said yes?'

'Would it be true?'

'It happened just the way I'm presuming you were told. She'd been warned plenty of times about reversing her wheelchair into the lift, but she would do things her way. Then one day, just as everyone feared, she reversed in without checking. The lift wasn't there and she plunged to her death. I was in Riga at the time.'

Andee stared at her, not sure what to say.

'It's easily checked,' Penny told her.

In silence, Andee started to the door.

Penny said, 'Are you going away feeling sorry for yourself because you don't have the sister you've always dreamt about?'

Andee turned round. 'It's you I feel sorry for,' she said, 'because you've lost sight of who you are and what means anything to you.'

Penny's lip curled.

'What you do know,' Andee continued, 'even if you don't want to admit it, is that you've made some terrible mistakes in your life and they started when you were fourteen years old,' and with a tender, sad smile she left.

Chapter Eighteen

On returning to her car Andee peeled the parking ticket from the windscreen and got into the driver's seat, oblivious to the sudden gusts sweeping the bay. Instead of returning to the hospital right away she remained where she was, her head resting on the steering wheel as she tried to process what felt like the most bizarre and difficult encounter she'd ever had.

She realised only too well that hard drugs had played a major part in distorting Penny's already irrational young mind, but knowing that didn't change how damaged it still was. The way Penny perceived the world and herself was as normal to her as it was crazy and upsetting to Andee. Even the good she was trying to do was being carried out in a convoluted and highly dubious way – this was presuming she'd told Andee the truth, and Andee was ready to believe that she had.

In fact, the more she thought about it, the more convinced she was becoming that Penny had been wanting to talk to someone for a very long time. She might claim that she had no interest in what people thought of her, but she did care what Andee thought, and realising that was making Andee want to cry.

Her sister, for all that she might deserve it, was quite possibly the loneliest and saddest person Andee had ever known. She might have been awkward and difficult when she was young, but by now she was so damaged by all that had happened to her that she had no proper sense of what was right or wrong, or even of who she really was any more. The way she'd shown signs of coming apart today, the guarded restlessness, the constantly changing moods, and cry for help that she hadn't even realised she was uttering, spoke more clearly than anything of how tormented she was inside.

For Andee, it was almost impossible to know how to go forward from here. What could she do to help Penny, or at least make her believe that she mattered and always had? Her defences were a solid wall of lies and delusions; her feelings were so deeply buried they might never be found.

Deciding she needed to speak to Sven, Andee gave herself no time to think it through, but simply connected to his number. There was no reply from either him or Selma. It didn't matter; with just these few seconds' grace she realised this wasn't a conversation to be had by phone.

Letting her head fall back against the seat, she closed her eyes and thought of how much she'd like to speak to Graeme right now. He might not have the answers, but he was such a good listener that things always seemed clearer after she'd discussed them with him. But it didn't feel like an option when she was having doubts about his relationship with Nadia. She'd have to confront them at some point, but right now she couldn't make herself and her feelings a priority.

Starting the engine, she turned the car around and drove back up the hill to the hospital. She was asking herself if she should have told Penny before she left that she was a grandmother now. Would it have meant anything to her? Or would she simply have continued to see the infant as belonging to the people who'd signed a contract they fully expected to be honoured?

Realising she needed some answers sooner rather than later, Andee put in a call to Helen Hall to find out what she'd learned so far. Then, remembering she'd left Gould at the hotel she rang to let him know where she was and, more importantly, that the baby was now in the world.

A while later Andee was holding the tiny newborn in her arms, wanting to bury herself in his irresistible baby smell and innocence. His eyes came wide and startled before closing again; his mouth was puckered and red. *Where am I?* he seemed to be saying. *What just happened?*

As she held him she felt herself understanding, far more than she had before, just how devastating it would be for the American couple to lose him. They probably didn't even know he'd been born yet; were no doubt even now waiting by the phone, more terrified than excited to hear the news.

However, how could she not support Jonathan and Juliette's need to keep him? He was theirs in every way. They had made him, he carried their genes and, like any other baby born to loving parents, he deserved to spend his life with them. Even if the Americans were rich beyond belief, could give him everything he could ever wish for and love him as deeply as he deserved, one day he would want to know his real parents, and how would he feel on learning that the law had forced them to give him up?

Still inhaling the intoxicating scent of him and remembering when her own children had been born, Andee felt her mother's hand on her arm and realised she was crying.

'It's because I'm happy for you,' she told a worried-looking Jonathan and Juliette. 'He's part of my family,' she reminded them, 'and he's so beautiful and sleepy and *big*.'

Coming to take him, Jonathan said softly, 'I want you to know that we won't give him up, not for anything. I don't care what the law says . . .'

'Sssh,' Andee soothed, seeing tears of anger and defiance in his eyes. 'Don't let's worry about that now. All that matters is that he's with us, we already love him and we're going to do everything we can to keep him.'

Jonathan was shaking his head. 'You don't understand,' he said. '*We are going to keep him.* It's not about trying, or fighting, or going through courts of law. He is my son. I am his father, Juliette is his mother and no piece of paper in the world is going to separate us.'

Admiring his passion, and desperately hoping he was right, Andee watched him go to sit with a drowsy Juliette and felt her heart overflowing in the way she knew it would the day she saw Luke or Alayna's newborn baby. Jonathan and Juliette still seemed so tenderly young, and nervous, but they were parents now, proud, overwhelmed, needing the support of their families, but determined to be everything to their son. That was what he deserved. Only hours old and already he was surrounded by his mother, father, great-aunt, great-grandma, and two grandparents on the way. He was going to know the richness of being Italian, British and Swedish; he'd no doubt speak all three languages, but most importantly of all he'd be where he belonged.

Meeting Jonathan's eyes, Andee felt her heart buckling with the sorrow of Penny not being a part of this. She had no idea if it might help to heal her, or at least make her see things differently, but as the baby's grandmother she deserved to know he was in the world.

How tragic it was that they'd then have to do everything they could to protect him from her.

By late the following morning Jonathan and Juliette had taken the baby to the coach house at the edge of the moor, and Juliette's startled parents had arrived from their village home in Piedmont. Apparently they'd had no idea their daughter was even pregnant until the call had come to tell them they were grandparents. They'd believed that Juliette was spending a year in London and the US learning English, before returning to continue her studies at the university in Turin. They'd now been informed, to their horror and despair, that their daughter had accepted Penny's offer of becoming a surrogate mother because her parents' bakery business had failed. She couldn't, she said, allow them to spend every last penny of their savings to give her the education they'd never had.

Though it wasn't possible for Andee to know exactly how they felt about their daughter's decision or the unexpected addition to their family, it was plain from the moment they arrived that they adored Juliette, and they couldn't have been more eager to hold and marvel over a baby that had come as a total surprise to them. They'd already decided that they must take this little family back to Italy, where they could help with the baby while Juliette continued her studies and Jonathan found work nearby. Exactly what kind of work was apparently to be discussed at a later date, but it was clear from the wryness of Jonathan's tone as he translated for Andee and Maureen that he was more than happy to go along with the plans. What no one had yet confessed to was the possible lawsuit that would very likely prevent the baby going anywhere.

She'd left them half an hour ago, with her mother and Jenny preparing to go and stock up at the supermarket while she took the same circuitous route she'd used to get there (just in case she was being followed) to go back into town where she was due to meet with the lawyer, Helen Hall.

'As you know, this isn't my area of expertise,' Helen told her as they settled down with coffees in Helen's office. She was a slight woman, a few years older than Andee, with unruly flame hair and porcelain skin. She was also the closest Andee had to a good friend outside her family. 'So I've been in touch with Henry Gibbs whose speciality is family law. He should be here any minute.'

'Have you already briefed him?' Andee asked.

'In so far as I could, but obviously you'll be able to explain better than I can. Ah, here he is,' and she got to her feet as the door opened for her secretary to show in a short, wiry man with spiky grey hair, endearingly rosy cheeks and red-rimmed spectacles. He was wearing a jaunty bow tie and baggy blue suit that made him look rather more like a clown than a lawyer.

'Sorry,' he said, shaking Andee's hand, 'dressed for the next client who's four and a half and afraid of men, so I'm trying to play up the unscary look. Trouble is, I don't think clowns are quite doing it these days.'

'I think you'll be fine,' Andee told him drily. 'It's good to meet you.'

After embracing Helen, he accepted a coffee and with a quick glance at his watch came straight to the point. 'Personally, I've never had to deal with surrogacy,' he said frankly, 'but I've spoken to a colleague in London, Jhanvi Best, who's had some experience, mostly in India, and she's willing to take a look at it for us. To get things started she's asked me to find out a few facts from you, such as which US state the contract was drawn up in. Do you have a copy of it? Who is acting for the intended parents in this country? And have social services been notified yet?'

Inwardly flinching at the mention of social services,

Andee said, 'I'm pretty sure the contract was drawn up in Texas, but I'll check. No, I don't have a copy of it, but I'll try to get one. I'll also find out who's acting for the intended parents over here, and no to the question about social services. If possible we'd like to keep them out of it for as long as we can.'

He nodded his understanding. 'I'm afraid the instant it goes before a judge, probably even before that, they'll have to know, but for now we'll keep it to ourselves.'

'How soon can you get the information?' Helen asked Andee. 'I'd imagine the sooner the better?' She glanced at Henry for confirmation.

'Indeed,' he agreed. 'I'll give you my card. You can call me any time. If I'm with a client or in court I'll get back to you as soon as I'm free. Can I ask where the baby is now?'

'With its birth parents and their families,' Andee replied.

'That's good. I should think having a good support network of blood relatives will help, but I don't want to give any false hope because Americans can be pretty tenacious, not to say ferocious, when fighting for their rights.'

'As can we,' Andee informed him.

Clearly liking the response, Henry finished his coffee and got to his feet. 'I'm sorry this was rushed,' he said, shaking her hand again, 'but I thought it better for us to meet in person rather than talk on the phone. As soon as you can get the information to me I'll pass it along and we'll decide what needs to be done next.'

'Of course it all depends on the intended parents

filing a lawsuit,' Helen pointed out, gently anchoring them.

Appreciating the reminder, for everything seemed to be going so fast, Andee turned back to Henry as he said, 'Do you think there's a chance they won't?'

Wishing she could give him some hope of that, Andee said, 'I wouldn't bet on it. They don't know yet that he's been born, but we can't keep it from them very much longer.'

'No,' he confirmed, 'you really can't. If you don't own up to the birth it could be read as the parents planning to abscond. I hope they're not, by the way, because they'll be found eventually and running from this won't help their case at all.'

Ten minutes later, with those words still echoing in her ears, Andee was driving through town when Penny finally called her back. 'Where are you?' Andee immediately asked.

'Still at the Grand, where I'll be staying until you go elsewhere.'

'What do you mean?'

'Well, Jonathan and Juliette must be around here somewhere or you wouldn't be. If you move them, I'm guessing you'll go with them, so I'll follow.'

'Penny, this is crazy. They could be anywhere. I don't have to be with them . . .' Realising there was no point in pursuing that, she said, 'We need to talk.'

'Again?'

'Yes, again. I'm not far away. I'll come to the hotel.'

'*No*, don't do that. I'm busy today trying to save everything my son and his girlfriend are so selfishly destroying. Do you have any idea what it's like dealing with American lawyers? No, of course you don't, well let me tell you it's nothing short of hell, and if they carry out their threats I'll be completely ruined. Everything will be over, the surrogacy, the clinics, the refuges, everything I've spent half my life creating. My lawyer's here, so please don't come, we have a lot to do.'

'OK, then email me a copy of the contract Jonathan and Juliette signed so I . . .'

'Why? What do you want it for?'

'What do you think? Jonathan and Juliette are going to fight for their baby. You already know that . . .'

'You have to talk them out of it.'

'I don't have to do anything, but you need to know that the baby's been born. They're calling him Alexander in honour of Jonathan's brother, your other twin.'

Penny was silent, and Andee immediately regretted the way she'd broken the news.

'Congratulations,' she said softly. 'You're a grandmother.'

'For God's sake, this isn't about me being a grandmother,' Penny cried frantically. 'You need to tell me where they are. If you won't talk sense to them then I have to . . .'

'I'm not letting you anywhere near them until this lawsuit is made to go away.'

'There's no point trying to blackmail me when it's not in my hands. The Blakemores want the child they've prepared and paid for . . .'

'The other thing I need from you,' Andee interrupted, 'is the name of the lawyer they've hired to handle things over here. Please put it in the email you send with the contract,' and before Penny could protest any further she ended the call.

It wasn't until she was talking to Gould a few minutes later that she realised her big mistake. Now that Penny knew the baby had arrived it was highly likely she, or more probably the American lawyers, would contact social services with a request that they remove him from his parents to prevent them from disappearing with him. Or from harming him in some way? God only knew what they'd tell the authorities in order to get Alexander away from Jonathan and Juliette.

'And when they know he's in care,' she told her mother later that evening, 'they'll begin the most vicious attack on Jonathan and Juliette's characters to try and prove they are unfit parents.'

Maureen looked both aghast and exhausted. 'We have to talk to Penny,' she said. 'Make her see sense. This baby is her flesh and blood . . .'

'I don't think that matters to her in the way it does to us.'

'Then we have to *make* it matter.'

Wishing it were as easily done as said, Andee went to let Blake and Jenny into the kitchen with the Chinese takeaway they'd ordered to save anyone having to cook. It was often hard for her to look at Blake and not think of Graeme, and as she did so now, for the first time in a few days Graeme rang.

Liking to think it was telepathy, she excused herself and took the phone out to the hall to sit at the foot of the stairs. 'Hi, how are you?' she asked softly.

'I'm fine,' he replied. 'How about you?'

She grimaced inwardly. 'Where to start?'

'So maybe this isn't a good time?'

Surprised by the stiffness of his tone, Penny's offer to show her photographs of him and Nadia immediately came to her mind. *You can see for yourself how close they are.*

'There's something I have to tell you,' he said. 'I've been trying to think of the right way . . .'

Deciding a protracted break-up was the last thing she needed to deal with right now, she said, 'It's OK. I already know. You don't have to explain, just be happy,' and quickly ending the call she swallowed hard on the emotions twisting her heart, turned off her phone and went back to the kitchen to try to eat some food.

It happened more or less as Gould had predicted. As soon as the American lawyers knew about the baby's existence they instructed someone from their London office to get straight on to social services. The only surprise was that Penny herself rang to inform Andee of this.

'Why the hell did you let it happen?' Andee raged. 'For once in your life can't you do the right thing?'

'Right for who? For you? For Jonathan? What about me and my clients, the Blakemores? I have to consider them . . .'

'Before your own son? Before your grandson? He has the right to be with his real parents . . .'

'I'm not arguing about this any more. You won't win

this. You can't, so why don't you just bring the baby to me, or you'll be the one responsible for him being taken into care. Think on that; I'm not making it happen, *you* are,' and the line went dead.

Ready to explode, Andee somehow resisted the urge to slam the phone against the wall, and used it to call Henry Gibbs instead.

'OK, it'll take social services a while to act,' Henry told her calmly. 'I know this, because it always does. Do you have a copy of the contract yet?'

'I've requested it, but I'm not confident the person I asked will send it.'

'Then get me the names of the American lawyers. Jhanvi will take care of it and we'll see where that ends us up.'

'But with the time difference between here and Texas . . .'

'Don't worry, it's likely to be days, not hours, before anyone gets their act together. They'll need the court's approval for an emergency care order, and we must try to be ready for them when they apply.'

Having no idea how they were going to manage that, Andee rang Jonathan. 'Are you sure you don't have a copy of the contract?' she asked.

'I'm sorry. If I'd known it was going to matter . . .'

'OK, just tell me the name of the Blakemore's lawyer.'

To her relief, he said, 'I don't know the actual lawyer's name but it's a firm in Houston called Feinstein and Beird. They do all the contracts . . .'

'That's great. Now, please don't any of you leave the

house for at least the next two days, OK? I don't want anyone to know where you are, least of all your mother. Blake and Jenny will bring everything you need, they'll tell the neighbours you're guests of Rowzee's, and I'll always be at the end of the phone . . .'

'She might have it bugged,' he said anxiously.

'I think you give her credit for more powers than she has,' Andee told him, 'but we know that she's having me followed, possibly my mother too, so we won't be able to come ourselves. Have you explained the situation to Juliette's parents yet?'

'We're hoping it'll get sorted before we have to.'

It was a lovely thought. 'I think you need to prepare them,' she cautioned.

Later in the day Andee was once again with Helen Hall when Gould rang.

'I've just had a call from one of our guys in child protection,' he told her. 'They've been contacted by social services asking if they know anything about a missing baby in a surrogacy case.'

'Oh Christ!' Andee muttered. 'They're obviously not wasting any time. What did you tell them?'

'I stalled, said I'd ask my team and get back to them.'

After relating the call to Helen, Andee said to Gould, 'I really owe you for this. I don't . . .'

'Just tell me what your next move is going to be,' he cut in.

'We're waiting for a copy of the contract to arrive from the States. Without that it's not possible for the lawyers here to know how to proceed.'

'Well, the other side obviously already has it, so you'd better make sure they don't get it in front of a judge before your guys have seen it, or the child will be gone and you'll be fighting to get him out of care instead of being put into it.'

After ringing off Andee said to Helen, 'Can the lawyers in Texas drag this out, make sure the contract doesn't get to us until after the authorities have acted?'

Helen nodded grimly. 'It's possible. The judge won't like it, but if they can show a legally binding contract to say that the child is the subject of a surrogacy case in the United States, the court will probably decide that the child has to be taken into care to prevent the birth parents from disappearing with him.' She paused, and looked Andee straight in the eye. 'Even if the contract arrived this minute,' she said, 'I don't see how it's going to help you. They'll still take the baby away until the case has been settled, and it's anyone's guess how long that will take. It could be years.'

Chapter Nineteen

Two days later with still no sign of a contract, and mercifully no word yet from social services, Andee was in the lobby of the Grand hotel, ready to force her way into Penny's suite if necessary, when Leo Johnson rang.

'I've just had a tip from a clerk at the family court,' he told her gravely. 'The application for an emergency care order is about to go in front of a judge.'

Furious and frightened, Andee thanked him, rang off and immediately called Henry Gibbs. 'Can you get there?' she implored. 'I know we don't have the contract, but someone has to represent the birth parents.'

'I'll do my best,' he promised. 'If I can get someone to cover . . . Where are you now?'

'About to make another attempt at getting the contract.'

'If you succeed bring it straight to the court. Otherwise, I'll be in touch as soon as I have some news.'

After being assured that Michelle Cross was still in the same suite Andee didn't bother announcing herself, she just took the lift to the tenth floor and hammered on the door.

'All right, all right,' Penny snapped as she opened up. 'Anyone would think there was a fire.'

Andee looked around, found no sign of a lawyer, only a stack of papers on a desk close to the window and a laptop computer showing a screen full of text that clearly wasn't English.

'I take it you know there's a court hearing this morning,' she said tightly.

Penny's nod was brief.

'What's the matter with you?' Andee cried, throwing out her hands. 'Why are you letting this happen?'

Penny regarded her steadily. She appeared far more composed than she had a few days ago. Her hair was neatly styled, her face carefully made up and she was wearing an expensive-looking black pantsuit – as though she were about to appear in court? 'How many times do we have to go through this?' she asked coldly. 'I'm honouring the contract . . .'

'Where is it?' Andee cut in harshly. 'I need a copy *right now*.'

'What makes you think I have it?'

'For God's sake, we both know you do . . .'

'Even if you're right, it won't help you. That child belongs to Abby and Donald Blakemore. The court here will see that . . .'

'Our lawyers need to examine it.'

'They'll get the opportunity . . .'

'You mean *after* the baby's been seized by the authorities?'

'I'm told that it has to happen that way.'

Suddenly seeing red, Andee grabbed Penny by her

shirt front and shoved her against the wall. 'I want that damned contract now,' she raged. 'I'm going to give your grandson the chance to grow up with his real family, even if you won't.'

'Violence isn't going to help you,' Penny gasped. 'You don't have right on your side and if you attack me again I'll call security.'

'I'll call them myself,' Andee shouted, letting her go. 'And after that I'll call the police, the press, the whole damned world to tell them exactly who you are and what you're doing.'

Penny turned away, took a few steps, and as her head fell forward it was as though the fight drained from her. She said nothing, did nothing, until her laptop signalled the arrival of an email. It was from Selma, Andee noticed, but her mobile started ringing and seeing it was Henry Gibbs she rapidly clicked on.

'I'm sorry, the order's been granted,' he told her, 'and I've been instructed to inform the court of the baby's whereabouts.'

Andee's eyes closed as she tried to think. If she hadn't asked him to go there he wouldn't be in this position, but it was too late to regret that now. She desperately wanted to refuse the information, or to tell Jonathan and Juliette to run, but she knew very well that defying the court would be just about the worst thing they could do.

'Andee?' Gibbs pressed gently. 'You have to tell me.'

Taking a breath she said, 'Do you know Rowzee Cayne?'

'Who doesn't?'

'They're at her house.'

With a sigh he said, 'I'm really sorry. It's up to you whether to call and prepare them. If you do, for God's sake tell them not to run.'

As she rang off Andee spun round, eyes blazing with rage, ready to lay into Penny again.

Penny was at her laptop, typing so furiously it was as though she'd forgotten Andee was in the room.

Slamming the lid down on her hands, Andee seethed, 'You've got your way. They're about to take the baby . . .'

'Stop, just stop!' Penny cried, clasping her hands to her head.

'What is it with you?' Andee raged. 'You're making your own son hate you, turning the whole world against you. You say you don't care what people think of you but I know *you do.* I know that in there,' she punched a hand to Penny's chest, 'is a heart that's broken into so many pieces it's forgotten how to feel, but that doesn't mean it isn't capable. You can hide that from yourself, but you can't hide it from me. So for God's sake, help your son. Your grandson. Me, your sister . . .'

Penny shot to her feet, almost pushing Andee over.

As she turned away Andee spun her back again. 'They're on their way to get him,' she cried. 'He's an innocent child, days old, and *you* are just letting it happen.'

Penny's face was stark, her eyes so clouded by the darkness inside her that it was impossible to know how much was reaching her.

Unable to spend another minute with her, Andee said bitterly, 'I don't want you ever to come near me again. Do you hear that? As far as I'm concerned you died at the age of fourteen and you're still dead.'

After slamming out of the room she raced to the lift, took it to the ground floor and ran out to her car. She'd have to put her foot down now if she was to get to the coach house before the social workers who'd been instructed to collect the baby.

As Andee approached the coach house her heart twisted and sank. She was already too late. Three, no four social workers were remonstrating with Juliette's parents at the front gate, no one understanding what the other was saying, and fists looking as though they were about to fly.

As Andee leapt out of her car Jonathan came out of the house, closing the front door behind him. 'They're trying to take him,' he shouted at Andee, 'but we're not going to let them.'

'We have an emergency care order,' one of the social workers told her. 'If they don't let him go we'll have to call the police.'

'You do that,' Andee told her. At least it would buy them some time. Taking Jonathan's hand she held it tightly as she connected to Gould. 'It's all kicking off,' she told him. 'We're up at Rowzee's. Is there anything you can do?'

'Like what?' he asked. 'We can't go against a court order.'

'But social services are calling for backup and the

Italian parents are about to cut up rough. I need some support.'

'I'll see what I can do.'

With Jonathan's help Andee took hold of Juliette's parents and steered them back into the house. 'We'll wait until the police arrive,' she told the social workers over her shoulder, and winced as Juliette's mother screamed at them in Italian. Since it was clearly abusive, Andee quickly closed the door behind them before she could say any more.

Juliette was in the kitchen, holding Alexander and looking so terrified that Andee longed to lie and tell her everything would be all right. Unfortunately, no one had ever accused Penny of forcing Juliette to become a surrogate mother. Juliette had entered into the agreement of her own free will, as had Jonathan, and now here they were.

'Have you heard anything from your mother's lawyer, or the lawyers in the States?' Andee asked Jonathan as he went to put an arm round Juliette.

'No. No one's been in touch today, until those people outside turned up.'

'I'm sorry. I came to warn you, but obviously I didn't make it in time.'

'So what is happening?' Juliette asked in a tormented voice.

Feeling as bad as she'd ever felt when breaking the news of a death, Andee said, 'I'm afraid you don't have a choice. You have to hand him over . . .'

'No! Never!' Juliette shouted, holding Alexander tighter and making him cry.

'We can't do that, he's ours,' Jonathan told her.

'I understand how you feel,' Andee responded, as the baby's screams got louder, 'but he's not being taken to the States, at least not yet. He'll be taken to someone who's experienced in looking after babies . . .'

'But I am breastfeeding,' Juliette protested furiously. 'Who is going to feed him?'

'It's possible they'll let you continue,' Andee said, 'but only under supervision. We have to get some advice,' and taking out her phone she connected to Henry Gibbs.

'Yes, I asked for feeding visits,' he confirmed, 'and they've been granted.'

'Thank you. I don't suppose the contract's turned up?'

'No, but it's not likely to overturn anything at this stage even if it does. Are you with them?'

'Yes, I am. Social services have called for police backup and a car's just arrived outside, so I'm guessing it's them.'

'Is Blake and Jenny,' Juliette's father said, turning back from the window.

Relieved beyond words at the prospect of having two level heads to support her, Andee went to let them in, and came to a sudden stop when she saw that Graeme was with them. To her dismay she felt heat burning her cheeks as her heart lurched like an adolescent's.

With a quick raise of his eyebrows he passed her and followed Blake along the hall into the kitchen.

'What the heck's going on?' Blake demanded, hefting two bags of shopping on to the island as Jenny brought in a fresh supply of Pampers. 'Who are those people outside?'

As Andee explained, forcing herself not to look at Graeme, Jenny went straight to Juliette and the baby to wrap them in her arms. 'Don't worry, we won't let them take him,' she assured her. 'Will we?' she pressed Andee.

Wishing she didn't feel like the villain of the piece, Andee said, 'I'm afraid we don't have a choice.' Her eyes went to Graeme and quickly moved away.

Juliette's parents started shouting again, rising to a crescendo as though trying to outdo their grandson's yells, and seeming to hold Andee responsible for everything.

Using his reasonable grasp of Italian Graeme did his best to calm them down, but it took a loud knock on the front door to silence them all.

Blake went to answer, with Andee close behind.

'The police are here,' a social worker told them. 'Please don't make us take him by force.'

Afraid it might well go that way, Andee turned back to Jonathan. 'For the baby's sake,' she implored, 'please don't resist. It'll frighten him and he's already frightened enough.'

'I can't let them do it,' he cried brokenly. 'If we let him go now we'll never see him again.'

'You have visiting rights,' she reminded him.

'But for how long? He needs to be with us. He knows us already.'

'Oh Jonathan,' she groaned, touching a hand to his cheek, 'I can't tell you how much I wish this wasn't happening.'

'Once he goes to America we'll never see him again.'

'You don't know for certain that he'll go. We're going to fight for him in the courts . . .'

'We won't win. She'll make sure we don't.'

Knowing he was referring to his mother, Andee said, 'She doesn't have the power to influence a British court.'

'But I'm not British, nor is Juliette.'

'Alexander is,' she said softly, hoping with all her heart that it would count for something. There was such a long way to go, so much to sort out, but right now they must deal with the police hovering on the doorstep and one of the social workers trying to push her way in.

Juliette's eyes were so murderous as the woman approached her, and Alexander was screaming so loudly, that Andee only just made out Juliette saying, 'I will kill him and myself before I let you have him.'

Juliette's parents began shouting again, and as the social worker tried to take the baby Juliette's mother would have slammed her over the head with a poker had Graeme not swiftly grabbed it from her hand. Then the police were inside, holding Juliette's screeching, struggling parents as Juliette, yelling and kicking too, fought to keep hold of her baby.

The noise was so deafening, the scene so heartbreakingly harrowing, that it took a while before anyone heard a man's voice roaring, 'Stop! All of you *stop*.'

As silence fell, Andee turned to find Gould standing at the door with . . . *Penny*?

'She was trying to make herself heard,' Gould explained, 'so I helped.'

Penny seemed reluctant to come forward, and was quick to look over her shoulder when another car arrived.

It turned out to be Henry Gibbs.

Appearing careful to avoid anyone's eyes, Penny said, 'I have the contract,' and taking it from an attaché case she handed it to Gould. 'You will see,' she went on, 'that the law in Texas requires the embryo to be transferred to a surrogate mother a minimum of fourteen days before the agreement with the intended parents is signed. The dates on the contract, and on the medical records, show that in Juliette's case it happened thirteen days before.'

When she'd finished no one spoke. Andee wasn't entirely sure any of them actually understood what had just been said.

Going for clarity, she said, 'Are you telling us that the contract is void?'

Penny's eyes still met no one's as she nodded.

Andee said to Jonathan, 'Was the baby not conceived in the normal way?'

He shook his head. 'We were both donors at the time. It happened in a laboratory. We didn't fall in love until after.'

Andee looked at Penny, not entirely sure what to make of this.

Penny's eyes were on Jonathan, but he wasn't looking at her.

'He's telling the truth,' Penny said, and turning around she began walking away.

'Wait!' Andee called after her, but Penny kept going.

'Does this mean we can keep the baby?' Juliette asked, looking from Jonathan to Andee and back again.

'We have an emergency care order,' a social worker reminded everyone.

Henry Gibbs took the contract from Gould.

No one moved, even Alexander fell silent, as Gibbs cast an eye over a highlighted clause of the agreement. When he'd finished, he held out a hand for the order, took it and tore it in half.

Still clearly unsure of events, Jonathan said. 'Is it all over?'

As Gould nodded for the police officers to leave, the social workers, deprived of their care order and backup, could only follow.

'We'll get it sorted with the court,' Henry Gibbs promised Jonathan and Juliette, 'but I think I can safely say that no one will be back to try and take your baby away.'

'I'll catch you later,' Graeme said softly to Andee as he left the house with Blake and Jenny.

Biting back words she hadn't even considered, Andee simply nodded, and after waiting for her mother to come inside, she closed the front door and hugged her.

'Are you all right?' Maureen murmured. 'I didn't realise Graeme was back.'

'I think he came to make sure his sister's house was still standing,' Andee told her, only half joking. 'Now go see your great-grandson. They're waiting for you.'

Maureen hesitated. 'Is it really all sorted?' she whispered. 'We don't have to go through some ghastly trial?'

Shrinking from how badly it would have affected her mother's health if they'd had to battle with Jonathan and the baby on one side and Penny on the other, Andee said, 'It's not looking likely.'

Maureen seemed to breathe. 'Where's Penny?' she asked.

Andee had been wondering the same. 'At her hotel, I suppose. Or she might be on her way back to London by now.' Seeing how anxious her mother looked, she added, 'I'll try calling her . . .'

'Maureen! You're here,' Jonathan cried, and coming to wrap her in his arms he hugged her so hard that Maureen started to gasp.

'Sorry,' he said, pulling back and wiping the tears on his cheeks.

'Oh, there, there,' Maureen soothed, clasping his handsome young face in her hands. 'It's all fine now, my love. You're keeping your baby and you're going to be such a good daddy.'

'I still can't believe it,' Jonathan choked, looking at Andee. 'I keep thinking it was a trick, and that she'll be back any minute laughing and poking fun at me for believing it . . .'

'Ssh,' Maureen chided. 'It's not going to happen.'

'You saw the lawyer tear up the care order,' Andee reminded him. 'He wouldn't have done that if he weren't confident that it has no worth.'

'But what if there's another contract and that one was a fake?'

Aching for how cruel his mother must have been to Jonathan for him to think like this, Andee recalled the way Penny had looked at him before she left. It had been impossible to know what she was feeling, but Andee knew it wasn't nothing. 'I swear I don't think she'd have come here to expose the mistake unless it was genuine,' she told him.

He turned round as Juliette appeared, and seeing Maureen she fell into the arms of her tiny son's great-grandmother.

Remembering how reassuring those arms had been for her over the years, Andee whispered to Jonathan, 'Come on, let's go outside.'

He followed her around to the back of the house where two swing chairs, a padded wicker sofa and a coffee table doubling as a backgammon board were absorbing the warmth of the early afternoon sunshine. The garden, stretching all the way to the stream that separated it from the Burlingford estate, was alive with colourful flowers. Only yesterday Rowzee had texted to say they should be cut and put in vases for her guests to enjoy.

'I'm not sure what we should do now,' Jonathan said, sitting next to Andee on a top step of the wooden deck. 'I'm afraid if we try to leave she'll suddenly spring out of nowhere and grab the baby before we know what's happening.'

Taking his hand, Andee said, 'I honestly don't think she's as bad as she tries to make out.'

Scoffing, Jonathan said, 'You don't know the half.'

'I realise things have been difficult . . .'

'She's my *real* mother. She's a *part of me*. That goes beyond difficult.' Disgust, shame, thickened his voice.

Realising that he still had a long way to go to recover from learning that Ana wasn't his birth mother, Andee searched for some words of comfort. They were hard to find when Penny had behaved the way she had, especially over the baby. He would understandably struggle to forgive that. Andee couldn't help wondering if Penny's ambivalence – to put it kindly – towards her son might in some way be connected to seeing how horrified he'd been to learn that she was his mother. No matter what she said, it must have cut very deeply to realise she was so despised.

'You're going to defend her, aren't you?' he accused.

Still holding his hand between both of hers, she said, 'I can't do that when I don't know enough about what's gone on between you, but I will say this: I truly believe she came here today to try and make you see that she's not all bad.'

Astonished, Jonathan cried, 'She fucked up a contract. That's what she came to tell us.'

'But she could have got the lawyers to do that. She didn't need to be here in person. I believe she came because she wanted you to know that *she* was making the court case go away, and that she was doing it for you.'

He clearly wasn't buying it. 'If there hadn't been a problem with that contract our son wouldn't be with us now, you have to know that. In fact, she's probably known all along that there was a problem, so she didn't need to put us through any of this. She could have made it known a long time ago.'

'Maybe she's only just checked the detail. OK, I can

see you're not ready to consider that either. Look, I can't make excuses for her, I don't know her well enough to do that, but during the short time I have known her, as an adult I mean, I've got a sense of the terrible conflict, even fear, that's raging away inside her. She's struggling badly, and what's been happening lately is clearly bringing it to a head. It's my belief that she loves you deeply, but she has no idea how to show it, she's probably even afraid to try.'

He turned to look at her, his eyes showing a tormented disbelief. 'You said it yourself, you haven't known her for long,' he replied. 'She's vindictive, sadistic . . . She's bloody *inhuman*. Even Pappa says that about her.'

'But he still cares for her?'

Since he couldn't deny that, he said belligerently, 'Alex is the lucky one. At least he got to die before he found out that she-devil . . .'

'Stop, please stop,' Andee came in gently, but forcefully. 'Your brother's death was a tragedy that you really can't use in that way. By the time your mother found out what had happened to him she had been through the kind of hell that made it impossible for her to think straight, or even know who she was any more, never mind how she should relate to anyone else. Frankly, I believe she's still suffering in ways she might not even realise herself. That's what serious drug addiction does to a person, and never forget those drugs were forced on her. Yes, she chose to leave home at fourteen because she felt unloved, unappreciated, and we are to blame for that, not her. Families, parents, get things wrong sometimes, but it doesn't mean they don't care, and in Penny's case, as a parent, she hardly knows where to begin. You know you wouldn't have been born if you hadn't been part of the surrogacy deal that Sven set up. He did the wrong thing for the right reason, and you still love him . . .'

'You have to stop now,' he protested. 'Pappa can never be compared to *her*.'

Putting an arm around him, Andee toyed with the idea of telling him that no girls had gone missing, that no one was trafficked or forced to do anything they didn't want to, but decided to save it for later. It still had to be checked, and he already had enough to process for one day. So all she said was, 'People are so complex, especially someone who's suffered the way your mother has, that we often can't even begin to understand them. I just want you to try to keep an open mind where she's concerned. I'm having to do the same, because I swear she's a mystery to me too, but as we all move forward from here one thing I know for certain is that we're going to need one another every step of the way.'

'That's just where you're wrong,' he told her, 'because she doesn't need anyone, and she never has.'

It was early evening when Graeme returned to the coach house, unannounced, and asked Andee to take a stroll with him. Knowing she'd look ridiculous to the others if she refused, Andee followed him outside, already planning to tell him that they really didn't need to have this conversation.

As they reached the hamlet, where they were greeted by the heady scents of freshly mown grass, honeysuckle and a neighbours barbecue, Andee said, 'I can only begin to imagine what a shock it was for you when you arrived here today, but at least they seem to be taking good care of the place.'

With a note of humour, Graeme said, 'I knew they would with you and your mother in charge of things, but you're right, it was a bit of a shock to walk into that chaos. I'm still not entirely sure I understand everything that happened.'

Andee had to smile. 'That makes two of us,' she confessed, 'but I guess the important thing is that the baby won't be going to the States. In fact, once Jonathan gets past the fear of this being one of Penny's cruel jokes, I think he'll be very happy to take his little family to Italy so they can be close to Juliette's parents.'

'And how do you feel about that, having only just met him?'

'Sad, because I'd like to get to know him better, and I know Luke and Alayna will want to meet him as soon as they find out they have another cousin. But we'll visit him in Italy, and hopefully he'll come to see us here. I guess my real concern right now is for Penny, and how she isn't figuring in Jonathan's plans for the future at all.'

'Mm,' he responded thoughtfully. 'There's obviously a lot of work to be done there, if they even want to do it.'

'I think she does, but heaven only knows how she'll go about it.'

'And what about your mother? How's she dealing with things?'

Andee wished she could give a proper answer to that, but all she could say was, 'I'm not sure. One minute she seems to be holding it together very well, the next she looks completely shattered – and lost, like she's not entirely sure what's happening or what she should be doing. It's been hard for her, and I'm not convinced that even the relief of Jonathan getting to keep the baby is making it much easier. Of course she's happy about that, she wouldn't have wanted it any other way, but . . .' She sighed heavily at the size of the but.

'Really it's all about Penny?'

Andee nodded, and they both waved to one of the neighbours as he returned from a walk on the moor with his dog. 'She truly doesn't know how to process the issues Penny's thrown up, and frankly I don't either. I'm not even sure we'll hear from her again now the struggle for Alexander is over.'

'But you've got her number.'

'Yes, that's true.'

After a while he said, 'Do you think she knew all along that the contract was invalid?'

'I've no idea. Jonathan's convinced of it, but if she did she'd have known we'd find out sooner or later, so why would she keep it to herself? My guess is she didn't realise until it was checked against the medical file, and that might only have happened in the last day or two.'

'Well, however it came to light, I dread to think of the kind of lawsuit she must be facing now.'

Dreading it too, Andee said, 'It won't be pretty, that's for sure, and to be honest I don't know how equipped she is to deal with it. She's not as . . . invincible as she likes to make out, and I got the feeling when I was with her the other day that she's afraid of something. Well, of course she is, given the mistake with the contract, but I wouldn't be surprised if it goes deeper than that.'

As they reached the picnic area at the end of the hamlet where a stunning view of the bay and sunset was glittering tantalisingly through the trees, Graeme offered her his hand as they descended the few rugged steps into the glade. When she was there, he kept hold of it and folded it through his arm.

'There's something I need to discuss with you,' he said, after a few moments of absorbing the beauty of their surroundings, 'and before you say you know what it is, I don't think you do . . . Why did you say that, by the way?'

Wishing she wasn't having to admit this, she attempted to sound wry as she said, 'Penny has photos of you with Nadia.'

Clearly startled, he turned to look at her. 'What photos?' he asked, apparently more perplexed than angry.

Starting to feel embarrassed now, Andee said, 'She told me you seem very close.'

His eyebrows rose with some sort of understanding as he nodded. 'And you saw these photos?' he wondered.

This was becoming more awkward by the second. 'She offered to show me, but I didn't really want . . .

She had someone following you, and I think that someone took Nadia to be me. You're going to tell me they don't exist?'

'If she had someone following me I'm sure they do, but they'd be no different to photos of me with my sisters or your mother. Affectionate, fun, although there hasn't been a lot of fun with Nadia lately, which brings me to what I want to discuss with you.'

Andee looked back at the view, preparing for the worst.

'There's no easy way of saying this,' he began, 'so I'll come straight to the point. Nadia doesn't want you working on the project any more.'

A beat after the shock, Andee felt the rejection like a slap.

'The reason,' he continued, 'is probably what you're suspecting . . . I don't mean that there's anything between us, but she would like there to be. I've told her many times that it's not going to happen, but there's so much at stake with this property – in that she's paying me so well – that she thinks she's calling all the shots. She knows now that she isn't.'

Andee was very still as she regarded him closely, not quite sure of what he was saying.

'If you're not able to work on Nadia's villa with me,' he said, 'I'm not going to do it.'

As understanding reached her, Andee's jaw almost dropped. 'But all that money,' she protested. 'It's over a hundred thousand pounds.'

'I won't deny it would be good to have, but frankly I'd rather have you.'

She continued to stare at him, still trying to take it in. 'But I'm not worth that much,' she objected.

Laughing, he brought her to him and lowered his mouth tenderly to hers.

Minutes passed, birds sang, the distant sea soughed as she put her arms around him and felt so relieved and so complete that she simply ignored the text that had just arrived on her phone.

When finally he let her go, he said, 'Considering all that's been happening lately, maybe you'd better check that message.'

Seriously hoping it was something that could wait, she opened up the text. Seeing it was from Penny, she became aware of a strange feeling stealing over her.

Have you given any thought to how the book ends?

'Oh my God,' she murmured, knowing exactly what this meant, and grabbing Graeme's hand she ran like the wind to her car.

Chapter Twenty

For the second time that day Andee was hammering on the door to Penny's suite at the Grand hotel. The only difference this time was that the manager and Graeme were with her.

Her heart was thudding with fear. *Have you given any thought to how the book ends?* Kate Trask had chosen to escape her crimes, her shame and the lack of her son's love by taking her own life.

'Penny!' she shouted fiercely. 'Please let me in.'

Since she'd already told the manager what she feared, he didn't hesitate in unlocking the door, and moments later she was bursting into the room.

She looked around, hardly able to see through her panic, until finally she spotted Penny sitting in one of the window seats, staring blankly out at the sea. She was clearly very much alive, and virtually collapsing with relief, Andee cried, 'Why didn't you answer? You must have heard me knocking.'

Penny said nothing, simply continued to gaze out at the horizon, seeming not to register anything beyond whatever she was seeing in her mind.

Turning to the manager, Andee said, 'Thank you. It'll be fine now. I'll meet you downstairs,' she told Graeme.

After they'd gone she closed the door quietly and went to sit in a chair close to the window. As she waited for her heart to settle, she looked around the room and saw Penny's suitcases stacked on the floor. Whether they were already packed it wasn't possible to tell. The desk was empty, no sign of the laptop or the files that had littered it earlier.

When it became clear that she'd have to break this strangely awful silence, Andee said, 'OK, you got me here. So what now?'

Without turning round, Penny said, 'You thought I'd killed myself.'

'Isn't that what I was meant to think?'

Penny didn't deny it. 'I will, of course, leave everything to Jonathan,' she said.

Her alarm increasing to fear, Andee said, 'Have you taken something? Do I need to call an ambulance?'

Penny inhaled a shaky breath and let it go slowly. 'No, you don't need to call an ambulance,' she replied.

'So what's this about?' Andee demanded, wanting to shake her out of this peculiar stupor.

'I have something for you,' Penny said. It's a USB stick containing all the files you'll need to show where the so-called missing girls are. You'll also find details of the refuges in Riga, Vilnius and Minsk and a list of the scouts who search out the vulnerable. Everything's there, right down to the details of the students who take the opportunity to make a lot of money during a gap year. You'll even discover how much they're paid. It's easier for the boys of course, so they don't receive anywhere near as much as the girls.' She smiled grimly. 'Some of them like our set-up so much that they decide to continue being donors while working as escorts from the apartments in London and Stockholm. You can interview them if you like, ask them how free they are to come and go. All their details are there.'

Feeling faintly disoriented, Andee took the memory stick and asked, 'Why are you doing this?'

Penny's expression had no warmth, only something that looked like sadness, or possibly resentment. 'Because I'm ruined, or I soon will be, and all those young people will have to find their own way from here. I'm not sure what will happen to the refuges; it's not easy to get state funding in those countries.'

'You're assuming the Blakemores are going to sue.'

'I know they are. I heard from their lawyers as soon as the problem with the contract was revealed.'

'Which was when?'

'When I received the medical file the day before yesterday. Until then I fully believed everything was as it should be.'

Having to ask the question, Andee said, 'Does that mean you'd still be trying to take the baby if all the conditions had been met?'

Penny sighed and turned her hands over as she looked down at them. As Andee looked at them too she felt an uneasy beat in her heart. Why hadn't she made this connection before? Kate Trask had worn gloves, not to cover eczema, but to mask her arthritic joints. Did it mean anything? Maybe it was just a bizarre or psychosomatic coincidence.

'No, I wouldn't be trying to take him,' Penny replied, 'but the Blakemores' lawyers wouldn't have stopped until they had him, no matter how old he might be by then.'

'You seem so sure of that.'

'I know the Blakemores. They're very determined and desperate people.'

'Can't you offer them another surrogate?'

'I have, but after this they don't trust me, so they're going to make sure that no one else makes the same mistake. They're already petitioning to have the clinics shut down, and it won't be long before they hit me with a ruinous claim for damages.'

'And where exactly do they think all this bitterness and litigation is going to end them up? Not with a baby, that's for sure.'

'Oh, I expect they'll get one eventually, and they'll be able to boast to their friends about what they did to me, so everyone will know that you cross the Blakemores at your peril.'

After a while, Andee said, 'I can't help wondering what they'd have done if the baby had been born with a physical or mental impairment. They don't sound like the kind of couple who'd accept anything less than what they would call perfection.'

'They wouldn't have. There's a clause in all the contracts to cover that. The baby has to be in full health or the intended parents will be entitled to a full refund.'

Shocked, disgusted, Andee said, 'What would happen to the baby?'

'I can't answer that because the problem's never arisen. If it did, I guess we'd find a home for it somewhere. We'd have to if the biological mother didn't want to keep it.'

Still having a difficult time with the ethics of it all, no matter whom it might be helping, Andee said, 'So what are you going to do next?'

Penny swallowed and raised one of her flaked hands to her face.

Seeing how badly it was shaking, Andee said, 'What is it? There's more, I can tell . . .'

Penny almost laughed. 'You think being ruined isn't enough?'

'It might be, but you're keeping something back, so why don't you tell me what it is?'

Pressing her hand to her head as tears flooded her eyes, Penny said, 'Sven has been taken to hospital. He's only got days to live and I don't know how to tell Jonathan.'

'Oh Penny,' Andee murmured, going to her. She felt oddly bony and stiff, clearly uncomfortable with the physical contact, even though she didn't resist it.

'He loves his father so much.' Penny's voice shook. 'We all do.'

Andee stopped herself from offering to break the news, feeling Jonathan had to hear it from Penny.

'His father's going to die and the only parent he'll have is me,' Penny stated bleakly. 'Imagine how he's going to feel about that. He'll hate me for not being the one to die. I don't blame him for hating me. I've never done anything to make him feel any other way. I didn't want him to be my son, I didn't want anyone to belong to me and I didn't want to belong to anyone. But I do belong to Sven. He's been everything to me for as long as I can remember . . . I'm terrified of a world without him in it. I don't know how I'm going to cope. I just don't know,' she gasped desperately.

With tears stinging her own eyes, Andee tried to comfort her, but Penny wasn't listening.

'Ever since he told Jonathan about me,' she ran on, 'it's been his dearest wish that Jonathan and I should find a way to work things out. I've told him so many times that it'll never happen, that I'm incapable of what he's asking and Jonathan's not willing, but he won't believe it. He has so much faith in us . . . He thinks we'll do it for him, and I want to, I want to so much, but we've left it too late.'

'That's not true,' Andee told her firmly. 'He's still alive, and you must talk to Jonathan. Does he know how Sven feels?'

Penny nodded. 'But he doesn't know that Sven's so close to the end.'

'Then I'll take you to Jonathan now, and I'll stay with you while you tell him. I'll hold both your hands and I'll even come to Stockholm if you think it'll help.'

Penny was shaking her head. 'Why would you do that for me after the way I've treated you?'

'Because you're my sister, and he's my nephew and because I want Sven's wish to come true as much as he does.'

Penny was still shaking, seeming unable to make

herself stop. 'I've left everything to Jonathan,' she repeated faintly. 'My lawyer has my will . . .'

'Penny!' Andee cried, suddenly realising that something was very wrong. 'Penny, what have you done?'

'I lied,' Penny murmured, slumping slightly. 'I always lie.'

Trying to hold her up, Andee whipped out her phone and called Graeme. 'We need to get her to hospital,' she told him. 'Please call an ambulance,' and forcing Penny to her feet she began urgently walking her around the room.

It was just after dawn the following morning that Andee, stiff and aching from spending the night in a chair, opened her eyes to find Penny watching her from the hospital bed. Apart from the redness and slight bruising around her mouth her face was colourless and pinched; her eyes were sunken and shadowed.

Struggling to sit straighter, Andee said, 'Hi. How are you feeling?'

Penny's voice was hoarse. 'Probably about as good as I look.'

Encouraged by the humour, Andee filled a glass with water and handed it to her. 'Do you remember what happened?' she asked.

After gingerly swallowing, Penny said, 'Do you want me to thank you for bringing me here?'

Andee shrugged. 'I didn't have anything else to do.'

Almost managing a smile, Penny shifted slightly and winced.

'Headache?'

Penny nodded.

'It could be a lot worse,' Andee reminded her.

As Penny's eyes closed she raised her peeling fingers to her head.

'Do they hurt?' Andee asked.

Penny glanced at her and realising what she meant, she said, 'It's worse some days than others.' She sighed shakily. 'It's funny, isn't it, that my hands should be a problem, not like Kate Trask's arthritic joints, but still an affliction.'

'You need to let it go,' Andee said softly. 'You're not her, and nor are you anything like her.'

Penny stared off into the distance, watching ghosts only she could see. 'Who knows I'm here?' she asked.

'No one, apart from me and Graeme.'

'So it's all . . . You're still together?'

Wondering if Penny had ever known what it was to be in a romantic relationship, Andee said, 'We are.'

Penny nodded as her eyes drifted again. 'No one else needs to know about this, do they?' she said after a while.

'Not if you don't want them to.'

Penny looked at the saline drip attached to her left hand, then removing it she swung her legs over the side of the bed and swayed.

'Too fast,' Andee said, steadying her. 'And you need to see a doctor before we leave.'

'They're not keeping me here. I have to get to Sven.'

'Don't worry, they'll be glad to have the bed back. There's a shower in there. I popped back to the hotel during the night and brought you some things. They're in that bag.'

Penny stared at the holdall and seemed unable to move.

Going to her, Andee slipped an arm around her and rested her head against hers. 'It'll be all right,' she whispered. This was a new feeling, comforting her little sister.

It was a while before Penny turned to look at her. 'I've screwed up so badly,' she said, gazing into Andee's eyes, 'and I've just gone on and on screwing up.'

'So maybe you're tired of it now?'

Penny gave a small nod.

'Good, then get in the shower and when you're ready we'll take the first steps towards trying to make some things right.'

Just over an hour later, complete with all the leaflets and helpline numbers the hospital insisted they take, Andee was driving them to Rowzee and Pamela's coach house. Graeme had gone on ahead to prepare the way, while Penny's chauffeur had been summoned from the hotel to follow Andee's car. It was making Penny feel more secure, Andee realised, to know that she'd be able to get away if she needed to.

Struck again by how lonely and vulnerable her sister really was behind the façade that was slowly but surely falling apart, Andee reached out to hold her hand.

Penny didn't respond. She sat rigidly in her seat, trying to battle whatever doubts and demons were assailing her. When Andee let her hand go, she said, belligerently, 'It's much easier when you don't care.'

Touched and amused by how like the child Penny she sounded, Andee said, 'Really?'

Penny continued to stare out of the window, registering only she knew what as they turned on to the coast road where block after block of affordable housing and holiday homes had replaced what had once been vast swathes of buttercup fields and bluebell woods. 'It's changed a lot since we were young,' she commented, sounding offended. 'Frankly, I'm not sure I like being here.'

Understanding that the resentment was far more to do with nerves than genuine disapproval, Andee wondered what memories were coming up for her, and how hard she was finding it to handle the complicated emotions they would be stirring.

'I'm not sure she's up to seeing Jonathan this soon,' Andee had said to Graeme earlier while Penny was in the shower, 'but with Sven having so little time left, I don't see there's a choice.'

'There isn't,' he agreed. 'I've looked into flights for this evening. There's plenty of availability at the moment, but I won't book anything until we know who's going. I'll leave now to make sure I'm at the coach house before you.'

After he'd gone Andee had called her mother to tell her about Sven's deteriorating condition, and to warn her that Alayna was intending to turn up later in the day. 'You know what she's like,' Andee said, 'she obviously knows something's going on and she's determined to find out what it is. So just in case I'm not around, will you be OK with explaining about Penny?' It was a big ask, too big, but maybe Blake and Jenny wouldn't mind being there to support her.

'I'll do my best,' Maureen promised, sounding daunted. 'How's Penny taking it about Sven?'

'She's very upset. We're just about to go and break it to Jonathan. I'll come and see you before I head off to the airport.'

'So you're going to Stockholm too?'

'I'm not sure yet. I'll let you know.'

Now, as she and Penny turned at Hope Cove and started up towards the moor, Penny was gazing hard at her phone as though willing it, or even daring it to ring. Though it was on silent Andee knew it had rung at least a dozen times in the past hour, and heaven only knew how many texts and emails had arrived throughout the night.

'I should be in the States,' Penny stated. 'I've got three girls due to give birth in the next couple of weeks. I'm always there for the handover. Everyone's wondering where I am, and what's going on.'

'Isn't there someone who can deputise for you?' Andee asked.

'Maria. She runs the clinics.'

'So why are you worried?'

'Because I should be there.' Pressing a hand to her head, she said, 'Why doesn't Selma call? Is that good or bad?'

'You could always call her.'

Penny turned away. Clearly she was afraid to. 'I want to send a text to let him know that Jonathan and I are on our way,' she declared angrily. 'If he knew that he'd definitely hold on, but I can't until I know it's true.'

'Why not?' Andee ventured. 'Even if it doesn't go the way you hope with Jonathan, it'll make Sven happy for a while to think you're both coming.'

Penny threw out her hands. 'Why do you always know the right thing to do?'

Drily Andee said, 'I'll try to get it wrong next time.'

Penny started to press in a message. When she'd finished she said, 'If Jonathan doesn't want to go with me, I'll let him go on his own. Sven will want to see him and it's important for him to say goodbye to his father.'

'It's important for you too,' Andee reminded her.

Penny nodded, and bit her lip as tears shone in her eyes.

Opening the glove box, Andee pointed her to the Kleenex.

Minutes later they were at the gates to the Burlingford estate, only yards from the coach house where Graeme's car was parked next to the Mini Jonathan and Juliette were using.

Andee turned to Penny. In spite of the freshly applied make-up her face was ashen as she stared with dark, haunted eyes into the next few minutes.

'Graeme came on ahead to explain about the contract and lawsuit,' Andee told her. 'He hasn't had much time, but he was going to try telling Jonathan about the missing girls who aren't missing at all.'

'He won't believe it,' Penny said hoarsely.

'He'll have to when we prove it.'

Penny looked at her. 'Have you been through the files?' she asked.

Andee shook her head.

'So you don't know if I was telling the truth.'

In spite of a beat of unease, Andee said, 'I trust you.'

Penny's gaze held on to hers. In the end, she said quietly, 'You're a good person.'

Reaching for her hand again, Andee felt its icy coldness and lifted it to her cheek to warm it. The hard flakes of skin, like little signs of vulnerability, moved her deeply. 'Are you ready?' she asked softly, knowing she wasn't.

Penny glanced in the side mirror to make sure the Mercedes was still behind.

'Do you know what you're going to say?'

'No. I . . . I guess I just have to tell him.'

By the time they reached the front door Graeme had already opened it. 'Juliette's upstairs with her parents and the baby,' he told them. 'Jonathan's outside on the terrace.'

'How much does he know?' Andee asked.

'Nothing about Sven. I'm honestly not sure how he's dealing with what I told him about you,' he said to Penny.

Penny took a breath but no words came.

'I did my best,' he promised.

Slipping an arm round Penny's waist, Andee eased her inside and along the hall to the kitchen. They could see Jonathan standing with his back to the open French doors.

He gave no indication that he'd heard them come in, but simply continued to stare across the garden to the fruit orchard beyond.

Letting Penny go, Andee gave her a gentle push forward.

After two steps Penny turned back, looking as though she might flee. Andee's heart went out to her. Of all the difficult, even harrowing situations she must have faced in her life, this was clearly right up there with the hardest.

'Jonathan,' Andee said.

She saw him stiffen and for a moment she thought he was going to ignore her, but finally he turned around. His eyes were harsh, defensive; his fists were clenching and unclenching at his sides. He didn't look at his mother, only at Andee. 'Whatever she's told you . . .'

Andee's hand went up. 'You need to listen,' she cautioned. To Penny she said, 'Go ahead.'

Before Penny could speak, Jonathan spat, 'If this is supposed to be an apology I'm not interested, because you won't mean it. You're only doing it to . . .'

'Jonathan,' Andee chided. 'You really do need to listen.'

Apparently catching on to the fact that there might be more going on than he realised, his eyes shot warily to his mother and back to Andee.

Penny attempted to clear her throat. Andee could see her lips trembling and moving, but no words were coming out.

'It's OK,' Andee murmured, going to her.

'I can't do it,' Penny gasped.

'Yes you can.'

'I told you,' Jonathan growled, 'I don't want an apology any more than I want *her* as a mother.'

Andee felt Penny flinch.

Realising she needed to take over, Andee said, as firmly but gently as she could, 'What she's trying to tell you is that Sven is in the hospital. He only has days to live and she'd like you to go with her to Stockholm . . .' She broke off as Jonathan backed away, shouting, 'No! I don't believe you. It's one of her tricks. This is the kind of thing she does.'

'Jonathan, you know he's sick,' Andee broke in. 'You knew this was coming . . .'

'No! I won't let it,' he cried. 'He can't go. It's her fault. She made him sick.'

'You know that's not true.'

'Oh God, oh God,' he wailed, clasping his hands to his head. 'You've got to stop it, please. Please stop it.'

Going to him, Andee held him as he twisted one way then another, sobbing into his hands and calling for his father. 'Pappa, Pappa,' he gasped, stooping low as though unable to take the pain of what he'd known was coming.

Andee rubbed his back, watching Penny as she looked on helplessly.

Suddenly his head came up. 'She's lying,' he raged desperately. 'I know she is.'

Andee caught him by the shoulders and turned him around. 'Look at her,' she said, 'does she look like someone who's lying? And would she, over something like this? He means the world to her too. You know that.'

Jonathan's head fell back as he tried in vain to contain his grief. He began stomping about the room, banging his fists into furniture, even himself.

'Jonathan, we . . . we need to go to him,' Penny said brokenly.

'Not with you,' he snarled.

'Jonathan!' Andee cut in. 'Think of how much it will mean to him to see the two of you together.'

'He knows I hate her.'

'And do you think he wants it to be like that? Please, go together . . .'

From the doorway, Juliette said, 'Jonathan, we will go and we must take the baby. Sven will want to meet his grandson.'

Struggling to control more tears, Jonathan went to bury his face against her. 'Yes,' he murmured into her hair. 'He'll want to meet his grandson.' To Andee he said, 'I have to call Selma. She'll tell me if this is true.'

Feeling Penny's pain, Andee said, 'It's true, Jonathan. If you won't take Penny's word for it, *Kate's* word for it, then please take mine.'

Still unable to look at Penny, he said to Andee, 'OK, then we should go today.'

Penny managed to say, 'If you'd rather I waited a day . . .'

'No, you must go too,' Andee insisted. 'Jonathan, please don't push her out. We've no idea how much time Sven has left. Don't make it too late for her.'

Jonathan turned his back, still holding on to Juliette. Andee could hear her whispering to him in Italian, seeming to soothe and encourage him until, finally, he turned to his mother.

'Do it,' Juliette murmured.

When he still didn't move, Juliette took his arm and walked him to Penny. 'Do it,' she repeated.

Obediently Jonathan lifted his head and said, *'Kom du ocksa.'* Come too.

Andee watched as Penny stood motionless, tears spilling from her eyes, until finally she was able to lift a hand and place it on his shoulder.

To Andee's relief he didn't shrink away.

'Tack,' Penny whispered.

Jonathan turned to Andee. 'And you?' he asked. 'Will you come too?'

Andee looked at Penny, and seeing how desperately unsure she was of being able to do the right thing, she said, 'Of course.'

Andee found Graeme outside talking to the chauffeur.

'I'm going with them,' she told him. 'Juliette and the baby are coming too.'

'OK, I'll get on to the flights,' he replied. 'We'll need to sort out what to do about the baby's passport, but I think I know someone who can help with that. Will Juliette's parents be staying here?'

'No, they're arranging to go back to Italy to start making things ready for when Jonathan and Juliette join them. There's a flight later today from Bristol airport.'

'OK, I'll organise a taxi for them unless Blake's free to do it. I'll take you to Heathrow, because you won't fit all the baby paraphernalia and five people into the Mercedes.'

Andee's heart swelled. 'It might be too much for Penny and Jonathan to be in the same car for such a long journey at this stage, so Penny ought to come with us.'

He nodded agreement and glanced at his watch. 'I should get on to it, make sure you can get on this evening's flight.'

'Before you go,' she said, putting a hand on his arm, 'why don't you come too? Maybe you could show me around Stockholm.'

Drawing her into his arms, he replied, 'I'd love nothing more, but your sister knows the city far better than I do, and I think it would be good for you both to spend some time together.'

In spite of feeling apprehensive about that, Andee didn't argue, because of course he was right.

'What are you going to do now?' he asked.

'I'm taking Penny to see my mother.'

He grimaced comically. 'OK. Good luck with that. I'll call when the flights are confirmed and come and pick you up from the Lodge.'

Maureen was waiting when Andee and Penny reached Bourne Hollow, fresh coffee already made for her and Andee, tea for Penny, remembering she didn't drink coffee, and some home-baked pinwheel cookies on the table. She looked and sounded as nervous as Penny clearly was, and Andee had to admit to feeling anxious too. There was so much to say, too much for the short time they had, but it wouldn't have been right to leave without them at least trying to make the first moves back to each other.

'You should eat,' Maureen said to Penny, and knowing

it was her mother's way of showing she cared, Andee wanted to hug her.

'It's a new cookie recipe,' Maureen told them, 'from one of the contestants on *Bake Off*.'

To Andee's relief Penny reached for a biscuit and broke it in two, in spite of looking as though food was the last thing she wanted.

'I'm going to take my coffee upstairs while I pack,' Andee informed them. 'You don't need me to help you with this.'

Looking as though they desperately did, they watched her carry her mug out to the hall and sat staring at the door long after she'd closed it.

Penny nibbled on a cookie. 'They're very good,' she told her mother.

As Maureen looked at her she felt so lost that she had no idea what to say. All the turmoil and torment of the last few weeks was still there, it couldn't just disappear. Yet seeing Penny as she was now, seeming helplessly exposed and needy, a shadow of the woman who'd come here a few short weeks ago, Maureen realised it was as if a missing piece of herself was trying to find its way back. It didn't quite fit, kept hurting and trying to get away, but at last it felt as though she might stand a chance of getting hold of it. In this moment it didn't matter that this woman, like the girl she'd once been, had caused her mother to question herself and her feelings in the most harrowing way; or that she'd created so much doubt in Maureen's heart that the shame, the fear had been impossible to bear. Right now that child, that woman, looked broken, frightened, and in desperate need of the kindness Maureen longed to give, if she only knew where to start.

In the end she said, 'I'm sorry to hear about Sven.'

Penny's eyes went down and Maureen saw the grief go through her like a shiver. 'Thank you,' Penny mumbled. 'He was . . . He is . . .' She shook her head, apparently unable or unwilling to say more.

'I'm sorry not to have known him,' Maureen said. 'He sounds a very special man.'

Penny nodded. At last her eyes came back to her mother's. She swallowed hard. 'It wasn't true what I said about Dad. I know you know that, but I think you need to hear me say it,' she told her.

It was true; Maureen had needed it very much.

'I'm sorry I hurt you so badly,' Penny continued, 'and that I didn't have the courage to come back when I should have.' Her hands closed into tight, painful fists. 'There are so many apologies that it's hard to know where to begin.'

'You just have,' Maureen said softly. 'And I'm sorry too. I should have been a better mother, should have understood and listened more . . .'

'I never really deserved to be loved anyway.'

Rocked by the statement, Maureen couldn't think what to say.

'It's OK, I don't . . .'

'It's not true,' Maureen interrupted. 'You were loved, very much. And you still are.'

'But . . .'

'Listen to me', Maureen said firmly, taking Penny's

hand, 'whatever you've done, wherever you've been and wherever you go, one thing will never change. I am your mother and I will always love you and want you in my life. That was always the case, it remains the case, and will forever be the case, so please don't ever doubt it.'

As Penny stiffened with pain Maureen went to hold her, tears running down her own cheeks as she felt her younger daughter pressing against her as though she was really, truly trying to find her way back.

'I know you have to go to Stockholm now,' Maureen went on, 'but promise me you'll stay in touch, and even come back to see us.'

'I promise,' Penny choked. 'As long as you're sure.'

'Of course I am. I don't want to lose you again.'

By the time Andee came to let them know it was time to go to the airport Penny was on her second biscuit, and sitting quietly in her chair looking for all the world like the child she'd once been as Maureen gently brushed her hair.

'She needs to look her best for Sven,' Maureen told Andee.

Andee looked at them both trying to take it in. This might feel like a dream, or something happening in a parallel world, but it really wasn't. Penny was back.

Penny was back.

She was actually here, no longer hiding behind the masks she'd created, for the moment at least she'd stopped pretending to be someone who didn't care. Maybe this was the real Penny Lawrence, the daughter and sister they'd have to get to know all over again, even as she got to know herself. Not that it was going to be easy, it would take a miracle to bring that about. With so many questions still to answer and damage to repair, it was sure to be a very long road. However, today wasn't the day to be troubling themselves with that, it was a time simply to feel thankful that things had got this far – because there was no doubt in Andee's mind that these past few weeks were just the beginning.

Acknowledgements

An enormous thank you to Gunnel Oscarsson for introducing me to the wonderful city of Stockholm. A fabulous experience and a city I'd love to visit again and again. Also thank you Gunnel for undertaking the Swedish translations.

More thanks to my dear friends Gill Hall and Ian Kelcey whose legal expertise once again guided my hand.

As usual my wonderful husband, James Garrett, provided unflinching moral support throughout the writing of this book, heroically withstanding the many highs and lows that come with creating an extreme and challenging story.